AMSCO®

ADVANCED PLACEMENT® EDITION

EUROPEAN
HISTORY

PERFECTION LEARNING®

AMSCO® Advanced Placement® European History: is one of a series of
Advanced Placement® social studies texts first launched with the book now titled
AMSCO® Advanced Placement® United States History.

© 2023 Perfection Learning®

Please visit our websites at:
www.perfectionlearning.com

When ordering this book, please specify:
Softcover: 978-1-6636-3972-1 or **T533301**
eBook: ISBN 978-1-6636-3973-8 or **T5333D**

2 3 4 5 DR 27 26 25 24 23

Printed in the United States of America

Contributors

Senior Reviewers

Lou Gallo
AP® European History Consultant
West High School, Knoxville, Tennessee
Dwight Global Online School, New York, NY

Robert Wade
AP® European History Consultant
John Paul II High School
Plano, Texas

Writers and Reviewers

Don Baeszler
AP® European History Consultant
Riverview High School
Sarasota, Florida

Alaina Brown
AP® European History Consultant
Novi High School
Novi, Michigan

Catherine Holden Desmond
AP® European History Consultant
Baltimore County Public Schools
Baltimore, Maryland

Sue Chaney Gilmore
College Board Consultant
Martin Luther King Academic Magnet
 High School
Nashville, Tennessee

Alice Grant
AP® European History Consultant
Pelham Memorial High School (retired)
Pelham, New York

Bryan Henry
AP® European History Teacher
Kingwood High School
Kingwood, Texas

Gerald Hurd
AP® European History Exam Selector
Olympic High School
Silverdale, Washington

Brian Jameson
AP® European History Teacher
AP® European History Exam Selector
Covenant Day School
Matthews, North Carolina

Jody Janis
AP® European History Teacher
J. Frank Dobie High School
Houston, Texas

Mark Klopfenstein
AP® European History Teacher
Palmer Ridge High School
Monument, Colorado

Ken LeSage
AP® European History Exam Table Leader
College Board Certified Consultant
Lewis-Palmer High School
Monument, Colorado

Jamie Oleson
AP® World History Teacher
Rogers High School
Spokane, Washington

Lenore Schneider
AP® National Leader
New Canaan High School
New Canaan, Connecticut

Clara Webb
AP® European History Exam Table Leader
Boston Latin School
Boston, Massachusetts

Pam Wolfe
AP® European History Consultant
Yeshiva of Greater Washington
Silver Spring, Maryland

Contents

UNIT 3 — Absolutism and Constitutionalism c. 1648 to c. 1815

UNIT 4 — Scientific, Philosophical, and Political Developments c. 1648 to c. 1815

UNIT 5 — Conflict, Crisis, and Reaction in the Late 18th Century c. 1648 to c. 1815

UNIT 6 — Industrialization and Its Effects c. 1815 to c. 1914

Preface

AMSCO Advanced Placement® European History provides a concise narrative, skills instruction and practice, multiple-choice questions, short-answer questions, long essay questions, and document-based questions designed to help students understand the significant content and develop the vital skills needed to master the subject. It can be used in classes as either the core textbook or along with other resources.

For teachers, an Answer Key is available from the publisher. It also includes correlations to standards identified by the College Board.

Upon publication, *AMSCO Advanced Placement® European History* was up to date with all standards and guidelines published by the College Board. For the latest information on Advanced Placement® European History courses and the exam, check the European history section of apcentral.collegeboard.com and advancesinap.collegeboard.org.

EUROPE TODAY

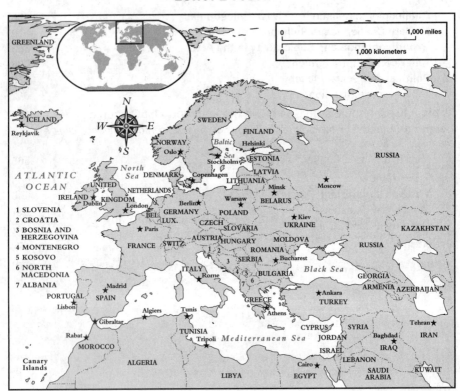

Introduction

Studying Advanced Placement® European History

Enrollment in AP® courses such as this one has grown over the years. Students cite many reasons they want to take courses such as AP® European History:

- They provide evidence that the student has the ability to succeed as an undergraduate.
- They increase eligibility for scholarships.
- They help strengthen a student's college applications.
- They help reduce college expenses by earning college credit.
- They allow students to test out of introductory college courses.
- They reflect the fact that AP® students have better college graduation rates.
- They help enrich students' high school experience.

The placement and credits offered will vary from college to college. The College Board's website provides a comprehensive list of colleges and universities that accept AP® examinations and the credits they award for passing scores.

Most students who take AP® courses report that they are more challenging than regular courses; they also report that AP® courses are more interesting and gratifying. The rewards of taking on the challenges of an AP® program go beyond the scores and placement. They include the development of lifelong reading, reasoning, and writing skills, as well as an increased enjoyment of history.

This introduction will provide you with background information that will help you understand the structure of the AP® European History exam.

Overview of the AP® European History Exam

This textbook was created to prepare you for the current AP® European History exam. The exam emphasizes the history practices and reasoning skills used by historians, with a strong focus on themes and related concepts to help deepen your understanding of European history. It includes readings, images, and other data sources and requires 3 hours and 15 minutes to complete. The AP® European History exam will include the components shown in the table on the following page.

SECTION	QUESTION TYPE	NUMBER OF QUESTIONS	TIMING	PERCENTAGE OF TOTAL EXAM SCORE
I	Part A: Multiple-choice questions	55 questions	55 minutes	40%
	Part B: Short-answer questions	3 questions: • Required Question 1: 1600–2001 • Required Question 2: 1600–2001 • Required Question 3: c. 1450–c. 1815 OR Question 4 c. 1815–present	40 minutes	20%
II	Part A: Document-based question	1 question: topics from 1600–2001	60 minutes (includes a 15-minute reading period)	25%
	Part B: Long essay question	1 question, chosen from three options on the same theme but different time periods: • 1450–1700 • 1648–1914 • 1815–2001	40 minutes	15%

Source: *AP® European History Course and Exam Description.*

Each of these exam components will be explained in this introduction, along with a guide to sequential skill development. AP® examinations, including the European History exam, score student performance on a five-point scale:

- 5: Extremely well qualified
- 4: Well-qualified performance
- 3: Qualified
- 2: Possibly qualified
- 1: No recommendation

An AP® score of 3 or higher is usually considered evidence of mastery of course content similar to that demonstrated in a college-level introductory course in the same subject area. However, the requirements of introductory courses may vary from college to college. Many schools require a 4 or a 5.

The AP® exams are built differently than typical classroom tests. For example, the developers of the AP® exams want to generate a wider distribution of scores. They also want higher reliability, which means a higher likelihood that test takers repeating the same exam will receive the same scores.

In addition, AP® exams are scored differently. The cutoff for a "qualified," or level 3, score varies from year to year depending on a multitude of factors.

The writers of the AP® exam also design it to be more difficult. If you take a practice exam before you have fully prepared for the test, don't be surprised if you have difficulty with many of the questions. More importantly, don't be discouraged. AP® European History is challenging. But like many challenges, people can master it by breaking it down into manageable steps.

How This Book Can Help

The goal of this textbook is to provide you with the essential content and instructional materials needed to develop the knowledge and the historical reasoning and writing skills needed for success on the AP® European History exam. You can find these in the following parts of the book:

- *Introduction* This section introduces the practices and historical reasoning skills, seven course themes, and four chronological periods of the history program. A step-by-step skill development guide provides instruction for answering (1) the multiple-choice questions; (2) the short-answer questions; (3) the document-based question; and (4) the long essay question.

- *Concise History* The 9 units (88 topics) of essential historical content and accessible explanation of events are the heart of the book.

- *Maps and Graphics* Maps, charts, graphs, cartoons, photographs, and other visual materials also are integrated into the text to help students practice analytical skills.

- *Historical Perspectives* Each unit includes one section that introduces significant historical issues and conflicting interpretations.

- *Key Terms* To assist reviewing, each topic ends with a list of key terms listed in order of appearance.

- *Multiple-Choice Questions* Each topic contains 3 multiple-choice questions to assess your historical knowledge and skills using a variety of sources.

- *Short-Answer Questions* Each topic contains a three-part short-answer question to provide practice writing succinct responses.

- *Document-Based Questions* Each unit includes a DBQ for practice.

- *Long Essay Questions* Each unit contains a long essay question.

- *Practice Examination* Following the final unit, the book includes a complete practice examination.

- *Index* The index is included to help locate key terms for review.

A separate Answer Key is available for teachers and other authorized users of the book and can be accessed through the publisher's website.

The Study of AP® European History

Historians attempt to give meaning to the past by collecting historical evidence and then explaining how this information is connected. They interpret and organize a wide variety of evidence from primary sources and secondary texts to understand the past. AP® European History should develop a student's ability to think like a historian: to analyze and use evidence and to deal with probing questions about past events. Often there is no one "answer" for such questions any more than one historical source can provide a complete answer for a question. AP® teachers and readers are looking for the student's ability to think about history and to support ideas with evidence.

AP® candidates should appreciate how both participants in history and historians differ among themselves in their interpretations of critical questions in European history. Each unit of this book includes one or more Historical Perspectives features to introduce some of the issues debated by historians. The AP® European History exam does not require an advanced knowledge of historiography—the study of ways historians have constructed their accounts of the past. Some people refer to historiography as "the history of history." Nevertheless, prior knowledge of the richness of historical thought can add depth to your analysis of historical questions.

Students planning to take the AP® European History exam also need to become familiar with and then practice the development of (1) historical thinking skills and reasoning processes, (2) thematic analysis, and (3) the concepts and understandings of the nine units that provide the organization of the content. These three components of the course are explained below for orientation and future reference.

Don't become overwhelmed with this introduction or try to comprehend all the finer points of taking the AP® exam in the first few days or weeks of studying. Mastery of these skills and understandings takes time and is an ongoing part of the study of AP® history. This introduction will become more helpful as a reference after you have studied some historical content and have begun to tackle actual assignments.

Historical Thinking Skills and Reasoning Processes

The study of AP® European History includes three basic components that shape the course: (1) the thinking skills and reasoning processes of history, (2) thematic analysis, and (3) the concepts and understandings of the nine units that organize the content. These three components are explained below for orientation and future reference.

How Historians Think

The Advanced Placement® History courses encourage students to think like historians. The practices and skills that historians use in researching and writing about historical events and developments are the foundation of the AP® European History course and exam. Learning these skills and reasoning processes can be developed over a course of study, but an introduction to them is a good place to start.

- Historians need to be able to **analyze historical evidence** found in a wide variety of **primary sources** from written records to historical images and artifacts. Historians also need to explain and evaluate the evidence from **secondary sources**, especially the work of other historians with differing points of view.

- As historians research the evidence, they look for **connections** and patterns among historical events and developments. They use reasoning processes, such as making **comparisons**, studying **causation**, and analyzing **continuity and change** to find and test possible connections.

- Most historians communicate their findings through publications and presentations. This creative process takes the additional practice of **argument development**, which includes making a defensible claim and marshaling relevant and persuasive evidence to support an argument. Writing about history also challenges one to clarify and refine one's thinking about the subject or the question under study.

Historical Thinking Skills

The study of history includes the use of many thinking skills. Of these, AP® courses focus on six.

1. **Developments and Processes** The ability to identify and explain historical concepts, developments, and processes is fundamental to the analysis of historical evidence. For example, "the Age of Enlightenment" has proved a useful concept to describe the period during the 18th century when enlightened ideas and thoughts began to spread throughout the continent. Students need to be able to explain the historical concepts and developments and provide specific historical evidence to illustrate or support such a historical concept or development. For example, a multiple-choice question on the AP® exam might ask "Which of the following is a result of new ideas during the Enlightenment?"

2. **Sourcing and Situation** The use of historical evidence involves the ability to explain and evaluate diverse kinds of primary and secondary sources, including written works, data, images, and artifacts. Students need to be able to explain (1) the historical setting of a source, (2) its intended audience, (3) its purpose, and (4) the point of view of the original writer or creator. For example, an AP® exam question might ask "Which of the following best reflects the point of view expressed by the author?" Another possible question is "Briefly explain ONE characteristic of the intended audience for this image."

    For secondary sources, this skill also involves understanding how particular circumstances might influence authors. Historians can "rewrite" history because their personal perspective or society's perspective changes, because they discover new sources and information, and above all, because they ask new questions.

3. **Claims and Evidence in Sources** The analysis of either primary or secondary sources also includes the ability to identify the author's argument and the evidence used to support it. For example, an AP® question might provide short quotations from two secondary sources about the causes of the French Revolution. The reading might be evaluated by a multiple-choice question such as "Which of the following would best support the argument of historian A?" A short-answer question might ask "Briefly explain ONE major difference between historian A's and historian B's historical interpretations." Questions can also ask students to discover patterns or trends in quantitative data found in charts and graphs.

4. **Contextualization** The skill of contextualization involves the ability to accurately and explicitly explain how a historical event, policy, or source fits into the broader historical picture, often on the regional, national, or global level. Placing the specifics of history into their larger context gives them additional usefulness and significance as historical evidence. Contextualization is evaluated through questions such as this: "[The excerpt] best reflects which of the following developments during the Renaissance?" or "The conditions shown in the image depict which of the following trends in the late 19th century?"

5. **Making Connections** This skill involves identifying and analyzing patterns and connections between and among historical developments and processes, and how one development or process relates to another. Making connections on the AP® exam will use the three reasoning processes of comparisons, causation, and continuity and change (see below). For example, liberalism, nationalism, socialism, and communism were growing in importance during the same period in the late 19th century. Are any patterns and connections common among these developments? The exam could ask an essay question such as this: "Evaluate the extent to which the spread of liberal ideas contributed to the growth of nationalism."

6. **Argumentation** Developing an argument includes the skill of using evidence effectively to make a point. Students need to recognize that not all evidence has equal value in support of a position. Writers need to select examples that are accurate and relevant to their argument. Making judgments about the use of relevant historical evidence is an essential skill in free-response questions on the AP® exam.

   Again, the focus of the question will be not on the simple recall of facts but on a conceptual understanding of the evidence and the ability to link that understanding to the argument. For example, to support the argument about the impact of technology from 1848 to 1914, it is not enough to describe the technologies of the period. In addition, one should explain the connection of specific new technologies, such as railroads or electric power, to the changes in the economy. The AP® exam also values the use of diverse and alternative evidence to qualify or modify an argument in order to develop a more complex insight into history.

Reasoning Processes

The study of history includes the use of several reasoning processes. Of these, AP® courses focus on three very important ones.

1. **Comparison** Thinking about comparison involves the ability to describe and evaluate similarities and differences between two or more historical developments. The developments might be in the same era or in different ones. This process also asks one to explain the relative significance of similarities and differences between historical developments and to study a given historical event or development from multiple perspectives.

    The ability to make a comparison is evaluated in questions such as "The ideas expressed in the excerpt were most similar to those of which of the following?" or "Evaluate the most significant difference between the unification of Italy and the unification of Germany." Expect AP® questions to test similarities and differences of conceptual understandings rather than simple recall.

2. **Causation** The study of causation is the primary tool of historians to explore the connections—both causes and effects—among events. Historians are often challenged to make judgments between primary and secondary causes and between short-term and long-term effects for developments such as the French Revolution or World War I.

    Students will need to not only identify causes and/or effects but also explain the relationship between them. For example, it will not be enough to state that either incompetent government policies or increases in bread prices led to the French Revolution. One must be able to explain the connections of specific evidence to one's position. At the AP® level, a causation question might ask "Which of the following most strongly influenced A?" or "B contributed most directly to which of the following trends?" The use of causation as a reasoning process is used with all historical thinking skills.

3. **Continuity and Change** The study of history also involves the ability to describe and explain patterns that reveal both continuity and change over time. The study of themes especially lends itself to discovering continuity and change in varying lengths of time from a few decades to hundreds of years.

    For example, one might argue that the role of women greatly changed during the 20th century because they gained political rights, had increased education, and attained executive positions in the corporate world. The AP® exam might evaluate the understanding of continuity and change by asking "Which of the following developments best represents the continuation of A?" or "Which of the following best represents a later example of the change B?" A more complex essay question can ask "Evaluate the extent to which C changed during D." Responding to this item involves understanding not only an event but also its significance in longer trends in European history.

Course Themes

Each AP® European History exam question also is related to one or more of seven course themes. These seven themes will help you think about the main ideas in European history. The themes include the study of interactions with the natural environment, the development and interaction of cultures, the building and expansion of states as well as the resulting conflict, the dynamics of economic systems, and the development and change of social structures and gender roles. Each theme covers cross-period and cross-cultural investigations. They help identify trends and processes that have developed throughout centuries in different parts of Europe and the world.

Each topic in this book includes Key Terms—a review list of important names, places, events, and concepts used in that topic. The entries in the Key Terms lists are arranged by the order in which they appear in the topic.

Theme 1: Interaction of Europe and the World (INT)

This theme focuses on Europe's growing interaction with the broader world after 1450. It focuses on the motivations that led to these interactions as well as the consequences for both non-European and European societies. The possible motivations were many, including the desire for economic gain, the broadening of each European nation's power, and the spread of Christianity. The consequences were even more numerous and wide ranging—and often devastating.

In the Americas, Europeans established colonies that would fundamentally and permanently alter both continents' people and societies. Civilizations were toppled, land was expropriated, and populations were decimated. Africa was profoundly affected by the European takeover of the Americas because millions of Africans were captured and sold into bondage to work on colonial plantations. Europeans, too, were affected by the interaction of peoples, cultures, and environments. Many left to live abroad, never to return. The exchange of foods and goods between the new and old worlds changed how Europeans lived irrevocably.

European colonialism and imperialism developed and spread throughout Asia and Africa in the 19th and 20th centuries, fueling resistance by subject peoples and competition among the European colonial powers.

Theme 2: Economic and Commercial Developments (ECD)

This theme explores the ways in which the new global commercial network, developed and dominated by Europeans, eventually led to profound impacts on the continent's social and political systems. The commercial wealth that resulted from colonization fueled a further economic revolution in the 17th and 18th centuries. The growth of large-scale agriculture during this era also led to significant change, including a rise in European populations and a gradual shift in populations from rural to urban.

Over time, these changes resulted in rising levels of material prosperity for some Europeans, particularly in the era of technological advances after 1850. But this prosperity was distributed unequally, with often-stagnant working-class wages and the exploitation of workers and resources from the less-developed world. These inequalities gave rise to ideologies such as socialism that sought greater equality through the reform, or even replacement, of the capitalist system.

Theme 3: Cultural and Intellectual Developments (CID)

This theme explores the ways in which knowledge has been created and transmitted throughout European history. Beginning in the 15th century, thinkers in multiple fields of inquiry tentatively began to question traditional sources of authority and knowledge, substituting a belief in direct inquiry and subjective truths.

With the advent of the Enlightenment in Europe, however, growing numbers of Europeans adopted a view of the world based on natural laws and objective scientific truths in place of traditional and religious beliefs. This led eventually to a blossoming of scientific and mathematical knowledge and the application of scientific methods to social and political issues and systems. The 20th century saw another shift, from a belief in objective knowledge and truths to the exploration of subjective paradigms and irrational forces (especially in psychology).

Theme 4: States and Other Institutions of Power (SOP)

This theme focuses on the cultural, economic, and social impact of changes within European government and social institutions over time. The rise of sovereign states and the success of the Protestant Reformation signaled a shift away from traditional church power and toward secular and state control of many societal and governmental institutions.

Intellectual, political, and social aspects born of the Enlightenment fueled movements away from monarchies and aristocracies and toward the rule of law and representative governments. The participation of everyday people in governance, chiefly through broadening suffrage, increased over time. However, mass politics and the political and economic crises of the early 20th century combined to fuel the rise of totalitarian regimes at the expense of parliamentary governments. The latter half of the century saw the rise of international (the UN and NGOs) and European (EEC and EU) organizations designed to promote worldwide and regional stability.

Theme 5: Social Organization and Development (SCD)

This theme focuses on changes to family and societal classes and groups across Europe. Movements such as the Protestant Reformation and the Industrial Revolution had massive consequences for European society. How and when people got married and started families changed, as did how those families functioned. Women's roles evolved markedly, with women seeking greater economic and legal rights by the 19th century. The development of middle and working classes fundamentally changed how people related to one another at home and otherwise.

World War I brought an end to the remnants of the old order as empires were disbanded and democracy expanded. After World War II, welfare states developed in Western Europe, providing increased family support, reproductive choices, and universal health care. The end of the Cold War brought about the EU, which, while highlighting the shared values of European society, has experienced difficulty particularly over the question of immigration.

Theme 6: National and European Identity (NEI)

This theme examines how Europeans' ideas of cultural, national, and regional identity have evolved over time. Early modern European identity was based on cultural elements such as shared language, history, and location, and it could be manifested in anything from a city-state to a small principality to an emerging nation-state.

While great 17th- and 18th-century monarchs built powerful nations around cultural and linguistic ties in places like France and Russia, England's continued growth was accompanied by the rise of an increasingly powerful Parliament. The ideas of the Enlightenment and the French Revolution gave rise to a European sense of shared values, based around citizenship, reason, and equality.

The growing sense of nationalism in the 19th century brought together new nations (Italy, Germany, and the Netherlands) but also served as a divisive force in multiethnic states, such as the Habsburg Empire. This nationalism carried through the 20th century, leading to the century's great conflicts and the eventual rise of independent nations and greater political fragmentation. This process was reversed, in a way, by the rise of the EU. But recent struggles within the EU show that European identity is ever changing.

Theme 7: Technological and Scientific Innovation (TSI)

This theme focuses on the positive and negative effects of technological and scientific innovations. The Renaissance ushered in new ways of thinking that led to a tremendous transformation in political-diplomatic actions, socioeconomic development, and cultural-intellectual life that continued through the 21st century.

The invention of the printing press in the 15th century radically changed Europe leading to increased literacy, the growth of strong centralized governments, the end of religious uniformity, and the Scientific Revolution.

This pattern continued and advances in technology and science contributed to increased life expectancy and standard of living as well as lower childhood mortality rates. Despite the positive demographic changes that occurred, new innovations also contributed to the horrors of industrialized warfare and the nuclear arms race.

Historical Periods

AP® European History also is based on a framework of four historical periods. According to the College Board, the instructional importance and assessment weighting for each period is equal. These periods are briefly described below, and each description includes the units of the book that address each period's content.

Period 1: c. 1450 to c. 1648 (Units 1–2) The period from the Renaissance to the Peace of Westphalia deals with the growth of science, mathematics, art, and philosophy in Europe. It also examines changes and conflicts brought about by major events and trends such as the Protestant Reformation, the Catholic Counter-Reformation, the overseas expansion of European power, and the Columbian Exchange. During this period, power in Europe was increasingly centralized and secular, and power also was increasingly open to men of talent and wealth, not just those who belonged to the hereditary nobility.

Period 2: c. 1648 to c. 1815 (Units 3–5) The period from the Peace of Westphalia to the Congress of Vienna deals with growth in Europe in a number of different avenues. In politics, a balance of power system between European states emerged and was generally challenged only when one or another state sought to upset the balance. (Revolutionary and Napoleonic France represent major upsets of the system.)

Overall economic strength and individual standards of living grew as well, particularly in Atlantic countries. Further, the Scientific Revolution and the Enlightenment altered Europeans' ways of thinking as reason increasingly challenged religion and literacy grew.

Period 3: c. 1815 to c. 1914 (Units 6–7) The period from the Congress of Vienna to the beginning of World War I saw industrialization grow and spread throughout Europe. This led to the growth of specific social classes, particularly the proletariat (working class) and the bourgeoisie (middle class). Rapid population growth and urbanization also followed, bringing their own challenges. During this period, responses to socioeconomic change led to increased liberalism and nationalism, eventually resulting in the revolutions of 1830 and 1848. Although most of the revolutions were quelled by authorities, liberalism and nationalism continued to grow even more after 1848.

Rising nationalism helped promote and consolidate state power, and led to the unification of both Germany and Italy. This nationalism spurred further imperial actions, and as a result, Africa was partitioned and came under the domination of European powers. At the same time, European emigrants sought better lives, chiefly in the Americas, and brought their cultures with them.

Period 4: c. 1914 to Present (Units 8–9) The period from the beginning of World War I to the present was dominated by conflict, namely the two world wars and the Cold War. Great areas of Europe were devastated by war and tens of millions of people, mostly civilians, perished. Nazi Germany's genocidal Holocaust alone marks the 20th century as a grim period in European history. The problematic resolution of World War I led to resentment in Germany and elsewhere, where fascist dictatorships arose. The Great Depression of the early 1930s also helped fuel dissatisfaction and anger.

After World War II, a more internationalist perspective emerged along with a more unified Europe, which culminated in the European Union. The union grew after the end of the Cold War as some former Soviet satellite countries joined. Nonetheless, there has been increased nationalism since the end of the Cold War resulting in regional wars in the former communist areas, and European Union members continue to balance national sovereignty with membership. Britain recently withdrew from the European Union.

In general, the nations of Europe became more secular and their governments became increasingly involved in citizens' economic lives. New Europeans—migrants from former colonies and world conflict zones—added diversity to the continent's culture and bolstered populations in a period of low birth rates. However, these immigrants often found inhabitants unwilling to accept them, and questions of social justice and identity remain.

Answering the AP® Exam Questions

History, like any field of study, is a combination of subject matter and methodology. The history practices, reasoning skills, and themes are methods or tools to explore the subject matter of history. One cannot practice these skills without knowledge of the historical content and understanding of specific historical evidence. The following section provides suggestions for development of another set of skills useful for answering the questions on the AP® exam. Again, the "mastery" of these skills, particularly writing answers to AP® questions, takes practice. This section will suggest how to develop the skills related to each different kind of question on the exam:

- multiple-choice questions
- short-answer questions
- document-based questions
- long essay questions

Answering the Multiple-Choice Questions

The College Board asks 55 multiple-choice questions (MCQs) on the AP® European History exam, and students have 55 minutes to complete this section. The value of the MCQs will be 40 percent of the student's score, and each MCQ will assess a historical reasoning skill and also will require historical knowledge from the Concept Outline of AP® European History. Questions will be related to the analysis of a stimulus—a primary or secondary source, such as a passage, image, map, or table.

Each question will have one best answer and three distractors. The questions will emphasize the ability to analyze the source and use the historical reasoning skill the question requires.

This textbook provides preparation for the multiple-choice questions section of the exam through items at the end of each topic and on the Practice Exam at the end of the book. The MCQs in this book are similar in form and purpose to those appearing on the AP® exam but also are designed to review the content and understanding of the topic.

Analyzing the Stimulus On the AP® exam, multiple-choice questions will be introduced with a stimulus. When analyzing a stimulus, ask yourself basic questions to spark your thinking: Who? What? When? Where? and Why? Beyond these questions, one of the most important questions to ask is "What is the point of view of the author, artist, or speaker?" Consider the following excerpt from the Nuremberg Charter, which defined war crimes and laid the foundation for trials following World War II:

> The following acts . . . are crimes coming within the jurisdiction of the Tribunal for which there shall be individual responsibility:
>
> . . . *Crimes against humanity:* namely, murder, extermination, enslavement, deportation, and other inhumane acts committed against any civilian population, before or during the war, or persecutions on political, racial or religious grounds in execution of or in connection with any crime within the jurisdiction of the Tribunal, whether or not in violation of the domestic law of the country where perpetrated.

The multiple-choice questions about this excerpt will test your understanding of it. (Answering this question will be easier after you have studied the World War II era.) In addition, the questions will focus on one or more historical reasoning processes. The following are topics of multiple-choice questions that could be asked about this excerpt:

- *Causation:* Why does the definition of "crimes against humanity" include the phrase "whether or not in violation of the domestic law of the country where perpetrated"?

- *Continuity or change over time:* Is the establishment of a postwar court to try officials of defeated nations an example of continuity or change?

Making a Choice You need to read the stem (the question or statement before the choices of possible answers) of any MCQ and all four choices carefully before you choose your answer. More than one choice may appear to be correct at first, but you must select the best answer. If you are not immediately confident which answer is best, start by eliminating answers you recognize as incorrect. Choices that include words that reflect absolute positions, such as always, never, or exclusively, are seldom correct, since historical evidence can rarely offer such absolute certainty. Keep in mind the need to make judgments about the significance of a variety of causes and effects.

Should you guess on the AP® exam? Yes: The exam format does not penalize for guessing, and points are not deducted for incorrect answers. So you should answer every question. Obviously, though, the process of first eliminating a wrong answer or two before guessing increases your chances of choosing the correct answer.

Budgeting Your Time The AP® European History exam allows 55 minutes to answer the 55 questions. Fifty-five minutes does not allow enough time to spend 2 or 3 minutes on difficult questions. For questions involving a passage, chart, or picture, read the question first. If you find a question is hard, make a guess and then come back to it later if you have time.

Recommended Activities Practicing sample multiple-choice questions is important before the exam, if for no reason other than to reduce the number of surprises about the format of the questions. However, for many students, the review of content through multiple-choice questions is not the most productive way to prepare for the exam. The purpose of the topic content in this text is to provide a useful and meaningful review of the essential concepts and evidence needed for the exam. By reviewing the essential facts in the historical content, you will better recall and understand connections between events, which is extremely important for applying the historical reasoning skills.

Answering the Short-Answer Questions

The AP® European History exam will include four SAQs. You will have 40 minutes to answer three of them.

Short-Answer Question	Required	Primary Practice or Skill Assessed	Stimulus	Time Period
1	Yes	Analyzing secondary sources	Secondary source	1600–2001
2	Yes	Analyzing primary sources	Primary source text or visual source	1600–2001
3	Either 3 or 4	Unspecified historical developments or processes	No stimulus	1450–1815
4	Either 3 or 4	Unspecified historical developments or processes	No stimulus	1815–2001

Source: AP® European History Course and Exam Description

Each question consists of three parts (labeled a, b, and c). A single part might ask for either ONE or TWO examples. No thesis is required. The following is a sample stimulus and question:

"In capitalist society we have a democracy that is curtailed, wretched, false, a democracy only for the rich, for the minority. The dictatorship of the proletariat, the period of transition to communism, will for the first time create democracy for the people, for the majority, along with the necessary suppression of the exploiters, of the minority."

— *The State and Revolution*, Vladimir Lenin, 1917

1. a) Describe one <u>similarity</u> between the ideas and actions of Vladimir Lenin prior to and during the Russian Revolution with those of the ideas and actions of Robespierre during the French Revolution

   b) Describe one <u>difference</u> between the ideas of Vladimir Lenin prior to and during the Russian Revolution withthose of the ideas and actions of Robespierre during the French RevolutionExplain a difference between the long-term effects of the French Revolution and the long-term effects of the Russian Revolution of 1917.

   c) Explain a difference between the long-term effects of the French Revolution and the long-term effects of the Russian Revolution of 1917.

Answering the Document-Based Question (DBQ)

The AP® European History exam consists of one document-based question (DBQ) that includes seven documents. It will focus on a topic from between 1600 and 2001. You will be given 60 minutes to answer the question, which includes 15 minutes for reading the documents.

For details on how responses are scored, see the Course and Exam Description. In short, you should state a clear thesis and provide support for it from the documents. To receive a top score, you will need to refer to at least six of the documents in your analysis. To strengthen the probability of earning the maximum point value for this question, however, use all seven documents. In addition, you should analyze one or more of these elements of three documents:

- the creator's point of view
- the creator's purpose
- the historical situation when the document was produced
- the intended audience for the document

Some teachers refer to this analysis of the elements as "sourcing" the document. Earning credit for sourcing a document requires more than a simple statement such as "The intended audience is the elite class." You also will need to state the significance of this analysis. In other words, give a reason or further explanation of the significance for the point of view, purpose, historical situation, or intended audience. To determine significance, ask yourself, "What is the creator's point of view?" "Why did the creator produce the document?"

"In what historical situation was the document created?" "What audience was the creator addressing?" The answers to these questions often are overlapping. Besides using evidence stated in the documents, you should include outside knowledge in your response. This consists of additional examples, details, and analysis that provide context or clarify what is in the documents or that provide new information that supports your thesis.

Answering a DBQ builds on the skills for writing responses to the essay questions. (These are discussed in more detail in the following section on the long essay question.) The same skills apply here:

- Write a thesis statement that addresses all parts of the question.
- Provide historical context for your argument.
- Build argumentation supported by relevant specific evidence.
- Use the historical reasoning skill targeted in the question.
- Use evidence in a compelling way.

The most important difference between a DBQ response and a long essay is that your DBQ response should refer to specific sources to support arguments. This sample DBQ prompt illustrates how important it is to identify and address all parts of the prompt. Read it closely.

Evaluate whether or not World War I greatly changed the role of women in Europe.

An effective answer will address the reasoning process and period: continuity and change in Europe during and after World War I.

A common mistake writers make in answering a DBQ is to write little more than a descriptive list of the documents. The order of the documents in the DBQ should not control the organization of the essay. Rather, group the documents based upon how they support your thesis. Analyze the documents for evidence they provide, and integrate them into an organized and persuasive essay.

In a strong essay, a writer groups pieces of evidence from the documents that relate to each other. However, grouping requires more than simply placing related evidence within the same paragraph. It also requires seeing commonalities and contradictions in the evidence and explaining how they both fit your argument:

- Words and phrases such as *similarly, in addition,* and *as well as* alert the reader that you see a common element among the documents.
- Phrases such as in *contrast to* or *this is different from* alert the reader that you see contradictory evidence in the documents.

As you use this textbook, you will find a DBQ in the review section at the end of each unit and another one in the Practice Exam at the end of the book. Use these practice DBQs to develop your historical reasoning skills as well as the writing skills needed for answering the DBQ on the exam.

Here are some tips for writing an effective DBQ:

1. Use the 15-minute reading period to make margin notes on the documents. Underline key parts of the prompt to help keep you on track. Before writing, formulate a thesis that addresses all parts of the question. The key historical reasoning skills to be developed for the successful writing of a DBQ answer are contextualization, comparison, causation, and continuity and change over time.

2. Keep references to the documents brief. Because the exam readers know the content of the documents, you do not need to quote them. A reference to the document's author or title is enough. Many writers simply cite the document number in parentheses, such as (Doc. 1). Readers like this system as well because it is simple and clear.

3. Use all of the documents. (The scoring guidelines call for students to use all or all but one of the documents.) However, recognize that each document represents a point of view, and some might contain information that is not accurate.

4. Address contradictory evidence. Your thesis should be complex enough to account for evidence that does not support your argument, and you should demonstrate that you understand other points of view and the context in which the documents were created. Demonstrate your judgment about the sources based on your knowledge of the historical period.

Recommended Activities As a prewriting activity for the DBQs, work with a small group of classmates to read and discuss a contemporary primary source document and two historical ones. For each, discuss the author's point of view, intended audience, purpose, and historical context.

Following is a practice scoring guide for DBQs based on the College Board's grading rubric. (Check apcentral.collegeboard.com for the full rubric and any updates.) Use this guide to evaluate your work and to internalize the criteria for writing a strong DBQ essay.

Practice Scoring Guide for the Document-Based Question

A. **Thesis: 0–1 Point**

- 1 point for a historically defensible thesis/claim that establishes a line of reasoning to address the question and does not merely restate it. The thesis must be at least one sentence and located in one place, either in the introduction or in the conclusion.

B. **Contextualization: 0–1 Point**

- 1 point to describe the broader historical context of the question, such as developments either before, during, or after its time frame. Describing the context requires more than a mere phrase or reference.

C. **Evidence: 0–3 Points**

   Evidence from the Documents: 0–2 Points
- 1 point for accurately describing the content of **three documents** that address the question.

   OR (Either the 1 point above or the 2 points below, but not both)

- 2 points for accurately describing the content of **six documents** and using them to **support the arguments** used in response to the question. Using the documents requires more than simply quoting them.
   Evidence Beyond the Documents: 0–1 Point
- 1 point for using at least one additional piece of specific historical evidence **beyond** those found in the documents that is relevant to the arguments for the question. The evidence must be different from evidence used for the contextualization point and more than a mere phrase.

D. **Analysis and Reasoning: 0–2 Points**

   (Unlike the long essay question scoring, both points can be gained)
- 1 point for using at least **three documents** to explain **how or why** the document's point of view, purpose, historical situation, and/or audience is relevant to an argument used to address the question.

- 1 point for demonstrating a **complex understanding** of the historical developments by analyzing the multiple variables in the evidence. This can include analyzing more than one cause, both similarities and differences, both continuity and change, and/or the diversity of evidence that corroborates, qualifies, or modifies an argument used to address the question.

Answering the Long Essay Question (LEQ)

Test takers will answer one of three questions with a long essay in 40 minutes. All three options will focus on the same theme and reasoning skill, but they will focus on different periods. The first will focus on Period 1, the second on Periods 2 and 3, and the third on Periods 3 and 4. Before you begin to write, take 5 to 10 minutes to identify key points and plan the structure of your essay. Your essay responses will be evaluated on the argument you present: provide a clear evaluative thesis and support it with evidence.

Development of Essay Writing Skills Begin developing your writing skills as soon as the course starts. Rather than simply writing and rewriting complete essays, break down the skills needed to write an effective AP® history essay into sequential steps and work on one of them at a time. Following are basic steps in writing an essay:

1. Analyze the question.

2. Organize the evidence.

3. Take a position and express it in a thesis and introductory paragraph.

4. Write the supporting paragraphs and conclusion.

5. Evaluate the essay.

1. Analyze the Question Some students rush to start writing and fail to grasp the question fully. Before writing, ask yourself two questions:

- What is the topic?
- What is the historical reasoning skill?

Read over the question or prompt two or more times. What are the key words or phrases in the question? Underline them. They could be verbs such as *evaluate, analyze, explain, support,* or *refute.* All questions have one thing in common: They demand the use of historical reasoning skills and analysis of the evidence. An essay answer will not receive full credit by simply reporting information: You need to demonstrate that you can use the targeted historical reasoning skill. For example, consider this sample long essay question:

Evaluate the reasons why Great Britain began industrializing in the mid-18th century, before any other country.

Note all of the parts of the prompt. What is the topic? Industrialization in Great Britain. What is the historical reasoning process? Causation. What does the prompt ask you to do? Evaluate reasons. What type of evidence do you need to provide? It must be significant and it must include an evaluation of the causes. An essay that fails to deal with all parts of the question will receive a lower score than one that addresses the entire question. The few seconds you take to identify the topic and key reasoning skills will help you avoid the mistake of writing a clear, information-rich essay that receives little or no credit because you answered a question that was not asked.

Recommended Activity As an initial skill-building activity, analyze the essay questions at the end of Period 1. Underline the key words that indicate what the writer should do, and circle the words that indicate the specific parts or aspects of the content that need to be addressed.

2. Organize the Evidence Directions for the AP® European History exam advise students to spend some time planning before starting to answer the essay question. This advice emphasizes how critical it is to first identify what you know about the question and then organize your information. A recommended practice is to spend five minutes to create a brief outline, table, or other graphic organizer summarizing what you know about the question. The following table shows one way to organize the information that could become the essay to answer the question about the Industrial Revolution in Great Britain.

WHY DID GREAT BRITAIN LEAD THE INDUSTRIAL REVOLUTION?	
Geographic Factors	**Nongeographic Factors**
Massive coal deposits, coal used to • power steam engines • boost iron/steel production Coal industry itself became huge	Investment capital accumulated during trans-Atlantic slave trade
An island nation, Britain's strong maritime tradition bolstered • importation of raw materials • export of finished goods	Well-established British legal system protected investors and private property
Enclosure movement eliminated most common farmlands • forced farmers off land and into cities • created low-cost industrial workforce	Agricultural Revolution improved diets, reducing infant mortality and prolonging lives • workers were healthier and could work more efficiently • population (number of industrial workers) grew
Network of rivers and streams for powering mills and transporting goods	Technological improvements • spinning jenny and water frame • gave rise to the factory system

Recommended Activity Practice identifying the type of evidence you will need to answer questions by creating an outline, table, Venn diagram, or other graphic organizer for each of the questions in Units 1 to 3.

3. Take a Position and Express It in the Thesis and Introductory Paragraph After you see the evidence that you know, you can write a thesis statement that you can support. A strong thesis, or argument, is an essential part of every AP® European History long essay answer. Writers usually state the thesis in the first paragraph (sometimes the second), and they often restate it in the final paragraph or final two paragraphs. A thesis must be more than a restatement of the question.

A thesis requires taking a position on the question. In other words, it must be evaluative. Many students have difficulty taking a position necessary to build a strong argument. Some are afraid of making a mistake. But think about the nature of history. History does not offer the certitude of mathematics or the physical sciences. Disagreement over the interpretation of historical evidence develops because of the limitations of the evidence available and the differing perspectives of both participants and historians. AP® readers are looking not for the "right answer" but for a writer's ability to interpret the evidence and use historical support for that interpretation. Consider this important advice for any AP® essay question: If you think that you can write an essay without making some judgment that results in a thesis statement, you have not understood the question.

Below is one example of a thesis statement based on the information in the table on the previous page.

Between 1750 and the early 19th century, Britain became the first European state to industrialize because it had a unique combination of geographic and political advantages, including access to coal, capital, workers, technology, shipping, and a supportive government.

This statement takes a position—Britain had unique characteristics—and it identifies causation for the events raised in the question. This interpretation will provide the organizing argument that guides the development of the essay.

Recommended Activity Work with one or two partners. Each of you should write a prompt that might appear on a test based on a current event in the news. Exchange prompts. Then write a thesis statement in response to your partner's prompt. Compare and discuss your thesis statements using these guide questions:

- Does the thesis take a position?
- Does the thesis offer an interpretation of the question?
- Does the thesis help organize ideas for an essay?

The main point of the first paragraph is to clearly state a thesis that addresses the question. Readers will look for a clear thesis that sets the organization for the rest of the essay. An effective introductory paragraph also may provide the context of the question and a preview of the main arguments that will be developed in the subsequent paragraphs. However, this additional information should not distract from the thesis statement.

You may have learned to write an argumentative five-paragraph essay: a one-paragraph introduction, three paragraphs of support, and a one-paragraph conclusion that ties back to the introduction. This model shows the importance of the introductory paragraph in shaping the full essay, including the arguments to be developed. However, the total number of paragraphs in your AP® essay is for you to determine. You are likely to need more than three paragraphs of support.

Recommended Activity Practice writing introductory paragraphs for the essay questions at the end of each unit. Next, follow up the introductory paragraph with an outline of the supporting paragraphs. For each paragraph, list historical evidence that you will link to the thesis. The exercise of writing an introductory paragraph and an outline of your supporting paragraphs helps in two ways. First, it reinforces the connection of the main points in the introduction to the supporting paragraphs. Second, it requires you to think in terms of historical evidence before you start writing a complete essay.

4. Write the Supporting Paragraphs and Conclusion The number and lengths of the paragraphs forming the body of the essay will vary depending on the thesis, the main points of your argument, and the amount of historical evidence you present. To receive the highest score, you also must explain how specific historical evidence is linked to the thesis. Each essay also will have a targeted historical reasoning skill that you should use to analyze the historical development or process you identified in your thesis. The chart that follows shows the main focus of an essay based on key words in the prompt.

Key Words in the Question	What an Essay Should Do
Cause, causation	Describe, analyze, and evaluate reasons why something happened, using specific examples.
Compare, comparison	Describe, analyze, and evaluate specific examples that show similarities and differences.
Continuity and change over time	Describe, analyze, and evaluate similarities (representing continuity) and differences (representing change across time) with specific examples.
Describe, identify	Describe or identify a significant, specific example of the essay topic.
Explain, analyze, evaluate	Identify and comment on the nature and relationship of the parts of a topic in order to explain why things happened.
Contextualization	Describe, analyze, and evaluate the extent to which other specific, relevant events influenced historical developments or process.

Besides your ability to address the targeted reasoning skill, your essay will be assessed on how well you develop your argument. Readers will consider how well you use specific historical evidence, recognize the historical context, and include evidence from outside the theme and time period of the question prompt. For example, in the sample question, the context of the Age of Discovery and the colonial markets it created is essential to understanding the industrialization of Britain.

Your goal is not to fill a specific number of pages but to write an insightful, persuasive, and well-supported answer. Many students fail to achieve the full potential of their essay because they simply list a few generalities or a "laundry list" of facts, and they do not answer the full question. Keep in mind that the readers of your essay are not looking for a retelling of history, or "stories." They will be grading you on your ability to craft an analytical essay that supports an argument with specific evidence. A short yet concise essay in which every word has a purpose is better than an essay bloated with fillers, flowery language, and interesting stories.

Your conclusion should restate the thesis. In addition, it should answer the larger question of "So what?" That is, the conclusion should provide the context and explain why the question is relevant in a broader understanding of history.

General Writing Advice Here are some tips to keep in mind as you start practicing the writing of history essays for the AP® exam:

- *Write in the third person.* Avoid using first-person pronouns (I, we). Write your essay in the third person (it, they, she, etc.).

- *Write in the past tense.* Use past tense verbs, except when referring to sources that currently exist (e.g., the document implies).

- *Use the active voice.* Readers prefer the active voice over the passive voice because it is more effective in explaining cause and effect. For example, "Factories were built in Britain" is in the passive voice. It is weak because it fails to say who built the factories. "Wealthy investors built factories in Britain" is in the active voice. It is stronger because it states who was taking action.

- *Use precise words.* Use words that clearly identify persons, factors, and judgments. Avoid vague verbs such as felt. Use stronger verbs instead such as insisted, demanded, or supported. Also, avoid vague references, such as they and others, unless you are clearly referring to people already identified. Use specifics, such as Louis XVI of France. Use verbs that communicate judgment and analysis, such as reveal, exemplify, demonstrate, imply, and symbolize.

- *Explain key terms.* The majority of questions will deal with specific terms (such as Agricultural Revolution or mercantilism), and an essential part of your analysis should be an explanation of these terms.

- *Anticipate counterarguments.* Consider arguments against your thesis to show that you are aware of opposing views. The strongest essays confront conflicting evidence by explaining why it does not undercut the thesis. The statement of counterarguments is known as the concession or the conciliatory paragraph. Writers often present it directly following the introduction.

- *Remain objective.* Avoid opinionated rhetoric. The AP® test is not the place to argue that one group was the "good guys," while another was the "bad guys." And do not use slang terms such as "bad guys"!

- *Communicate your organization.* Each paragraph in your essay should develop a main point that is clearly stated in the topic sentence. It is also good practice to provide a few words or a phrase of transition to connect one paragraph to another. Each paragraph also should include a sentence that links the ideas in the paragraph to the thesis statement.

- *Return to the thesis.* Writers often restate their thesis in the final paragraph in a fresh and interesting manner or explain its significance. The conclusion should not try to summarize all the data or introduce new evidence. If you are running out of time but have written a well-organized essay with a clear thesis that is supported with evidence, your conclusion can be very short. As noted earlier, including your thesis in the first and the last paragraph helps you make sure you have stated it clearly.

Recommended Activity Your first effort to write an AP® European History essay will be a more positive experience if it is an untimed assignment. After gaining confidence in writing the essay, you should try your hand at a timed test similar to that of the AP® exam (40 minutes for the essay). The purpose of such practice is to become familiar with the time constraints of the exam and to learn ways of (1) improving the clarity as well as the efficiency of your writing and (2) gaining insight into the type of information needed. The feedback from these practice tests—whether from teachers, peers, or self- evaluation—is essential for making progress.

5. Evaluate Your Essay More essay writing does not necessarily produce better essays. Breaking down the process into manageable steps is one key for improvement. Peer evaluation as well as self-evaluation also can help you internalize the elements of an effective essay and learn ways to improve. The activity on the next page provides a set of questions about how effectively an essay achieves the elements that the AP® readers look for in their grading. The use of the essay-evaluation techniques can help AP® candidates better understand the characteristics of an excellent essay.

Activity: Evaluation of the Essay

1. **Introductory Paragraph** Underline the thesis and circle the structural elements identified in the introduction. How effectively does the introductory paragraph prepare the reader for the rest of the essay? How might you improve the introductory paragraph?

2. **Thesis** Is the thesis clear? Does it take a position and address all parts of the question?

3. **Analysis** Does the body of the essay provide analysis of the question? Does the body reflect the argument and controlling ideas stated in the introductory paragraph? Does the body acknowledge opposing points of view? How could the analysis be improved?

4. **Evidence** Is the thesis supported clearly with substantial, relevant information? Is the evidence clearly connected to the stated thesis through strong paragraph topic sentences? What significant additional information or evidence could have been used for support?

5. **Errors** What minor or major errors in fact or analysis does the essay display?

6. **Presentation** How well organized and persuasive is the essay? Do the supporting paragraphs and their topic sentences address all parts of the essay prompt and stated thesis? Does paragraph composition, sentence

structure, word choice, or spelling add to or detract from the essay? Identify areas that need improvement.

Recommended Activity Evaluation by a teacher and self-evaluation of essay work is initially less threatening than peer evaluation, but once a level of confidence is established, peer evaluation can help you become a better writer and is often the most useful form of feedback.

This scoring guide for the long essay question is based on the College Board's grading rubric. (Check apcentral.collegeboard.com for the full rubric and any updates.) Use the guide to evaluate your work and internalize the characteristics of a strong long essay.

Practice Scoring Guide For Long Essay Questions

A. Thesis: 0–1 Point

- 1 point for a historically defensible thesis/claim that establishes a line of reasoning to address the question and not merely restate it. The thesis must be at least one sentence and located in one place, either in the introduction or in the conclusion.

B. Contextualization: 0–1 Point

- 1 point to describe the broader historical context of the question, such as developments either before, during, or after its time frame. Describing the context requires more than a mere phrase or reference.

C. Evidence: 0–2 Points

- 1 point for identifying specific historical examples of evidence relevant to the question.

OR (Either the 1 point above or the 2 points below, but not both)

- 2 points for using specific and relevant historical examples of evidence that support the arguments used to address the question.

D. Analysis and Reasoning: 0–2 Points

- 1 point for using historical reasoning to frame or structure the arguments that address the question, such as causation, comparison, or continuity and change over time. Reasoning may be uneven or not as complex as needed to gain two points.

OR (Either the 1 point above or the 2 points below, but not both)

- 2 points for using historical reasoning and demonstrating a complex understanding of the historical developments by analyzing the multiple variables in the evidence. This can include analyzing more than one cause, both similarities and differences, both continuity and change, and/ or the diversity of evidence that corroborates, qualifies, or modifies an argument used to address the question.

Review Schedule

Plan how you will prepare to take the AP® European History exam. Set a schedule for your review of each period of history. You might spread your review over a long or a short amount of time. Many AP® candidates find that study groups are helpful. The following is a sample of a review schedule using this text. It assumes the review will take place over six weeks:

- Week 1: Review writing skills
- Week 2: Period 1 (Units 1–2)
- Week 3: Period 2 (Units 3–5)
- Week 4: Period 3 (Units 6–7)
- Week 5: Period 4 (Units 8–9)
- Week 6: Complete and review the Practice Exam

Staying with a schedule requires discipline. A study group that chooses a specific time and place to meet and sets specific objectives for each meeting can reinforce the discipline of all its members. Some individuals may find it more productive to create a review schedule for themselves. If this review text has been used in conjunction with a history course, your familiarity with the essential content and skills developed in this book should make it an even more convenient and efficient review tool.

UNIT 1: Renaissance and Exploration
c. 1450 to c. 1648

Topic 1.1

Contextualizing Renaissance and Discovery

Essential Question: What was the context for the development of the Renaissance and Age of Discovery?

The Roman Empire provided most of Europe with unity and order that promoted trade, transportation, and art and scholarship until its fall in the early 5th century. The resulting disunity from its fall led to a period called the Middle Ages, which had no significant scientific achievements, no great works of art, and few noteworthy leaders. During this time, there was no government or entity that united the people of Europe. Rather the dominant culturally unifying force was the Roman Catholic Church, which exerted a conservative and rigid influence on European society at all levels. The church supported the feudal system of noble lords who owned land and their serfs who were bound to the land and whose lives and labor were largely controlled by the lords.

Several important developments in Europe paved the way for a loosening of the grip of both the church and feudal system:

- The Crusades made the exchange of ideas between European and Islamic scholars possible.

- The massive population declines from the Black Death destroyed Western European serfdom by drastically improving the bargaining power of peasants.

By the 1300s, however, changes in European society signaled a new era of thought, reason, and artistic expression that came to be known as the Renaissance (which means "rebirth"). Beginning in Italy, a resurgence in the study of Classical learning, arts, and values—those of Greek and Roman antiquity—took hold and eventually spread. Over time, this movement would act as a catalyst for fundamental changes in how Europeans produced art, developed technology, farmed, traded, and governed.

Rediscovery of the Classical and Natural Worlds The great rebirth in Europe known as the Renaissance was marked by important transitions. Europe emerged from the Middle Ages to a time of increasing individualism and nonreligious (although not antireligious) scholarship inspired by classical Greek and Roman writing and culture.

Technological innovations also helped spur advances during the Renaissance. Inventions, such as the printing press, helped further new approaches to scholarship that challenged previously established institutions, such as the Catholic Church. As Europe rediscovered so much of its own past and reconnected with the natural world, education began a shift toward some nonreligious avenues and the classics.

Exploration and Territorial Expansion This new, more open way of thinking also encouraged Europeans of the Renaissance to think beyond their own physical borders. Developments in navigation and cartography led to the establishment of overseas colonies, expanded trade networks, and connections among cultures.

Nations that were once bound to their country's borders established vast empires in other parts of the world, searching for gold, spices, and other goods. In these far-flung empires, exchanges of some greatly beneficial plants and animals occurred. However, the exchange of diseases would prove devastating to indigenous people. Another tragic outcome of exploration and colonization was the trade in enslaved Africans.

Despite the waning influence of the Church during this period, Christianity was still a significant impetus for such vast exploration. European explorers and missionaries attempted to spread Christianity to the native populations, even if it had to be done coercively.

Commercial and Agricultural Capitalism Changes in farming and commerce affected economic systems and also impacted social structure. For many Europeans, daily life still revolved around the changing seasons as they farmed and worked at the will of the lord in the manor. Agricultural developments and the growth of a money economy allowed for a shift to larger-scale farming over time. Advances in banking and finance contributed to the success of urban financial centers and the rise of a new economic elite class of merchants and bankers.

Struggle for Sovereignty Financial innovations during the Renaissance also helped pave the way for the modern state. Political leaders began to streamline tax collection and to use newly expanded military powers to redraw boundaries. This strain led to fragmentation throughout Europe and marked the beginning of centuries of struggles for territory and sovereignty.

ANALYZE THE CONTEXT

1. Explain how colonization impacted both citizens of Europe as well as indigenous populations in other parts of the world.

2. Describe how the shift from the Middle Ages to the Renaissance affected the European economy.

Topic 1.2

Italian Renaissance

The noblest pleasure is the joy of understanding.

—Leonardo da Vinci (1452–1519)

Essential Question: How did the revival of classical texts contribute to the development of the Italian Renaissance?

Essential Question: What were the political, intellectual, and cultural effects of the Italian Renaissance?

Beginning in the mid-1300s, Europe entered a period of transition between the Middle Ages and the modern world. Since the 19th century, historians have called this period the **Renaissance**, from a French word meaning "rebirth."

During the Renaissance, many intellectuals showed a renewed interest in the civilizations of Greece and Rome during the **classical era**, roughly 800 B.C.E. to 500 C.E. Scholars of the 15th century first used the term *Middle Ages* to mean the period between the end of the classical era and their own time.

The Renaissance began in northern Italy and spread throughout Europe. It was a time when scholars began to break free of the religion-based thinking of medieval times toward a belief in human dignity and limitless potential.

Revived Interest in the Classical World

Throughout the Middle Ages, monks had preserved and studied many classical texts in monasteries throughout Europe. Yet during the Renaissance, the revived interest in classical texts took a new form. One major change was that many Renaissance scholars were not members of the clergy. In addition, they approached the texts in new ways.

group of religious officials

Italian Renaissance Humanists

Renaissance intellectuals who studied classical civilization and its texts were later called **humanists** because they focused on human beings and their inherent dignity. Humanists began to break free of the medieval philosophy known as scholasticism, which focused on Roman Catholicism and religious inquiries, such as proving the existence of God.

Shift in Ideas about Religion Although humanists remained Christians, they tended to emphasize different values than did medieval scholars. The content of classical texts was **secular**, or worldly, rather than religious.

Humanists emphasized living a good earthly life rather than a life of penance (sorrow for or action to atone for sins) aimed toward an afterlife. In addition, there was growth of **individualism,** or a focus on personal rather than religious or political interests.

Petrarch One of the earliest humanists, sometimes called the Father of Humanism, was an Italian poet and scholar named **Petrarch** (1304–1374). He saw the Middle Ages as a period of darkness when knowledge of classical civilization was in decline. (Later historians would call this time the Dark Ages.)

A lover of language, Petrarch searched for forgotten Latin manuscripts in monastery libraries and private collections of the wealthy throughout Europe. One key discovery was *Letters to Atticus* by the Roman statesman and orator **Cicero** (106 B.C.E.–43 B.C.E.), which gave insights into political life in classical Rome. Petrarch, followed by many later humanists, adopted Cicero as a model for writing in Latin. Though he appreciated Latin, Petrarch was among the first scholars of his era to write in the Italian **vernacular,** or everyday language of his region.

Stemming from his work with ancient manuscripts, Petrarch developed new **philological** approaches, or scholarly methods of analyzing texts with a focus on the history of language. One famous use of philology occurred in 1440 when **Lorenzo Valla** demonstrated that an important Roman Catholic document, the *Donation of Constantine*, supposedly written by the Emperor Constantine in the 4th century, was a forgery, because its language was not the 4th-century Latin the emperor would have used.

Petrarch also admired Cicero's life as an engaged citizen. As a humanist, Petrarch focused on how people behaved. He criticized medieval thinkers who focused more on scholarly issues of logic than on everyday concerns of ethics.

Marsilio Ficino Another important Italian Renaissance humanist was **Marsilio Ficino** (1433–1499). In a similar way to how Petrarch intensely studied Latin and the works of Cicero, Ficino studied Greek and the works of Plato (c. 428 B.C.E.–c. 348 B.C.E.). Ficino connected Plato's philosophy to more recent Christian theology. He translated Plato's known writings into Latin, and scholars used those translations for hundreds of years.

Ficino was interested in the idea of Platonic love—an intense, spiritual love that is unconcerned with money, power, or romance. "Artists in each of the arts seek after and care for nothing but love," Ficino wrote. To finance his studies and translation projects, Ficino had the backing of the rich and politically powerful Medici family. (See Topic 1.5 for more about the Medici family.)

Pico della Mirandola The goal of **Giovanni Pico della Mirandola** (1463–1494) was to take philosophical views (often competing views) and blend them. This goal was made possible by his remarkable education, which saw him study philosophy and languages (including Greek, Hebrew, and Arabic) in the major learning centers of the day: Paris, Bologna, Padua, and Florence. His famous humanist work "Oration on the Dignity of Man" wove together many ideas from other and earlier schools of thought to describe his idea of the place of humans and their relationship to God in the order of the world.

New Connections, New Challenges

Many classical Greek texts in philosophy and science had nearly disappeared in Europe during the Middle Ages. However, Arabic-speaking Islamic scholars in the Middle East, North Africa, and Spain preserved these works. These scholars had translated the works into Arabic, and from Arabic into Latin.

As Europeans came into increased contact with the Islamic world during the Crusades of the 12th century, the texts again became available in Europe. However, since books were still copied by hand at that time, access to them was limited.

After the invention of the printing press around 1450, many more copies of books were available. With the spread of books and literacy, the dominance of universities and the Catholic Church over intellectual life declined. Classical texts and new methods of scientific inquiry, rather than theological writings, became the focus of education.

Changes in Education Scholars in the 15th century expanded the revival of interest in Greek and Roman texts to include literature, drama, and history. These works had been unavailable or of little interest to medieval scholars who were primarily concerned with theological questions. During the 15th century, the liberal arts (areas of study required for general knowledge rather than for specific professional skills, such as becoming a lawyer or church official) of the Middle Ages began to be called the humanities. Humanists were known as teachers of the humanities. The chart shows that despite some similarity in medieval and Renaissance higher education, there was a different emphasis.

LIBERAL ARTS CURRICULUM AT EUROPEAN UNIVERSITIES	
Medieval Universities, c. 13th century	Renaissance Universities, c. 15th century
• Grammar • Logic • Arithmetic • Geometry • Astronomy • Music • Rhetoric (guiding an audience to a specific conclusion)	• History • Moral philosophy • Eloquence • Letters (grammar and logic) • Poetry • Mathematics • Astronomy • Music
Instructors read aloud from Latin texts because few books were available.	Students were required to know Classical Latin and Greek to read those works directly.

Humanists believed that education could help people achieve their full human potential and would prepare them to be active, productive citizens. Therefore, they created secondary schools to teach the humanities to students at younger ages. In addition, while universities continued to focus on traditional fields of study, they also began to include the humanities. The goal for humanists was not the preparation of scholars in theology, law, or medicine, but the development of an individual who excelled in many areas. A few women of the period, such as Isotta Nogarola, also trained as humanists. However, most scholars and all Catholic priests were male.

Many important thinkers of the time enthusiastically supported increased study of ancient Greek and Latin texts:

- **Leonardo Bruni** translated Greek and Latin works and wrote biographies of poets from the 1300s.

- Leon Battista Alberti (1404–1472) wrote books in Italian so that a broad range of people would understand them. Like Petrarch, Alberti was strongly influenced by Cicero.

- Niccolò Machiavelli (1469–1527) studied the works of the Roman historian Livy.

Challenges to the Catholic Church As popes became more concerned with their political and financial power and with secular Renaissance culture, they lost some of the spiritual authority they once held. This shift happened at the same time many Christian humanists, especially in northern Europe, began to focus on texts of the early Catholic Church. These humanists advocated a return to a simpler and more humane form of Christianity. They criticized religious practices that they believed were not based on Scripture.

Revival of Civic Humanist Culture

In the 15th century, a single, unified country did not control the Italian peninsula. Instead, it was a collection of small regional kingdoms and self-governing communities called **city-states**. Large city-states, such as the northern Italian cities of Florence, Venice, and Milan, also controlled the surrounding regions. Some of the city-states were ruled by local dukes and others by powerful families. Invasions by French, Spanish, and Germanic forces only added to the political instability and rivalry among city-states.

Greek and Roman Political Institutions As humanists studied classical texts, they developed renewed admiration for Greek and Roman political institutions. For example, the city-state itself was the common form of government in classical Greece, with Athens and Sparta as the two best-known examples. Athens had been the site of the birth of **democracy**, government in which the people hold power either directly or by electing representatives. The Roman Republic was a **representative government**, or one elected by and representative of the people.

Roman politicians such as Cicero became secular models of active, engaged citizenship and eloquent leadership. Humanists saw in the classical examples a **civic humanist culture** that they sought to promote in their own era.

Baldassare Castiglione One secular model for individual behavior by the aristocratic class came from a writer in Milan. **Baldassare Castiglione** (1478–1529) wrote *The Book of the Courtier* (1528), which outlined how to act as a proper gentleman or lady. The book remained influential for centuries. According to Castiglione, the ideal courtier, or person who often spent time at the court of a ruler, was similar to a medieval knight but was also classically educated, skilled in the arts, and engaged in civic life by serving that ruler. He also wrote about the ideal female courtier, who was educated, a patron of the arts, and above all helped her husband to rise to his fullest potential.

Niccolò Machiavelli In 1498, **Niccolò Machiavelli** began serving as a diplomat for the republic of Florence, thus also becoming familiar with French and German politics. While earlier generations of diplomats had represented the Christian empire, Machiavelli observed that Renaissance diplomats worked on behalf of their own states.

The early 16th century was a time of violence and instability in Florence. In 1512, a shift in political power caused the exile of Machiavelli and others who supported a republic. Hoping to demonstrate his insight and persuade another leader to hire him, Machiavelli turned to political writing.

Machiavelli's most famous work, *The Prince* (1513), provided advice for rulers. The book is still required reading in many high schools today. Unlike medieval political teachings that focused on morality, *The Prince* separated politics from morality. Perhaps written as a satire on contemporary Italian politics, *The Prince* stressed the need for an absolute ruler to use any means to achieve political unity and independence from foreign control.

Machiavelli presented a cynical view of human nature that required the prince to be feared rather than loved. This secular approach was contrary to Christian beliefs about the importance of love. He emphasized maintaining the power of the state to provide citizens with peace and safety. To create and maintain stability, Machiavelli explained, leaders often had to commit acts such as lying and bribery but should still appear virtuous. A leader unwilling to act in such ways would weaken the state and lose power.

In a later work, *The Discourses* (1531), Machiavelli pointed to the Roman Republic as a model of a government under law, rather than under an authoritarian prince. Yet, whether Machiavelli himself favored republicanism or despotism (the exercise of oppressive and absolute power), his ideas were influential. The principles for achieving and maintaining power in *The Prince* became a guide for later authoritarian regimes. *The Prince* has become identified with the belief that "the ends justify the means," or that any methods, however evil or dishonest, may be used to achieve positive results. People still use the word *Machiavellian* to mean ruthless and crafty.

Francesco Guicciardini Machiavelli's friend and neighbor **Francesco Guicciardini** (1483–1540) also wrote about politics and government. However, his works were based on his own extensive real-life experiences as a governor, a representative of two popes, and a lieutenant general. Guicciardini shared Machiavelli's dark view of human nature. He once wrote, "There is nothing so fleeting as the memory of benefits received."

Religion, philosophy, and politics were all vital to this period. Yet when most people think of the Italian Renaissance, they think of paintings, sculptures, and other works of art.

Renaissance Ideas in the Visual Arts

The revived interest in classical civilizations affected the visual arts just as it had affected other aspects of Renaissance culture. Artists of the Middle Ages had emphasized religious messages rather than realistic portrayals of their subjects. Paintings lacked depth and often had odd proportions. Renaissance artists, however, studied examples of classical art, and along with the influence of humanist ideas, brought a fresh emphasis and style to the visual arts. Renaissance artists promoted not only religion, but also personal, political, and religious goals of the artists and their patrons.

In addition to using classical themes and styles and focusing on human beings, Renaissance painters and sculptors incorporated new techniques and trends in their work. In contrast to the heavy use of symbolism in medieval painting, Renaissance artists tried to be more realistic in two ways:

- As artists observed the natural world more closely, they began to aim for **naturalism** in their works. Artists wanted to imitate nature.

- Artists mastered the technique of **geometric perspective**, which used mathematics to help them create the appearance of space and distance in two-dimensional paintings.

Artistic developments in the city-states of Italy led the way in the development of Renaissance art and architecture.

Source: Getty Images

Medieval paintings, such as this one of Mary holding Jesus, often appear flat and somewhat out of proportion (left). This Renaissance painting of Mary, the mother of Jesus, shows the depth and complexity of art from that period (right).

The Medici Family and Florence

Italian Renaissance patrons of the arts were rulers and popes who commissioned works of art mainly to increase their own prestige. Among the most prominent of these patrons were members of the Medici family, which controlled Florence for decades. Their commissions of paintings, sculptures, and architecture made Florence the early center of much of the greatest Renaissance art.

For example, Cosimo de' Medici commissioned **Filippo Brunelleschi** (1377–1446) as architect for the rebuilding of the Church of San Lorenzo in Florence. The church reflects the influence of Roman architecture with its use of classical columns and rounded arches. Further, it is built to a more human scale than medieval Gothic cathedrals. Brunelleschi also incorporated into the church the largest dome built since classical Rome. This engineering feat exemplifies the Renaissance ideal of reaching one's potential.

The cathedral in Cologne shows the impressive scale and complexity of Gothic churches (left). The Church of San Lorenzo reflected the human-scale church architecture during the Renaissance (right).

Cosimo de' Medici's grandson, Lorenzo de' Medici (ruled Florence 1469–1492), kept a large group of artists at his court, including Sandro Botticelli (1445–1520). Botticelli's famous painting from 1482, *Primavera (Spring),* displays the artist's interest in classical mythology, featuring the figures of Venus, Cupid, Flora, and Mercury.

Italian Sculpture and Painting

In the late 15th century, Rome was quickly becoming the prominent artistic center of Europe. Several Italian painters and sculptors dominated the period and continue to influence artists today.

Donatello One of the greatest Italian Renaissance artists, **Donatello** (c. 1386–1466) sculped in marble and bronze. He often used ancient sculptures as inspiration, but he had his own distinctive style. Donatello created a new type of sculpture. Instead of three-dimensional panels that a viewer could walk around from all angles, he sculpted marble panels that were shallow and yet gave the illusion of depth. The faces on Donatello's sculptures were far more detailed and expressive than sculptures created by artists of the Middle Ages.

Source: Wikimedia Commons

The Last Supper was a fresco painted by Leonardo da Vinci between 1495 and 1498.

Leonardo da Vinci The remarkable range of talent is a defining characteristic of **Leonardo da Vinci** (1452–1519). He studied nature and conducted experiments, dissected human bodies to learn more about their structure, and drew designs for machines that were far ahead of his time.

Leonardo urged artists to move beyond the earlier emphasis on realism to a portrayal of human beings that reflected their idealized or divine qualities. Two of his most famous paintings are the portrait *Mona Lisa* and *The Last Supper*, a **fresco**, or wall painting using watercolor on wet plaster. *The Last Supper* demonstrates Leonardo's mastery of geometric perspective (the representation of three-dimensional objects in two-dimensional art) as well as his skill at depicting idealized human figures with psychological insight.

Michelangelo Another renowned Italian sculptor, painter, architect, and poet was **Michelangelo** (1475–1564). In 1501, the government of Florence commissioned (paid) him to create the marble sculpture *David*, in which he portrays the biblical figure of David to reveal the splendor of the human form.

Michelangelo is probably best known for his painting the ceiling of the Sistine Chapel in the Vatican, which was commissioned by the pope. In the paintings, Michelangelo focused on scenes from the biblical book of Genesis, showing humans as reflections of the divine. In this commission and others, including plans to rebuild St. Peter's Basilica in Rome, the pope sought to revitalize the prestige of the papacy and the Papal States, the lands in central Italy that the pope ruled from 756 to 1870.

Raphael The painter **Raphael** (1483–1520) created many paintings of the Virgin Mary that idealized her beauty. In 1508, Pope Julius II commissioned Raphael to paint a series of frescoes in the Vatican Palace. Perhaps the most famous is *School of Athens*. In this work, Raphael portrayed a gathering of classical scholars, including Aristotle and Plato, using geometric perspective and other Renaissance techniques to demonstrate harmony, balance, and order—all principles central to both classical and Renaissance art. Because of these artists and others, many experts consider the Italian Renaissance a period of tremendous innovation and creativity.

In *School of Athens* (painted c. 1510–1511), Raphael created an image of almost perfect balance. The viewer's eye tends to go to the two central figures, the ancient Greek philosophers Plato and Aristotle.

Architecture of the Italian Renaissance

Unlike architects of later periods, Italian Renaissance architects often excelled in many subjects besides architecture. Many modern buildings have features that echo the design of structures from this artistic period.

Leon Battista Alberti Mathematics fascinated **Leon Battista Alberti**. His book *On Painting* transformed visual arts in Italy because it explained how to make a two-dimensional image look three-dimensional.

Alberti was also a skilled architect. He looked to classical architecture for inspiration, just as he looked to classical literature to inspire him in his writing. He designed Santa Maria Novella, which still stands in Florence. The front of the building mimics ancient Roman temples.

Alberti's creation, Santa Maria Novella (left), has similar elements to classical Roman temples (right).

Andrea Palladio Author and sculptor, **Andrea Palladio** (1508–1580), was known for creating many palaces. He visited Rome and measured its ancient structures. Like Alberti, Palladio created buildings that looked similar to ancient Roman architecture but were adapted to the materials and needs of his time period.

REFLECT ON THE ESSENTIAL QUESTIONS

Essential Question: *How did the revival of classical texts contribute to the development of the Italian Renaissance?*

Essential Question: *What were the political, intellectual, and cultural effects of the Italian Renaissance?*

Contributions of Classical Texts	Effects of Classical Texts

KEY TERMS

Renaissance	Marsilio Ficino	naturalism
classical era	Giovanni Pico della Mirandola	geometric perspective
humanists		Filippo Brunelleschi
secular	Leonardo Bruni	Donatello
individualism	city-states	Leonardo da Vinci
Petrarch	democracy	fresco
Cicero	representative government	Michelangelo
vernacular	civic humanist culture	Raphael
philological	Baldassare Castiglione	Leon Battista Alberti
Lorenzo Valla	Niccolò Machiavelli	Andrea Palladio
	Francesco Guicciardini	

Questions 1–3 refer to the passage below.

"The foundations of all true learning must be laid in the sound and thorough knowledge of Latin: which implies study marked by a broad spirit, accurate scholarship, and careful attention to details...Without it the great monuments of literature are unintelligible, and the art of composition impossible. . . .

But we must not forget that true distinction is to be gained by a wide and varied range of such studies as [lead] to the profitable enjoyment of life. . . .

First amongst such studies I place History: a subject which must not on any account be neglected by one who aspires to true cultivation...For the careful study of the past enlarges our foresight in contemporary affairs and affords to citizens and to monarchs lessons of incitement or warning in the ordering of public policy. . . .

The great Orators of antiquity must by all means be included. Nowhere do we find the virtues more warmly extolled, the vices so fiercely decried. . . .

I come now to Poetry and the Poets. For we cannot point to any great mind of the past for whom the Poets had not a powerful attraction."

—Leonardo Bruni, *On Learning and Literature*, c. 1405

1. The passage most clearly shows the influence of which development?
   (A) The use of the scientific method to critique traditional knowledge
   (B) The development of mandatory systems of public education
   (C) A renewed interest in classical Greek and Roman texts
   (D) The increase of publications questioning papal authority

2. The methods of learning described in this passage reflected most directly which change in thinking?
   (A) Political revolutions based on the idea of natural rights
   (B) The application of geometrical perspective in art and architecture
   (C) New ideas about government and individual behavior
   (D) A shift in emphasis from religious to secular ideas

3. Based on the information in the passage, which word most accurately describes Bruni's intellectual interests?

(A) Humanism

(B) Scholasticism

(C) Despotism

(D) Naturalism

SHORT-ANSWER QUESTION

Use the passage below to answer all parts of the question that follows.

"But since my intent is to write a thing that is useful for whoever understands it, it seemed to me more appropriate to go after the effectual truth of the thing than the imagination of it. And many have imagined republics and principalities that have never been seen or known to exist in truth. For there is such a distance from how one lives to how one ought to live that he who abandons what is done for what ought to be done learns what will ruin him rather than what will save him, since a man who would wish to make a career of being good in every detail must come to ruin among so many who are not good. Hence it is necessary for a prince, if he wishes to maintain himself, to learn to be able not to be good, and to use this faculty and not to use it according to necessity.

Thus, leaving behind the things that have been imagined about a prince, and discussing those that are true, I say that all men, when they are spoken about, and especially princes, because they are placed higher, are noted for some of the following qualities, which bring them either blame or praise. That is to say that one man is held liberal, one a miser; one is held a giver, one rapacious [greedy]; one cruel, one compassionate. The one is held a breaker of faith, the other faithful; the one effeminate and pusillanimous [timid], the other fierce and spirited . . ."

—Niccoló Machiavelli, *The Prince*, 1513

1. a) Describe ONE argument the author makes regarding the methods a ruler should use to achieve political goals.

b) Explain how Machiavelli's argument was influenced by classic Greek and Roman political beliefs.

c) Explain how the writings of Machiavelli and other Humanists challenged traditional political beliefs.

Topic 1.3

Northern Renaissance

. . . so sweet a thing it is not to be wise, that on the contrary men rather pray against anything than folly.

— Desiderius Erasmus, *Praise of Folly*, 1509

Essential Question: How were Renaissance ideas developed, maintained, and changed as the Renaissance spread to northern Europe?

Renaissance humanism and art spread to the regions north of the Alps in the late 15th century in a movement known as the **Northern Renaissance**. Northern humanists focused more on religion than their counterparts of the Italian Renaissance. The naturalism of their art was more human-centered, and artists often showed ordinary individuals and scenes from everyday life. In addition, some artists in the north were less focused on the beauty of the human form and realistic settings and more on rendering exquisite details in smaller works, such as illuminated manuscripts and altarpieces painted on wooden boards. Like many Italian Renaissance artists, Northern Renaissance artists depended on wealthy patrons to buy their art and support their work.

Possibly influenced by Renaissance ideas, Christians started to become critical of the growing secular spirit of the Church. They wanted to restore what they considered purer Christian practices.

Visual Arts in the Northern Renaissance

Flanders, a region in what is now part of France and Belgium, became the leading center of art in the north in the 15th century. Northern artists observed nature closely in order to depict details accurately, but they did not display the skill of Italian artists in the use of perspective and proportion. After the spread of Protestantism in northern Europe, the number of religious works of art declined.

Albrecht Dürer To improve his skills, the German master **Albrecht Dürer** (1471–1528) traveled to Italy to study in 1494. He even exchanged works of art with Raphael. In addition to paintings, Dürer created prints and woodcuts. In a woodcut, the artist carves an image into a block of wood and then uses ink and paper to reproduce the image on paper.

Jan van Eyck One of the first artists to excel at the new medium of oil painting was **Jan van Eyck** (c. 1390–1441). He signed many of his paintings with the notation "As best I can."

Van Eyck's painting *Arnolfini Portrait* (1434) is believed to be of a wealthy merchant and his wife. The portrait shows home furnishings, clothing, and even a pet. These details help us understand how some people lived during this period in history.

Pieter Bruegel the Elder Another Northern Renaissance artist was Flemish (from Flanders) artist **Pieter Bruegel the Elder** (1525–1569). He painted scenes from the Bible and scenes from the lives of peasants—ordinary people who worked the land. Like Dürer, Bruegel traveled to Italy to learn more about the techniques employed by artists there, especially Raphael.

Pieter Bruegel the Elder's oil painting *Peasant Wedding* (c. 1567) shows a celebration by peasants of the 16th century.

Rembrandt A painter from a slightly later time, **Rembrandt** (1606–1669), was a Baroque artist, which means he created bold, dramatic, complex artworks. (See Topic 2.7 for more about Baroque art.) Rembrandt's most famous (and largest) painting is *The Night Watch*, which shows soldiers getting ready to defend a city.

Today, people remember Rembrandt for his dramatic use of light and shadow and his dedication to realism—which some of his critics called ugliness.

Source: Wikimedia Commons

This 1657 self-portrait of Rembrandt includes light and deep shadows. It shows him realistically instead of trying to make him look more handsome or younger than he actually was.

In response to his critics, Rembrandt said, "Life etches itself onto our faces as we grow older, showing our violence, excesses, or kindnesses."

Christian Humanists Seek Religious Reform

The growing Renaissance interest in secular matters strongly affected the Roman Catholic Church in Europe. The desire for fine art and material wealth caused the Church to be a patron for painters, such as Michelangelo, and to build grand cathedrals. Thus, in the view of reformers, many church officials had turned away from their true religious responsibilities. In response to this and other practices, **Christian humanists** called for religious reform. Their motto was *"Ad fontes"* ("back to the source"). Christian humanists began reading the Bible in Greek and Hebrew and studying writings of early Christian leaders.

Erasmus Pleads for Reform One of the best representatives of Christian Humanism was the Dutch scholar **Desiderius Erasmus**. He received a traditional education as well as a new liberal arts education at the University of Paris.

Erasmus called for literate people to read the Bible themselves. He encouraged the reading of the New Testament in Greek, Latin, and Hebrew in order to understand its original meaning. With a deep understanding of Roman Catholic teachings, Erasmus began writing extensively about the need for reform. Particularly important was his book *Praise of Folly* (1509). In the title, Erasmus used folly to mean foolishness. In it, he satirized the lack of knowledge among much of the clergy and the focus of the papacy on money and power rather than spiritual concerns.

While Erasmus called for reform, he feared splintering the Roman Catholic Church. Although Erasmus agreed with concerns raised by another church critic, Martin Luther, he felt Luther's manner was too harsh and his action too defiant. (See Topic 1.4 for more about Martin Luther.)

Thomas More Calls for a Utopia An English Christian humanist and close friend of Erasmus's, **Thomas More,** studied at the University of Oxford. This helped him gain government positions such as a member of Parliament and advisor to Henry VIII, king of England. In 1516, More wrote the book *Utopia* about an imaginary land that possessed a perfect, orderly society. Calling for the creation of a more just society, More argued in favor of education for women and abolition of private property.

Essential Question: *How were Renaissance ideas developed, maintained, and changed as the Renaissance spread to northern Europe?*

Characteristics of the Northern Renaissance	Renaissance Reflected in Religious Reform

KEY TERMS

Northern Renaissance
Albrecht Dürer
Jan van Eyck

Pieter Bruegel the Elder
Rembrandt
Christian humanists

Desiderius Erasmus
Thomas More

MULTIPLE-CHOICE QUESTIONS

Questions 1–3 refer to the image below.

Source: Wikimedia Commons

In this 1435 painting, Dutch artist Jan van Eyck shows Nicolas Rolin, a wealthy contributor to the Catholic Church, seated with the Virgin Mary, who is holding Jesus.

1. This painting reflects how the Northern Renaissance artists commonly portrayed

    (A) individuals interacting with nature

    (B) merchants and their trade goods

    (C) stories from classical mythology

    (D) religious content as the subject matter

2. Based on the image and its intended audience, the inclusion of Rolin in the painting was most likely a reflection of
   (A) the artist's belief in the divine right of kings
   (B) the desire of secular rulers to control church institutions
   (C) the effort of elites to enhance their prestige by supporting art
   (D) the use of art to promote civic virtue

3. In what way is this painting similar to works by artists of the Italian Renaissance?
   (A) It shows landscapes rather than people as the focal point.
   (B) It portrays ordinary people carrying out everyday activities.
   (C) It includes an extraordinary number of small details, skillfully painted.
   (D) It uses harsh light and deep shadows to show people as they really looked.

SHORT-ANSWER QUESTION

Answer all parts of the question that follows.

1. a) Describe ONE difference between the Italian Renaissance and the Northern Renaissance in the period from 1450 to 1550.

   b) Describe ONE similarity between the Italian Renaissance and the Northern Renaissance in the period from 1450 to 1550.

   c) Using a specific example from the period 1450 to 1648, explain how classicism influenced the work of Northern Renaissance artists or scholars.

Topic 1.4

Printing

If God spare my life, ere [before] many years I will cause a boy that driveth the plow shall know more of the Scripture than thou doest [than you religious leaders do].

—William Tyndale (c. 1490–1536), religious reformer who believed all people should be able to read the Bible in their native language

Essential Question: What influence did the printing press have on cultural and intellectual developments in modern European history?

Today, books are plentiful and often inexpensive. In the Middle Ages, though, they were so rare and costly that few people had ever seen a book, and fewer had learned to read one. The development and spread of the mechanical printing press was a technology that changed learning forever, much as the Internet has in the 20th and 21st centuries. As people read more and learned more, they began to develop their own ideas—sometimes shocking or rebellious ideas.

The Printing Press Revolution

One key feature of the Renaissance was access to written works. During the Middle Ages, books had been copied by hand. Printing from carved wooden blocks began in Europe toward the end of the 14th century. Such blocks were first used to print religious pictures and then small amounts of text. Renaissance scholars needed new technologies to make their ideas available beyond Italy.

Invention of the Printing Press A revolutionary printing technology—**movable type** made of metal—was developed by printers over the first half of the 15th century in Europe. With this new development, printers could compose whole pages of text by creating lines of type from individual letters. Once a page was printed, the printer could take the type apart and reuse it.

German printer **Johannes Gutenberg** devised a usable form of the new process between 1445 and 1450. In addition, Gutenberg developed a **printing press** that differed from earlier technology. The hand-operated wooden press was the beginning of a process of mechanizing printing and producing large quantities of books. The **Gutenberg Bible**, completed in 1456, is one of the first known examples of a book produced from movable type.

Printing then spread rapidly throughout Europe, and within a few years there were printers throughout the Germanic states of the Holy Roman Empire. By the 1470s, printing had spread throughout Europe. By 1500, Europe had more than 1,000 printers, and Venice alone had nearly 100. Cities in present-day Germany and Italy were hotbeds of early printing. Later, printers launched businesses in Sweden, France, England, and what is now Poland.

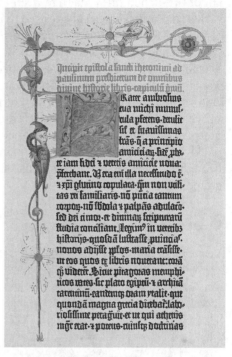

Source: Getty Images

A page from a Gutenberg Bible with Latin text

One of the earliest printers in Venice was Aldus Manutius the Elder (1449–1515). He printed works by dozens of ancient writers in Greek and Latin. Within a century, he and his descendants printed editions of nearly 1,000 different books. Having accurate, relatively inexpensive copies of these works changed how scholars of the 1400s and 1500s saw the world. He wrote in an introduction to one of his books, "Those who cultivate letters [want to learn] must be supplied with the books necessary to their purpose; and until this supply is secured I shall not rest."

With all the different printers and editions, book buyers often relied on printers' marks to ensure quality. These were simple symbols representing a particular printer's work. Book buyers could recognize and remember these marks easily, much like the corporate logos of today. Printer Charlotte Guillard (c. 1485–1557) used such marks when she issued more than 200 different books.

Many earlier printed works had been religious or classical and were often in Latin. However, the printing press made **vernacular literature**, written in the everyday language of a region, increasingly available. The availability of books in the language that ordinary people used increased the number of lay readers (people who could read even though they had little or no religious training). Over the following centuries, people reading books in their own language continued and accelerated the development of unique national cultures throughout Europe.

The Printing Press and Religious Reform Renaissance humanism spread to northern Europe in the late 15th century, and northern humanists focused more on religious concerns than did their Italian counterparts. By 1500, about half of the 40,000 titles that had been published were Bibles or other religious works. Humanists especially desired to reform the Catholic Church. (See Topic 1.3.) Such calls for reform spread slowly at first because they were written in Latin and had to be copied by hand.

However, by 1517, printing had become well established and would have extensive impacts on Europe. That year, German monk **Martin Luther** (1483–1546) called for religious reform. Luther emphasized the Bible as the main source of religious truth and believed that people should be able to read and interpret the Bible themselves without the aid of priests. Luther's ideas were quickly translated into German, printed into pamphlets, and distributed throughout German-speaking lands. A local protest by one unknown scholar ignited a raging controversy.

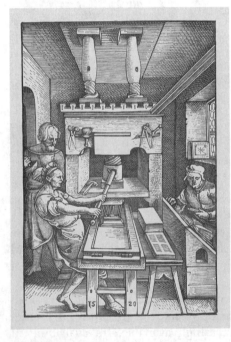

This wood engraving from 1879 shows printers operating a press in 1520.

Soon, additional reformers added to the debate sparked by Luther. The printing press allowed them to spread their ideas faster and more widely than ideas had ever spread before.

Within a decade, a revolutionary shift in European Christianity and politics, known as the Protestant Reformation, had begun. (See Topic 2.3 for more information on the Protestant Reformation.) Scripture readings became an important part of the Protestant religious services that were replacing the Catholic mass. Since most people did not read Latin, if they were going to read the Bible, they needed one in their vernacular, or local language. With the spread of printing, affordable Bibles appeared in many vernaculars for the first time.

Essential Question: *What influence did the printing press have on cultural and intellectual developments in modern European history?*

Secular Effects of Printing Press	Religious Effects of Printing Press

KEY TERMS

movable type	printing press	vernacular literature
Johannes Gutenberg	Gutenberg Bible	Martin Luther

MULTIPLE-CHOICE QUESTIONS

Questions 1–3 refer to the passages below.

"At first, he [John Fust, a partner of Gutenberg's, who took Bibles to Paris to sell] sold copies for so high a sum as 500 or 600 crowns, the prices usually demanded by the transcribers. He afterwards lowered his price to 60 crowns, which created universal astonishment; but when he produced copies as fast as they were wanted, and lowered the price to 30 crowns, all Paris was agitated. The uniformity of the copies increase the wonder; information was given to the police against him as a magician; his lodgings were searched; and a great number of copies being found, they were seized; the red ink with which they were embellished, was said to be his blood; it was seriously adjudged that he was in league with the devil, and if he had not fled, most probably he would have shared the fate of those whom ignorant and superstitious judges condemned in those days of witchcraft."

—John Platts, *A New Universal Biography*, 1826

"[The early reactions to printed books] that are most frequently cited associate printing with divine rather than diabolic powers. But then the most familiar references come either from the blurbs and prefaces composed by early printers themselves or from editors and authors who found employment in print shops. Such men were likely to take a more favorable view than were the guildsmen who made a livelihood from manuscript books. . . . Whether the new art was considered a blessing or a curse; whether it was consigned to the Devil or attributed to God; the fact remains, that the initial increase in output did strike contemporary observers as sufficiently remarkable to suggest supernatural intervention."

—Elizabeth L. Eisenstein, *The Printing Press As an Agent of Change*, 1979

1. Which of the following best describes the context of the time in which the events discussed by Platts occurred?

   (A) People were fascinated by new technology and eager to understand how it worked.

   (B) People were mostly interested in works of literature and philosophy written by Cicero, Aristotle, and other classical authors.

   (C) People assumed that forces more powerful than humans caused events that seemed impossible.

   (D) People feared that the printing press would make more books available to scholars, leading to a return of scholasticism.

2. As shown by the shifts in prices Fust charged for copies of the Bible, the changing cost of printing a book contributed to which of the following developments in Europe?

   (A) The demand for copies of the Bible increased so much that more people studied it as a work of literature than as a religious text.

   (B) The demand for non-religious books increased so much that people became less committed to their faith.

   (C) The demand for books in Latin increased so much that cultures became more similar throughout Europe.

   (D) The demand for books in vernacular language increased so much that national cultures became more distinct from each other.

3. According to Eisenstein, one limit on the value of the early reactions to printed books as a source is that most reactions were written by

   (A) scribes who made their living copying books

   (B) people with an interest in selling printed books

   (C) religious leaders who wanted to spread Christianity

   (D) printers who had been threatened by mobs

SHORT-ANSWER QUESTION

Answer all parts of the question that follows.

1. a) Describe ONE way in which the printing press influenced the spread of ideas in Europe from 1450 to 1550.

   b) Describe ONE way the printing press influenced religion in Europe in the period from 1450 to 1550.

   c) Using a specific example from the period 1450 to 1550, explain ONE way the printing press influenced language in Europe.

Topic 1.5

New Monarchies

If I had two heads, then one should be at the King of England's disposal.

—Christina of Denmark, Duchess of Milan (c. 1521–1590), refusing to
marry Henry VIII of England who had a wife beheaded

Essential Question: What were the causes and effects of the
development of political institutions from 1450 to 1648?

People have always craved power and struggled to possess it. The beliefs and
actions of people in Europe who wielded power greatly influenced political
institutions. Three major changes in the early modern period—approximately
the 15th century through the 18th century—shaped political development:

- the shift from **decentralized power** spread among many groups and
  individuals to **centralized power** in which a small group held control
- the shift in influence from the landed nobility who had inherited their
  position to people with education, skills, and wealth
- the shift from law and justice dictated by religion to rules of law
  dictated by a secular system

State Power and Religion

In some places, leaders and religious groups used the religious changes of the
Reformation to promote political unity. In others, such changes led to partisan
turmoil and challenges to a leader's authority.

Top-Down Religious Reform in England

In Central Europe, religious reforms started from the bottom up, with a variety
of monks and preachers. Gradually, it spread to the upper reaches of society.
However, in England, reform was top down. The king of England changed the
religious practice of his subjects by edicts and laws.
└→ an order issued by someone

    Henry VIII Breaks with the Pope In 1509, Henry VIII assumed the
throne of England. While he first supported the papacy and the Catholic
Church, this came to an end in dramatic fashion.

    In 1527, after more than 20 years of marriage, Henry VIII wanted to
end his marriage to Katherine of Aragon. She was the youngest daughter of
Ferdinand and Isabella of Spain and the aunt of Holy Roman Emperor Charles
V. During their marriage, Katherine gave birth to six children, but the only one
who survived to adulthood was female, **Mary Tudor**.

Henry wanted an annulment + wanted the Pope's permission but didn't receive it

Without a male heir, Henry VIII feared for the stability of the Tudor Dynasty after his death, especially since he was only the second Tudor king. He asked Pope Clement VII for an annulment, or cancellation, of his marriage, claiming that it should never have been allowed. Katherine had been married to Henry's brother before he died, and Henry argued that his marriage to her was improper. The pope, pressured by the Holy Roman Emperor Charles V (who was also Katherine's nephew) and unwilling to offend Spain's Catholics, refused to grant the annulment.

In 1533, Anne Boleyn, the mistress of Henry VIII, became pregnant. Henry VIII divorced Katherine—knowing the pope would object—so he could marry Boleyn, who gave birth to Elizabeth, another female. Pope Clement VII declared Henry and Anne Boleyn's marriage illegal.

In a show of power as much as it was a religious reform, Henry VIII responded by denouncing the authority of the pope. In November 1534, the English Parliament passed the **Act of Supremacy**, making the king of England the head of the Church of England. England was no longer a Catholic country.

Only three years after they were married, Henry had Anne Boleyn executed for adultery. He later married Jane Seymour, who gave birth to Edward, the son and heir Henry had long sought. Seymour died shortly afterward due to complications from the birth. Henry married three more times (six in total) but had no more children. *← Denounced the Pope to marry Anne Boleyn and later execute her*

Results of the Break with Rome While the Church of England was no longer officially part of the Roman Catholic Church, many people in England remained loyal Catholics. To enforce his power, Henry VIII created more religious reforms. One of these was the Treason Act, which made refusing to recognize the Church of England as the state religion an act of treason. Violating this act was punishable by death. Refusal to recognize Henry as head of the church cost the famous humanist thinker and author (and Henry's lord chancellor) Sir Thomas More his life in July 1535.

While Henry broke away from the control of the pope, he continued to support most of the doctrines of the Roman Catholic Church. In 1539, the government reaffirmed core Catholic doctrines:

Source: Getty Images

Henry VIII of England was known for his strong will and self-confidence. He was perhaps even better known for beheading two of his six wives.

- Members of the clergy would stay unmarried.
- Confession of sins to a priest (rather than directly to God) remained vital.
- The idea of transubstantiation, or that during communion the bread and wine consumed by chuch members actually became the body and blood of Jesus Christ (rather than being a symbol of Jesus' sacrifice) was still an official belief.

High church: More Catholic
Low church: More Protestant

These beliefs divided Catholics and Protestants.

The Church of England became known as the Anglican Church. Anglicans did not all agree with how closely they should keep to Catholic traditions and doctrine. Those who wanted to remain close to Catholic doctrine were known as "High Church," while those who were more influenced by Protestant doctrines and practices were known as "Low Church."

Two Brief Reigns Following Henry's death, his young son Edward became king. He reigned for only six years (1547–1553) before dying at age 15. During these years, the government became more Low Church.

However, his successor, Mary Tudor (reigned 1553–1558), took the country in the opposite direction. She tried to restore Catholicism to England. Those in England who had not wanted to break with Rome supported her, as did her powerful husband, the Spanish king Philip II. Mary's persecution of some Anglican bishops earned her the nickname "Bloody Mary."

Mary Tudor reigns after Edward dies at 15

Elizabeth Takes Control After Mary Tudor's death, her half-sister, Elizabeth I (reigned 1558–1603), tried to find a middle ground, sometimes called the Elizabethan Settlement or the Anglican Compromise, that would end religious turmoil. She returned to Anglicanism, rejecting both Roman Catholicism and Calvinism (Puritanism). During her long reign, she avoided harsh persecution of people who practiced their own beliefs quietly.

Elizabeth was determined to restore the Anglican Church in England and keep England from returning to Catholicism. At the same time, she wanted to prevent more radical reform movements from growing. One such radical group, the Puritans, wanted to "purify" the Church of England, demanding the elimination of clerical dress and removal of Catholics from England. These Puritans became a serious source of discontent and opposition to the Church of England, and therefore the crown. Some sought freedom to practice their religion in North America. But those who stayed in England would later directly threaten the power of the monarchy. Overall, however, during her long reign, Elizabeth established a number of official acts that helped solidify control over the religious life and morality of the English people.

Elizabeth wanted a more Anglican community but let people practice their own religions

LEGAL SUPPORT FOR THE CHURCH OF ENGLAND UNDER ELIZABETH I		
Act	**Year**	**Provisions**
Act of Supremacy	1558	• Redeclared the King of England the head of the Church of England • Acknowledged Elizabeth as the head of the Church of England

LEGAL SUPPORT FOR THE CHURCH OF ENGLAND UNDER ELIZABETH I		
Act of Uniformity	1559	• Reestablished the *Book of Common Prayer*, which provided religious instructions while avoiding criticism of Catholicism or the Pope • Noted the need for subjects to attend church services once a week
Thirty-Nine Articles	1571	• Reestablished English as the language of the Church of England

Many people of the time believed that a woman could not rule a country effectively. In a rousing speech to her troops, Elizabeth I said, "I know I have the body but of a weak and feeble woman; but I have the heart and stomach of a king, and of a king of England, too."

The Emergence of New Monarchies

Some states emerged during the early modern period that featured greater royal control and centralization and were known as **new monarchies**. They laid the groundwork for the centralized **modern state**. These monarchies established bureaucratic methods of tax collection, created strong military forces, implemented systems of justice, and even determined their subjects' religion. Especially in Spain, France, and England, monarchs controlled nearly every aspect of people's lives.

Spain For most of the 15th century, the Spanish region of Aragon, home to **King Ferdinand**, was one of the most important areas of Europe. It was the main maritime power of the western Mediterranean, with an impressive fleet of ships. The Castile region of Spain, home to **Queen Isabella**, was the other great power on the Iberian Peninsula. The marriage of Ferdinand and Isabella in 1469 began the process of unification and consolidation of power in Spain.

Using national taxes such as the *alcabala* (a tax on the sale or exchange of property), Ferdinand and Isabella began to centralize power. To limit the power of nobles in Castile, they used *coreregidores* (magistrates who worked to strengthen royal authority) to carry out justice in the name of the monarch.

The king and queen also used the Inquisition, a Catholic judicial body established to root out heresy, as a tool to consolidate their power. Spain's Jewish population, one of the largest in Europe and relatively prosperous, was targeted as a threat to the expanding kingdom's religious unity. Antisemitic (anti-Jewish) persecution forced Chrisian conversion upon many Jews (known as *conversos*), but some (known as *marranos*) continued to secretly practice Judaism. Both groups were among the principal targets of the Spanish Inquisition, which routinely used torture as a means of gaining confession. As many as 2,000 individuals were burned at the stake at the height of the Inquisition, and 3,000 to 5,000 were executed over the course of the Inquisition.

Ferdinand's forces defeated Muslim Granada in 1492, which completed the *Reconquista*, or the driving of Muslims from Spain. Jews who had not converted to Christianity (estimated at as many as 250,000) were expelled at the same time, creating a uniformly Christian population.

One of the most important parts of Ferdinand and Isabella's union was the consolidation of military power. The couple's success in several military campaigns (such as the victory in Granada) resulted in more political and economic strength for their kingdom. This allowed Ferdinand and Isabella to provide financial backing for the voyages of Christopher Columbus and other explorers, which eventually elevated Spain to a world power.

France For more than a century, England and France intermittently battled in what was called the Hundred Years' War (1337–1453). The extended conflict left France in shambles. Yet the economic and military changes caused by the war allowed French kings to use their positions to centralize state power. Using the *taille* (a land tax organized under King Charles VII), French kings gathered royal income to establish an army, thus increasing royal power. To carry out the law, the king sent officials known as bailiffs into the provinces. Later kings also brought the duchy of Burgundy as well as the provinces of Anjou, Provence, and Maine under royal control, adding valuable land and income to the crown. Ruling from 1461 to 1483, Louis XI, son of Charles VII, helped France recover from the damage of the Hundred Years' War. He also succeeded in weakening the power of the aristocracy (wealthy landowners with titles such as marquis, comte, baron, and so on), thereby strengthening the power of the king.

The power of the French king also increased through an agreement between France's Francis I and Pope Leo X in 1516. The **Concordat of Bologna** permitted the pope to collect all the income that the Catholic Church made in France. However, it also gave King Francis I more direct control over French Catholic leaders. He could restrict their ability to communicate directly with Rome. The concordat also confirmed the king's right to nominate church leaders, such as archbishops, bishops, abbots, and priors.

In 1598, after 50 years of religious war, King Henry IV of France promoted French unity by issuing the **Edict of Nantes**. This order granted the Calvinist Protestants of France, known as **Huguenots**, new rights. By no longer treating Huguenots as heretics, or individuals who reject the faith of the church, the edict helped unify France. It gave Huguenots civil rights, including the rights to worship as they chose, work in any field, work for the state, and bring complaints directly to the king. The edict marked the end of the religious wars that had been fought in France throughout the second half of the 16th century.

England King Henry VII became the first Tudor monarch through his family's victory in the Wars of the Roses (which pitted Tudor's family, the Lancasters, against the House of York for the English throne). Henry then married Elizabeth of York to help legitimize his position. Over time, he further increased royal power by:

- using diplomacy to avoid expensive wars
- avoiding overtaxing the landed **gentry**—wealthy landowners who did not have inherited titles—and the middle class

- sending justices of the peace into the various counties to hear cases and "dispense justice in the name of the king"
- creating the advisory Royal Council, made up mostly of the gentry

Henry VII also used the Court of the Star Chamber to control the actions of irresponsible nobility. Named for the pattern of stars on the ceiling of the room, the **Star Chamber** was an English law court created in the late 15th century. It was run by advisors to the monarch and judges. When created, its purpose was to hear cases against wealthy and powerful individuals whom regular courts might have been unwilling to convict. It gradually changed into an appeals court, or courts that could overturn decisions of lower courts. Appeals courts are an important part of the judicial system for most countries today.

However, the Star Chamber became increasingly powerful and subject to political influence. It used its unchecked power to oppress social and political enemies without any real trial. Friends of the monarch were encouraged to bypass lower courts to receive a favorable judgment from the Star Chamber. The body was disbanded in 1640. People still use the term *star chamber* today. Now it refers to secretive, upper-level government meetings in which powerful people act without considering what is just or fair.

German Territories and the Peace of Augsburg The Holy Roman Empire came into existence in 800 C.E. By the 16th century, it was a collection of kingdoms, principalities, and cities that occupied a large portion of Central Europe, as well as parts of modern-day Italy. A meeting in 1530, known as the **Diet of Augsburg** (*diet* meaning a formal meeting) was held to try to settle differences between Catholic and Protestant regions of the Holy Roman Empire—which was then ruled by Charles V of the Austrian Habsburg family. The result instead was that Protestants were given a deadline for returning to Catholicism. As a result, Protestant princes and cities formed a defensive alliance called the **Schmalkaldic League**.

This Protestant league was tolerated for years by Charles for fear that any move against it would push the territories (and their armies) into an alliance with France, with which the Holy Roman Empire was at war. When Charles was able to gain the upper hand against France, he moved against the Schmalkaldic League, defeating it in battle in 1547. In spite of this victory, Charles found that he was unable to force Catholicism on his Protestant subjects. In 1555, the Augsburg settlement, also called the **Peace of Augsburg**, was agreed. It allowed individual rulers to choose whether their subjects would practice the Lutheran or the Roman Catholic form of Christianity.

Merchants, Lawyers, and Nobles Increase Power

During the rule of the Holy Roman Empire, the Catholic Church was the main influence on daily life because it controlled so much wealth. For example, it had enough money to commission artwork, which is why so much of the art produced before the Renaissance was religious art. Innovations in banking and finance helped create urban financial centers and a money economy. In other words, people mainly exchanged items and services for money rather than bartering (exchanging items and services for other items and services).

As a result of these changes, commercial and professional groups gained increasing power in many countries. These groups included merchants, lawyers, and other educated and skilled individuals. Often, they made deals directly with monarchs. So, while owning land could still bring money and power, having education or expertise also became important.

In Northern Europe, the development of commerce and finance led to a golden age of art. For example, in the Netherlands, Dutch artists painted for private collectors rather than the Catholic Church. These private individuals supported many painters and a wide range of styles. While many artists continued to use religious themes, they often showed the influence of Protestantism. Others portrayed wealthy individuals.

Guilds Merchant groups called **guilds**, which first began in the Middle Ages, continued to wield significant power. Although kings and queens controlled state governments, these guilds often controlled local governments. Usually, guilds and their members stayed loyal to their king or queen. Doing so helped guild members stay in control on the local level.

Power of the Medici Family Merchants and financiers also led developments in Renaissance Italy. One of the most prominent families based in what is today Italy was the Medici family of Florence. (See Topic 1.2.) The Medicis were independent patrons of the arts, providing artistic freedom that was previously unknown. The Medici family itself also produced three popes and two queens and founded the Medici Bank, one of the most prosperous institutions in Europe at that time. ← very impressive + important

Gentry Reform in England also led to noble titles becoming rewards for personal or professional accomplishments. The gentry was the class of prosperous families who made their money through commercial ventures rather than inheritance, though they did sometimes include rural aristocrats, which were called landed gentry. The gentry in England often allied with the king to increase their political standing.

Nobles of the Robe In France, some nobles gained power by holding important state offices. People called them **nobles of the robe** because of the robes they wore while carrying out these duties. This was a change from the past, when power usually come from military service, not from carrying out official duties. There was often tension between nobles of the sword (military leaders) and these new nobles of the robe. Eventually, nobles of the robe were able to transmit their titles and power to their children, thereby increasing their families' status for generations.

Secular Political Theories

As the Catholic Church began splintering and losing some of its power, monarchs, nobles, and merchants were starting to gain power. In Central Europe, the Holy Roman Empire began to shrink in territory and influence.

In Italy, warring city-states competed for power and territory. This political fragmentation allowed for new political ideas to emerge throughout Europe.

Several writers developed theories to support the emerging secular state, or a government not primarily based on religion. In Renaissance Italy, Niccolò Machiavelli in *The Prince* (see Topic 1.2) provided for new concepts of the state. As power transferred away from traditional religious bodies and toward secular states, such political theories strengthened the state institutions.

These political theories focused on two types of relationships—those between individuals and those between individuals and the state. The theories also explored the responsibilities inherent in such relationships, especially the state's duty to take care of its people.

NEW IDEAS ABOUT POLITICS		
Writer	**Theory**	**Significance**
Niccolò Machiavelli Florentine 1469–1527	**Machiavellianism**: Rulers should be willing to use cunning and deceit to keep themselves in power. Doing so will also help society by providing security and stable government. His most famous work, *The Prince*, was written as a handbook for rulers and aspiring political leaders.	• He is considered the father of modern political science. • He argued that ambition and therefore conflict are an inevitable part of human nature. • He advocated for republicanism—the belief in states ruled by the consent of citizens through elected leaders rather than monarchs.
Jean Bodin French 1530–1596	**Absolute Sovereignty**: Rulers of the sovereign state, operating by the doctrine of the divine right of kings, maintain peace by issuing laws and dictating religion, regardless of whether the people consent. His book *Colloquium of the Seven* is a conversation about truth among men from seven religious and intellectual traditions, including skepticism.	• He spread the idea of the modern state as different from the personal holdings of the monarch. • He viewed families (patriarchy) as the model for the state. • He was an early advocate for religious tolerance.
Hugo Grotius Dutch 1583–1645	**Natural Law**: Humans are born with certain innate rights. Leaders should govern by rational laws or ethical principles based on reason. His book *On the Law of War and Peace* outlined the rules of war. Grotius argued that there are three just causes of war: self-defense, reparation of injury, and punishment.	• He laid the foundation for international law and diplomacy, including freedom of the seas and humane treatment of civilians during war. • He defined the idea of one society of states, governed by laws and agreement, not by force and warfare. • His vision of an international society influenced the Peace of Westphalia (1648), which ended some conflicts among the Spanish, Dutch, and Germans.

REFLECT ON THE ESSENTIAL QUESTION

Essential Question: *What were the causes and effects of the development of political institutions from 1450 to 1648?*

Causes	Effects

KEY TERMS

decentralized power	Concordat of Bologna	Niccolò Machiavelli
centralized power	Edict of Nantes	Machiavellianism
Henry VIII	Huguenots	Jean Bodin
Mary Tudor	gentry	absolute sovereignty
Act of Supremacy	Star Chamber	Hugo Grotius
Elizabeth I	Diet of Augsburg	natural law
new monarchies	Schmalkaldic League	
modern state	Peace of Augsburg	
King Ferdinand	guilds	
Queen Isabella	nobles of the robe	

MULTIPLE-CHOICE QUESTIONS

Questions 1–3 refer to the following passage.

> "The first attribute of the sovereign prince therefore is the power to make law binding on all his subjects in general and on each in particular. But to avoid any ambiguity one must add that he does so without the consent of any superior, equal, or inferior being necessary. If the prince can only make law with the consent of a superior he is a subject; if of an equal he shares his sovereignty; if of an inferior, whether it be a council of magnates [powerful individuals] or the people, it is not he who is sovereign…
>
> But because law is an imprecise and general term, it is as well to specify the other attributes of sovereignty comprised in it, such as the making of war and peace. This is one of the most important rights of sovereignty, since it brings in its train either the ruin or the salvation of the state…
>
> The third attribute of sovereignty is the power to institute the great officers of state…
>
> The fourth attribute of sovereignty, and one which has always been among its principal rights, is that the prince should be the final resort of appeal from all other courts."
>
> —Jean Bodin, *Six Books of the Commonwealth*, 1576

1. Which of the following best describes the historical context in which the theory of sovereignty expressed in the passage emerged?

    (A) The shift in military power from states' armies to monarchs' private armies

    (B) The shift in economic power from merchants to large landowners

    (C) The shift in religious power from local priests to Roman Catholic Church leaders

    (D) The shift in political power from local rulers to central governments

2. Which of the following books most clearly argued for similar claims to those made by Bodin in this passage?

    (A) *The Prince* by Niccolò Machiavelli because it argued that states needed a powerful individual ruler

    (B) *The Discourses* by Niccolò Machiavelli because it argued in favor of a republican form of government

    (C) *On the Law of War and Peace* by Hugo Grotius because it argued that countries should follow international laws

    (D) *The Leviathan* by Thomas Hobbes because it argued that political power came from an agreement among people

3. Based on this passage, which power of a monarch would Bodin consider most significant?

    (A) To reflect the will of the people of the country

    (B) To issue laws that governed all citizens

    (C) To follow the guidance of the state church

    (D) To carry out the decisions of the governing council

SHORT-ANSWER QUESTION

Answer all parts of the question that follows.

1. a) Describe how religious conflict influenced the development of political institutions in England from 1509 to 1547.

    b) Identify ONE cause for the centralization of political power from 1450 to 1648.

    c) Explain ONE effect of the centralization of political power from 1450 to 1648.

Topic 1.6

Technological Advances and the Age of Exploration

We Spaniards know a sickness of the heart that only gold can cure.

—Hernán Cortés (c. 1485–1547)

> **Essential Question:** What were the technological factors that contributed to European exploration and expansion from 1450 to 1648?

> **Essential Question:** What were the motivations and effects of European exploration and expansion from 1450 to 1648?

During the Renaissance, Europeans became more interested in the world around them. Intellectuals of the time studied classical texts and observed the natural world in order to understand it better. By the late 15th century, educated Europeans knew that the earth was round. Yet, they had little understanding of the size of their world, as few Europeans had traveled beyond their own region. This new era of exploration and expansion had profound effects on Europe and the rest of the world. However, it was more than curiosity that sparked the era of exploration and colonization beginning in the 15th century and continuing well into the 19th century.

Motives for Exploration

In the 15th century, Europe was not a particularly wealthy or intellectually advanced region of the world. Two overarching reasons historians sometimes give to explain why European states took the lead in exploration were "God and gold." Yet behind these reasons also was the desire to gain power and glory for monarchs and emerging centralized states.

Christianity Stimulates Exploration

The desire of Europeans to spread and strengthen the Christian faith affected events both within and beyond the continent. Between the birth of Jesus and 1492, Christians had spread the faith throughout the Mediterranean world and into northern and eastern Europe.

Catholics React to the Reformation As Europeans began to explore the world, many wanted to spread Christianity. The split in Europe resulting from the Protestant Reformation (see Topic 2.2) increased the desire of some countries to spread their faith. Portugal, Spain, and France, which remained largely Catholic, were interested in both commerce and spreading their beliefs. For those countries, particularly Spain, religion was a powerful factor in exploration and colonization. A Catholic religious group called the **Jesuits** eventually performed missionary work around the world. The Jesuits were and are largely focused on education and expanding human knowledge. (See Topic 2.5 for more about the Jesuits.)

Protestants Seek Refuge—and Profit However, people from England and the Netherlands, mostly Protestant, focused more on commerce. Dutch explorers traveled through the East Indies and parts of Asia, competing with the Portuguese, British, and Spanish. In the 17th century, English groups sought refuge in North America from the Anglican Church—Puritans in Massachusetts, Catholics in Maryland, and Quakers in Pennsylvania.

As Christians carried their faith throughout the world, some used it as justification for subjugating the indigenous peoples they encountered. Some Christians believed that it was acceptable to dominate, profit from, and even enslave others if they also forced those others to become Christian. In letters to Spain, Christopher Columbus described the indigenous people he met (whom he called Indians) as having "very subtle wit" and being skilled at "navigating all these seas." However, he also wrote, "Let us in the name of the Holy Trinity go on sending all the slaves that can be sold."

Commercial Motives for Exploration

Though Europeans were geographically confined during the Middle Ages, they were exposed to goods and ideas from Asia and Africa. For example, Venetian merchant **Marco Polo** published an account of his travels throughout Asia in the late 13th century, giving medieval Europeans their most detailed information about that region.

Search for New Routes to the East Europeans were aware of exotic products and luxury goods such as gold, spices, silk, and jewels from Asia and Africa. Knowledge of these products increased as a result of the religious wars called the Crusades. Yet, European access to such products was limited.

In the 14th century, the Muslim rulers of the **Ottoman Empire** gained control of trade routes connecting Asia to Europe both by land and by the Mediterranean Sea. Traders from Venice were the only Europeans who had direct access to the Muslim ports. Therefore, Europeans had to purchase spices, such as ginger and cinnamon, and other foreign goods from Muslim traders at very high prices. For example, in Spain, nutmeg was as expensive as gold.

Quest for a Water Route Europeans hoped to discover an all-water route connecting Europe to Asia. This would not only bypass Ottoman-controlled lands, but it also would be less expensive. Transporting heavy goods over water was much cheaper and easier than transporting them over land.

Europe's monarchs also hoped to find an all-water route to Asia in order to enhance the power of their states and increase their personal wealth. Countries explored different paths to Asia:

- The Portuguese traveled south along the coast of Africa and then east across the Indian Ocean.
- The Spanish tried to reach Asia by sailing west across the Atlantic and Pacific Oceans.

Mercantilism One important economic idea that motivated the search for a route to the East was **mercantilism**. This measured the wealth of a country by how much gold and silver it accumulated. Mercantilism developed in 16th-century Europe, particularly England and France, and began to lose supporters in the 18th and 19th centuries. It includes these principles:

- The world's wealth is like a pie. It is a limited size, and the only way to get a larger share is for another state to get a smaller share. This belief reflected the world as it existed before the 19th century. Life changed very little from one generation to the next, and economic growth was normally slow. In contrast today, people assume that technological change will make the global economic pie larger and larger.

- A country grows wealthier if it has a **favorable balance of trade**, which means it **exports** (sells to other countries) more than it **imports** (buys from other countries). If it does, then it will receive more in payments of gold and silver than it pays out. Today, economists rely less on balance of trade to measure a country's wealth. A wealthy country might have an unfavorable balance of trade because it can afford to import many goods.

- A **colony**, or a separate land controlled by a parent country, can enrich the parent country by providing precious metals, crops, and other products. Colonies also served as markets for the parent country's goods.

Governments that followed mercantilist policies tried to regulate trade to encourage exports, discourage imports, and justify seizing colonies. However, starting in the late 1700s, people began to believe that countries could prosper with fewer restrictions on trade. In particular, consumers benefited by the opportunity to buy less expensive products made in other countries. An ideology of free trade began to replace the belief in mercantilism.

Economic and Political Motives Converge Governments spent money on exploration and trade for a blend of reasons. For example, the French politician **Jean-Baptiste Colbert** (1619–1683) came from a family of merchants. As finance minister for King Louis XIV (see Topic 3.7), he reformed the French tax system to make the country richer and more politically stable. However, another primary reason he wanted France to have strong international trade was to weaken the rival Dutch economically and politically.

Exploration and Advances in Knowledge

European interest in finding new trade routes and establishing overseas colonies converged with growth of knowledge about geography and **navigation**, the science of plotting the course of a ship. In the 13th and 14th centuries, European navigators had developed detailed charts (which were actually early maps) called **portolani**. These gave ship captains accurate information about the location and distances between European ports. These charts, however, were not accurate or detailed enough for extended ocean voyages.

Advances in **cartography**, or the making and study of maps, grew in the 15th century. Early explorers created detailed maps based on their observations as they traveled. The invention of printing in the mid-15th century made more copies of maps available to navigators in different countries.

To sail long distances in unknown waters, Europeans adopted Middle Eastern and Chinese navigational technology:

- Europeans developed a new type of ship, the caravel, that was faster and provided more cargo space than previous ships. They also began replacing their traditional square sails with triangular **lateen sails**, developed by Arab sailors. Lateen sails allowed more flexibility for sailing regardless of wind direction.

- Europeans adopted the **sternpost rudder** from China. It was a steering device attached to the ship's main beam at the rear that made the ship more maneuverable.

- To navigate a seemingly endless ocean, with no landmarks in sight, sailors used the **astrolabe** and the **quadrant** (a smaller lighter version of the astrolabe) to determine where they were at sea based on the altitude of the sun or a star above the horizon.

- Sailors used the **compass**, which likely came from China in the 12th century, to aid in directional location by indicating which way is north.

Advances in military technology, such as gunpowder weapons and steel swords, also helped Europeans establish overseas colonies and empires. Caravels were large enough to support mounted cannons and maneuverable enough to fight naval battles. Horses gave Europeans an advantage when colonizing the Americas, where there had been no horses before Europeans arrived. Perhaps most importantly, Europeans brought smallpox and other diseases that killed millions of indigenous people, making European conquest more feasible.

Source: Getty Images

Astrolabes were a type of technology that helped keep voyagers safe by improving seaborne navigation.

REFLECT ON THE ESSENTIAL QUESTIONS

Essential Question: *What were the technological factors that contributed to European exploration and expansion from 1450 to 1648?*

Essential Question: *What were the motivations and effects of European exploration and expansion from 1450 to 1648?*

Technology and Motivations	Effects

KEY TERMS

Jesuits	imports	lateen sails
Marco Polo	colony	sternpost rudder
Ottoman Empire	Jean-Baptiste Colbert	astrolabe
mercantilism	navigation	quadrant
favorable balance of trade	portolani	compass
exports	cartography	

MULTIPLE-CHOICE QUESTIONS

Questions 1–3 refer to the following passage.

> "From Christ, the eternal truth, we have the command 'You must love your neighbor as yourself'….Christ seeks souls, not property. He…thirsts not for riches, not for ease and pleasures, but for the salvation [saving] of mankind….
>
> If you seek Indians so that gently, quietly, mildly, humanely, and in a Christian manner you instruct them in the word of God, [you] will receive an imperishable crown of glory… But if it be the order that by sword, fire, massacre, trickery, and an inhumanity that is greater than barbaric you may destroy and plunder utterly harmless peoples who are ready to renounce [turn against] evil and receive the word of God, you are children of the devil and the most horrible plunderers of all."
>
> —Bartolome de las Casas, *In Defense of the Indians*, 1548

1. According to de las Casas, what should be the main reason for Europeans to contact indigenous peoples?

   (A) To provide them with religious instruction

   (B) To learn about their religion or religions

   (C) To dominate them militarily

   (D) To help them find gold and other luxuries

2. Which of the following people would most likely have disagreed with the point of view de las Casas expresses in the passage?

   (A) An indigenous person

   (B) A Jesuit priest

   (C) Christopher Columbus

   (D) The pope

3. In this passage, what evidence does de las Casas provide to support his claim?

   (A) Accounts from Jesuit priests

   (B) A quotation from the Bible

   (C) The opinion of the king of Spain

   (D) Examples of mistreatment of indigenous peoples

SHORT-ANSWER QUESTION

Use the passage below to answer all parts of the question that follow.

"Too often, we historians tend to tell our story with the knowledge of the end result to come... But it is strangely liberating to look at the old maps, and see the vast stretches not-yet-filled-in, and populated instead with mermaids and unicorns and other figments of Europe's overheated imagination. Champlain's earliest and supposedly scientific renderings of the new world include a large winged dragon, ready to take flight. Well into the 18th century, maps of the Atlantic continued to include completely fictitious islands that had been legends for centuries, but never existed— the Sunken Land of Buss, St. Brendan's Isle, Hy-Brazil, the Island of the Seven Cities, and a dozen others."

—Ted Widmer, *Navigating the Age of Exploration*, 2007

1. a) Describe ONE piece of historical evidence (not specifically mentioned in the passage) that would support Widmer's interpretation about the Age of Exploration.

   b) Describe ONE piece of historical evidence that would refute Widmer's interpretation about the Age of Exploration.

   c) Explain how the Age of Exploration reflected the broader context of changes in ideas about individuals and society in 15th- and 16th-century Europe.

Topic 1.7

Rivals on the World Stage

The plague lasted for seventy days, striking everywhere in the city and killing a vast number of our people....We were covered with agonizing sores from head to foot.

—Aztec eyewitness to the smallpox plague that explorer Hernán Cortés accidentally brought to the Americas

Essential Question: How and why did trading networks and colonial expansion affect relations among European states?

The desire for power, resources, and luxury goods caused military and trade interactions between many states around the globe. As existing and emerging powers established control in new territories, they brought their languages, religions, and cultures with them. In many cases, they also brought disease and destruction.

Overseas European Empires

As Europeans established new trade networks, they sometimes negotiated agreements that benefited both themselves and local people in Africa, Asia, and the Americas. However, Europeans often used coercion to establish overseas empires by subduing native populations or enforcing trade monopolies.

Spanish Colonies

The Reconquista (see Topic 1.5) meant that Spain had become a more unified and powerful nation. This unity and power had come at tremendous cost—in lives lost in battle and for Jews and Muslims who either had to flee the country or convert to Christianity. Once Spain's rulers had stabilized their country, they turned their attention to the outside world.

Spain wanted direct access to the Asian spice trade. Spain had the wealth and resources not only to compete for trade but also to establish a vast empire of colonies. This empire would generate great wealth. It would also spread Christianity, either by persuasion or force, throughout the Americas and parts of Asia.

Early Explorations Italian explorer **Christopher Columbus** (1451–1506) was a devout Christian and an experienced sea captain. From his study of sea charts and other sources, he concluded that the earth was small enough that the shortest route to Asia from Europe was by sailing west across the Atlantic Ocean. He tried to persuade Portugal to support his plan, but the Portuguese realized that Columbus had miscalculated the size of the earth and was planning on the longer route. Portugal had already begun to develop a thriving trading empire by this time. As you will see in Topic 1.8, by the time of Columbus's westward voyage, Portugal's navigators had already been exploring the west coast of Africa for half a century. They had also rounded the Cape of Good Hope and begun to explore the Indian Ocean.

Columbus then approached the Spanish monarchs, King Ferdinand and Queen Isabella of Spain (see Topic 1.5) who ruled from 1469 to 1516. They were willing to take a risk on his plan. They backed his first expedition, and he set sail in August 1492. After a two-month voyage, he landed in the Bahamas and also explored parts of Cuba and Hispaniola (present-day Haiti and the Dominican Republic) in the Caribbean Sea. Columbus believed he had reached Asia and claimed the lands for Spain. Because he thought the land he had reached was the Indies, he called the area the **West Indies** and referred to the people as **Indians**. The indigenous people he met called themselves the Arawaks (peaceful) and the Caribs (brave).

Treaty of Tordesillas Columbus made three later voyages between 1493 and 1502 trying to find a way to reach the Asian mainland. However, he was unsuccessful. He never acknowledged that he had found a landmass that was previously unknown to Europeans. Columbus did explore all the major islands of the Caribbean and what is now Central America. Spain gained control of all these lands because they were west of a line established by an agreement between Spain and Portugal that created separate spheres of colonial influence called the **Treaty of Tordesillas**. The treaty separated their interests along a line that divided the world through eastern South America. East of the treaty line, Portugal received control of trade routes around Africa's Cape of Good Hope and a portion of South America that became eastern Brazil.

Italian explorer **Amerigo Vespucci**, who traveled along the eastern coast of South America between 1499 and 1504, was the first to refer to this area as the **New World**. A mapmaker used Vespucci's first name to refer to the lands he explored, and people have called them the Americas ever since.

Mexico In the early 16th century, Spanish **conquistadors**, or conquerors, began subduing the indigenous populations in the Americas. Conquistadors led expeditions that were sponsored by the government but privately funded.

Conquistador **Hernán Cortés** (1485–1547) first reached what is now Veracruz on the Gulf of Mexico in 1519, when the **Aztec Empire** ruled most of the region. The Aztecs had an advanced civilization. Yet Cortés conquered them and destroyed their capital, Tenochtitlán, within two years. Though he had a small force of soldiers, Cortés had horses and guns. He also had help from native groups who were enemies of the Aztecs. Perhaps the most important factor helping Cortés was disease, which killed millions of native people.

By 1550, the Spanish controlled northern Mexico and part of Central America. They built Mexico City on the ruins of Tenochtitlán. It became the capital of **New Spain**, which included Mexico, Central America, and the Caribbean.

THE IMPACT OF THE TREATY OF TORDESILLAS

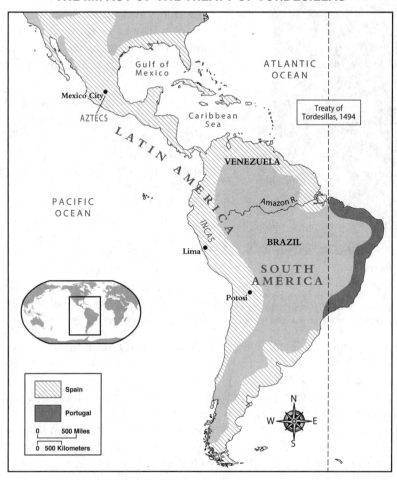

In 1494, Spain and Portugal decided to divide up the Americas for themselves, without asking the people who lived there or any other countries. Portugal got the lands east of the dotted line on the map, and Spain got the lands west of the line. Pope Alexander VI brokered the deal. This is the reason Portuguese is the main language of Brazil and Spanish is the main language of most of the rest of Latin America.

Forced Labor To ensure a labor supply, the Spanish under Queen Isabella had established the **encomienda** system. Large landowners, *encomenderos*, forced indigenous people to work on plantations for food and shelter. The Spanish also forced indigenous groups to do the dangerous work in gold and silver mines. With this supply of labor, tremendous wealth flowed to Spain. As part of the encomienda system, encomenderos were bound to instruct their subjects in the ways of Christianity and keep them faithful.

Jesuit missionaries tried to save the indigenous people from some of the horrors of the conquistadors. Spanish priest **Bartolomé de las Casas**, a member of a religious order called the Dominicans, insisted that the encomienda system and forced labor were unjust. The arguments of de las Casas persuaded Charles V to call the Council of Valladolid in Spain. This was the first time that any

Source: Getty Images

Our Lady of Guadalupe is a depiction of Mary, the mother of Jesus. To many people, she also represents aspects of indigenous faiths practiced in Mexico before the arrival of Christianity.

European colonizer publicly debated the rights and treatment of indigenous peoples. The arguments of de las Casas are seminal texts in the field of human rights, but they did little to change Spanish policy.

Asiento System An **asiento** was a contract between the government of Spain and either another country, a private company, or an individual. The agreement was that this other party would supply Spain with enslaved Africans to work in the Americas, and Spain would pay for this service. The Spaniards lacked a base in Africa and found it easier to contract this process. Historians estimate that 450,000 Africans were captured and forced to go to the Americas as part of this system from the late 16th century to 1750.

South America Spanish explorer **Vasco Nuñez de Balboa** crossed the Isthmus of Panama in 1513. He was the first European to reach the eastern shore of the Pacific Ocean.

Spain then became interested in the western coast of South America. Conquistador **Francisco Pizarro** (c. 1475–1541) arrived in the region in 1530 and found the **Inca Empire** in a weakened condition. European disease had already killed a large proportion of the population, including the emperor. The empire then became embroiled in civil war and Pizarro took advantage of the situation. With his force of fewer than 200 men and his superior weapons, he defeated the Inca and took control of their capital.

Within five years, Pizarro established a new Spanish capital in Lima that governed Peru, the part of the empire covering much of western South America. The Spanish used a similar system to control the indigenous population and extract wealth as they had in New Spain.

The Pacific A Portuguese explorer sailing for the Spanish named **Ferdinand Magellan** (1480–1521) set out in 1519 to explore the eastern coast of South America and the Pacific Ocean. Magellan and his crew survived the storm-ravaged straits at the southern tip of South America and headed west. Because of the lack of wind to push them westward, they nearly starved to death on the voyage. But in 1521, they reached the islands later named the Philippines after the Spanish king Phillip II. Magellan died while on the islands, but one of his ships continued the voyage across the Indian Ocean and around Africa. It completed the first voyage around the world.

At first, the Spanish saw the Philippines primarily as a stop on the way to the **Spice Islands**—the islands east of present-day Indonesia and south of the Philippines with rich soil that is ideal for growing sought-after spices such as nutmeg and cinnamon. The Spanish did not establish a permanent settlement there until 1565, and they did not found the capital of Manila until 1571. As in the Americas, Catholic missionaries set out to convert the native people, many of whom had embraced Islam shortly before the Spanish arrived. Manila became a center of commerce, as traders exchanged Chinese silk for Peruvian and Mexican silver. The trade drew Chinese merchants along with a growing number of Spanish settlers.

The size and wealth of the Spanish Empire made Spain a dominant power in Europe in the 16th century. Between 1492 and the mid-1500s, Spain established an empire that stretched from northern Mexico through much of South America and the Caribbean islands, and into the Philippines. By the 17th century, Europeans had begun to build a global trade network. Over time, they pushed out the Muslims and Chinese who had dominated trade in the Indian Ocean and the western Pacific.

THE SPANISH IN THE AMERICAS AND THE PACIFIC: 16TH CENTURY			
Territory	Explorer	Economic Activities	Religious Issues
Mexico	Hernán Cortés	Plantation agriculture; gold and silver mines	Imposition of Catholicism strengthened hold of Spanish over natives as cheap labor
Peru	Francisco Pizarro	Plantation agriculture; silver mines; trade for Inca gold products and fabrics	Imposition of Catholicism strengthened hold of Spanish over natives as cheap labor
Philippines	Ferdinand Magellan	Trade (Chinese silk for Mexican silver); other commercial activities	Conversion to Catholicism after many had previously adopted Islam

Competition Among Atlantic States

Spain administered a vast empire in the Americas. The Spanish explored parts of what later became the United States, including Florida and several southeastern and southwestern states. Spain wanted to claim all North America for its empire. However, the Atlantic states of France, England, and the Netherlands challenged this plan in the early 17th century.

Shortly after the voyages by Columbus, explorers of other states doubted his conclusion that he had reached Asia. The sea routes to Asia controlled by the Portuguese and the Spanish were long and difficult. Therefore, these explorers sought alternative routes, sailing north and then either west or east looking for a passage to Asia. In their explorations, they found and claimed other parts of the New World.

The Netherlands The Dutch became the leading maritime power around 1600 and dominated 17th-century European trade. They were the first to benefit from a weakening of Spain and Portugal and later faced challenges from France and England. Like the Portuguese, the Dutch focus for expansion overseas was on developing a trade network rather than a colonial empire. They established two trading companies:

- The Dutch East India Company (see Topic 1.10), founded in 1602, focused on Asian trade and established a strong presence in the Spice Islands.

- The Dutch West India Company, created in 1621, focused on the Americas and established the colony of **New Amsterdam** in 1624. The colony stretched from the mouth of the Hudson River north to present-day Albany, New York. The only Dutch North American colony, New Amsterdam was taken over by the English in 1664 and became **New York**.

England One of the early explorers for England was the Venetian **John Cabot**. Sailing across the North Atlantic in 1497, Cabot reached the eastern coast of Canada. His explorations gave England a basis for claiming land in North America.

After Cabot's voyages, the English became consumed with domestic issues and colonizing Ireland. They did little exploring of the Americas for the next century. By the time they did, the Spanish controlled the most profitable regions: the sugar islands, gold mines, and silver mines in the south.

English Colonies Finally, in 1607, the English established their first permanent settlement in North America—**Jamestown**, Virginia. By 1670, England had established colonies in eastern Canada and several smaller islands in the West Indies, including Barbados and Bermuda. They had also founded 11 of the 13 colonies along the Atlantic coast of North America that would later be part of the United States.

The English were also interested in expanding their trade to compete with the Portuguese and the Dutch in Asia. For this reason, they established the British East India Company in 1601. (See Topic 1.10.)

France The French sent out early expeditions to explore the Americas, looking for a passage to Asia:

- In 1524, the Italian navigator **Giovanni de Verrazano** sailed on behalf of France. He explored the Atlantic coast from North Carolina to Newfoundland.

- From 1534 to 1536, **Jacques Cartier** became the first European to explore the St. Lawrence River in Canada.

Neither explorer found a passage to Asia. However, Cartier's explorations established French claims to the territory.

It took decades before the French established a permanent North American settlement. In 1608, **Samuel de Champlain** founded Quebec as a prosperous fur-trading post in eastern Canada. He continued to explore the surrounding region and strengthened French claims to Canada, then called **New France**.

France also established colonies in the West Indies beginning in the 1620s. While the islands such as Martinique and Guadeloupe that the French colonized were small, the sugar these islands produced made them very valuable.

THE ATLANTIC STATES IN THE AMERICAS AND ASIA, 15TH TO 17TH CENTURIES			
Atlantic Nation	Explorers	Lands Claimed	Economic Activities
England	John Cabot	Parts of Canada; Jamestown; smaller islands in West Indies (including Barbados and Bermuda); by 1670, 11 of the 13 colonies that would become the United States	British East India Company, established 1601; competed with Portuguese and Dutch for trade in Asia
France	Giovanni Verrazano, Jacques Cartier, Samuel de Champlain	Area of St. Lawrence River in Canada; established trading post at Quebec, 1608; established New France in Canada; colonies in West Indies, including Martinique and Guadeloupe	Fur trading in Quebec; sugar plantations in West Indies
The Netherlands	Willem Schouten (discovered route to Pacific around southern tip of South America, 1615–1616)	Established colony of New Amsterdam, which was taken over by England and renamed New York	Focused on developing trade network; established Dutch East India Company (1602) for Asian trade and Dutch West India Company (1621) for trade in the Americas

Rivalries Among European Powers

As European states competed for trade, rivalries and conflicts developed among them in the 17th and 18th centuries. Because countries adopted the mercantilist idea that the amount of worldwide wealth was limited, they believed that their wealth could grow only at the expense of their neighbors.

Growing Trade Rivalries Competition for wealth and resources took place all over the globe. For example, the Portuguese had first sought to dominate the trade in spices and silk from Asia in the early 16th century. When the Spanish colonized the Philippines after 1570, they began to compete with the Portuguese. At the beginning of the 17th century, the Dutch successfully challenged the Portuguese for dominance of the spice trade when they established a strong presence in the Spice Islands. While Portuguese military efforts had been successful against Muslim traders in the region, they were less successful against the Dutch. In addition, even though the British East India Company had been established before the Dutch came to the region, the Dutch were strong enough economically to force the British to cede the trade in the islands and to shift their focus to India, which was ruled by the Mughal Empire.

During the 18th century, Britain became the dominant European power in Asian trade. France also established trading companies in Asia in the 17th century, but it had little success with them.

Conflict over American Colonies Based on the Treaty of Tordesillas of 1494, Spain and Portugal tried to avoid conflicts by dividing their colonizing efforts. Each wanted to monopolize trade and colonize based on explorations in their assigned regions. However, other European states such as England, France, and the Netherlands did not consider themselves bound by the treaty. They soon began their own explorations that led to the establishment of trading companies and colonies in the early 17th century.

Wars in Europe and the Americas Rivalries over land in the Americas led to conflicts later in the 17th and 18th centuries. When the Spanish king Charles II died childless, the **War of the Spanish Succession** erupted. From 1701 until 1714, rival claimants to the throne fought bitterly. Fighting spilled over to the North American colonies. In the end, Britain gained the most in the New World, while Spain and France were weakened. (See Topic 3.6.)

Great Britain and France fought a series of wars in the 18th century that included battles over North American colonies. One of those wars, the **Seven Years' War** (1756–1763), resulted in France giving up claims to large amounts of land east of the Mississippi River and in Canada. (See Topic 5.3.) After this war and others, France controlled very little land on the North American continent.

REFLECT ON THE ESSENTIAL QUESTION

Essential Question: *How and why did trading networks and colonial expansion affect relations among European states?*

European Power	Actions That Influenced Relations with Other Powers

KEY TERMS

Christopher Columbus	encomienda	John Cabot
West Indies	Bartolomé de las Casas	Jamestown
Indians	asiento	Giovanni de Verrazano
Treaty of Tordesillas	Vasco Nuñez de Balboa	Jacques Cartier
Amerigo Vespucci	Francisco Pizarro	Samuel de Champlain
New World	Inca Empire	New France
conquistadors	Ferdinand Magellan	War of the Spanish
Hernán Cortés	Spice Islands	Succession
Aztec Empire	New Amsterdam	Seven Years' War
New Spain	New York	

Questions 1–3 refer to the following passage.

"Upon which assurance of your royal love I have given my general command to all the kingdoms and ports of my dominions to receive all the merchants of the English nation as the subjects of my friend; that in what place soever they choose to live, they may have free liberty without any restraint; and at what port soever they shall arrive, that neither Portugal nor any other shall dare to molest their quiet; and in what city soever they shall have residence, I have commanded all my governors and captains to give them freedom answerable to their own desires; to sell, buy, and to transport into their country at their pleasure.

For confirmation of our love and friendship, I desire your Majesty to command your merchants to bring in their ships of all sorts of rarities and rich goods fit for my palace; and that you be pleased to send me your royal letters by every opportunity, that I may rejoice in your health and prosperous affairs; that our friendship may be interchanged and eternal."

—Jahangir, ruler of the Mughal Empire, letter to
King James I of England, 1617

1. Which of the following concepts is this letter most clearly describing?
   (A) The colonization of England by Jahangir
   (B) A trade agreement between England and the Mughals
   (C) The establishment of an encomienda system
   (D) The establishment of an asiento system

2. Which of the following most likely explains why Jahangir mentions Portugal?
   (A) The Portuguese and the English were rivals in trade.
   (B) The Portuguese and the Mughals established rival colonies.
   (C) Portugal took over Spanish colonies in India.
   (D) The king of England was about to become king of Portugal.

3. Which of the following is the most important part of the broader historical context in which Jahangir wrote this letter?

(A) The Dutch and other Europeans had successfully prevented English trade with the Spice Islands.

(B) The Portuguese and other Europeans had little interest in trade with India because of its climate.

(C) The English were already the dominant colonial power in the Americas and wanted to expand their empire.

(D) The English produced goods such as wool and coal that would be more highly valued in India than in the rest of Asia.

SHORT-ANSWER QUESTION

Use the passage below to answer all parts of the question that follows.

"While women suffered the usual indignities to which they were subject anywhere, several dimensions of their life separated their New World existence from that of their counterparts in Europe. The competitive relations among European communities and the infeasibility of tight village control led to increased opportunities for women to move to new locations and to adopt new economic roles.

While women in Europe often found themselves tied to the region of their birth, the mobility available to New World women in some areas provided greater potential for independence. . . . The physical mobility possible in the New World could provide . . . women the chance for a fresh start.

Black women escapees from Curaçao [an island in the Caribbean] who became liberated by taking this journey [to Venezuela] often turned to commerce in their new homeland. . . . The occupation more available to European women in the New World than in the old was trading.

Mixed-race May Musgrove Matthews Bosomworth operated a trading post in Georgia supplying both Englishmen and Native Americans. In New France, Elizabeth Bertrand Mitchell, Madelaine and Josette Laframboise, Elizabeth Mitchell and Agatha Biddle all played important roles in the fur trade coming through the island of Mackinac [in the Great Lakes]."

—Patricia Seed, "Women in the Atlantic World," in *Gender, Race and Religion in the Colonization of the Americas*," 2007

1. a) Describe ONE historical development Seed describes.

   b) Identify ONE type of evidence Seed uses in this passage to support her claim.

   c) Explain ONE type of evidence that would refute Seed's claim.

Topic 1.8

Colonial Expansion and Columbian Exchange

And afterwards I did send for a cup of tea (a China drink) of which I never had drank before.

—Samuel Pepys, diary entry Tuesday, September 25, 1660; this is the first written record of an English person drinking tea

Essential Question: What were the economic, social, and cultural impacts of European colonial expansion and the development of trade networks?

As new trade networks developed and countries increased their colonization efforts, cultures around the globe began to influence one another in new ways:

- Economic changes led to poverty for many and vast wealth for some. For example, the international banking industry grew more powerful and profitable, and the insurance industry emerged.

- Social changes led to improved nutrition as plants and animals were transported to new places. New leisure activities emerged. For example, coffee is not native to Europe, but coffeehouses became popular there.

- Cultural changes included the spread of languages and religions— sometimes voluntarily, but other times by force.

Global Exchanges Reshape the World

Before the era of expansion, the Mediterranean Sea was the center of European maritime trade and naval power. States that bordered the Mediterranean— such as the Italian city-states, Spain, and France—were the most powerful. Foreign trade around the Mediterranean focused on the region to the east controlled by the Ottoman Empire. For example, the Italian city-state of Venice had been an especially significant port where trade from Asia entered Europe. But beginning in about 1420 with the settlement of the Madeira Islands off the coast of North Africa, Portugal began its era of exploration, international trade, and overseas empire and would eventually challenge Venetian dominance.

Portuguese Trading Network

The Portuguese were the first to begin systematically exploring to increase overseas trade. Under the leadership of **Prince Henry the Navigator**

(1394–1460), the Portuguese wanted to spread Christianity and obtain direct access to gold, ivory, and slaves from sub-Saharan Africa. Henry was known as "the Navigator" for his support of sailing on the open seas. However, he never sailed beyond the sight of land. Henry established a school for navigators on the country's southwest coast in 1419. The work there formed the basis of Portuguese explorations of the 15th and 16th centuries.

Africa Beginning in the 1430s, Portuguese sailors explored the western coast of Africa looking for gold. The combination of winds and currents and a lack of natural harbors made traveling along this coast dangerous. Finally, in 1471, the Portuguese found a source of gold in western Africa. Europeans later referred to the area as the **Gold Coast**.

Trade in gold, ivory, and enslaved people grew, and the Portuguese developed a trading network based in forts along the African coast. The Portuguese negotiated with local landowners to get land for their forts.

The Portuguese usually didn't capture enslaved people. African leaders along the coast realized their kingdoms could benefit economically by selling captives, and sometimes their own people, as slaves to the Portuguese. By the 1480s, Portuguese were already shipping enslaved Africans abroad to work on sugar plantations. In the 1500s and 1600s, the Spanish, English, and French also began to export enslaved Africans.

South Asia The Portuguese heard that there was a possible trade route to Asia around the southern tip of Africa, then called the Cape of Storms. In 1488, the explorer **Bartolomeu Dias** (c. 1450–1500) was the first European to sail around the Cape. But Dias turned back as his crew refused to go on against powerful currents.

Ten years later, **Vasco da Gama** (c. 1460–1524) rounded the Cape, which he renamed the Cape of Good Hope, and explored the coast of East Africa. Da Gama then sailed to the southeastern coast of India by crossing the Indian Ocean, then called the Arabian Sea. There, in the port of Calicut, he acquired a cargo of spices that would yield huge profits.

In later years, the Portuguese sought to dominate the spice trade and eliminate Muslim traders from the market. In 1510, Portugal used its maritime strength to defeat the Muslim kingdom that ruled the city of Goa on the western coast of India and set up a port and trading operation there.

Pressing Eastward After reaching South Asia, the Portuguese continued eastward. They started to travel more extensively throughout Asia, seeking to expand their access to the spice trade. In 1511, they captured the city of Malacca on the Malay Peninsula from its Muslim inhabitants. The Portuguese used that port as a base to extend their lucrative trading network to China and the Spice Islands. In the Spice Islands, the Portuguese negotiated a treaty that allowed them to export cloves to Europe. However, they did not have the desire, population, or political power to establish colonies in Asia.

Dividing the World In the 1494 Treaty of Tordesillas (see Topic 1.7), Spain and Portugal agreed to establish separate spheres of colonial influence.

The explorer **Pedro Álvares Cabral** (c. 1467–1520) claimed Brazil as a colony for Portugal in 1500. The Portuguese began to establish settlements there in the 1530s and eventually set up large sugar cane **plantations**, or large farms that usually grows a single cash crop such as sugar, tobacco, or cotton.

Plantations need large workforces. At first, the colonists enslaved the native people and forced them to work on the plantations. Later, they imported enslaved people from Africa as well. The sugar that was exported from Brazil and sold in Europe created tremendous wealth for Portugal, which ran its colony in Brazil along mercantilist principles. Eventually, coffee also became a valuable export from Brazil.

Shifts in Economic Power

Before the discovery of new trade routes that originated on the Atlantic Ocean, Europeans had thought there was little benefit to having ports on the Atlantic coast. They had believed that there was little value that could come from the West. But Portuguese and Spanish explorations opened their eyes to a far different possibility. In the 17th century, the Dutch were the first to grasp this possibility and dominate the new global trading network. Yet by the early 18th century, the English had surpassed the Dutch.

Leading Atlantic Ports

The transtition of economic power to the northern Atlantic states is clear in the shifting location of leading port cities. Cities expanded as new markets developed.

Lisbon The Portuguese began their exploration and trade from the port city of **Lisbon** in the 15th century. It became clear in the early 16th century that Lisbon's distance from northern and central Europe made it less than ideal as a place from which to ship goods from Asia throughout the continent.

Antwerp The Portuguese then set up a trading center in the city of **Antwerp** on a river near the North Sea in what is now northern Belgium. At that time, this region was part of the Netherlands, then under the control of Spain. Antwerp was the financial and commercial center of northern Europe. The city benefited from the emerging trade from Spanish and Portuguese overseas colonies. Portuguese traders faced stiff competition in the city from other European traders.

Amsterdam By the early 17th century, the northern parts of the Netherlands had become independent of Spain. The Dutch port city of **Amsterdam** then surpassed Antwerp and became the major trading port in Europe. The Dutch had large fleets of ships that traded both regionally and internationally.

Bristol As the English grew in political, social, and economic power, a city on the west coast of England also grew. As a port city, **Bristol** easily allowed for the import and export of many goods. But it was also a manufacturing center, which made it even more prosperous than many other port cities. People in or near Bristol imported wool and made it into cloth. They also imported sugar and cacao and made them into chocolate.

London Another port city, this one in southeastern England, became more powerful during this period. **London** became a cultural center, with many theaters and coffeehouses. It became a business center, with the first fire insurance company forming in 1680. And gradually, London became (and still is) a center for international banking. By the late 1800s, more than half the world's trade was completed in British currency.

Though the Atlantic states became part of an expanding world economy, trade within Europe still accounted for most of European trade volume even at the end of the 17th century. However, the goods that were traded from overseas, such as pepper, spices, sugar, tea, and coffee, tended to be more valuable.

The Columbian Exchange

The **Columbian Exchange** received its name because it began with the voyages of Columbus. It refers to the exchange of plants, animals, and diseases between the *Old World*—Europe, Africa, and Asia—and the New World.

American historian Alfred Crosby first explained the concept in the 1970s. A vast ocean separated the Old World from the New World, so different plants, animals, and germs evolved in each region. The exchange thus had enormous consequences in both regions, both positive and negative.

Food and Other Goods As Europeans established colonies around the world, they began to trade goods between Europe, the Americas, Asia, and Africa. These goods included spices, luxury goods, precious metals, crops, and livestock. Tomatoes, potatoes, corn, and squash were introduced to Europe from the Americas, while Europeans brought cattle, horses, pigs, and sheep to the Americas and introduced the cultivation of wheat.

The exchange of foods throughout the world led to better nutrition and increased population. High-calorie foods, such as corn and especially potaotoes, which are able to grow in poor soil, led to a population boom in Europe. Tea from Asia, coffee from Africa, and chocolate from Mexico, along with sugar and tobacco from the Americas, changed European life.

Cultural Exchanges and Clashes Cultural practices were also exchanged. Spanish colonization in the Americas and the Philippines brought a new language and religion, including the institutions of the Catholic Church, along with its churches, schools, and hospitals. The introduction of enslaved Africans and the ideas they brought with them from their homelands caused changes in language, religion, foods, and other aspects of culture as well.

Furthermore, the relative ease with which Europeans conquered indigenous populations reinforced Europeans' belief that they had a superior civilization. European expansion marked a shift toward European dominance beyond the continent.

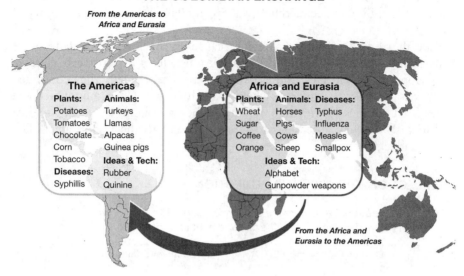

THE COLUMBIAN EXCHANGE

From the Americas to Africa and Eurasia

The Americas

Plants:	Animals:
Potatoes	Turkeys
Tomatoes	Llamas
Chocolate	Alpacas
Corn	Guinea pigs
Tobacco	**Ideas & Tech:**
Diseases:	Rubber
Syphillis	Quinine

Africa and Eurasia

Plants:	Animals:	Diseases:
Wheat	Horses	Typhus
Sugar	Pigs	Influenza
Coffee	Cows	Measles
Orange	Sheep	Smallpox
	Ideas & Tech:	
	Alphabet	
	Gunpowder weapons	

From the Africa and Eurasia to the Americas

Economic Opportunities Europeans profited in many ways from the Columbian Exchange. For example, by establishing plantations to grow sugar cane, coffee, tobacco, and cotton in different parts of the Americas, Europeans cultivated lucrative cash crops that could be sold directly to a growing European market. Because Europeans relied largely on forced labor of indigenous peoples and enslaved Africans, their costs to grow the crops were low. In addition, the slave trade itself was a source of profit.

Livestock—including cattle, sheep, pigs, and horses—provided another economic opportunity for Europeans. Settlers brought animals from the Old World to the New World, where they had lots of space to graze and few natural predators. Herds were raised for their meat, hides, and wool, which could all be sold at a profit.

Ecological Disasters Old World plants, animals, and diseases came to the New World along with European settlers. The results were often devastating. Plants and animals in the New World were destroyed, as the introduction of Old World plants, including weeds, often edged out native species.

Extensive grazing by European livestock eroded the soil in many areas and made it difficult for native species to grow. Some areas began to look like deserts as the soil eroded. Europeans also cleared forests, often by large-scale burning to create open land for settlements, grazing, and crops, further damaging the environment.

Diseases By far, the worst disaster was the introduction of European diseases, such as **smallpox** and **measles**. Peoples of the Americas had never been exposed to these diseases. As a result, their bodies had not built up **immunity**, or resistance, to them as Europeans had over several centuries. As soon as Europeans arrived, epidemics began devastating the native population.

Historians estimate that because of epidemics caused by European diseases, the native population declined between 50 and 90 percent within a century of contact.

Death from disease was a major reason Europeans dominated Native Americans as quickly as they did. The deadly effects of European diseases first happened in the West Indies, where Columbus landed. They continued in Mexico and South America when Spanish conquistadors conquered the Aztecs and the Inca. By the time the English began colonizing North America in the 17th century, diseases had already spread to the region and killed many Native Americans.

REFLECT ON THE ESSENTIAL QUESTION

Essential Question: *What were the economic, social, and cultural impacts of European colonial expansion and the development of trade networks?*

Economic Impacts	Social and Cultural Impacts

KEY TERMS

Prince Henry the Navigator	plantation	London
Gold Coast	Lisbon	Columbian Exchange
Bartolomeu Dias	Antwerp	smallpox
Vasco da Gama	Amsterdam	measles
Pedro Álvares Cabral	Bristol	immunity

HISTORICAL PERSPECTIVES: *WHAT WAS THE IMPACT OF EUROPEAN EXPLORATION?*

European exploration caused dramatic changes in the Americas and Africa. The native population of the Americas plummeted, and millions of Africans were enslaved and forcibly relocated.

Advantages for Western Europe To dispel the belief that western Europeans dominated the world due to their superior culture, Jared Diamond explained in his book *Guns, Germs, and Steel* (1997) that Europeans benefited from geography. They had better access to the animals, innovations, and ideas of the more advanced societies in eastern Asia. European access to horses and cows improved the efficiency with which they could use the land and travel and trade across it. Guns and steel in European hands became more advanced, and this, combined with years of plague, led to the development of a well-armed and resistant group of people that was ready to dominate a part of the world that lacked these advantages.

Helen Nader, an expert in medieval history, argued in the article "The End of the Old World" (1992) that Europeans couldn't just impose their ideas on others. They had to adapt to the weather, people, and the environment. This meant developing new ways of trading. From the beginning, success and profit in the Americas was about innovation. For the Spanish monarchs Ferdinand and Isabella to profit from the Americas, they had to infuse it with a strong competitive spirit.

Early explorers obscured this goal by following tradition and maximizing their own wealth. But by 1504, the Spanish crown saw the need for high-volume trade, which required many investors rather than single explorers. As a result, Spanish America was full of family farms, run by households with a degree of local control, and acceptance of free trade. This brought the Spanish their wealth, at least in the short term. Their acceptance of competition, trade, and sometimes self-rule would soon be seen as a characteristic of the modern world.

Impact on the World Andre Gunder Frank challenged explanations of history that he found too centered on Europe. In *ReOrient: Global Economy in the Asian Age* (1998), he argued that exploration changed the world because European capitalism provided the needed wealth (in the form of crops, silver, and gold) for Europe to rise simultaneous to the decline of the East. Ultimately, European exploration established a new world system that placed Europe at the center. This system became so much a part of the western worldview that it has taken historians the past 60 years to break with the Eurocentric tradition and explain the realities and complexities of Europe's rise and the resulting impact.

1. Why did Europeans succeed in establishing trade networks, according to Jared Diamond? How does Helen Nader's opinion on this issue differ?

2. Which of the historians discusses social issues in addition to economic issues?

3. Which historian's view makes the most sense to you? Why?

MULTIPLE-CHOICE QUESTIONS

Questions 1–3 refer to the following passage.

"Because it will be necessary to use Indian labor in mining gold and other tasks We have ordered done, you are to require the Indians to work in the things of Our service, paying to each the salary that seems just to you...

Because it is necessary to found some towns on Hispaniola...you are to establish new towns in the numbers and at the sites that seem best to you, after careful inspection.

Because it Our will that the Christians in the abovesaid island of Hispaniola live together from now on rather than being scattered through the countryside, [you should make sure that] no one lives outside the towns than are established on the island. . . .

Since the security of the land requires the construction of some forts, you are to determine the manner of building these forts and build up to three. . . .

Since We have been informed that good practice has not been followed in the cutting of brazilwood, many trees being cut down so that more dye can be obtained, you are to give orders that no one is to cut down the tree. . . .

In order that Christians and Indians shall live together in peace, friendship, and harmony, and that there be no fights or quarrels among them, you shall order that no one give or sell offensive or defensive weapons to the Indians nor exchange such weapons with them. . . .

Since there will be other things that cannot now be acted on from here as they should be, you are to inform yourself as soon as you arrive of what problems need to be dealt with and how."

—King Ferdinand and Queen Isabella, letter to the governor of Hispaniola (present-day island of Haiti and Dominican Republic), 1501

1. Which of the following provides evidence that modifies or refutes the argument that all Spaniards wanted what the monarchs called "peace, friendship, and harmony" in the colonies?

   (A) The encomienda system established by the Spanish

   (B) The Treaty of Tordesillas signed by Spain

   (C) The goods and diseases transferred in the Columbian Exchange

   (D) The techniques used by some missionaries to spread Christianity

2. Which of the following best identifies the historical context for the directions in the last paragraph of the passage?

   (A) The technology of the period meant that communication between Spain and its colony took many weeks.

   (B) The political views common in the period led European monarchs to try to decentralize power.

   (C) The religious beliefs dominant in the period caused the monarchs to trust that the governor would follow God's will.

   (D) The racial attitudes shared in the period made the monarchs realize that they did not know how to interact with indigenous people.

3. Which of the following individuals had an accomplishment most similar to the goal desired by Ferdinand and Isabella in this passage?

(A) Prince Henry the Navigator because he traded with a region Europeans had not traded directly with before

(B) Bartholomeu Dias because he sailed around a geographic barrier that Europeans had not passed before

(C) Vasco da Gama because he acquired spices from a land Europeans had not reached by an all-water route before

(D) Pedro Cabral because he established a permanent colony in a land Europeans had not colonized before

SHORT-ANSWER QUESTION

Use the image below to answer all parts of the question that follows.

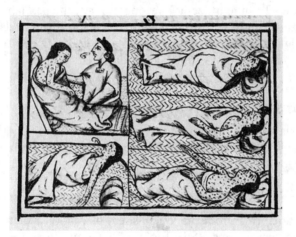

Source: Wikipedia Commons/the Florentine Codex, c. 1585

This drawing shows a smallpox victim in the Americas. The original artist is unknown.

1. a) Describe the historical situation portrayed in this drawing.

b) Describe ONE effect of the historical situation portrayed in this drawing.

c) Explain why this drawing might be intended for a particular audience.

Topic 1.9

The Slave Trade

The men...on being brought aboard ship, are immediately fastened together two and two, by handcuffs on their wrists, and by irons riveted on their legs. . . . They are frequently stowed so close as to admit of no other posture than lying on their sides.

— Alexander Falconbridge, former surgeon on a slave ship, 1788

Essential Question: What caused the slave trade to develop?

Governments, individuals, and businesses all saw advantages to increased overseas trade. To maximize the economic advantage, labor had to be inexpensive and plentiful. This need led to the beginning and development of the slave trade which brought power, profits, and luxury goods to developed countries. It also brought suffering to enslaved people and centuries of inequality.

Origins of the African Slave Trade

The African slave trade was another result of the expanding Atlantic trading system and the colonization of the Americas. When the Portuguese brought their first cargo of enslaved Africans to Europe in 1441, they sold the enslaved people within European countries. The slave trade grew gradually as the Portuguese continued to explore and trade along the west coast of Africa.

Planter Society Europeans established plantations that used a large work force to farm crops. (See Topic 1.7.) Common to plantations were labor-intensive crops such as rice, sugar cane, coffee, and cotton that required hundreds or even thousands of workers. Members of **planter society** organized and profited from this labor.

In the 16th and 17th centuries, as Europeans began establishing a plantation economy in the Americas, plantation owners first turned to indigenous peoples as slave laborers and forced them to work under cruel conditions. Deaths from European diseases and harsh treatment created a **demographic catastrophe** among indigenous peoples. *Demographic* means "having to do with populations of large groups of people with a shared characteristic," such as a certain nationality.

Because so many indigenous people died of disease or overwork, Europeans looked for another form of labor. They decided to use enslaved Africans, which meant a significant change to the Atlantic slave trade.

Work on plantations was backbreaking. This drawing shows enslaved people harvesting sugar cane.

Development of the African Slave Trade

Profits from slave trading and plantations were enormous. As plantations produced more crops, the average prices for those crops decreased. More people were able to try sugar, coffee, and other plantation crops—and more people began to crave these items, which increased the demand for goods produced by enslaved people. As a result, the demand for labor and subsequently the slave trade grew larger and more complex.

The Triangle Trade Slave traders, importers, exporters, and smugglers all took part in the triangle trade. They bought, shipped, and sold raw materials, finished goods, and human beings. Because enslavement and plantation labor happened in faraway places, many ordinary consumers never considered the human costs of the products they bought. (For more about the Triangle Trade, see Topic 3.4.)

The Middle Passage Captured people working on plantations were only part of the human cost of the triangle trade. Before these enslaved people began work, they had to travel hundreds or even thousands of miles under inhuman conditions. The **Middle Passage** was one part of the triangular trade. It involved shipping enslaved Africans to the Americas and the West Indies. It was the largest sea-going forced migration in human history.

THE TRIANGLE TRADE

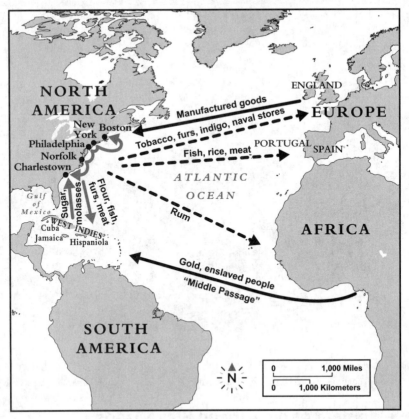

The triangle trade was a complex trading network that lasted from the 14th century until the early 19th century. It led to great wealth for some and death and suffering for many Africans.

Millions of men, women, and children made this trip on overcrowded ships between about 1518 and the mid-19th century. The trips took between 21 days and 90 days depending on several variables. Disease, mistreatment by crew members, starvation, severe weather, and suicide were all risks to African captives. Crew members threw the bodies of dead or dying captives off the boat for sharks to eat. Today, historians estimate that 13 percent of Middle Passage captives died on the voyage.

Continued Growth of the Slave Trade Europeans realized that supplying labor to plantations in South America and the West Indies and later in North America could be extremely profitable. The Portuguese and the Spanish brought slaves to the Americas, especially to Brazil and the islands of the West Indies in the early 16th century. The first English slave-trading expedition of 1562 sold slaves to the Spanish West Indies. English slave-trading voyages increased after the establishment of the English colonies in North America. The first enslaved Africans were brought to Virginia in 1619. The slave trade continued to expand throughout the 17th and 18th centuries.

IMPORTS OF ENSLAVED AFRICANS		
Colonial Region	Select Modern Countries in Region	Percentage of Total Imported Slaves
Portuguese colonies	Brazil	39%
British West Indian colonies	Jamaica, Barbados	18%
Spanish colonies	Dominican Republic	18%
French colonies	Haiti	14%
British Mainland colonies	United States	6%
Other	Suriname	5%

Source: Adapted from Stephen D. Behrendt, et al. *The Encyclopedia of the African and African American Experience*

Even people who were not directly involved in the slave trade sometimes benefited from it. For example, they were able to buy cotton, furs, rum, and sugar at much lower prices than they would have if plantation owners had used hired workers. Beginning in the late 1700s, some members of religious groups began to refuse to buy goods made by enslaved people.

REFLECT ON THE ESSENTIAL QUESTION

Essential Question: *What caused the slave trade to develop?*

Origins	Development

KEY TERMS

planter society   demographic catastrophe   Middle Passage

MULTIPLE-CHOICE QUESTIONS

Questions 1–3 refer to the passage below.

"I was not long suffered to indulge my grief; I was soon put down under the decks, and there I received such a salutation in my nostrils as I had never experienced in my life; so that with the loathsomeness of the stench, and crying together, I became so sick and low that I was not able to eat, nor had I the least desire to taste any thing. I now wished for the last friend, Death, to relieve me; but soon, to my grief, two of the white men offered me eatables; and, on my refusing to eat, one of them held me fast by the hands, ... and tied my feet, while the other flogged [whipped] me severely.

. . . In a little time after, amongst the poor chained men, I found some of my own nation, which in a small degree gave ease to my mind. I inquired of them what was to be done with us? They gave me to understand we were to be carried to these white people's country to work for them."

—Olaudah Equiano, *The Interesting Narrative of the Life of Olaudah Equiano; or, Gustavus Vassa, the African, Written by Himself*, 1789

1. The conditions on the slave ship that Equiano described were most directly a result of which of the following developments?

   (A) Planters in European colonies desired low-cost labor.

   (B) Planters in European colonies had success using Indigenous American laborers.

   (C) Europeans had a high demand for plantation products such as tobacco and sugar.

   (D) Africans had overpopulated some regions so many were forced to leave.

2. In this passage, Equiano is most likely describing an example of which historical event?

   (A) Ethical consumption

   (B) Demographics

   (C) Planter society

   (D) The Middle Passage

3. The significance of Equiano's point of view is best stated by which of the following explanations?

   (A) By providing basic factual information, he shows the role of the slave trade.

   (B) By describing historical trends, he provides the context for the slave trade.

   (C) By giving a first-person account, he expresses the human cost of the slave trade.

   (D) By summarizing data, he analyzes the economic causes and effects of the slave trade.

SHORT-ANSWER QUESTION

Use the passage below to answer all parts of the question that follows.

"In spite of the fact that most slave ships were equipped with pistols, muskets, . . . cannons, and around-the-clock guards, slave revolts were still a recurring part of the Atlantic crossing. Although most revolts were put down, several slave mutinies were successful. In June 1730, Captain George Scott of the sloop, Little George, sailed from the Guinea Coast (in route to Rhode Island) with a cargo of some ninety-six slaves. Several days into the voyage, at four-thirty in the morning, several slaves slipped out of their irons and killed the three watchmen who were on the deck. Totally taken by surprise, the captain and his crew were forced down into the cabin, where they were imprisoned by the revolting slaves. For several days the slaves controlled the ship and managed to sail it back to the Sierra Leone River. Nonetheless, after a failed attempt to scare the slaves with a bottle bomb and threats of sinking the ship, the captain and the crew of the Little George finally resolved to make a deal with the slaves. Accordingly, both parties agreed to grant the other their freedom. Then, after making it to the shore the slaves abandoned the ship. Incidentally, the captain did try to recapture the slaves, but was too weary and malnourished to pursue them."

—A. T. Bly, "Crossing the Lake of Fire: Slave Resistance during the Middle Passage, 1720–1842," *The Journal of Negro History*, 1998

1. a) Describe ONE historical concept that this passage demonstrates.

   b) Explain ONE long-term cause that led to the development described in the passage.

   c) Explain ANOTHER long-term cause that led to the development described in the passage.

Topic 1.10

The Commercial Revolution

I want to gain while I can.

—Jakob Fugger (1459–1525), German
merchant and financier

Essential Question: Between 1450 to 1648, what European commercial and agricultural developments took place and what were the economic effects?

Modern Europe emerged in the period that began around 1500 with European expansion through trade and colonization. As European society became more closely connected to the wider world, many aspects of daily life were shaped more and more by commercial and agricultural capitalism:

- **Capital** is wealth in the form of money that can be invested to create more wealth.

- **Capitalism** is an economic system that includes private ownership of the **means of production**, such as tools, buildings, and machines.

- In economic terms, the **market** is where buyers and sellers freely exchange goods and services.

In capitalism, the market, rather than the government, determines what to produce, how to produce it, and who produces it. Thus, capitalism is sometimes called a **market economy**.

Forms of capitalism emerged in the 15th century. At that time, **entrepreneurs**, individuals who assumed the risk of a business venture, generally acquired capital for their ventures as merchants. For example, the European woolen industry emerged in the 1400s. Entrepreneurs bought raw wool from many sources. Then they hired home-based workers to process it and sold the finished products throughout northern Europe. This is sometimes referred to as "cottage industry." Other kinds of work, such as mining or shipbuilding, required workers to come to a place of employment to work.

In the 16th century, this system of producing goods was spread over a wider area, especially in rural England and the western Holy Roman Empire. Commercial capitalism, or capitalism used for large-scale trade or business, that emerged in the 16th and 17th centuries extended to more-distant international markets. At the same time, traditional economic and social structures remained important throughout Europe.

Economic Patterns

Economic changes that came to Europe after 1500 had widespread consequences for the economy and society. New patterns emerged while traditional hierarchies and status relations continued to define the roles of individuals in many groups.

Changes in Banking and Finance

To handle the global trade market, banking and finance needed new tools. In the 15th and early 16th centuries, prominent families such as the **Medici** in Italy and the **Fuggers** in central Europe mostly controlled Europe's banking. (See topic 1.2 for more about the Medici family and Topic 1.5 for the nobles of the robe.) But as ever-larger amounts of capital flowed into Europe in the form of trade profits and precious metals from the Americas, banks needed to meet the new requirements of commercial capital markets.

Such changes helped grow the **money economy**, an economy based on cash for investment, for wages, and for buying and selling goods. The money economy replaced the earlier economy, in which people grew or made most of what they used. A money economy is more convenient because it can be used by anyone to purchase any good, not just by an individual who produces a specific good and can only barter for that good. Also, money doesn't spoil as many agricultural products do, is simple to divide, and easy to store.

Double-Entry Bookkeeping As business deals became more complex, merchants needed a better way to keep track of where their money went. **Double-entry bookkeeping** is a type of accounting where both sides of each transaction is tracked in a ledger, or book where the information is recorded. For example, if you sell a wool blanket for one coin, you write down what you no longer have (the blanket) and what you now have (the coin).

Venetians used double-entry bookkeeping by the early 1300s. Because Venice was a center of printing and publishing, authors created manuals on this topic, and those manuals spread throughout Europe.

Joint-Stock Companies One important financial innovation of the late 16th and early 17th centuries was the **joint-stock company.** This type of business venture raised large amounts of capital for international trade and colonization ventures. In this enterprise, many investors bought **stock**, or shares, in a company. Because many investors buy stock, the risk is distributed among the stockholders and is limited to any individual investor. They received **dividends**, or payments, as a return on their investment based on the company's profits.

Investors could receive high returns from such ventures. For example, the **Dutch East India Company** was a joint-stock company formed in 1602 to finance Dutch trade in Asia. During the first ten years of its operation, the company paid investors a return of about 30 percent. To put that in perspective, in the last century, modern U.S. stocks have paid investors a return of about 10 percent a year. If the company existed today, it would be worth almost $8 trillion.

The **British East India Company** also made significant profits as its agents bought and sold spices, cotton, silk, tea, and eventually a drug called opium. At its peak, this organization controlled one-fourth of the world's trade. As with the Dutch East India Company, part of these profits came from using the labor of enslaved people.

Urban Financial Centers As banking and finance changed, new capital markets emerged based in several urban financial centers, such as **Genoa**, **Amsterdam**, and **London**. Bankers in these centers could make deals throughout Europe.

URBAN FINANCIAL CENTERS IN THE 16TH AND 17TH CENTURIES		
City	Location	Economic Importance
Genoa	On the Mediterranean Sea near the current border of Italy and France	Genoa gained new importance in the later 16th and 17th centuries as the center of capital for the Spanish empire. Through central trading fairs and letters of exchange (authorizations of payments), bankers helped money flow from Spain to Spanish soldiers in the Netherlands.
Amsterdam	On the North Sea along the Amstel River	In 1609, the Dutch formed the Bank of Amsterdam, owned by many investors. Individuals, companies, and governments could deposit money in the bank and transfer capital to one another. The Dutch also established the Amsterdam Exchange for stock trading. It was the center of European business by the mid-17th century, as Amsterdam became Europe's financial capital.
London	In southeast England along the Thames River, inland from the English Channel	London became England's financial center as trade expanded with the establishment of joint-stock companies starting in the middle of the 16th century. As the Dutch weakened late in the 17th century, London's importance grew as a European financial center.

New Economic Elite

The growth of towns and **commerce**, or large-scale buying and selling, made merchants and bankers more powerful in some places than nobles who owned land. In some states, rulers granted titles of nobility to the most powerful merchants and bankers, such as the Fuggers in central Europe. Over several generations, the Fuggers rose from the peasantry to the merchant class and eventually made fortunes in goldsmithing, mining, and banking.

In 17th-century Amsterdam, wealthy merchants, manufacturers, and shipyard owners were at the top of the social scale. These elites controlled the city government and the nation's legislative body. Nobles who owned land were a step below the city's new economic elite, although there were intermarriages between these groups.

London was similar to Amsterdam in this period, as a small number of wealthy merchants controlled the city. Increase in wealth could improve a person's rank in society. Despite London's growing importance in international trade, England was still about 80 percent rural by the early 17th century. The landed nobility had the highest status in the English countryside. However, a growing number of gentry—wealthy landowners who did not have inherited titles—were gaining in influence.

Subsistence Farming and Commercial Agriculture

In pre-industrial Europe, most people lived in rural communities and made their living from agriculture. For landowners and agricultural workers, social customs and class relations had mostly stayed the same since the Middle Ages. By the 1600s, however, the economic changes of commercial capitalism reached the countryside of Western Europe, where they began to transform the traditional way of life.

Subsistence Agriculture

In the Middle Ages, the social **hierarchy**, or ranking, and economic patterns in Western Europe still revolved around the system of feudalism. In this system, a lord would grant land (a fief) to a vassal, a person who accepted the land in exchange for loyalty and military service. Life in the European countryside revolved around the **manor**, a large agricultural estate under the control of a noble, or lord. The term **landlord** originally meant the lord who owned and controlled a certain amount of land. Although the nobility made up a small minority of the population, they owned most of the land and kept their power through a system in which land and titles were inherited from one generation to the next. **Peasants**, who made up the vast majority of the population, farmed the land and occupied the lowest rung of the social order.

Changing Status of Peasants During the early Middle Ages, the majority of European peasants labored under **serfdom**. This meant they were legally bound to the land and subject to the authority of their landlord. Many peasants, or serfs, worked three days a week for the lord and paid rent for the land that they farmed. Often this payment came in the form of a portion of crops they grew or products made from livestock grazed on the lord's land. Serfs had some rights, unlike slaves who were considered property and had no rights.

Source: Getty Images

Although the plow was a valuable piece of technology, an English peasant still had to labor long hours.

Subsistence Economy A scarcity of suitable land for farming and a lack of scientific knowledge limited how much food peasants could produce. From the Middle Ages through the 17th century, **subsistence agriculture**, or farming for survival, was the norm in most of Europe. Peasants worked hard just to grow enough food to feed themselves and their families. They had very little food in reserve. Therefore, a bad harvest could lead to food shortages and, at worst, deadly famine (which happened on average every seven years in most of Europe's history).

For example, Europe began to experience changes in the weather in the early 14th century, a period sometimes called the **Little Ice Age** that lasted until about 1850. Cooler temperatures, frequent storms, and heavy rains led to shorter growing seasons. These conditions resulted in famines throughout northern Europe. Social effects of such situations led to smaller families and later marriages. Also, widespread hunger and malnutrition likely made the surviving population more susceptible to diseases, such as the plague that arrived in 1347.

Devastating Disease During the late Middle Ages, the status of peasants did improve, though, particularly in Western Europe. Economic and demographic changes altered the balance of power between peasants and lords and contributed to the decline of serfdom.

One of the main demographic factors was the **Great Plague** or **Black Death**, an outbreak of bubonic plague. It began in 1347 and reduced the population of Europe by as much as one-third, with around 25 million people dying of the disease.

The plague basically ended serfdom in Western Europe, although in Eastern Europe, serfdom continued until the mid-1800s. It caused a severe labor shortage and thus freed many peasants from serfdom. These free peasants could move, marry, and sell their land without their lord's permission. The decrease in the labor pool also allowed the remaining laborers to demand higher wages.

The Open-Field System Farming methods that developed in the Middle Ages continued to organize rural food production well into the 1600s. Most villages adopted the **open-field system**, in which farmland was divided into two or three large fields. Within each field, land was further divided into narrow strips. Individual peasant families owned or rented several strips scattered in different places throughout the fields. The fields were "open" in the sense that there were no fences separating individual plots, and the scattering of plots ensured that areas of good and poor soil were evenly distributed.

A portion of land was also set aside as common land, known as **the commons**. Everyone could use this land for livestock grazing. So the open-field system had some elements of private land ownership and some elements of communal land ownership. Villagers had to make collective decisions about what to grow and when. The survival of the village thus depended on community cooperation.

Crop Rotation A major problem on farms was soil exhaustion. Planting the same crop, such as wheat, many seasons in a row depleted the soil of nutrients and resulted in smaller harvests. To confront this challenge, a system of **crop rotation**, or planting crops in different fields at different times, developed during the Middle Ages. In the traditional **two-field system**, half the land lay fallow, or empty and unused, in each growing season, so the soil could recover nutrients.

In northern Europe, the **three-field system** became widespread. In the fall, the villagers planted grains such as wheat or barley in one field. In the spring, they planted crops such as oats, beans, or peas in a second field. They left the third field fallow. During the next planting season, the village rotated the crops to different fields. Two-thirds of the land was always in use, and one-third was recovering. This system resulted in bigger harvests than the two-field system.

However, the three-field system was not practical in all parts of Europe. The Mediterranean region did not get enough spring and summer rainfall for a second spring planting, so the less-productive two-field system continued.

Commercialization of Agriculture

The growth of colonization and overseas trade in the 16th century helped cause the rise of commercial capitalism in Europe. Rather than getting wealth from inherited land, merchants made their money from trade, the profits of private investment, and the selling of goods to a market of consumers.

The Price Revolution Beginning in the early 16th century, vast quantities of gold and silver entered Western Europe from the Spanish colonies in the Americas. That influx of precious metals and the resulting greater circulation of money, along with population growth, led to rising prices of food and other basic necessities in Europe. The widespread rise in prices over an extended time period, known as **inflation**, also contributed to the growth of commerce in the 16th century. This inflationary period, the **price revolution**, lasted from the late 15th century to the mid-17th century and was pivotal in the commercialization of agriculture.

While rising prices made life difficult for ordinary people, merchants and bankers benefited tremendously from the higher returns on their investments and loans. As they gained more capital, they looked for new ways to invest—and found them in the agricultural countryside.

As peasants migrated to towns, an increasing number of Europeans no longer grew their own food. They needed to buy it. Starting in the 1600s, middle-class investors and large landowners began a series of changes intended to shift the rural economy toward **commercial agriculture**. That means producing food and livestock products, such as wool, for profit rather than subsistence. These changes had a profound impact on the peasant way of life.

The Enclosure Movement From the viewpoint of a large landowner or capitalist investor, **the open-field system** of peasant agriculture was inefficient and wasteful. With limited land available, commercial farmers needed to find other ways to increase crop yields.

England passed laws that allowed investors and commercial farmers to buy land—including previously public land, the commons. **Enclosure** (also called inclosure) involved combining the various strips into larger fenced-in fields and establishing individual titles of ownership for each field. Most widespread in England, enclosures had started as early as the 12th century and developed rapidly from the 15th to 18th centuries. Land that used to be communal was now privately owned.

Effects of Enclosure Over time, enclosure increased agricultural productivity and benefited the large landowners. The creation of privately owned, fenced-in fields made it easier for investors to buy more land and expand their holdings. In doing so, landowners could engage in large-scale production of crops and livestock, adopt new farming practices, and generate a surplus that they could sell. As the cost of food declined due to the efficiency of larger farms, diets expanded in their variety and the frequency of famines was reduced. All this led to a population increase.

However, the enclosure movement also profoundly disrupted traditional village life and created hardship for many peasants. Enclosure increased rural poverty and led to a growing population of landless peasants. Some became laborers or tenant farmers on large estates owned by wealthy landowners. Others, hoping to find enough work to survive, migrated to towns and cities, leading to rapid urbanization. In some cases, peasants tried to reassert their traditional rights by resisting enclosure. Peasant revolts swept through England in the 1500s and 1600s.

Serfdom, Peasants, and Revolts

The growth of commercial agriculture often harmed Western Europe's peasants. However, most were no longer legally under the control of a landlord. That meant they could choose how to adapt to the new economy. These choices included the freedom to move from one place to another and to change jobs.

Serfdom in Eastern Europe

As serfdom declined in Western Europe, an opposite trend occurred in Eastern Europe. By the early 16th century, the status of peasants in the east deteriorated, and serfdom became more entrenched.

Powerful, centralized states emerged in Austria, Prussia, and Russia during the 17th century as monarchs persuaded aristocrats to cooperate by making them part of the state bureaucracy or administrative structure. Landlords became tax collectors, judges, and military officers. In turn, the state protected the serfdom that benefitted the the aristocracy. In Russia, serfdom became official law in 1649 and was not abolished until the 1860s.

Peasant Revolts

Peasants had long fought against attempts by landlords to become wealthier at the expense of peasants' rights. In the late Middle Ages, peasants revolted in France and England when landlords tried to reimpose conditions that existed before the Great Plague had devastated the population. The landed nobility ultimately put down the revolts revealing the limit of what the peasants could achieve.

More than a century later in 1525, a much larger revolt occurred in the Holy Roman Empire. Serfs, influenced by the teachings of Martin Luther, revolted to gain greater economic and social freedom. Artisans and craftspeople joined the revolt. The forces of the nobility crushed the revolt, massacring thousands.

Commerce and the Growth of Cities

As commercial capitalism grew in the 16th and 17th centuries, the population began to shift slowly from rural to urban areas. In 1500, less than 6 percent of the population lived in cities of 10,000 people or more. By 1650, more than 8 percent made their homes in large cities.

Some peasants took advantage of their increased mobility and moved to towns to find work. Artisans, merchants, and professionals had regularly been based in towns, and their numbers continued to grow. Wealthy nobles also began to establish homes in growing cities, especially the urban financial centers. Such changes placed stress on the traditional political and social structures of cities.

Population and Prices

In the mid-16th century, Europe's population finally reached levels that had existed before the Great Plague that began in 1347. Population estimates increased from around 60 million people in 1500 to about 80 million in 1600.

The Dutch, English, and French experienced the most growth. Much of the growth occurred in cities, which grew to unprecedented sizes for post-classical European cities. In 1500, only the largest cities in Europe—including Paris, Constantinople, and four Italian cities—had populations of more than 100,000. By 1600, Naples was up to 300,000, and more Italian cities, including Rome, had reached 100,000. Paris was the largest city, with a population of 500,000.

As populations grew, prices increased unevenly. Prices of **agricultural commodities**, such as wheat, rose more rapidly than workers' wages. larger populations meant a greater demand for food, which led to higher food prices. However, the greater number of workers meant competition for jobs, so wages stayed low. The resulting difference between wages and the prices of food and other necessities reduced the standard of living for wage earners, including agricultural laborers and urban salaried workers. Also, rulers increased taxes to build up their military forces.

Migrants and Cities

From the 12th to the 15th century, merchant and craft guilds had been the economic and political leaders in European communities. While merchants were wealthier, craft workers were more numerous. The two groups competed for influence.

However, with the growth of commercial capitalism, the power of guilds declined. Merchants became entrepreneurs, and guilds had a difficult time keeping control of the production of goods as changes in manufacturing and trade occurred. Non-guild migrants in the cities challenged the merchant elites and the craft guilds for power. Merchants resented the influx of both the landed nobility and lower-wealth classes into the cities.

As more people migrated into cities, population density increased dramatically. This led to crowded and difficult living conditions for members of the lower classes. Cities generally lacked the resources to deal with this rapid growth and the problems that came with it, such as insufficient housing. Also, people who moved to cities often struggled with unemployment. Lots of new city dwellers meant more competition for jobs.

London In the early 17th century, city leaders in London tried to limit the city's population by outlawing the subdivision of older buildings into smaller and smaller dwellings. Their efforts were unsuccessful. Many people had to live in crowded and unsanitary conditions, which brought outbreaks of deadly diseases, such as plague and tuberculosis, as well as generally poor health. More than one-third of London's children died before the age of six.

In 1666, the Great Fire of London burned for four days. It ravaged much of the city because of the overcrowded conditions and shoddy construction. In addition, the lack of clean water and food combined with high food prices and unchanging wages made it difficult for people to thrive in the city.

Source: Getty Images

This engraving shows the fire that devastated London in 1666.

THE GREAT LONDON FIRE.

Many new businesses came into existence throughout this period. The businesses that caused the most pollution, such as slaughterhouses, were set up outside the city walls. Building new shipping docks along the river led to the construction of poorly built huts nearby to house workers.

London's population grew steadily. In 1600, it was 250,000. By 1815, it reached 1.5 million.

Paris In the 14th century, the Great Plague and the Hundred Years' War prevented Paris from developing rapidly. As France became increasingly centralized, its larger cities—such as the capital, Paris—became increasingly important and prestigious. In the 16th century, nobles and merchants began building elaborate mansions there. The first theater in Paris was established in 1548. By 1702, the population of Paris had risen to almost 600,000.

However, life in Paris could be hard for someone without much wealth. A committee that met in the city in 1666 noted problems with violence, a lack of clean drinking water, and price gouging (sellers charging unfairly high prices) for bread and meat. But the worst problem was pollution. There was little plumbing and no garbage collection, so people threw human waste, animal waste, and trash in the streets. Although the committee made rules and imposed fines to improve city life, poverty and overcrowding in Paris and other large cities of the time made life challenging.

REFLECT ON THE ESSENTIAL QUESTION

Essential Question: *What were European commercial and agricultural developments and their economic and social effects from 1450 to 1648?*

Economic Effects	Social Effects

KEY TERMS

capital	Dutch East India Company	Great Plague (Black Death)
capitalism	British East India Company	open-field system
means of production	Genoa	the commons
market	Amsterdam	crop rotation
market economy	London	two-field system
entrepreneurs	commerce	three-field system
Medici	hierarchy	inflation
Fuggers	manor	price revolution
money economy	landlord	commercial agriculture
double-entry bookkeeping	peasants	enclosure
joint-stock company	serfdom	agricultural commodities
stock	subsistence agriculture	migrants
dividends	Little Ice Age	

Questions 1–3 refer to the following passage.

"For in whatever parts of the land sheep yield the finest and thus the most expensive wool, there the nobility and gentry, yes, and even some abbots [heads of monasteries] though otherwise holy men, are not content with the old rents that the land yielded to their predecessors. Living in idleness and luxury without doing society any good no longer satisfies them; they have to do positive evil.

For they leave no land free for the plough: they enclose every acre for pasture; they destroy houses and abolish towns, keeping only the churches—and those for sheep-barns.... Thus one greedy, insatiable glutton, a frightful plague to his native country, may enclose many thousands of acres within a single hedge. The tenants are dismissed and compelled, by trickery or brute force or constant harassment, to sell their belongings. One way or another, these wretched people—men, women, husbands, wives, orphans, widows, parents with little children and entire families ... are forced to move out. They leave the only homes familiar to them, and can find no place to go. Since they must leave at once without waiting for a proper buyer, they sell for a pittance [almost nothing] all their household goods .... When that little money is gone (and it's soon spent in wandering from place to place), what remains for them but to steal, and so be hanged—just, you'd say!—or to wander and beg?....

'To make this hideous poverty worse, it exists side by side with wanton [uncontrolled] luxury.... If you don't try to cure these evils, it is futile [pointless] to boast of your severity in punishing theft. Your policy may look superficially [on the surface] like justice, but in reality it is neither just nor practical.' "

—Thomas More, *Utopia* (1516), revised edition, George M.
Logan and Robert M. Adams, 1989

1. The passage describes developments resulting most directly from which trend in 15th-century Europe?
   (A) The long tradition of subsistence agriculture
   (B) The increase in peasant revolts in Western Europe
   (C) The exploration of lands beyond Europe
   (D) The beginnings of the commercialization of agriculture

2. Which of these individuals would most likely have agreed with More?
   (A) An owner of a cloth manufacturing company
   (B) An entrepreneur in commercial agriculture
   (C) A peasant who depended on subsistence agriculture
   (D) A noble who gained control of more land because of an enclosure

3. Based on what you have read in the topic, where would "these wretched people" most likely have gone after selling their belongings?
   (A) To southern Europe, to avoid the Little Ice Age
   (B) To a large city, to look for work
   (C) To eastern Europe, to become serfs
   (D) To a small town, to buy a farm or business

SHORT-ANSWER QUESTION

Use the passage below to answer all parts of the question that follows.

> "The orthodox [standard] view of the causes of the Price Revolution points to the large quantity of the precious metals, at first of gold, but later and principally of silver, shipped from Spanish possessions in the New World to Europe, and links this with the behavior of prices in European countries."
>
> —J. D. Gould, "The Price Revolution Reconsidered,"
> *Economic History Review*, NS, 17: 2 (1964)

1. a) Describe ONE specific piece of evidence that supports the orthodox view of the causes of the Price Revolution.

   b) Describe ONE specific piece of evidence that modifies or refutes Gould's explanation about the causes of the Price Revolution.

   c) Explain ONE effect of the Price Revolution on the social or economic structure in Europe.

1.11

Causation in the Renaissance and the Age of Discovery

O stupendous Necessity . . . thou dost compel every effect to be the direct result of its cause, by the shortest path. These are miracles.
—Leonardo da Vinci (1452–1519)

Essential Question: What were the causes and consequences of the Renaissance and the Age of Discovery?

Italy was a natural place for the rediscovery of Classical Greek and Roman culture to take place. It was a frequent staging and return point for Crusaders heading to the eastern Mediterranean. In the East (including Constantinople) and in nearby Spain, Muslim scholars had preserved troves of Greek and Roman scholarship. Contact with these regions through warfare, diplomacy, and trade helped bring this ancient knowledge back to Western Europe. Knowledge and study of Classical texts, art, and values ultimately served as the cause of the Renaissance. The Renaissance, in turn, began a kind of chain reaction that helped cause multiple, wide-ranging changes in European society.

Society, Religion, and the Arts For centuries, the power of the Roman Catholic Church had dominated culture. But access to the ideas of the Classical, pre-Christian era invited an interpretation of society and life that went beyond the church's strict teachings. Humanists became emboldened to study such worldly topics as history, philosophy, natural sciences, and mathematics, and inventions such as the printing press caused information to be shared much more easily. The consequence of all this freely shared information was not a quick abandonment of Christianity, but rather a more rational approach to theology that would have far-reaching effects not only within the church, but also for everyday Europeans. Even in the northern Renaissance, where the church still had a stronger influence, human-centered naturalism was a consequence of the Renaissance. Renaissance painters and sculptors still generally chose religious subjects, but they were portrayed in an increasingly realistic and naturalistic fashion. Over time, their subjects became increasingly secular.

Exploration and Colonization Causation can also be seen clearly between the learning and inquiry of the Renaissance and the Age of Exploration. Scientific and mathematical learning brought about technological advances in shipbuilding and increased sailors' navigational abilities. As a consequence, Europeans gained the ability to seek spices in Asia by sea, and their attempts to do so brought them into contact with previously unknown lands and peoples. Invariably, these lands were overtaken, and these peoples were subjugated. Colonization in Asia, Africa, and the Americas brought riches to Europe, new converts to the Christian church, and warfare and new diseases to the indigenous populations. The consequences of colonization differed vastly between those who colonized and those who were colonized. Colonization also led to the trade in enslaved people from Africa, as European settlers in the Americas sought an inexpensive labor source for their new American plantations.

Economic Power and Rising Capitalism As the establishment of colonies shifted Europe's gaze from east to west, causation is again seen clearly at work. Europe's focus and its centers of power began to shift from the Mediterranean to the Atlantic. As a result, trading powers such as Venice waned while England and the Netherlands began to take the lead. Additionally, the booming trade in goods between the old world and the new brought increasing riches into Europe, spurring the spread of commercial capitalism. Cities such as London and Amsterdam became banking powers. The influx of capital from colonial trade also helped cause changes in agriculture in many parts of Europe. Increasing land ownership among the economic elite caused changes in agriculture and the demographics of rural and urban areas.

Political Power and Increasing Secularism The increase in trade and the competition between nations for colonies and wealth caused changes in who held political power, why they held it, and how it was gained. In medieval Europe, members of the nobility who owned land held most of the wealth and power. But in nations that became involved in increased trade, wealth and power began to shift to people with education and skills who were not necessarily nobles. The waning of power among the nobility helped monarchs gain power, giving rise to more recognizably modern states. The bureaucratic structures of capitalism could be exercised by the educated, skilled middle class to benefit these new monarchies. Organized systems of taxation, increasingly professional armies, and structured legal systems took shape.

QUESTIONS ABOUT CAUSATION

1. How was religion one of the causes of the Age of Exploration?

2. How are the rediscovery of Classical ideas and shift of power from the Mediterranean world to the Atlantic causally linked?

3. How did the establishment of colonies help lead to the new monarchies that began to arise in Europe?

WRITE AS A HISTORIAN: *UNDERSTANDING THE PROMPT*

Historians use many types of sources to help explain the past. They range from very personal diaries to works of later scholars analyzing events. One way to think about this range of sources is to distinguish between primary and secondary sources.

A primary source is a first-hand account of an event or of what a person thought. For example, a legal charter for the British East India Company. A secondary source is a later description of an event or of what a person thought. This might be the book of a 21st century historian.

Determining which type of source is used can help a reader understand a prompt by more clearly identifying the author's main point and point of view. Also, when answering an essay question, try to think as a historian does by understanding complex relationships and analyzing information to support a position. Read the prompt slowly. Circle direction words, such as *explain*, *evaluate*, *validate* or *refute*, and *compare*. Each of these words has its own meaning:

- *Explain* means to use evidence and reasoning to provide information about how or why a particular event, outcome, pattern, relationship, or situation comes into being.

- *Evaluate* means to identify positive and negative aspects or determine something's significance.

- *Validate* means to show support for an idea. *Refute* means to argue against it.

- *Compare* means to explore similarities and/or differences between ideas or things.

Examine *continuity and change over time* means to understand how and why some things have changed in a given period of time while others have remained the same.

Direction: Complete the series of questions below.

Identify each item as either a primary or a secondary source.

1. *Representations of Slavery*, by historian Douglas Hamilton, which analyzes how museums, movies, and websites have portrayed slavery as it developed in European colonies

2. The journal kept by Christopher Columbus of his voyages to the Americas

3. De *varietate fortunae*, an account of the voyages of Nicolò de Conti, who travelled in the Indian and Pacific Oceans in the 15th century

4. Drawings and other artwork in the *Sino-Spanish Codex*, created in 1590, showing people in Japan, China, and the Philippines as portrayed by Spanish explorers, missionaries, and traders

Identify the reasoning skill that each statement requires.

5. Evaluate the extent to which increased wealth from overseas trade transformed European society and economics.

6. Compare Spain and the Dutch Republic in terms of their motivations for exploration.

Writing notes in the margins is one way to plan your response to a question. If you use accurate historical evidence and clearly organize your thoughts, writing will be easier, and your argument will be easier for readers to identify.

For each of the following prompts, which statement below it would be most useful in the argument answering it.

7. Explain the ways in which the revival of classical texts influenced Italian society during the Renaissance.

   a. Classical Greek and Roman texts were written by people such as the playwright Euripides, the epic poet Homer, and the satirist Horace.

   b. The intellectuals of the Renaissance, later known as humanists, used their knowledge of Greek and Latin to revive classical ideas that put humans at the center of all things.

8. Explain the ways in which the invention of the printing press affected European society during the Renaissance.

   a. The printing press spread Renaissance ideas beyond Italy and created more vernacular literature, which led to a rise in national cultures and a lasting challenge to the power of the Catholic Church.

   b. Europe was affected by a movement called the Protestant Reformation, started by Martin Luther in Germany in 1517.

LONG ESSAY QUESTIONS

Directions: Suggested writing time is 40 minutes. In your response, you should do the following:

- Respond to the prompt with a historically defensible thesis that establishes a line of resoning.
- Describe a broader historical context relevant to the prompt.
- Support an argument in response to the prompt using specific and relevant examples of evidence.
- Use historical reasoning (e.g., comparison, causation, continuity and change over time) to frame or structure an argument that addresses the prompt.
- Use evidence to corroborate, qualify, or modify an argument that addresses the prompt.

1. Evaluate the extent to which changes in technology influenced European life in the 14th to 16th centuries.

2. Evaluate the extent to which changes in how people viewed history influenced European life in the 14th to 16th centuries.

3. Evaluate the extent to which competition between Spain and Portugal affected overseas exploration in the 15th and 16th centuries.

4. Evaluate the extent to which the interactions with Europeans affected native peoples during the Age of Exploration.

DOCUMENT-BASED QUESTION

Directions: Question 1 is based on the accompanying documents. the documents have been edited for the purpose of this exercise. You are advised to spend 15 minutes planning and 45 minutes writing your answer. In your response, you should do the following:

- **Thesis:** Make a defensible claim that establishes a line of reasoning and consists of one or more sentences found in one place.
- **Contextualization:** Relate the argument to a broader historical context.
- **Document Evidence:** Use content from at least six documents.
- **Outside Evidence:** Use one piece of evidence not found in the documents.
- **Document Sourcing:** Explain how or why the point of view, purpose, situation, or intended audience is relevant for at least three documents.
- **Analysis:** Show the relationships among pieces of historical evidence and use them to support, qualify, or modify an argument.

1. Evaluate the extent to which the beliefs and attitudes of Europeans during the Age of Discovery and Exploration affected both the indigenous peoples of the Americas and the Europeans.

Document 1:

Source: Christopher Columbus, letter to the King and Queen of Spain, 1494

[All gold shipped from the island to Spain] should be taken on board the ship, both that belonging to your Highnesses and the property of everyone else; . . . that there should come with the gold, for a testimony, a list of all that has been put into the said chest, properly marked, so that each owner may receive his own; and that, for the faithful performance of this duty, if any gold whatsoever is found outside of the said chest in any way, be it little or much, it shall be forfeited to your Highnesses.

That all the ships that come from the said island shall be obliged to make their proper discharge in the port of Cadiz, and that no person shall disembark or other person be permitted to go on board until the ship has been visited by the person or persons deputed for that purpose, in the said city, by your Highnesses, to whom the master shall show all that he carries, and exhibit the manifest of all the cargo, it may be seen and examined if the said ship brings anything hidden and not known at the time of lading [loading]. That the chest in which the said gold has been carried shall be opened in the presence of the magistrates of the said city of Cadiz, and of the person deputed for that purpose by your Highnesses, and his own property be given to each owner.

Document 2

Source: Amerigo Vespucci, letter to Lorenzo di Medici, 1503

They have no cloth, either of wool, flax, or cotton, because they have no need of it; nor have they any private property, everything being in common. They live amongst themselves without a king or ruler, each man being his own master, and having as many wives as they please. The children cohabit with the mothers, the brothers with the sisters, the male cousins with the female, and each one with the first he meets. They have no temples and no laws, nor are they idolaters.

What more can I say! They live according to nature, and are more inclined to be Epicurean than Stoic. This statement implies that the inhabitants pursue pleasure rather than consider philosophical matters. They have no commerce among each other, and they wage war without art or order. The old men make the youths do what they please, and incite them to fights, in which they mutually kill with great cruelty. They slaughter those who are captured, and the victors eat the vanquished; for human flesh is an ordinary article of food among them.

(continued on next page)

You may be the more certain of this, because I have seen a man eat his children and wife; and I knew a man who was popularly credited to have eaten 300 human bodies. I say further that they were surprised that we did not eat our enemies, and use their flesh as food, for they say it is excellent. Their arms are bows and arrows, and when they go to war they cover no part of their bodies, being in this like beasts.

Document 3:

Source: Alfonso de Albuquerque, "Lion of the Sea," the Algarve History Association

The island of Goa is also fertile and could supply food to the Portuguese navy; it has a good harbour and was a centre for shipbuilding. The timing was perfect since the new Khan was away on the mainland establishing his authority... After an extraordinary piece of reconnaissance under fire by a junior officer, Albuquerque sailed into the harbour and the city quickly surrendered. But within weeks, the new Khan returned and, overwhelming the Portuguese defence, forced them back into their ships. The summer monsoon had arrived and Albuquerque found that his ships could not cross the harbour bar. From 1 June to 16 August, Albuquerque and his fleet were immobilised in the river and the Portuguese were subjected to surprise attacks, lack of food and water and the heat of an Indian summer. They finally managed to emerge from the river after 77 uncomfortable days and gathering his forces, a determined Albuquerque renewed his attack three months later. The new Khan was again away and Albuqerque's victory was swift and his reprisals terrible. His captains were told to 'reconnoitre the whole of the island and to put to the sword all Mohammedans, men, women and children'. Christians and Hindus joined the slaughter and for four days 'they poured out the blood of the Moors'. The Khan tried for three years to reoccupy his city but after a campaign of 33 months, the Muslims finally accepted the permanent loss of Goa.

Document 4:

Source: Charles V, Emperor and King of Spain, Instructions for the Viceroy Mendoza, a Spanish colonial official, 1535

Also, you should see if the towns are able to pay more gold, silver, and other things of value than they currently pay; [and if so], you should inform them that their assessment will be increased, payable in silver, gold, or its equivalent.

Since I have been informed that the Indians of that country pay their tributes in blankets, corn, and other local goods that are difficult to turn

(continued on next page)

into revenue, you should find a manner in which their tributes can be paid by converting all those things into a certain quantity of gold or silver yearly. This should be accomplished in such a manner that it increases Our revenue but not their labor, and since this is a very important matter, you should place great care in it, listing what they pay in tribute presently and what Our officials get for it when they sell it or use it in payment, and what its value would be if commuted to gold or silver; and you should send this list along with your report on the first ship to come...

Also, We are informed that in many places in the said province there are large and wealthy mines of gold, silver, and other metals, and that in addition to the fifths paid by private individuals who mine them with Our license and permission, We could increase Our revenues greatly if Our officials in the said mines purchased for Us a large number of slaves, either blacks or people purchased from the Indians who are held and reputed to be slaves. And because this is a matter of great importance and We could receive great benefit if it is correct.

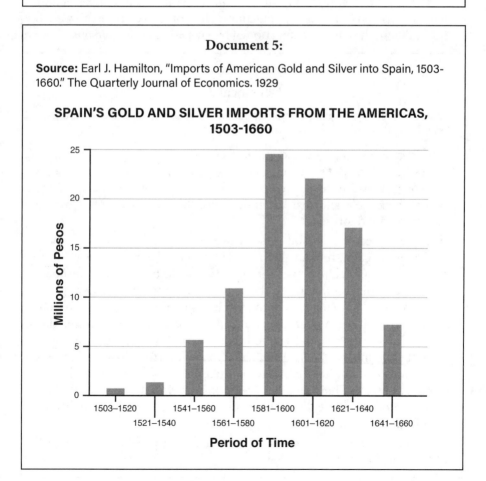

Document 5:

Source: Earl J. Hamilton, "Imports of American Gold and Silver into Spain, 1503-1660." The Quarterly Journal of Economics. 1929

SPAIN'S GOLD AND SILVER IMPORTS FROM THE AMERICAS, 1503-1660

Document 6:

Source: Bartolomé de Las Casas, "The Devastation of the Indies," 1542

They are very clean in their persons, with alert, intelligent minds, docile and open to doctrine, very apt to receive our holy Catholic faith, to be endowed with virtuous customs, and to behave in a godly fashion. Some of the secular Spaniards who have been here for many years say that the goodness of the Indians is undeniable and that if this gifted people could be brought to know the one true God they would be the most fortunate people in the world....Yet into this sheepfold, into this land of meek outcasts, there came some Spaniards who immediately behaved like ravening wild beasts, wolves, tigers, or lions that had been starved for many days. And Spaniards have behaved in no other way during the past forty years, down to the present time, for they are still acting like ravening beasts, killing, terrorizing, afflicting, torturing, and destroying the native peoples, doing all this with the strangest and most varied new methods of cruelty, never seen or heard of before, and to such a degree that this Island of Hispaniola once so populous (having a population that I estimated to be more than three million), has now a population of barely two hundred persons.

Document 7:

Source: St. Francis Xavier, writing from Japan to the Society of Jesus in Europe, 1552

[The Japanese said,] God therefore, if He were good, could never have done such a thing as create beings so evil (as Devils). To these arguments we replied that the devils were created good by God, but became evil by their own fault, and that in consequence they were subject to eternal punishment and torment.

Then they objected that God, who was so severe in punishing, was not at all merciful. Again, how could He, if He created the human race in the manner we taught, allow men sent into the world to worship Him to be tempted and persecuted by the devil? In like manner, if God were good, He ought not to have made man so weak and so prone to sin, but free from all evil. Again, it could not be a good God, they said, who had created that horrible prison of hell, and was to be forever without pity for those who suffer therein the most fearful torments from all eternity. Lastly, if He were good, He would not have imposed on men those difficult laws of the Ten Commandments. Their religious traditions, on the contrary, taught that all who should invoke the authors of their religion would be delivered even from the torments of hell.

They were quite unable to digest the idea that men could be cast into hell without any hope of deliverance.

UNIT 2: The Age of Reformation
c. 1450 to c. 1648

Topic 2.1

Contextualizing 16th- and 17th-Century Challenges and Developments

Essential Question: What was the context in which the religious, political, and cultural developments of the 16th and 17th centuries took place?

From its beginning, the Catholic Church dealt with discontent and challenges to its doctrine, hierarchy, and politics. Even before the Middle Ages, dozens of Christianity sects existed. The Church fought to stamp out these sects, which it considered heresies. In the 11th century, fundamental differences in religious and political beliefs resulted in the division of Christianity into Eastern Orthodoxy and Roman Catholicism.

This spirit of independence and challenge carried into the 14th century, when the English cleric and scholar John Wycliffe publicly challenged numerous doctrines and practices of Roman Catholicism. Also, he translated the Bible into English in the 1380s—a radical act for the time. Wycliffe inspired the ideas of reformers such as Jan Hus (who was burned at the stake in 1415 for his opposition to certain Church beliefs). These men and others influenced Martin Luther and other reformers to question the Catholic Church during the Protestant Reformation.

The Challenge of Religious Pluralism to a Unified Europe Starting in the 16th century, a religious revolution known as the Reformation changed and divided Europe. Protestant reformers questioned Catholic practices and doctrines. Such concerns fractured the unity of Christianity in Central and Western Europe, bringing the emergence of religious pluralism—differing, and often competing, sects of Christianity. The Catholic Reformation followed, rejuvenating Catholicism, but allowed no reconciliation with Protestants. This division in religion began to affect ideas about culture and wealth, including the concept that God's favored people would be rewarded with affluence.

In addition, some reformers confronted secular, or nonreligious, institutions and governments that had historically controlled religious institutions. Some Protestants refused to accept the secular state's power over the church. Europe's religious tension heightened the existing political conflicts between the nobility and monarchy. The religious conflicts fragmented relationships among states, both politically and economically. Wars were fought to establish, protect, or defeat the ability of people to worship according to the dictates of individual conscience. The Reformation shook up the established order in nearly every aspect of society.

Commercial and Agricultural Capitalism During the 16th and 17th centuries, commercial and agricultural capitalism emerged in Europe and slowly began to replace traditional economic institutions of the Middle Ages. As commerce grew, cities expanded and populations migrated more. The Renaissance and the Reformation began to change work roles of men and women, even as the nuclear family remained the primary social unit. Women's education became an issue of debate as they joined the male-dominated workforce in minor roles. Culture and leisure activities continued to revolve around religion and the traditional agricultural calendar. People clung to traditional folk ideas for their community standards.

Struggle for Sovereignty The new development of European secular systems of law brought about sovereign states to replace the medieval universal Christendom. New local governments gave power to local leaders rather than religious institutions. This fragmentation throughout Europe began centuries of struggles for territory and sovereignty.

ANALYZE THE CONTEXT

1. Was the Protestant Reformation a continuity or a change in European historical thought and practice? Explain.

2. How did the ending of medieval universal Christendom throughout Europe affect governments?

Topic 2.2

Luther and the Protestant Reformation

I cannot and will not recant anything, for to go against conscience is neither right nor safe. Here I stand, I can do no other, so help me God. Amen.

—Martin Luther, Diet of Worms, 1521

Essential Question: How and why did religious beliefs and practices change from 1450 to 1648?

One early reason for Martin Luther's demands for religious reform stemmed from concerns over the Catholic Church's policy of selling **indulgences**, a practice that had come to mean the buying of forgiveness for sin, which added to the enormous wealth of the Catholic Church. Indulgences were sold to all classes and the more wealth one had, the more one paid. While peasants paid less for indulgences, this practice still drained the little money these impoverished people had. However, over time, many reformers called into question other Catholic practices and doctrines, such as papal infallibility—the belief that the word of the pope, when speaking on matters of faith, is incapable of error. Such concerns fractured the unity of Christianity in Central and Western Europe, bringing the emergence of differing and often competing sects of Christianity in the 16th century. This religious revolution became known as the **Reformation**.

Martin Luther Establishes New Doctrine

As Christian Humanists called for Church reform. (See Topic 1.3.) One of them, **Martin Luther**, demanded change so strongly that he threatened Christian unity. Growing up, Luther had attended a school run by the Brethren of the Common Life, a group that taught Christian Humanism. He later attended the University of Erfurt, receiving a liberal arts education and embracing the religious slogan "back to the source," referring to the Bible as the source. Studying the book of Romans in the Bible, Luther was struck by the emphasis on God's grace—an emphasis he believed the Catholic Church had lost.

Luther Presents Religious Grievances Luther argued that any religious practices encouraging the belief that good works led to salvation were misleading. For example, he strongly disagreed with the practice of seeking salvation through the buying and selling of indulgences. Luther presented his document known as the *95 Theses* after Pope Leo X proclaimed a Jubilee

Indulgence to raise money for the restoration of St. Peter's Basilica. The most famous indulgence preacher was Johann Tetzel. He was hired to sell indulgences in the German states of the Holy Roman Empire. According to legend, Tetzel said, "As soon as the gold in the casket rings, the rescued soul to heaven springs." In response, according to legend, an angry Luther nailed his theses to the door of the Wittenberg church, denouncing indulgences and other Church practices. More likely, according to the custom of the time, Luther simply wanted to prompt his archbishop and other scholars to discuss possible reforms within the Catholic Church. Luther wrote the theses in Latin, but the document's translation into German and the printing press made it widely available throughout Europe within months. Luther quickly became the key figure of a rapidly growing protest movement that objected to:

- *simony*—the buying and selling of Church appointments and offices
- *pluralism*—the holding of multiple Church positions at the same time
- *nepotism*—the appointment of family and friends to Church positions
- *immorality*—the decline in moral standards of clergy and monks

The Catholic Church Responds Catholic officials responded forcefully, accusing Luther of heresy. Luther defended his positions in 1518 at a diet (assembly of leaders) in the city of Augsburg but was ordered to recant by Church leaders. Luther refused and returned to Wittenberg. A 1519 debate between Luther and Church scholars at Leipzig, Germany, further set the Reformation in motion.

The pope issued a decree demanding that Luther recant or be excommunicated—exiled from the Catholic Church. In April 1521, Luther appeared before a diet that convened in the city of Worms with the choice to either recant or affirm his beliefs. Luther's case was so important that presiding over the Diet of Worms was the newly chosen emperor of the Holy Roman Empire, Charles V. According to legend, when confronted with his writings, Luther refused to back down, declaring, "Here I stand. I can do no other." Because he refused to recant, the Catholic Church excommunicated Luther, and Charles V declared him an "outlaw of the empire."

Lutheran Doctrines and Practices In an age when religious dissent could mean death, Luther's strong stand took courage. However, he was supported by many German rulers. Some cared little about theology, but hoped the religious controversy would help them reduce Rome's political power. Frederick III, the prince of the German state of Saxony, where Luther was born and returned after being excommunicated, protected Luther at Wartburg Castle. There, Luther began to work out his ideas more fully such as:

- **Primacy of scripture**: Luther insisted on the importance of the Bible over church traditions as the source of authority. He noted that the pope, church officials, and church councils could make errors while the Bible was infallible. This is known as *sola scriptura*. Luther translated the New Testament into common German to make it more accessible to more people (which other reformers had argued in favor of for centuries).

- *Salvation:* Luther argued that faith in God was a Christian's only way to salvation because of the power of God's grace. While in a monastery, Luther arrived at his belief in *sola fide*—that people gained eternal **salvation by faith alone**. He argued that attending church and helping the poor were good works but believed that they did not in themselves bring salvation.

- *Access to God:* Luther insisted that all Christians had access to God without the assistance of priests, bishops or the pope. This idea would be further developed by later Protestant theologians in the Reformation and become known as **"the priesthood of all believers."**

Luther and traditional Catholics had some shared beliefs but even in those beliefs there were fundamental differences. The presence of Christ in the communion, for example. Luther believed that the communion's bread and wine were both bread and wine *and* the body and blood of Christ (consubstantiation). In the traditional Catholic belief, the bread and wine of communion actually *became* the body and blood of Christ (transubstantiation).

While many of Luther's religious ideas were radical for his time, his ideas on social reform were not. He called for harsh treatment of the peasants who revolted during the Peasants' War of 1524-25, and late in his life, expressed strongly antisemitic views.

LUTHER VERSUS THE CATHOLIC CHURCH		
Issue	Luther's Beliefs	Catholic Teachings
How God judges people for salvation	Faith alone, although faith leads to good works	Faith and good works
Source of religious authority	The Bible alone; primacy of scripture	The Bible, the pope, and centuries of religious interpretation
Organization of the clergy	Pastors are independent	Strict hierarchy
Role of Mary, mother of Jesus	Honored, but not considered holy	Revered as holy

Calvin Bring New Interpretations

Huldrych Zwingli, a Swiss pastor, was key in starting the Reformation in Switzerland. Like Martin Luther, Zwingli criticized the Catholic Church on numerous issues. Zwingli met with Luther at the Marburg Colloquy (religious discussion) but the men differed on the presence of Christ in the Eucharist. Zwingli believed the the bread and wine were symbolic—similar to the beliefs of John Calvin, who took over the reform movement upon Zwingli's 1531 death.

Calvinism Takes Root In 1536, French-born theologian **John Calvin** published his book *Institutes of the Christian Religion*, calling for religious and political reform. Calvin had studied the ideas of Luther and other dissidents, and he agreed with many of their criticisms of the Catholic Church. However, Calvin developed two unique ideas: **predestination** and his concept of **the elect.** In predestination, Calvin believed that an omnipotent (all-knowing) God already knew who would be saved and that, even at birth, a person's eternal fate was set. From this belief, Calvin later developed his concept of the elect—those chosen by God to be saved—in order to ensure people would live according to God's law. Their pious behavior would be an outward sign that such people were part of the elect.

Calvinism and Wealth The Age of Discovery transformed the western European economy by shifting the economic power to the Atlantic states, producing new economic opportunities for the middle class, and creating innovations in financial practices. (See Topic 1.10.) During this period, Calvin's Christian teachings addressed how the accumulation of wealth through hard work was a sign of God's favor.

Calvin's teaching encouraged the development of banks and moneylending as long as ethical banking practices were employed. Calvin believed that God called individuals to complete a certain job in the community. Thus, by working hard, Christians helped the community and served God. These Calvinist teachings took root in banking centers like Geneva and Amsterdam since his ideas complemented the rise of capitalism and the growth of the middle class. The ideas of wealth and God's favor were later advanced by Puritans in England.

Source: Getty Images

Calvinist churches were often plain so they would not distract people from worshipping God (left). Roman Catholic churches were often ornate so that the beauty would inspire people to worship God (right).

Responses to Luther and Calvin

The teachings of Luther and Calvin sparked unintended responses by religious radicals and other groups. Many religious radicals like the Anabaptists believed Luther and Calvin had not gone far enough and demanded more reforms. Groups like the German peasants applied the teachings of Martin Luther to create social change in select German states.

German Peasants' War Martin Luther's challenge to the established religious order inspired peasants in many German states to contest their society's social and political hierarchy. German people in the countryside and in towns had long felt overburdened by taxes, rents, and ever-increasing demands for labor. Landowners worsened the situation by seizing more and more common pastureland. Hardships brought on by crop failures in the region made the situation even more volatile.

In 1524 and 1525, peasants in various German states formed bands that quickly swelled as they traveled the countryside, sacking abbeys, burning the homes of nobles, and battling nobles' armies. A confederation of peasants' groups created The Twelve Articles, which called for more control of their churches, fewer restrictions on hunting and forest use, and reduced workloads, fines, and taxes. In the end, the German Peasants' War was short and unsuccessful. The nobles, with their greater military abilities and resources, maintained their control, and the peasants gained little, if anything. It is estimated that 100,000 peasants lost their lives in this short but brutal conflict.

Although the peasants cited Luther's teachings as a basis for their rebellions, Luther did not support them. He relied on the protection of a noble after being excommunicated by the church. As the conflict intensified, Luther advised the nobles to swiftly and aggressively end the rebellion.

Anabaptists and the Radical Reformation In 1525, another strand of Protestantism emerged in Zurich. **Anabaptists** believed the teachings of Luther and Calvin had not gone far enough in their reforms to religious practices and beliefs. Anabaptist leaders such as Jakob Hutter and Menno Simons called for more radical changes and looked to the New Testament of the Bible for religious truth. Anabaptists held numerous beliefs that challenged Catholic and Protestant beliefs:

- They rejected the baptism of infants. Anabaptists stressed that only adults could make the decision to believe.
- They believed sin existed throughout the secular world. Anabaptists attempted to avoid sin by living a more secluded, simple life.
- They avoided involvement in government affairs.
- They strictly followed scripture over any secular authority.

Both Catholics and other protestant groups persecuted Anabaptists for their beliefs. Some Anabaptists groups also allowed women to preach, which was deemed heretical by other religious groups at the time. Persecution of Anabaptists was widespread in Europe and caused many to later migrate to North America.

REFLECT ON THE ESSENTIAL QUESTION

Essential Question: *How and why did religious beliefs and practices change from 1450 to 1648?*

Catholic Beliefs	Challenges to Catholic Beliefs

Indulgences
Reformation
Martin Luther
95 Theses
Diet of Worms

Charles V
Primacy of Scripture
Faith Alone
"the priesthood of all
    believers"
John Calvin

Predestination
The Elect
Geneva
German Peasants' War
Anabaptist

HISTORICAL PERSPECTIVES: *HOW GERMAN WAS LUTHER?*

Just over 500 years ago, Martin Luther posted his *95 Theses* at the University of Wittenberg, inviting his fellow scholars to a debate. Luther's relationship with German culture and politics has been controversial ever since.

Unintentionally Political Writing a few years after World War II, the British historian, G. R. Elton, portrayed Luther as strongly shaped by his cultural heritage as a German. In *The New Cambridge Modern History, Vol. II, The Reformation*, Elton argued that Luther saw a Roman-based church exploiting Germans and rebelled against it. Elton focused on political rather than cultural aspects, pointing out that the Reformation took root only where princes and lords supported it. To Elton, Luther was a benefactor of the German princes seeking to establish modern states independent of Rome's influence. Luther himself may not have been interested in politics, but his ideas provided support for those who were.

A Friend of Germans By the early 21st century, the focus on German pride shifted. Germany had evolved into a solid member of an internationalist, integrated Europe that downplayed particular national identities. In *Martin Luther: Renegade and Prophet* (2016), another British historian, Lyndal Roper, portrayed Luther as a man neither looking backward toward a German past nor as a tool of political leaders. Roper focused on the personal life of Luther as a man. She saw significance in Luther's friendship with those who were proud to be German. Protestant artist friends such as Albrecht Dürer, Hans Holbein, and Lucas Cranach surrounded him. Luther was part of an intellectual trend to see pride in their identity as Germans as the answer to their problems. In the words of one reviewer, "Luther's campaign to 'restore' Biblical Christianity to 16th-century Germany was a battle for land and national supremacy."

1. What is one piece of evidence that supports G.R. Elton's interpretation of the political nature of Martin Luther?

2. What is one piece of evidence that supports Lyndal Roper's interpretation of the intellectual nature and German identity of Martin Luther?

Questions 1–3 refer to the passage below.

"Since the message of the Reformation, like that of the earlier religious movements, meant a loosening of hierarchies, it had a particular appeal to women. By stressing the individual's personal relationship with God and his or her own responsibility, it affirmed the ability of each to find truth by reading the original Scriptures. Thus, it offered a greater role for lay participation by women, as well as men, than was possible in Roman Catholicism. . .

[Nevertheless], the Reformation did not markedly transform women's place in society, and the reformers had never intended to do so. To be sure, they called on men and women to read the Bible and participate in religious ceremonies together. But Bible-reading reinforced the Pauline [St. Paul's] view of woman as weak-minded and sinful. When such practice took a more radical turn in the direction of lay prophesy, as occurred in some Reform churches southwest of Paris, or in the coming together of women to discuss "unchristian pieces," as was recorded in Zwickau [a city in eastern Germany], reformers—Luther and Calvin alike—pulled back in horror."

—Marilyn J. Boxer and Jean H. Quataert, *Connecting Spheres*, 1987

1. The historians' statement most directly supports which interpretation?
   (A) The most important causes of the Reformation were economic and political, rather than religious.
   (B) The Reformation idea of spiritual equality failed to spark a profound social transformation.
   (C) The Reformation primarily expanded the power of the existing elite and state authorities.
   (D) The ideas of the Reformation were rooted in earlier efforts to reform the Catholic Church.

2. Which statement provides the strongest evidence to support the authors' argument in the first paragraph?
   (A) Luther believed in social equality for men and women.
   (B) Women served as assistants in Protestant religious education.
   (C) Luther opposed clerical celibacy.
   (D) Women were encouraged to preach in Anabaptist churches.

3. The authors' argument in the second paragraph is most strongly supported by the claim that Protestants often

   (A) rejected papal authority on the role of women

   (B) wanted to legalize divorce

   (C) called for primary education for both boys and girls

   (D) emphasized marriage and obedience by wives

SHORT-ANSWER QUESTION

Use the passage below to answer all parts of the question that follows.

"The repudiation of ordination as a sacrament demolished the caste system of clericalism and provided a sound basis for the priesthood of all believers since, according to Luther, ordination is simply a rite of the Church by which a minister is installed to discharge a particular office. He receives no indelible [permanent] character, is not exempt from the jurisdiction of the civil courts, and is not empowered by ordination to perform the sacraments. At this point what the priest does any Christian may do, if commissioned by the congregation, because all Christians are priests."

—Roland H. Bainton, *Here I Stand: A Life of Martin Luther*, 1950

1. a) Describe ONE way Bainton thought that Luther's view on ordination challenged the structure of the Roman Catholic Church.

   b) Describe ONE specific piece of evidence that supports the view that Luther did not want to challenge all structures of the Roman Catholic Church.

   c) Explain ONE response by the Roman Catholic Church to Luther's teachings that it thought challenged traditional doctrines.

Topic 2.3

Protestant Reform Continues

No Estate [social class] shall try to persuade the subjects of other Estates to abandon their religion nor protect them against their own magistrates.

—Peace of Augsburg, 1555

Essential Question: How and why did religious beliefs and practices change from 1450 to 1648?

As the printing press allowed for more information related to the Reformation to be disseminated, individuals challenged the practices and beliefs of the Roman Catholic Church. However, some of these religious reformers confronted secular institutions and governments. Groups such as the Puritans and Huguenots objected to the role of monarchy in determining the state's religious practices and customs. In some cases, groups rejected the secular world and sought to live a life of seclusion. The Reformation may have begun as a religious reform movement, but as it evolved, it began challenging the secular state.

The Printing Press Spreads Reformation Ideas

Renaissance humanism spread to northern Europe in the late 15th century, and northern humanists focused more on religious concerns than did their Italian counterparts. (See Topic 1.4.) By 1500, about half of all titles that had been published were Bibles or other religious works. Humanists especially desired to reform the Catholic Church, but such calls had spread slowly at first, because they were written in Latin and had to be copied by hand.

However, by 1517, the printing press had become well established and would have explosive impact on Europe. Martin Luther's call for religious reform emphasized the Bible and that people should be able to read and interpret it themselves, without the aid of priests. (See Topic 2.2.) Luther's ideas were quickly translated into German, printed into pamphlets, and distributed throughout German-speaking lands.

Luther himself translated the New Testament, the part of the Christian Bible that deals primarily with the life of Jesus, into German in 1521. The resulting printed Bible sold rapidly when it was published in September 1522. A popular French version of the New Testament appeared in 1523, and an English version was printed in Germany in 1526. Although all of these **vernacular Bibles**, Bibles printed in the everyday spoken language of European peoples, were suppressed by political authorities in Catholic states, the books and their ideas spread broadly over time and furthered Reformation ideas of religious reform.

Religious Challenges to Monarchical Power

Martin Luther published the *95 Theses* to prompt religious reform. He had little interest in politics. However, religion and politics were thoroughly intertwined in Europe during his lifetime. His challenges to religious authority created an environment that prompted others to challenge political authority.

Puritans Challenge the English Crown In 1534, with the Act of Supremacy, the English King Henry VIII broke with the Roman Catholic Church. The king of England became the head of the Church of England, or the Anglican faith. England continued to move toward more Protestant doctrines during Henry's son, Edward's brief reign (1547–1553). Edward's successor, Mary Tudor (1553–1558) who had been raised Catholic, reversed course and attempted to return the Catholic Church to power in England. (See Topic 1.5.)

After Mary's death, her half-sister Elizabeth I (1558–1603) became queen and the leader of the Church of England. She embraced many Protestant beliefs and practices. In the late 16th century, **Puritans** believed the Church of England needed to remove lingering Catholic traditions and further purify Anglicanism of all Catholic beliefs and practices. Puritans were English Calvinists who embraced John Calvin's most fundamental ideas, such as predestination.

During her reign, Elizabeth attempted to calm the religious turmoil between Catholics and Puritans. The Elizabethan Settlement (1559) and Thirty-Nine Articles (1571) modified religious practices attempting to appeal to both groups, but these attempts did not go far enough for Puritans.

After Queen Elizabeth I died in 1603, the Stuart monarchy (a succession of English rulers of Scottish descent) dealt with continued tensions between the Catholic Church and Church of England. Puritans feared several Stuart monarchs, James I (1603–1625) and Charles I (1625–1649), would direct the country back toward Catholicism.

The struggle between the Puritans and the Stuart monarchy culminated with the English Civil War (see Topic 3.2) when the Puritans supported the Parliamentarians against the Royalists. In 1649, the Parliamentarians successfully overthrew the Stuart monarchy and executed Charles I.

Nobles in Poland In the 16th century, the ideas of Calvin, Luther, and Zwingli came to Poland, in large part through Polish nobles—many of whom had traveled and studied throughout Europe. The Polish monarchy initially rejected these new religious teachings. Yet, **Polish nobles** continued to follow numerous Protestant paths, challenging the king's control of religious institutions. In 1573, the Warsaw Confederation Act was enacted by a gathering of Polish nobles, who convinced the newly elected Polish monarch, Henry of Valois, to accept it. The act allowed for religious toleration in the kingdom, but was short lived as the Catholic Reformation reversed the spread of Protestantism.

Monarchs Initiate Religious Reform and Control

While Henry VIII and Elizabeth I responded to the Reformation by establishing and strengthening a new state religion in England, other rulers made different choices. Some loosened restrictions to allow religious pluralism. Others, such as Philip II of Spain, became strong advocates for Catholicism.

France's Agreement with the Pope In France, King Francis I (reigned 1515–1547) signed the Concordat of Bologna in 1516 which allowed the Catholic Church to collect income from French churches, while the king gained the power to tax the clergy and appoint Catholic bishops in France. (See Topic 1.5 for more about the Concordat of Bologna.) The Concordat of Bologna worked for several decades, since nearly all French were Catholics.

However, by 1562, French Calvinists, known as **Huguenots**, had grown to represented 10 percent of the country's population, or about 2 million people. More importantly, an estimated 40 percent of the French nobles identified as French Calvinists and sought to gain more political rights. The Huguenots' struggle for greater political power, and the established Catholic order's desire to head off this struggle, led to nearly three decades of bloodshed in France. (See Topic 2.4 for about French wars of religion.)

The Holy Roman Emperor Implements Peace By the reign of Holy Roman Emperor Charles V (1506–1556), the Habsburg Dynasty encompassed about 1.5 million square miles of territory throughout Europe and the Americas. Charles focused much of his attention on fighting a series of conflicts with the Ottoman Empire and France.

These concerns prevented him from dealing more forcefully with Lutheranism, and by the time he tried to do so, it had become strongly entrenched. After failing to eradicate Lutheranism in the Schmalkaldic Wars, Charles decided on a political approach and established the Peace of Augsburg in 1555 with German states. This legal agreement allowed each German ruler to determine whether residents of that state would be Catholic or Lutheran. (See Topic 1.5.) The faith of the ruler would become the faith of all. This agreement did not acknowledge Calvinism or Anabaptism as options.

Protestants and the State

While some monarchies were able to consolidate power during this era of religious strife, other Protestant denominations refused to allow the subordination of the church to the state. In particular, the Anabaptists desired to live independent of the state while Calvinists acknowledged the interdependence of the church and state. Yet, both refused to make religion inferior to the secular state.

Anabaptists Reject the Secular World Anabaptists excluded themselves from society because they believed that sin existed everywhere. This seclusion placed them in direct conflict with many governments because Anabaptists refused to serve in the government or the military. Thus, Anabaptists became detached from the state and elected to live a non-violent, communal life. Largely because of the Anabaptists' unique doctrine and solitary lifestyle, both Catholics and Protestants targeted them for persecution. Nevertheless, the Anabaptists maintained their desire to live independent of the secular world.

Calvin in Geneva In 1536, the year Calvin published *Institutes of the Christian Religion*, the leaders in the Swiss city of **Geneva** invited him there to live and preach. In Geneva, Calvin's doctrines transformed not only the practice of Christianity but also the role of the government. The Bible served as the highest law in Geneva, and sinning was a civil offense. Calvin established the Genevan Consistory to enforce Calvinist doctrine and required residents to denounce the Catholic faith and to attend church services five times a week. People could be punished for missing church. Failing to follow religious laws could could result in a person forced to leave the city. Other cities with Calvinist populations enacted similar laws to those in Geneva. These laws also required churches to provide social services for the city's poor and sick.

REFLECT ON THE ESSENTIAL QUESTIONS

Essential Question: *How and why did religious beliefs and practices change from 1450 to 1648?*

Religious Reforms	Outcome of Reforms

KEY TERMS

vernacular Bibles	Polish nobles	Geneva
Puritans	Huguenots	

MULTIPLE-CHOICE QUESTIONS

Questions 1–3 refer to the image below.

Source: Wikimedia Commons

Printing press, c. 1568

1. Based on the year this image was created, which of the following most likely describes the historical development it shows?

   (A) Writing novels for general readers

   (B) Creating commercial advertisements for guilds

   (C) Producing religious pamphlets

   (D) Censoring political broadsides

2. Which of the following allowed the activity shown in this image to have greater impact on the spread of ideas advocated by leaders of the Reformation?

   (A) The use of vernacular in printing texts

   (B) The printing of books in Latin

   (C) The support of the Catholic Church

   (D) The rising power of the central governments

3. Which of the following groups relied most heavily of the technology shown in this image when it was first developed?

   (A) Monks in the early Middle Ages

   (B) Scholastics in the late Middle Ages

   (C) Artists before the Renaissance

   (D) Humanists in the Renaissance

SHORT-ANSWER QUESTION

Answer all parts of the question that follows.

1. a) Explain ONE similarity between Puritans and Huguenots.

   b) Explain ONE difference between Puritans and Huguenots.

   c) Explain ONE difference between Huguenots and Anabaptists.

Topic 2.4

Wars of Religion

The right to the public or private exercise of religion, as well as those who . . . adopt a confession of faith different from that of their territorial lord, shall be tolerated with clemency.

—Treaty of Westphalia, 1648

Essential Question: How did religious and political factors influence each other from 1450 to 1648?

Religious tension in Europe in the 16th century heightened the conflict between the nobility and monarchy as well as the established order in Europe. Monarchs throughout Europe were consolidating power and centralizing the state while the emerging middle class contributed more to the economy.

The nobility's role in the economy and government was becoming threatened and they used religion to protest their diminished role. As monarchies were challenged, some individuals like Henry IV of France embraced religious pluralism to quell unrest. Other monarchs, such as those of Spain and the Holy Roman Empire, unsuccessfully attempted to maintain complete control and were forced to abdicate some of their authority in various regions.

Conflicts Among Religious Groups

The growing religious tension between Catholics, Lutherans, Calvinists, and Anabaptists throughout Europe, combined with political rivalries that often fell along religious lines, brought nearly a century of warfare. Between 1562 and 1648, millions would be slaughtered or would die from hunger and disease related to internal rebellion, civil war, and other conflicts.

The French Wars of Religion

In the 16th century, the struggle intensified between Huguenots and the Catholic Church in France.

Origins of the Religious Conflict The French monarchy persecuted the Huguenots in order to diminish the power of the nobility and protect Catholicism. (See Topic 2.3.) In 1559 and 1560, France suffered the death of two monarchs, which brought 11-year-old Charles IX to the throne. His mother, **Catherine de' Medici**, acted as regent and ruler. She used harsh and sometimes misguided tactics to ensure the throne for her sons. The ascension of Charles IX caused a power vacuum in which religious and political persecution flourished.

DOMINANT FAITHS IN WESTERN EUROPE, 1560

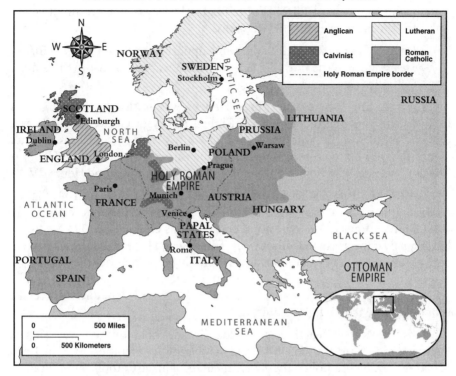

With religious and political motivations, the French Wars of Religion continued to escalate, leading to nine civil wars from 1562 to 1589.

Religious Violence In 1562, after a massacre of Huguenots at Vassy, French Calvinists took to the streets and looted Catholic churches, destroying artwork and breaking stained-glass windows.

Tensions between Catholics and Huguenots reached a peak in 1572 at the marriage of Margaret of Valois, the sister of King Charles IX of France, to **Henry of Navarre**, a leading Calvinist and second in line for the throne. Henry of Navarre invited many wealthy and influential Huguenots to the wedding in Paris. Although she originally arranged the marriage to calm tensions, Catherine de' Medici, in collaboration with the reactionary Catholic Guise family, ordered the massacre of the Huguenots, which pleased the pope and other reactionary Catholics. Starting in Paris and spreading outward, an estimated 10,000 to 20,000 people were killed in an event known as the **St. Bartholomew's Day Massacre**.

Political Rivalry As civil war persisted in France, three men, each named Henry, vied to be king:

- **Henry III** of Valois was a Catholic. He was the fourth son of King Henry II and supported by his mother, Queen Catherine de' Medici, who was Italian. Henry III became king of France in 1574 after the death of Charles IX and ruled until 1589. Catherine was influential throughout his reign.

- Henry of Navarre, the husband of Margaret of Valois, was a Huguenot with support from Elizabeth I of England. He was heir-presumptive to the throne after Henry III of Valois.

- Henry of Guise was a Catholic with support from Philip II of Spain. He established the Catholic League, which wanted to ensure that only Catholics ruled France.

The resulting **War of the Three Henrys** was settled by assassinations. In 1588, the bodyguards of Henry III killed Henry of Guise. A year later, a Catholic monk, on the orders of Henry of Guise's brother Louis, assassinated Henry III, who left no direct male heir to the throne. The Huguenot Henry of Navarre ascended the French throne in 1589 and took the name **Henry IV**.

Political Ending Henry IV took power in a French society torn by religious conflict. Raised as a Protestant but ruling a majority-Catholic country, he looked for a compromise that would end religious conflict. In 1593, he took a bold step by converting to Catholicism. This angered his Huguenot supporters, but reassured Catholics. His conversion demonstrated that he was a Politique, a French moderate who valued unity and peace more than any particular religious group. Henry IV wanted control of the government and a successful economy more than religious uniformity.

Edict of Nantes Reacting against four decades of bloodshed over religion, Henry IV took a historic step in 1598 toward religious toleration with the **Edict of Nantes**. Under this policy, the government recognized Catholicism as France's official religion. However, the policy also allowed Huguenots to worship freely in certain provinces and this **religious pluralism**, or the toleration of multiple religious views, promoted political stability. The Edict of Nantes ended much of the religious violence in France allowing Henry IV to bolster the economy, particularly in Paris. He regulated the state economy, invested in public works, and supported agriculture.

However, many people rejected toleration of beliefs they found not just wrong but dangerous. In 1610, Henry IV, like Henry III and Henry of Guise before him, was assassinated. His killer was a Catholic extremist. The efforts of Henry IV to promote religious toleration were eventually eradicated by the absolutist power of Louis XIV. (See Topic 3.7.)

The Habsburg Dynasty

The Habsburg Dynasty was a prominent ruling family throughout Europe starting in the Middle Ages. By 1520, **Charles V**, the head of the dynasty, had assumed control of territories throughout Europe such as the Holy Roman Empire, Austria, Spain, Northern Italy, and the Netherlands when he ascended to the throne upon the death of his father, King Philip I of Spain. Spain's acquisition of colonies in the Americas made the Habsburg's power even greater. Nevertheless, towards the end of his reign, Charles V recognized the size of the Habsburg Dynasty was unmanageable and divided his dominion in 1556.

Following Charles V's abdication (largely due to poor health), Philip II, his son assumed control of the Spanish Habsburgs and reigned from 1556 to 1598. Ferdinand, Charles's brother, took control of the Austrian Habsburgs and reigned from 1558 to 1564. The Habsburgs faced deadly political and religious tensions in the 16th and 17th centuries like France and England.

Confronting the Ottoman Empire The **Ottoman Empire** completed its conquest of the Byzantine Empire with the capture of Constantinople in 1453. The Ottomans then turned their attention to lands in Central and Eastern Europe.

A series of wars over two centuries between Habsburg controlled countries and the Ottoman Empire reached a crucial point when the Ottomans besieged Vienna in 1683. An army combining the forces of the Holy Roman Empire, the King of Poland, and the Duke of Lorraine (in present-day eastern France) defeated the massive Ottoman force. This loss marked the end of Ottoman expansion into Europe and signaled the beginning of a two-century decline in dominance.

Confronting Christian Disunity Philip II was fiercely anti-Protestant, and he devoted his rule to making all of Europe Catholic again. This led to wars with the Netherlands and England.

Philip's first conflict over religion emerged in the Spanish Netherlands. Many members of the Dutch middle class there had converted to Calvinism. They embraced the Calvinist emphasis on hard work. While Philip's father, Charles V, had maintained the loyalty of the Dutch, Philip II ignored the local customs, demanded strict adherence to Catholicism, and raised taxes to fund exploration in the Americas and Asia. In 1566, Philip began to persecute Dutch Calvinists as heretics after groups called iconoclasts—a person who destroys religious images—destroyed statues of saints in Catholic cathedrals. In response, William of Orange took leadership of the Dutch resistance movement.

In 1581, the seven northern provinces of the Netherlands declared their independence and established the Calvinist Dutch Republic. While Calvinism emerged as the dominant religion, Lutheranism, Anabaptism, and Judaism were permitted. Religious pluralism became the standard in the Netherlands.

Philip II's desire for universal Christendom also led him into conflict with England. England's Protestant queen, Elizabeth I, supported the Protestant rebellion in the Netherlands. Moreover, Elizabeth had encouraged British sea captains to interrupt Spanish trade with the Americas, and even raid Spanish vessels.

Encouraged by the pope, Philip II responded by attacking England. He sent the Spanish Armada (a large fleet of ships) to invade England in 1588. Because of bad weather and the use of English fire ships (ships filled with explosives, set on fire, and floated toward enemy ships), the armada was defeated. The English victory and the Dutch rebellion enabled Protestant groups to gain both religious and political strength in Europe.

Habsburg-Valois Wars A series of wars were fought between the Spanish Habsburgs and France from 1494 to 1559 for control of the Italian peninsula. Each side wanted to use the economic strength and location of Italy to bolster their position as the primary European power. After initial victories, France gave up most of its claims on the Italian peninsula to Spain.

The Thirty Years' War

Religious conflicts continued in central Europe in the 17th century because of a weakness in the 1555 Peace of Augsburg. That agreement allowed the German princes the power to determine whether their state would be Catholic or Lutheran. However, it excluded other Protestants, particularly Calvinists, from the agreement.

The Events of the Thirty Years War In 1618, upon the death of the king of Bohemia (present-day Czech Republic) who had no heirs, the kingdom reverted to the Holy Roman Emperor Ferdinand II. The Bohemians, who were Protestant, preferred a German Calvinist leader, Frederick I, as king. The conflict between Frederick I and Ferdinand II touched off the **Thirty Years' War**. The war had four phases as other countries took sides for religious, political, and economic reasons:

- During the Bohemian Phase (1618–1625), armies of Ferdinand II defeated Frederick I at the Battle of White Mountain, allowing the Holy Roman Empire to reimpose Catholicism in many of the empire's German states.

- During the Danish Phase (1625–1630), Christian IV, the Lutheran king of Denmark, took up the Protestant cause, while also hoping to gain territory in the German states. Danish invading forces were defeated, and Ferdinand II's forces advanced to occupy part of Denmark for a time. The Treaty of Lubeck (1629) ended Danish involvement. Also, Ferdinand issued the Edict of Restitution, which forced Protestant princes to return to Catholicism or pay huge sums of money to control Catholic lands.

- During the Swedish Phase (1630–1635), King Gustavus Adolphus of Sweden, a brilliant military leader, took control of Protestant forces. Adolphus had been consolidating power in the Baltic region and sought greater influence in central Europe. His army was funded to a large degree by **Cardinal Richelieu**, who was the chief minister to French King Louis XIII. Winning several important victories, Adolphus and his German allies were able to reverse many of the gains previously made by the Catholic forces.

- During the French Phase (1635–1648) and with the death of Gustavus Adolphus, the French entered the war directly, on the side of the Protestants. The Spanish entered on the side of the Catholic Holy Roman Empire. This phase saw a continuation of the France-Habsburg rivalry (as seen the Habsburg-Valois wars) with the French now fighting the Spanish primarily in northern German states. This time, the French gained the upper hand. As in the Swedish Phase, France—a Catholic nation—supported Protestant nations, choosing political and economic motives over religious unity.

The Peace of Westphalia

ruined HRE

The Thirty Years' War ended with the **Peace of Westphalia** in 1648. This was a set of treaties that effectively weakened the Holy Roman Empire while also ending any lingering hopes that Europe might again be unified under a single Christian faith. The terms of the Peace of Westphalia had the following provisions and effects:

- The independence of the Netherlands and the Swiss Confederation from Spain and the Holy Roman Empire were officially recognized.

- French, Swedish, and German rulers gained strength. France replace Spain as the primary European power. The Swedes gained territory and started building a lucrative trade network. The German territories of Brandenburg and Prussia were united to form a state that would soon rival Austria.

- Italian regions were removed from the Holy Roman Empire, which caused the empire to focus on its traditional holdings in Central and Eastern Europe.

- The terms of the Peace of Augsburg were confirmed. By confirming that local leaders had control of religious questions and loyalties in their respective areas, the power of the Holy Roman Empire was diminished.

- Calvinism became an officially recognized religion.

Source: Wikimedia Commons

The Swedish painter Carl Wahlbom's *The Battle of Lutzen*, 1632, (National Museum of Sweden) dramatically portrays the turmoil and violence of the Thirty Years' War.

The Changing Nature of War While the Thirty Years' War was a religious conflict between Protestants and Catholics, it was also a political and economic conflict. Rulers exploited the fight over beliefs in order to strengthen themselves. For example, France was led by a Catholic king, Louis XIII, and his chief minister was Cardinal Richelieu. However, they sided with the German Protestants against the Catholic Habsburgs of Austria. France was more concerned with weakening their political foes, the Habsburgs, than with rolling back Protestantism. ~~changed Europe, ended last large religious war~~

The Thirty Years' War, which cost between three and six million lives, was the last large religious war in Europe. The Peace of Westphalia was a turning point in European history. France became the dominant continental power, and Calvinism joined Catholicism and Lutheranism as a major force. European rulers accepted that the continent would be home to various types of Christians. These rulers accepted religious pluralism—but not religious freedom.

REFLECT ON THE ESSENTIAL QUESTION

Essential Question: *How did religious and political factors influence each other from 1450 to 1648?*

Conflicts	Outcome of Conflicts

KEY TERMS

Catherine de' Medici	War of the Three Henrys	Ottoman Empire
Henry of Navarre	Henry IV	Thirty Years War
St. Bartholomew's Day Massacre	Edict of Nantes	Cardinal Richelieu
Henry III	religious pluralism	Peace of Westphalia
	Charles V	

MULTIPLE-CHOICE QUESTIONS

Questions 1–3 refer to the passage below.

> "So it was determined to exterminate all the Protestants and the plan was approved by the queen. They discussed for some time whether they should make an exception of the king of Navarre and the prince of Condé. All agreed that the king of Navarre should be spared by reason of the royal dignity and the new alliance. The duke of Guise, who was put in full command of the enterprise, summoned by night several captains of the Catholic Swiss mercenaries from the five little cantons, and some commanders of French companies, and told them that it was the will of the

king that, according to God's will, they should take vengeance on the band of rebels while they had the beasts in the toils. Victory was easy and the booty great and to be obtained without danger. The signal to commence the massacre should be given by the bell of the palace, and the marks by which they should recognize each other in the darkness were a bit of white linen tied around the left arm and a white cross on the hat."

—Jacques de Thou (1553–1617), French historian describing the
St. Bartholomew's Day Massacre, August 24, 1572

1. What was the "new alliance" made by the king of Navarre that is referred to in the passage?
   (A) A marriage between the Protestant king and a Catholic princess
   (B) A treaty between the French monarch and Swiss mercenaries
   (C) A pledge by the royal family to grant more power to each region
   (D) An agreement between the king and nobles to end religious toleration

2. Which statement describes the historical context in the 16th and 17th centuries in Europe most associated with the events described in the passage?
   (A) Conflicts between monarchs and local leaders
   (B) Conflicts between landowners and peasants
   (C) Conflicts between clergy and lay people
   (D) Conflicts between Roman Catholics and Protestants

3. What was the relationship between the events of 1572 described in the passage and the Edict of Nantes issued in 1598?
   (A) Both were examples of deadly religious persecution.
   (B) Both were examples of greater religious toleration.
   (C) Reaction against the events of 1572 led to more persecution in 1598.
   (D) Reaction against the events of 1572 led to more toleration in 1598.

SHORT-ANSWER QUESTIONS

Use the passage below to answer all parts of the question that follows.

"[The Thirty Years' War] was not primarily a religious war. Religion certainly provided a powerful focus for identity, but it had to compete with political, social, linguistic, gender and other distinctions. Most contemporary observers spoke of imperial, Bavarian, Swedish, or Bohemian troops, not Catholic or Protestant, which are anachronistic [not appropriate for the time period] labels used for convenience since the nineteenth century to simplify accounts.

The war was religious only to the extent that faith guided all early modern public policy and private behavior. To understand the conflict's true relationship to the disputes within Christianity, we need to distinguish between militant and moderate believers. All were religious and we should not see moderates as necessarily more rational, reasonable or secular [without a base in spirituality]. The difference lay not in their religious zeal, but how they related faith and action. All were convinced their version of Christianity offered the only true path to salvation and the sole correct guide to justice, politics and daily life. Moderates, however, were more pragmatic, regarding the desired reunification of all Christians within a single church as a general, rather distant objective. Militants saw this goal as within their grasp and were not only prepared to use force rather than persuasion but also felt personally summoned by God to do so."

—Peter H. Wilson, *The Thirty Years War: Europe's Tragedy*, 2011

1. a) Describe ONE piece of evidence not in the source that supports Wilson's argument.

   b) Describe ONE piece of evidence not in the source that modifies Wilson's argument.

   c) Explain how the results of the Thirty Years' War might support or modify Wilson's argument.

Topic 2.5

The Catholic Reformation

To praise vows of Religion, of obedience, of poverty, of chastity and of other perfections of supererogation [to go beyond what duty requires].

—Ignatius Loyola, "The Spiritual Exercises," c. 1524

Essential Question: What are the continuities and changes in the role of the Catholic Church from 1450 to 1648?

The Reformation challenged the beliefs and practices of the Catholic Church. Protestant groups gained increasing support throughout all of Europe, which created religious as well as political tensions. Many Catholics were unhappy with some of the practices of the Church—such as indulgences, pluralism, and simony—and others were alarmed by the increasing power of secular rulers to interfere in church matters.

In response, the Roman Catholic Church evaluated its practices and beliefs in a movement known as the **Catholic Reformation**. By forming energetic new religious orders, reforming orders that had lost their direction, and holding councils to examine church doctrine, the Catholic Church sought to revive itself. In the end, the Catholic Reformation further ensured religious division in Europe.

Division Among European Christians

During the Middle Ages, the Catholic Church had established institutions, known together as the Inquisition, to defend its official doctrines. The Inquisition searched for and punished heretics, Christians who denied important Church doctrines. In 1542, the pope introduced the **Roman Inquisition** to stop Catholics from converting to Protestantism. Seventeen years later, the pope took another step to stop the spread of Protestantism, establishing the *Index of Prohibited Books*, a list of books that Catholic printers were not to print and Catholics were not to read. Being caught in possession of any of these books was evidence of heresy and was punishable by death. Together, the Inquisition and the *Index* helped cement the growing religious divide in Europe.

The Catholic Reformation Revives the Church

The Catholic Church's responses to the Reformation included the creation of new religious orders and the reforming of misguided orders. New leaders and doctrines arose to challenge the established order of the Church.

New and Revamped Orders

The energy of the Protestant Reformation transferred to the Catholic world during the early 16th century. Inspired individuals attempted to breathe new life into Catholic society through bold action and reform.

The Jesuits In 1540, **Ignatius Loyola** established the **Jesuits**, an all-male order that emphasized a life of poverty, obedience to authority, prayer, and communal living. The Jesuits served as missionaries in the Americas and East Asia and are considered by many to be the most influential religious order of this period as they converted millions to Roman Catholicism. For example, Francis Xavier sailed to India and the Spice Islands seeking to convert people to Catholicism. At the same time, the Jesuits became famous for their rigorous scholarship. Many of the most prestigious universities in Europe were founded and staffed by Jesuits (Loyola University and Georgetown University examples still in existence today). This commitment to research and learning would later bring them into conflict with other Roman Catholics who disliked their willingness to question traditional teachings.

The Ursulines Another influential order, the Company of St. Ursuline, or the **Ursulines**, was also established in the 16th century. This all-female order focused on the Christian education of girls, which it saw as crucial to rejuvenating the family and society. During the following centuries, the Ursulines established convents throughout Europe. Some Ursulines shared the Jesuits goal of spreading the Catholic faith to other continents. In 1639, French Ursulines established their first overseas convent in Quebec in New France. They quickly began to teach the faith to indigenous First Nations girls, who also were taught to read and write.

Teresa of Avila and the Carmelites Saint **Teresa of Avila** addressed the need for reforms within the Carmelite Order, which many thought had become careless and materialistic. She confronted the growing secular nature of the Catholic Church by insisting on the importance of personal prayer. She reformed the Carmelite Order by demanding complete poverty and the rejection of property. By restoring and maintaining strict rules within the convent, she gradually won the respect of church leaders.

Council of Trent Confirms Catholic Doctrine

To promote the unity of the Catholic faith, Pope Paul III convened the **Council of Trent**. Meeting three times between 1543 and 1563, the council was responsible for reaffirming traditional Catholic doctrine while addressing Church issues. The Council addressed simony (the holding of multiple church positions at the same time), pluralism (the buying and selling of church appointments and offices), indulgences (buying the forgiveness of sins), and it condemned clerical immorality. Church officials discussed the official beliefs of the Catholic Church and the criticisms of Protestant reformers. The Council of Trent mostly reaffirmed established Catholic doctrine by:

- emphasizing the need for the seven sacraments (baptism, confirmation, communion, penance, anointing the sick, matrimony, and holy orders)
- stressing the role of both faith and good works
- affirming Latin as the language of the Church
- continuing clerical celibacy
- maintaining the art in churches
- upholding the power of the papacy

The Council of Trent did make some minor reforms related to pluralism, celibacy, and education of the priesthood.

The actions of the Catholic Reformation revived Catholicism and some regions that had rejected the religion, returned to the church. This is particularly true in Southern and Central Europe, in what are today the countries of Spain, Italy, Austria, and Poland.

REFLECT ON THE ESSENTIAL QUESTION

Essential Question: *What are the continuities and changes in the role of the Catholic Church from 1450 to 1648?*

Continuities	Changes

KEY TERMS

Catholic Reformation	Ignatius Loyola	Teresa of Avila
Roman Inquisition	Jesuits	Council of Trent
Index of Prohibited Books	Ursulines	

MULTIPLE-CHOICE QUESTIONS

Questions 1–3 refer to the passage below.

"Let no one think that this Commandment entirely forbids the arts of painting, engraving, or sculpture. The Scriptures inform us that God Himself commanded to be made images of Cherubim [a category of angel], and also the brazen serpent. The interpretation, therefore, at which we must arrive, is that images are prohibited only inasmuch as they are used as deities to receive adoration, and so to injure the true worship of God. . . .

He [the pastor] will also inform the unlettered of the use of images, that they are intended to instruct in the history of the Old and New Testaments, and to revive from time to time their memory; that thus, moved by the contemplation of heavenly things, we may be the more ardently inflamed to adore and love God Himself. He should, also, point out that the images of the Saints are placed in churches, not only to be honored, but also that they may admonish us by their examples to imitate their lives and virtues."

—Council of Trent: *Catechism for Parish Priests*, 1566

1. Who among the following leaders or groups would most strongly disagree with the passage?
   (A) Charles V because he was focused on stopping Muslim advances in Europe
   (B) Anabaptists because they opposed ornate church buildings
   (C) The pope because the Council of Trent tried to weaken his authority
   (D) King Henry VIII because he rejected the leadership of the papacy

2. Which of the following best explains the purpose this passage was written to achieve?
   (A) To revise traditional practices to include some reforms proposed by Protestants
   (B) To propose compromises that would persuade Protestants to accept papal authority
   (C) To demonstrate that Roman Catholics and Protestants shared beliefs on many issues
   (D) To defend Roman Catholic practices against the challenges posed by Protestants

3. Who is most likely the primary audience for this passage?
   (A) People who are not Christians but want to learn about the faith
   (B) Protestants who might want to join the Roman Catholic Church
   (C) Roman Catholic bishops who are considering leaving the Church to become Lutherans or Calvinists
   (D) Members of Roman Catholic congregations who want to understand the teachings of the church better

Answer all parts of the question that follows.

1. a) Explain one way in which new religious orders contributed to the Catholic Reformation during the sixteenth century.

   b) Explain one way in which the Council of Trent reaffirmed traditional Catholic doctrine.

   c) Explain one way in which the Council of Trent addressed church abuses.

Topic 2.6

16th-Century Society and Politics

Since the people is a body with several heads, it is divided by orders, Estates, or particular occupations.

—Charles Loyseau, *A Treatise on Orders and Simple Dignities*, 1610

Essential Question: How did economic and intellectual developments from 1450 to 1648 affect social norms and hierarchies?

The Renaissance, Reformation, and Age of Exploration had profound impacts on economic and intellectual movements within Europe. These major historical developments created a ripple effect that altered some of the social norms and hierarchies in urban and rural areas in early modern Europe. Households functioned as economic units, with husbands and wives contributing with tasks that, together, accomplished the needed work.

16th Century Families and Households

Families were the basic social unit throughout 16th century Europe. The nuclear family was the main institution for reproduction and the raising of children, both essential elements of the economy of rural areas. Property also was primarily transferred through families, which passed on land and possessions through inheritance. Family units provided needed services, such as the care of land and resources, as well as tending to the sick, young, and aged. Every family member contributed labor and resources to the individual family economy. Family structure during the early modern period reflected the patriarchal structure of the larger social order.

Rural Households In rural areas, men and women were responsible for different but complementary tasks to make the family unit self-sufficient. Most Europeans were simple farmers at this time. In parts of eastern Europe, they were still serfs, but in Western Europe many were tenant farmers, meaning they worked on land that was owned by someone else. Men generally worked in the fields, tending to the major crops such as wheat, barley, rye, and oats, or they worked with livestock like cattle, sheep, and poultry. Women generally raised children, preserved food, and prepared the meals. Women also spent some of their time keeping a small, family garden, curing meat, and milking cows. Children also had work to do, collecting wood and water, and helping their parents with chores. As they grew older, boys joined their fathers in the fields, learning to be farmers.

Urban Households Towns were generally small in the 16th and 17th centuries. Merchants, business owners, and lawyers did nonphysical labor and had more options in how to structure their lives than did poorer people. Men were also often employed as craftsmen or artisans— workers in a skilled trade. They were engaged in metalworking (blacksmiths), preparing leather (tanners), barrel production (coopers), and other tasks that provided goods for other town residents—and for rural residents looking for specific services and goods. Women often worked beside their husbands at these tasks, since the workplace was generally the home. Women in urban areas performed similar tasks to their rural counterparts. They were responsible for maintaining the household—raising children, buying food from the market, and preparing and preserving food. More items, however, could be bought from other merchants, so less time was spent making soap, candles, spinning, and weaving.

Source: Getty Images

The Merry Family, a Dutch painting from the 17th century by Jan Steen, portrays a lively scene in the home of a prosperous family.

Established Hierarchies

Even with the growth of new economic elites, people in 16th-century Europe understood their places in established hierarchies that had long been based on class, religion, and gender. These hierarchies determined the ways people viewed each other's status in urban and rural settings.

Class Traditionally, class was determined by birth and wealth, which placed monarchs and the nobility with inherited titles at the top of the scale. States also regulated how family property could be divided, supporting the traditional model of a father passing land and other forms of wealth to his oldest son, a practice called **primogeniture**. For example, in England, in wealthier families, the father had to ensure that the family's wealth remained intact, which meant his oldest male child inherited most of his estate through primogeniture. This family structure caused younger sons to become members of the clergy or artisans. After the Reformation, fewer men sought lives within the church, leading to an increase in artisans that would eventually help fuel an emerging capitalistic structure.

The expanding commercial economy created opportunities for some social mobility, or movement among classes, as wealthy merchants, manufacturers, and bankers rose in class in some societies. In France, for example, some Nobles of the Robe (see Topic 1.5), people holding administrative or judicial offices, were not landowners and could pay for their positions to become hereditary. Yet some privileges and perceptions remained attached to ownership of land, as the composition of Britain's Parliament of the time illustrates:

- Nobles served in the **House of Lords**, the upper house of Parliament, and were often close advisers to the king. They were also the leaders of the counties where their vast estates were located.

- The wealthy but untitled gentry made up about five percent of the rural population and could be chosen to serve in the **House of Commons**, the lower house of Parliament. They also served as local magistrates.

Religion While religious pluralism was an emerging idea, many regions embraced one faith and used it to control the people. If an individual challenged the established religion, they were often exiled or discriminated against, accused of witchcraft, or killed. For example, Michael Servetus was burned at the stake as a heretic by the city council of Geneva for not supporting the Calvinist teachings on the trinity. Catholics, too, were known to kill those whose views diverged from accepted teaching. Jews were expelled from many countries or forced to practice their religion in secret. Amsterdam was an exception. The city had a diverse population, which encouraged religious toleration, which also boosted trade and economic growth.

Gender European society remained generally **patriarchal**, as men controlled government and public life as well as private households, while women were under the authority of their fathers or husbands. This gendered male-dominated structure existed most typically in the upper class, dominated by the nobility

In limited instances women had some economic independence and status. For example, in Amsterdam, widows of skilled craftsmen could take their husband's place in a guild and engage in business. The only claim a daughter would have to her parental estate would come with her **dowry**, or the transfer of property or money that she would receive upon marriage. Wives could usually determine who should receive their dowry upon their death, and husbands typically could not claim ownership to more than one-third of the dowry during the marriage. Women even had the right to sue their husbands if they thought the dowry was being used improperly.

Women's Intellect and Education

Before the Reformation, Catholic convents were havens for unmarried women, offering them a chance to study, write, and lead. However, unmarried women still had few other options. After the Reformation, women in Protestant countries lost many of the opportunities provided by convents but, the Protestant emphasis on literacy allowed some women freedom to explore other options. For example, many women used their homes to teach the gospel and feed the hungry. Some took to writing—from poems to theology to memoirs. Divorce become an option for married women in some places, though typically with many restrictions.

As women's roles started to change, the traditional family unit became even more important. The family—not a church or a monastery—was now the center of Christian life. Both men and women were thought to be able to communicate directly with God. No one needed a male priest or other intermediary to pray or confess sins. Women were encouraged to gain education, though typically mainly as a means of raising educated children who were good Christians and citizens. The question of how much education women should receive became an ongoing discussion, primarily in Italy and England in the mid-17th century.

The Woman Question An academic debate began in France in the 1530s over whether women were fit to attend university. It expanded into broader questions about gender relations, and became known as *La Querelle des Femmes*, or the Woman Question:

- One side argued that women were naturally inferior to men, and this was unchangeable. They cited three reasons: God created man first, men were physically stronger, and Eve—the woman created from Adam—deceived him and ultimately brought on humanity's downfall.

- The other side argued that men oppressed women to maintain their own social status and power. Eve was actually the one who was deceived. Women's inferior position was due to a lack of education and was therefore changeable.

This became the fundamental question regarding the limits placed on women: Were the limits set by God or by humans? In limiting the opportunities for women, was the male-dominated society maintaining an unchangeable sanctified order, or was it oppressing women?

Limitation on Women Though this period provided more options for women than they were afforded previously, there were still many restrictions. Single women might have been able to choose to live outside a convent, but they were still not allowed to serve as preachers. They also were not allowed to hold positions of authority within the church. Instead, even single women were expected to serve as models of obedience and Christian charity. Most importantly, they were expected to be quiet.

Anabaptists Compared to Catholic, Lutheran, and Calvinist churches, Anabaptist churches were less patriarchal. For example, women held some leadership positions—even as preachers. They led worship services, taught the Scriptures, and were regarded as elders and prophets. Because of this stark contrast to the accepted practices of the time, many Anabaptist women were punished for their behavior.

Marriage and Childbirth

The 14th century had been among the hardest on Europe's population. War, famine, and disease killed millions. In contrast, the 15th and 16th centuries were a period of growth. France's population doubled from 10 million to 20 million from 1450 to 1550. Europe still relied on human power to produce goods, so the increased population helped bring economic growth. Europe's population growth also meant farmers and artisans had greater incentive to bring more food and other essentials, as well as luxury items, to market.

Population growth affected marriage patterns also. Europeans in the early modern period typically did not marry out of love. Rather, they married for economic reasons, such as to run a farm and have children to assist with farm work.

Strains on Resources

After catastrophic periods of famines or epidemics, when large numbers of people died from starvation and disease, marriage rates typically rose. During the **Black Death**—or plague—in the mid-14th century, more than 20 million people, or one-third of the population of Europe, died. Immediately afterward, Europe desperately needed to repopulate. The marriage rate rose and the age at marriage fell. During times of prosperity, however, couples typically waited for land and employment opportunities before marrying. As a result, the marriage rate fell and the age at marriage rose.

By the early modern period, Europe's population had rebounded from the Black Death so sufficiently that economic resources could no longer keep pace with demand for products. Couples married at an increasingly older age (between 26 and 27 for men and between 24 and 25 for women), as they waited to obtain land and opportunity. Acquiring a plot of land usually depended upon the death of the man's father, so some couples waited even longer.

Harsh Winters and Poor Harvests As part of the Little Ice Age, beginning around 1300 (see Topic 1.10), a series of unusually harsh winters led to poor harvests in the 1600s. Scarcity of food brought malnutrition and widespread disease. To cope with their poverty, members of the agricultural class started to have smaller families. They waited until they could become financially established before marrying, and thus married at a later age.

Decline of Multigenerational Households While it was once common to find several generations of one family living in the same household, this practice became increasingly less common in western Europe during the early modern period. In fact, a family would likely look very similar to today's nuclear family—two parents marrying in their late-twenties and raising a small number of children.

Influences on Family Size

A number of factors contributed to the low rate of live births and high infant mortality in the early modern period. These included cultural and economic factors, as well as scientific and medical knowledge of the time:

- When women married at a later age for economic reasons, they had fewer childbearing years.

- The number of miscarriages and stillbirths was high, reflecting both to lack of medical knowledge and extreme working conditions that strained a woman's body.

- Infant mortality was high. About one in four babies died in infancy, while another one in four died before puberty. A woman in the early modern period would see roughly two children survive to adulthood.

Persistence of Folk Ideas

Folk ideas and celebrations varied greatly throughout Europe, ranging from festivals marking rites of passage, such as births and marriages, to feasts at a specific time of year such as harvests, saints' days, or religious holidays. When the Protestant Reformation brought religious upheaval, it also changed many traditions. Hoping to maintain their way of life, many held tightly to folk ideas and customs, especially in Germany, where the Reformation began and where its effects were felt most.

Carnival

The Christian period of Lent spans the six weeks before Easter, and **Carnival** is the three- to six-day period of celebration immediately before Lent. In the early modern period, Carnival's lavish feasting and celebrations served as a balance to Lent's fasting and purification. Carnival and Lent were polar opposites, but they were also meant to mutually support each other. The extreme feasting and celebrating during Carnival emphasized humans' multitude of sins from the previous year. It also was a way to release impulses by allowing people to live all those sins simultaneously. Carnival also helped reinforce the social order by temporarily allowing individuals to live outside that order: women posing as men, for example, peasants as aristocrats, and people as animals. Lent, in contrast, was a time of fasting and purification to serve **penance**—the voluntary self-punishment or confession for having done wrong.

After the Reformation, Protestant leaders rejected penance as a sacrament. Carnival, therefore, quickly became another target for anti-Catholic attacks. Even the Catholic Church came to reject Carnival when it did away with public confession.

Still, individuals fought to maintain the folk tradition of Carnival, especially in rural areas where the reach of the church and state was less strong. Carnival continues to exist today—most notably in the cities of Rio de Janeiro, Brazil, and New Orleans, Louisiana—but it has virtually no religious significance.

Blood Sports

Some popular entertainment in the early modern period were **blood sports**, also called "butcherly sports" because of their violent nature. These activities pitted humans against each other in jousting matches. Though not intended as deadly events, many participants did die in them. Other activities pitted animals against each other in dogfights or cockfights.

Saints' Day Festivities

Traditionally, Catholic celebrations took place to honor the patron saint of a town or state. For example, the Feast of Saint Mark (*Festa di san Marco*) honors the patron saint of the Italian city of Venice.

Additionally, All Saints' Day, also known as the Feast of All Saints, is celebrated every year on November 1 to commemorate all saints. It is preceded by All Hallow's Eve, from which modern Halloween is descended. All Hallow's Eve was celebrated at the same time as a pagan holiday.

Enforcement of Communal Norms

The success of the Reformation promoted the spread of humanism, with its increased emphasis on critical thinking rather than acceptance of traditional beliefs. While people adapted many folk ideas and maintained them beyond the early modern period, the Reformation and humanism challenged other practices that eventually became obsolete. However, certain forms of control and punishment survived from earlier times and were used by both local and church authorities.

PUNISHMENT AND CONTROL DURING THE EARLY MODERN PERIOD	
Method	**Description**
Charivari	• Charivari was a loud, public mock parade, with clanging pots and pans to make rough music. It was a form of social intimidation or shaming, particularly in small communities in Western Europe to enforce social norms. • As populations grew and capitalism began to replace subsistence agriculture, the social structure that supported charivari eventually disappeared with the rise of more official forms of social control, such as police and courts.
Stocks, pillory and pranger	• The stocks were a form of public punishment from medieval times. The offender sat on a bench with ankles closed into holes in boards for several hours. The wrists and neck might similarly be restrained. Townspeople might throw waste at the prisoner. • The pillory, also with medieval roots, entrapped the victim's head and wrists as he stood or walked around an upright wooden bar. Passersby often threw waste and otherwise tortured the prisoner, depending on the severity of the crime. • In a similar device, the pranger, the victim's neck was chained to restraints around the ankles, placing the victim in an uncomfortable half-kneeling position. In a less ominous form, the offender was chained to a column in the town center. • Public punishment with these devices remained common until at least 1748.
Whipping and branding	• Whipping, or flogging, was often accompanied by punishment in the stocks, pillory or pranger. Like the blood sports and executions of the period, it drew many spectators. • Branding was used to identify people who did not support a particular set of beliefs—sometimes used by the Catholic Church to mark individuals who openly disagreed with its teachings.

Witchcraft

The many changes brought about by the religious and social upheaval of the Protestant Reformation contributed to increased accusations of witchcraft. Before Europeans used science to understand causes of illnesses, famines, and other misfortunes, they often attributed such events to witchcraft. Accusations of witchcraft peaked between 1580 and 1650, years of religious turmoil following the Reformation. As many as 100,000 people were accused and 40,000 executed on charges of practicing witchcraft. Exact numbers are not available, because detailed records were not kept. Most of the accused were women. As religious controversies became less deadly and knowledge of science spread, fear of witches declined.

Religious Upheaval The Reformation brought the church into people's homes, but it also brought thoughts of the devil and witchcraft. After the Reformation, Catholic rituals to defeat evil lost much of their perceived effectiveness. Many Protestants and Catholics were left feeling powerless against evil, so some invented ways to regain control. The medieval belief that the devil could assume a physical form became more prevalent as individuals saw the devil in other people and accused them of witchcraft.

Social and Economic Upheaval Witchcraft accusations were also a result of social and economic upheaval. In the county of Essex in England, for example, most accusations were brought after a dispute regarding charity. The alleged witch, usually an older, poorer woman, would come to a wealthy home to ask for money, food, or work. The family might turn her away, with the woman muttering angry words as she left. If an unexplained illness or some other disaster later came upon the wealthy family, they would accuse the woman of witchcraft.

Accusations also came between members of poorer classes. In fact, the major peasant concern throughout Europe at this time was with **maleficium**, the harm supposedly brought on by witches. Accusations usually came after arguments over land use or resources. These disputes, many of which seemed petty, always had been a normal part of village life. They rose to a level of concern as Europe changed from an agriculture economy to a capitalistic one. Individuals did not have the same control over their land and resources as they once did. In this way, witchcraft accusations also highlighted the breakup of the traditional village community and economy.

Prominence of Women Roughly 80 percent of those killed for witchcraft were women, and many of them were elderly. Midwives were also accused of witchcraft to provide blame when a couple lost a pregnancy or because they practiced a science that was unfamiliar at the time.

Women were not only more likely to be accused of witchcraft, but they were also more likely to be accusers. Some historians believe this happened because so many of the issues surrounding witchcraft related to women's concerns— child rearing, issues within the home, and the politics of reputation. Many accusations came after the death of a child, usually with the mother as accuser. Postmenopausal women, or those of an older age, often were the accused.

Regional Variation Witch hunts were not uniform throughout Europe. Witchcraft in French lands was less intense, but still provided some of the most dramatic trials of the era, as in 1634 in the town of Loudun in western France. In the countries of the British Isles, witch hunts occurred frequently in Scotland, seldom in England, and almost never in Ireland.

The death rates from witch hunts were the highest by far in the German-speaking states of the Holy Roman Empire and their immediate neighbors, especially Poland. About three-fourths of all executions for witchcraft occurred in the Holy Roman Empire. In some places, executions became widespread. For example, in the late 1670s, about 140 beggars and poor children were executed for witchcraft in the Austrian city of Salzburg alone. The Reformation had started in Germany, and individuals in these areas felt its effects most intensely. Their way of life changed most quickly and most dramatically, so they had the strongest incentive to try to regain control over what was lost, lashing out at suspected witches.

REFLECT ON THE ESSENTIAL QUESTION

Essential Question: *How did economic and intellectual developments from 1450 to 1648 affect social norms and hierarchies?*

Economic and Intellectual Developments	Effects on Social Norms and Hierarchies

KEY TERMS

primogeniture	Black Death	pillory
House of Lords	Carnival	pranger
House of Commons	penance	whipping
patriarchal	blood sports	branding
dowry	charivari	maleficium
La Querelle des Femmes	stocks	

MULTIPLE-CHOICE QUESTIONS

Questions 1–3 refer to the passages below.

Passage 1

"You brashly and publicly not merely wonder but indeed lament [express sorrow] that I am said to possess as fine a mind as nature ever bestowed upon the most learned man. You seem to think so learned a woman has scarcely before been seen in the world. You are wrong. . . . The explanation is clear: women have been able by nature to be exceptional, but have chosen lesser goals. For some women are concerned with parting their hair correctly, adorning themselves with lovely dresses. . . . But those in whom a deeper integrity yearns for virtue, restrain from the start their youthful souls, reflect on higher things, harden the body with sobriety and trials, and curb their tongues, open their ears, compose their thoughts in wakeful hours, their minds in contemplation to letters bonded to righteous. For knowledge is not given as a gift, but [is gained] with diligence. Nature has generously lavished its gifts upon all people. . . . You pretend that I alone am admirable because of the good fortune of my intellect."

—Laura Cereta, letter to Bibulus Sempronius, writing in response
to his praise of her intellect, 1488

"To promote a woman to bear rule, superiority, dominion, or empire above any realm, nation, or city, is repugnant to nature; contumely [humiliating insult] to God, a thing most contrary to his revealed will and approved ordinance; and finally, it is the subversion of good order, of all equity and justice... And first, where I affirm the empire of a woman to be a thing repugnant [disgusting] to nature, I mean not only that God, by the order of his creation, has spoiled woman of authority and dominion, but also that man has seen, proved, and pronounced just causes why it should be. Man, I say, in many other cases, does in this behalf see very clearly.... For who can deny but it is repugnant to nature, that the.... weak, the sick, and impotent persons shall nourish and keep the whole and strong.... And such be all women, compared unto man in bearing of authority. For their sight in civil regiment is but blindness; their strength, weakness; their counsel, foolishness; and judgment, frenzy, if it be rightly considered."

—John Knox, *The First Blast of the Trumpet Against the Monstrous [Unnatural] Regiment of Women*, writing in response to the rule of Queen Mary in Scotland, 1558

1. The most important element of the historical context in which Cereta and Knox made their arguments was that

   (A) global exploration had made Europeans aware of societies in which women held greater power than did men

   (B) England had defeated the Spanish Armada during the reign of female monarch

   (C) women were more commonly working for wages in jobs outside of the home

   (D) an increasing number of women were becoming educated, and a few had served as monarchs

2. Which of the following is the most important difference in the main ideas expressed in these two passages?

   (A) Cereta focuses on the intelligence of females while Knox focuses on the power held by females.

   (B) Cereta is responding to a compliment while Knox is responding to the idea of female monarchs.

   (C) Cereta admits that some women focus on trivial issues while Knox admits that some women could be strong rulers.

   (D) Cereta is writing before 1500 while Knox is writing after that date.

3. What evidence do Cereta and Knox both cite in their passages to support their arguments?

(A) Both appealed to God's commands about different roles based on gender.

(B) Both appealed to how they thought nature had intended for women to act.

(C) Both appealed to the opinion of past thinkers they considered wise.

(D) Both appealed to specific examples of women who demonstrated their point.

SHORT-ANSWER QUESTION

Use the passage below to answer all parts of the question that follows.

"Since the beginning of the early modern era, family formation processes in most western European societies . . . have been linked to the assumption of the headship of a household . . . newly marrying couples were not absorbed into pre-existing households, but instead set up their new residence apart from their [birth] families. [F]or western Europeans, achieving independence entailed carrying all of the start-up costs associated with acquiring housing and equipping the household with the necessary material possessions. . . .

[B]oth marriage and headship occurred relatively late in the life-cycle, when the couple had been able to accumulate capital through many years of living outside the parental homes and working as servants. . . . By contrast in east-central and eastern Europe, new couples generally [went] to live with the groom's [birth] family. Here, the key feature was not only that marriage took place at a younger age, but that it hardly ever led to the establishment of a new independent householding unit, but rather resulted in the enlargement of the existing parental household."

—Mikolaj Szoltysek, *The Oxford Handbook of Early Modern European History, Vol. 1,* 2015

1. a) Describe ONE difference between the family formation process in Western Europe and that in Central and Eastern Europe.

   b) Explain ONE piece of historical evidence that would support the explanation of the family formation process in Western Europe.

   c) Explain ONE piece of historical evidence that would show a difference in family patterns in Western and Eastern Europe in the early modern period.

Topic 2.7

Art of the 16th Century: Mannerism and Baroque Art

In the seventeenth century, ... Baroque architects, artists, and urban planners so magnified and invigorated the classical and ecclesiastical traditions of the city [Rome] that it became for centuries after the acknowledged capital of the European art world.

—art historian Jean Sorabella, 2003

Essential Question: How and why did artistic expression change from 1450 to 1648?

During the Renaissance, artists and sculptors valued ideal, life-like forms because of the impact of classicism and humanism. Throughout the 16th century, two new artistic styles emerged that were influenced by religious strife and self-promoting monarchs. While religion and classicism remained important subjects, artists placed a greater emphasis on displaying emotion and showing wealth in Mannerism and Baroque art.

Mannerist and Baroque Artists

In the 16th century, monarchies, city-states, and the Catholic Church commissioned works of art to exhibit their power and prestige. Artists continued to follow some of the High Renaissance principles but also began expressing themselves in new ways.

Mannerism

The term **Mannerism** started as a criticism. It came from 16th-century critics who thought contemporary artists were painting in the "manner" of Michelangelo and Raphael but lacked the same substance. Mannerists wanted to replace the traditional principles of balance and harmony with more distortion and illusion to add drama to their works. These artists exaggerated the lighting and form of the body to create a unique artistic movement between the Renaissance and Baroque periods. Mannerism reflected the spiritual and political turmoil following the Protestant Reformation in the 1520s and 1530s. Mannerism spread from Italy to other parts of Europe.

Tintoretto Born Jacopo Robusti, **Tintoretto** (1518–1594) challenged the perfection of Renaissance art by using bold brush strokes and dramatic gestures. He spent most of his life in Venice and became the leading painter of the city-state following the death of Renaissance painter, Titian. He typically painted large narrative dramas, such as *The Miracle of Saint Mark*.

El Greco Perhaps the best example of Mannerism was the work of Doménikos Theotokópoulos, who was known as **El Greco** (1541–1614). He was originally from Crete and studied in Venice and Rome. Inspired by the works of Michelangelo and Tintoretto, he desired to break from traditional methods. The emotion of the Counter Reformation and Inquisition intensified his work. He embraced elongated figures and dark, eerie colors creating feelings of intense emotion in his portraits and religious paintings. An example of his unique perspective and style can be seen in *The Disrobing of Christ*. His contemporaries criticized his work as overly dramatic, yet future artists became inspired by his work. (See Topic 7.8.)

Source: Wikimedia Commons

El Greco's *The Disrobing of Christ* (1577–1579) shows his powerful use of color in the robes of Christ and others in the painting.

Baroque

Around 1570, Mannerism gave way to the **Baroque**, which also began in Italy. Baroque art and architecture brought together Renaissance classical traditions and the strong religious feelings stirred up by the Reformation. However, it departed from the realism and naturalism of Renaissance works in its dramatically complex appeal to the senses. The term *baroque*, like *mannerism*, was initially a criticism. It referred to what some thought was the style's exaggerated look.

Baroque architecture and sculpture became important to Catholic rulers and clergy in central and northern Europe, who resisted the Reformation and commissioned dramatic Baroque architecture and sculpture to stimulate religious devotion in their followers.

The courts of Madrid, Vienna, Prague, and Brussels were patrons of Baroque artists. The grand scale and splendor of their palaces, including elaborate decorations, were intended to reflect their power and evoke awe. In the same way, the Catholic Church wanted to reflect the power of the faith in its new churches. Baroque art spread beyond central and southern Europe and included painting, sculpture, and architecture by a number of recognized artistic masters.

Protestant artists of the Baroque period, such as Rembrandt and Vermeer, tended to paint indoor scenes showing people doing work or going about their daily lives. Commissioned mainly by wealthy merchants, Protestant Baroque art shows the restrained wealth of Calvinist believers while at the same time highlighting the fact that they were members of the wealthy middle and upper classes.

Caravaggio Born in Milan, **Caravaggio** (1571–1610) reinvigorated Italian artists by emphasizing the ordinary and using dramatic lighting. Spending most of his career in Italian city-states, Caravaggio painted large, religious works for the Catholic Church. The focus of the painting sat in the light while the rest of the painting remained in the shadows as seen in *The Calling of Saint Matthew*. He did not idealize the religious subject but rather portrayed them as everyday men or women. He also sought to capture the drama and tension of the moment. Caravaggio's unique artistic style points to him being something of a bridge from mannerism to the baroque.

Source: Wikimedia Commons

One of Caravaggio's most famous paints is *The Calling of Saint Matthew* which uses dramatic lighting and shadows.

Artemisia Gentileschi Caravaggio's followers were called "the Caravaggisti" because of their use of dramatic lighting. **Artemisia Gentileschi** (1593–1653), a pupil of Caravaggio, became one of his most successful followers as well as the first widely known female painter of the era. She painted mostly female subjects, specializing in women from the Bible and mythology. In her works, she used lighting to dramatize the emotion of the female figures.

Gian Lorenzo Bernini Considered the most famous Italian Baroque architect and sculptor, **Gian Lorenzo Bernini** (1598–1680) left a mark of the cityscape of Rome through his numerous fountains, artworks and facades. As a sculptor, his figures appeared to be in motion as their muscles flexed and faces showed emotion. For example, unlike Michelangelo's *David* who stands in place, Bernini's sculpted David's body is in motion slaying Goliath. He shows the drama and the emotion of the figure or event. In addition, he completed the work on St. Peter's Basilica, begun during the High Renaissance.

Peter Paul Rubens The most prominent Baroque painter of northern Europe was **Peter Paul Rubens** (1577–1640). His paintings, which exemplified Baroque style, were dramatic in their use of light and color and dynamic movement. The Catholic Church employed him in cathedrals, such as Antwerp, to show their grandeur and wealth. He traveled throughout European courts painting monarchs, princes, and dukes. He used bold brushstrokes and vibrant colors in his works making the individual come alive. He was also known for sensual nude forms in his work.

REFLECT ON THE ESSENTIAL QUESTION

Essential Question: *How and why did artistic expression change from 1450 to 1648?*

Changes in Mannerism	Changes in Baroque

KEY TERMS

Mannerism	Baroque	Gian Lorenzo Bernini
Tintoretto	Caravaggio	Peter Paul Rubens
El Greco	Artemisia Gentileschi	

Questions 1–3 refer to the painting below.

Source: Wikimedia Commons

Pieter Brueghel the Elder, a Dutch painter, *The Fight Between Carnival and Lent*, 1559

1. Which artistic style does this painting most represent?
   (A) Italian Renaissance because of its idealized human figures and sense of balance
   (B) Northern Renaissance because of its emphasis on detail and human activities
   (C) Mannerism because of its use of dark colors and distorted figures
   (D) Baroque because of its combination of classical traditions and religious feeling

2. The painting provides evidence that most supports which of the following claims about 16th century society?
   (A) The Christian religious calendar continued to influence social norms and traditions.
   (B) The Reformation ended the practice of celebrating religious holidays.
   (C) The Counter Reformation led to religious upheaval and public executions.
   (D) City councils began selecting religious practices and customs.

3. Which of the following might limit the use of this painting as a source of information about the Renaissance?

(A) Because it was painted by someone in northern Europe, it might not reflect events or attitudes in southern Europe.

(B) Because it was painted long after the Renaissance, it is a secondary rather than a primary source.

(C) Because it portrays mostly people of one gender, it tells little about gender relationships in the Renaissance.

(D) Because it portrays people in an agricultural setting, it does not reflect life in villages or cities.

SHORT-ANSWER QUESTIONS

Use the passage below to answer all parts of the question that follows.

> "Baroque art (derived from the Portuguese word "Barrocca," meaning rough or imperfect pearl) originated in Italy and a few other countries as an imperceptible passage from the late Renaissance, which ended about 1600. It was occasionally seen as a variation and brutalization of the Renaissance style and sometimes conversely as a higher form of its development, and it remained dominant until approximately the middle of the 18th century. Conventionally, Baroque style is not emphasized in the global history of art because the time period when it flourished—between 1550 and 1750— is correctly viewed as an enclosed time period in which various directions were expressed."
>
> —Klaus Carl and Victoria Charles, *Baroque Art*, 2009

1. a) Explain how ONE piece of evidence supports the argument by Carl and Charles regarding the *change* in art in the Baroque period.

   b) Explain how ONE piece of evidence supports the argument by Carl and Charles regarding the *continuity* in art in the Baroque period.

   c) Explain how Baroque art reflected the political context of its time.

Topic 2.8

Causation in the Age of Reformation and the Wars of Religion

A dog barks when his master is attacked. I would be a coward if I saw that God's truth is attacked and yet would remain silent.

—John Calvin (1509–1564)

Essential Question: How did the religious, political, and cultural developments of the 16th and 17th centuries affect European society?

Starting in the 16th century, both the Protestant and Catholic Reformations shook up the established order of society. Protestant reformers questioned Catholic practices and doctrines. The Catholic Reformation followed with moves to secure the religion's adherents. But on both sides of the divide, there was little desire for understanding or acceptance. The religious conflicts fragmented relationships within and among states, both politically and economically. Conflicts intensified and wars were fought—all in the name of promoting one religion over another.

At the same time, commercial and agricultural capitalism emerged in Europe and slowly replaced traditional economic institutions of the Middle Ages. The resulting growth of commerce caused cities to expand and populations to migrate more readily. The work roles of men and women changed as the nuclear family remained the dominant social unit and people clung to traditional folk ideas for their community standards. Even as new ideas and realities caused change, a degree of continuity was always present.

Religious Pluralism Causes a Divided Europe The religious reformations forever changed traditional European Christianity, culture, and attitudes toward wealth and prosperity. Protestant reformers, including Martin Luther and John Calvin, protested what they viewed as the flawed doctrine, greed, and amorality of much of the Roman Catholic Church. New Christian doctrine and practices developed by these reformers became the mandate of the new Protestant churches. One of the Protestant beliefs was that people who were favored by God gained wealth as a reward. Religious radicals, including the Anabaptists and other groups, in turn protested both the ideas of the Catholics and of other Protestants. At the same time, Catholics began their own Reformation in an attempt to root out corruption, bring revived hope and faith to adherents, and regain those who had turned to one of the Protestant groups.

Reformers, including the Jesuit Order, succeeded to some degree in breathing new life into Catholicism. However, reconciliation with the Protestants was not part of their plan.

The Reformations made it increasingly possible for secular state control of religious institutions. However, Protestant leaders resisted monarchs who tried to maintain rule over religious institutions. These conflicts resulted in wars, such as the French wars of religion among the nobility and the monarchy. The competitions among religious groups grew into political and economic conflicts within and among states.

The Religious Wars Cause a Struggle for Sovereignty The development of secular systems of law brought about sovereign states to replace religious universal law throughout Europe. The Thirty Years' War for religious power ended with the Peace of Westphalia in 1648. This was a set of treaties that effectively weakened the Holy Roman Empire while also ending any lingering hopes that Europe might again be unified under a single Christian faith.

New local governments gave power to local leaders—both nobles and church leaders—rather than religious institutions. This fragmentation throughout Europe began centuries of struggles for territory and sovereignty.

Commercial and Agricultural Capitalism Causes Societal Changes Over the 16th and 17th centuries, emerging commercial and agricultural capitalism in Europe slowly caused the traditional economic institutions of the Middle Ages to fade away. This new commerce caused cities to expand and populations to move, thereby causing traditional politics and societies to evolve as well. These changes were occurring as the authority of religion became weaker during the Reformation, and as a result, traditional political and social structures were placed under stress.

Culture and leisure activities continued to revolve around religion and the traditional agricultural calendar. With so much religious upheaval, people clung to traditional folk ideas and rituals for their community standards. This period saw European society on the threshold of stepping into the modern era, while still having one foot in the Middle Ages.

QUESTIONS ABOUT CAUSATION

1. How did religious pluralism divide Europe in the 16th and 17th centuries?

2. What political changes came about in Europe as a result of emerging commercial capitalism in the 16th and 17th centuries?

3. How did the religious wars of the 16th and 17th centuries affect Europe?

UNIT 2 REVIEW: The Age of Reformation
c. 1450 to c. 1648

WRITE AS A HISTORIAN: *USE EVIDENCE*

Evidence is specific information based on facts or reasons, not a generalized or unsupported opinion. The most accurate evidence for an essay uses specific names of people, places, and events.

Which evidence below each question would be most useful in answering it? Explain your choice.

1. How did Protestant Reformation change Christian teaching?

   a. Martin Luther and John Calvin criticized Catholic teachings, leading to new beliefs such as the priesthood of all believers, the primacy of scripture, predestination, and salvation by faith alone.

   b. Protestant leaders charged that the Catholic Church was corrupt and that its leaders used their positions to gain wealth and power.

2. How did religious reform result in increased state control of religious institutions in England?

   a. One Reformation idea was to implement a top-down approach to centralize power and bring about religious reform.

   b. The English monarchs initiated reform that gave them more control over religious life.

Evidence must be relevant. It should focus on the right culture, time period, and topic. For example, if a question asks about religious intolerance in France, facts about the persecution of the Huguenots would be more relevant than facts about the Versailles palace.

For each claim below, evaluate the relevance of the evidence.

3. Conflicts among religious groups overlapped with political and economic competition among states.

   a. The Thirty Years' War was Europe's most deadly religious war, but it became also a rivalry between France and the Habsburgs for political domination of the European continent.

   b. Members of the House of Habsburg ruled the Holy Roman Empire for three centuries. During this time, they fought off both foreign challengers and domestic opposition.

4. The principle of religious toleration emerged over time.

    a. The Peace of Augsburg (1555) allowed princes in the Holy Roman Empire to choose Catholicism or Lutheranism for their subjects, but not Calvinism or Anabaptism.

    b. Groups like the Huguenots, the Puritans, and the nobles of Poland all challenged the monarchs' control over religious institutions in the regions they lived in.

LONG ESSAY QUESTIONS

Directions: Suggested writing time is 40 minutes. In your response, you should do the following:

- Respond to the prompt with a historically defensible thesis that establishes a line of reasoning.
- Describe a broader historical context relevant to the prompt.
- Support an argument in response to the prompt using specific and relevant examples of evidence.
- Use historical reasoning (e.g., comparison, causation, continuity and change over time) to frame or structure an argument that addresses the prompt.
- Use evidence to corroborate, qualify, or modify an argument that addresses the prompt.

1. Evaluate the extent to which nation-states or individual rulers differed in their attempts to resolve the conflicts between Protestants and Catholics during the 16th and 17th centuries.

2. Evaluate the extent to which reform movements transformed Christian beliefs or practices during the 16th and 17th centuries.

3. Evaluate the extent to which family structure, social interaction, and community norms changed during the 15th and 16th centuries.

4. Evaluate the extent to which religion influenced gender roles and family demographics during the period from 1450 to the mid-1600s.

DOCUMENT-BASED QUESTION

Directions: Question 1 is based on the accompanying documents. The documents have been edited for the purpose of this exercise. You are advised to spend 15 minutes planning and 45 minutes writing your answer. In your response, you should do the following:

- Respond to the prompt with a historically defensible thesis that establishes a line of reasoning.
- Describe a broader historical context relevant to the prompt.

- Support an argument in response to the prompt using at least six documents
- Use at least one additional piece of specific historical evidence (beyond that found in the documents) relevant to an argument about the prompt.
- For at least three documents, explain how or why the document's point of view, purpose, historical situation, and/or audience is relevant to an argument.
- Use evidence to corroborate, qualify, or modify an argument that addresses the prompt.

1. Analyze the extent to which women's lives were affected by the Reformation.

Document 1:

Source: John Knox, Protestant reformer, *First Blast of the Trumpet Against the Monstrous Regiment of Women*, 1558

To promote a woman to bear rule, superiority, dominion [control], or empire above any realm, nation, or city is repugnant to nature, contumely to God, a thing most contrarious [contrary] to his revealed will and approved ordinance, and, finally, it is the subversion [ruin] of good order, of all equity and justice....For those that will not permit a woman to have power over her own sons will not permit her, I am assured, to have rule over a realm; and those that will not suffer her to speak in defense of those that be accused, neither that will admit her accusation intended against man, will not approve her that she shall sit in judgment, crowned with royal crown, usurping [seizing] authority in the midst of men.

Document 2

Source: Martin Luther, German reformer, *Table Talk* (a collection of Luther's saying as compiled by his students), 1566

Men have broad and large chests, and small narrow hips, and more understanding than women, who have but small and narrow breasts, and broad hips, to the end they should remain at home, sit still, keep house, and bear and bring up children.

Document 3

Source: Pieter Bruegel the Elder, Flemish painter, *The Peasant Wedding*, 1567

Document 4

Source: John Jewel, Anglican Bishop, *On the State of Matrimony* from *The Second Book of Homilies*, a book authorized by Elizabeth I in 1571

The woman ought to have a certaine honour attributed to her, that is to say, she must be spared and borne with, the rather for that she is the weaker vessel, of a frail heart, inconstant, and with a word soon stirred to wrath. And therefore considering these her frailties, she is to be the rather spared. By this means, thou shalt not only nourish concord: but shalt have her heart in thy power and will…. Ye wives, be ye in subiection to obey your own husbands (1 Peter 3.1). To obey, is another thing then to control or command, which yet they may do, to their children, and to their family: But as for their husbands, them must they obey, and cease from commanding, and perform subiection. For this surely doth nourish concord very much, when the wife is ready at hand at her husband's commandment.

Document 5

Source: Moderata Fonte, Italian writer and poet, *The Worth of Women: Wherein Is Clearly Revealed Their Nobility and Their Superiority to Men*, published after her death in 1592

It really is something ... that men disapprove even of our doing things that are patently good. Wouldn't it be possible for us just to banish these men from our lives, and escape their carping and jeering once and for all? Couldn't we live without them? Couldn't we earn our living and manage our affairs without help from them? Come on, let's wake up, and claim back our freedom, and the honour and dignity that they have usurped from us for so long. Do you think that if we really put our minds to it, we would be lacking the courage to defend ourselves, the strength to fend for ourselves, or the talents to earn our own living? Let's take our courage into our hands and do it, and then we can leave it up to them to mend their ways as much as they can: we shan't really care what the outcome is, just as long as we are no longer subjugated to them.

Document 6

Source: Bernard Picard, *Assemby of Quakers*, shows a female Quaker preacher and her congregation, 1723

ASSEMBLÉE des QUAQUERS à Londres
A. Quaqueresse qui prêche

Document 7

Source: Gian Lorenzo Bernini, Italian sculptor, *The Ecstasy of St Teresa*, located in the Church of Santa Maria della Vittoria, Rome, 1652

UNIT 3: Absolutism and Constitutionalism
c. 1648 to c. 1815

Topic 3.1

Contextualizing State Building

Essential Question: What was the context in which different forms of political power developed from 1648 to 1815 in Europe?

The religious reformations of the 16th century brought conflicts that resulted in widespread instability and fragmented relationships politically and economically—both within and among states. At the same time, commercial and agricultural capitalism emerged in Europe and slowly replaced traditional economic institutions of the Middle Ages. As commerce grew, cities expanded and populations migrated more. Politically, the development of European secular systems of law resulted in new local governments, which led the transition of power away from religious institutions and toward local and regional entities.

All of the changes and struggles for sovereignty brought different forms of political power to 17th- and 18th-century Europe. New states were built with the new political structures.

Struggles Against Political Centralization In 17th-century Europe, factions of individuals began to challenge their monarchs and resist political centralization. Conflicts emerged and grew between absolute rulers with centralized power and developing secular governments with new political institutions. Struggles to rule erupted between monarchs who wanted more power and nobles who wanted to maintain their traditional shared power and regional autonomy. Competition between monarchs and nobles became fierce and long-standing.

Some absolute monarchs adapted to maintain their control. Whether by political maneuvering, military strength, internal improvements, Europe's monarchs dealt with challenges to their power from aristocracy and other classes.

Developments of the Agricultural Revolution added another layer of complexity to the struggle for power. As fewer peasants and farm workers were needed to produce food for the population, the power of landowning nobles shifted to merchant and middle-class city dwellers. Additionally, in regions where a nation or imperial power held sway over linguistically and/or culturally different communities, these groups began to resist the dominant national group in an attempt to gain some level of self-governance. This resistance often had far-reaching consequences, including intensifying already violent conflicts.

These conflicts and the subsequent Peace of Westphalia established a new balance of power. This complex system of diplomacy as well as advances in warfare developed and prevented any state from gaining too much power. Among other developments that contributed to this balance, France challenged the dominance of the Habsburg Empire, the Ottoman Empire bagan to decline, and Prussia grew in strength.

Differing Sovereignty Models During the 17th and 18th centuries, absolute monarchies solidified their hold over much of Europe. These monarchies were based on the idea that kings and queens had a divine right to rule. Due to the turmoil within European Christianity, ideas changed, and absolute monarchies began to be challenged. Slowly, armed with emerging ideas from European intellectuals, some people came to the conclusion that monarchs actually did not have this divine right. Instead, they had a social contract with their subjects, in which the ruler had obligations to provide certain rights and security to subjects. In return, subjects had to give up some freedoms for the protections provided by the monarchy. These Enlightenment ideas greatly influenced the relationship between states and individuals.

From the growing challenges to absolute monarchy grew different models of political sovereignty. One model was a constitutional monarchy, which gave a parliament shared power with a monarch, as was seen after the English Civil War and the delicate balance that was reached after the war. Power was shared, although not equally, among the crown, Parliament, the aristocracy, and the people. Another political model that emerged was an oligarchy, or a legislative body from a select societal class that ruled the state. For example, the Dutch Republic was created so that power was held by urban gentry and rural landholders.

ANALYZE THE CONTEXT

1. How did struggles against political centralization affect Europe in the late 17th and 18th centuries?

2. How did religious reformations lead to the evolution of new sovereignty models in Europe?

Topic 3.2

The English Civil War and the Glorious Revolution

The state of monarchy is the supremest thing upon earth; for kings are not only God's lieutenants upon earth, and sit upon God's throne, but even by God himself they are called gods.

—King James I to Parliament, 1610

Essential Question: What were the causes and consequences of the English Civil War?

England was distinct from other European nations in that it had both a strong monarchy and a powerful Parliament. In governments on the European continent, different groups, or estates, shared influence. Each estate's influence corresponded to the desires of a special interest group, such as the clergy. England's two houses of Parliament more closely represented the country as a whole and served as a check on the monarch's power. This system was tested during the English Civil War (1642–1651), a series of bloody and expensive battles pitting royal forces against Parliament.

The English Civil War

The **English Civil War** erupted as a result of the Stuart monarchs' efforts to make England an **absolute monarchy**—that is, a government in which the king or queen rules with absolute, or unlimited, power. Queen Elizabeth I died without a direct heir, and the Stuart monarchy, distant relatives of Elizabeth, assumed the crown. As a result, James IV of Scotland became King **James I** of England. Because of his absolutist beliefs, James clashed with the English Parliament, specifically the House of Commons (where non-noble members sat), almost from the beginning of his reign.

King **Charles I**, James's son and heir, shared his father's belief in the divine right of kings and, therefore, began on a similar path to James when he assumed the throne in 1625. When Parliament convened in the first years of his reign, it refused to grant the king taxation powers and funds without recognition and advancement of its rights. The House of Commons was also dominated by Puritans, many of whom objected to the increasingly "popish" direction of the Church of England. In March 1629, Charles adjourned the increasingly radical Parliament and did not call it again for 11 years. When he did, to raise funds for war in Scotland, Parliament sought to reprimand him for illegal taxation and his rejection and suppression of the Puritan movement.

Source: Getty Images

Contrast the appearance of King Charles I (left) and Oliver Cromwell (right). These differences reflected not just ideas about clothing and hairstyle but deep-seated religious views as well. *parliment*

Charles did allow ppl to control church

The new Parliament tried to wrest control of the army from the king, as well as assume control of the future direction of the Anglican Church. Charles's rejection of Parliament's demands led to civil war in 1642. On one side were the **Parliamentarians** who wanted change. (They were also called Roundheads, a derisive name referring to the short haircuts of many Puritans who were a part of this group.) On the other side were the **Royalists**, also called Cavaliers, who supported the monarchy.

The Parliamentarian army, under **Oliver Cromwell**, was victorious, and in 1649, Parliamentary forces executed Charles I. Cromwell established a Commonwealth but spent much of his energy putting down Royalist revolts. In 1653, he became lord protector and ruled until his death in 1658. After Cromwell's death, his son Richard ruled briefly as lord protector.

Restoration and Abdication

In 1660, Parliament restored the monarchy, in a period known as the **Restoration**, with Charles II as king. After Charles II's death, his brother James II, a Roman Catholic, became England's monarch.

Upon assuming the throne in 1685, James began suspending the law to appoint Catholics to positions in the church and government, thus ignoring the will of Parliament. When James II's wife gave birth to a son, anti-Catholic nobles rebelled in response to James's growing absolutism and Catholic sympathies. They called on James II's Dutch son-in-law **William of Orange**, a Protestant, to invade and depose the king. In 1688, James II fled, abdicating the throne. William of Orange ruled as King **William III** with his wife **Mary II**. The accession of William and Mary to the throne became known as the **Glorious Revolution**.

TIMELINE OF THE ENGLISH CIVIL WAR

Date	Event	Significance
1603	James I succeeds Elizabeth I	• James believed in the divine right of kings, which caused conflict with Parliament. • James I spent extravagantly with little oversight from Parliament.
1625	Charles I succeeds James I	• Charles I tried to fulfill his father's wish to unite England with Ireland, which made Parliament suspicious that such a move would strengthen royal power and weaken the power of Parliament.
1629–1640	Charles I dissolves Parliament	• Charles dissolves Parliament because of its objections to his taxation and imprisonments without trial. Charles raises revenue with non-Parliamentary taxes, which makes him increasingly unpopular.
1642	Civil war begins	• Supporters of Charles I fought supporters of the **Long Parliament**, so called because it lasted from 1640 until 1660.
1648	Parliament is purged	• In December 1648, Cromwell's army expelled 121 members deemed unacceptable. The remaining **Rump Parliament** carried out Cromwell's wishes, charging Charles I with treason and putting him on trial.
1649	Charles I executed	• Most of the population opposed the execution of the king by a small minority of English Parliamentarians.
1649–1653	England, Scotland, and Ireland become a republic known as the Commonwealth	• Parliament and the Council of State replaced the monarchy with Oliver Cromwell as lord protector of the Commonwealth (protectorate).
1651	Charles II crowned king of the Scots	• Scottish support for Charles II had grown, causing a greater divide with the Commonwealth.
1651	Civil war ends	• English, Scottish, and Irish Royalists who supported Charles II continued to fight for the restoration of the monarchy. Fighting ended with the Parliamentarian victory at the Battle of Worcester on September 3, 1651.
1653–1658	Protectorate governs	• England was ruled for a short time as a republic, not a monarchy. • Oliver Cromwell was named lord protector over the commonwealth of England, Scotland, and Ireland. • Over time, Cromwell was criticized by republicans as tyrannical. • When Oliver Cromwell died, his son Richard became lord protector. He was unable to carry on his father's policies, and the protectorate failed.
1660	Charles II resumes the throne and the Restoration begins	• Parliament's New Model Army removed Richard and reinstated the Rump Parliament and the monarchy. • English, Scottish, and Irish monarchies were restored under Charles II.

The English Bill of Rights

before they could become king + queen, they had to sign it

When William and Mary took power in 1689, Parliament required that they accept a **Bill of Rights**. This document, also known as the Declaration of Right, established **parliamentary sovereignty** by limiting the monarchs' powers while extending some of Parliament's:

- Parliament had the power to meet frequently.
- Parliament needed to approve any change in the law.
- Parliament needed to approve taxes.

In addition, the Bill of Rights declared that some members of Parliament would be chosen through elections (by a small part of the population), that the monarch could not keep a standing army, and that government could not use excessive fines or cruel punishments. However, it did not grant equality for Catholics. By forcing the monarch to share power with Parliament, this document created a **constitutional monarchy**. It had a major impact on the writing of the United States Constitution and Bill of Rights.

REFLECT ON THE ESSENTIAL QUESTION

Essential Question: *What were the causes and consequences of the English Civil War?*

Causes of the English Civil War	Consequences of the English Civil War

---

KEY TERMS AND PEOPLE

English Civil War	Oliver Cromwell	Long Parliament
absolute monarchy	Restoration	Rump Parliament
James I	William of Orange	Bill of Rights
Charles I	(William III)	parliamentary sovereignty
Parliamentarians	Mary II	constitutional monarchy
Royalists	Glorious Revolution	

MULTIPLE-CHOICE QUESTIONS

Questions 1–3 are based on the following document.

- The pretended [assumed] power of suspending the laws or the execution of laws by regal authority without consent of Parliament is illegal; . . .

- It is the right of the subjects to petition the king, and all commitments and prosecutions for such petitioning are illegal;
- The raising or keeping a standing army within the kingdom in time of peace, unless it be with consent of Parliament, is against law;
- The subjects which are Protestants may have arms for their defense suitable to their conditions and as allowed by law;
- Election of members of Parliament ought to be free;
- Freedom of speech and debates or proceedings in Parliament ought not to be impeached or questioned in any court or place out of Parliament;
- Excessive bail ought not to be required, nor excessive fines imposed, nor cruel and unusual punishments inflicted;
- Jurors ought to be duly impaneled and returned; . . .
- And that for redress of all grievances, and for the amending, strengthening and preserving of the laws, Parliaments ought to be held frequently. . . .

—English Bill of Rights, 1689

1. The creation of this document resulted most directly from which of the following developments?
   (A) The crowning of King James VI of Scotland as King James I of England
   (B) The rise to power of Oliver Cromwell as lord protector of the Commonwealth
   (C) The overthrow of James II during the Glorious Revolution
   (D) The decline in power of the British aristocracy relative to the monarchy

2. What type of government does the excerpt reflect?
   (A) Republic because it was led by elected leaders
   (B) Constitutional monarchy because it limited the power of the king
   (C) Absolute monarchy because it weakened the power of wealthy landowners
   (D) Despotism because it was based on the exercise of absolute power

3. Which individual would likely be most supportive of the provisions of the English Bill of Rights?
   (A) King James I
   (B) King Charles I
   (C) Oliver Cromwell
   (D) King James II

SHORT-ANSWER QUESTION

Use the passages below to answer all parts of the question that follows.

Passage 1

"This interpretation is that the English Revolution of 1640–60 was a great social movement like the French Revolution of 1789. The state power protecting an old order that was essentially feudal was violently overthrown, power passed into the hands of a new class, and so the freer development of capitalism was made possible. The Civil War was a class war, in which the despotism of Charles I was defended by the reactionary forces of the established Church and conservative landlords. Parliament beat the King because it could appeal to the enthusiastic support of the trading and industrial classes in town and countryside, to the yeomen and progressive gentry, and to wider masses of the population whenever they were able by free discussion to understand what the struggle was really about."

—Christopher Hill, *The English Revolution, 1640*, 1940

Passage 2

"Charles's personal rule reads like a 'how to annoy your countrymen for dummies'. His introduction of a permanent Ship Tax was the most offensive policy to many. Ship Tax was an established tax that was paid by counties with a sea border in times of war. It was to be used to strengthen the Navy and so these counties would be protected by the money they paid in tax; in theory, it was a fair tax against which they could not argue.

Charles's decision to extend a year-round Ship Tax to all counties in England provided around £150,000 to £200,000 annually between 1634 and 1638. The resultant backlash and popular opposition however proved that there was growing support for a check on the power of the King.

Through the study of money, religion and power at this time it is clear that one factor is woven through them all and must be noted as a major cause of the English Civil War; that is the attitude and ineptitude of Charles I himself, perhaps the antithesis of an infallible monarch."

—Victoria Masson, "The Origins & Causes of the English
Civil War," *Historic UK*

1. a) Identify ONE piece of evidence not in the source that would support Hill's argument.

   b) Identify ONE piece of evidence not in the source that would support Masson's argument.

   c) Explain ONE important difference between Hill's and Masson's historical interpretations of the causes of the English Civil War.

Topic 3.3

Continuities and Changes to Economic Practice and Development

... the free-market system distributes the fruits of economic progress among all people. That's the secret of the enormous improvements in the conditions of the working person over the past two centuries.

—economist Milton Friedman, *Free to Choose: A Personal Statement*, 1980

Essential Question: What were the continuities and changes in commercial and economic developments from 1648 to 1815?

The Agricultural Revolution that took place in Britain was a major turning point and helped lead, in turn, to an Industrial Revolution. As farm workers became more productive, fewer were needed to feed the nation. Faced with a lack of rural employment, many people left the countryside for cities, where they worked for wages in new industries. The development of modern notions of private property and job specialization, or division of labor, helped create a market economy. (See Topic 1.10.)

The Agricultural Revolution

One of the most significant periods of change in history deals with people's ability to produce enough food to feed entire populations. The Agricultural Revolution that began in Britain in the 18th century gave it the most productive farms in Europe. By the 19th century, British agricultural production was as much as 80 percent higher than the average European country.

In Britain, fewer and fewer people worked on farms because they were migrating to cities, yet farm output nearly tripled between 1500 and 1700. In 1500, one farmer could feed approximately 1.4 people. By 1700, one farmer could feed 3.0 people. Most other countries in Europe needed twice as many farmers to feed a comparable population.

Increased Food Production

There were numerous reasons why Britain's food production increased so dramatically. One reason was Britain's climate. Atmospheric patterns changed in the 17th century, so the weather became drier and warmer. Also, Britain utilized science and technology. For example, scientific breeding of livestock (selective breeding) practiced by British beef cattle and sheep farmers improved agricultural production.

With so many people leaving the countryside to take urban jobs, the remaining farmers had to use all the tools at their disposal to create enough food for a growing population. British farmers, out of necessity, utilized several farming methods to increase output.

Crop Rotation Most crops pull nutrients out of the soil, so fields were traditionally allowed to recover by lying fallow, or unused. Farmers discovered that rotating crops such as turnips, alfalfa, and clover over successive seasons would restore depleted nitrogen to the soil. This practice of **crop rotation** greatly improved soil quality and the amount of food that farmers could produce. *led to increase in food production*

Mixed Farming British farmers began to utilize a **mixed farming** system where they raised livestock and crops on the same land. Crops common to Britain made excellent grazing for the country's many sheep. As the animals grazed, they deposited manure, which further enhanced the soil. When the manure and cover crops were tilled under, fields became even more productive.

Source: Getty Images

The Dishley breed of sheep was developed using the techniques of scientific breeding.

Advances in Farm Machinery Until the early 18th century, all farm tasks—from tilling the soil to sowing seeds to harvesting crops—were done manually by people and/or using animals. That began to change as British farmers met the challenges of providing food for domestic consumption and for export to other nations by creating technological solutions:

- In 1701, Jethro Tull invented a **seed drill** and **mechanical hoe**. The seed drill metered out the seeds in straight lines and then covered them with dirt. The horse-drawn mechanical hoe removed weeds from between the seed rows.

- In 1730, Joseph Foljambe created a cast-iron plow based on earlier Chinese and Dutch designs. These were much more durable and efficient than wooden plows. Soon Foljambe's plows were being fashioned by blacksmiths throughout Europe and North America. The smiths used interchangeable parts and standard patterns.

- In 1784, Andrew Meikle invented the **thresher**—a machine that separated grains from plants.

Enclosure Movement

Another change to farming was the **enclosure movement**—a series of laws allowing for the sale of public lands. During this movement, the often collectively owned and used public land (known as the commons) was purchased, usually by large landowners. Small fields were consolidated into larger landholdings surrounded by hedges or fences.

The enclosure movement contributed to a growing population of landless peasants. Some worked on the new larger farms, while many others migrated to towns and cities in search of work. Whether by choice or by force, more and more small farmers lost access to land as it was enclosed by prosperous independent **yeoman farmers**. As grain prices rose, these yeomen were able to recover the costs of enclosure. This led to more efficient and profitable farms with professional managers to keep up with the latest developments.

National Markets

Because farmers no longer supplied only their families and immediate communities, agricultural products needed to be transported to and sold in cities, spurring an entirely new realm of economic activity involving merchants, middlemen, transporters, lines of credit, insurance, and banks. New legislation addressed weights and measures and ways to prevent price-fixing.

Trade was also affected by the elimination of **internal tariffs** and the implementation of **customs barriers**:

- Internal tariffs were taxes on items or properties sold within the country. These hurt the average person by raising the price of essential goods. Eliminating internal taxes lowered prices and gave people more money to spend. In France, finance minister Jean-Baptiste Colbert (1619–1683) reduced internal tariffs as part of his mercantilist policies to decrease France's debt and revitalize its industries.

- Customs barriers were measures designed to protect trade. One example was the **external tariff** imposed by Britain on French wines. This tariff made importing wine very expensive, which is one reason the British became beer brewers and whiskey distillers.

Transportation and Land Conversions

To provide better infrastructure for farming and commerce, the British borrowed several kinds of technology from the Dutch, who had developed these technologies after working with flooded lowlands for centuries. The following ideas improved British transportation and land usage:

- Between 1500 and 1700, the British expanded inland waterways through a canal system and tripled the number of usable roadways, helping move products to market more efficiently.

- Britain drained and reclaimed lands to make them arable for farming, adding from 10 to 30 percent additional farmland.
- They created **water meadows**, or fields of grass near rivers. Using planned irrigation, they could periodically flood the meadows. The river nutrients improved the grasses. This allowed farmers to move animals onto these pastures earlier in the spring. As a result, farmers who raised animals, produced more meat, milk, and hides. The manure from the pastured animals then improved the summer grasses, which were cut to make hay for winter feeding.

Agricultural Exchanges and European Nutrition

After England established colonies in North America, a host of new foods from the New World became part of Europeans' diets. While Europeans once had only wheat as a major source of carbohydrates, after the late 15th century they had corn, potatoes, and cassava. An acre of any one of these New World crops yielded twice as many calories as wheat. Other new foods included avocados, beans, cacao, chilies, papayas, peanuts, pineapples, pumpkins, squashes, sweet potatoes, peppers, tomatoes, and turkeys. This exchange of crops across the Atlantic and around the world, known as the Columbian Exchange (see Topic 1.8), enriched both Europe and its colonies and provided the following benefits:

- Starvation, which had previously limited Europe's population growth, largely disappeared. The productive and plentiful potato crop helped alleviate the famines that had plagued Europe for centuries. A half-acre planted with potatoes could feed a family for a year.
- People's tastes and dietetic diversity expanded, contributing to better health and longevity.
- Europe's soaring population resulted in greater immigration to the New World and more agricultural trade.
- Old World crops thrived in the Americas, giving the colonists even better food choices than their counterparts in Europe.

Expanding the Cottage Industry System

[handwritten: goods out of your house]
[handwritten: need for banks bc money going back & forth]

Before the widespread growth of factories during the Industrial Revolution, the main production system in the 17th and first half of the 18th centuries in Western Europe was the **putting-out system** or **cottage industry**. Merchants employed people such as spinners and weavers to work from home making finished products, and the workers were paid on a piece basis. This system expanded as increasing numbers of laborers in homes or workshops produced for markets. Historians call this time period **proto-industrialization**. (The prefix *proto* means "first" or "original.") The system was the earliest example of industrialization in Europe.

The advantages for the workers were that they could remain in their rural villages while bringing in wages. They needed no investment other than their own time and labor. For the first time, women and children earned money on a widespread basis, and rural economies prospered.

The advantages for merchants were lower wage costs and greater efficiencies because workers specialized in the tasks they did best. Merchants could now sell finished goods at higher prices than they had been able to charge for raw wool.

Developments in Labor and Trade

Nowhere did commercial changes occur as dramatically as in Britain. Britain enjoyed a combination of factors that created **self-sustaining growth** as it developed a market economy and achieved a high level of prosperity. Self-sustaining growth is an economic cycle in which a nation produces goods that then drive more economic activity. Britain's woolens market provides one example.

The Textile Industry

Britain's wool was by far the finest in Europe. Britain's excellent grazing lands resulted in long, healthy fleeces on the sheep and the finest wool in Europe. British wool was so superior that most of its competitors on the continent dropped out of business. The more that Europeans desired British wool, the more the country produced.

Farmers specialized in raising sheep or producing wool. Merchants bought the wool. As a part of the putting-out system, spinners wove it into thread. Weavers used looms to join the threads into bolts of fabric. Dyers added color and patterns to the fabric. Seamsters turned the bolts of woolen cloth into garments. Warehouse workers stored clothes and fabrics in warehouses. Clerks and agents provided insurance for all the goods and buildings. People invested money in several of these steps of production.

At every stage of the textile industry, these newly created jobs paid relatively high wages, leading to a money-based economy. This step toward prosperity was all based on well-fed sheep.

Britain's woolen industry paid wages directly to workers. Being paid wages by the number of pieces produced gave workers an incentive to increase productivity. No longer working as subsistence farmers, people used their wages to purchase food and household goods. These changes created more new, specialized jobs—often in fast-growing cities—where urban laborers also earned and spent wages. London's population grew from 50,000 in 1500 to 1 million in 1800. Workers in London earned three times as much as workers in Vienna or Florence, cities that had not experienced a switch to wage-based jobs.

Revolutionizing Industry

In 1700, industry was a rarity. However, growing demand drove innovation. New technologies allowed investors to move production out of cottages and into mills and factories.

In particular, the burgeoning cotton textile industry grew rapidly, making use of several new inventions. Thus, during the mid-18th century, entrepreneurs began processing textiles in factories, which were first run by water-powered machines. Changes such as this challenged the growing cottage industry of spinners and weavers.

Other industries spurred even more inventions. **Steam engines** powered machinery for extracting coal from the mines and crushing iron ore. Across England, industrial centers sprang up, specializing in textiles, mining, tools, toys, hats, stockings, shipbuilding, and other products. All these goods had to be transported and marketed. As more opportunities emerged, the need arose for financial supports, such as business legislation, insurance, and banks.

NEW TECHNOLOGIES IN THE TEXTILE INDUSTRY, 18TH CENTURY		
New Technology	Main Inventor	Significance
Spinning jenny 1765	James Hargreaves	Spun multiple spools of thread simultaneously
Water frame 1769	Richard Arkwright	Used water power to drive spinning wheels
Spinning mule 1779	Samuel Crompton	Enabled a single worker to operate more than 1,000 spindles at a time
Cotton gin 1793	Eli Whitney	Separated cotton fibers from seeds

The Le Chapelier Law

During the period when Britain's industrial economy was booming, places such as France and the German states did not have governments that were as business-minded as Britain's; therefore, they did not industrialize at the same pace. At the start of the French Revolution, the National Assembly passed the **Le Chapelier Law** (1791), which banned workers' associations such as guilds and trade unions and established free enterprise as the new norm in France. The law also banned the right to strike in the belief that workers should not demand wage increases during a time of national crisis. The law was overturned in 1884, and the rights of workers to associate and strike were restored.

Development of Market Economies

During the Middle Ages, Italian merchants and bankers had dominated international trade and finance. Genoese bankers served as venture capitalists, financing the endeavors of foreign nations. For example, they provided credit to Spain as it built an overseas empire in return for silver from the Americas. These changes, and other later changes, stimulated the economy and helped change from a subsistence or barter economy to a market economy. (See Topic 1.10.) As this economic transition took place, new financial practices and institutions emerged. During the Reformation, Protestant kings like Henry VIII had seized property from the Catholic Church, enriching themselves and their supporters and increasing the amount of gold available.

Property Rights and Protections

During the 17th and 18th centuries, European lawyers and philosophers began to formulate theories of property ownership and rights:

- In a 1625 legal treatise, the Dutch lawyer Hugo Grotius argued that the state has eminent domain, or "supreme ownership," of all property. Under this theory, the state had the power to condemn private property, but it could do so only for public use and when accompanied by payment of just compensation to property's owner.

- In the late 17th century, the German lawyer Samuel von Pufendorf refined an ancient theory of property rights asserting that individual ownership of property must be sanctioned by the state.

- Pufendorf's contemporary, the English philosopher John Locke, held a different view of property rights: It is what an individual produces through their labor (or ideas and ingenuity) that guarantees the right to property. The right to property earned by an individual is a natural right and does not need to be sanctioned by the state. Indeed, the state should protect individuals' right to ownership.

During the Glorious Revolution of 1688, the British government committed to protecting and preserving private property. With this assurance, the elites felt confident that they could own land, add to it, or make improvements on it without the risk of having it confiscated. This meant that they had an incentive to find new ways to profit from their land, which was another factor driving economic growth.

With a representative Parliament, Britain's wealthy class shared power with the monarch. The Glorious Revolution had created an economic aristocracy made up of both landed nobles and the commercial class. Unlike the French aristocracy, these British aristocrats invested in commercial and industrial ventures. They were thus willing to tax themselves and fund public works if those choices meant they could somehow profit. They profited from cheaper transportation costs because of better roads and from a stronger navy that protected shipping lanes during the import and export of their wares.

Britain's financial and political stability stood in direct contrast to France's during this period. France had no viable national parliament, and taxes often went to subsidize the luxurious lifestyle of the king and his court at Versailles. Stability was an important factor that gave Britain economic advantages and a head start during the Commercial and Industrial Revolutions.

Insurance

Property insurance—especially fire insurance in an era of wooden buildings—was integral to economic success. Insurance offered security to entrepreneurs and encouraged them to accumulate wealth in the form of factories and inventories. In an era of extensive maritime trade, insurance also offered security to merchants engaged in commercial shipping. Joint-stock companies issued insurance in case of damage to shipments.

However, the insurance industry itself also provided investment opportunities. Private investors insured other people's businesses in exchange for premium payments. As long as the premiums were larger than the payouts, the insurers made money. This required them to develop special skills to assess risks and price their products. One of the earliest insurers was Lloyd's of London, founded in 1688. It is still one of the world's largest and most respected insurance companies.

Banking

Prior to the start of the Industrial Revolution, most major business transactions were conducted in gold or silver. Copper was used for smaller daily commerce. When people needed a business loan, they turned to merchants or family members because a more organized system for investment capital had not yet been required.

The modern banking industry emerged in Italy during the Middle Ages and Renaissance, where they functioned originally as moneylenders. Banking families such as the Medici wielded great political power, while Genoa's banks helped fund the Spanish empire. Banking firms such as the Fugger company in Augsburg (southern Germany) were based on the Italian model and helped finance the wars of the Holy Roman emperors. English, German, and Portuguese merchants began to rely on banks in the Netherlands for credit during the 16th and 17th centuries. (See Topic 1.10 for more on banking changes in 16th century.)

As commerce boomed, entrepreneurs needed loans to meet short-term operating expenses. Private industrialists and governments needed loans to expand the infrastructure of roads and canals. Merchants needed a place to deposit their profits. Specialty banks arose to serve various industries. These banks made money by keeping cash reserves on hand from deposits and then lending money out at a certain rate of interest. This availability of capital fueled expansion by allowing new and varied businesses to start.

The Bank of England In England, banking grew from goldsmiths, who moved and stored precious metals as part of their business. The **Bank of England**, chartered by William and Mary in 1694, was privately owned by stockholders until 1946. Its original mission was to gather enough subscriptions from wealthy investors that the cash-poor government could borrow £1.2 million at 8 percent interest, with a service charge of £4000 per year. Half of this loan went to rebuild the British navy following a major defeat by the French navy in 1690.

Because the British developed this financial resource, the nation experienced several advantages:

- The navy quadrupled in size and positioned Great Britain to become a world power and to build an overseas empire during the 18th and 19th centuries.

- The resulting industries—ironworks for ship equipment and agriculture to feed sailors, for example—drove increased economic expansion.
- The bank became a **limited-liability corporation** that had the sole right to issue government notes, which were used as readily available paper money secured by either government bonds or gold deposits. *Limited liability* refers to the principle that an investor was not responsible for a corporation's debts or other liabilities beyond the amount of the original investment, thus making investment safer.

The bank was such a profitable venture that George Washington remained a stockholder, even during the Revolutionary War. However, the fact that banknotes were tied to gold reserves meant that growth was limited to the amount of gold in the vaults. For this reason, most banks went off the gold standard in the 1930s.

REFLECT ON THE ESSENTIAL QUESTION

Essential Question: *What were the continuities and changes in commercial and economic developments from 1648 to 1815?*

Continuities	Changes

KEY TERMS AND PEOPLE

crop rotation	customs barrier	spinning jenny
mixed farming	external tariff	water frame
seed drill	water meadow	spinning mule
mechanical hoe	putting-out system or	cotton gin
thresher	cottage industry	Le Chapelier Law
enclosure movement	proto-industrialization	Bank of England
yeomen farmer	self-sustaining growth	limited-liability corporation
internal tariffs	steam engine	

MULTIPLE-CHOICE QUESTIONS

Questions 1–3 refer to the passage below.

"[T]he Manufacturer sends the poor Woman combed Wool, or carded Wool every Week to spin, and she gets eight Pence or nine Pence a day at home; the Weaver sends for her two little Children, and they work by the Loom, winding, filling quills . . . and the two bigger Girls spin at home with their Mother, and these earn three Pence or four Pence a Day each: So that put it together, the Family at Home gets as much as the Father gets Abroad, and generally more . . . [T]he Family feels it, they all feed better, are cloth'd warmer, and do not so easily nor so often fall into Misery and Distress; . . . and as they grow, they do not run away to be Footmen and Soldiers, Thieves and Beggars . . . but have a Trade at their Hands, and every one can get their Bread."

—Daniel Defoe, *A Plan of the English Commerce*, 1728

1. Which of the following best identifies the historical development that Defoe describes in this passage?
   (A) The emergence of the cottage industry system in Western Europe
   (B) The spread of mixed farming that increased agricultural productivity
   (C) The migration of people to towns for jobs caused by the enclosure movement
   (D) The use of new technology that created more jobs in textile factories

2. The system described here is an example of
   (A) entrepreneurship
   (B) natural rights
   (C) subsistence economy
   (D) proto-industrialization

3. A historian could best use this excerpt as a source as evidence for which of the following features of the early 18th century?
   (A) The emergence of new class divisions as a result of industrialization
   (B) The increase in tariffs passed by Parliament
   (C) The improved standard of living brought about by new economic practices
   (D) The development of new upper-class attitudes toward the poor

SHORT-ANSWER QUESTION

Answer all parts of the question that follows.

1. a) Describe ONE reason for the growth of a modern banking industry.
   b) Describe ANOTHER reason for the growth of a modern banking industry.
   c) Using a specific example from the period 1648 to 1815, explain an effect of the creation of the Bank of England.

Topic 3.4

Economic Development and Mercantilism

We cannot force foreigners to buy their goods, as we have done our own countrymen. The next best expedient . . . is to pay them for buying. . . . The mercantile system proposes to enrich the whole country, and to put money into all our pockets, by means of the balance of trade.

—Adam Smith, *The Wealth of Nations*, 1776

Essential Question: What were the continuities and changes in commercial and economic developments from 1648 to 1815?

Adam Smith used the term *mercantile system* to describe an economic system designed to build the economic and political strength of a nation. This was the dominant system in Western Europe from the 16th through the 18th centuries. It was based on a belief that the world's wealth was finite, and the nations of Europe competed to gain the greatest possible share of that wealth. Mercantilist nations wanted to export more goods than they imported to acquire gold and silver and to establish colonies to use for resources and markets.

gold = nation's wealth

A Worldwide Economic Network Develops

Modern Europe began to emerge around 1500 with the expansion of trade and colonization. During the 17th and 18th centuries, life for ordinary Europeans changed even more dramatically because of the **Commercial Revolution**, a period of unprecedented expansion of commerce and trade. The seeds for this expansion were originally sown by a desire for silks and spices from Asia, which drove advances in shipping and exploration during the 15th and 16th centuries. Countries bordering the Atlantic Ocean took advantage of their port cities to conduct trade that sent them around the southern tip of Africa to Asia and across the Atlantic to the Americas. The nations that prospered most during this period were those that established colonies in these far-flung regions.

Mercantilism and Colonies

Europe dominated the developing worldwide economic network, beginning with its voyages of discovery in the 16th century and continuing through the 19th century. Two major factors enabled it to do so—mercantilism and colonization.

Mercantilism From the 16th through the 18th centuries, European nations believed that their economic growth and well-being were best served by following a policy of **mercantilism**, which limited imports by using tariffs (taxes on foreign products) and maximized exports by forcing its colonies to trade only with the ruling nation. Such policies brought a positive balance of trade and thus boosted monetary reserves—the accumulation of gold and silver in the treasury. The increase in reserves enabled a country to pay for a strong military. The economic and military strength of mercantilist nations allowed them to exploit cheap labor and extract raw materials from colonies in order to secure advantages over rival nations.

Colonization Mercantilism drove European nations to colonize large swaths of the globe. **Colonization** permitted nations to increase their power by gaining political or economic control of other territories—often through force. In general, colonial empires were established through settlements in the Americas and through trading empires in Asia and Africa. Five nations—England, Spain, Portugal, the Netherlands, and France had both settlements and trading empires. These colonial powers divided the world:

- Portugal claimed Brazil.
- Spain claimed Latin America (other than Brazil) and the Philippines.
- The Netherlands claimed parts of Indonesia.
- France claimed parts of Canada and the central part of the present United States.
- England claimed parts of eastern North America, eastern Australia, and New Zealand.
- All five colonial powers had trading posts in Africa and Asia and claimed islands in the Caribbean.
- Russia did not colonize, but it did expand its borders significantly eastward over time, eventually reaching the Pacific Ocean.

Colonies in Latin America were mined for silver and gold. Those in parts of North America were a source of timber, fish, and furs. Colonies in the Caribbean and what is now the southern United States provided plantation crops such as sugar, tobacco, and cotton. Those in Asia and Africa supplied silks, teas, spices, and minerals. Everywhere, native peoples were used for cheap labor and as a market where colonizing powers could sell finished goods.

Greater Prosperity

Colonies provided new opportunities for trade. They provided resources for European manufacturing and markets for Europe's finished goods. This new system of commerce allowed businesses to thrive in the 17th and 18th centuries. Institutions such as charter companies, insurance companies, and national banks evolved to provide investment capital and spread the risks inherent in overseas trade. Governments passed laws to regulate trade, protect property rights, and manage taxation. (See Topic 3.3.)

Over a remarkably short time, economies shifted from a feudal model of traditional farming to a system driven by wages and consumer demand. The more demand for products grew, the more quickly technology advanced to supply that demand. This, in turn, fed further consumption as goods became cheaper, more plentiful, and more easily transported.

The physical and material well-being of Europeans rose to a level never before seen, but these changes came at a price. As European nations competed to conquer and colonize, they came into conflict with native populations and with one another. The transatlantic slave trade resulted in the deaths and dislocation of millions of Africans. Europe became more sharply divided between the wealthier Atlantic nations engaged in overseas trade and the more traditional central and eastern European nations that had less economic growth. Despite these challenges, the European Commercial Revolution laid the groundwork for the Industrial Revolution and modern society.

THE WORLD IN 1750

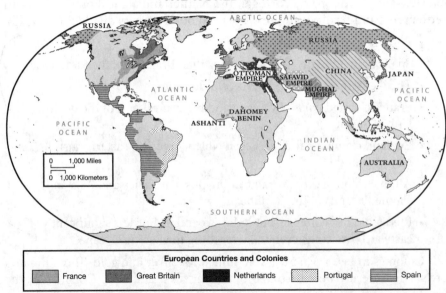

The Transatlantic Slave-Labor System

When European explorers landed in the Americas, they targeted native populations as a source of labor. Native Americans were not well suited to the hot, exhausting labor of plantation farming or mining. As many Native Americans died, often from disease brought from across the Atlantic Ocean, Europeans looked for a new source of labor. They turned to Africa.

From the 15th to the 19th centuries, an estimated 12.5 million Africans were forcibly transported to the Western Hemisphere. About 10.7 million people survived the journey across the ocean. Millions more Africans died during raids and wars to obtain people to sell and enslave. Approximately 5 million Africans were taken to Brazil and another 5 million went to the sugar plantations of the Caribbean. About 400,000 were transported to North America. Britain engaged in more slave trading than the other major European colonial powers, transporting 2 million to 3 million enslaved people in the 18th century alone. However, in 1807, Britain became one of the first European states to ban slave trading.

The Middle Passage

The **Middle Passage** was the name given to the transatlantic slave-trade journey from West Africa to the West Indies. Raiding parties led by Europeans and Africans captured free people and forced them into captivity. The enslaved people were held in dungeons at different points along the coast of Africa, sometimes for up to a year, until a ship could carry them to the New World. While awaiting their fate, the captives were subject to epidemics, physical and sexual abuse, pirate raids, storms, and raids by hostile tribes.

Once aboard ships, enslaved people were packed in rows below decks. Chained to platforms stacked in tiers, each person had a space about the size of a coffin—6 feet long, 16 inches wide, 3 feet high. It was impossible for them to stand up or turn over in these bunks where they stayed nearly 24 hours a day. Many grew sick from dysentery and other diseases because of poor sanitation and dangerous fumes from a lack of ventilation in the hold. Others mutinied or tried to commit suicide by jumping overboard or by refusing to eat. If the ship's progress stalled because of bad weather or a lack of wind, water and food rations were cut so much that many captive Africans starved. In one case, when water ran low, the British captain of the slave ship *Zong* threw 133 enslaved Africans overboard to save the remaining captives and then filed an insurance claim on his "cargo."

Triangle Trade

The trade linking Europe, Africa, and the Americas is known as the **triangle trade** because the three parts of the route—from Europe to Africa, from Africa to the Americas, and from the Americas back to Europe— traced a triangular shape. From the 16th through the early 19th centuries, the name became synonymous with a form of colonial commerce that managed imports and exports to enrich European slave-trading nations.

Source: Shutterstock

The murder of enslaved people on the *Zong* was among the most infamous events of the transatlantic slave trade.

trade triangle explained

European ships took advantage of the trade winds to sail south before trying to cross the Atlantic Ocean. This became the first leg of history's most well known triangular trade route, as traders picked up captive people in Africa. On the second leg of the journey, the ships transported enslaved people from Africa to the New World, where they were sold or traded for the products that other enslaved individuals had produced—sugar, molasses, cotton, rice, indigo, tobacco, hemp, and rum. These items were then shipped from the Americas back to Europe on the final leg of the journey. The raw materials and crops were sold, and the profits used to purchase finished goods, such as cloth, knives, guns, tools, copper, and brass items, which were sold back to the colonies or traded in Africa for additional enslaved people.

Plantation Economies in the Americas

Primogeniture was common in many European societies. It was a remnant of feudalism meant to keep estates intact. Based on the system, the oldest son inherited the family's estate. One result was that ambitious younger sons left home to seek their fortunes. Many emigrated to the Americas to acquire farmland and some eventually established **plantations**, or agricultural estates that used mostly slave labor to produce cash crops. In the Caribbean, this meant sugar production. Because the production of sugar was so labor intensive, operating expenses were high. Many plantation owners believed that working enslaved people to death was more profitable than providing humane living conditions. During the 18th century, one-third of newly imported enslaved people died within three years of their arrival.

Plantations helped build family fortunes and dictated social and economic roles on the islands. Plantation owners controlled the legislature and militia and even the public calendar, all of which revolved around sugar production. By the 1830s, Britain acquired additional plantation territories following the Napoleonic Wars. The increased supply from these territories forced sugar prices down. That, along with reduced demand and increased antislavery sentiment, eventually weakened Caribbean plantation economies.

Impact on European Consumers and Markets

The effect of a steady flow of raw materials from trade with the Americas, India, and Asia changed life for European consumers. Slave labor kept the cost of many goods low. Improved technologies converted these raw materials into plentiful finished goods. Affordability and abundance led people to desire improved social status—which they could display by having beautiful furnishings and clothes and all the latest available conveniences.

New Products

The products that made the greatest contribution to the development of a European consumer culture were sugar, silks and other fabrics, tobacco, rum, tea, and coffee.

Sugar More than any other product, sugar drove transatlantic trade, colonialism, and slavery. It was a rare commodity for Europeans before 1492. But as Britain established Caribbean plantations, it became more and more available. Europeans started to consider sugar a necessity, so plantation owners reaped huge profits. British manufacturers and exporters benefited as well since the Caribbean plantations needed manufactured goods and other provisions from the home country.

Britain protected its sugar growers with mercantilist policies. For example, the 17th-century **Navigation Acts** protected the monopoly to sell British goods, such as sugar, within the empire. Sugar tariffs helped enrich the British government but were a source of controversy as they raised consumer prices. The Navigation Acts and the tariffs were not repealed until the mid-1800s.

Fabrics Britain came to specialize in the mass production of cotton and wool, spurring the Industrial Revolution. Brightly colored printed cotton textiles from India were very popular until the 1790s, when European mills began to produce them. France had its own textile industry, geared toward the wealthy. France became Europe's leading silk producer. Silk had long been a closely guarded treasure in China until the Silk Roads linked China to the Roman Empire in the 2nd century B.C.E. But it was not until the Industrial Revolution that weaving silk became more feasible for the French. In 1801, **Joseph-Marie Jacquard** (1752–1834) invented a machine to create patterned silk textiles for luxury clothing and furnishings.

Tobacco Spanish and Portuguese sailors helped spread tobacco from the Americas throughout the world. By the end of the 16th century, tobacco use had spread across Europe. The Spanish and the British originally grew tobacco in the Caribbean, where it became a key item in the triangle trade. Later, Spain and Portugal expanded operations into Cuba and Brazil. In the early 17th century, **John Rolfe** (1585–1622) planted tobacco in Virginia, where it became an economic force for colonial development—so much so that it was used as currency to purchase enslaved people, pay taxes, and buy goods from England. In 1624, the Jamestown colony sold 100 tons of tobacco to England. By 1680, the yearly total was more than 100 times that. European governments levied tariffs on tobacco to maintain trading monopolies.

Rum Britain and France first made rum—a profitable alcohol made from sugar by-products—in the 17th century on their sugar islands, and European colonists quickly started drinking it. By the 18th century, British rum makers sold their product throughout Europe and North America. However, three developments made Britain's rum trade less profitable:

- The American Revolution halted trade between Britain and its colonies.

- Competition from other European nations and the United States in rum production reduced demand for British rum.

- The growing tide of antislavery sentiment turned some people against goods produced using slave labor.

At the same time, rising demand in France's cities helped the Caribbean Island of Martinique become a major rum producer. Rum production led to a second trade triangle—New England merchants bought molasses from the Caribbean and distilled it into rum. They shipped the rum to Africa in exchange for enslaved individuals, and then traded those people in the Caribbean for more molasses.

Tea In the early 1600s, limited amounts of tea were first imported from China. However by 1750, the consumption of tea in Britain had increased two hundredfold. The British government levied a tax on tea that accounted for about 10 percent of the nation's annual revenues. British mercantilist policies prevented competition from Dutch and Russian tea producers but also brought protests. In the American colonies and elsewhere, tea smuggling became widespread to avoid taxes. In 1773, Britain tried to help the struggling British East India Company by passing the Tea Act, which allowed the company to sell directly to North America, which eliminated colonial merchants from the process. Colonists, however, were still required to pay a tax on the tea. Their famous tax protest—the Boston Tea Party—was a significant act of defiance and is one of the causes of the American Revolution.

Coffee Venetian merchants introduced coffee to Europe in the late 16th or early 17th century, and it quickly spread throughout the continent. The Dutch founded the first European-owned coffee estate in Ceylon (Sri Lanka) in 1619. The French grew coffee in the Caribbean, and the Spanish and Portuguese grew it in Central and South America. Following the protests against Britain's tea monopolies, coffee became the more popular drink in the Americas.

Opportunities from Foreign Trade

Colonial expansion and trade fueled economic and social growth in Europe from the 16th through the 19th centuries. On the import side, European factories and industries benefited from the influx of raw materials, and people's health improved with new food crops. Cheap labor—whether from enslaved people or indentured servants—helped generate massive fortunes and huge amounts of taxable wealth. On the export side, mercantilist monopolies and tariffs secured ready markets for European finished goods. Europe was growing into an economic powerhouse. In particular, the characteristics on the following page propelled Britain, and eventually other countries, into the Industrial Revolution.

EUROPE'S COMMERCIAL REVOLUTION OF THE 17TH AND 18TH CENTURIES	
Diet	Europeans experienced increased food supplies and better nutrition thanks to food products imported from the Americas, Asia, and Africa beginning in the 16th century.
Weather	By the early 17th century, the weather became warmer and drier, and this, along with new crops, led to improved health and a population growth.
Demography	Although Europe in 1700 was still largely rural and somewhat depopulated from waves of plague, Britain (and, to a lesser extent, the Dutch Republic) used trade within Europe and overseas to begin a Commercial Revolution.
Education	The growing population became more literate and was inspired by Enlightenment ideals to manipulate their world through scientific discoveries and technological innovation.
Machinery	After a brief period of proto-industrialization, factories and mines powered by machines and engines spread rapidly throughout Britain, generating jobs in urban centers. The Industrial Revolution started around 1750.
Agriculture	Urbanization meant that remaining farmers had to become even more efficient, leading to the Agricultural Revolution.
Money	A money-based economy emerged, and the standard of living improved (in Britain especially), so that for the first time, people used wages to purchase food and factory-made consumer goods.
Trade	Increasing trade among European nations and with overseas colonies led to increased wealth because of mercantilist policies. The growing merchant middle class wanted to share power with the elites and the monarchy.
Colonies	Nations that created colonial empires experienced increased political power and economic prosperity. Particularly, Britain's successes in the colonial phases of the wars of the 18th century expanded its profitable colonial empire and made Britain the foremost world power.

REFLECT ON THE ESSENTIAL QUESTION

Essential Question: *What were the continuities and changes in commercial and economic developments from 1648 to 1815?*

Continuities	Changes

KEY TERMS AND PEOPLE

Commercial Revolution	Middle Passage	Navigation Acts
mercantilism	triangle trade	Joseph-Marie Jacquard
colonization	plantation	John Rolfe

Questions 1–3 refer to the passage below.

"And in regard his Majesty's plantations beyond the seas are inhabited and peopled by his subjects of this his kingdom of England; for the maintaining a greater correspondence and kindness between them, and keeping them in a firmer dependence upon it, and rendering them yet more beneficial and advantageous unto it in the further employment and increase of English shipping and seamen, vent [sale] of English woolen and other manufactures and commodities, rendering the navigation to and from the same more safe and cheap, and making this kingdom a staple, not only of the commodities of those plantations, but also of the commodities of other countries and places, for the supplying of them; and it being the usage of other nations to keep their plantations trade to themselves. Be it enacted . . . that . . . no commodity of the growth, production, or manufacture of Europe shall be imported into any land, island, plantation, colony, territory, or place to his Majesty belonging, or which shall hereafter belong unto or be in the possession of his Majesty, his heirs and successors, in Asia, Africa, or America . . . but what shall be bona fide, and without fraud, laden [loaded] and shipped in England, Wales, . . . and in English built shipping . . .; and whereof the master and three fourths of the mariners at least are English, and which shall be carried directly thence to the said lands, islands, plantations, colonies, territories, or places, and from no other place or places whatsoever. . . ."

—British Parliament, Navigation Act, July 27, 1663

1. What type of system does this passage describe?

   (A) Capitalism

   (B) Mercantilism

   (C) Triangle trade

   (D) Colonialization

2. What was the main purpose of the directions described in this passage?

   (A) To keep England's overseas possessions loyal to the king

   (B) To promote trade between England's colonies and other colonies

   (C) To protect the English manufacturing and shipping industries

   (D) To prevent fraudulent business practices throughout England and Wales

3. One result for European countries from the process described in the passage was to increase

(A) the economic power in the world held by them

(B) the economic independence of their colonies from them

(C) the growth of free trade among them

(D) the growth of economic freedom within them

SHORT-ANSWER QUESTION

Use the table below to answer all parts of the question that follows.

NUMBER OF SHIPS SAILING TO ASIA FROM SELECTED EUROPEAN COUNTRIES, 1500-1800			
Country	1500–1599	1600–1699	1701–1800
Portugal	705	371	196
Dutch Netherlands	65	1,770	2,950
England	—	811	1,865
France	—	155	1,300
Denmark, Sweden, and Austrian Netherlands	—	54	350
Total	770	3,161	6,661

Source: Compiled in Angus Maddison, *The World Economy, Volume 1: A Millennial Perspective*, OECD Development Centre Studies, 2006.

1. a) Describe ONE development that contributed to the patterns shown in the table.

b) Explain ONE way the patterns on the table reflect technological changes from 1500–1800.

c) Explain ONE way the patterns on the table reflect economic changes from 1500–1800.

Topic 3.5

The Dutch Golden Age

All these considerations give us more than sufficient reason to renounce the King of Spain ... [we] the inhabitants were not treated as subjects, but enemies, enslaved forcibly by their own governors.

—Dutch Act of Abjuration, 1581

Essential Question: What factors contributed to the development of the Dutch Republic?

With the Act of Abjuration, the Netherlands formally declared independence from Spain. For much of the 16th century, the Dutch had grown increasingly unhappy with taxation and forced religious uniformity from Spain. During the Reformation, Calvinism had become the dominant religion in the seven northern provinces of the Netherlands. In the 1500s, Habsburg rulers, such as Charles V and his son Phillip II, used the Inquisition to try to stamp out Protestantism in the Netherlands, and the quest for independence began. Dutch leadership united against Spanish control during several stages of this conflict, which ultimately led to the creation of the Dutch Republic.

The Dutch Republic

The Dutch Republic (1588–1795) was formed during the **Eighty Years' War** (1568–1648), when the Dutch battled for independence from Spain. Stemming from the military agreement known as the **Union of Utrecht** (1579), the Dutch Republic consisted of the northern provinces of the Netherlands that won independence from Spain between 1568 and 1609. The remaining provinces, the Spanish Netherlands, united under Spanish rule.

THE DUTCH REPUBLIC AND THE SPANISH NETHERLANDS, C. 1598

After gaining its indepence, the Dutch Republic developed into a world power in the 17th century. It was Europe's leading cargo shipper, and it engaged in an ongoing rivalry with Britain that sometimes led to maritime wars. The Dutch Republic also fought land wars, in particular in the latter half of the 17th century and usually against the French. The republic generally fared well in these conflicts. It was a wealthy center of shipping and finance with a profitable trade empire in the Americas and Asia and throughout the Indian Ocean. (See Topic 4.4.)

Dutch Oligarchy

The Dutch Republic did not have a monarch. Instead, estates representing the seven provinces each selected a provincial leader, or *stadholder*. The estates sent these delegates to meet in a legislative body called the Estates-General, which decided military and foreign policy issues. However, this was not truly a representative body but an **oligarchy**, or a select class within a society controlling the government. The Dutch oligarchy was made up of rural landholders and **urban gentry**. *Urban gentry* refers to upper-class townspeople who were often professionals or merchants. The policies supported by oligarchs are designed to maintain and increase their status and wealth—in this case of the Dutch Republic, the wealth that had been gained through trade.

Merchants and financiers held most of the power in the Dutch Republic. Governments of other European powers attempted to squeeze the Dutch out of increasingly lucrative trade in Asia in the late 1500s. The influence of merchants and financiers was strong enough to convince the Estates-General to act and charter the Dutch East India Company to protect the nation's interests.

Dutch East India Company

To promote trade, the Estates-General formed the **Dutch East India Company** in 1602 as a private enterprise. Known by its Dutch initials, VOC, it was a **joint-stock company**, similar to a modern corporation, in which shareholders could buy stock. The company was professionally managed by a board of directors, enabling it to raise capital and spread risk across a wide pool of investors.

The profits of the VOC made Amsterdam one of the richest cities in the world. The influx of wealth helped keep the Dutch Republic peaceful and stable, in part because it offered upward mobility for workers and peasants. Even though the lower classes did not share in political power, their standard of living was higher than that in other European countries. However, when investors dumped their VOC shares in the 18th century because of worries about British competition, the company went into bankruptcy. As a result, the Dutch Republic declined in power and world influence.

Dutch Civilization in the Golden Age

The Dutch Republic experienced a golden age from 1609 until the early 18th century, when economic and political stagnation brought it to an end.

Dutch Society There was less disparity between classes in the Dutch Republic than elsewhere in Europe. Landed nobles made up a smaller portion of the elite in the Dutch Republic than in other European nations at the time. The majority of the upper social class was made up of wealthy townspeople who had made their fortunes as merchants and financiers. Below them was a large class made up of prosperous artisans and small business owners. There was also a very large working class, which was generally well paid. Most farmers prospered by producing cash crops for the nation's urban population.

Religion The official religion of the Dutch Republic was the Calvinist Reformed Church, but there were also other Protestant sects, including Lutherans and Anabaptists (Mennonites). Many Spanish and Portuguese Jews settled in the Netherlands and were influential in the intellectual, social, and economic life of the country. Jews from Eastern Europe, on the other hand, made up a class of impoverished workers. In spite of the general religious toleration, the public practice of Roman Catholicism was forbidden. Nevertheless, there were sizable islands of Catholicism in most of the provinces.

The Arts The economic prosperity of the Dutch Republic was accompanied by a cultural flowering. Dutch artists such as Rembrandt (1609–1669) and Johannes Vermeer (1632–1675) painted their masterpieces during this time. (See Topic 4.5.) Dutch literature rivaled the literature of England and France, although its influence was limited because of the relatively small number of people who read Dutch. The Calvinists considered music frivolous, but the organ playing of the leading Dutch composer of the era, Jan Pieterszoon Sweelinck (1562–1621), influenced both Bach and Handel.

Philosophy and Science Philosophy and science also flourished. The Dutch-born Jewish philosopher Benedict de Spinoza (1632–1677) was one of the leading exponents of rationalism and a key figure of the Enlightenment. French philosopher René Descartes (1596–1650) spent two decades in the Netherlands. There he found the freedom to engage in the studies that would help him revolutionize thought. The physicist Christiaan Huygens (1629–1695) formulated the wave theory of light and discovered the shape of Saturn's rings. The pioneering microbiologist Antonie van Leeuwenhoek (1632–1723) laid the groundwork for the sciences of bacteriology and protozoology.

REFLECT ON THE ESSENTIAL QUESTION

Essential Question: *What factors contributed to the development of the Dutch Republic?*

Factors	Developments

Eighty Years' War	oligarchy	Dutch East India Company
Union of Utrecht	urban gentry	joint-stock company

MULTIPLE-CHOICE QUESTIONS

Questions 1–3 refer to the passage below.

"Furthermore, as men's habits of mind differ, so that some more readily embrace one form of faith, some another, for what moves one to pray may move another only to scoff, I conclude, in accordance with what has gone before, that everyone should be free to choose for himself the foundations of his creed, and that faith should be judged only by its fruits; each would then obey God freely with his whole heart, while nothing would be publicly honoured save justice and charity.

Having thus drawn attention to the liberty conceded to everyone by the revealed law of God, I pass on to another part of my subject, and prove that this same liberty can and should be accorded with safety to the state and the magisterial authority—in fact, that it cannot be withheld without great danger to peace and detriment to the community.

In order to establish my point, I start from the natural rights of the individual, which are co-extensive with his desires and power, and from the fact that no one is bound to live as another pleases, but is the guardian of his own liberty. I show that these rights can only be transferred to those whom we depute to defend us, who acquire with the duties of defence the power of ordering our lives, and I thence infer that rulers possess rights only limited by their power, that they are the sole guardians of justice and liberty, and that their subjects should act in all things as they dictate: nevertheless, since no one can so utterly abdicate his own power of self-defence as to cease to be a man, I conclude that no one can be deprived of his natural rights absolutely, but that subjects, either by tacit agreement, or by social contract, retain a certain number, which cannot be taken from them without great danger to the state."

—Benedict de Spinoza, *Tractatus Theologico-Politicus*, 1670 (translated as
A Theologico-Political Treatise by R. H. M. Elwes)

1. Which of the following would most likely have agreed with the ideas in this passage?
   (A) Charles V of the Holy Roman Empire because of his actions toward Protestants
   (B) Philip II of Spain because of his policies on his overseas empire
   (C) Charles I of England because of views on the monarchy
   (D) William III of England because of his position on the Declaration of Right

2. How would Spinoza's heritage as a Jew have shaped his perspective on religion as expressed in the first paragraph?
   (A) He was not part of the conflict between Catholics and Protestants.
   (B) He knew that religious discrimination was a new development in history.
   (C) He had benefited from the religious toleration of the Dutch Republic.
   (D) He believed that people of different religions could not coexist peacefully within one country.

3. How did Spinoza's view of religion inform his attitude toward government?
   (A) He favored an authoritarian government since God demands complete obedience.
   (B) He used religion to back his support for the theory of the divine right of kings.
   (C) He believed that governments had the power to require people to adopt the same basic religious beliefs.
   (D) He believed that God endows people with natural rights that are limited only by social contracts with rulers.

SHORT-ANSWER QUESTION

Answer all parts of the question that follows.

1. a) Describe ONE action or event in England from 1600 to 1700 that challenged absolutism by providing an alternative political system.
   b) Describe ONE action or event in the Netherlands from 1600 to 1700 that challenged absolutism by providing an alternative political system.
   c) Explain ONE similarity in the actions or events discussed in parts a and b.

Topic 3.6

Balance of Power

The absolute power of princes and sovereign lords does not extend to the laws of God and of nature. . . . His yoke is upon them, and they must bow their heads in fear and reverence before His divine majesty.

—Jean Bodin, *On Sovereignty,* 1576

Essential Question: How did European states establish and maintain a balance of power on the continent from 1648 to 1815?

By signing the Treaty of Westphalia in 1648, Europe's monarchs ended centuries of religious conflict that had taken a terrible toll on human life and financial resources. Between 1648 and 1815, the nation-state was well on its way to becoming the principal form of political organization across Europe. Catholic and Protestant political leaders alike agreed that the object of statecraft was a **balance of power** maintained through diplomacy—a system in which no one empire, kingdom, or country would dominate, either on the continent or in the New World.

In this period, monarchs advanced the needs of their sovereign states through the political system known as **absolutism**. Many, though not all, absolute monarchs believed that they ruled by **divine right**—that their power derived directly from God, as the French political philosopher Jean Bodin had asserted. They amassed power by creating bureaucracies with enough resources to wage wars intended either to maintain the balance of power or to disrupt it. States that centralized control and expanded their borders generally fared better than those that did not. States that failed to centralize control tended to break down.

New Diplomacy and New Warfare

The **Peace of Westphalia** in 1648 brought the end of the wars of religion in Europe. With the end of those wars, a new concept, balance of power, started affecting how European states interacted and their diplomatic and military objectives. A nation or group of nations maintains a balance of power by assuring that its strength equals that of potential adversaries, usually through military might or the formation of alliances.

Advances in military technology and tactics also changed warfare. The development of artillery and mobile cannons was revolutionary. Sword-carrying knights riding on horseback gave way to troops with firearms and marching in lines. Armed forces became professional organizations under control of a sovereign, not a noble aristocrat. Larger units fighting for a single state replaced small militias fighting for their local leader. These changes gave more power to the states and state leaders willing to adopt these advancements.

THE MILITARY REVOLUTION DURING THE WARS OF RELIGION		
Development	**Replaced**	**Effect**
Gunpowder artillery (using cheap and reliable firearms)	Longbows and crossbows	Enabled high-intensity warfare using volley fire and artillery barrage
Siege cannon	Trebuchet catapults	Rendered existing fortresses obsolete
Star fort (or bastion fort)	Existing castles	Protected against attacks by besieging ordnance with angled walls that were thicker and flatter than traditional forts
Bayonet	Pike	Allowed a spear to be attached to a firearm, which was more efficient than carrying both
New light cavalry, such as the dragoon or hussar	Armored lancers riding armored horses	Provided option for mounted soldiers to attack or dismounted soldiers to defend

This great military revolution favored the rulers who could acquire and manage the resources necessary to build increasingly complex fortifications, or defenses. Successful leaders were also skilled at managing increasingly complex groups of troops. Monarchs who were able to increase taxes enough to build a military outmaneuvered those who could not. This was especially true by the end of the 18th century in Spain, Sweden, and France.

Spain Under the Habsburgs

Spain under the Habsburgs dominated Europe politically and militarily for much of the 16th century and the early part of the 17th century. The Habsburg family created a dynasty, producing emperors and kings for the Holy Roman Empire and throughout Europe, including Phillip II of Spain. Under the Habsburgs, Spain was made up of several smaller kingdoms, including Aragon, Castile, León, Navarre, and Portugal (from 1580 to 1640). It also ruled the Netherlands and large parts of what is now Italy, in addition to a large overseas empire.

In 1648, Spain suppressed revolts in Naples and Sicily, two of its Italian territories, over excessive taxes to support Spain's war efforts. In that year, it also recognized the full independence of the United Provinces of the Netherlands. During the second half of the 17th century, Spain suffered a sharp economic and political decline. In three successive wars with France (1667–1668, 1672–1678, and 1689–1697), Spain lost territory as well as influence throughout Europe. When Charles II, the last Habsburg king of Spain, died childless in 1700, he left the throne to a grandson of Louis XIV of France, sparking the War of the Spanish Succession.

Sweden Under Gustavus Adolphus

When he came to the throne of Sweden at the age of 16, **Gustavus Adolphus** (1594–1632) inherited a constitutional crisis as well as wars with Denmark, Poland, and Russia. He was able to settle the crisis between the nobility and the monarch by enlisting them in his government, which also provided them many economic benefits. His reign saw the creation of a supreme court, a national treasury, and a war office, making Sweden's central administration the most modern in Europe.

Gustavus Adolphus ran his military units like machines. A master of organization, he gave his infantry and cavalry the capacity for offense, providing increased firepower so they could strike first. He made his artillery mobile, and he organized linear formations of soldiers to be more flexible and responsive to commands. By the end of the 17th century, infantry units in Sweden resembled those that would persist well into the 20th century: large, more-permanent, standing armies.

France

After the Thirty Years' War, the French army became Europe's dominant land force. Up until then, Spain had been the prevailing military power. The French army adopted the basic infantry formation from Gustavus Adolphus's Swedes, but in much greater numbers.

Louis XIV helped make the French army superior to others of the time. He enacted reforms to bring individual field commanders under control, built 33 new fortresses, and remodeled 3,000 others. These fortresses were fully equipped. An army on the march could make camp at any of them and find everything they needed, including food and heavy artillery.

Challenges to Monarchs

Throughout Europe, factions of individuals challenged their monarchs and resisted political centralization, a form of government in which a single person or small group exercises control. This struggle for power ultimately produced varied types of government systems across Europe.

In eastern and southern Europe especially, monarchies seeking enhanced power faced challenges from traditional elites—often the landed nobility— who wished to retain traditional forms of shared governance and regional autonomy. Competition between monarchs and nobles was fierce and ongoing, particularly in the Netherlands, Spain, and France.

Dutch Resistance in the Spanish Netherlands

The decline of Spain as an economic power partially resulted from growing competition with the Netherlands, a region under Spain's control. The **Dutch Revolt**, also known as the Dutch War for Independence or the Eighty Years' War (1568 to 1648), ending when Dutch independence was officially recognized by the Peace of Westphalia. (See Topic 3.5.)

The Netherlands had already achieved a central role in inter-European trade as a result of its geographic position and large merchant marine fleet. For example, the Netherlands provided a connection between the Baltic region of north-central Europe and the rest of the continent. Increasingly, the Netherlands' capital of Amsterdam outstripped Spanish-controlled Antwerp as northern Europe's center of commerce.

The Catalan Revolt in Spain

In 1640, Spain faced increased military threat from France, its neighbor to the north. Spain's King Philip III therefore attempted to centralize his power and raise taxes to fund the ongoing wars. He also sent Count Olivares, one of his favored ministers, into the Spanish region of Catalonia with roughly 9,000 troops to enlist the region's people and resources to fight the French. Instead, he was met with fierce Catalan backlash. The **Catalan Revolt** ultimately caused the downfall of Olivares.

The Fronde in France

Violent civil uprisings against the French monarchy erupted between 1648 and 1653 to check the growing power of France's royal government. This series of uprisings were known as the **Fronde** (French for "sling," which was used to cause damage to French noble's property during the uprising). The Fronde was a reaction to the policies intended to weaken the influence of the nobles and reduce the power of the **Parlements**, or judicial bodies, by chief minister Cardinal Jules Mazarin. Mazarin and Louis XIV's mother, Queen Anne, ruled until the young king came of age.

There were two phases of the Fronde. In the first phase, the Parlement of Paris refused to approve the government's revenue measures in 1648, while France was at war with Spain. The government initially gave in to many of the demands because its military was occupied with fighting Spain. During the second phase, from January 1650 to September 1653, members of the nobility tried to gain political power. Eventually, the French government was able to suppress the rebel factions and restore order.

The Fronde was not successful, but it ultimately scarred young Louis XIV so deeply that he intensified his absolutism for the rest of his reign. The failure of the Fronde did reveal the inability of the French nobility and Parlements to resist royal absolutism. This stands in contrast to the growing power of England's Parliament, evident in its ultimately successful challenge to royal absolutism in the Glorious Revolution. (See Topic 3.2 for more about the English Civil War and the Glorious Revolution.)

Conflicts Among Identity-Based Minorities

While the English Civil War and the conflicts in the Netherlands, Spain, and France pitted nobles against monarchies, groups of citizens fought among themselves in conflicts in other areas of Europe. Minority groups with identities based on a unique language or culture resisted the dominant national group, often with far-reaching consequences, including inflaming conflicts that led to the Thirty Years' War.

Czech Identity in the Holy Roman Empire In the 17th century, the Bohemian estates—located in modern-day Czech Republic—were under control of the Habsburgs and represented the different regions and interests of the Czech people. Czech nobility also dominated the region. The Bohemian estates tried to maintain their Czech identity and social status, despite the Habsburgs' attempts to mandate Catholicism and centralize their power. In 1618, the Bohemian estates rose against the Habsburgs, signaling the start of the Thirty Years' War, but they were defeated in 1620 at the Battle of the White Mountain.

One of the primary influences in this movement was Jan Hus, though he had lived two centuries earlier. (Hus was condemned by Catholic authorites and burned at the stake for heresy in 1415.) Hus was a voice for reforming the Catholic Church long before the Protestant Reformation led by Martin Luther and John Calvin. His teachings had a strong influence and resulted in increased Bohemian resistance to the Catholic Church and the formation of a Bohemian national identity that continued through the Thirty Years' War. (See Topic 2.4.)

Celtic Regions of Scotland, Ireland, and France Clashes between traditional Celtic societies in modernizing European states began in the 17th century and stemmed from both religious and economic conflicts. Traditionally religious people, Celts were affected by various states' attempts to limit religious nonconformity. Celtic farmers were removed from their land as militaries expanded their infrastructure, such as the fortifications built by Louis XIV in France.

European Wars and Diplomacy

Following the Peace of Westphalia in 1648, the Holy Roman Empire split into about 300 sovereign principalities, each with its own dynastic, political, and ethnic interests. Because of the competition for territory and resources both in Europe and in colonies worldwide, these states frequently found themselves at war. Attempts at diplomacy often failed, and alliances shifted as countries tried to keep a precarious balance of power. New nations arose while old empires, such as the Ottomans, saw their power decline in a changing political landscape.

The End of Ottoman Expansion in Europe

The Ottoman Empire spread quickly out of Asia Minor in its early centuries and engaged in wars with the Habsburg Empire for 300 years. The Ottomans first reached the outskirts of Vienna, capital of the Habsburg Empire, in 1529. They wanted the city in order to control trade routes along the Danube River to the Black Sea and overland to Germany. They already controlled much of Hungary and southeastern Europe.

In 1681–1682, border skirmishes escalated between the Ottomans and the Habsburgs over control of Hungary. The Ottomans attacked Vienna in 1683, causing the Holy Roman Empire, the Habsburg monarchy, and the

Polish-Lithuanian Commonwealth to unite against the invaders. The Ottomans lost the **Battle of Vienna** (1683), and over the next 16 years, they lost control of the rest of Hungary. The Battle of Vienna marked a turning point in history—the beginning of the end of Ottoman domination of Eastern Europe.

The Wars of Louis XIV

Source: Getty Images

According to legend, bakers in Vienna celebrated the victory over the forces of the Muslim Ottoman Empire by making rolls in the shape of the crescent moon. The crescent moon is a symbol of Islam.

During Louis XIV's long reign (1643–1715), he kept France engaged in a series of wars. He challenged Britain, the Dutch Republic, Spain, the Habsburg rulers, and their allies in his quest to expand his power. The wars were expensive, and Louis left his successors large debts.

Wars Against the Dutch and Others France, aided by England, fought the **Dutch War** (1672–1678) to gain the Spanish Netherlands (now Belgium and a portion of northern France). The Dutch stopped French advances, though, and France eventually made peace. Still, Louis XIV remained the most powerful monarch in Europe.

The **Nine Years' War** (also known as the War of the Grand Alliance, 1688–1697) pitted France against the Dutch Republic, Spain, England, Austria, the Holy Roman Empire, and the Duchy (a region ruled by a duke or duchess) of Savoy. It was fought in multiple places including northern Europe, Ireland, and Scotland, as well as in colonial areas. Unprepared for a protracted war on multiple continents, all parties signed a treaty in 1697. While this treaty stopped the fighting, it did not end the ambitions of Louis XIV and other monarchs to expand their territories.

War of the Spanish Succession One of Louis XIV's goals in fighting the Nine Years' War was to weaken and even conquer the Habsburgs. His other goal was to establish the right of his grandson **Philip, Duke of Anjou**, to rule Spain as **Philip V** (reigned 1701–1746; left throne briefly, January–August 1724) following the death of the childless Charles II. Emperor Leopold I of Austria had an equally strong claim to the Spanish throne by birth and marriage. Alarmed by the power Louis XIV's plans would gain for France, England and the Dutch Republic allied with Austria in the **War of the Spanish Succession** (1702–1713). Spain and France, both Catholic countries, were allies, along with Savoy and Portugal (both of which later changed sides). Throughout most of the war, the English and Dutch (both Protestant countries) prevailed over the French, both on land and at sea.

The war ended with the **Peace of Utrecht** (1713), a series of treaties that altered the balance power established with the 1648 Treaty of Westphalia. The Peace of Utrecht only partially accomplished the goals of the countries involved:

- Britain won territories in Spain and the Americas, as well as the sole right to import enslaved Africans into Spanish colonies in the Americas for 30 years.
- Other states recognized Philip V as the king of Spain.
- Spain retained control of Milan and Naples.
- The southern Netherlands (modern Belgium and Luxembourg) were ceded to Austria.
- France acknowledged the Protestant succession in England.

These treaties assured a period of peace and balance of power between Britain and France in Europe. However, conflicts between the rivals continued in North America.

Prussian and Habsburg Rulers

One nation to arise at this time was Prussia, made up of areas in eastern and central Europe. From 1701, the Hohenzollern dynasty ruled Prussia, after Frederick III of Brandenburg gained the title "king of Prussia" from the Holy Roman Emperor and became Frederick I of Prussia (reigned 1701–1713).

Frederick William I The son of Frederick I, **Frederick William I** (reigned 1713–1740), expanded Prussia's territories by creating a large and powerful army financed by taxation. He persuaded the Prussian estates—legislative bodies composed of representatives from cities and towns—to allow him to impose taxes at will on the peasants. In exchange, he promised leaders of the estates that peasants would work the land for minimal pay. Peasants were also conscripted into the army. Prussia's army numbered 38,000 soldiers in 1713, but by 1740, it had grown to 83,000. By the time of his death in 1740, Frederick William I had turned Prussia into a prosperous and efficient nation.

Frederick the Great The son of Frederick William I was Frederick II, known as **Frederick the Great**. He inherited his father's prosperous nation and turned it into Europe's leading military power.

When the Habsburg Holy Roman Emperor Charles VI died in 1740, he left as his heir a daughter, the Archduchess **Maria Theresa**. Frederick the Great sensed the empire's weaknesses—a disorganized army and poor finances—and decided to attack its territories. First, he invaded Silesia, an area in Central Europe to which his Hohenzollern dynasty had weak claims. Facing a hostile alliance, Maria was forced to cede Lower Silesia to Prussia. Time after time, if Frederick II saw that Maria Theresa's armies were growing stronger or forming new alliances, he preemptively attacked Habsburg territories.

Frederick II's own alliances, especially with France, were based mostly on mutual hatred of the Habsburgs. When Britain and Russia agreed to protect the electorate of Hanover against a possible French or Prussian attack, it resulted in a new Franco-Austrian alliance. A worried Frederick II invaded Saxony and Bohemia in 1756, beginning the **Seven Years' War** (1757–1764). Prussia found itself facing opposition from France, Russia, Sweden, and several small German states. Only two things saved it: subsidies from Britain and the death of the Russian empress Elizabeth, Frederick II's archenemy. Her successor, Peter III, admired the Prussians and signed a Russo-Prussian armistice, even as Berlin itself was besieged by the armies of France, Austria, and Russia.

The war cost Prussia 180,000 men and devastated its countryside. Prussia signed a peace agreement with Russia that lasted until 1780.

Partitions of Poland

While Prussia continued to rise as a great military power under Frederick II, the Commonwealth of Poland moved toward collapse. In addition to Poland, the Commonwealth included Lithuania, Belarus, and Latvia, as well as large parts of Ukraine and Estonia. This ethnic diversity led to divisions in the Commonwealth among landed elites who controlled the representative assemblies and key leadership positions in government. These elites defied the king, exempted themselves from taxation, and exploited the peasantry. Poland had neither a powerful monarchy (like France's) nor an effective government bureaucracy (like Britain's) to unite the country. People felt more connection to their region than to the abstract idea of a country called Poland.

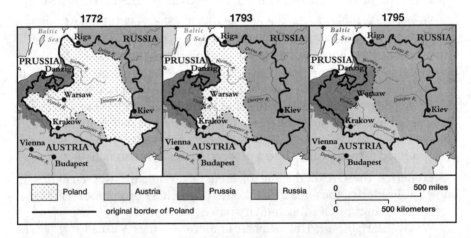

In 1652, the Polish legislature, or **Sejm**, adopted the practice of liberum veto, under which a single negative vote could block proceedings. This was meant as a safeguard against tyranny. In reality, the liberum veto could paralyze the functioning of the state. In 1764, the Russian empress Catherine II engineered the election of her former lover, Stanisław Poniatowski, as King **Stanisław II** of Poland. His attempts to strengthen the monarchy and modernize the nation were opposed by many members of the Polish elite, and civil war broke out in 1768. Poland's neighbors took advantage of its weakness. The first **partition**, or division, marked the beginning of a change in the balance of power in Europe. By the end of the 17th century, Poland would experience two more partitions and would be completely annexed by neighboring counries. Poland did not again appear as a nation on European maps until 1918.

THE THREE POLISH PARTITIONS, 1772-1797		
Partition and Causes	**Losses**	**Empires That Gained Land**
First Partition of Poland, 1772 Frederick II suggested the partition to resolve a conflict between Russia and Austria over Russia's annexation of Ottoman territories. Austria originally opposed the partition but annexed some Polish border areas.	About 80,000 square miles, which was almost one-third of the country and home to more than one-third of the population	Russia received the largest area, in the northeast. Austria acquired the densely populated Little Poland, which was renamed Galicia. Prussia gained the least territory, part of Great Poland, cutting Poland off from the Baltic Sea.
Second Partition of Poland, 1793 In the 1790s, in response to an attempt by conservatives to overthrow Poland's new liberal constitution, Russia intervened. Russia and Prussia each seized more land from Poland.	About 115,000 square miles	Russia gained most of Lithuania, Belarus, Podolia, and western Ukraine. Prussia acquired the rest of Great Poland.
Third Partition of Poland, 1795 Russia and Prussia put down a 1794 uprising for Polish independence.	About 45,000 square miles, which was all the remaining land	Russia and Prussia split the rest of Poland, except for the remaining land of Little Poland, which went to Austria.

REFLECT ON THE ESSENTIAL QUESTION

Essential Question: *How did European states establish and maintain a balance of power on the continent from 1648 to 1815?*

Political Efforts to Establish and Maintain Power	Military Efforts to Establish and Maintain Power

KEY TERMS AND PEOPLE

balance of power	Parlements	Peace of Utrecht
absolutism	Battle of Vienna	Frederick William I
divine right	Dutch War	Frederick the Great
Peace of Westphalia	Nine Years' War	Maria Theresa
Gustavus Adolphus	Philip V (Philip, Duke of	Seven Years' War
Dutch Revolt	Anjou)	Sejm
Catalan Revolt	War of the Spanish	Stanisław II
Fronde	Succession	partition

Questions 1–3 refer to the map below.

"In 1648, the settlement of the Peace of Westphalia marked the end of the Middle Ages and of the universalist world of Emperor Charles V. Among the few who clearly discerned what had happened was the pope. At first he hesitated to approve or disapprove. But in the end, his verdict was a definitively [decline] of the Peace of Westphalia. The pope's verdict reverberated even three hundred years later in a letter from Pope Pius XII to the Bishop of Münster on the occasion of the 300th anniversary of the Peace of Westphalia. . . . In 1648 Counter-Reformation Europe did not accept tolerance, but at least had established confessional pluralism and refrained from any kind of religious war."

—Wilhelm Ribhegge, "Counter-Reformation Politics, Society and Culture," *Journal of Neo-Latin Studies*, 2000

1. Which of the following statements best explains the broader historical context of the 16th and 17th centuries for the events described by Ribhegge?

   (A) The support these events gave to the Counter Reformation resulted in peace between Protestants and Roman Catholics.

   (B) The events described led to greater European unity under the Roman Catholic Church.

   (C) The compromise these events included on religion removed the primary cause of deadly wars since the Reformation began.

   (D) The rejection of full religious tolerance in these events enabled Calvinists to continue to practice their beliefs about Christianity.

2. In the first sentence, Ribhegge uses the phrase "the universalist world of Charles V" to mean that leaders such as Charles V believed that

   (A) people were all equal and hence should have the same rights

   (B) Europeans should all aspire to share the same religion

   (C) one emperor should rule over all countries in Europe

   (D) conflict would always exist between people somewhere in Europe

3. Which of the following claims most directly modifies or refutes Ribhegge's argument about the relationship between the Peace of Westphalia and the Middle Ages?

(A) Traditional elites still dominated the politics of much of Central and Eastern Europe such as the landed elites in Poland.

(B) Many vernacular languages in western Europe grew out of or were heavily influenced by Latin.

(C) Much of the art produced during the Italian Renaissance featured religious themes.

(D) The Counter Reformation reasserted the power of the Roman Catholic Church after the Reformation.

SHORT-ANSWER QUESTION

Use the map below to answer all parts of the question that follows.

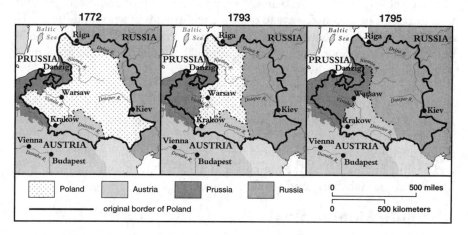

1. a) Explain ONE way the map provides evidence that Russia benefited the most from the three partitions.

   b) Explain ONE way the map provides evidence of a new geographic relationship between Russia and Prussia.

   c) Explain ONE way the map shows how the balance of power in Europe changed because of the partitions of Poland.

Topic 3.7

Absolutist Approaches to Power

The Sovereign is absolute; for there is no other Authority but that which centers in his single Person, . . . The Extent of the Dominion requires an absolute Power to be vested in that Person who rules over it.

—Catherine the Great, "Instructions to the Commissioners for Composing a New Code of Laws," 1767

Essential Question: How did absolutist forms of rule affect social and political development from 1648 to 1815?

Though absolute monarchs believed they wielded unlimited power, in reality they did not. They needed ways to pay for their unending wars, and they faced challenges from key elite groups within their regimes. The monarch-elite relationship determined the nature of a monarch's reign. As one grew more powerful, the other was weakened.

These challenges facing absolute monarchies both on the European continent and in the Americas ultimately weakened absolutism. As a result, Britain was poised to dominate Europe and much of the rest of the world for 150 years. Britain's strength came from its constitutional government, with its constrained monarchy, strong Parliament, religious and intellectual toleration, and healthy finances. It had advantages that the absolute monarchies of France, Spain, and the Habsburg lands could not match.

Absolute Monarchies

Absolutism arose in Europe's new states as the old medieval order broke up. It began in 16th-century Western Europe with monarchs who held absolute power over both church and state. Absolutism became widespread in the 17th and 18th centuries, and several factors contributed to its general acceptance:

[handwritten margin note: weakened catholic church growing acceptance of protestants]

- The Catholic Church was weakened by growing Anglican, Calvin, and Lutheran movements, so it provided limited resistance to the increasing authority of monarchs. However, in France, Louis XIV gained the power to appoint bishops and therefore control of the French Catholic Church.

- The expansion of trade led to the rise of cities, whose merchant and middle classes hoped absolutism would bring stability and prosperity.

- Absolutist rulers favored the merchant class and middle class and weakened the nobility as a result.

- New weaponry, such as gunpowder, gave monarchs greater power to destroy nobles' lands and castles, keeping them in check.

Because monarchs claimed a divine right to rule, no one was permitted to argue against their decisions, which were often tyrannical and threatened the financial stability of their nations.

Monarchs and the Aristocracy

Under absolutism, a state's power was directly connected to the strength of its ruler. Strong monarchs did not accept restrictions on their authority—not by nobles, legislatures, churches, citizens, the courts, the military, or agencies, such as a finance ministry. Absolutism posed problems for several reasons:

- Incompetent absolute monarchs could lead their nations into chaos.

- Without checks on the ruler from other forces, royal decisions could be based on whims and favoritism rather than on the choices of an efficient government bureaucracy staffed by public servants.

- The nobility, who stood the best chance of limiting the monarch's power, did not represent the needs and viewpoints of the vast majority of subjects.

When France's Louis XIV said that he *was* the state *("l'état, c'est moi")*, he meant that he alone had the authority to rule the kingdom. In contrast, modern nations belong to "the people," with power divided in a system of checks and balances among a chief executive, a law-making body, and the courts—all of which are meant to serve the public good. Some examples of absolute monarchs who reigned with varying degrees of success were Philip II of Spain, James I of England, Louis XIV of France, and Peter the Great of Russia.

Philip II of Spain

During **Philip II**'s reign (1556–1598), Spain reached the height of its power. Philip succeeded in solidifying the unity of Spain, begun under Ferdinand and Isabella, and even united the Iberian Peninsula by gaining control of Portugal. Philip's forces (along with Venice and the Papal States) checked Ottoman expansion in the Mediterranean by winning an important naval victory at the Battle of Lepanto (1571). However, the ongoing revolt in the Netherlands and the loss of the Spanish Armada in its attempted invasion of England (1588) pointed to Spain's weaknesses and signaled its coming decline.

Philip II disliked travel, so he stayed in Spain and made all decisions based on reports from his ministers. Because he ruled on all matters both grand and trivial, the work of government slowed down, especially when he failed to make decisions. He was notoriously suspicious and condoned the murder of his enemies, so his court was filled with factions and treachery. Philip wanted glory and power for both Spain and Catholicism, but he earned the enmity of most of the rest of Europe in the process. After the death of Philip II, Spain began a slow period of decline.

less time

James I of England

Unlike France or Spain, England during the Middle Ages developed a participatory system of government at both the local and parliamentary levels. England's Parliament had two chambers:

- the **House of Lords**: the upper chamber, made up of nobles and bishops of the Church of England
- the **House of Commons**: the lower chamber, made up of members elected to represent boroughs, or legislative regions

There were frequent conflicts between monarchs and Parliament over taxation and royal powers. **James I** (reigned 1603–1625) believed in the divine right of kings, meaning he was answerable only to God—not Parliament. James believed his spending could not be checked. He overspent and wanted Parliament to cover his personal debts. The members of Parliament (MPs) disapproved and set a precedent by implementing stringent rules over the king's finances and establishing their own greater independence.

James I also needed tax money to pay for war against Spain. Because the MPs were anti-Catholic and anti-Spanish, they agreed to his request but drew up a petition that said James's son, Charles, would have to marry a Protestant. James felt Parliament had overstepped its bounds. In defiance of Parliament, he had Charles marry a Catholic, Henrietta Maria, the sister of the French king. James's conflicts with Parliament laid the groundwork for a rebellion against his son and successor, **Charles I**, and for the English Civil War. (See Topic 3.2.)

Louis XIV of France

taxed everyone excessively

No monarch embodied the concept of absolutism better than **Louis XIV** of France (1638–1715), known as the Sun King. Louis XIV inherited the throne when he was five years old and ruled for 72 years. Until he was proclaimed of age to rule in 1651, his mother, Anne of Austria (1601–1666), and godfather, **Cardinal Jules Mazarin** (1602–1661), ruled a country that was fractured and unstable. To counter such problems, Louis XIV followed a system in which royal representatives called intendants went into the countryside to run the country on behalf of the king. **Cardinal Richelieu**, chief minister of the previous king, Louis XIII, had stripped provincial officials of their power when he divided the country into districts, each administered by an intendant. Because the king appointed the intendants, they displaced local authorities.

Eventually, the local authorities and the nobility fomented an unsuccessful uprising called the **Fronde** (see Topic 3.6), but its lasting effect was to convince the young king that his power must be absolute.

French Society Louis XIV surrounded himself with **courtiers**—wealthy, powerful nobles who vied for his favor. In doing so, he eventually brought them under his control. Louis lived lavishly, building the opulent and expensive **Palace of Versailles** 12 miles outside of Paris, as well as several other costly *chateaux,* or castles.

His military campaigns made France both powerful and multicultural. His army seized land in the north (Flanders), the east (Lorraine and Alsace), and the south (in the Pyrenees). By the end of his reign, many of his subjects spoke Spanish, Dutch, German, or a less-common regional language.

Source: Louvre, Paris, photo by Leemage/Corbis via Getty Images (Charles); Uffizi Gallery, Florence, photo by DeAgostini/Getty Images (Louis)

Two absolute monarchs: Charles I of England (painted by Anthony van Dyck, 1635) and Louis XIV of France (painted by Hyacinthe Rigaud, 1701) in similar poses. (Charles was an uncle by marriage to Louis, as his wife, Henrietta Maria, was a sister of Louis' father, Louis XIII.)

The French Economy To expand France's borders, Louis XIV needed a strong army, which meant he also needed a strong economy that generated tax revenues. Finance minister **Jean-Baptiste Colbert** (1619–1683) instituted mercantilist policies to decrease France's debt and revitalize its industries. He worked to expand France's colonies and create a favorable balance of trade. (For more about mercantilism and colonialism, see Topic 3.4.) However, most of Colbert's work was undone by Louis XIV's endless wars. Louis XIV also renewed France's war against its own Protestants, the Huguenots, revoking in 1685 the rights they had been granted in the Edict of Nantes. This loss of rights caused up to 800,000 Huguenots to flee the country. Some historians believe that their departure depleted the French middle class and further hurt the economy.

Absolutist rule in France was costly. During Louis XIV's riegn, France supported a modern army of up to 350,000 in wartime. He also involved France in numerous wars. Paying for this military resulted in crippling taxation for the poorer classes. In contrast, for most of Louis' reign, the nobility was taxed very lightly. In 1695, Louis' wars and debts led to the institution of a new tax, the *capitation*, which in theory applied to all French citizens. However, the nobility quickly found ways around payment. Louis' policies left the treasury in very poor conditions—a state of affairs that would continue and even worsen.

The Westernization of Russia

Russia, which had broken free of Mongol control in the 1400s, was a multiethnic empire with its capital in Moscow. The empire grew as it conquered people of many nationalities and languages. Russian monarchs, called **tsars**, or czars, established control over all these varied peoples by granting the land back to local elites, or nobles (called boyars), in exchange for their support. In order to build loyalty and familial relationships, the tsars married their children into the families of these nobles, who were given positions of trust and power. In turn, the nobles agreed to cede control to the central government.

Studying Western Europe Tsar **Peter the Great** (reigned 1682–1725) saw Russia as a medieval state that had not learned from technological, social, and commercial advances made by the Western European powers. He believed that these differences threatened Russia's strength and independence. In 1697, Peter traveled to Europe with the **Grand Embassy**, a group of about 250 boyars, mainly to see firsthand how the more advanced Western European countries operated. In disguise as Sergeant Pyotr Mikhaylov, Peter visited arsenals, factories, museums, schools, and shipyards, as well as experiencing Parliamentary sessions. He returned home convinced Russia had to modernize.

As one way to accomplish this modernization, he allied with Saxony and Denmark-Norway in the **Great Northern War** (1700–1721) against Sweden. His goal was to gain access to the Baltic Sea and acquire a seaport so that Russia could compete for trade and naval power. Peter's main prize from his victory in the war with Sweden became the seaport city of St. Petersburg, which he began planning and building as his "window on Europe." He brought architects and artisans from around the world to help build his magnificent new capital. He also rerouted trade through the new capital, and by 1726, the city hosted 90 percent of Russia's foreign trade.

RUSSIAN EXPANSION

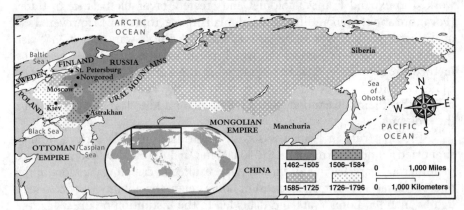

In addition to building the new capital, Peter the Great instituted reforms to modernize science, technology, industry, and education:

- promoting science and technology so that Russia's military, industry, transport, and trade could compete with those of Western Europe
- founding the St. Petersburg Academy of Sciences (later the **Russian Academy of Sciences**)
- inviting foreign experts to teach at the St. Petersburg Academy
- establishing guilds with special privileges to increase economic activity
- sponsoring secular education

Reorganizing Institutions In his quest to Westernize and strengthen his empire, Peter the Great reorganized government, the Church, and the military under his absolute rule. To pay the great expenses for warfare and modernization, Peter tripled taxes. He conscripted peasants into lifetime service in the army and forced them to work in mines or manufacturing. The nobles had to serve for life in either the army or in government. To modernize the Russian bureaucracy, Peter created the Table of Ranks so that nobles could achieve status in either the military or government service. The ancient landed aristocracy, known as the **boyars**, and the clergy resisted Peter's changes, and both groups were severely punished. For example, Peter required all his courtiers and officials, leading merchants, and military personnel to wear Western-style clothes and shave off their beards and mustaches.

Peter also reorganized the Russian Orthodox Church. He abolished the patriarch, the Orthodox Church's traditional leader, and established the **Holy Synod**, made up of officials and priests obedient to the tsar. Church lands were disposed of at the tsar's will, occasionally to placate the aristocracy.

Catherine the Great Peter's work was carried on by the empress Catherine II, who came to be known as **Catherine the Great** (1729–1796). Catherine began life as a minor German princess, but she was selected to marry Peter the Great's grandson, the grand duke Peter, in 1745. Peter and Catherine disliked each other intensely, but Catherine found comfort in reading and preparing herself to rule. Months after her husband assumed the throne as Peter III at the beginning of 1762, she forced him to abdicate and had herself proclaimed empress. Eight days later, Peter was assassinated.

One of Catherine's first tasks was to replenish the state treasury, which was empty. She did this by seizing the property of the clergy, who owned one-third of the land and serfs in Russia. The clergy lost what power they still had, becoming state-paid functionaries. Two years later, she placed a former lover on the throne of Poland. (See Topic 3.6.)

Catherine had read the works of English and French liberal philosophers, such as Montesquieu and Rousseau, and became a disciple. She is often referred to as an "enlightened despot." In 1767, she convened a commission made up of delegates from all the provinces and social classes, excluding serfs, to frame a constitution, but it was deemed too liberal and never adopted. Catherine had planned to emancipate the serfs but gave this up as a result of the Pugachev Rebellion. This widespread uprising posed a serious threat to Catherine's regime and convinced her that the peasants posed a real threat that she must continue to neutralize or control.

Catherine's final years were darkened by the execution of the French king, the advance of revolutionary armies, and the spread of radical ideas. By the end of her reign, she had reorganized 29 provinces under her administrative reform plan. Catherine succeeded where Peter had failed in adding more than 200,000 square miles to Russia's territory, including Crimea from the Ottoman Empire and more than half of Poland.

	EXAMPLES OF ABSOLUTE MONARCHS		
State	Leader	Reign	Accomplishments
England	James I	1603–1625	• Believed monarchs ruled by divine right • Dissolved Parliament • Married his son to a Catholic
Spain	Philip II	1556–1598	• Controlled Spanish Netherlands • Launched Spanish Armada against England • Worked tirelessly and conscientiously • Controlled political appointments
France	Louis XIV	1643–1715	• Used intendants to spread his control • Brutally suppressed rebellions • Increased the military • Extended France's borders • Levied high taxes on the peasants
Russia	Peter the Great	1682–1725	• Conscripted peasants into the military and supporting industries • Forced nobles to serve for life in the military or government • Westernized Russia • Controlled the Orthodox Church • Built a new capital, St. Petersburg

[Handwritten annotations: "England believed in divine right wanted to expand"; "Spain to expand"; "Cared abou military"; "Russia didn't believe in divine right"]

REFLECT ON THE ESSENTIAL QUESTION

Essential Question: *How did absolutist forms of rule affect social and political development from 1648 to 1815?*

Social Effects	Political Effects

KEY TERMS AND PEOPLE

Philip II	Cardinal Richelieu	Grand Embassy
House of Lords	Fronde	Great Northern War
House of Commons	courtier	Russian Academy of
James I	Palace of Versailles	Sciences
Charles I	Jean-Baptiste Colbert	boyar
Louis XIV	tsar (czar)	Holy Synod
Cardinal Jules Mazarin	Peter the Great	Catherine the Great

HISTORICAL PERSPECTIVES: *WHY DID RUSSIA AND WESTERN EUROPE DIVERGE?*

As the question in the title suggests, historians debate over whether Russia ever made a definitive break from the rest of Europe. Arguments often reflect whether a particular historian's perspective is based on beliefs tied to the Cold War, a broader world-history perspective, or the viewpoint of the post-Cold War period.

The Mongol Influence Historian Robert Strayer credited the Mongols with helping to establish modern Russia and the founding of Moscow. Strayer explained how Russians adopted Mongol weapons, diplomatic rituals, court practices, taxation, and the military draft.

Richard Pipes went further to suggest that Mongol influence in Russia was critical because it cut Russia off from Catholic Western Europe, the Byzantine Empire, and the Islamic Empire. This break established a patrimonial system in which nobles answered only to the tsar and lacked exposure to the cornerstones of Western political thought—Roman law, Catholic theology, feudalism, and commercial culture. This break was critical, Pipes believed, because it prevented the rise of an independent noble or middle class and respect for private property that would allow for the rise of the state as a public institution. To Pipes, this cemented a separate, conservative past and future for Russia.

Divergence or Similarity Angela Rustemeyer, a German historian writing during and after the Cold War, tried to find greater similarity between Russia and the West. In her article in the journal *Kritika* (2010), Rustemeyer traced recent historiographical shifts, highlighting four historians discussing closer Russian ties to Europe than previously understood.

As a result, Rustemeyer directly challenged the arguments popularized by Pipes. First, she demonstrated not the absence of feudalism but the evolution of a system in which the Russian nobles, much like their Western European counterparts, owed loyalty to the tsar. And much like Western Europeans, the tsar increasingly responded to the nobles' demands—thus establishing a public sphere of interaction. Second, Rustemeyer compared the support of Russian abbots for economic expansion to that of the Calvinists and Peter the Great's control of religion to that of Henry VIII.

Third, Rustemeyer cited the work of historian Donald Ostrowski as she noted a direct and intentional shift by Russia away from the Mongols toward Western Europe. Ostrowski had explained, for example, how the shift from bows and arrows to gunpowder weapons represented a reorientation not only of Russian foreign policy but also military practices and structure. Rustemeyer's conclusion was that Russia had already embarked on a path of modern state-building much like that of the rest of Europe but that it was accelerated by Peter the Great.

A Contextualization Challenge The historiography of Russia from the Western perspective always faces a challenge. Classifying a vast territory that covers one-sixth of Earth, spanning Europe and Asia, has never been easy for historians. The challenge was complicated by Cold War tensions and uncertainty of the motivations of leaders such as Vladimir Putin. The result leaves historians trying to remain objective on a topic and goal that very much reflects crucial issues of their time. Historical viewpoints about Russia present an important lesson in contextualization, as the questions historians ask and the answers they develop are shaped by the times in which they write.

1. In your view, did Russia make a break from Western Europe, or were the two regions ever really linked? Explain your answer.

2. How successful do you think the Russians were in adopting Western ways starting with Peter the Great?

3. How might the differences between Russia and the West account for the persistence of autocratic regimes such as that of Vladimir Putin?

MULTIPLE-CHOICE QUESTIONS

Questions 1–3 refer to the passages below.

Passage 1

"A well conducted government must have an underlying concept so well integrated that it could be likened to a system of philosophy. All actions taken must be well reasoned. . . . Laziness, hedonism [pursuit of pleasure] and imbecility, these are the causes which restrain princes in working at the noble task of bringing happiness to their subjects. . . . A sovereign is not elevated to his high position, supreme power has not been confined to him in order that he may live in lazy luxury, enriching himself by the labor of the people. . . . The sovereign is the first servant of the state . . . one demands that he work efficiently for the good of the state. . . .

Catholics, Lutherans, Reformed, Jews and other Christian sects live in this state, and live together in peace. If the sovereign, actuated by a mistaken zeal, declares himself for one religion or another, parties spring up, heated disputes ensue, little by little persecutions will commence and, in the end, the religion persecuted will leave the fatherland, and millions of subjects will enrich our neighbors by their skill and industry."

—Frederick the Great of Prussia, *Political Testament*, 1752

Passage 2

"33. The Laws ought to be so framed, as to secure the Safety of every Citizen as much as possible.

34. The Equality of the Citizens consists in this; that they should all be subject to the same Laws.

35. This Equality requires Institutions so well adapted, as to prevent the Rich from oppressing those who are not so wealthy. . . .

39. The political Liberty of a Citizen is the Peace of Mind arising from the Consciousness, that every Individual enjoys his peculiar Safety; and in order that the People might attain this Liberty. . . .

123. The Usage of Torture is contrary to all the Dictates of Nature and Reason; even Mankind itself cries out against it and demands loudly the total Abolition of it."

—Catherine the Great of Russia, the instructions of Catherine II to the Legislative Commission of 1767

1. The main idea of both sources is that the writers want their government
   (A) to establish a republican system of choosing leaders
   (B) to follow an economic policy of mercantilism
   (C) to adopt reforms to make them more tolerant and humane
   (D) to become more like the Dutch government

2. These sources could be used to support the arguments about religion that led people to issue which document?
   (A) the Concordat of Bologna 1516 because of its position on income from French churches
   (B) the Peace of Augsburg because of its position on religion in German kingdoms
   (C) the Edict of Nantes because of its position on religious pluralism in France
   (D) the English Bill of Rights because of its position on the rights of Roman Catholics

3. Which of the following might limit the use of each source in helping historians understand the 18th century?

(A) Both leaders are describing their goals, which might have been different from their behavior.

(B) Both are writing private letters, in which they might have unfairly tried to portray their own actions positively.

(C) Both are repeating views that most people had at the time, so these might have been just what they were expected to say.

(D) Both are writing before they had come to power, so they had no experience as rulers.

SHORT-ANSWER QUESTION

Use the passage below to answer all parts of the question that follows.

"In the 17th century, European governments devoted more attention to the public image of the ruler than at any time since the later Roman Empire. Among these governments, it was the French who were the most concerned with the ways in which the king was represented. . . . The most elaborate and self-conscious attempts at projecting a favorable image of the ruler were those made by a group of officials, artists and men of letters . . . in the reign of Louis XIV, especially in the period of his personal rule, which lasted for more than half a century (1643–1715). The term 'propaganda' is all the more appropriate [to describe these favorable images] because the government was concerned not only to present the king in a heroic light but also to spread official interpretations of specific events of the reign."

—Peter Burke, "Fabrication of Louis XIV," 1992

1. a) Describe ONE piece of evidence that supports Burke's argument regarding the power of absolute monarchs in Europe.

   b) Describe ONE piece of evidence that undermines Burke's argument regarding the power of absolute monarchs in Europe.

   c) Explain ONE example of a new monarch in the 15th or 16th centuries that provoked a similar political system to those described by Burke.

Topic 3.8

Comparison in the Age of Absolutism and Constitutionalism

Laws are the sovereigns of sovereigns.

—King Louis XIV of France

Essential Question: How were different forms of political power that developed from 1648 to 1815 similar and different?

Europe during the 17th and 18th centuries endured many power struggles. Through these fights for sovereignty, different types of political power and structures were created for different states.

Comparing Changing Governments In some 17th-century European states, there began a move from absolutism and centralized political structures to more secular and regional governments. On one side of the struggle for sovereignty were monarchs who wanted to increase their powers. On the other side were nobles who wanted to keep and even build on traditional shared power and regional autonomy. Below are examples comparing the different political struggles for sovereignty in several European states.

An example of the many struggles between monarchs and nobles was a violent struggle for political control in France under the rule of King Louis XIV. Cardinal Richelieu, chief minister of the previous king, Louis XIII, had stripped provincial officials of their power when he divided the country into districts, each administered by a royal representative. Because the king appointed the representatives, they displaced local authorities. Eventually, the local authorities and the nobility carried out an unsuccessful series of uprisings called the Fronde, but its lasting effect was to convince Louis XIV that his power must be absolute. France's result contrasted with the growing power of England's Parliament, evident in its ultimately successful challenge to royal absolutism in the Glorious Revolution.

In another political struggle to compare, some minority groups with identities based on a unique language or culture began to fight for self-governance. For instance, beginning in the 17th century, battles took placed between traditional Celtic societies and national governments in the modernizing European states of Scotland, Ireland, and France. Traditionally religious people, Celts were affected by various states' attempts to limit religious nonconformity. Celtic farmers were removed from their land as militaries expanded their infrastructure.

Another example was the growing competition between Spain and the Netherlands, a region under Spain's control. This resulted in the Dutch War for Independence lasting 80 years (1568 to 1648) and ending when Dutch independence was officially recognized.

In the 17th century, the Bohemian estates (located in modern-day Czech Republic) were under control of the Habsburgs. The Bohemian estates tried to maintain their Czech identity and social status, despite the Habsburgs' attempts to mandate Catholicism and centralize their power. In 1618, the Bohemian estates rose against the Habsburgs, signaling the start of the Thirty Years' War, but they were defeated in 1620.

Comparing Different Sovereignty Models In much of 17th- and 18th-century Europe, the established type of government was absolute monarchy. Due to the religious Reformations, the idea that monarchs had a divine right to power began to change. Slowly, many people came to the conclusion that monarchs had a social contract with their subjects, not a divine right to rule. The social contract included the concept that monarchs were to provide certain rights and protections to their subjects, while the subjects gave up some freedoms for the monarchy's protections. Below are examples comparing the different sovereignty models in several European states.

New models of political sovereignty grew out of the idea of the social contract as opposed to an absolute monarchy. One model was a constitutional monarchy. In which, a monarch shared power with a parliament. England was distinct from other European nations in that it had both a strong monarchy and a powerful Parliament. England's Parliament more closely represented the country as a whole and served as a check on the monarch's power.

Another political model that evolved was an oligarchy. This was a legislative body from a select societal class that ruled the state. The Dutch oligarchy was made up of rural landholders and urban gentry, or upper-class professionals and merchants. The policies of oligarchs are designed to maintain and increase their status and wealth through trade.

QUESTIONS ABOUT COMPARISON

1. How did Europe's absolute monarchies compare to constitutional monarchies?

2. How did the Dutch oligarchy differ from a monarchy?

UNIT 3 REVIEW: Absolutism and Constitutionalism
c. 1648 to c. 1815

Writing in chronological order means structuring an essay by presenting the supporting evidence in the order it occurred. (In Greek mythology, the god *Chronos* governed linear, orderly, predictable time.) Chronological organization helps the reader of a historical essay in several ways. First, it organizes the material sensibly. Second, it helps explain cause and effect, or how things built upon each other. Third, it can aid a smooth transition into the next main idea.

Which words in the sentences below cue the reader that the writer is using chronological order?

1. In the early 17th century, the English King James I believed in a divine right monarchy. His son and successor, Charles I, continued this absolutism by dissolving Parliament and attempting to rule without it for 11 years.

2. As a result of the Glorious Revolution in the late 17th century, English co-monarchs William of Orange and his wife, Mary, accepted a limited monarchy and Parliament's Bill of Rights.

3. After sending Russians to study in the West and bringing foreigners to Russia, he effected changes such as forcing men to shave, adopting Western court processes, and creating an Academy of Sciences.

4. In 1697, he traveled incognito to the West and learned about Western science and industry. He was credited with moving Russia from the medieval world into the modern world.

5. Peter was an absolutist who governed by subduing the nobles. Later, in the second half of the 18th century, Catherine the Great continued Peter's program of growth through conquest and diplomacy, but she gave increased freedom back to the nobles and was considered an enlightened despot.

Based on cue words and transitions, put the following ideas into chronological order.

6. During the 17th and 18th centuries, absolute monarchies were established throughout much of Europe, but they were not equally successful.

   a. Other examples of absolute monarchies were those of England's James I of England and Phillips II, III, and IV of Spain.

b. Eventually, challenges to absolutism led to alternative political systems.

c. However, not all monarchies were absolutist. Weak leadership and poor policies, like the liberum veto, plagued Poland. Poland also suffered uprisings that led to massacres of noblemen, Jews, and Catholic priests. A weak monarchy led to Poland's partition by Prussia, Russia, and Austria and its disappearance from the map of Europe for 123 years.

d. Two results of these alternative systems were the English Bill of Rights, which gave Parliament sovereignty, and the Dutch Republic, established by a Protestant revolt of urban gentry and rural landholders to promote trade and protect traditional rights.

e. Louis XIV epitomized the idea of absolute monarchy. Even though his finance minister, Jean-Baptiste Colbert, improved French manufacturing, Louis bankrupted France with his incessant wars.

LONG ESSAY QUESTIONS

Directions: Suggested writing time is 40 minutes. In your response, you should do the following:

- Respond to the prompt with a historically defensible thesis that establishes a line of reasoning.
- Describe a broader historical context relevant to the prompt.
- Support an argument in response to the prompt using specific and relevant examples of evidence.
- Use historical reasoning (e.g., comparison, causation, continuity and change over time) to frame or structure an argument that addresses the prompt.
- Use evidence to corroborate, qualify, or modify an argument that addresses the prompt.

1. Evaluate the extent to which the governmental structure of France during the 17th and 18th centuries differed from that of England/Britain during the same period.

2. Evaluate the extent to which religious and economic reasons led to England's Glorious Revolution.

3. Evaluate the extent to which slavery in the Americas influenced the economies of Europe.

4. Evaluate the success of two European countries in establishing a mercantilist empire.

DOCUMENT-BASED QUESTION

Directions: Question 1 is based on the accompanying documents. The documents have been edited for the purpose of this exercise. You are advised to spend 15 minutes planning and 45 minutes writing your answer. In your response, you should do the following:

- Respond to the prompt with a historically defensible thesis that establishes a line of reasoning.
- Describe a broader historical context relevant to the prompt.
- Support an argument in response to the prompt using at least six documents.
- Use at least one additional piece of specific historical evidence (beyond that found in the documents) relevant to an argument about the prompt.
- For at least three documents, explain how or why the document's point of view, purpose, historical situation, and/or audience is relevant to an argument.
- Use evidence to corroborate, qualify, or modify an argument that addresses the prompt.

Document 1

Source: Joost van den Vondel, Dutch poet, poem written to celebrate a visit of the Queen Mother of France to the East India House, 1639

Twas not enough they'd won the field in Netherlands;

They sailed the earth to distant and exotic lands.

As far as shines the sun, resolved the sun would see

Their mighty deeds. Our Holland serves as granary

For all the Indies grow. The North has filled its ships

With Eastern crops. The Winter Prince who warms his lips

With pepper, guards in these domains the boast

Of all that heavenly fires of summer cook and roast. . . .

Great Java shares with us her treasures fair,

And China, porcelain. We Amsterdammers journey

Where Ganges casts its waters down into the sea:

Wherever profit leads us, to every sea and shore,

For love of gain the wide world's harbours we explore.

Document 2

Source: Jean Baptiste Colbert, Finance Minister to Louis XIV, *Memoir of 1663*

It is almost certain that every State, in proportion to its grandeur and extent, is sufficiently provided in its own territory with the means of subsistence; provided that these means are well and faithfully administered.

Document 3

Source: Joseph Van Aken, *An English Family at Tea*, 1720

Document 4

Source: Jethro Tull, British agriculturalist, *Horse-Hoeing Husbandry*, 1733

All sorts of dung and compost contain some matter which, when mixed with the soil, ferments therein; and by such ferment dissolves, crumbles, and divides the earth very much. This is the chief and almost only use of dung. . . . This proves, that its (manure) use is not to nourish, but to dissolve, i.e., divide the terrestrial matter, which affords nourishment to the Mouths of vegetable roots. His underestimate of the value of manure.

Document 5

Source: Lémery, Louis, *A Treatise of all Sorts of Foods, Both Animal and Vegetable*, 1745

Coffee fortifies the Stomach and Brain, promotes Digestion, allays the Head-ach, suppresses the Fumes caused by Wine, and other spirituous Liquors; promotes Urine and Womens Terms, opens some Peoples Bodies, makes the memory and Fancy more quick, and People brisk that drink it: This last Effect has been observed, say they, by the Shepherds of *Africa*, who took Notice, that before Coffee was used, and that their Sheep fed upon this Kind of Pulse, that they skipped about strangely.

Document 6

Source: Bill of Sale for One Slave: Beth, eight-year-old girl; sold by Lawrence Lancaster to Thomas Cook for 32 pounds, 10 shillings, in the American colonies March 18, 1757

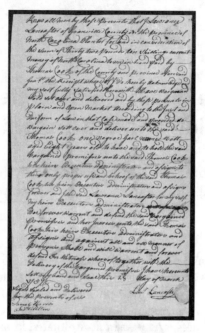

Document 7

Source: David Hackett Fischer, *The Great Wave*, 1996

THE PRICE REVOLUTION OF THE 16TH CENTURY
(price relatives in England, 1450-1650)

Years	Grain	Stock	Wood	Manufactors	Wages
1450-69	99	100	102	101	101
1470-89	104	101	102	101	98
1490-09	105	105	88	98	101
1510-29	135	128	98	106	104
1530-49	174	164	108	119	114
1550-69	332	270	276	202	169
1570-89	412	344	227	227	105
1590-09	575	433	312	247	219
1610-29	788	649	500	294	296

1450.99-100

Grain
Livestock
Wood
Manufacturer
Farm Wages

800
700
600
500
400
300
200
100
0

1450-1469 1510-1529 1570-1589 1630-1649

UNIT 4: Scientific, Philosophical, and Political Developments
c. 1648 to c. 1815

Topic 4.1

Contextualizing the Scientific Revolution and the Enlightenment

Essential Question: What was the context in which the Scientific Revolution and Enlightenment developed in Europe?

The great thinkers of antiquity considered and tried to solve the same questions that challenge people even today: What is life? What is Earth and the visible universe? Why do things interact with each other the way they do? And so on. And though they took on these questions admirably and left a fascinating legacy that spurred the Renaissance, their conclusions were often limited by existing beliefs, a dearth of accumulated knowledge, and relatively primitive technology. *scarcity*

After the advent of Christianity *religious rule + law* and through the Middle Ages, the thinkers of Europe were limited by the dogma of the Catholic Church. Challenging the worldview of the Catholic hierarchy could easily lead to charges of heresy, which could have deadly outcomes. But as you have read, the Renaissance boosted inquiry and creativity, allowing artistic, social, religious, scientific, and political ideas to begin to evolve. By the 17th and 18th centuries, this growing spirit of intellectual exploration and freedom developed into what became known as the Enlightenment and the Scientific Revolution.

Renewed Interest in Classical World Ideas During the Renaissance, European thinkers rediscovered art and ideas from ancient Greece and Rome. These classical values were developed further during the Enlightenment. Philosophers saw critical thinking and classical views as the best means of improving politics, economics, and societies. They believed that applying reason to community problems could produce positive outcomes and people and societies could experience progress unlike that seen in earlier times.

European thinkers applied reason and the scientific method to all aspects of life, especially nature, producing a huge change in the established conceptual framework that became a movement known as the Scientific Revolution. The scientific method, consisting of observation experimentation, and the use of advanced forms of mathematics, challenged traditional ideas about astronomy, nature, and biology.

Europe Moves toward Emphasizing Reason The viewpoints and practices of the Scientific Revolution and the Enlightenment created a new, although not unchallenged, emphasis on reason in European life. Traditional patterns of thought from the Middle Ages gave way to empiricism, skepticism, rationalism, and classical knowledge. These changes affected governments, religion, and the social order. The use of the printing press and new and growing forms of print media helped spread Enlightenment ideas. Enlightenment theories on politics and economics evolved to the point of threatening absolutism and mercantilism. The Scientific Revolution brought about a new rational view of religion, which moved people to an appreciation of natural phenomena and calls for religious tolerance.

Changes to Day-to-Day Life Over time, life in Europe changed due to the Scientific Revolution. It affected populations, the environment, medicine, commerce, and technology. For example, on the one hand, European population growth was slowed by new marriage patterns and by new birth control methods. But on the other hand, better medicine helped to decrease child mortality and increase lifespans. In addition, some families had more wealth for raising their children and purchasing new items that made life more comfortable.

ANALYZE THE CONTEXT

1. How did the Renaissance set up conditions for the Enlightenment and the Scientific Revolution to develop during the 17th and 18th centuries?

2. How did the Enlightenment and the Scientific Revolution affect political, social, and religious issues?

Topic 4.2

The Scientific Revolution

Nature is relentless and unchangeable, and it is indifferent as to whether its hidden reasons and actions are understandable to men or not.

—Galileo Galilei (1564–1642)

Essential Question: How did understanding of the natural world develop and change during the Scientific Revolution?

The scientific advances that began during the Northern Renaissance in the 16th century laid the groundwork for a dramatic shift in thinking about the universe and humanity's place in it. Before that, the accepted view of the universe was determined mostly by the Catholic Church. People accepted the seemingly obvious geocentric (Earth-centered) view. From the late 17th century and through the 18th century, advances in scientific thought and processes, known as the Scientific Revolution, changed the views of many.

The Scientific Method

As part of the **Scientific Revolution**, some scholars promoted a more systematic approach to acquiring knowledge about the natural world. They laid the foundations for the **scientific method**, an approach based on observation, experimentation, and reasoning.

Two Types of Reasoning

An English lawyer named **Francis Bacon** (1561–1626) encouraged scientists of his time to build their knowledge on the foundation of **inductive reasoning**, which moves from the specific to the general. For example, a scientist might observe many individual flowers and then come up with a general conclusion about flowers based on those observations. Bacon believed that scholars should combine careful observation and systematic experimentation to collect small bits of information. Then they could use the information to support valid general conclusions. Bacon encouraged the growth of an international community of natural philosophers who would share the information from their research. The area of work of these scholars came to be called natural science.

In contrast, **deductive reasoning** moves from the general to the specific. A leading advocate of this approach was the French philosopher **René Descartes** (1596–1650). He wanted scientists to think like students of geometry. They should start with general principles, similar to geometric axioms, and then apply them using strict logic to understand particular cases.

EXAMPLES OF INDUCTIVE AND DEDUCTIVE REASONING		
Starting Point	Conclusion	Type of Reasoning
Greek, Roman, and Italian republics all failed.	Therefore, republican governments do not work.	Inductive
The paths of Mercury, Venus, Mars, and Earth through space do not form perfect circles.	Therefore, the orbits of the planets are not circles.	Inductive
All humans are rational. Descartes is a human.	Therefore, Descartes is rational.	Deductive
Humans are born with natural rights.	Therefore, England should pass laws that respect the rights of individuals.	Deductive

Developing the Scientific Method

The English mathematician and physicist **Isaac Newton** (1643–1727) brought these two complementary forms of reasoning together into the scientific method. A scientist might begin by conducting experiments that involved observation and data collection. Over time, general conclusions could be drawn from this data. Then these general conclusions might be extended by deductions that led to new hypotheses that could be tested through further experimentation. The goal of this new scientific endeavor was the formulation of general principles about the way the world worked, called **natural laws**, often based on mathematical proofs or expressed as mathematical formulas. Newton's universal law of gravitation provides one example of a natural law.

When laying out his method of inductive reasoning, Francis Bacon clearly stated that his goal was for humans to gain practical benefits from scientific knowledge and "conquer nature in action." An example of this scientific approach can be seen in Europeans' encounters with the Western Hemisphere that began in the late 15th century. These encounters provided new impetus to formulating natural laws based on a wealth of data gained through direct observation, including new information about geography, types of plants and animals, and different races and cultures in the New World.

Observation-Based Science

Renaissance humanism and art laid the groundwork for new ideas in science to emerge in the 16th and 17th centuries. Humanists' emphasis on learning Greek led later scholars to read a broader range of classical texts, providing a source of ideas that challenged the existing worldview. In addition, artists' close observations of the natural world and use of **mathematics** to develop techniques, such as perspective, established a new way to learn about the world. Mathematics is a science of structure and order that developed from counting and measurement. Later thinkers expanded the use of experimentation that Leonardo da Vinci and others developed in the late 15th century. These new methods for studying the natural world were the core of the Scientific Revolution.

New Ideas in Astronomy

Since ancient times, scholars have tried to understand their world and the cosmos, or the universe. The word **astronomy** comes from the ancient Greek word meaning "arrangement of the stars." It is a general term for the study of the universe beyond the Earth. **Cosmology** is the branch of astronomy concerned with the origins and structure of the universe.

Medieval Worldview The classical cosmology of the Greek philosopher Aristotle and astronomer Ptolemy (2nd century C.E.) went unchallenged for more than 1,400 years, forming the basis of the worldview of medieval scholastic philosophers. Aristotle and Ptolemy portrayed a geocentric universe—one with Earth at the center of a system of concentric spheres, including the sun, circling around it. According to this worldview, the planets were bodies of light. Medieval scholastic philosophers accepted this view and, in line with their Christian beliefs, taught that God and the souls of those who had been saved existed beyond the outermost sphere of the system.

Copernicus's New System Among the first Europeans to challenge the classical view was **Nicolaus Copernicus** (1473–1543), a Polish mathematician and natural philosopher, a scholar who studied the physical world. In classical writings, Copernicus found references to ancient Greeks who questioned the geocentric views of Aristotle and Ptolemy and believed instead in a **heliocentric**, or sun-centered, universe.

Copernicus then applied advanced mathematics to earlier astronomical observations to confirm the idea that the planets, including Earth, revolved around the sun. He proved that the perceived motion of the sun came from the Earth spinning on its axis and its annual orbit around the sun. Although he still accepted many of Aristotle's ideas, Copernicus feared criticism of his heliocentric system. Therefore, he only published his work, *On the Revolution of the Heavenly Spheres*, shortly before his death.

Building on Copernicus Later natural philosophers built on Copernicus's work, including German astronomer **Johannes Kepler** (1571–1630). By analyzing precise measurements of planetary orbits, Kepler found them to be elliptical rather than circular. By demonstrating these elliptical orbits, Kepler further supported Copernicus's still-controversial heliocentric model and disputed the religious belief (which even he had originally held) that the circle was the "perfect shape" and reflected the Divine order.

Kepler shared his published work with the Italian mathematician **Galileo Galilei** (1564–1642) in 1597. Galileo then extended Kepler's ideas through use of a new method to observe the planets. He became the first European to build and use a **telescope**, an optical instrument, for this purpose and thus discovered details that had never been known, such as the moons that circled Jupiter as well as the craters on Earth's moon. With these observations, Galileo showed that the planets were not ethereal bodies but were similar to Earth in their composition. Galileo's book *The Starry Messenger*, published in 1610, reaffirmed the heliocentric system and brought attention to these new ideas.

The Catholic Church rejected Galileo's work and found him guilty of heresy. They placed him under house arrest until his death. Although Galileo retracted his ideas publicly, his works continued to circulate. Later, Galileo's work on bodies in motion further challenged Aristotle's views of the universe.

A New Worldview The Catholic Church's condemnation of Galileo diminished the growth of science in Italy. The scientist who later brought together the ideas of Copernicus, Kepler, and Galileo was Isaac Newton. Among Newton's many accomplishments was the discovery of the universal law of gravitation. Newton published his proofs for this law in *Principia* (1687), demonstrating that gravity applied to objects on Earth and in space and was the force that held the planets in orbit around the sun.

Newton saw the universe as a giant machine with God as the prime mover who set the planets in motion. While Newton's ideas were accepted rather quickly in England, it took almost a century after *Principia* was published before they were generally accepted on the continent of Europe.

During a period of approximately 200 years, astronomers had developed a radical new cosmology, challenging the ideas of Aristotle and Ptolemy that were so widely held for about 1,400 years. Such rapid change in such fundamental beliefs shook the foundations of knowledge, but it was just an early step in replacing trust in tradition with reliance on observations and data.

Anatomical and Medical Discoveries

Much like medieval astronomy, medicine of medieval times was dominated by ideas from ancient Greece and was transformed in the 16th and 17th centuries. The work of the Greek physician **Galen** (2nd century C.E.) dominated the fields of anatomy and physiology. *Anatomy* refers to the structure of the bodies of humans, animals, and plants. *Physiology* refers to how those systems function.

Traditional Theory of Medicine Because Galen dissected animals rather than humans, his ideas about human anatomy were often incorrect. He thought two different systems of blood that flowed through the arteries and veins which controlled different bodily systems. According to Galen's humoral theory of the body and disease, the body was composed of four humors, namely blood, yellow bile, phlegm, and black bile. Galen believed disease was caused by an imbalance of the humors.

Challenges to Galen's Ideas Three physicians were most notable in challenging Galen's theories:

- **Paracelsus** (1493–1531) used observation and experiments to develop a theory of disease based on chemical imbalances in specific organs that could be treated with chemical remedies in exact dosages.

- **Andreas Vesalius** (1514–1564) emphasized anatomical research, including dissection of the human body. His book *On the Fabric of the Human Body* (1543) was a seminal work in the field of human anatomy.
- **William Harvey** (1578–1657) corrected Galen's ideas on the circulatory system, describing the body instead as an integrated system. Harvey's experiments demonstrated that the heart was the starting point for the circulation of a single system of blood that makes a complete circuit through the body's arteries and veins. Modern physiology is based on Harvey's ideas.

SCIENCE BEFORE AND AFTER THE RENAISSANCE		
	Medieval Science	**Post-Renaissance Science**
Goal	To demonstrate the truth of traditional Christian beliefs	To understand the natural world
Background of Natural Philosophers	Most were clergy members	Most were nonclerical
Classical Sources	Relied on Aristotle, Ptolemy, and Galen	Drew on a broad range of classical sources
Methods	Relied primarily on logical analysis	Combined observation and experiments with logic and mathematical calculations
Relationship with Religious Authorities	The Catholic Church judged the validity of scientific ideas	Science and religion were separate paths of inquiry

Persistence of Traditional Views

The acquisition of knowledge through inductive and deductive reasoning makes up an inquiry-based theory of knowledge, or epistemology—a way of understanding what we know and how we know it. While this new method dominated the thinking of natural philosophers during the 16th and 17th centuries, it did not generally clash with more traditional ideas about how people learned. Europeans continued to believe that spiritual forces governed the cosmos. Most scientists of the time believed in God and accepted a role for religion. Only later, in the 19th century, did people disagree over the boundary between science and religion.

Scientists of the 16th and 17th centuries also continued to accept two other traditional explanations about the world—alchemy and astrology:

- **Alchemy** was a medieval and Renaissance approach to chemistry primarily focused on discovering a method to turn common metals into gold. In a broader sense, alchemy was concerned with transformation and saw the world as filled with divinity.
- **Astrology** was originally synonymous with astronomy, but during the Renaissance it came to mean the study of the heavenly bodies as they influenced human activity.

These traditional ideas continued to appeal to elites and to some natural philosophers. For example, Kepler studied astrology and was interested in the idea of a sacred geometry in the universe. Newton wrote extensively about his experiments in alchemy. Paracelsus's view that a human being was a small reflection of the larger universe was similar to the basis of astrology. These traditional views persisted partly because, like the new science, they supported the idea that humans could understand the universe and make predictions about it.

LEADERS IN THE SCIENTIFIC REVOLUTION

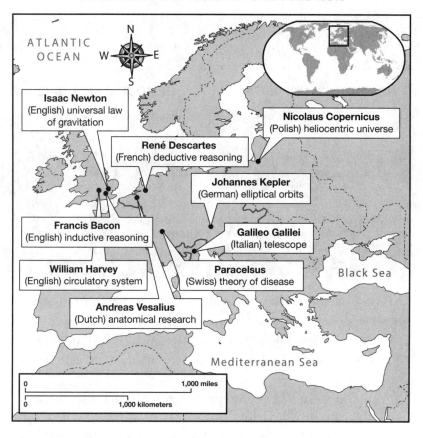

REFLECT ON THE ESSENTIAL QUESTION

Essential Question: *How did understanding of the natural world develop and change during the Scientific Revolution?*

Change Due to the Scientific Revolution	Explanation of Change

KEY TERMS

Scientific Revolution	mathematics	Galen
scientific method	astronomy	Paracelsus
Francis Bacon	cosmology	Andreas Vesalius
inductive reasoning	Nicolaus Copernicus	William Harvey
deductive reasoning	heliocentric	alchemy
René Descartes	Johannes Kepler	astrology
Isaac Newton	Galileo Galilei	
natural law	telescope	

MULTIPLE-CHOICE QUESTIONS

Questions 1–3 refer to the diagrams below.

GEOCENTRIC UNIVERSE   **HELIOCENTRIC UNIVERSE**

1. The two diagrams of the cosmos above illustrate the contrast between the ideas of

    (A) most Calvinists and most Lutherans in the late 16th century

    (B) most astrologers in the early 16th century and most astronomers of that time

    (C) most northern Europeans such as Kepler and most southern Europeans such as Galileo

    (D) most ancient scholars such as Aristotle and most 16th- and 17th-century scientists such as Copernicus and Galileo

2. Part of the context in which the change in thinking represented by the diagrams above occurred was an increase in

    (A) the use of experimentation to test ideas

    (B) the use of science to prove religion

    (C) the percentage of scientists who were also clergy members

    (D) the acceptance of Galen's theories about anatomy and physiology

3. Which of the following explains how the shift in ideas represented by the images influenced the study of astrology?

   (A) It became more popular because the new ideas provided evidence to support it.

   (B) It remained accepted as another way for humans to understand the universe.

   (C) It began to decline because religious leaders began to criticize it.

   (D) It quickly died out because it conflicted with the new ideas.

SHORT-ANSWER QUESTION

Use the passage below to answer all parts of the question that follows.

"Amidst other discourse, he [Isaac Newton]told me, he was just in the same situation, as when formerly, the notion of gravitation came into his mind. "Why should that apple always descend perpendicularly to the ground?" thought he to himself, occasioned by the fall of an apple, as he sat in a contemplative mood. "Why should it not go sideways, or upwards? But constantly to the earth's center? Assuredly, the reason is, that the earth draws it. There must be a drawing power in matter, & the sum of the drawing power in the matter of the earth must be in the earths center, not in any side of the earth. Therefore does this apple fall perpendicularly, or toward the center. If matter thus draws matter, it must be in proportion of its quantity. Therefore the apple draws the earth, as well as the earth draws the apple."

That there is a power like that we here call gravity, which extends its self through the universe & thus by degrees, he began to apply this property of gravitation to the motion of the earth, & of the heavenly bodies: to consider their distances, their magnitudes, their periodical revolutions: to find out, that this property, conjointly with a progressive motion impressed on them in the beginning, perfectly solved their circular courses; kept the planets from falling upon one another, or dropping all together into one center. And thus he unfolded the Universe. This was the birth of those amazing discoveries, whereby he built philosophy on a solid foundation, to the astonishment of all Europe."

—William Stukeley, (1687–1785) *Memoirs of Sir Isaac Newton's Life*, 1752

1. a) Describe the historical context regarding scientific thought when Stukeley wrote this passage.

   b) Explain ONE way in which the developments discussed in the passage challenged medieval scientific beliefs.

   c) Explain ONE effect scientific developments such as those discussed in the passage had on European intellectual development.

Topic 4.3

The Enlightenment

To love truth for truth's sake is the principal part of human perfection in this world, and the seed-plot of all other virtues.

—John Locke, letter to philosopher Anthony Collins, 1703

Essential Question: What were the causes and consequences of Enlightenment thought on European society, and what was its impact on intellectual development from 1648 to 1815?

The **Enlightenment**, or the Age of Reason, was the period of intellectual history set in motion by the application of the scientific method to political, social, economic, and religious institutions. It transformed many aspects of European society. Enlightened thinkers believed that applying reason to community problems would produce positive progress and people would become enlightened. Although the Enlightenment took different forms in various nations, two unifying themes emerged:

- a rational questioning of prevailing institutions and patterns of thought
- a general belief that human progress was possible

Old ideas were open to question. However, developments of the Enlightenment did not go unchallenged. Feudal, despotic, and religious restrictions continued to exist, and clerics in particular remained bulwarks of the old ways of thought.

Rational and Empirical Thought

Beyond the field of science itself, the Scientific Revolution had its greatest impact in the area of philosophy, where it led to two schools of thought—**rationalism** and **empiricism**. The two schools differed in their understanding of how people know what they know.

- Rationalism focused on innate reason, the concept that people are able to gain knowledge independently of what they observe. It emphasized that humans have the ability to recognize and understand the world through reason. Rationalism was very strong in France, led by philosopher René Descartes and his use of deductive reasoning.

- Empiricism was based on the idea that all human knowledge comes through what the senses can experience. Empiricism became prominent in England, led by Francis Bacon who advocated using inductive reasoning. (See Topic 4.2 for more on deductive and inductive reasoning.)

Proponents for both rationalism and empiricism argued that what people *knew* was more important than what they *believed,* and that investigation and reflection were more important than faith. In their emphasis on rational thought, both groups of thinkers were influenced by the classical Greek thinkers such as Socrates and Aristotle.

While this belief in the use of logic and reason undermined superstition and prejudice, it also set up a conflict with religious authorities. Revolutionary advances in physics and mechanics brought about a new concept of God as the creator of a universe that operated deterministically, like a machine. This creator does not intervene in the universe.

The workings of natural law could be investigated by anyone, while religious teachings relied on faith-based hypotheses. Obedience, fear, and dependence on ritual gave way to open-mindedness and autonomy. Enlightenment thinkers questioned religious institutions, arguing that human reason, not faith, was the key to improving society. The goal of many Enlightenment thinkers was to reduce the power of the church in society.

The emphasis on human reason led to a high value on human dignity. Many intellectuals denounced slavery. Some argued for an end to the use of torture of criminals and reserving capital punishment for the most abhorrent crimes, as well as for making prisons more humane.

The British Empiricists

Political philosophers tried to use the methods of the Scientific Revolution to analyze society's problems. Like mathematicians, they established basic facts as a starting point and systematically built upon them. People such as philosopher Thomas Hobbes believed that just as the natural world followed natural law so did human society. *Natural laws* were laws that applied to all humans and could be discovered and understood through observation and reason Both Hobbes and John Locke were empiricists who emphasized the importance of knowledge gained through experience, but because of when they lived, they reached radically different conclusions about how governments should operate.

Hobbes's *Leviathan* Like many philosophers, **Thomas Hobbes** (1588–1679) wrote in reaction to events he witnessed. He lived during the violent upheaval of the English Civil War and was appalled by the execution of King Charles I in 1649. In his book *Leviathan* (1651), Hobbes wanted to create a government that could guarantee peace and security for citizens. He argued that in a state of nature—in a society without government—humans would pursue their own survival and self-interest with no respect for the needs or rights of others. Each individual's life would be "solitary, poor, nasty, brutish, and short." In order to form "society," individuals would give up some of their rights to a sovereign authority. This authority must be very powerful—similar to a great sea monster from the Bible called a *leviathan.*

Hobbes espoused that once this new government was created, the people must live under the rules of that government. He favored an absolute monarchy, although not one based on divine right. He feared that a government with limits on its power could not command the respect and fear necessary to tame and control humans' naturally violent, self-seeking nature.

John Locke and Natural Rights Philosopher **John Locke** (1632–1704) believed that since humans are governed by natural law endowed by a creator, they possess **natural rights** that come from the creator as well. These rights are independent of any particular society or government. Many of his beliefs were shaped by his Puritan upbringing. Unlike Hobbes, who saw the horrors of the English Civil War, Locke lived through the peaceful transformation of power brought about by the Glorious Revolution in which absolute monarchy gave way with minimal bloodshed to Parliamentary sovereignty. Locke thus presented a more positive view of human nature than Hobbes.

In his most important work, *Two Treatises of Government* (1689), Locke argued that people are born with basic and inalienable rights, including life, liberty, health, and property. Like Hobbes, Locke argued that people willingly came together to form governments, forming a **social contract**—a mutually beneficial agreement struck between the people and those who would govern them. Unlike Hobbes, however, Locke believed that the purpose of such government was to protect people's natural rights. Should the government fail in this regard, the people could replace it with a new government. In fact, government only exists because of the tacit consent of the governed, and it is answerable to the people. Civil and political rights reside with the people and are not bestowed upon them by God or king. Locke's ideas about natural rights and limited government were influential with the American founders who wrote the Declaration of Independence and the Constitution.

Blank Slate In contrast to Hobbes, Locke argued that people are not naturally dangerous to each other. In his *Essay Concerning Human Understanding* (1690), Locke insisted that a person's mind at birth is a blank slate, often referred to by its Latin name, *tabula rasa.* According to Locke, people are neither bad nor good, but are motivated by self-interest. They derive all knowledge from what they experience with their senses, and they are thus capable of learning and improving themselves. Therefore, Locke emphasized the importance of education in creating a stable society.

The French Philosophes

The 18th-century intellectuals who popularized Enlightenment beliefs toward reason were known as the **philosophes** (French for "philosophers"). In the spirit of the Enlightenment, they criticized France's *ancien régime*—the country's feudal social and political systems under which the monarch, church, and nobility controlled society for their own benefit.

The philosophes sought social reform of the systems by applying the principles of the Scientific Revolution to them. They believed that natural laws governed social institutions similarly to those laws that governed the physical universe. Their task was to discern these natural laws and use them as the basis for reform. With their faith in reason and belief in fundamental natural laws, philosophes for the most part embraced progress, earthly happiness, and liberty as innate rights.

Source: Wikimedia Commons/ Maurice Quentin de La Tour

A 1753 portait of Jean-Jacques Rousseau

Jean-Jacques Rousseau One of the most influential French philosophes was the Geneva-born thinker **Jean-Jacques Rousseau** (1712–1778). Rousseau is famous for his treatise *The Social Contract* (1762), with its striking assertion that "man is born free, but everywhere he is in chains." Although the words seem like a call to revolution, Rousseau's next sentence went on to say he would now "show how they [the chains] are legitimate."

In contrast to those philosophers who saw education as a key to happiness, Rousseau viewed people in their natural state as free and happy. He argued that humanity enters into civil society to secure this freedom and happiness. His concept of the social contract was of an agreement among free individuals that gives government its legitimacy. The state exists to promote the liberty and equality of its citizens, and its laws should be respected only when they are supported by the general will of the people. Rousseau strongly opposed the idea of a republican form of government. Instead, he insisted that citizens should make laws directly, and the ideal state would be small enough that an assembly of all citizens would be possible.

Some politicians and historians have interpreted Rousseau's beliefs as upholding the principle that all citizens are bound by the general will with no possibility of dissent; in other words, they are "forced to be free." This interpretation could lead to a tyranny of the majority, and his ideas were later used to justify the French Revolution's Reign of Terror. (See Topics 5.4 and 5.5 for more about the French Revolution.)

Rousseau's views on education were distinctive for his time. While other thinkers saw education as training, he did not. In his book titled *Emile, or On Education* (1762), he defined the proper role of education as fostering the innate curiosity of each child, who should not be regarded simply as a small adult. They should not be harshly punished but should learn from the consequences of their actions. Children should learn by following their interests and reaching their own conclusions. Society's institutions corrupted humans and the aim of education should be to preserve the original, perfect natural state of the child.

Unlike many of his contemporaries, Rousseau maintained an ambivalent attitude toward reason and emphasized human emotion and sentiment—ideas that would connect him to the origins of Romanticism. (See Topic 5.8.)

Rousseau's Beliefs on Women Rousseau's views on women's roles in society were traditional—even conservative. Like many before him, he believed that the biological differences between the genders created distinctly different capabilities in all areas of life. Rousseau believed women should marry and stay at home to nurture children, rather than go out into the community to conduct business or participate in politics. He held the age-old idea that females should be subordinate to their husbands and fathers. According to Rousseau, women lacked the intelligence and characteristics to work side by side with men. To him, these beliefs were the natural laws of life that should not be challenged.

The prominent female English Enlightenment thinker and philosopher **Mary Wollstonecraft** (1759–1797), challenged Rousseau's position on women. In works such as *A Vindication of the Rights of Woman*, she advanced the idea that only through equal access to education, citizenship, and financial independence, could women's full potential be reached.

Voltaire One of the most influential philosophes was François-Marie Arouet (1694–1778), known by his pen name **Voltaire**. He was a brilliant writer and an accomplished historian. Voltaire fiercely advocated tolerance and freedom of religious belief and was known for his witty satirical critiques of the French clergy and aristocracy, which he deemed ignorant and corrupt. Voltaire coined the slogan *écrasez l'infâme*, meaning "crush the loathsome thing," a reference to the Roman Catholic Church. In his *Treatise on Toleration* (1763), Voltaire criticized religious fanaticism and superstitious lack of rationality. As did other philosophes, he held that the thought processes of the Scientific Revolution also should be applied to social institutions.

Voltaire was exiled from Paris for a time and was twice imprisoned in Paris's infamous prison, the Bastille. Upon his release, he moved to England, where he received a warm welcome from the leading literary figures of the day. He was fascinated with English society, with its greater tolerance of freedom of thought, and he learned English in order to read the works of John Locke. Voltaire was so impressed by English society that during his exile he wrote *Letters on the English* (1734), a biting satire that extolled the virtues of the English while demeaning French society.

Eventually Voltaire returned to France, where he published his masterwork, the short novel *Candide* (1759). It was his bitter commentary on the hope for progress. The new scientific discoveries had led to widespread optimism that social progress was inevitable. Many Enlightenment intellectuals argued that if God was not controlling human society, then humans could shape their future. Through reason, they could improve it. However, given the evidence of widespread human suffering, Voltaire rejected this optimism as unrealistic and unwarranted.

Denis Diderot Another French philosophe, **Denis Diderot** (1713–1784) was fascinated by the idea that everything in the natural world could be catalogued and described. He spent 26 years gathering contributions from more than 150 writers on science, technology, politics, religion, art, and virtually every other human endeavor. The result was a 28-volume work, the *Encyclopédie*—literally, "the circle of teachings." Diderot's *Encyclopédie* (1746) was controversial by its very premise, because it placed human reason as the foundation of all knowledge. All other forms of knowledge, including theological, were mere branches. Despite attempts at censorship, the *Encyclopédie* was widely disseminated across Europe and the Americas.

Montesquieu The Baron de Montesquieu, better known as simply **Montesquieu** (1689–1755), was a French lawyer and writer. As an aristocrat, Montesquieu was critical of the monarchs' usurpation of the traditional privileges of the aristocracy. Unlike other philosophes, he espoused a more favorable view of the Middle Ages, a time when the king's powers were balanced by nobility and clergy.

Inspired by the achievements of scientists in explaining the natural world, Montesquieu, like Voltaire and Diderot, attempted to apply scientific principles to political institutions and theory. In particular, he focused on the law. Montesquieu argued that the best system of government featured a separation of powers, a division of governmental authority into separate branches, such as the legislative, executive, and judicial. To Montesquieu, the British constitutional monarchy was a prime example of this: having a king, parliament, and judiciary. Each branch was granted specific powers, creating a system of checks and balances, the ability of each branch to limit the power of the other branches. This concept influenced the American founders, especially James Madison, the father of the Constitution.

Montesquieu explored such ideas in *The Spirit of Laws* (1748), a groundbreaking study of comparative law and political theory. He made the case for greater civil liberties, abolition of slavery, the elimination of religious persecution, and limits on the arbitrary application of state power. Montesquieu's work inspired modern political science and sociology.

Cesare Beccaria One of the most influential Enlightenment thinkers from Southern Europe was an Italian lawyer and philosopher **Cesare Beccaria** (1738–1794). Beccaria sparked a criminal justice reform movement when he brought scientific reasoning to bear in the field of criminal justice in his influential treatise *On Crimes and Punishments* (1764), inspired by Montesquieu and published with a detailed introduction by Voltaire. In this essay, Beccaria called for an end to the use of torture, a common tactic of the time used on suspects to obtain confessions. He argued that torture was irrational, because it might lead an innocent person to confess. He also denounced capital punishment as not only unnecessary but also a violation of basic rights, since the state does not have the right to take lives. His deterrence theory was based on Enlightenment views of man: As men are rational beings, punishment should be just severe enough to outweigh the possible rewards derived from committing the crime. Beccaria is considered the father of modern criminal law and criminal justice.

COMPARING AND CONTRASTING MAJOR ENLIGHTENMENT THINKERS		
Individual	Key Idea	Major Writings and Legacy
Hobbes	People give up individual freedoms for security Government must be powerful to keep peace	*Leviathan* Established the concept of the social contract
Locke	Government duty to protect citizens' natural rights to life, liberty, and property People's right to revolt if government abuses its power	*Second Treatise on Civil Government* Influenced Thomas Jefferson and the Declaration of Independence
Rousseau	The social contract between government and people The concept of general will (but intolerant of dissent from the general will, an attitude later used to justify tyranny)	*The Social Contract* Influenced the French Revolution and the doctrine of socialism
Wollstonecraft	Women's equality	*A Vindication of the Rights of Woman* Led to formation of women's rights groups
Voltaire	Freedom of religion Freedom of speech Defense of enlightened despotism	*Letters on the English* Supported the separation of church and state Advocated for individual freedoms
Montesquieu	Three branches of government The separation of powers to check absolutism	*The Spirit of Laws* Influenced the U.S. Constitution
Diderot	Tried to articulate the essential principles of every art and science	*Encyclopédie* Changed the way society views, organizes, and accesses knowledge Spread Enlightenment thinking across Europe
Beccaria	Criminal justice; abolition of torture Punishment consistent with crime committed, regardless of class	*On Crimes and Punishments* Led to criminal law reform and limits on the use of torture in parts of Europe

Spread of Enlightenment Ideas

Spurred by the Enlightenment's intellectual community that crossed beyond national boundaries, the 18th century saw the creation and growth of new civic institutions outside of government and the traditional university setting for the purpose of spreading and debating new social and political concepts.

The Growth of Civil Society

Coffeehouses and **salons** were popular and important new institutions that spread Enlightenment ideas. For a penny, coffeehouse customers could buy coffee, read newspapers, and discuss news and ideas. Political groups and societies often formed and met in coffeehouses. For the most part, coffeehouses were a male sphere. On the other hand, French discussion groups known as salons were often mixed gatherings, frequently hosted by an influential woman in her own home. Female *salonnieres* often provided crucial financial support and protection to intellectuals promoting reform.

One famous mathematician and philosophe who attended many salons was the **Marquis de Condorcet** (1743–1794). He was an early champion of social science and human rights. His advocacy of women's rights was extreme even among Enlightenment thinkers in the salons. While he believed that men and women had natural differences in addition to the biological ones, he held that justice and reason demanded equal education and political rights.

Other new civic institutions appeared during the Enlightenment. **Academies** were specialized groups, sometimes funded or protected by wealthy individuals or royalty, to investigate and promote knowledge, often in the areas of science, technology, and the arts. The Royal Society, founded by England's King Charles II, and the French Academy,

Source: Getty Images

Salons reflected both the intellectual passions driving French culture and the expanding opportunities for women during the Enlightenment.

begun by Louis XIV, allowed scientists to meet, share, and build upon one another's work. In addition, the first modern **lending libraries** emerged across Europe and the Americas, with the goals of collecting information and educating the citizenry, a condition seen as crucial to democracy.

As the power of the church diminished, secret organizations such as the fraternal brotherhood of Freemasonry became popular and members met in chapters known as **masonic lodges**. The all-male Freemasons grew from stonemasons' guilds of the Middle Ages to become the world's largest secret society. They eventually adopted rites of ancient religious orders, but they had no official Christian affiliation. Freemasonry sought to provide a moral and ethical framework that encouraged personal growth. It also grew into a worldwide network of like-minded men who relied on each other for comradeship, advice, and personal and business connections. The movement spread from Europe to the United States, where at least nine signers of the Declaration of Independence were Freemasons.

The Spread of the Printed Word

What made the spread of ideas possible during this time was not only new urban institutions where people could meet and discuss ideas, but also a revolution in print culture brought about by technology and supported by improved transportation. As the literacy rate rose significantly during the Enlightenment, there was widespread demand for books, engravings, pamphlets, periodicals, newspapers, and novels.

Not surprisingly, the new freedom of expression often met with censorship. Conservative religious and political institutions sought to prevent the spread of ideas they considered radical and dangerous. For example, Voltaire's printer was arrested, while Diderot desperately edited page proofs of the *Encyclopédie* on his own in an attempt to avoid censorship. Both philosophes were jailed for their writings.

Often, authorities tried to be discreet in their efforts to censor, as bans were both difficult to enforce and likely to stir public opposition. However, the Republic of Letters—the network of letters, journals, and other publications exchanged among Enlightenment thinkers—transcended national boundaries and thus disrupted censorship. Books banned in one country were printed in another and smuggled to where they were prohibited. French authorities were unable to destroy the print plates of the *Encyclopédie* as they were housed in Switzerland.

Challenges of New Cultures

During the Scientific Revolution, as European natural scientists and explorers traveled across the globe, their discoveries sparked new ways of thinking about humanity, religion, and nature, and led to the establishment of new fields such as anthropology. Yet there was disagreement about the nature of the societies these scientists and explorers were encountering. Rousseau proposed the idea of the "noble savage," who lived in a joyful state of nature that was as yet unspoiled by civilizing forces. While others, such as the French naturalist Georges-Louis Leclerc de Buffon, depicted the "ignoble savage," living in a backward condition, intellectually and morally inferior to European society. Although enlightened thinkers professed the belief in the equality of men, slavery was still a powerful economic force which would prove hard to abolish, and science would often be used to justify ill treatment of non-Europeans.

Religion and Toleration

As the Scientific Revolution progressed, a secular, or nonreligious, culture began to expand across Europe. The Enlightenment can be characterized, in fact, by its strong aversion to the institutions of the church. This is not to say, however, that Enlightenment thinkers opposed religion entirely, even if they opposed its distinguishing characteristics.

Natural Religion and New Ideas

Whereas traditional Christianity saw God as beyond human comprehension, most philosophes believed that human reason provided a path to understanding God. This natural religion argued that God exists in nature, not separate from it. His laws are natural laws that can be discovered through scientific study. Natural religion represented a challenge to the revealed religion of the church, in which God could be known only through revelation, faith, and miracles.

Deism The French philosophe Voltaire is well-known for using satire and wit in fighting religious hypocrisy. Voltaire argued (at least for a time) that there must be a God. He espoused **deism**—the belief that God had created the world and set it in motion (as a watchmaker may make a watch and wind it up) and then left it to run on its own according to natural law. While deists, like Voltaire, accepted God, they rejected organized religion and its insistence that those who disregarded its boundaries would face eternal damnation. Deism became widely accepted by the educated elite during the Enlightenment. For a brief time during the terror of the French Revolutionary period, it became the national religion of France. Among European nations, France was especially drawn to deism after centuries of religious wars and domination by the Catholic Church.

Atheism Voltaire's writings were highly influential on the evolving religious attitudes of Enlightenment intellectuals, among them was Denis Diderot. Diderot received a Jesuit education but turned to deism, following Voltaire's example, and then to **atheism**—the complete rejection of God and religion.

One of the first and most outspoken atheists of the Enlightenment was **Baron d'Holbach** (1723–1789), a French philosopher and contributor of science articles to the *Encyclopédie*. In his 1770 book, *The System of Nature*, d'Holbach proposed a materialistic godless universe in which everything could be understood through scientific reasoning—particularly physics. God, he thought, was an invention created by human ignorance and fear.

Skepticism The Scottish philosopher **David Hume** (1711–1776) advocated **skepticism**, which asserted that all knowledge and beliefs should be approached with doubt. In *An Enquiry Concerning Human Understanding* (1748), Hume undermined the religious texts by using logic to argue against miracles. In *Dialogues Concerning Natural Religion* (published after his death in 1779), he argued that human reason was not sufficient to prove the existence of God. He also disputed the idea of an afterlife and made a strong case that religion corrupts rather than contributes to morality. His critiques provided a systematic argument against religious authority.

Hume's skepticism was more radical than deism or atheism. In fact, it threatened not only religious authority but also the prevailing principles of the Enlightenment. To Hume, the fact that human senses were fallible called all experiences into question. Therefore, it was by no means certain that human reason could reveal universal truths, or that any universal truths even existed.

EMERGING BELIEF SYSTEMS OF THE 17TH AND 18TH CENTURIES		
Idea	Main Proponents and Influential Works	Beliefs
Deism	Voltaire • *Candide* (1759) • *Dictionnaire Philosophique* (1764)	• Believed that God had created the world, set it in motion, and then left it to run on its own according to natural law • Rejected organized religion
Atheism	Baron d'Holbach • *Christianity Unveiled* (1761) • *The System of Nature* (1770)	• Completely rejected God and religion • Proposed a materialistic godless universe in which everything could be understood through scientific reasoning
Skepticism	David Hume • *An Enquiry Concerning Human Understanding* (rev. 1758) • *Dialogues Concerning Natural Religion (1779)*	• Argued that all knowledge and beliefs should be approached with doubt • Argued that human reason was not sufficient to prove the existence of God • Argued against religious authority • Threatened both religious authority and Enlightenment principles

An Emphasis on Private Revelation

As deism, atheism, and skepticism were taking firm root in 18th-century Europe, new faith movements developed in reaction. Under the influence of Enlightenment thought, religion—formerly a matter of public allegiance to the established church—was held to be a matter of individual conscience. The new religious movements embraced this distinction, as it meant every conversion was proof of "true" belief.

Methodism Among those troubled by the new nonreligious -*isms* was the British Anglican priest **John Wesley** (1703–1791). Wesley experienced an intense personal revelation that led him to form the **Methodist** movement, which spread across England and beyond. Methodism is a Protestant Christian theology that focuses on a personal experience with God, through which any individual can earn salvation. This concept had great appeal to the working classes, as did Methodism's stress on the importance of charitable works. Wesley preached nearly anywhere so all people could hear his message. (See Topic 5.8 for more about Wesley and Methodism.)

Pietism Around the same time, another Christian religious movement, also responding to the desire for a personal relationship with God, sprang up in Germany and spread across Northern Europe. **Pietism**, which began among German Lutherans, emphasized mystical personal experience and the primacy (importance) of the Bible. This emphasis on personal piety predated and paved the way for the acceptance of Lutheranism in Northern Germany.

However, in keeping with the Enlightenment view of humans as creatures of reason, Pietism also regarded individual moral behavior as the key to salvation and considered all believers as lay priests of the church. Pietism was known for its enthusiastic and emotional religious services that welcomed members of every social class. The pietist movement promoted many educational reforms in 18th-century German-speaking Europe. Its members were encouraged to undertake evangelizing missions. John Wesley was influenced by the pietist movement when he encountered it in the American colonies, where he spent two years as a missionary.

FAITH MOVEMENTS OF THE 18TH CENTURY		
Faith Movement	Main Proponents	Beliefs
Methodism	John Wesley (British Anglican priest)	• Considered religion a matter of individual conscience • Focused on personal experience of God and salvation • Stressed charitable works
Pietism	German Lutherans	• Sought personal relationship to God • Emphasized mystical personal experience and importance of the Bible • Regarded individual moral behavior as the key to salvation and considered all believers as lay priests of the church • Promoted educational reforms • Encouraged members to undertake evangelizing missions

Mercantilism During the Enlightenment

From the 16th to the 18th centuries, mercantilism was bound to the belief that power equals wealth. A key goal of mercantile policy was the accumulation of monetary reserves, particularly gold and silver. Without a reserve of such wealth, a nation would be unable to maintain an army or navy, weakening its influence. To prevent wealth from flowing out of the country, protectionist policies were put into place imposing high tariffs on imports, unless they were raw materials to be transformed into finished goods for export. The goal was to produce a favorable balance of trade.

Mercantilism encouraged the establishment of colonies, which could be a source of precious metals and raw materials, as well as a captive market for manufactured goods from the home country. Laws such as the British Townshend Acts regulated trade in the colonies, which led to anger and protest in America. Production was regulated and monopolies enforced by officials such as Colbert, the French finance minister under Louis XIV.

The Challenge of New Economic Theories

Like absolutism in the political sphere (see Topic 3.7), mercantilism required strong state power to regulate economic activity so a nation could compete against other nations for the Earth's fixed supply of gold and silver. And like absolute monarchs, proponents of mercantilism considered the interests of subjects as subservient to the interests of the monarchy, an attitude that would be called into question by the Enlightenment concepts of natural rights and the social contract.

Physiocrats Challenges to the importance of the monarch also came from French thinkers who focused on the economy. **Physiocrats** argued that land and labor were sources of wealth. Like Locke, they saw government's function as the protection of life, liberty, and property.

Early physiocrat, **Anne Robert Jacques Turgot** (1727–1781), was an advisor to King Louis XV of France. He advocated for *laissez-faire*, a French phrase that means "leave alone." He thought government should not interfere in the economic sector by imposing regulations, particularly on trade. Turgot thought the economy would work best when all individuals were free to determine what goods they wanted and what work they would contribute. He rejected the mercantilist theory about the importance of building up gold reserves in the treasury.

Another physiocrat, **François Quesnay** (1694–1774), was a doctor and economic theorist. He believed that a state's economic strength was derived not from gold and silver but from agriculture. Industry and manufacturing, he felt, were "sterile" activities that ultimately did not produce wealth. While this idea would prove misguided, Quesnay demonstrated how to apply scientific reasoning to studying the economy. Quesnay called for reduced taxes, elimination of tolls, and an end to government restrictions on trade.

Adam Smith The most influential economic reformer was Scottish philosopher **Adam Smith** (1723–1790). Paralleling the scientists of his day who searched for natural laws governing the physical world, Smith searched for natural laws governing economic behavior. One of these laws, Smith believed, was that people were naturally social. For example, they cared if others suffered, and they were inclined to gather with each other and to trade goods.

Based on these beliefs, Smith laid out a series of principles of economic behavior that together formed a single, complete system. His 1776 book, *An Inquiry into the Nature and Causes of the Wealth of Nations* (commonly called *The Wealth of Nations*), marked the start of modern economic thought. Smith tried to answer basic economic questions, such as why some countries were wealthier than others. Like physiocrats, Smith attacked mercantilism for overregulating trade in an attempt to accumulate gold. Smith argued that the wealth of a nation came not from gold, but from the productivity of its workers.

He believed that Great Britain and other countries would be wealthier if they had fewer restrictions on trade. Unlike physiocrats, who thought agriculture was the primary source of wealth, Smith thought all forms of labor were valuable.

Another question Smith tried to answer was how an economy worked at all. Without any central authority allocating resources, raising or lowering prices, or setting wages, economies somehow adjusted to changing desires of people. It was as if an **invisible hand**, a force that no one could see, guided all economic decisions. Individuals made choices such as to buy or sell goods or to take or leave jobs based primarily on their own self-interests. When everyone did so, the competing self-interests balanced each other.

Smith recognized an important role for government in protecting property rights, preventing powerful businesses from misusing their influence, taking care of the disadvantaged, and promoting trade. But he is best remembered for his attacks on the excesses of government regulation under mercantilism. The system he described became known as **capitalism.**

REFLECT ON THE ESSENTIAL QUESTION

Essential Question: *What were the causes and consequences of Enlightenment thought on European society, and what was its impact on intellectual development from 1648 to 1815?*

Causes of the Enlightenment	Consequences of the Enlightenment	Influence on Intellectual Development

KEY TERMS

Enlightenment	Montesquieu	David Hume
rationalism	*The Spirit of Laws*	skepticism
empiricism	Cesare Beccaria	John Wesley
Thomas Hobbes	*On Crimes and Punishments*	Methodist
John Locke		Pietism
natural rights	coffeehouse	mercantilism
social contract	salon	physiocrats
philosophes	Marquis de Condorcet	Anne Robert Jacques Turgot
Jean-Jacques Rousseau	academy	
The Social Contract	lending library	*laissez-faire*
Mary Wollstonecraft	masonic lodge	François Quesnay
Voltaire	deism	Adam Smith
Denis Diderot	atheism	invisible hand
Encyclopédie	Baron d'Holbach	capitalism

Questions 1–3 refer to the passages below.

Passage 1

"If a covenant be made wherein neither of the parties perform presently but trust one another, in the condition of mere nature, which is a condition of war of every man against every man, upon any reasonable suspicion, it is void: but, if there be a common power set over them both with right and force sufficient to compel performance, it is not void . . . . . . in a civil estate, where there is a power set up to constrain those that would otherwise violate their faith, that fear is no more reasonable, and for that cause he which by the covenant is to perform first is obliged [morally required] so to do."

—Thomas Hobbes, *Leviathan*, 1651

Passage 2

"Where-ever therefore any number of men are so united into one society, as to quit everyone his executive power of the law of nature, and to resign it to the public, there and there only is a political, or civil society. And this is done, where-ever any number of men, in the state of nature, enter into society to make one people, one body politic, under one supreme government; or else when anyone joins himself to, and incorporates with any government already made: for hereby he authorizes the society, or which is all one, the legislative thereof, to make laws for him, as the public good of the society shall require; to the execution whereof, his own assistance (as to his own decrees) is due. And this puts men out of a state of nature into that of a commonwealth, by setting up a judge on earth, with authority to determine all the controversies, and redress the injuries that may happen to any member of the commonwealth."

—John Locke, *Two Treatises of Government*, 1690

1. Both Hobbes and Locke agree with which of the following ideas?
   (A) Absolute monarchies are the most efficient form of government because they keep order and provide stability to the population.
   (B) Parliamentary governments are the most efficient form of government because they represent the wishes of the people.
   (C) Social contracts are necessary to society because they mutually benefit government, individuals, and the entire community.
   (D) Governments should have very limited power and they should use that power with great restraint.

2. Hobbes' ideas in the first passage were most influenced by the

(A) English Civil War

(B) Glorious Revolution

(C) Stuart Restoration

(D) Act of Supremacy

3. Locke's ideas in the second passage were most influenced by which of the following?

(A) The English Civil War

(B) The Glorious Revolution

(C) Louis XIV's religious policies

(D) Elizabeth I's religious policies

SHORT-ANSWER QUESTION

Use the passage below to answer all parts of the question that follows.

"It is helpful to . . . think about the Enlightenment as a series of interlocking, and sometimes warring problems and debates. These were problems and debates which affected how the Enlightenment worked not only in Europe, but also in the rest of the world. . .This presentation of the Enlightenment sees this movement as a group of capsules or flashpoints where intellectual projects changed society and government on a world-wide basis.

However, this is a new interpretation. Until quite recently, it was normal to understand the Enlightenment as ultimately a unitary phenomenon, as if there was an entity called the Enlightenment. This version of Enlightenment saw it as a desire for human affairs to be guided by rationality, rather than faith, superstition or revelation, a world view based on science, and not tradition."

—Dorinda Outram, *The Enlightenment*, 2013

1. a) Describe ONE example that supports the author's argument that the Enlightenment was "guided by rationality."

b) Describe ANOTHER example that supports the author's argument that the Enlightenment was "guided by rationality."

c) Explain ONE way that events of the 18th century contradicted the view that the Enlightenment was "guided by rationality."

Topic 4.4

18th-Century Society and Demographics

The agricultural revolution transformed the earth and changed the fate of humanity. It produced an entirely new mode of subsistence, which remains the foundation of the global economy to this day.

—Robyn Davidson, *No Fixed Address: Nomads and the Fate of the Planet*, 2006

Essential Question: What factors contributed to demographic changes from 1648 to 1815, and what were the consequences of those changes?

The economy of preindustrial Europe had been based on cottage industry, merchant guilds, and subsistence agriculture produced on small landholdings and dependent on peasant labor. Most people lived in villages rather than cities. The population, slowly increasing for centuries, had been held in check by periods of epidemic, disease, and war. Low-productivity agricultural practices and poor or nonexistent transportation caused periodic disruptions to the food supply, leading to deadly famines.

By the 18th century, the population of Europe began to increase because of significant changes in agriculture and the economic transition toward industrialization. This burgeoning populace would experience life much differently from previous generations. Overall, levels of prosperity and material well-being rose, reflected in changing social and cultural behavior. At the same time, there was a vast increase in the numbers of poor, as displaced agricultural workers **migrated** to cities for work, cutting them off from traditional extended-family networks.

Population Growth

One revolution in modern history was the shift in demographic patterns, the trends in birth and death rates and population size, that emerged during the 18th and 19th centuries. One was a dramatic increase in population. In preindustrial Europe, the growth rate averaged less than 1 percent per decade. In the 1800s, that rate jumped to nearly 10 percent per decade.

In 1700, roughly 110 million people lived on the European continent. By 1800, the figure was about 190 million; in 1900, it was 423 million. Demographers measure population growth by comparing birth rates to death rates (mortality). In 1700, birth rates were slightly higher than death rates. However, by 1750, while birth rates remained stable, death rates began to plummet. Infant mortality decreased and life expectancy became significantly higher. By 1820, the birth rate was substantially greater than the death rate, creating a population explosion.

The new demographic pattern alarmed political economist Thomas Malthus (1766–1834). Like other Enlightenment thinkers, Malthus tried to apply scientific tools to what he observed around him. In 1798, he published *An Essay on the Principle of Population*, in which he demonstrated that while populations grew geometrically (by a constant multiple), the food supply could only increase arithmetically (by a constant amount). As the population grew at higher rates, it would inevitably run out of food. Malthus argued for severe limits to be placed on population growth to prevent famine.

The population continued to grow, yet Malthus's predictions didn't occur for several reasons. A revolution in how food was farmed was the primary contributor. This included land use, advances in farming technology, new crops, fencing land, and improved food transportation systems. Also, improvements in the health of many people, changes in European marriage patterns, and migration to cities were contributing factors for population growth.

The Agricultural Revolution

For centuries, most Europeans had experienced chronic undernourishment, living on a subsistence diet—just enough food to sustain life. This was a major cause of the high mortality rate. During the Enlightenment, thinkers used science to approach the problem of food shortages and famine. As a result, the late 17th and 18th centuries saw a second revolutionary transformation in Europe, the **Agricultural Revolution**, a series of breakthroughs that increased agricultural production.

Changes in Farming

The Agricultural Revolution changed how people farmed. It greatly increased food production, reducing the number and frequency of food-related crises.

Land Use Additional land became available for agricultural use through **land reclamation**, the process of changing lands to make them suitable for other uses—often farming. In England and the Netherlands, reclamation often required building dikes, or walls to prevent flooding from the sea. The engineering of dikes in the Netherlands was so successful that England hired Dutch engineer Cornelius Vermuyden (1595–1677) to drain the marshy fens in East Anglia. The resulting farmland was some of the most productive in the country. Other European states followed the same methods to clear and plant their woodlands and forests and drain their wetlands.

The Dutch led the way in **crop rotation**, the practice of growing different crops in a specific area so that the land could remain in continuous use without depleting the soil. This contrasted with traditional farming techniques in use since the Middle Ages, when land was left fallow, or uncultivated, for a period to restore nutrients. First, farmers in Flanders (a Dutch-speaking area in what is today Belgium) discovered that a four-year, four-crop rotation of wheat, barley, turnips, and clover would result in dramatically higher crop yields. Turnips and clover were rich in nitrogen, which replenished the soil. Turnips were especially important because they could remain in the ground in winter and their tops provided food for grazing livestock.

The idea of crop rotation then spread throughout Europe. For example, the British aristocrat Charles Townshend (1674–1738) observed crop rotation when he served as ambassador to the Netherlands. He established the process in Britain, starting on his own estates.

Advances in Technology and Science Advances in farming combined to create the Agricultural Revolution. Improved technology allowed for more food to be produced by fewer workers. Also, selective breeding techniques of British engineer Robert Bakewell (1725–1795) improved the size and health of livestock. (See Topic 3.3 for more scientific and technological improvments of the Agricultural Revolution.)

New Crops The effects of the Columbian Exchange—the interchange of plants, animals, diseases, and culture between the Americas and Europe—had been reflected in European diets since the 16th century. The exchange brought important new crops, including tomatoes, corn, and, perhaps most importantly, potatoes, which became a staple in Ireland by the 1750s. The potato had a shorter growing season than most grains, grew well in poor soil and cold climates, and was highly nutritious. (See Topic 1.8 for more information about the Columbian Exchange.)

Enclosures The **enclosure movement** was a new method of organizing and using land. The open field system ended with the enclosure movement of the late-18th century. In Britain, the **Enclosure Acts** allowed wealthy landholders to purchase the common areas, consolidate them into single farms, and enclose those farms with fences. Before long, much of the agriculture in Great Britain took place on commercial farms. (See Topics 1.10 and 3.3 for more on the open-field system and the Encolsure Acts.)

With enclosure, large-scale farmers could now plow and plant huge parcels of previously uncultivated land, greatly increasing the amount of food produced. On the other hand, enclosure brought ruin for small-scale farmers and peasants since many depended on the commons for survival. The enclosure movement forced many peasants out of farming and into cities in search of work (providing a low-wage source of labor for the Industrial Revolution).

Transportation

To transport their increasing supply of food, Britain and other countries of Western Europe were improving their internal transportation systems. Nations built new roads and widened existing ones, creating turnpike networks suitable for wheeled transportation. They strengthened bridges, linked canals and waterways, and gradually lifted road tolls—a remnant of feudal times. Eventually, European nations established railroad networks. All of these developments made it easier and less expensive to transport food to urban areas. Food transportation also was facilitated by the widespread adoption of a sterile canning process developed by French chef Nicolas Appert (1749–1841) at the request of Napoleon Bonaparte, who desired to improve the food supply for his field troops.

Improvements in Health

Along with the Agricultural Revolution, Europe's growing population was better-nourished and healthier for two additional reasons:

- Advancements in medical science included new understanding of disease transmission and the development of inoculation.
- Developments in engineering resulted in cleaner water, safer food, better sewage disposal, and improved hygiene.

The Danger of Infectious Diseases

Recurrent episodes of infectious disease had caused major rises in Europe's death rates. For some diseases, such as tuberculosis, the bacteria that caused them could be found all over Europe. Other diseases, such as malaria, were confined to certain regions or climates. Widespread diseases, or **epidemics**, swept through the continent in periodic waves and then mysteriously subsided, only to reappear later. Some epidemics, such as typhus and typhoid fever, spread as a result of unsanitary conditions and primarily affected the poor.

The epidemic of the **bubonic plague**, or Black Death, wiped out a third of the European population in the 14th century and then reappeared at approximately 20-year intervals until the early 18th century. In 1665, plague reduced the population of London by 16 percent, and in the years between 1710 and 1720, it killed a third of Marseilles, half the city of Danzig (modern-day Gdansk in Poland), and almost half of the cities of Prague, Copenhagen, and Stockholm. Historians do not know why the plague ended. Theories include immunity through repeated exposure, decline in the rats that carried the disease, isolation of infected individuals or areas, improved sanitation, and genetic mutations in the bacteria responsible for the disease.

The most devastating epidemic disease was **smallpox**, affecting all levels of society and changing the course of history as it killed off members of royal families. In the late 17th and 18th centuries, smallpox epidemics were a leading cause of death in Europe and Britain, eliminating as much as 13 percent of the population of each generation. Those who survived the disease were left disfigured and often blind.

The Anti-Epidemic Campaign

In the 17th century, the Scientific Revolution inspired many physicians to apply new techniques to investigating and treating infectious diseases. By looking at not only the patient but also the patient's environment, scientists discovered that unsanitary conditions, particularly in crowded urban areas, were connected to epidemics, and public health campaigns arose.

Near the end of the 19th century, smallpox was still killing as much as 10 to 20 percent of Europe's population. To combat it, variolation—an inoculation procedure of infecting someone with live smallpox virus taken from a blister of someone with a mild form of the disease—was introduced in Britain by **Lady Mary Wortley Montagu** (1689–1762), who had learned about it when she lived in Turkey. However, Edward Jenner (1749–1823) developed a safer alternative—the world's first vaccine—in 1796. Jenner had noticed that milkmaids who had cowpox, a similar but less virulent disease, did not get smallpox. He determined that giving people cowpox protected them from smallpox. With his new vaccine, Edward Jenner became known as the "father of immunology." Thanks to his treatment, smallpox soon declined across Europe and has since been eradicated worldwide.

Other Health Practices

Additional practices against disease became important during this period, including quarantining and improved personal hygiene. Rising standards of living and the increased food supply led to improved overall health, which meant stronger resistance to disease. The availability of silk and cotton cloth meant more sanitary bedding and clothing. A growing preference for tea and coffee meant that people often boiled water before drinking it. On the other hand, increased urbanization facilitated the spread of disease and new public health and sanitation concerns.

Marriage and Children

The European **marriage pattern** tended to limit population growth, at least for non-nobility. Its main features were late marriage age, small age difference between husband and wife, and the establishment of a nuclear household after marriage that is separated from both spouses' parents. People often waited to marry until they had enough resources to start their own independent households. Those unable to acquire such resources might never marry at all.

Consequently, the European marriage pattern represented an important check on population growth rates. However, this situation began to change, depending on social position. More and more rural peasants were forced to migrate to urban areas looking for work. This also released them from some of the social constraints imposed by families and village traditions. At the same time, the growing middle class was less troubled by financial considerations, making it possible for men and women to marry for status, companionship, or even love.

Children of Unwed Parents By the second half of the 18th century, the rate of babies born to parents not married to each other (sometimes called illegitimate births) began to show a rapid and dramatic increase. In Britain, France, and Germany, statistics suggest that fewer than 1 percent of babies were born out of wedlock in 1600; by 1800, this had increased to around 3 to 6 percent; by 1850, it was 20 percent or even higher. These figures indicate increased sexual activity between unmarried people, particularly those in urban areas who were removed from the control of family and community authorities. Despite the surge in births outside of marriage, unwed mothers still suffered brutal social stigma that in some cases left them with no recourse but prostitution and the abandonment of their children.

Foundling Hospitals Despite opposition from both the Catholic Church and the Church of England, some couples practiced birth control to avoid pregnancy. However, unwanted pregnancies continued to occur. No public financial support was available for unwed mothers. Killing an infant was a capital crime for which a number of women were hanged in the 18th century. The first foundling hospital—an institution that cared for unwanted children— was established in 1739 in Britain. Parliament announced that the hospital would accept all abandoned children it received, but that policy was quickly overturned when almost 15,000 arrived within the first year. Conditions at the hospital were harsh, with only about a quarter of children surviving to adulthood.

Birth and Infancy Childbirth, which almost always took place in the home, was dangerous, with high maternal and fetal mortality rates. However, more and better food and less infectious disease meant that once born, more children survived infancy. By the end of the 18th century, the traditional family pattern of many births and many infant deaths was shifting toward a pattern of fewer births and fewer infant deaths.

There was considerable variation in infant care both among different social classes and among different countries. Particularly in France, but also in Scandinavia, many women chose not to breastfeed, believing it to be unpleasant and bad for the mother's health. Instead, they hired other women called wet-nurses to breastfeed their infants. Wealthy women hired wet-nurses to live in their homes, while working women who could not maintain a live-in wet-nurse might send their babies off to live with hired wet-nurses, often for years.

Wet-nursing was popular even though it greatly increased the risk of infant mortality. Some women preferred it, while some women had no alternative. Either way, it was standard practice. In his influential novel *Emile*, the Enlightenment philosopher Jean-Jacques Rousseau urged mothers to breastfeed their own infants as one important step in a comprehensive plan for nurturing and educating children.

Changing Views of Childhood Before the 18th century, the concept of childhood as a developmental stage did not really exist. Children were regarded as small adults. In the upper classes, children were strictly disciplined, while in the lower classes, children were expected to work just as adults did.

The Enlightenment elevated childhood and coincided with the rise of a middle class possessing more resources to devote to children. John Locke discussed the development of children in his concept of *tabula rasa*, or blank slate, which included the belief that behavior and personality were learned.

In *Emile*, Rousseau similarly argued that children were born innocent and childhood should be a privileged period before the hardships of adulthood.

Young children should focus on play, exercise, fresh air, and freedom. Boys should then learn a craft to nurture hand-eye coordination. Formal education should be delayed until they reached their teens. Education for girls should focus on the skills they would need to be wives and mothers.

Source: Getty Images/ H. Armstrong Roberts

The Age of Innocence by Sir Joshua Reynolds

Artistic representations of children from this period reflected this Enlightenment attitude toward children. Portraiture of innocent, sweet children became popular. The painting *The Age of Innocence* by Sir Joshua Reynolds (1723–1792), which shows a barefoot young girl sitting outside absorbed by the natural beauty, was deeply admired by the public. *The Portrait of Isabelle Bell Franks* by Thomas Gainsborough (1727–1788) is another example of a painting of an angelic-looking child. One of the most famous works of the 18th century is Gainsborough's painting *The Blue Boy*. It is believed to be a portrait of the son of a wealthy London business family.

Education Before the Enlightenment, education had been mostly a privilege of the upper class, and university education focused on certain professions, such as law or medicine. The Scientific Revolution led to increased interest in education. As print materials became widely available during the Enlightenment, the demand for literacy rose. The 17th-century Czech educator John Amos Comenius (1592–1670) developed the first comprehensive system of universal education, and his ideas were extremely influential on Enlightenment thinkers.

In the late 18th century, Prussia became the first nation to implement compulsory universal education. The Prussian education system provided free compulsory public education for boys and girls ages 6 to 13; it also required teacher training, a universal curriculum, and mandatory kindergarten. The Prussian system was widely seen as effective and efficient and became a model for many other nations. The curriculum, which included folk tales and national history all taught in a common language, encouraged the development of a shared national identity.

France's educational system dated to the Roman Empire, but it served a small part of the populace and remained under church control. As early as the 17th century, convent schools, operated by orders of nuns such as the Ursulines, educated girls from the lower class as well as from the aristocracy.

During the French Revolution, rebels seized church properties, including schools. Enlightenment intellectual and politician Marquis de Condorcet (see Topic 4.3) developed a plan for a universal state educational system. The revolutionary government did establish new public schools for young men.

However, it could afford to maintain them only briefly. Not until 1802 did Napoleon lay the foundation for a modern school system in France. His goal was to produce loyal, unquestioning citizens. He left many elementary schools in the control of the church but established state-supported secondary schools that used a common curriculum taught in French. A system of universal secular elementary education was not fully in place in France until the 1880s.

Austrian **Empress Maria Theresa** (ruled 1740–1780) mandated in 1775 that all children ages 6 to 12 must attend school. Schools shared a unified curriculum and required teachers to complete training. The system was two-track, permitting only upper-class boys to continue on to secondary school.

Life in Cities

The Agricultural Revolution meant fewer workers were needed to produce food and many people could no longer make a living farming. European cities offered economic opportunities, and people seeking work flocked to them.

In the 18th century, these cities had growing populations consisting of many young people. They migrated to urban areas for jobs and entertainment that could not be found in rural areas. The migrants left behind their traditional communal values handed down for generations in the villages where they were born. Urban areas had shops, theaters, and other leisure activities for those who could afford them.

Urban Growth Patterns

In 1500, very few European cities, mostly in the Mediterranean area, had populations of more than 100,000. For the next 150 years, the growth of towns and cities was slow but steady. Between 1650 and 1750, however, a few major cities began to expand rapidly, notably Paris, Naples, Amsterdam, and London. In Amsterdam, the capital city of the Netherlands, many immigrants from Germany, France, Spain, and Portugal greatly increased the population. Large urban areas became concentrated in the north of the continent. Certain negative features of 18th-century city life confronted everyone:

- Cities were overcrowded and congested. There was not enough housing. Streets were too narrow for all the carts, carriages, and pedestrians.

- Cities were dirty. Human and animal waste was poured out of windows. Horse manure filled the streets. Sanitation was poor. Sewage systems, if they existed, were rudimentary. Water was impure and air was polluted from coal and wood that heated and lit homes and shops.

- Cities were noisy. Streets swarmed with noisy horse-drawn carriages, vendors, and even livestock.

Though city dwellers had higher incomes and more dependable food supplies than rural dwellers, their mortality rates were higher. This resulted from infectious disease, which spread rapidly in crowded and unsanitary areas.

The Seine River, which runs through Paris, France, was heavily polluted with sewage and was a health threat to citizens.

Nonetheless, urban populations continued to grow with the steady arrival of new migrants. And city life did improve over time as cities made efforts to provide drainage, light outdoor areas at night, and clean public streets regularly. Cities also undertook large-scale public works projects to build new sewage systems and roads. These works required higher taxes.

The Wealthy and the Poor

In the 18th century, city life also held many attractions. There was the allure of cultural and social activities. Lisbon, Portugal, was one of the wealthiest cities anywhere in the 1700s. Its location on the Atlantic Ocean became the most important trading port in the world. Likewise, Vienna, Austria, became a cultural center. European musicians and composers such as Mozart and Beethoven flocked to Vienna to find patrons to support their careers. The flourishing market economy of these and other European cities meant shops and vendors with captivating new fashions, foods, and consumer goods. The urban wealthy could enjoy a luxurious lifestyle.

Such pleasures were not available to the urban poor, however. They lived in crowded, unheated, and filthy slums. Their constantly growing population meant a chronic labor glut; competition for work pushed wages down. Poverty was widespread and severe. The close conditions of urban living made it obvious that wealth and opportunity were not equally available to all.

Unsurprisingly, there was great discontent among the urban lower classes. Many urban areas experienced riots in response to events that increased the misery of the poor, such as an increase in the price of bread, the main item in their diet. For example, Amsterdam's economy stagnated in the mid-1700s and there was a rebellion of citizens against the government's taxation system. Philanthropic groups, such as the Society for Public Welfare (1784) that promoted education, eventually were organized to aid needy citizens.

As cities continued to grow, so did the problems of the urban poor. Crime was rampant. Prostitution was prevalent, as was begging. Many poor city dwellers turned to drinking gin, relatively inexpensive and readily available, to assuage their suffering.

Evaluating Urbanization

Historians evaluating urbanization of the early industrial period have engaged in a standard of living debate. Economic historians focus on the steady overall rise in living standards and greater life expectancy. Social historians look instead at the destruction of centuries-old village traditions and the misery of the urban poor. Both agree that mass migration created a potential large-scale inexpensive urban workforce that would be crucial to support the beginnings of the Industrial Revolution. (See Topics 6.2 through 6.4 for more on industrialization.)

Essential Question: *What factors contributed to demographic changes from 1648 to 1815, and what were the consequences of those changes?*

Factors That Led to Demographic Changes	Consequences of Factors

KEY TERMS

migrate	Enclosure Acts	marriage pattern
Agricultural Revolution	epidemic	Nicolas de Condorcet
land reclamation	bubonic plague	Empress Maria Theresa
crop rotation	smallpox	
enclosure movement	Lady Mary Wortley Montagu	

MULTIPLE-CHOICE QUESTIONS

Questions 1–3 refer to the table below.

AVERAGE AGE OF FIRST MARRIAGE IN ENGLAND			
Period	Men	Women	Difference
1600–1649	28.1	25.6	2.5 years
1650–1699	28.1	26.2	1.9 years
1700–1749	27.2	25.4	1.8 years
1750–1799	25.7	24.0	1.7 years

Source: E. A. Wrigley and R. S. Schofield, *The Population History of England, 1541–1871* (Cambridge, England: Cambridge University Press, 1989). Averages are the mean based on data from 13 communities.

1. Which argument about marriage age from 1600 to 1800 does the table most clearly provide evidence to support?

   (A) Marriage age for men steadily increased.

   (B) Marriage age for women changed more than marriage age for men.

   (C) The age difference between men and women stayed pretty constant.

   (D) Marriage age for both men and women generally declined.

2. Which of the following changes was occurring at the time as the changes shown in the table?

   (A) Migration from cities to villages was increasing because people wanted to escape the unhealthy conditions in cities.

   (B) Landowners were relying more on serfs as an agricultural workforce because they felt they were losing too much of their labor force.

   (C) Families in both rural and urban communities were having more children because people felt they needed children to provide for them as they aged.

   (D) Unmarried couples were having children more commonly because urban residents felt fewer restrictions on their behavior than did rural residents.

3. European marriage patterns during the 17th and 18th centuries resulted in which of the following?

   (A) An increase in multigenerational households

   (B) An important check on population growth rates

   (C) More emphasis by religious leaders on increased birth control

   (D) Less importance placed on the development of children

SHORT-ANSWER QUESTION

Answer all parts of the question that follows.

1. a) Explain ONE cause of the decrease in child mortality in Europe during the 18th century.

   b) Explain ONE effect on family structures of the decrease in child mortality in Europe during the 18th century.

   c) Explain ONE effect on demographic patterns of the decrease in child mortality in Europe during the 18th century.

Topic 4.5

18th-Century Culture and Arts

The strongest principle of growth lies in the human choice.

—George Eliot (1819–1880)

Essential Question: How was European cultural and intellectual life maintained and how did it change from 1648 to 1815?

During the 18th and early 19th centuries, the reduction in child mortality and increase in life expectancy formed the demographic foundation for new attitudes toward marriage, children, and families. The growing money economy was creating a new middle class with education and financial means.

There was a new, powerful desire for consumer goods and an unfamiliar ability to afford at least some of them, particularly among wealthier city dwellers. Art, architecture, and music began to shift to express Enlightenment ideas, as well as the values of a growing middle class.

Advancing a Market Economy

The population explosion in the late-18th century occurred because of improvements in the food supply and reductions in infectious disease. Occasional famines still occurred, but for the most part, there was sufficient food to sustain the population by the mid-18th century.

The subsequent demographic changes brought great social change. Lower mortality and better nutrition meant Europeans, particularly in Western Europe, were healthier than ever. In addition, education levels were rising, and culture was becoming more accessible to a greater number of people.

The Consumer Revolution

By the end of the 18th century, a high proportion of Western Europeans experienced unprecedented levels of relative material prosperity. For centuries, life for most Europeans had been dominated by scarcity. Now a **Consumer Revolution**, propelled by the disposable income of the growing middle class, swept across Europe, bringing both a powerful desire for consumer goods and an unfamiliar ability to afford at least some of them, particularly among city dwellers.

Increase in Commercial Production In preindustrial Europe, the household had traditionally been the site of production for most people. Now, however, a population of merchants, financiers, and wage earners—people no longer dependent on the land for livelihood—shared a common bond. They embraced consumption to satisfy *desire* rather than *necessity*, and the wealthy saw luxury items and fashion as a way to display their economic status. This attitude was emulated by the masses but with cheaper fashions and edibles, ensuring that the consumer revolution carried through to all levels of society.

Household goods and products began to shift from being mostly homemade to mostly commercially produced. Consumerism, in turn, brought jobs and stimulated commerce, creating even more wealth. The new consumer economy eventually became a permanent feature of capitalist economies worldwide.

Consumer Goods for the Home A number of factors, such as increased trade both within Europe and with Asia and the American continents, resulted in an increased supply and variety of consumer goods. Those who could not afford imported luxury goods made up a market for lower-cost domestic imitation items, allowing the lower classes to emulate the upper classes. Asian-imported ceramics, particularly Chinese porcelain, were so popular that importers could not keep up with demand, sparking a domestic ceramic industry. Entrepreneur Josiah Wedgwood (1730–1795) developed less expensive imitation ceramics that became very popular. Wedgwood's success was built not only on quality but also on his understanding of the new consumer market. He realized that items used by the upper class would become desired by the middle class. When Queen Charlotte, wife of George III, purchased some of his ceramics, he convinced her to let him use her name in advertising.

OCEAN TRADE BY EUROPEANS IN THE 19TH CENTURY

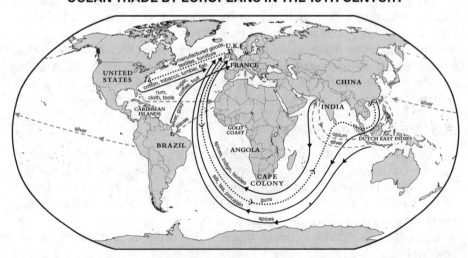

In addition to porcelain dishes, other household consumer items in great demand included mirrors, cotton and linen goods, silks, decorative prints, and jewelry. These took on increasing importance as status symbols for the owner. Consumers desired these items for their usefulness but even more for their ability to confer social status. Demand for such consumer items inspired domestic glass making as well as silk and cloth manufacturing.

Food and Drink Some of the most popular commodities of the 17th and 18th centuries were consumables. Europeans were able to obtain coffee, hot chocolate, tea, and liqueurs. Sugar, once an exotic luxury item, became widely available and inexpensive as a result of slavery in the New World, and the consumption of sugar skyrocketed among all social classes.

New Leisure Venues Soon, coffeehouses and other public spaces sprang up, allowing the shared social consumption of these new beverages. Located mostly in urban areas, these venues served as a meeting place for all classes of male society, encouraging a healthy exchange of ideas. Women sometimes were proprietors or servers at coffeehouses, but otherwise they were unwelcome. The coffeehouse began to decline in popularity during the 1800s as homes grew increasingly comfortable and privacy became more desirable; some coffeehouses later evolved into private men's clubs while tea shops became popular with women.

In villages and more rural areas, taverns and alehouses were places to socialize, converse, dine, and drink alcohol. Taverns that offered sleeping accommodations to travelers were called *inns*. In fact, until the end of the 18th century, when the first restaurants began to appear in France, inns and taverns were the only places to dine outside of the home. They were popular meeting places to conduct business affairs and hold meetings, so they were sometimes referred to as "public houses" or "pubs."

As Europe grew increasingly urban, there was a dramatic increase in the number of **theaters** and **opera houses**, designed to cater to a new and broader audience—the growing middle class.

New Printed Materials As an alternative to coffeehouses, lending libraries opened, making books and other printed materials available to those who could not afford to buy them. This promoted the exchange of ideas begun in the new leisure venues. This led to the concept of a "public opinion," or shared viewpoint on an issue. In spite of attempted censorship by religious and political leaders, the public was becoming increasingly literate throughout the 18th century.

Many varied printed materials became available to communities. These included newspapers, periodicals (magazines), books, pamphlets, and Denis Diderot's 28-volume *Encyclopédie*, the collection of contributions from more than 150 writers on science, technology, politics, religion, art, and virtually every other human endeavor.

Changing Attitudes and Identities

The growing desire for consumer goods changed not only spending behavior but also society's attitude toward labor since individuals—particularly women—needed money to purchase the new goods they desired. Work outside the home—wage-earning labor—was necessary to maintain the household and purchase the consumer items.

Spurred by demographic growth in the 18th century, the Consumer Revolution resulted in a new type of social identity. Once people had the opportunity to choose from a variety of consumer goods, those goods became more than just functional items. The goods began to represent one's individuality and social position. The family unit, in general, had shifted from a unit of production to one of consumption. Consumer goods became increasingly important in the home, the locus of domestic life.

"HA, HA! YOU MUST LEARN TO LOVE ME."
Vide " The Bottle In

Source: Getty Images

The expressions on the faces of the family in this British cartoon suggests that not everyone was pleased with the food they were importing.

Family and Private Life

The Enlightenment had brought a rethinking of old attitudes toward home life, childhood, and education. During this period, many long-held social patterns were rethought though others remained in place.

Concern for Privacy

A new concept of the home reflected the shifting attitudes of consumers. Formerly, a typical home might consist of a few rooms that served multiple functions. With the advent of the Consumer Revolution, homes began to be designed with specific rooms for specific functions, each decorated appropriately. Privacy became a central focus, leading to developments such as the **boudoir**. Originally intended as a quiet space for prayer, by the second half of the 18th century, the boudoir became a private retreat set aside specifically for the wife—a place for her to dress, read, relax, and entertain, "free" from her husband and from the traditional role assigned to her. The evolution of the boudoir reflects the emerging concept of **domesticity**, the idea of the home as a private sphere distinct from the encroachments of the public world. It served as a refuge from outside influences.

This new concept of domestic space was reflected in the sentimental novel, a popular 18th-century literary genre that celebrated feeling as opposed to reason. It sought an emotional response from readers. The main characters were often females, and virtue was a main theme. The women were either virtuous or their virtue was imperiled or lost.

- The novels of **Samuel Richardson** (1689–1761), such as *Pamela* and *Clarissa*, emphasized the vital role private domestic spaces served in the lives of his female characters.

- Jonathan Swift (1667–1745), in the poem "The Lady's Dressing Room," used a fragrant boudoir as a metaphor for the female body.

- Later examples include the works of **Jane Austen** (1775–1817), Charlotte Brontë (1816–1855), and George Eliot (1819–1880). Their heroines followed the social rules of the time, but their observations and private emotions were refreshingly acute and independent. (George Eliot was actually a woman, Mary Ann Evans. She used a man's name for her books since it was easier for a man to publish and sell works of literature.)

Source: Getty Images

Jane Austen wrote books for a popular audience. Her books and movies based on them remain so popular that she was portrayed on modern British currency.

The Private Life and the Public Good in Art

During the 17th and 18th centuries, a new artistic movement spread. In painting, architecture, and music, the focus became grandeur, ostentation, and unimaginable opulence.

The Baroque Movement

In the 17th and early-18th centuries, the **Baroque movement** that had been inspired by the religious fervor of the Protestant and Catholic Reformations dominated European art. Royal courts and religious leaders, hoping to awe viewers and listeners with the power of art, provided patronage to support painters, architects, and musicians. Some states established official "academies" to exhibit the works of artists judged suitable.

Baroque Music Baroque composers also depended on the patronage of royalty and aristocrats, and they wrote many compositions to be performed either as part of church services or at the royal court. **Johann Sebastian Bach** (1685–1750) wrote numerous *cantatas,* vocal pieces featuring instrumental accompaniment, for the Leipzig church that supported him. He received a commission from a Brandenburg nobleman to compose his famous *Brandenburg Concertos.*

Along with the cantata, the Baroque period saw the development of other musical forms, particularly opera and oratorio, large-scale dramatic concert pieces based on religious subject matter. The prolific composer **George Frideric Handel** (1685–1759) wrote nearly 50 operas and 30 oratorios. He composed *Water Music* at the behest of King George I of England, who desired a concert on the Thames River. Handel's masterpiece, *Messiah* (1741), is renowned for its dramatic and stirring "Hallelujah Chorus."

Source: Getty Images

This sculpture by Bernini of an angel holding a cross is one of a series of ten he planned for a bridge in Rome. Like other Baroque sculptors, he tried to portray energy and movement in his works.

Baroque Art and Architecture Baroque architects constructed royal palaces, such as the Palace of Versailles in France with its impressive entrance halls, magnificent staircases, lavish reception rooms, and extravagant decorative gilding. In painting, Baroque artists concentrated on religious themes and portraits of royalty. King Philip IV appointed the great Spanish artist **Diego Velásquez** (1599–1660) as the official painter of the Spanish court. Velásquez's work includes numerous portraits of members of the royal family, including his masterpiece *Las Meninas.*

The creator and master of baroque sculpture **Gian Lorenzo Bernini** (1598–1680) was also an accomplished architect. He was commissioned by Pope Urban VIII to renovate Saint Peter's Basilica and create several ornate chapels and piazzas near the Vatican. His designs included monumental open spaces flanked by sculptures in marble and bronze.

The Evolution Away from Baroque Style

Particularly in Protestant countries, the middle class began to grow in the 18th century. These people could now afford luxuries such as art and books for their homes. As a result, art and literature increasingly reflected the values of these growing middle-class consumers, moving the Baroque in new directions.

Dutch Golden Age While appearing during the Baroque period, the art from the "Golden Age" of Dutch painting highlighted the increasing emphasis on private life and the growing importance of the middle class:

- Frans Hals (1582–1666) created realist paintings of a wide swath of humanity. He portrayed wealthy and influential aristocrats, clerks and members of guilds, colorful entertainers, and typical working-class men and women.

- The prolific Dutch painter and printmaker **Rembrandt van Rijn** (1606–1669) painted mainly portraits and biblical scenes, including such figures as Jesus and David, early in his career, but many of his most respected works focus on common people in everyday domestic settings or in nature. His paintings reveal a deep sense of humanity, regardless of the subject's station in life.

- **Johannes Vermeer** (1632–1675) painted mostly domestic interiors, often, as in *The Milkmaid,* showing women engaged in simple chores. *Girl with the Pearl Earring* is another of his famous paintings.

None of these artists received royal patronage, as perhaps is indicated by their broad choice of subject matter. Regarded today as among the finest artists in history, all three men had difficulty earning a living and died in poverty.

Source: Wikimedia Commons
The Milkmaid by Johannes Vermeer

Rococo By the mid-18th century, the Baroque style had begun to evolve, and a looser, more graceful art form known as Late Baroque, or **Rococo**, spread across Europe. In contrast to Baroque glorification of churches and castles, Rococo art was secular, exuberant, and hedonistic. It reflected a general shift in emphasis from the public to the private sphere. This made it well-suited to the private interiors of upper-class homes and salons. It featured fluid lines; light, airy colors with gilt touches; painted ceilings; decorative mirrors; small sculptures; and a fascination with Chinese figurines and screens. Representative artists working in this style included the French artists Jean-Antoine Watteau (1684–1721) and Jean-Honoré Fragonard (1732–1806).

Neoclassicism

The Rococo period was short-lived. Near the end of the 18th century, as the Enlightenment focus on the individual continued to grow, the Rococo movement gave way to **Neoclassicism**. In contrast to Baroque glorification of church and court, Neoclassicists honored the secular values of reason and order and upheld the classical ideals of simplicity and symmetry. Neoclassicism was inspired by the cultural values of ancient Greece.

Neoclassicism in Art and Architecture Neoclassic artists and architects avoided ornamentation, preferring simple harmonious forms that revealed an underlying proportion and harmony. The French artist **Jacques-Louis David** (1748–1825), whose works inspired many during the French Revolution, produced perhaps the quintessential expression of Neoclassical ideals in *Oath of the Horatii*, painted in Rome and based on an ancient Roman legend. The painting, which depicts three brothers saluting their father as he hands them their swords before a deadly battle, forcefully evokes stoic self-sacrifice, calm inner strength, and devotion to duty.

Source: Wikimedia Commons
Oath of the Horatii by Jacques-Louis David

The Neoclassic influence in architecture can be seen in the **Pantheon** in Paris, which is modeled on the ancient Pantheon in Rome. Originally intended as a Jesuit church, it was given new secular purpose during the French Revolution as a mausoleum for great French citizens, among them Voltaire and Rousseau.

Neoclassicism in Music In the 18th century, music also went through a profound stylistic transition. Composers such as **Wolfgang Amadeus Mozart** (1756–1791) reflected the ideas of the Enlightenment. His music often focused on secular rather than religious themes, and it emphasized order and balance rather than drama and emotion.

Neoclassicism in Literature England produced the most influential writers of this period, also known as the Augustan Age for its imitation of the classical Roman writers Horace and Virgil. It also saw the development of a number of literary forms, including political satire, melodrama, and the modern novel (including many new subgenres).

NEOCLASSICAL AUTHORS	
Author	Selected Works and Style
Daniel Defoe (1660–1731)	• Written as a series of letters, the story *Robinson Crusoe* describes the adventures of a shipwrecked man on a deserted island who learns to survive and finds redemption in nature without guidance from the church. • The novel explores economic issues of that time.
Samuel Richardson (1689–1761)	• *Pamela* and *Clarissa* feature women who defend their chastity. • Richardson originated the *epistolary novel*, a fictional work written in the form of letters.
Henry Fielding (1707–1754)	• Fielding was a novelist and dramatist famous for the humorous novel *Tom Jones*, in which the protagonist faces a colorful cross-section of social classes. • The major theme of *Tom Jones* is the struggle to maintain one's virtue when confronted with rogues, hypocrites, and villains.
Johann Wolfgang von Goethe (1749–1832)	• Goethe portrayed idyllic pastoral life and emphasized emotions over reason. • *Faust* is a play about a man who sells his soul to the devil for knowledge and wealth, also addresses man's search for meaning.
Jane Austen (1775–1817)	• Her novels included *Sense and Sensibility*, *Pride and Prejudice*, and *Emma*. • Austen focused on the morals and social behavior of the English middle and upper classes at the turn of the 19th century.

REFLECT ON THE ESSENTIAL QUESTION

Essential Question: *How was European cultural and intellectual life maintained and how did it change from 1648 to 1815?*

Cultural and Intellectual Changes	Effects of Changes

KEY TERMS

capitalism	Baroque movement	Neoclassicism
Consumer Revolution	Johann Sebastian Bach	Jacques-Louis David
theater	George Frideric Handel	Pantheon
opera house	Diego Velásquez	Wolfgang Amadeus Mozart
boudoir	Gian Lorenzo Bernini	Daniel Defoe
domesticity	Rembrandt van Rijn	Henry Fielding
Samuel Richardson	Johannes Vermeer	Johann Wolfgang von Goethe
Jane Austen	Rococo	

MULTIPLE-CHOICE QUESTIONS

Questions 1–3 refer to the painting below.

Source: Gallery of Honous, Rijksmuseum

In the Rembrandt painting, *The Syndics of the Amsterdam Drapers' Guild* (1662), six men are a committee responsible for inspecting the quality of the clothe produced in Amsterdam.

1. The painting above best reflects what artistic development of the period?

   (A) Dutch Golden Age art often portrayed common domestic settings.

   (B) Neoclassic art often depicted religious scenes.

   (C) Baroque art included lavish portraits of royalty.

   (D) Romantic art returned to works of harmony and balance.

2. Which of the following historical developments enabled artists such as Rembrandt to create paintings such as the one shown?

   (A) The conflict between Roman Catholics and Protestants resulted in competition among religious groups to support artists.

   (B) The rise of commercial elites in centers of trade created a new economic class of people who could support artists.

   (C) The development of the concept of the divine right of kings caused monarchs to believe they had a duty to support artists.

   (D) The division of the Holy Roman Empire into about 300 sovereign principalities produced more rulers with resources to support artists.

3. The style of this painting demonstrates a shift from earlier works of art because it

(A) focused on everyday life more than did Italian Renaissance paintings

(B) portrayed distorted people and objects more than did Mannerist paintings

(C) reflected religious themes more than did the Baroque paintings

(D) emphasized proportion and harmony more than did Neoclassical paintings

SHORT-ANSWER QUESTION

Use the passage below to answer all parts of the question that follows.

"Happily for him, a love of the theatre is so general, an itch for acting so strong among young people, that he could hardly out-talk the interest of his hearers. From the first casting of the parts to the epilogue, it was all bewitching, and there were few who did not wish to have been a party concerned, or would have hesitated to try their skill . . . .

[The] inclination to act was awakened, and in no one more strongly than in him who was now master of the house; and who having so much leisure to make almost any novelty a certain good, had likewise such a degree of lively talents and comic taste as were exactly adapted to the novelty of acting. The thought returned. 'Oh for the Ecclesford theatre and scenery to try something with'...Henry Crawford, to whom, in all the riot of his gratifications it was yet an untasted pleasure. Was quite alive at the idea... 'Let us be doing something. Be it only half a play, an act, a scene; what should prevent us? Not these countenances, I am sure,' looking towards the Miss Bertram; 'and for a theatre, what signifies a theatre? We shall only be amusing ourselves. Any room in this house might suffice.' . . .

[N]othing in the world could be easier than to find a piece which would please them all. [Edmund] was determined to prevent it, if possible, though his mother, who equally heard the conversation which passed at table, did not evince the least disapprobation."

—Jane Austen, *Mansfield Park*, 1814

1. a) Describe ONE way this passage could be used as evidence to support the claim for the growth of leisure venues.

   b) Describe ONE sentence or phrase in this passage that provides evidence that some people resisted the growth of leisure venues.

   c) Explain ONE part of the context in which this passage was written.

Topic 4.6

Enlightened and Other
Approaches to Power

All religions must be tolerated. . . .
[E]very man must go to heaven in his own way.

—Frederick the Great (1712–1786)

Essential Question: How were political power and religious toleration influenced by Enlightenment thought from 1648 to 1815?

New political theories based on Enlightenment ideals challenged the existing system of European absolutism in the 17th and 18th centuries. These new ideals spurred a number of rulers to consider themselves enlightened, using their power to promote industrial, educational, societal, and legal reforms. In addition, a new tolerance of religious differences began to take hold.

Challenges to Absolutism

As philosophes reevaluated the political realm in light of the new ideas of the Enlightenment, movements in favor of limits on government power swept across Europe and the Americas. However, **absolutism** still dominated European nations in the 1600s and 1700s. Under this system, monarchs held total, or absolute, power, which many claimed as a divine right granted to them by God. Therefore, they saw themselves as answerable only to God and not to the people they ruled.

New Ideas

Some Enlightenment philosophers believed that a strong monarchy was a good form of government. However, for the most part, they rejected the idea that the monarch had a divine right to power. Instead, even the more conservative Enlightenment thinkers tended to agree that monarchs were entrusted with power by means of the social contract and that the state originated from the consent of the governed.

Such thinkers believed that as long as both the ruler and the ruled followed the social contract, the government was right. But what was the recourse if the monarch did not act for the good of the people? People are born with certain civil and political rights, the philosophers believed. Once formed, government's role was to secure its citizens' liberty and happiness—rights derived from natural law before the formation of government. Humans had an inalienable right to pursue their own happiness. These beliefs about human nature, in particular John Locke's ideas of the social contract and the political ideologies derived from them, were used to justify many revolutions, beginning with the Glorious Revolution of 1688 in England. Thomas Jefferson, in the Declaration of Independence, set the beliefs forth as the rights of "Life, Liberty, and the pursuit of Happiness."

Enlightened Absolutism

While the ideals of the Enlightenment found voice in political revolution, most philosophes advocated not revolution, but political reform—and unsurprisingly, considering their education and sophistication, they tended to look for this reform from above (rulers and monarchs), not below (citizens). Many European rulers looked to the philosophes for fresh ideas about how to strengthen state control and streamline bureaucracy, reform and modernize social institutions, better manage resources, and increase national prosperity.

Known as **enlightened monarchs**, or enlightened despots, these 18th-century rulers embraced Enlightenment ideals to the extent that they could further their goals while rejecting concepts that expressly limited their own political power. The philosophes were not hostile to **enlightened absolutism**, as this approach to governing came to be known, since most did not oppose monarchy unless the monarch violated the social contract.

Enlightened Rulers The attitudes of rulers toward Enlightenment thinkers varied considerably from country to country. Ironically, the monarchies of Britain and France, nations with the most visible and influential public intellectuals, regarded the movement with indifference (Britain) or hostility (France, which in many cases censored or exiled movement leaders). In contrast, Catherine the Great of Russia, Frederick II of Prussia, and Holy Roman Emperor Joseph II welcomed Enlightenment ideas into their courts, providing financial support and embracing reforms.

Important Reforms While each enlightened monarch focused on concerns specific to his or her nation and interests, common threads link their achievements. In general, the enlightened despots were drawn to reforms that weakened the church and the aristocracy, whose power they recognized as a potential threat to their own. To this end, they limited the ability of the nobles to punish the peasants, abolished certain tax exemptions for the clergy and nobility, established a measure of legal protection for religious toleration, worked to codify laws, and supported internal improvements. For example, King Frederick of Prussia ordered the cultivation of potatoes to help the soldiers' diet and also to respond to rising bread costs. Frederick reportedly described his reforms by saying "I am the first servant of the state." When contrasted with Louis XIV's declaration a century earlier that "I am the state," Frederick's words neatly summarize the shift in attitude during the Age of Reason.

18th-Century Monarchs

During the 18th century, Enlightenment ideals spurred a number of rulers to engage in enlightened absolutism. Enlightened monarchs, including Frederick II of Prussia and Joseph II of Austria, maintained absolute power but often used it to promote industrial, educational, societal, and legal reforms.

Prussia Gains Power

King **Frederick William I** (reigned 1713–1740) reformed the Prussian military structure and technology with original methods. (See Topic 3.6.) He had a professional standing army of highly-trained soldiers who used state-of-the-art muskets and cannons. However, to maintain the support he needed for his modern military, Frederick William continued to uphold traditional rural aristocracy, which controlled and taxed peasants. Despite his skillful leadership in making Prussia a force in Europe, Frederick William is not a true example of an enlightened monarch.

Frederick William I's son, **Frederick II** (reigned 1740–1786), also known as Frederick the Great, believed the king's duty was to protect and serve his people through efficient government and prosperity:

- He expanded Prussia's territories (especially into Silesia), which enabled the treasury to collect more taxes and thus pay for a strong army.

- He created new departments to manage mines, forests, and commerce.

- He reformed the judiciary and initiated competence exams for judges and other civil servants.

- He began the work that would become the Prussian Common Law.

However, despite being enlightened in the sense of instituting important reforms, Frederick II believed that only the nobility had a sense of honor, and during his reign, the peasants continued to live in a state of serfdom.

Frederick II also believed that a good ruler must be personally involved and not simply rely on his ministers. His mistrust of allowing others to govern had its downside. Though people in his administration were honest and hardworking, they avoided taking initiative. Decisions and ideas came from the top and thus were limited.

Though remembered as a successful military leader, Frederick was more interested in the arts than in war. He was considered an excellent flute player, and he composed sonatas and symphonies that are still played by orchestras today. Frederick was so impressed with French culture that when he built a new palace, he gave it a French name, *Sanssouci*, which means "without concerns." Among his friends were Voltaire, Rousseau, and other French thinkers.

Reforms in Austria

The Habsburgs were the most powerful Catholic family across Europe in the 17th century. Habsburg dominance was challenged by the **Peace of Westphalia** (see Topic 2.4), which ended the Thirty Years' War (1618–1648). In the 18th century, the Habsburgs continued to hold power in Austria, although the empire's focus shifted eastward.

Additionally, changes within the Habsburg dynasty took place in the 1700s. **Maria Theresa** (ruled 1740–1780), while not considered a truly enlightened monarch, made some reforms. For example, she limited landlords' power and was the first European monarch to mandate public education. However, she still was a traditional Catholic who did not believe in religious toleration.

Maria Theresa's son, **Joseph II** (reigned 1765–1790), became Austrian Emperor upon the death of his father. Because his mother was ruler of the Habsburg Empire, Joseph II became her co-regent.

The two rulers were often at odds. Joseph II was an enlightened absolutist who believed in religious toleration, but his mother did not. After her death in 1780, Joseph II issued numerous royal decrees to speed reform. These reforms included the following:

- limiting the power of the Catholic Church
- providing more freedom for the press
- abolishing serfdom
- signing the **Edict of Toleration** (1782), which protected religious freedom for Jewish, Protestant, and Greek Orthodox citizens

Joseph II ran into opposition, though, because he did not seek the approval of the nobles or the clergy before making these rapid reforms. He alienated citizens in the Austrian Netherlands by trying to trade their land to regain control of Bavaria, a move that was stopped by Frederick II of Prussia (Maria Theresa's bitter enemy). He heavily taxed the peasants, who were more concerned about the high taxation than about what was gained through Joseph's reforms.

As domestic unrest mounted, Joseph II forged a military alliance with Catherine II of Russia to counter Prussia's growing strength. However, the alliance brought his empire into conflict with Turkey and the Ottomans, who wanted to control Hungary. With his resources stretched thin and his health failing, Joseph II abolished his own reforms in Hungary in order to regain more absolutist control.

Joseph II died alone, feeling his reign had been a failure. However, his actions paved the way for the abolition of feudalism in 1848. His views on religious toleration were progressive for his time. They were embraced by much of the rest of Europe after his death.

A New Toleration

Enlightenment influence could be seen in a new **religious tolerance**. The influential John Locke argued the concept of fundamental natural rights, which were seen by many to include freedom of religion. Furthermore, Locke's advocacy of separation between church and state naturally promoted tolerance as the state was no longer tethered to a single religion. The growing sentiment that religion was a matter of individual private conscience rather than public concern was only one of many factors that led to greater religious tolerance in the Enlightenment era.

A related Enlightenment influence was the growth of nationalism, the belief that an individual's primary loyalty should be to the nation. Nationalism thus deemphasized religious differences as devotion to the church declined and devotion to the state increased. In addition, a general sense of fatigue had set in after centuries of religious warfare. Lastly, a shift in the relationship between state and church authority took place under both democratic governments and enlightened despots.

Many governments implemented policies of religious toleration:

- England passed a Toleration Act in 1689. It included most Protestants but excluded Roman Catholics and Unitarians.

- France issued the Edict of Tolerance signed by Louis XVI in 1787. It gave Protestants the freedom of worship and other legal protections. During the French Revolution, the *Declaration of the Rights of Man and Citizen* (1789) proclaimed complete freedom of religion across France. In 1791, the French National Assembly offered full civil equality to Jews, setting a model for the rest of Europe.

- Prussia, during the reign of Frederick the Great of Prussia (1740–1786), accepted exiled religious groups, such as Polish Jews, from elsewhere in Europe.

- Austria, under Joseph II, enacted religious toleration for Christians of any denomination. The following year, he issued an edict extending this tolerance to Jews.

By 1815, most European nations had enacted legal protections for religious toleration for Christian minorities, and some had included Jews as well. Despite this, the progress toward full religious freedom and civil equality for Jews was gradual and uneven. They were still prohibited from entering some occupations and living in some areas. It was not until the 20th century that Jews were extended full citizenship everywhere in Europe.

JEWS IN EUROPE, C. 1800

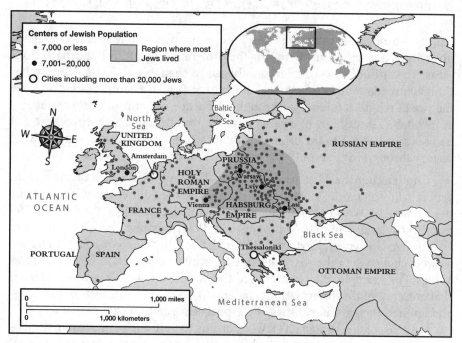

Source: Information adapted from a map created for the International Institute for Jewish Genealogy by Sandra Crystall based on the research of Laurence Leitenberg, iijg.org.

REFLECT ON THE ESSENTIAL QUESTIONS

Essential Question: *How were political power and religious toleration influenced by Enlightenment thought from 1648 to 1815?*

European Leaders Influenced by the Enlightenment	Practical Effects of Enlightenment Influence

KEY TERMS

absolutism	Frederick II	Edict of Toleration
enlightened monarchs	Peace of Westphalia	religious tolerance
enlightened absolutism	Maria Theresa	
Frederick William I	Joseph II	

During the long wars over religion in Europe, to say someone tolerated religious diversity was a criticism. It meant they tolerated untruthful and dangerous ideas. The attitude toward toleration began to change with Voltaire and other Enlightenment thinkers. In the 19th century, British historians began to see the rise of religious toleration throughout Europe not only as positive but also as inevitable. It was part of a general march toward human improvement that had reached its peak in the present. In other words, the historians were viewing history through the lens of their own beliefs, not on its own terms.

Challenging the March of Progress That optimistic view of the past in general and toleration in particular changed in the 20th century. The horrific destruction in World War I caused many intellectuals to rethink the belief that history was a march of progress. In 1931, a young British historian at Cambridge University, Herbert Butterfield, published *The Whig Interpretation*, a direct challenge to the rosy view of earlier historians, whom he identified as Whigs. For example, they had praised the development of religious toleration that grew out of the Reformation—because it was a value the historians held—and ignored the painful realities of the post-Reformation world.

One cost of this Whiggish view, according to Butterfield, was that historians judged people by the values of the historians' time rather than of the historical period. For example, historians condemned rulers such as the 16th-century Queen Mary for trying to uphold the long tradition of religious unity as a way to keep the state together and at peace.

Political Necessity By 2000, Butterfield's ideas were widely accepted. Historians tried to understand the past on its own terms, without making it a story of progress that led to the present. Cary J. Nederman, a professor of political science at the University of Arizona, pointed out that the Protestant Reformation and the resulting fragmentation of Christian Europe did not provide a direct line toward greater toleration. Luther and Calvin, the most influential leaders of the Reformation, did not advocate for religious toleration. For Nederman, early steps toward toleration such as the Peace of Augsburg (1555) and the Edict of Nantes (1598) were the result of political necessity. During the 17th century, writings by Thomas Hobbes and John Locke that supported religious toleration were ratifying a belief that it was a sensible policy. There was nothing inevitable about it.

Centralized Government More recently, economist Mark Koyama focused on how political conditions after the Reformation led to religious toleration. Once a monarch no longer needed the pope's blessing, persecuting heretics became politically irrelevant and economically unwise. They could allow religion to become a private matter. They did not need to expend money and lives trying to enforce religious unity. In addition, as the state became centralized and standardized, rulers found it more efficient and economically advantageous to treat everyone the same regardless of their faith. Centralization and standardization drove equality and toleration slowly but steadily. Religious toleration was not part of the story of a steady progress in human history nor part of an improvement in human morality. Rather, it was just a practical response to changes in political structures.

1. Explain how and why religious toleration became more widespread, according to Cary Nederman.

2. Explain why Mark Koyama maintained that religious toleration was NOT a result of people making steady progress as better people.

MULTIPLE-CHOICE QUESTIONS

Questions 1–3 refer to the passage below.

"One must attempt, above all, to know the special genius of the people which one wants to govern in order to know if one must treat them leniently or severely, if they are inclined to revolt . . .

[The Prussian nobility] has sacrificed its life and goods for the service of the state; its loyalty and merit have earned it the protection of all its rulers... In such a state no factions or rebellions need be feared . . . it is one goal of the policy of this state to preserve the nobility.

A well-conducted government must have an underlying concept so well integrated that it could be likened to a system of philosophy. All actions taken must be well reasoned . . . However, such a system can flow but from a single brain, and this must be that of the sovereign.

Catholics, Lutherans, Reformed, Jews and other Christian sects live in this state, and live together in peace. If the sovereign, actuated by a mistaken zeal, declares himself for one religion or another, parties spring up, heated disputes ensue, little by little persecutions will commence and, in the end, the religion persecuted will leave the fatherland, and millions of subjects will enrich our neighbors by their skill and industry.

It is of no concern in politics whether the ruler has a religion or whether he has none. All religions, if one examines them, are founded on superstitious systems, more or less absurd."

—Frederick the Great of Prussia, "Political Testament," 1752

1. The ideas expressed in this passage best illustrate which of the following 18th century developments?

   (A) The establishment of representative government based upon a social contract

   (B) The conservative reaction to the French Revolution

   (C) The expansion of the commercial economy

   (D) The application of rational principles to government

2. The third paragraph of the excerpt best reflects which element of Frederick the Great's point of view on governing?

   (A) The ultimate decision-making must come from the monarch.

   (B) The ultimate decision-making must come from the honorable nobles.

   (C) Representatives of the peasantry should be involved in all important decisions.

   (D) All decisions should be arrived at democratically, even if the monarch disagrees.

3. Which other political leader would be most likely to support the ideas expressed in this source?

   (A) Charles I of England

   (B) Philip II of Spain

   (C) Henry IV of France

   (D) Louis XIV of France

SHORT-ANSWER QUESTION

Answer all parts of the question that follows.

1. a) Describe ONE way the Enlightenment influenced the development of religious tolerance.

   b) Describe ONE way political institutions expanded religious tolerance in Europe in the 1700s.

   c) Explain ONE way in which ideas toward religious pluralism changed as a result of the Enlightenment.

Topic 4.7

Causation in the Age of the Scientific Revolution and the Enlightenment

Finally we shall place the Sun himself at the center of the Universe.
—Nicolaus Copernicus (1474–1544)

Essential Question: How and why did the Scientific Revolution and Enlightenment challenge the existing European order and understanding of the world?

During the Enlightenment and the Scientific Revolution of the 17th and 18th centuries, European thinkers applied reason and the scientific method to many aspects of life, especially nature, producing significant changes to established and accepted concepts of the world. The scientific method, consisting of observation, experimentation, and mathematics, challenged traditional religious ideas about astronomy, nature, and biology.

Renewed Classical World Ideas Causes Changes and Challenges During the Renaissance, European thinkers had rediscovered art and ideas from classical times of ancient Greece and Rome. As an example, the traditional view of a geocentric universe—one with the earth at the center of a system of concentric spheres, including the sun, circling around it, was challenged by Nicolaus Copernicus, a Polish mathematician and natural philosopher, a scholar who studied the physical world. In classical writings, Copernicus found references to ancient Greeks who questioned the geocentric views of Aristotle and Ptolemy and believed instead in a heliocentric, or sun-centered, universe. Copernicus then applied advanced mathematics to prove that these ancient thinkers were, indeed, correct.

Enlightenment-era thinkers believed that questioning old ideas and applying classical thought and modern scientific methods to community problems would produce progress. However, this new thinking was challenged by traditional institutions. Feudal, despotic, and religious restrictions continued to exist, and clerics in particular clung to the old ways of thought and fought the new ways. Also, most Europeans continued to believe that spiritual forces governed everything in the universe. Even most scientists of the time believed in God and found a role for religion within their reasoning.

New Emphasis on Reason Causes Change The viewpoints and practices of the Scientific Revolution and the Enlightenment created a new emphasis on reason in European life. Traditional patterns of thought from the Middle Ages gave way to rationalism, empiricism, and skepticism. Rationalism was very strong in France, led by philosopher René Descartes and his use of deductive reasoning, or drawing conclusions from general principles. Empiricism was based on the idea that all human knowledge comes through what the senses can experience.

Scottish philosopher David Hume provided some of the most radical thought of the period. His belief in skepticism, all knowledge and religion should be approached with doubt, was strongly opposed by Church authority. Rationalism, empiricism, and skepticism argued that what people knew was more important than what they believed, and that investigation and reflection were more important than faith.

These changes in viewpoint affected social order, government, and religion. Enlightenment theories on politics and economics evolved to the point of challenging the rule of absolute monarchs and economic systems. The Scientific Revolution brought about a new rational view of religion, which moved people to an appreciation of natural phenomena and calls for religious tolerance. By 1815, most European nations had enacted legal protections for Christian minorities.

Scientific Revolution and Enlightenment Cause Changes to Day-to-Day Life The concentrated application of reason and experimentation to a broader range of issues that plagued society led to numerous improvements. In the Netherlands, engineers developed improved drainage methods to open up new land for planting. From this same country came the idea of crop rotation, which allowed farmers to plant on all of their land every year. New agricultural innovations—the seed drill, the threshing machine, and selective breeding—came into use, as well. These advances, along with development of canals and improved roads caused the amount of food produced to increase throughout Europe, which lead to healthier people and longer life expectancies.

The Scientific Revolution caused a leap forward in the medical sciences. One example was a greater understanding of how diseases were transmitted. The development of vaccines to inoculate people against deadly infectious diseases, such as smallpox, saved countless lives. Advances in medical thought worked in tandem with developments in engineering to help supply more people (especially in cities) with cleaner water, better sewage disposal, and improved hygiene. Safer and more plentiful food, protection against some infectious diseases, and cleaner water caused the population of Europe to increase.

QUESTIONS ABOUT CAUSATION

1. How did renewed classical world ideas during the Enlightenment cause changes and challenges to the existing European order?

2. How did a new emphasis on reason during the Scientific Revolution cause changes and challenges to the existing European order?

UNIT 4 REVIEW: Scientific, Philosophical, and Political Development
c. 1648 to c. 1815

WRITE AS A HISTORIAN: *STRUCTURE THE ESSAY*

Most essays written for AP® exams follow the same basic structure:

- The first paragraph sets the context and ends with the thesis statement.
- Each body paragraph starts with a topic sentence that introduces the main idea of the paragraph and includes evidence to support the thesis.
- The last paragraph recaps the evidence and restates the thesis.

For each thesis statement, choose the best topic sentence that supports it.

1. In its early stages, modern Europe developed a market economy that provided the foundation for its global role.

   a. Trade was freed from traditional restrictions, and wages and prices became more market-driven.

   b. Because workers had more geographic mobility, they were not as tied to traditional family and community traditions.

2. European domination of the worldwide economic network had several negative social consequences.

   a. Products such as sugar, tea, tobacco, and rum were widely enjoyed by Europeans.

   b. Triangle trade among Europe, Africa, and the Americas caused the slave trade to increase.

For each of the topic sentences below, choose the best supporting evidence.

3. The importation and transplantation of agricultural products from the Americas contributed to increases in food supply and trade.

   a. France's growing climate was hospitable to crops from the Americas such as beans, peppers, corn, squash, tomatoes, and potatoes.

   b. England's plantations produced crops such as rice, tobacco, and sugar that enriched a growing merchant class.

4. England's mercantilist policies provoked rebellion in its American colonies.

   a. The majority of profits from plantations flowed back across the sea to absentee owners in England.

   b. The colonists, in many ways, enjoyed a higher standard of living as a result of their greater economic opportunities.

LONG ESSAY QUESTIONS

Directions: Suggested writing time is 40 minutes. In your response, you should do the following:

- Respond to the prompt with a historically defensible thesis that establishes a line of reasoning.
- Describe a broader historical context relevant to the prompt.
- Support an argument in response to the prompt using specific and relevant examples of evidence.
- Use historical reasoning (e.g., comparison, causation, continuity and change over time) to frame or structure an argument that addresses the prompt.
- Use evidence to corroborate, qualify, or modify an argument that addresses the prompt.

1. Evaluate the extent to which the medieval worldview differed from the modern worldview of the Scientific Revolution and Enlightenment.

2. Evaluate the extent to which the Scientific Revolution and Enlightenment altered how people perceived education and the discovery of knowledge.

3. Evaluate the most significant change in the interaction between religion and science in Europe in the three centuries following the Reformation.

4. Evaluate the most significant impact the Scientific Revolution had on religious tolerance.

DOCUMENT-BASED QUESTION

Directions: Question 1 is based on the accompanying documents. The documents have been edited for the purpose of this exercise. You are advised to spend 15 minutes planning and 45 minutes writing your answer. In your response, you should do the following:

- **Thesis:** Make a defensible claim that establishes a line of reasoning and consists of one or more sentences found in one place.
- **Contextualization:** Relate the argument to a broader historical context.
- **Document Evidence:** Use content from at least six documents.
- **Outside Evidence:** Use one piece of evidence not in the documents.
- **Document Sourcing:** Explain how or why the point of view, purpose, situation, or intended audience is relevant for at least three documents.
- **Analysis:** Show the relationships among pieces of historical evidence and use them to support, qualify, or modify an argument.

1. To what extent did the ideas of the Enlightenment influence European society?

Document 1:

Source: *Memoir of Marmontel*, by Jean-Francios Marmontel, published 1805, here describing a salon held by Madame Geoffrin in Paris, c. 1775

The circle was formed of persons who were not bound together. She had taken them here and there in society, but so well assorted were they that once there they fell into harmony like the strings of an instrument touched by an able hand….Nowhere was conversation more lively, more brilliant, or better regulated than at her house. It was a rare phenomenon indeed, the degree of tempered, equable heat which she knew so well how to maintain, sometimes by moderating it, sometimes by quickening it. The continual activity of her soul was communicated to our souls, but measurably; her imagination was the mainspring, her reason the regulator. Remark that the brains she stirred at will were neither feeble nor frivolous…[her] talents, I say, were not those of an ordinary woman. It was not with the follies of fashion and vanity that daily, during four hours of conversation, without languor and without vacuum, she knew how to make herself interesting to a wide circle of strong minds.

Document 2

Source: *The Blue Bottle Coffee House*, by an unknown artist c. 1900, painting of the first coffee house opened by Jerzy Francieszek Kulczycki in Vienna in 1686

Credit: Wikimedia Commons

Document 3

Source: Society of the Friends of Blacks, address to the National Assembly, 1790

You have declared them (the rights of man as expressed in the Declaration of Rights of Man and Citizen, August, 1789) that all men are born and remain free and equal in rights; you have restored to the French people these rights that despotism had for so long despoiled;...we are not asking you to restore to French blacks those political rights which alone, nevertheless, attest to and maintain the dignity of man; we are not even asking for their liberty...it is therefore not yet time to demand that liberty [of emancipation]; we ask only that one cease butchering thousands of blacks regularly every year in order to take hundreds of captives; we ask that one henceforth cease the prostitution, the profaning of the French name, used to authorize these thefts, these atrocious murders; we demand in a word the abolition of the slave trade...

Document 4

Source: Thomas Paine, British citizen, fought in the American War of Independence, member of the French Convention 1792–1793 (from *Age of Reason*, published 1794)

The circumstance that has now taken place in France of the total abolition of the whole national order of priesthood, and of everything appertaining to compulsive systems of religion, and compulsive articles of faith, has not only precipitated my intention, but rendered a work of this kind exceedingly necessary, lest in the general wreck of superstition, of false systems of government, and false theology, we lose sight of morality, of humanity, and of the theology that is true....

I believe in one God, and no more; and I hope for happiness beyond this life. I believe in the equality of man; and I believe that religious duties consist in doing justice, loving mercy, and endeavoring to make our fellow-creatures happy. I do not believe in the creed professed by the Jewish church, by the Roman church, by the Greek church, by the Turkish church, by the Protestant church, nor by any church that I know of. My own mind is my own church. I do not mean by this declaration to condemn those who believe otherwise; they have the same right to their belief as I have to mine. But it is necessary to the happiness of man, that he be mentally faithful to himself.

Document 5

Source: Cesare Beccaria, economist and criminologist, *On Crimes and Punishments*, published in Italy, 1764

- What will be the penalty suitable for such and such crimes?
- Is death a penalty really useful and necessary for the security and good order of society?
- Are torture and torments just, and do they attain the end which the law aims at?
- What is the best way of preventing crimes?
- Are the same penalties equally useful in all times?
- What influence have they on customs?

The torture of a criminal during the course of his trial is a cruelty consecrated by custom in most nations...the dilemma is frequent. Either he is guilty, or not guilty. If guilty, he should only suffer the punishment ordained by the laws, and torture becomes useless, as his confession is unnecessary. If he be innocent his crime has not been proved...[T]hat pain should be the test of truth, as if truth resided in the muscles and fibres of a wretch in torture. By this method the robust will escape and the feeble be condemned.

Document 6

Source: Frederick the Great, ruler of Prussia from 1740–1786, quote from "Political Testament," 1752

Catholics, Lutherans, Reformed, Jews and other Christian sects live in this state, and live together in peace. If the sovereign, actuated by a mistaken zeal, declares himself for one religion or another, parties spring up, heated disputes ensue, little by little persecutions will commence and, in the end, the religion persecuted will leave the fatherland, and millions of subjects will enrich our neighbors by their skill and industry. It is of no concern in politics whether the ruler has a religion or whether he has none. All religions, if one examines them, are founded on superstitious systems, more or less absurd. It is impossible for a man of good sense, who dissects their contents, not to see their error; but these prejudices, these errors and mysteries, were made for men, and one must know enough to respect the public and not to outrage its faith, whatever religion be involved.

Document 7

Source: Olaudah Equiano, abducted in Nigeria as a child—later bought his freedom, autobiography, 1789

Tortures, murder, and every other imaginable barbarity and iniquity, are practised upon the poor slaves with impunity. I hope the slave trade will be abolished. I pray it may be an event at hand. . . . In a short time one sentiment alone will prevail, from motives of interest as well as justice and humanity. Europe contains one hundred and twenty millions of inhabitants. Query—How many millions doth Africa contain? Supposing the Africans, collectively and individually, to expend 5l. a head in raiment and furniture yearly when civilized, &c. an immensity beyond the reach of imagination! This I conceive to be a theory founded upon facts, and therefore an infallible one. If the blacks were permitted to remain in their own country, they would double themselves every fifteen years. In proportion to such increase will be the demand for manufactures. Cotton and indigo grow spontaneously in most parts of Africa; a consideration this of no small consequence to the manufacturing towns of Great Britain. It opens a most immense, glorious, and happy prospect—the clothing, &c. of a continent ten thousand miles in circumference, and immensely rich in productions of every denomination in return for manufactures.

UNIT 5: Conflict, Crisis, and Reaction in the Late 18th Century
c. 1648 to c. 1815

Topic 5.1

Contextualizing 18th-Century States

Essential Question: What is the context in which European states experienced crisis and conflict in the 18th century?

During the Enlightenment and the Scientific Revolution of the 17th and 18th centuries, European thinkers applied reason and the scientific method to many aspects of life, especially nature. This produced monumental changes to the established and accepted concepts of the world that had come before. These changes led to major social, cultural, political, and economic transformations, as well as to crises and conflicts in European states from 1648 to 1815.

Relationship Among European States The rivalry between Europe's powers intensified during the 17th and 18th centuries. Alliances shifted as European nations chose sides based their own needs at any particular time. Occasionally, conflicts among European nations spilled over to other continents such as North America and Asia. The hostilities between Britain and France were especially intense.

During this period, Britain became the dominant European power as long-term social and political issues weakened France. The British parliamentary monarchy proved to be more responsive to problems and willing to change than was the absolutist monarchy of France.

Impact of the French Revolution In France, widespread discontent with economic inequality, in combination with poor governance by the French monarchy, produced a population ready for change. Over several phases of the French Revolution, the government recognized some rights for the country's peasants and lower classes. Years of violence and political upheaval allowed for Napoleon Bonaparte to come to power as a champion of revolutionary ideals. After establishing numerous reforms in France, Napoleon's efforts to maintain power made his government look more like a dictatorship. Also, his imperialistic intentions led many European leaders to turn against him, and he was forced to leave France. Ultimately, the French Revolution inspired countless changes in France and Europe and around the globe.

Worldwide Economic Network As a result of the Age of Exploration and rapid progress in technology, Europe's commercial success grew quickly through trade. A worldwide economic network grew via sea trade and branched out from Portugal, the Netherlands, England, and France. These European states traded with what are today India and the Philippines, as well as countries and peoples in East and Southeast Asia, Africa, and North America. The commercial competition among European states resulted in diplomatic crises and warfare over control of territories.

Reason Versus Romanticism Between 1648 and 1815, the rationalism of the Scientific Revolution and the Enlightenment continued to influence all aspects of Europe. Enlightenment thinkers continued to question religious and royal authority. Their confidence in humanity led to a new emphasis on reason, rationalism, and skepticism. However, there was a strong reaction against these Enlightenment ideals by the early 19th century. This rejection came about through religious revivals and a turn toward emotion expressed through the art and literature of a movement known as Romanticism. This movement clashed with the Enlightenment's "heartless" rationalism. The expressive emotions of Romanticism burst forth in mass political movements and expressions of nationalism, which brought about war and revolutions in Europe and its colonies.

ANALYZE THE CONTEXT

1. How did Europe's worldwide economic network provide a context for crises and conflict between 1648 and 1815?

2. How did the clash between Enlightenment ideals and Romanticism provide a context for conflicts?

Topic 5.2

The Rise of Global Markets

All the countries and territories, which may have been conquered. . . by the arms of their Britannick and Most Faithful Majesties [the kings of Great Britain and Portugal], as well as by those of their Most Christian and Catholick Majesties [the kings of France and Spain]. . . shall be restored without difficulty, and without requiring any compensations.

—Article XXIII, Treaty of Paris, 1763

Essential Question: What were the causes and consequences of European maritime competition from 1648 to 1815?

With European nations engaged in ongoing wars for land and power on the continent, it was no wonder that these struggles spilled over in a quest to control the rest of the world. The Age of Exploration had been driven by the European quest for a direct route to the Spice Islands of the East Indies. The Portuguese were the first to reach India in 1498 by sailing around the southern tip of Africa. Portugal dominated the lucrative Indian Ocean trade with the East Indies—in this context, present-day India, Indonesia, Malaysia, and Southeast Asia—through most of the 16th century. During the 17th century, however, its dominance was challenged by the Dutch, the English, and the French.

European Competition and Commerce

Portuguese control over sea trade routes and ports in the Indian Ocean was first contested by the Dutch Republic, which would become the leading maritime power in the region in the 1600s. Increasingly, other European powers jockeyed for control over sea trade across the globe.

Rivalries Develop During the 15th and 16th centuries, Spain and Portugal were rivals in colonizing and exploiting resources around the world. The Spanish ruled Mexico and Central America, most of South America, parts of Africa, and the Philippines. The Portuguese ruled Brazil, parts of Africa, and key ports in Asia. These overseas holdings often changed hands as a result of treaties that ended European wars.

During the 17th century, rivalry between England and the Dutch Republic resulted in three wars. Hostility between the two nations came to an end in 1689 when the Dutch leader William of Orange became King William III of England, and the two nations became closely allied as the Maritime Powers.

From 1701 to 1763, the greatest seaborne rivalry was between Britain and France. By establishing colonial settlements and trade outposts, they vied for control—either directly or by controlling trade—in North America and the Caribbean, as well as in Africa, India, and eastern Asia.

Commercial Rivalries A combination of military and economic factors influenced commercial rivalries in the 18th century:

- the worldwide growth of trade and mercantilism
- the dominance of Europe's growing industrial power
- a rising need to find markets for machine-made goods
- a reliance on the use of Africans to ensure European wealth and industrialization
- the build-up of the British and French navies to control the seas, resulting in an increase in naval wars
- the declining naval dominance of Spain, Portugal, and the Netherlands

Rivalries in the East Indies

With the land routes connecting Europe with India and East Asia long controlled by the Ottomans, European powers turned to the sea. By the end of the 18th century, the British controlled the Indian subcontinent and the Dutch controlled most of the islands of the East Indies.

The Portuguese Beginning in the early 16th century, the Portuguese controlled European trade with India, China, and the East Indies. The intention was to make trade with the East Indies a royal monopoly, but the profits went to private merchants rather than to the royal treasury. In 1580, the Spanish king seized the vacant Portuguese throne, and by the time Portugal regained independence in 1640, Spain's European enemies had begun to encroach on its East Indian holdings. As other European nations chartered East India companies, Portugal lost its hold on the East Indies after more than a century of dominance.

The French King Louis XIV authorized the first **French East India Company** in 1664 at the behest of his chief minister of finance, Jean-Baptiste Colbert. Although the company acquired several trading posts in India, its progress was slowed by the British East India Company. The two companies backed warring native rulers as each jockeyed for domination of the Indian subcontinent. During the War of the Austrian Succession, France seized Madras, the center of British power, and appeared to be poised to control all of India. However, the peace treaty returned Madras to British control, and the French turned their focus to the West Indies. The French East India Company began to decline in 1769 when it lost its monopoly over trade with India and the company ended during the French Revolution.

The Dutch In the 17th century, the Dutch Republic rose to power with a strong fleet of ships and the creation of the **Dutch East India Company**, known by its Dutch initials as the VOC. The VOC sold shares to stockholders and was considered the first transnational corporation. Through a series of confrontations with the Portuguese, the VOC established the principle of freedom of the seas for trade. They instituted a trading monopoly in the Indonesian archipelago as well as in hundreds of other places. However, by 1799, the VOC had collapsed, in part because of competition from a strong British fleet, although the Netherlands continued to rule the Dutch East Indies as a colony.

The British In 1600, the British established an **East India Company** to compete with the Portuguese for the East Indies spice trade. In 1612, after defeating the Portuguese in India, the company concentrated on trade in Indian textiles and spices. The company acquired several trading centers, including Madras and Bombay. The beginning of the collapse of the Mughal Empire in the early 18th century led to armed conflict between the British and French East India companies for control of the

Source: Wikimedia Commons
Both sides of a 1735 coin made by the VOC

Indian subcontinent. The British East India Company eventually triumphed, gaining nearly total control of India at the end of the Seven Years' War in 1763. Parliament intervened to establish government control of political policies in India in 1773 and 1784. A combination of taxation, control of the local textile and shipbuilding industries, and trade restrictions helped Britain support its own industrial and economic growth, but the British presence in India devastated Indian economy and autonomy.

THE WORLD IN 1750

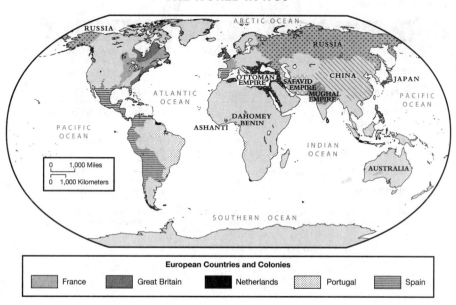

The Costs of Wealth

Throughout this period of history, Europe's commercial dominance grew because of **human capital** and rapid advances in technology. Human capital refers to the skills and resources of people and groups in a society. Europe's commercial success accelerated the growth of a worldwide economic network. However, growth came at a steep human cost for native peoples.

REFLECT ON THE ESSENTIAL QUESTION

Essential Question: *What were the causes and consequences of European maritime competition from 1648 to 1815?*

Causes	Consequences

KEY TERMS

French East India Company
Dutch East India Company

East India Company
human capital

MULTIPLE-CHOICE QUESTIONS

Questions 1–3 refer to the table below.

CARRYING CAPACITY OF MERCHANT FLEETS			
Fleet	**1570**	**1670**	**1780**
Netherlands	232	568	450
Germany	110	104	155
Great Britain	51	260	1,000
France	80	80	700
Italy, Portugal, and Spain	—	250	546
Denmark, Norway, and Sweden	—	—	555
North America	—	—	450

Source: Angus Maddison, *The World Economy,* Volume 1: A Millennial Perspective. (OECD, 2006). Adapted from Table 2-15, page 79. Data for some regions and years was not available or not significant.

Carrying capacities given in thousands of metric tons.

1. The data in this table best supports which of the following arguments about economic power as measured by capacity to engage in global trade between 1570 and 1780?

   (A) The most heavily Roman Catholic countries became poorer.

   (B) Northern European countries grew more powerful at an equal rate.

   (C) Countries increased their economic power most in periods of political conflict.

   (D) The countries with the largest colonial empires became the most powerful.

2. Which of the following is the most likely explanation for the change in the data for Great Britain?

   (A) The British focused largely on building its military vessels at the expense of building merchant vessels through the 18th century.

   (B) The British government supported the expansion of its merchant fleet to promote colonial growth.

   (C) Conflicts with other imperial nations left the British weakened and unable to expand it merchant fleet.

   (D) Conflicts with Indian nationalists forced the British to abandon its most valuable colonial possession.

3. Which of the following is the most likely explanation for the continuity in the data for Germany provided in this table?

   (A) Germany was already a sea power by 1570, so it did not need to expand its fleet for global trade.

   (B) Germany lacked a strong central government, so promoting global trade was difficult.

   (C) Germany was divided by religion, so it was not united enough to be active in global trade.

   (D) Germany had no direct access to the sea, so participating in global trade was difficult.

Use the passage below to answer all parts of the question that follows.

"The roots of this predatory corporate culture go back 400 years to the foundation and the global rise of the East India Company. Many modern corporations have attempted to match its success at bending state power to their own ends, but the Company remains unmatched for its violence and sheer military might.

The East India Company, which was established in London in 1599, was authorized by its charter to wage war, and from its maiden voyage in 1602, it used corporate violence to enhance its trade. In the mid-18th century, the Company began seizing by brute military force great chunks of the most prosperous provinces of the Mughal Empire, which then embraced most of India, Pakistan and Bangladesh and half of Afghanistan. . . . An international corporation was, for the first time, transforming itself into an aggressive colonial power.

Using the looted wealth of Mughal Bengal, the Company started ferrying opium east to China, then fought the Opium Wars [1839–1842] to seize an offshore base at Hong Kong and safeguard its profitable monopoly in narcotics. To the west, it shipped Chinese tea to Massachusetts.

Such was the reputation of the East India Company that in the cold winter of 1772–3, a panic spread across the 13 Colonies that the Company would be let loose on America. . . .

As a result of this panic, and the slapping of British taxes on tea, some 90,000 pounds of Company tea, worth £9,659 (more than $1.2 million today), was dumped in Boston Harbor. The Revolutionary War broke out soon after.

The Company had become, as one of its directors said, "an empire within an empire," with the power to make war or peace anywhere in the East. . . . Its armies were larger than those of almost all nation-states and its power now encircled the globe."

—William Dalrymple, "The Original Evil Corporation,"
New York Times, September 4, 2019

1. a) Describe ONE historical development that Dalrymple describes in this passage.

   b) Explain the significance of the words Dalrymple uses that indicate his point of view on the British East India Company.

   c) Explain another example of European dominance over a non-European area with conditions similar to those described by Dalrymple.

Topic 5.3

Britain's Ascendency

That the two Kingdoms of Scotland and England, shall, upon the first Day of May next ensuing the Date hereof, and for ever after, be united into one Kingdom by the Name of Great-Britain, . . .

—Article I of the Acts of Union, 1707

Essential Question: What were the economic and political consequences of the rivalry between Britain and France from 1648 to 1815?

Both England and Scotland had been ruled by the same Stuart monarchs for over 100 years before the two nations united formally into a single kingdom. The Stuarts had come into conflict with England's Parliament more than once, and Parliament had prevailed, executing one king and forcing another into exile. Queen Anne was the last of the Stuarts, and the English had reason to believe that France might try to place a Catholic Stuart back on the throne. The **Acts of Union** were meant not only to unify England and Scotland but also to ensure a peaceful transfer of power to a Protestant successor. Thus, England avoided the dynastic struggles that plagued other nations, most notably Spain.

Rivalry Between England and France

In 1688, France had the strongest army in Europe; its navy was larger than the combined navies of England and the Dutch Republic. With Austria engaged in a war against the Ottoman Turks on its eastern border, Louis XIV decided to invade the Rhineland—an area along the Rhine River that included parts of France, the Netherlands, and the Holy Roman Empire. His chief opponent was **William of Orange**, stadtholder of the Dutch Republic. William was the leader of Protestant opposition to Louis' attempts to strengthen his influence in the German principalities.

William, who became King William III of England in 1689, was one of the major architects of the Grand Alliance, which consisted chiefly of England, the Dutch Republic, and Austria, and served as an effective counterforce to France. The War of the Grand Alliance (1689–1697) temporarily blocked Louis' plans to expand into German lands. It did not, however, end the conflict between the Bourbon rulers of France and the Habsburg rulers of Austria nor the rivalry between England and France. Both of these rivalries would erupt again in the War of the Spanish Succession (1701–1714). (See Topic 3.6 for more on the War of the Spanish Succession.)

Source: Getty Images

An engraving of William of Orange and Mary Stuart, the future King William III and Queen Mary of England, 1677

The Rise of Britain

Following the Glorious Revolution (see Topic 3.2), plans began to formally join the kingdoms of England and Scotland, which had remained separate nations although they had the same monarch since 1603. With the Acts of Union in 1707, England and Scotland were joined as the kingdom of Great Britain. The union provided economic security for Scotland and political safeguards for England, which feared French attempts to place a Catholic ruler back on the English throne. The last Catholic king was James II, who ruled England prior to William and Mary and the Glorious Revolution.

Queen Mary's sister Anne became queen of England and Scotland in 1702, after the death of William III. Because Anne had no surviving children, the throne would pass to the nearest Protestant descendant of the Stuart monarchy—King James I's daughter Elizabeth. However, she died only weeks before Anne, so the throne went to Elizabeth's son, who was the ruler of the Electorate of Hanover—a territory of the Holy Roman Empire in present-day northern Germany. The first Hanoverian king was Anne's son, George I (reigned 1714–1727).

By the time King George I took the throne, Great Britain had become a major European imperial power as a result of the treaties of Utrecht. The War of the Spanish Succession had left Britain's rivals France and Spain, as well as the Dutch Republic, seriously weakened. It took France a decade to recover, but Spain and the Dutch Republic continued to decline both economically and militarily.

The War of the Austrian Succession

Holy Roman Emperor Charles IV died in 1740 with no male heir, leaving his daughter Maria Theresa to rule Habsburg lands. Shortly after the death of Charles VI, **Frederick II** of Prussia (also known as Frederick the Great) invaded the province Silesia, one of the wealthiest Habsburg lands. He also challenged Maria Theresa's right to rule any of the Habsburg dominions. Frederick's invasion of Silesia is viewed as the beginning of the **War of the Austrian Succession** (1740–1748).

Seeing an opportunity to weaken Habsburg power, France, Bavaria, and Spain sided with Prussia. Maria Theresa was backed by Britain, the Dutch Republic, and Hanover (the Pragmatic Alliance). Thus, it became yet another struggle between two alliances during a series of campaigns. In the end, the Treaty of Aix-la-Chapelle (1748) concluded the war and Frederick II agreed to recognize Maria Theresa's husband as the Holy Roman Emperor Francis I.

The War of Austrian Succession also became a struggle between Great Britain and France for control of North America and India. The American phase, known as King George's War (1744–1748), was characterized by bloody border raids that had no lasting effect. The hostilities between Great Britain and France would continue on the North American continent.

The Seven Years' War

The **Seven Years' War** (1756–1763) began with an attempt by Austria to regain the province of Silesia, which it had lost to Prussia in the War of the Austrian Succession. However, it soon involved all of the great powers of Europe, although in new alliances. This time, France sided with Austria, a development known as the Diplomatic Revolution, essentially ending the Habsburg-French rivalry that had existed since the 15th century. Saxony, Sweden, and Russia also sided with Austria in opposition to Prussia, Hanover, and Great Britain.

Prussia positioned itself as the defender of Protestantism in Europe against a Catholic French and Austrian alliance. Both France and Prussia were interested in expanding their holdings in Europe.

France and Prussia had traditionally been allies in opposition to Austria, while England (and later Great Britain) had traditionally allied itself with Austria in opposition to France. Britain had gained little as a direct result of its support of Austria, however. Now Great Britain's chief aim in allying itself with Prussia was to protect Hanover, which was still ruled by Britain's Hanoverian king, from the possibility of being taken over by France.

In the end, there were essentially two wars: one between Britain and France and the other between Austria and Prussia. Britain and France had been fighting for control of India since 1740, but by 1761 British naval superiority had brought a temporary end to the French threat in India. In the meantime, French aggression in North America had led to an undeclared war with Britain by 1754 known as the French and Indian War.

At the end of the war in Europe, Prussia had emerged as a great power, while Austria's prestige was further diminished. Prussia retained Silesia. Great Britain made enormous territorial gains, mostly at the expense of its old enemy France, which aroused the envy and hostility of much of the rest of Europe and would have major repercussions in the future.

British and French Rivalry in North America

At the end of the War of the Spanish Succession (as a result of Queen Anne's War), France had ceded portions of what is now Canada to Great Britain. However, France still claimed vast territories in North America. New France extended west from the Appalachian Mountains through the Mississippi Valley, south to Louisiana, and north through the Great Lakes and through Canada to the Atlantic Ocean.

The French and Indian War

The Seven Years' War in Europe spilled over to North America, where it became known as the **French and Indian War** (1754–1763). Britain and its American colonists wanted to counter French expansion along the western frontier of the Ohio River Valley. In the war, both sides allied with different Indian tribes, each making promises to the Indians that would be broken. Britain won the war, and territorial changes resulted under the **Treaty of Paris**:

- Britain received all lands east of the Mississippi River plus Canada from France.
- Britain received Florida from Spain.
- Spain received Louisiana and France's lands west of the Mississippi.
- France kept its sugar-producing islands, including Haiti, in the Caribbean.

The war's end marked the beginning of Britain's world dominance and resulted in North America becoming a mainly English-speaking continent.

The American Revolution

However, the British-French rivalry in North America was not over. During the **American Revolution** (1775–1783), one important factor in the colonists' success was their alliance with France. The French took advantage of the rebellion to gain revenge for losses in the Seven Years' War. The American colonial government sent representative Benjamin Franklin to negotiate a treaty that kept Spain out of the war and prevented any European powers from entering into secret alliances with Britain. The French provided arms, ammunition, military training, and troops to the Americans. French naval support assured American victory at the Battle of Yorktown, where the British finally surrendered in 1781.

In spite of this setback, Britain had established itself as the dominant power of Europe, and during the next century, the British Empire would expand dramatically. France, having helped the Americans achieve freedom, was about to experience its own quest for democracy. But that experiment would soon descend into chaos that would ultimately involve all of Europe.

FRENCH TERRITORIAL LOSSES TO BRITAIN IN NORTH AMERICA, 1713-1763

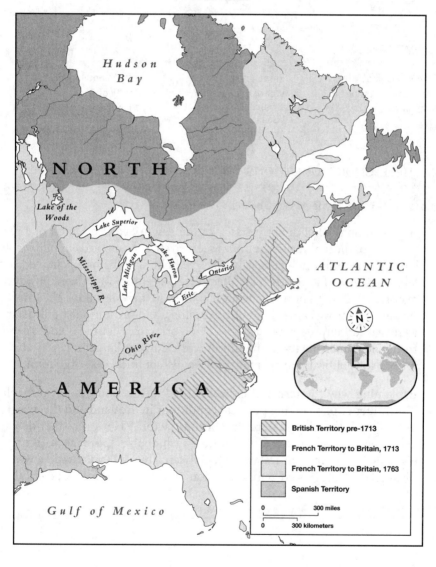

Essential Question: *What were the economic and political consequences of the rivalry between Britain and France from 1648 to 1815?*

Economic Consequences	Political Consequences

KEY TERMS

Acts of Union	Frederick II	French and Indian War
William of Orange	War of the Austrian	Treaty of Paris
Maria Theresa	Succession	American Revolution
	Seven Years' War	

MULTIPLE-CHOICE QUESTIONS

Questions 1–3 refer to the passage below.

"In 1907, on the 200th anniversary of the Anglo-Scottish Union of 1707, the story of the making of the union seemed straightforward enough. Scots look on the union in a generally positive light, and historians lauded the farsightedness of its Scottish architects. Half a century or so later, however, historians began to promulgate a very different view of union. The tone of this new work was anything but celebratory, and pro-unionist politicians were witheringly depicted as devoid of principle, courage, and vision. In the new interpretation, the union was a corrupt bargain; it was also a victory for political management and English political determination.

Explaining why the terms of debate shifted at this point is not difficult. The influence of changing political conditions in Scotland and the growth of nationalist feelings were important factors. However, the debate also reflected the pressure of the then-fashionable approach to writing eighteenth-century political history, pioneered by Sir Lewis Namier, which dismissed ideology and public opinion as important factors in political life. . . .

[More recent views] were informed by perceptions of events not just in Scotland but in a Europe confronting the threat of French 'universal monarchy', a threat that carried menacing consequences for European Protestantism and the balance of European military, political, and economic power. Against the background of the War of Spanish Succession, which Britain joined in 1702, Louis XIV's drive for European and global hegemony was readily seen as representing a direct challenge to Scottish and British national interests and integrity."

—Bob Harris, "The Anglo-Scottish Treaty of Union, 1707 in 2007: Defending the Revolution, Defeating the Jacobites," *Journal of British Studies*, 2010

1. According to Harris, compared to historians in 1907 who wrote about the Act of Union, historians in 1957 were more

    (A) opposed to the ideology of the leaders of Scotland in 1707

    (B) concerned about the growth of French power in 1707

    (C) committed to the idea of Scottish nationalism

    (D) focused on the self-interest of politicians in general

2. Historians writing in 1907 could point to which of the following developments as the most direct evidence to support their argument about whether Scotland was wise to unite with England in 1707?

    (A) The Spanish-Portuguese rivalry in the Americas in the 16th century

    (B) The success of the Dutch Republic in the 17th century

    (C) The fall of the Mughal Empire in the 18th century

    (D) The focus of the French on the West Indies in the 18th century

3. Harris argues that historians in 2007 writing about the Act of Union focused on more than did historians in 1907 and 1957 on the desire to

    (A) maintain an international balance of power

    (B) unite all people living on the island of Britain under one king

    (C) protect Roman Catholics from religious discrimination

    (D) celebrate the culture similarities between England and Scotland

SHORT-ANSWER QUESTION

1. a) Describe ONE similarity between the War of the Austrian Succession and the Seven Years' War.

    b) Describe ONE difference between the War of the Austrian Succession and the Seven Years' War.

    c) Explain one factor that accounts for the difference you described in part b.

The French Revolution

The representatives of the French people, organized as a National Assembly, believing that the ignorance, neglect, or contempt of the rights of man are the sole cause of public calamities and of the corruption of governments, have determined to set forth in a solemn declaration the natural, unalienable, and sacred rights of man. . . .

—Declaration of the Rights of Man, 1789

Essential Question: What were the causes, events, and consequences of the French Revolution?

The **French Revolution** (1789–1799) was a period of dramatic change that posed a fundamental challenge to Europe's political and social order. Before the Revolution, absolute monarchs ruled France as an extension of their own private property. They answered to no one, waged wars to increase their power and wealth, and heavily taxed the poorest people. The aristocracy and the Catholic Church had privileges and riches unknown to the common people, including exemption from taxation.

As Enlightenment ideals took hold in France, support grew for individual rights and a republican form of government. A republic is a state in which the people create the government, give it authority, and elect representatives. The representatives as well as civil servants run the government for the public good—not simply to build another palace for a king or subsidize the lavish lifestyles of nobles. France's revolutionaries found inspiration from the successes of the American Revolution and the United States Constitution.

Causes of the French Revolution

Many of the root causes of the French Revolution stemmed from economic crises. During the reign of Louis XIV, France fought many expensive wars. To finance these wars, the king raised money through taxation and borrowing. The nobility had exempted themselves from taxation, but they were willing to lend money to the crown at high interest rates. Up to 60 percent of all tax revenues—collected from commoners—went to repay these rich creditors. The remaining budget was still not nearly enough to govern a country of 25 million people and to fight its endless wars.

France had colonized many parts of the world, and while these colonies did generate wealth through trade, it was not enough to offset the costs of defending and managing them. During the Seven Years' War (1756–1763), the French crown lost vast territories in the Americas and India to Britain. Britain had now become the dominant trading power in Europe. (See Topic 5.3.)

France's Involvement in the American Revolution

France saw a chance for revenge when the American colonies declared their independence from Great Britain. After the American victory at Saratoga, the French began to provide money and weapons to the colonies. This aid helped the American colonies win the war, but France ended up in a deepening financial crisis. (See Topic 5.3.)

Problems with the Estates-General

France was on the verge of collapse, in large part because it still operated in the same fashion as it had since the Middle Ages. This was referred to as the *ancien régime*, France's feudal social and political system from the 15th century until 1789. Under this system, the Catholic Church and the nobility, who made up a small percentage of the population, controlled the economic, political, and social systems, including taxes and the courts, for their own benefit. Yet, like much of Europe, France had changed greatly during that time.

To deal with this financial crisis, King **Louis XVI** (ruled 1774–1792) was forced to call into action the **Estates-General**, which had been inactive for almost 200 years. The Estates-General was made up of three bodies:

- First Estate: the Catholic clergy—1 percent of the population, which owned 10 percent of the land

- Second Estate: the nobility—2 percent of the population, which owned 35 percent of the land

- Third Estate: everyone else in French society—97 percent of the population, which owned 55 percent of the land

As an unpopular ruler of a bankrupt state, Louis XVI felt he had to agree to revive the Estates-General. The people resented the wasteful extravagance of the Palace of Versailles, personified by the queen, **Marie Antoinette** (1755–1793), who spent lavishly on frivolous things when many of her subjects were starving. It became popular to blame Marie Antoinette, but in reality, France's problems began long before her arrival.

Though many in France hoped the Estates-General would resolve the country's problems, the governing body was ineffective for several reasons:

- Each of the three estates had one vote, even though the vast majority of French citizens were members of the Third Estate.

- The First Estate, the clergy, had already lost public confidence with the rise of secular and scientific beliefs during the Enlightenment.

- The Second Estate, the nobility, did not want to give up its privileges and power, which would involve taxing itself.

- The First and Second Estates always voted together since their interests were similar.
- Members of the Third Estate were forced to wear black robes and enter the meetings through a side door, reinforcing the perception that they were less important than the other two estates.

Eventually, the Third Estate realized that it could use its greater size to pressure the rest of the government to make significant changes.

Peasant and Bourgeois Grievances

The First and Second Estates feared mass rebellion by the peasants, who lived in poverty under feudal conditions. Outbreaks of rioting and looting by peasants were not unheard of. The **bourgeoisie** of the Third Estate—the urban middle class who lacked noble titles and therefore weren't exempt from taxation—also spoke out against the excesses of the system. However, rioting and looting did not serve their aims. Some members of the bourgeoisie were wealthier than the nobility, but they lacked the same status. They were able to dress and act like nobles, but the nobility wanted to preserve class distinctions. The aristocrats refused to share their titles or their tax exemptions.

Many of the bourgeoisie were well educated and familiar with the writings of major figures of the Enlightenment, such as John Locke, Jean-Jacques Rousseau, and Montesquieu. They were also familiar with Britain's constitutional system of government, where royal power was limited by Parliament, as well as the successful revolt of Britain's American colonies against tyrannical laws. They drew inspiration from these ideas and examples and dared to hope that they could bring about a change in their social and political position.

Between March and April of 1789, each of the three estates had compiled their grievances and their hopes for change. The people of the Third Estate asked for the following changes:

- a fairer taxation system
- a fairer voting system—by head, rather than estate
- an end to the requirement (known as the corvée) that peasants provide unpaid labor to landowners
- the elimination of the old feudal fees levied by nobles on peasant land holdings
- a halt to tithes, a 10-percent tax paid to the Church

After six weeks of negotiations that started May 5, 1789, nothing was resolved. The Third Estate walked out and declared itself the official representative government, called the **National Assembly**, insisting that the French people deserved liberty, equality, and fraternity. As a start, the National Assembly granted themselves authority over taxation.

REASONS FOR THE FRENCH REVOLUTION		
Category	Short-Term Causes	Long-Term Causes
Economic	• In the French budget for 1789, 40 percent was for interest on loans and 30 percent was for the military. • The urban poor spent 80 percent of their income on bread. • Nobles and clergy were exempt from taxation, so the burden fell on farmers and workers.	• Taxes were not increased to repay debts and military expenditures. • Nobles and clergy were exempt from taxation and thus, a burden on commoners. • The wars of Louis XIV, Louis XV, and Louis XVI had drained the economy without material gains.
Social	• Bad harvests of 1787–1788 hurt the poor. • The divide between bourgeoisie and the peasants was growing. • People disliked Queen Marie Antoinette.	• Land ownership was concentrated in the hands of the clergy and nobles. • Most people were peasants but had little status.
Political	• Few reforms helped the growing number of poor. • King Louis XVI was not a strong leader. • The bourgeoisie demanded reforms. • Each estate, regardless of size, had one vote in the Estates-General.	• Provincial Parlements wanted more power after the death of Louis XIV. • Kings refused to address basic problems of inequality. • The ideas of the philosophers and criticism of privileges and institutions grew during the Enlightenment.

The Tennis Court Oath

In June 1789, the National Assembly met at an indoor tennis court after being locked out of its traditional meeting hall, and the members swore an oath not to disperse before achieving a new constitution. Some members of the clergy and liberal nobles joined the cause. Louis XVI grudgingly accepted this new government, but secretly, the army was mobilizing around Paris and Versailles to disband it. To some historians, the Tennis Court Oath marked the beginning of the French Revolution—though most people at the time did not realize it.

Bread Shortages

All of this political maneuvering took place during France's worst economic conditions in decades. People were starving and unable to find one of the staples of their diet—bread. Bread shortages began as a result of a drought in 1788. Louis XVI decided to remove price controls on grain, thinking that if farmers could get higher prices, they would choose to grow more wheat, thus increasing the supply and keeping prices stable.

However, France's antiquated farming system didn't have the technology and efficiency to produce any additional food. As a result, prices skyrocketed. In addition, the king also allowed more grain to be exported. The exports, along with several years of bad weather, further reduced the grain supply and created a crisis.

Pamphleteers distributed written articles denouncing the king and queen. Some claimed that Marie Antoinette's response to learning of the peasants' bread crisis was unsympathetic. She reportedly said, "Let them eat cake." She did not, however, make that statement. But people believed the propaganda, and their anger at the gap between the hardships of the poor and the luxury of the wealthy grew.

The Liberal Phase of the Revolution

In the first phase of the French Revolution (1789–1791), the National Assembly produced liberal reforms—abolishing hereditary privileges for the aristocracy, increasing popular participation in voting, nationalizing the Catholic Church, and establishing a constitutional monarchy. However, as the people continued to express their rage, the Revolution became increasingly violent and intolerant of moderate opinions and actions.

Events of the Summer of 1789

On July 14, 1789, only a few weeks after the Tennis Court Oath, a group of rebels redirected the course of events. They were known as *sans-culottes* (French for "without knee-breeches") because they could not afford to buy the style of pants worn by more prosperous men. Hearing that the king was going to forcibly disband the National Assembly, the rioters stormed the Bastille, a prison in Paris. While the prison held only seven inmates (five forgers and two criminally insane), it symbolized the repression exercised by the French government. July 14, known as **Bastille Day**, has become France's equivalent of the Fourth of July in the United States. It is widely celebrated as the start of the French Revolution.

Throughout the summer of 1789, peasants rose up, destroying the manorial records and looting and burning the homes of tax collectors and elites. Nobles fled the country during what became known as the Great Fear. These actions were, however, mostly crimes against property, not people.

Source: Getty Images

The Bastille was often used to house political prisoners, although it was nearly empty when it was seized by revolutionaries on July 14, 1789.

On the night of August 4, the National Assembly officially abolished feudalism by voting to end seigniorial rights (authority as a feudal lord) and fiscal privileges of the nobility, clergy, and towns. Interestingly enough, this marked the end of the Revolution for the vast majority of French peasants, who only wanted freedom from traditional ties to the outdated manorial system.

On August 26, the National Assembly took matters a step further by issuing the **Declaration of the Rights of Man and of the Citizen**. Much like the American Declaration of Independence, it affirmed the Enlightenment ideals of "natural rights of man" so important to John Locke and Thomas Jefferson. It also incorporated the ideas of major French Enlightenment thinkers, such as Jean-Jacques Rousseau. Rousseau's idea of the social contract, that the state should represent the general will of its citizens, formed the basis for the French Declaration. It called for equality, free speech, representative government, and popular sovereignty. The day was a turning point in history. In just a few years, these ideals would spread throughout the rest of Europe.

Women's March on Versailles

In October 1789, nearly 7,000 women marched 14 miles from Paris to Versailles in the pouring rain. Carrying pitchforks, pikes, and other weapons, they chanted, "Bread! Bread!" Upon arrival, they broke into the palace searching for Marie Antoinette. Eventually, Marie Antoinette—using her children as a human shield—stood on a balcony before the angry crowd and allowed them to scream their frustrations at her.

The women didn't kill the queen, though they had beheaded two of her guards and stuck their heads on pikes. As a result of this turmoil, the king was forced to agree to the following terms:

- distribution of all the bread the palace had hoarded
- acceptance of the Declaration of the Rights of Man and of the Citizen
- agreement to accompany the women back to Paris to see how real citizens lived

The king saw no choice but to accept the demands. The October march by the women of Paris ended the days of the king's reign from the lavish Palace of Versailles. From that point until their executions (Louis in January 1793 and Marie Antoinette in October of the same year), the king and queen lived as virtual prisoners of the Revolution.

Civil Constitution of the Clergy

One issue facing the new government was the role of the Church. Already, the National Assembly had abolished all monastic orders and confiscated the Catholic Church's lands within France. The **Civil Constitution of the Clergy** (1790) expanded the law in the following ways:

- The Catholic Church was placed completely under the authority of the state.
- All of the clergy (not just the upper clergy) was told it owed its primary allegiance to France.
- The 10-percent tithe (tax) paid by the peasants was eliminated.
- Church dioceses were aligned with new administrative districts.
- In the future, bishops and priests would be elected by assemblies.

The new government sold church property to raise money for the government. France was largely a Catholic nation, so all these acts restricting the Church angered its strongest supporters, and many turned against the French Revolution.

Abolition of Provinces and Division of France into Departments

In 1790, the National Assembly abolished the provinces of the *ancien régime* to achieve greater national unity. After 1792, the country was divided into 83 *départements*, or **departments**, based on geographical features more than on historical territories that had their own loyalties. The departments established in 1792 still exist today.

Constitution of 1791

France's first constitution established a constitutional monarchy that placed lawmaking power in the hands of the new legislative assembly. It also gave the king a limited veto and allowed him to appoint his own ministers. However, many French citizens did not trust that their monarch would abide by the terms of the constitution.

The War of 1792

Louis XVI and his family had been forced to move from Versailles to the Tuileries Palace in Paris, where they could be more easily monitored. One night in June 1791, in what became known as the Flight to Varennes, they disguised themselves and attempted to flee the country. After they were caught and forced to return to Paris, their captors discovered that the king had written a letter denouncing the Revolution. In addition, a group of émigrés, or people who had left the country, and much of the French army loyal to the king had urged Prussia and Austria to invade France to restore the monarchy to its previous power. Despite its internal struggles, the new French government declared war on those nations in 1792.

The Revolution's leaders convinced the French people that defending the country and supporting the Revolution were tied together. Working-class Parisians stormed the Tuileries Palace, where the king's family lived in constant terror. The rioters killed approximately 600 members of the king's guard and threatened the legislative assembly.

The Radical Revolution

By 1790, political parties had begun to spring up, organized as clubs. Foremost among these were the **Jacobins**. The Jacobins included members of the National Assembly and radical leaders such as **Maximilien de Robespierre** (1758–1794).

Following the summer violence of 1792, the National Assembly dissolved itself, calling for elections to form a new parliament called the **National Convention**. All adult men, but no women, would be permitted to vote. However, rumors had spread that prisoners planned to join up with the approaching Prussian army. Radical *sans-culottes* such as **Jean-Paul Marat** (1743–1793) whipped the people into a frenzy of violence known as the September Massacres, in which crowds attacked the prisons and slaughtered more than 1,000 inmates.

The Jacobins seized control of the National Convention from the more moderate **Girondins** and implemented the following changes in 1792–1793:

- the elimination of the French monarchy—both Louis XVI and Marie Antoinette were executed by guillotine in January and October 1793, respectively
- the declaration of the Republic of France
- the adoption of a new calendar
- the de-Christianization of France

The De-Christianization of France

The National Assembly pursued a policy of de-Christianization as part of its attempt to establish a new order based on Enlightenment reason rather than faith. *Saint* was removed from all street names, the cathedral of Notre Dame was renamed the Temple of Reason, and a new republican calendar was adopted with year one beginning on September 22, 1792, the day on which the National Convention had proclaimed France a republic. Each year would have 12 months of three 10-day weeks. The remaining days were designated as festival days. The calendar reduced the number of nonworking days from 56 to 35, eliminating Catholic holidays. The new calendar faced much opposition from the beginning and eventually it was abandoned.

The Reign of Terror

The other nations of Europe, horrified by the overthrow of the French monarchy and the subsequent killing of the monarchs, allied against France. France stood alone against its enemies, but it could not unite. The Jacobins and Girondins couldn't compromise to rule the country and quell the violence. Fearful that the Revolution was in danger, the Jacobins began the **Reign of Terror**, a 10-month attempt to quash or kill the opponents of the Revolution, during which they guillotined approximately 16,000 citizens in Paris alone. Across France, the number of people executed by guillotine and otherwise reached somewhere near 50,000.

The Committee of Public Safety When the Reign of Terror began, the **Committee of Public Safety** was created. It suspended the new constitution and controlled the National Convention. Robespierre and **Georges Danton** (1759–1794) headed the Committee. Its job was to defend against foreign attacks and domestic rebellions. Because of the threats to France from across Europe and from within its own borders, the Committee assumed great powers. As Robespierre's vendettas against the counterrevolutionaries grew more extreme, people began to denounce the Committee for acting like a dictatorship. Those critics were arrested and executed. Danton, who strongly disapproved of the suppression of dissent, retreated from public life. However, soon Danton was drawn back into politics as a leader of the moderate opposition. For example, he argued against the complete elimination of Christianity. Robespierre had Danton arrested on charges of corruption and executed. At the guillotine, Danton said, "Show my head to the people. It is worth the trouble."

Revolutionary Armies and Mass Conscription

The Jacobins were an unstable force, but they did change French society. They promoted a strong sense of patriotism and created an enormous army. All able-bodied unmarried men aged 18 to 25 were conscripted to serve in a draft called the **levée en masse** (mass levy). Despite some draft evasions and desertions, the army grew to more than 1,000,000 men by 1794—the largest Europe had seen. Previous wars had been fought by professional soldiers of governments or dynasties. But this French force was an army created by a people's government, and the entire nation was involved in the war. Civilians were killed on a larger scale than ever before, and the door was opened to the total war of the modern world.

The French army was responsible for not only preserving the Revolution in France but also for spreading its ideals through Europe. With fair pay and benefits, soldiers and their families were committed to the revolutionary movement to spread wealth more equally and to end poverty. Families of soldiers received stipends. Men injured in battle were given generous veterans' benefits. France's goal became not only to reinvent itself but also to spread its beliefs throughout Europe using its army of believers.

Women in the French Revolution

The Declaration of the Rights of Man and of the Citizen was aptly named since the French Revolution did not extend equal rights to women. Women couldn't vote, own property, make a will, file a lawsuit, or serve on a jury. However, in the early stages of the Revolution, women were hopeful about gaining rights. They participated by forming clubs and debating politics.

Olympe de Gouges

Writer and reformer **Olympe de Gouges** (1748–1793) fought for the rights of women and minorities during the Revolution. Her most famous work was the "Declaration of the Rights of Woman and of the Female Citizen" (1791)—a

response to the failure of revolutionary ideals to extend to women. She once said, "Women have the right to mount the scaffold; they should likewise have the right to mount the rostrum [a podium for political speeches]." She herself often made speeches advocating divorce rights for women and the right of children whose parents were not married (as hers were not) to inherit parental property.

Though de Gouges was initially enthusiastic about the Revolution, its excesses dismayed her. As with many famous figures during this time, her death date gives a clue to her fate. She was beheaded by guillotine during the Reign of Terror for aligning herself with the moderate Girondists.

Source: Alexander Kucharsky
Portrait of Olympe de Gouges, c. 1790

Society of Republican Revolutionary Women

The group known as the **Society of Republican Revolutionary Women** lasted only five months, but it raised issues important to women of the time. Founded in 1793, it consisted largely of working-class women who vowed to "rush to the defense of the Fatherland" and "to live for the Republic or to die for it." Women of the group wore decorated red bonnets to signal their membership, which often provoked violence against them. During during the Reign of Terror in 1793, when the Jacobins turned against one of the women's leaders, the society dissolved itself.

The End of the Reign of Terror

By the end of June 1794, the people of France had grown weary of the seemingly endless executions—there had been 1,300 in June alone. On July 26, Robespierre gave a speech full of threats, and the next day deputies of the National Convention arrested him in what became known as the Thermidorian Reaction (named for the month of Thermidor in the revolutionary calendar).

Robespierre's Execution and the Establishment of the Directory

Robespierre was challenged by opponents on the Committee of Public Safety, many of whom worried that they might be next on his execution list. He was sent to the guillotine in 1794. After the execution of Robespierre, the Reign of Terror subsided. The moderate Girondins who had survived returned to power and wrote a new constitution that did the following:

- established France's first bicameral (two-house) legislature
- gave executive power to a five-member committee called the *Directoire*, or Directory
- allowed Parliament to appoint the members of the Directory

The Directory was yet another unsuccessful attempt at government. It lasted only four years and was riddled with corruption. It came to rely on the French army to enforce its authority. When radical factions such as the Jacobins protested, they were shut down by the army, now led by a young general named **Napoleon Bonaparte** (1769–1821). Napoleon and other generals wielded much of the national power as the French army pacified the country and also defeated the Prussians, Austrians, Spanish, and Dutch.

The Consulate

In 1799, Napoleon staged a coup d'état, a sudden overthrow of the government. He abolished the Directory. He replaced it with a governing system called the Consulate in which three consuls, or chief magistrates, would lead the French government. Napoleon appointed himself one of the consuls. The system lasted just five years, from 1799 to 1804.

REFLECT ON THE ESSENTIAL QUESTION

Essential Question: *What were the causes, events, and consequences of the French Revolution?*

Causes	Events	Consequences

KEY TERMS

French Revolution
Louis XVI
Estates-General
Marie Antoinette
bourgeoisie
National Assembly
Bastille Day
Declaration of the Rights of Man and of the Citizen

Civil Constitution of the Clergy
department
Jacobin
Maximilien de Robespierre
National Convention
Jean-Paul Marat
Girondin
Reign of Terror

Committee of Public Safety
Georges Danton
levée en masse
Olympe de Gouges
Society of Revolutionary Women
Napoleon Bonaparte

MULTIPLE-CHOICE QUESTIONS

Questions 1–3 refer to the passages below.

Passage 1

"Mothers, daughters, sisters [and] representatives of the nation demand to be constituted into a national assembly. Believing that ignorance, omission, or scorn for the rights of woman are the only causes of public misfortunes and of the corruption of governments, [the women] have resolved to set forth in a solemn declaration the natural, inalienable, and sacred rights of woman in order that this declaration, constantly exposed before all the members of the society, will ceaselessly remind them of their rights and duties; in order that the authoritative acts of women and the authoritative acts of men may be at any moment compared with and respectful of the purpose of all political institutions; and in order that citizens' demands, henceforth based on simple and incontestable principles, will always support the constitution, good morals, and the happiness of all."

—Olympe de Gouges, preamble to the "Declaration of Rights of Woman and the Female Citizen," 1791

Passage 2

"Consider, sir, dispassionately these observations, for a glimpse of this truth seemed to open before you when you observed, 'that to see one-half of the human race excluded by the other from all participation of government was a political phenomenon that, according to abstract principles, it was impossible to explain.' If so, on what does your constitution rest? If the abstract rights of man will bear discussion and explanation, those of woman, by a parity of reasoning, will not shrink from the same test; though a different opinion prevails in this country, built on the very arguments which you use to justify the oppression of woman — prescription.

Consider . . . when men contend for their freedom, and to be allowed to judge for themselves respecting their own happiness, it be not inconsistent and unjust to subjugate women, even though you firmly believe that you are acting in the manner best calculated to promote their happiness? Who made man the exclusive judge, if woman partake with him of the gift of reason?"

—Mary Wollstonecraft, introduction, *A Vindication of the Rights of Woman*, 1792

1. The passages are best understood in the context of which of the following events?
   (A) The Women's March on Versailles, which promoted ideas of women's suffrage
   (B) Lack of political rights for women during the revolutionary era
   (C) Rousseau's support for gender equality prior to the French Revolution
   (D) The debate over women's suffrage prior to the convening of the Estates-General

2. Both arguments reflect which of the following developments during the early phases of the French Revolution?
   (A) More women than men were executed during the Reign of Terror.
   (B) Lafayette proposed including women in the National Assembly.
   (C) Napoleon opened lycées for both men and women.
   (D) Women were active in political debates concerning the revolution.

3. Which of the following was a result of the ideas expressed in the passage?
   (A) The implementation of universal suffrage by the National Convention
   (B) The creation of the Society of Republican Revolutionary Women
   (C) The execution of Louis XIV and Marie Antoinette
   (D) The elimination of the Girondists during the Reign of Terror

SHORT-ANSWER QUESTION

Use the passage below to answer all parts of the question that follows.

" 'The evil which besets us,' declared Jeanbon Saint-André on 1 August, 'is that we have no government.' As a member of the Committee of Public Safety, he ought to have known. But when Danton proposed, in the same session, that the Committee be recognized formally as France's provisional government, the Convention would not agree. . . . It never did become the government, or enjoy undisputed executive authority. But in the course of the next twelve months it was to give the country the leadership to mobilize its resources with unprecedented assurance, and put the crisis of 1793 behind it."

—William Doyle, *Oxford History of the French Revolution*, 1989

1. a) Describe ONE specific argument used by people who thought Jacobin policies expressed the ideals of the French Revolution.
   b) Describe ONE specific argument used by people who thought Jacobin policies undermined the ideals of the French Revolution.
   c) Explain how Doyle views the Committee of Public Safety.

Topic 5.5

The French Revolution's Effects

So then, as you cannot deny what you have sworn, we are within our rights, and you ought to recognize yourselves as perjurers; by your decrees you recognize that all men are free, but you want to maintain servitude for 480,000 individuals who allow you to enjoy all that you possess.

—François Dominique Toussaint (Toussaint L'Ouverture),
letter to colonial leaders of Saint-Domingue, 1792

Essential Question: How did the events and developments of the French Revolution influence political and social ideas from 1789 to 1815?

In his letter to the colonial leaders of Saint-Domingue, Toussaint L'Ouverture accuses them of hypocrisy. He points out that the Declaration of the Rights of Man and of the Citizen states that "men are born and remain free and equal in rights" and that their "rights are liberty, property, security, and resistance to oppression," yet they continue to rely on the labor of enslaved people. His letter is an impassioned appeal for the abolition of slavery in keeping with the spirit of revolutionary France.

The Revolution Outside of France

Napoleon's coup ended the era of the French Revolution and ushered in the Napoleonic era. Under Napoleon's military leadership, France dominated the European continent and spread its revolutionary ideals across the world. This sometimes resulted in France's own colonies fighting for independence against their colonial rulers.

The Haitian Independence Movement

As Napoleon was rising through the military ranks, the French Revolution inspired rebellions in other regions of the world. Partly, people felt inspired by the power of the Revolution's egalitarian ideals. In addition, while France was embroiled in domestic strife, its colonies were vulnerable to unrest. One major uprising began as a slave revolt in the French colony that would become the nation of Haiti.

Toussaint L'Ouverture (c. 1743–1803) was a Black man born enslaved on Saint-Domingue, the western half of the Caribbean Island of Hispaniola. Today the island is composed of Haiti and the Dominican Republic. L'Ouverture's master taught him to read and later freed him in 1776. L'Ouverture possessed several traits that made him a great leader. He was intelligent and literate and could speak several languages. Further, he was a skilled military commander and a shrewd diplomat. Like Napoleon, L'Ouverture was influenced by the Enlightenment and ascended to power during a revolution.

Slave Revolt Saint-Domingue was perhaps the world's most lucrative colony. The sugar it grew and exported made plantation owners very wealthy. However, 89 percent of its inhabitants were enslaved Africans. Owners often worked enslaved people to death and used torture to punish them. One owner said it was more profitable to work an enslaved person to death and buy another one than to treat a slave humanely.

In 1791, a slave rebellion started to spread through the colony. Though L'Ouverture was already free, he shared the enslaved people's rage and took command of the revolt. First, he shipped his wife, sons, and former master off the island and to safety. Then, he trained his troops in guerrilla warfare tactics. Guerrilla warfare involves quick, small military actions against larger regular army or police units.

Source: Getty Images

Toussaint L'Ouverture, the leader of the Haitian Revolution, used guerrilla tactics effectively against the French colonial rulers.

While France fought its own Revolution, Spain and Britain invaded and tried to seize the profitable Saint-Domingue. Initially, the Black rebel commanders joined with the Spaniards from the eastern side of Hispaniola, while the British occupied the island's coasts. France's hold on its most profitable colony was in danger. However, in 1794, the French National Convention did what neither Spain nor England would: they declared the enslaved people free. L'Ouverture returned to the French side.

Haiti After the Revolt The French governor of Saint-Domingue appointed L'Ouverture lieutenant governor. The British began losing ground, and the Spaniards were expelled from Saint-Domingue. L'Ouverture became a popular figure who advocated for reconciliation between the races. Though L'Ouverture forced people to work, the laborers were free and shared in plantation profits. European plantation owners were permitted to return and run their businesses.

L'Ouverture pushed his rivals aside and appointed himself military governor over the newly renamed nation of Haiti. First, he signed trade treaties with Britain, much to the displeasure of France. Then, his forces invaded the Spanish portion of the island and freed all the enslaved people there. Napoleon distrusted L'Ouverture and began plotting against him. A French army arrived on the island, and L'Ouverture was tricked and arrested. He died in a French prison in 1803. However, his trusted followers feared France would reestablish slavery. They fought the French army and won, leading to Haiti's independence in 1804.

Opponents of the French Revolution

The French Revolution was initially received with enthusiasm by many intellectuals and revolutionaries, including the German Friedrich Schiller and Americans such as Thomas Jefferson and Thomas Paine. It gave hope to people throughout Europe who wanted change. Because France's Enlightenment ideals didn't match the violent reality of its actions, however, many of these early supporters eventually condemned the French Revolution. And there was always opposition to the Revolution, both within France and abroad.

Opponents Within France

Not everyone in France supported the French Revolution. While many conservative opponents of the Revolution met their end on the guillotine, some survived the turmoil by emigrating. Joseph de Maistre (1743–1821) and Louis-Gabriel-Ambroise, Viscount de Bonald, were two of the leading opponents of the French Revolution. Maistre was an author and diplomat who opposed both the scientific ideas of Francis Bacon and the Enlightenment ideas of Locke, Voltaire, and Rousseau. He believed in the supremacy of Christianity and the absolute rule of the monarch and the pope. Bonald was a politician who resigned in 1791 in protest against the Civil Constitution of the Clergy and emigrated to the German city of Heidelberg. He was condemned by the Directory for his royalist writings but was later allowed to return to France.

Opponents Outside of France

The monarchs of Britain, Austria, and Prussia opposed the French Revolution and threatened to invade France. Queen Marie Antoinette had encouraged her brother, Holy Roman Emperor Leopold II, to invade France in 1792. He joined Prussia in calling on other European rulers to save the French monarchy, but he died before France declared war on Austria.

One of the most influential writers of the time was the Englishman **Edmund Burke** (1729–1797). Burke wrote *Reflections on the Revolution in France*. In it, he cautioned Britain against engaging in the types of excesses occurring in France. Burke began writing his book in 1789 before the Reign of Terror;

however, his warnings of anarchy came to pass. Britain managed to subdue its own radical reformers who demanded greater freedoms both at home and for British subjects in India. Britain's stable representative government and healthy economy allowed it to remain peaceful.

REFLECT ON THE ESSENTIAL QUESTION

Essential Question: *How did the events and developments of the French Revolution influence political and social ideas from 1789 to 1815?*

Political Influences	Social Influences

KEY TERMS

Toussaint L'Ouverture   Edmund Burke

MULTIPLE-CHOICE QUESTIONS

Questions 1–3 refer to the passages below.

"It is Toussaint's supreme merit that while he saw European civilization as a valuable and necessary thing, and strove to lay its foundations among his people, he never had the illusion that it conferred any moral superiority. He knew French, British, and Spanish imperialists for the insatiable gangsters that they were, that there is no oath too sacred for them to break, no crime, deception, treachery, cruelty, destruction of human life and property which they would not commit against those who could not defend themselves. . . .

The cruelties of property and privilege are always more ferocious than the revenges of poverty and oppression. For the one aims at perpetuating resented injustice, the other is merely a momentary passion soon appeased."

—C.L.R. James, *The Black Jacobins: Toussaint L'Ouverture and the San Domingo Revolution*, 1938

1. What part of European civilization did Toussaint find "valuable and necessary"?
   (A) Christian emphasis on compassionate treatment of the defenseless
   (B) Enlightenment emphasis on reason and rights
   (C) Neoclassical emphasis on order and balance
   (D) Romantic emphasis on individualism

2. Based on these passages, the best summary of James's point of view toward the Haitian rebels is that he is

(A) opposed to them because of their use of violence

(B) opposed to them because they supported imperialism

(C) sympathetic to them despite their use of violence

(D) sympathetic to them despite their support for imperialism

3. James claims that one contrast between Haitians and Europeans is that Haitians were more likely to use violence

(A) briefly in order to achieve goals quickly

(B) consistently in order to maintain power

(C) cruelly in order to inflict suffering on others

(D) purposely in order to force people to change their religious beliefs

SHORT-ANSWER QUESTION

Use the image below to answer all parts of the question that follows.

Source: Wikimedia Commons/Anne-Louis Girodet de Roucy-Trioson

Jean-Baptiste Belley was a leader in the Haitian Revolution who also served in the French government. In this portrait, he is standing in front of a bust of Guillaume-Thomas Raynal, a writer who supported the French Revolution.

1. a) Describe ONE way that the above image shows the influence of the French Revolution on the Haitian Revolution.

b) Describe ONE way that conditions in Haiti were a cause of one of the events Belley was involved in.

c) Explain ONE effect of the Haitian Revolution on Europe's existing political order.

Topic 5.6

Napoleon's Rise, Dominance, and Defeat

The ideas that underpin our modern world—meritocracy, equality before the law, property rights, religious toleration, modern secular education, sound finances, and so on—were championed, consolidated, codified and geographically extended by Napoleon.

—Andrew Roberts, *Napoleon the Great*, 2014

Essential Question: What were the effects of Napoleon's rule on European social, economic, and political life?

Essential Question: What were the nationalist responses in Europe to Napoleon's rule?

Napoleon himself believed that he would be remembered longer for the code of civil law that bears his name than for the many battles he won as he conquered most of Europe. The Napoleonic Code was not just the law of France but of all the parts of Europe under French control. It was also adopted by many other European and Latin American countries, and the laws of Louisiana are based on it. It is still the law in a great many nations, confirming Napoleon's foresight.

Napoleon's Rise to Power

Born on the island of Corsica, Napoleon Bonaparte came from humble circumstances. He went to French schools and the military academy in Paris, graduating 42nd in a class of 58 at the age of 16. Upon graduation, he began his military career as a second lieutenant. He read Voltaire and Rousseau, and in 1791 he joined the Jacobin Club, which began as a debating society that favored a constitutional monarchy. During the Revolution, he rose quickly as an officer, achieving the rank of brigadier general in 1793 at age 24.

Napoleon was in Paris in October 1795 when the National Convention submitted a new constitution. Supporters of the monarchy staged an insurrection, and Napoleon was placed in charge of the troops that opened fire on the rebels. After saving the National Convention from the Parisian mobs, he defeated the Austrians in Italy. Returning to France as a hero, Napoleon was given command of an army to invade Egypt. After attacking and occupying the

Nile Delta, Napoleon's army was stranded when his fleet was destroyed by the British. Napoleon eventually returned to France, leading a successful coup to overthrow the Directory in November 1799.

First Consul and Emperor

A new governing body, the three-member Consulate, replaced the Directory. Napoleon was first consul along with two former members of the Directory. One of the Consulate's first acts was to draw up a new constitution. It gave most of the power to the first consul, who could appoint most members of the government. The Consulate also undertook administrative reforms that would outlast the constitution.

In 1800, Napoleon led the French army against Austrian forces in Italy and won. This victory cemented his power. He signed a peace treaty with Britain. By 1802, he had the government name him first consul for life, but that title was not enough to satisfy his desire for power. In 1804, he crowned himself Napoleon I, emperor of France.

Domestic Reforms Under Napoleon

Napoleon wanted to stabilize France after the violent excesses of the Revolution. One important step he took was to create the **Civil Code** (also called the Napoleonic Code), a body of law governing people, property, and civil procedures. Prior to the Code's adoption in 1804, France had a confusing, disorganized set of regional regulations based on feudal traditions. The Civil Code reinforced revolutionary principles by recognizing the equality of all male citizens under the law, guaranteeing religious toleration, and protecting property rights.

Centralized Government and the Merit System Napoleon also created a centralized national government, in which merit, rather than ancestry or social position, determined advancement. Since careers were now based on talent, the French bureaucracy grew more efficient. For the first time, it applied a tax system fair to all. When Napoleon became first consul, the government had a debt of 474 million francs, and it had only 167,000 francs in the treasury. Napoleon hired professional tax collectors who maintained accurate records and didn't skim from the money they collected. Gradually, indirect taxes increased on various items. Reducing expenses and increasing revenues helped stabilize the government's budget.

Educational System Under Napoleon, France opened schools called *lycées* (lee-sayz) for boys ages 10 to 16. The middle class now had more educational opportunities, with the idea that these young men would then move into the military and the government. Scholarships were given to those who could not afford to attend. The *lycées'* primary purpose was to indoctrinate an entire generation into the Napoleonic way of thinking.

Religious Reforms The **Concordat of 1801**, an agreement between Napoleon and representatives of the Catholic Church in Paris and Rome, reconciled some of the hostility caused by the earlier eradication of Christianity and confiscation of Church lands:

- The Catholic Church was reestablished in France, but it gave up claims on its former land holdings (which had already been sold by auction).
- Napoleon would nominate bishops, who would appoint priests, but the government would pay both Catholic and Protestant clergy.
- Napoleon recognized that Catholicism was the religion of the majority of French citizens without making it the official state religion.

Economic Reforms Napoleon's goals to promote economic health were straightforward—increase foreign trade and strive for full employment. Agriculture was a key to achieving both ends. Before the Revolution, France's agricultural system was so antiquated that the country imported staples such as butter and cheese. By 1812, France had become an exporter of these goods. Textile exports boomed as well. Napoleon discouraged unions and closely regulated the trade guilds, thinking that unhappy workers in unions could plant the seeds of rebellion. Instead, he focused on improving worker conditions to preempt any desire to unionize.

Curtailment of Rights Under Napoleon

Napoleon succeeded in creating national laws, reforming the economy, and affirming the redistribution of land once held by the Catholic Church. However, he was no longer a proponent of "liberty, equality, and fraternity"—the slogan of the French Revolution. To maintain power and build his empire, he used secret police, censored free speech, and limited individual rights. Abroad, he reinstituted slavery on the French islands of Martinique and Guadalupe in the Caribbean. In name, France was a republic that became an empire. In reality, it was a dictatorship.

Secret Police During Napoleon's reign, royalist and radical plotters threatened the government and its leaders. The man responsible for uncovering these plots was Minister of Police Joseph Fouché (1759–1820), who acted as chief of espionage. Fouché ran a vast network of spies and was adept at gathering and using information. He even kept a dossier on Napoleon.

Fouché, a former priest, hated the Catholic Church and refused to support the Concordat of 1801. His strong views cost him his job at one point, but his skill in discovering dissenters made him valuable to Napoleon. Fouché assured Napoleon that all possible threats to the emperor were eliminated—either publicly or privately. Some innocent people were assassinated simply to send a message to potential plotters. Napoleon didn't worry about these deaths. He believed that the ends of maintaining order justified such means.

Censorship and Restrictions Press censorship became more and more important to Napoleon as he came under increased public criticism. Paris had four major newspapers, each of which was required to maintain an on-staff censor to suppress criticism of Napoleon's politics or resistance to his military expansions across Europe.

Limitation of Women's Rights Under Napoleon's reign, women did not have the same rights as men. For example, a husband had the legal power to:

- control his wife's wages
- control the property his wife brought into marriage
- divorce his wife for adultery (even have her imprisoned)
- control all jointly held property
- control his wife's ability to file suits in civil court, take loans, or sell property

Further, while men could obtain a divorce easily, women could do so only with difficulty. All these rules were part of the Napoleonic Code.

The Napoleonic Wars

Napoleon was one of the most influential generals in history. He transformed the French army, combining ideas of leading military theorists with the study of great generals of the past. Among the new military tactics he adopted were:

- conscripting many men to provide a large army
- intense drilling of soldiers organized in units that could operate independently but come together for battle
- training soldiers to live off the land so that they would not be slowed by the need to transport large quantities of supplies
- adopting lighter field guns than those used by other armies
- using quicker battlefield movement
- delivering a decisive blow for total destruction of enemy armies
- cutting off the enemy's lines of communication and ability to retreat with a "move to the rear"

Between 1799 and 1815, Napoleon fought a shifting alliance of European countries during the period of the **Napoleonic Wars**. Using his large army of patriotic citizens, Napoleon won nearly all his early battles. His 1805 defeat of the Austrian and Russian armies at Austerlitz, in Moravia, is considered one of his greatest victories. Later that year, however, the French suffered a rare defeat at the Battle of Trafalgar, off the southern coast Spain, when the British navy under Horatio Nelson put an end to Napoleon's plans to invade England. The next year, Napoleon defeated the Prussians at Jena and Auerstädt.

Spread of Revolutionary Ideals Across Europe

By 1806, much of central and southern Europe was under French control, and Napoleon's armies spread the ideals of the Revolution. They proved that ordinary citizens could overthrow a monarchy and strip the aristocracy of their traditional privileges. Peasants now owned lands formerly controlled by the Church. When enlaved Haitians rebelled, France abolished slavery there. When the Haitians learned that the French had reintroduced slavery on the nearby island of Guadeloupe, they revolted against French rule and in 1804 won their independence. Despite setbacks and missteps, the trajectory was clear: the old order was ending and the time of the common people had arrived. This notion changed European politics and societies forever.

NAPOLEON'S EMPIRE AT ITS HEIGHT, 1812

Nationalistic Responses

The period from 1804, when Napoleon crowned himself emperor, until 1814, when he abdicated for the first time (but soon returned to power), became known as the First Empire. Napoleon abolished the Holy Roman Empire and redrew the map of Europe. The armies of Napoleon spread the ideas of the French Revolution, abolishing feudalism as they conquered territory. He heavily taxed conquered peoples to spare the French while he continued his wars. Unable to defeat Britain militarily, Napoleon created the **Continental System**, a blockade of British goods being shipped to European ports.

Napoleon's actions awakened a new identity in the people he conquered. People began to feel a stronger sense of nationalism, a pride in one's cultural heritage that later led to a desire to have a single political state for that culture. Before the spread of nationalism, people identified more with their city or region than with all people who shared their culture. Their political loyalty was more to an individual ruler, such as a king, than to the state in general. People often were loyal to a ruler who did not even speak their language.

Guerrilla War in Spain Napoleon invaded Spain in 1808, forcing King Charles IV to abdicate and placing his brother on the throne. The British joined Spanish forces in fighting the French. The British effectively used small bands of Spanish fighters to harass the French army. These small groups used guerrilla tactics to harass and indefinitely occupy the French army of 200,000 men, keeping them from joining Napoleon's Grand Army in its struggles elsewhere. By 1814, Napoleon had lost what was called the Peninsular War.

Nationalism in German States Nationalism also arose in German states, especially Prussia, where intellectuals called for cultural nationalism based on the unity of the German people. Prussia, which had been crushed by the army of Napoleon, undertook a series of political and military reforms. These included the abolition of serfdom and the creation of a larger standing army.

Following Napoleon's final defeat in 1815, students began the *Burschenschaft* ("Youth Association") movement at the University of Jena. The movement, which soon spread throughout the German states, embraced liberal constitutionalism and the unification of Germany. After student demonstrations in 1817 at Wartburg and a politically motivated assassination in 1819 by a *Burschenschafter*, alarmed German governments issued the Carlsbad Decrees to suppress the movement. The decrees merely succeeded in driving the movement underground.

Russian Scorched-Earth Policy Declaring that he wanted to free Poland from Russian power and hoping to end Russian support for Great Britain, Napoleon invaded Russia in June 1812 with an army of about 600,000. Russia had an army of about equal size but had the advantage of knowing the land and how to survive the harsh Russian winter.

As French forces moved deeper into Russia, the Russian army made the strategic choice to retreat, never giving the French the opportunity to defeat them decisively. Further, the Russians burned everything behind them, preventing the French army from living off the land. Napoleon managed to reach Moscow, but the city had been evacuated and was ablaze. Lacking food and supplies, Napoleon began to retreat in October. However, his decision to retreat came too late. As the Russian winter set in, French troops and their horses began dying from cold and starvation. Fewer than 40,000 French soldiers returned home. French hegemony, or authority over others, had ended.

End of the Napoleonic Era

As his army retreated during the Russian winter, Napoleon learned of an attempted coup back in France. He also faced a revived alliance of Austria, Russia, Prussia, and Great Britain. Napoleon was forced to abdicate in 1814 and exiled to the Mediterranean island of Elba. His return to France during the "Hundred Days" in 1815 was received enthusiastically among the French but rejected by other European countries. Napoleon raised another army, only to be defeated at the **Battle of Waterloo** in present-day Belgium. He abdicated a second time and this time was exiled to St. Helena, a remote island in the South Atlantic Ocean, where he remained until his death in 1821. Approximately 750,000 French soldiers and citizens died as a result of warfare during the time Napoleon pursued his dreams of domination.

MONUMENT TO NAPOLEON!

Source: Getty Images

Napoleon was portrayed by artists in contrasting ways—as a noble Roman emperor (top left), a tyrannical murderer (bottom left), or an inspiring general (right)—depending on which aspect of his life certain people wanted to emphasize.

REFLECT ON THE ESSENTIAL QUESTIONS

Essential Question: *What were the effects of Napoleon's rule on European social, economic, and political life?*

Essential Question: *What were the nationalist responses in Europe to Napoleon's rule?*

Effects on Social, Economic, and Political Life	Nationalist Responses

KEY TERMS

Civil Code	Napoleonic Wars	Battle of Waterloo
Concordat of 1801	Continental System	

Napoleon's historical importance is undeniable. But different historians depict him as various combinations of hero, tyrant, military genius, and heir to the French Revolution.

An Opportunist Conservative British historian and journalist Paul Johnson argued in a 2002 biography that Napoleon was merely an opportunist. Though Johnson gave him credit for his early military successes, he ascribes Napoleon's ultimate political and diplomatic failures to continued military campaigns.

A Machiavellian French historian and journalist Laurent Joffrin concluded in a 2004 article that "despite the blood and death, despite the wars and repression, his taste for rule and his mania for state building have meant that the despot [Napoleon] is seen as the favorite dictator of the French republic," meaning they like him better than Robespierre, best remembered for subjecting the French to the Reign of Terror. Joffrin explained that Napoleon accomplished more in three years than any of his predecessors. However, the beneficial results came from Napoleon's anger "more suited to the boxing ring" than an administrative office. He once threatened an opponent with a whip. Joffrin also noted Napoleon's use of repression to reestablish rule of law. In conquered territories, this meant executions without trials, burning villages, and imprisoning opponents. In France, repression included setting up spy networks in order to manipulate opinion and keep Napoleon informed.

Despite Napoleon's flaws, Joffrin saw some positive accomplishments. He explained that the Civil Code was Napoleon's proudest achievement and that "if he made war, it was only in order to govern better." But in the end, according to Joffrin, Napoleon's rationalism broke down and personal glory took root.

A Complex Hero By 2004, with the publication of Napoleon's complete correspondences, an even more complex picture of the French leader emerged. Oxford historian Michael Broers attempted to revisit the story of Napoleon, after having already written *Europe Under Napoleon* (1996) and analyzing Napoleon's elite paramilitary force—the *Gendarmerie*—in 1999 with the publication of the article "The Napoleonic Police and Their Legacy." In these earlier works, Broers described a Europe that only knew the horrors of war. French soldiers were hated because they were seen as not fighting for universal revolutionary ideals but for the nation of France, a France that had an ugly history of war with its neighbors. But as Napoleon took charge, the battle lines moved, and the "inner empire" (France) was free from war, and from 1801–1812, it remained stable and secure, leaving Napoleon free to establish stable civilian administration, expand his prefect system, implement the Napoleonic Code, end guilds, and protect freedoms.

However, the "outer empire"—Spain in particular—resisted stability despite the efforts of the *Gendarmerie* and remained unstable, even after the defeat of

Napoleon, whereas the inner empire quickly recovered and continued pursuing the ideas of the Napoleonic Code. Life in the inner empire was regulated by a clear, rational, and usually fair legal code. All these characteristics of the Napoleonic Empire are still at work in Europe because they remain effective. Broers even suggested that Napoleon ingrained these ideals and values so successfully that they remain central to the values of the European Union today.

Already noted for fair treatment of Napoleon, with new sources at his disposal, Broers described the political philosophy of Napoleon as based on the goal of persuading reactionaries to support the new regime (*ralliament*) and joining it (*amalgame*). While Joffrin did credit Napoleon for listening to his advisers early, he stressed Napoleon's desire to be the one to always make decisions and how he increasingly did so with little advice, whereas Broers used the letters to document Napoleon's consistent effort to seek the counsel of his advisers, govern by committee, and promote based on talent. Much like Johnson, Broers concluded that Napoleon's success was military, but not because of the land conquered; instead, it was because of his successful political policies of *ralliament* and *amalgame*.

1. Explain how Napoleon might be viewed as the heir to the French Revolution.

2. In what ways could Napoleon be considered a tyrant?

3. What do you consider to be Napoleon's legacy?

MULTIPLE-CHOICE QUESTIONS

Questions 1–3 refer to the following passage.

"Chapter VI: Of the Respective Rights and Duties of Married Persons

214. The wife is obliged to live with her husband, and to follow him to every place where he may judge it convenient to reside: the husband is obliged to receive her, and to furnish her with every necessity for the wants of life, according to his means and station. . . .

217. A wife, although . . . separate in property, cannot give, . . . pledge, or acquire by free or chargeable title, without the concurrence of her husband in the act, or his consent in writing. . . .

267. The provisional management of the children shall rest with the husband, petitioner, or defendant, in the suit for divorce, unless it be otherwise ordered for the greater advantage of the children, on petition of either the mother, or the family, or the government commissioner. . . .

1421. The husband alone administers the property of the community. He may sell it, alienate and pledge it without the concurrence of his wife. . . .

1427. The wife cannot bind herself nor engage the property of the community, even to free her husband from prison, or for the establishment of their children in case of her husband's absence, until she shall have been thereto authorized by the law. . . .

1549. The husband alone has the management of the property in dowry. . . . He has alone the right . . . to enjoy the fruits and interest thereof, and to receive reimbursements of capital. Nevertheless, it may be agreed, by the marriage contract, that the wife shall receive annually . . . a part of her revenues for her maintenance and personal wants."

—Code Napoleon, 1804

1. Which of the following statements best explains the historical context for understanding the creation of this document?
   (A) Napoleon thought women should have the same property rights as men, but not the same political rights.
   (B) Napoleon hoped to overturn advances in women's rights made during the Revolution.
   (C) Napoleon believed that granting rights to women would undercut positive changes made in the Revolution.
   (D) Napoleon planned to push for rapid progress in gaining rights for French women.

2. Which of the following best describes France's system of laws just before the implementation of the Napoleonic Code?
   (A) A disorganized set of laws and regulations based on feudal traditions
   (B) A compromise set of laws and regulations that maintained special rights and privileges for the monarch
   (C) An organized system of laws and regulations based on revolutionary principles
   (D) A system of laws and regulations that recognized the complete equality of men and women in France

3. The passage represents the continuation of which view of women that was commonly held prior to the French Revolution?
   (A) The wife can take over the family business if the husband dies.
   (B) The wife is economically dependent on the husband.
   (C) The wife is at the level of an enslaved person in the family.
   (D) The wife is an equal economic partner in marriage.

Use the passage below to answer all parts of the question that follows.

"New schools are being opened, and inspectors have been appointed to see that the instruction does not degenerate into vain and sterile examinations. The *lycées* and the secondary schools are filling with youth eager for instruction. The polytechnic school is peopling our arsenals, ports, and factories with useful citizens. Prizes have been established in various branches of science, letters, and arts, and in the period of ten years fixed by his Majesty for the award of these prizes there can be no doubt that French genius will produce works of distinction."

—Napoleon's statement to the legislative body, December 31, 1804

1. a) Describe ONE way that Napoleon changed the educational system in France.

   b) Explain ONE economic reason Napoleon wanted to change the educational system in France.

   c) Explain ONE political reason Napoleon wanted to change the education system in France.

Topic 5.7

The Congress of Vienna

Doubtless, at no time of the world's history had more grave and complex interests been discussed amidst so many fêtes [parties]. A kingdom was cut into bits or enlarged at a ball; an indemnity was granted in the course of a dinner; a constitution was planned during a hunt. . . .

—Count Auguste La Garde-Chambonas, *Anecdotal Recollections of the Congress of Vienna*, 1901

Essential Question: How did states respond to Napoleonic rule in Europe, and what were the consequences of these responses?

After Napoleon's defeat, the victors hoped to restore peace and order in Europe. The map of Europe had been greatly altered, and France's delegate agreed with the allies' desire to return nations to their pre-Napoleonic borders and to restore their legitimate monarchs and traditional institutions. This, they all hoped, would halt the forces of change that had been unleashed by the French Revolution and bring lasting peace and stability to Europe.

The Treaties of Chaumont and Paris

In November 1813, Napoleon rejected a peace treaty offered by Austria's foreign minister, Prince **Klemens von Metternich**. On March 9, 1814, Austria, Great Britain, Prussia, and Russia signed the Treaty of Chaumont promising to remain allies for the next 20 years and not to negotiate separately. The allies announced that they were fighting Napoleon, not the French people. By the time the allied armies arrived in Paris on March 30, 1814, France's provisional leader, Prince Charles-Maurice de Talleyrand, announced that Napoleon had been deposed as emperor. Napoleon abdicated on April 6. The four allies, along with Sweden, Portugal, and Spain, signed the 1814 Treaty of Paris with France. One of the treaty's stipulations was that all eight of the former warring nations should send representatives to meet in Vienna.

The Congress Convenes

Delegates to the **Congress of Vienna** began to arrive toward the end of September. Each nation sent its most important statesman. Metternich represented Austria, and Talleyrand was sent to represent France. Many of the rulers of minor European states also attended, lured in part by Vienna's glittering social life. Even Metternich sometimes found it difficult to subordinate pleasure to business.

Preliminaries

This was the first meeting to bring together all the major nations of Europe to try to determine the future of the continent and reestablish peace and stability by restoring the balance of power. Before the main meetings began, the four allies discussed territorial problems. Representatives of Germany drew up a constitution for their country. The real work of the Congress began after Talleyrand was allowed to join the four allies as the Congress's core group. Between January 7 and February 13, 1815, they settled the boundaries of all the lands north of the Alps and had started their work on Italy.

Redrawing the Map of Europe

During the Napoleonic wars, several members of Napoleon's family had been placed on the thrones of subjugated countries. One of the Congress's tasks (and one of Metternich's guiding principles) was to restore the old "legitimate" ruling dynasties to power. This included installing a constitutional monarchy in France, with the revolutionary laws and a parliament. The Bourbons regained the throne in the person of King Louis XVIII. France lost all the territory it had gained under Napoleon.

A number of territorial measures were put in place by the Congress. (See Topic 6.5 for a map of Europe after the Congress of Vienna.)

TERRITORIAL CHANGES FROM THE CONGRESS OF VIENNA

Changes to hinder future French expansion:

- The German Confederation, a loose alliance of 39 German states dominated by Austria, replaced the old Holy Roman Empire.
- The northern Italian kingdom of Lombardy-Venetia came under the rule of Austria.
- The Papal States in central Italy were restored to the pope.
- Prussia gained new territories in western Germany.
- Russia took over most of the Grand Duchy of Warsaw (Poland).

Other changes:

- The former Dutch Republic was combined with the former Austrian Netherlands (now Belgium) as the United Kingdom of the Netherland.
- Sweden took over Norway from the king of Denmark-Norway.
- Great Britain took over some former French, Spanish, and Dutch colonies, including the islands of Malta and Ceylon (Sri Lanka) and the Cape Colony in what is now South Africa.

Other Decisions

The Congress also dealt with other international problems, such as navigation on international rivers and the abolition of the slave trade. To help carry out its objectives, it codified rules of diplomacy.

Navigation The Congress established the principle of the freedom of navigation and created a Central Commission to regulate it and set uniform tolls. Freedom of navigation was guaranteed for many rivers, most notably the Rhine and the Danube: "The navigation of the rivers, along their whole course . . .

from the point where each of them becomes navigable, to its mouth, shall be entirely free, and shall not, in respect to commerce, be prohibited to any one."

Abolition of the Slave Trade The British Parliament had passed the Act for the Abolition of the Slave Trade in 1807. At the Congress, Britain pushed for a multilateral (or many-sided) ban on the slave trade but met opposition from France, Spain, and Portugal. Finally, however, eight leading powers did sign a declaration condemning the slave trade as "repugnant to the principles of humanity and universal morality." It stopped short, however, of abolishing the slave trade.

Diplomacy The Congress of Vienna established the principle of multilateral diplomacy, with frequent meetings of the representatives of major powers, as opposed to the bilateral (or two-sided) diplomacy that had prevailed. It established a diplomatic hierarchy with four classes of heads of diplomatic missions. Only great powers exchanged ambassadors; lesser states exchanged ministers. Treaties were to be signed in alphabetical order by country, using the French spellings. (French was the language of diplomacy throughout the world.) Rules that were drawn up by the Congress of Vienna still form the basis for diplomatic relations today.

The Final Act

On June 9, 1815—nine days before the Battle of Waterloo—all but one of the major participants signed the Final Act of the Congress of Vienna, which brought together all of the individual treaties and agreements that had been made since the Congress convened. (Spain refused to sign to protest the loss of its former territories in Italy.) The Congress succeeded in working out a balance of power, and most of the new boundaries lasted for more than 40 years, even though the new map ignored nationalities and the wishes of the inhabitants.

REFLECT ON THE ESSENTIAL QUESTION

Essential Question: *How did states respond to Napoleonic rule in Europe, and what were the consequences of these responses?*

Responses to Napoleonic Rule	Consequences

KEY TERMS

Klemens von Metternich   Congress of Vienna

Questions 1–3 refer to the passage below.

"I was not long suffered to indulge my grief; I was soon put down under the decks, and there I received such a salutation in my nostrils as I had never experienced in my life; so that with the loathsomeness of the stench, and crying together, I became so sick and low that I was not able to eat, nor had I the least desire to taste any thing. I now wished for the last friend, Death, to relieve me; but soon, to my grief, two of the white men offered me eatables; and, on my refusing to eat, one of them held me fast by the hands, and laid me across, I think, the windlass, and tied my feet, while the other flogged me severely. . . . In a little time after, amongst the poor chained men, I found some of my own nation, which in a small degree gave ease to my mind. I inquired of them what was to be done with us? They gave me to understand we were to be carried to these white people's country to work for them."

—Olaudah Equiano, describing conditions on a slave ship, *The Interesting Narrative of the Life of Olaudah Equiano; or, Gustavus Vassa, the African, Written by Himself*, 1789

1. The conditions on the slave ship described by Equiano were most directly a result of which of the following historical developments?

   (A) The conflict between Africans in Africa and the Americas

   (B) The demand among Africans for sugar and tobacco from the Americas

   (C) The rivalry among Europeans for control of American colonies

   (D) The conquest by Europeans of vast tracts of land in the Americas

2. The Congress of Vienna addressed the issue described by Equiano in the passage by

   (A) codifying the rules of trade and diplomacy that could cause conflicts

   (B) preventing the rise of another powerful military leader such as Napoleon

   (C) punishing France for spreading revolutionary ideals across Europe

   (D) settling boundary disputes among neighboring countries

3. Which of the following countries would have been most sympathetic to the ideas Equiano was describing?

   (A) France, which was the strongest supporter for the principles of universal natural rights

   (B) Germany, which had no colonies in the West Indies that relied on enslaved African labor

   (C) Great Britain, which had already passed an act banning the trade Equiano described

   (D) Spain, which had already imported all the enslaved Africans it needed for its colonies

Use the passage below to answer all parts of the question that follows.

"Given the current challenges to European unity, . . . Europeans should remember that, two hundred years ago, they celebrated together a long-awaited peace, as their statesmen collaborated on a lasting settlement to solve territorial questions and ensure international stability. . . . The Congress was so successful in solving the existential problems of Europe that Europeans would not fight a comparable war against each other for another century—until the Great War in 1914. The challenges that Europe faced in the twentieth century suggest, in fact, that the type of collaborative diplomacy developed at the Vienna Congress remains essential to limit conflict.

If the Congress produced a framework for a lasting peace, contemporary publicists often maligned its gatherings, and most nineteenth-century historians remained critical of its legacy. The assembly of aristocratic elites—with their dazzling festivities and hard-nosed territorial negotiations that trade populations among states—generated scorn, ridicule, and ammunition for political caricatures. . . . This contrast between the demonstrated success of and the coexisting prejudice against the Congress underscores the need to emphasize its origins in two decades of highly destructive warfare that annihilated states while expanding the French Empire."

—Katherine B. Aaslestad, "Serious Work for a New Europe: The Congress of Vienna after Two Hundred Years," *Central European History*, 2015

1. a) Explain how ONE historical event, situation, or development not in the source supports the point of view of Aaslestad as stated in the first paragraph.

   b) Explain how ONE historical event, situation, or development not in the source supports the point of view of historians described by Aaslestad in the first sentence of the second paragraph.

   c) Identify how Aaslestad connects the developments at the Congress of Vienna with developments in the 20th century.

Topic 5.8

Romanticism

To say the word Romanticism is to say modern art—that is, intimacy, spirituality, colour, aspiration towards the infinite, expressed by every means available to the arts.

—Charles Baudelaire, *The Salon of 1846*, 1846

Essential Question: How and why did the Romantic Movement and religious revival challenge Enlightenment thought from 1648 to 1815?

During the 17th and 18th centuries, the rationalism of the Scientific Revolution and the Enlightenment penetrated all aspects of European society. Whereas the previous age had exalted church and monarchy, Enlightenment intellectuals now questioned religious and royal authority. Their confidence in humanity led to an increase in toleration after centuries of crushing religious warfare. The new emphasis on reason also transformed culture, as artists and writers turned away from narrow religious focus to rediscover the ideals embodied in classical civilization.

Enlightenment rationalism thus produced a host of new ideas, including deism, skepticism, and neoclassicism. Inevitably, a backlash followed, in the form of a series of religious revivals and a growing use of feelings and emotion in art and literature. By the start of the 19th century, this **Romantic Movement**, or **Romanticism**, had displaced the "cold" rationalism of the Enlightenment.

The Revival of Public Emotion

Until the late 18th century, Enlightenment ideals of reason and science were the central theme of European culture. But rationalism was falling out of favor as society experienced the seductive appeal of passion, danger, intensity, drama, emotion, and the lure of the sublime. The Age of Reason was giving way to the Romantic Age.

Historians debate the sources of this transformative shift. Some suggest that the cataclysm of the French Revolution led to a loss of faith in humankind's ability to solve problems by reason alone. Others argue that industrialization and agrarian reform had created a new social class untethered by convention or traditional historic roles. Some argue that Romanticism was less a reaction against the Enlightenment than a natural outgrowth of the Enlightenment's emphasis on the individual.

Rousseau and the Challenge to Reason

Like other Enlightenment philosophes, **Jean-Jacques Rousseau** (1712–1778) criticized the existing social order and argued vehemently for individual freedom. Unlike the others, however, Rousseau did not put all his faith in reason. Instead, he managed to alienate deists, atheists, skeptics, and Catholic leaders alike by rejecting both deism's concept of an impassive "clockmaker" God and the Church's emphasis on dogma and obedience. Instead, Rousseau envisioned God as a benevolent force that one could experience subjectively through personal experience and inner feelings.

An eclectic figure, Rousseau was involved with the *Encyclopédie* but also composed music and wrote novels and poetry. His writings celebrate nature, spontaneity, individualism, and passion. This, along with his emphasis on the subjective, has led many historians to describe him as the "father of the Romantic movement."

The Romantic Movement

The Romantic Movement spanned roughly the last decade of the 18th century through the first half of the 19th century. Romantics departed in key ways from the orderly, rational, science-based thinking of the Enlightenment. They did not entirely reject reason but considered it inadequate by itself. Humans, they insisted, not only thought rationally but also felt with emotion. Thus, sentiment and imagination were vital for a truer understanding of the world.

This explains to some degree why this period is famous for an outpouring of genius in the fine arts. Beyond mere sensual pleasure, fine arts represented the expression of personal truth and spiritual experience. Artists and writers were no longer content to catalog the world, as in the *Encyclopédie*; their aim was to mine the depths of imagination and personal experience to produce a new vision. The Romantics were particularly preoccupied with the beauty of nature and the sense of wonder and awe it produced. Their art favored wild landscapes, exotic peoples, fantastic and spiritual experiences, and heart-stirring deeds of heroism and romance, often set in the Middle Ages. (See Topic 7.8 for more about Romantic artists.)

A New Religious Revival

The Romantic era's emphasis on feeling and intuition fed into a widespread **religious revival**. The very magnificence of the natural world, many felt, was proof enough of the existence of God. Generally, these revival movements shared a belief in the truth of personal spiritual experience, mysticism as a gateway to ultimate truth, and an emotional yearning for connection with God. At the same time, the Enlightenment ideal of religious tolerance and the view that religion was a matter of private conscience had taken hold and now became part of the fabric of the new movements.

An Emphasis on Private Revelation

As deism, atheism, and skepticism were taking firm root in 18th-century Europe, new faith movements developed in reaction. Under the influence of Enlightenment thought, religion—formerly a matter of public allegiance to the established church—was held to be a matter of individual conscience. The new religious movements embraced this distinction, as it meant every conversion was proof of "true" belief.

Evangelical Movements

As the focus of faith moved from the state church to voluntary associations of believers, evangelical movements began to spring up across Europe, especially in England, Germany, and France. Members actively shared their religious message in an effort to persuade outsiders to voluntarily and sincerely commit to Christianity.

Methodism In 1729, **John Wesley** (1703–1791), a priest in the Church of England, joined his brother Charles and two others in a religious study group at Oxford called the Holy Club. Because of their emphasis on methodical study and devotion, the group's approach was ridiculed as **Methodism**—a name that stuck. Wesley and his followers began offering social services in 1730, helping prisoners and the poor. In 1735, John Wesley went to Georgia, where for two years he tried unsuccessfully to minister to Native Americans and colonists alike. Back in England, Wesley published *The Nature, Design, and General Rules of the United Societies* (1743)— a guide for Methodist societies. Wesley believed that humans may be assured of their salvation and of the perfect love of God in this life. His brother Charles wrote more than 6,000 hymns to spread the messages of Methodism. The Methodist Society remained a part of the Church of England until 1795, four years after John Wesley's death.

Methodism became a mass movement, sometimes drawing crowds of up to 25,000 to outdoor tent "revivals." Its fervent adherents were sometimes regarded as extremists. However, they were also leading the charge in many social causes, including the abolition of slavery, prison reform, relief for the poor, improvements in education, and the creation of libraries. Poverty and disease were widespread in England, and the charitable work of the Methodists earned them respect.

Germany A similar situation existed in Germany, where the rationalism of the Enlightenment era gave way to a new personal religiosity that emphasized emotion, feeling, and the mysteries of the spirit. Pietist revivals competed with a neo-Lutheran movement focused on liturgy (prescribed religious service) and confession. (See Topic 4.3.)

France In France, religious fervor was tempered by political events. One of the primary goals of the French Revolution was ending the corruption and greed of the Catholic Church. As the Revolution progressed, policies were put in place to achieve these goals, ranging from confiscation of Church wealth to the nationalization of Church-owned property to fully outlawing the

Church and deporting or murdering many of its priests and clerics. However, as a reaction to the anticlericalism of the Enlightenment and the religious persecution during the Revolution, France experienced a Catholic revival in the early 19th century, as reflected in the writing of François-Auguste-René, Vicomte de Chateaubriand.

Nationalism and Mass Uprisings

Inspired by Enlightenment ideals, modern nationalism emerged during the late 18th century. It was ushered in by the ideals of the French Revolution:

- individual liberty rather than subordination to government
- equality among all citizens rather than special privileges for aristocrats
- fraternity among all people of a state rather than loyalty to a small local region

As Napoleon's army cut through Europe after the French Revolution, it undermined the old feudal structure. In some areas, Napoleon essentially liberated people from the control of nobles. In others, particularly in German-speaking areas where people were divided into hundreds of separate states, people united around a national identity to resist Napoleonic domination.

Another distinguishing feature of the late 18th century were **mass uprisings**. They were the driving force propelling the French Revolution forward, beginning with the storming of the Bastille and on through the march on Versailles, the peasant revolts of the Great Fear of 1789, and the massive national mobilization for the war effort. For the first time in history, a mass movement of the people had formed to overthrow an authoritarian regime and replace it with a representative government.

Both of these emerging forces were fueled by the emotions and sentiment the Romantic movement held in high value. These forces would become increasingly powerful in Europe in the decades to come.

REFLECT ON THE ESSENTIAL QUESTION

Essential Question: *How and why did the Romantic Movement and religious revival challenge Enlightenment thought from 1648 to 1815?*

Changes	Challenges to Enlightenment Thought

KEY TERMS

Romantic Movement	religious revival	mass uprising
Romanticism	John Wesley	
Jean-Jacques Rousseau	Methodism	

Questions 1–3 refer to the passage below.

"Up! up! my Friend, and quit your books;
Or surely you'll grow double:
Up! up! my Friend, and clear your looks;
Why all this toil and trouble?

The sun, above the mountain's head,
A freshening lustre mellow
Through all the long green fields has spread,
His first sweet evening yellow.

Books! 'tis a dull and endless strife:
Come, hear the woodland linnet [a type of bird],
How sweet his music! on my life,
There's more of wisdom in it.

And hark! how blithe the throstle [a type of bird] sings!
He, too, is no mean preacher:
Come forth into the light of things,
Let Nature be your Teacher."

—William Wadsworth, "The Tables Turned," 1798

1. Wordsworth's poem best demonstrates which of the following intellectual trends of the 18th and 19th centuries?

   (A) The emphasis on reason rather than tradition to make decisions

   (B) The spread of deism and atheism among many writers

   (C) The use of satire to criticize governmental authorities

   (D) The assumption that imagination is the best way to understand the world

2. The poem's themes are most directly a Romantic Movement's response to

   (A) peasant movements to revive agriculture

   (B) the spread of industrialization and urbanization

   (C) demands for suffrage and Parliamentary reform

   (D) higher literacy rates among the working class

3. The ideas expressed in this poem are a reaction against
   (A) Enlightenment rationalism
   (B) the French Reign of Terror
   (C) the expansion of Napoleon's Empire
   (D) Rousseau's entries in the *Encyclopédie*

SHORT-ANSWER QUESTION

Answer all parts of the question that follows.

1. a) Describe ONE way that Romanticism influenced how people thought about religion.

   b) Explain ONE way that deism, atheism, and skepticism provided the historical context for the rise of evangelical movements such as Methodism in Great Britain and pietism in Germany.

   c) Explain ONE way that the anticlericalism of the Enlightenment and the religious persecution during the French Revolution provided a context for a revival of Catholicism in France.

Topic 5.9

Continuity and Change in 18th-Century States

In politics . . . never retreat, never retract . . . never admit a mistake.
—Napoleon Bonaparte (1769–1821)

Essential Question: How did the developments and challenges to Europe's political order result in change from 1648 to 1815?

Europe in the 18th century continued to hold onto some aspects of earlier centuries. For example, long-fought conflicts among states continued through the 1700s. Also, expansion of trade begun in the Age of Exploration continued through the 1700s. In addition, earlier traditional beliefs were held onto by some Europeans as a rejection of the rationality of Enlightenment ideals. However, along with this continuity came many major changes.

New Political Institutions and Wars Between 1648 and 1815, continuity can be seen in the ongoing rivalries and armed struggles among European states. In 1756, the long-standing rivalry between Britain and France flared up again—this time over colonial claims. The British East India Company and the French East India Company began a war over control of India, known as the Seven Years' War. The British won control of India at the end of the conflict in 1763. The American phase of this conflict, known as the French and Indian War (1754–1763), also ended with a British victory. One major change brought about by this conflict was France's loss of all of its continental North American territories, with Britain taking all of the land east of the Mississippi and parts of Canada. Due to these changes and a weakening of France during the French Revolution, Britain became the dominant colonial power, not only in North America but around the globe by the early the 19th century.

The rivalry between France and Britain continued during the American Revolution (1775–1783). The French took advantage of the rebellion to ally with the American colonies and fight once again against Britain. The French supplied naval support, troops, arms, and military training to the American side and were instrumental in its victory over Britain.

Impact of the French Revolution Change occurred as Europe created new political institutions that got much of their impetus from Enlightenment thought. The French Revolution (1789–1799) was inspired by the republic that resulted from the successful American Revolution. The French wanted to create a similar new republic that replaced their absolute monarchy with a government for the people. Although the French Revolution began as a popular uprising against the tyranny of kings and aristocracy, it devolved into a chaotic, violent Reign of Terror. The republic that was sought did not last.

Worldwide Economic Network The Age of Exploration and the rapid technological advances that accompanied it caused Europe's seafaring trade to grow dramatically in the 17th century. Between 1648 and 1815, a worldwide economic network developed starting from Portugal, the Netherlands, Britain, and France trading with the East Indies (present-day India, Indonesia, Malaysia, Southeast Asia, and the Philippines), Africa, and North America.

This network set up a commercial competition among European states, which resulted in diplomatic clashes and warfare over sovereignty of territories. For example, the Portuguese had control over trade with China and the East Indies in the 16th century. But as other European states had begun their own East India companies, those states took control of trade away from Portugal by the end of the 17th century.

Reason Versus Emotion Between 1648 and 1815, Enlightenment ideals and Scientific Revolution concepts continued to impact European society, culture, and politics. Even so, strong movements against Enlightenment ideals such as rationalism and skepticism gained strength by the early 19th century. This movement came about through religious revivals and a renewed valuing of emotion expressed in art and literature known as Romanticism.

The movement away from Enlightenment ideals led Europe to a growth in nationalistic sentiment. During this period in Europe, nationalism became a basis for war. For example, French emperor Napoleon Bonaparte's efforts to control most of Europe in the early 1800s failed due to the nationalistic responses of those he meant to conquer.

QUESTIONS ABOUT CONTINUITY AND CHANGE

1. How did the continuing conflicts between Britain and France result in change in the period from 1648 to 1815?

2. How did the rise of nationalism in Europe result in change in the period from 1648 to 1815?

UNIT 5 REVIEW: Conflict, Crisis, and Reaction in the Late 18th Century
c. 1648 to c. 1815

WRITE AS A HISTORIAN: *CONCLUDE THE ESSAY*

A strong conclusion should summarize how evidence supports a thesis and demonstrate a complex understanding of the topic. A writer has some options in how to accomplish these goals in an effective conclusion:

- Restate the thesis in a broader chronological context. That is, remind the reader how the point made in the essay was connected to, or distinctive from, what came before or what would come later in history. For example, an essay on the French philosophes might compare them to Montaigne (1533–1592) or John-Paul Sartre (1905–1980).

- Restate the thesis in a broader geographical context. That is, remind the reader how the point made in the essay was similar to or unlike events elsewhere in the world. For example, the French philosophes were less focused on empirical data than were thinkers in Great Britain.

Another way to strengthen the conclusion is to expand on the thesis without taking the essay in a new direction. For example, if your thesis is that Enlightenment beliefs brought new optimism to European thought, you could conclude, "The Enlightenment philosophes' belief that science would result in progress brought renewed optimism to Europe after two centuries of religious conflicts."

Another method is to lay the groundwork for what came next as a result of the topic you've written about. This is called causation. For instance, "Ultimately, Enlightenment thinking laid the groundwork for the French Revolution."

It's also possible to end your essay by putting your argument into the framework of continuity and change over time. How is it part of a larger historical theme? An example of this is, "If history is a pendulum swinging back and forth between emotion and reason, the Enlightenment fully embodied the latter."

Yet another way to end an essay is with a quotation (or a paraphrase of one) that summarizes your thesis statement. In this case, a direct quote by Voltaire easily ties back to the thesis: "Voltaire captured the Enlightenment spirit when he urged people to judge men by their questions rather than their answers."

Choose the three sentences that best conclude an essay on the topic of "The Philosophes' Impact During the Enlightenment," and then identify which concluding method these sentences use.

1. Although the Enlightenment initially reached only the intellectual elite, it eventually spread to change European society at all levels.

2. Philosophers, such as Voltaire, Smith, Kant, and Hume, had major impacts on Europe during the Enlightenment.

3. The philosophes might not have brought about a paradise of reason and toleration, but they successfully challenged powerful institution.

4. Hume questioned whether a tree falling in a forest made a sound if no one was there to hear it; the world continues to hear the philosophes.

LONG ESSAY QUESTIONS

Directions: Suggested writing time is 40 minutes. In your response, you should do the following:

- Respond to the prompt with a historically defensible thesis that establishes a line of reasoning.
- Describe a broader historical context relevant to the prompt.
- Support an argument in response to the prompt using specific and relevant examples of evidence.
- Use historical reasoning (e.g., comparison, causation, continuity and change over time) to frame or structure an argument that addresses the prompt.
- Use evidence to corroborate, qualify, or modify an argument that addresses the prompt.

1. Evaluate the success of two European countries in establishing a global mercantilist empire.

2. Evaluate how new Enlightenment ideas were used during the French Revolution to challenge existing hierarchies in France.

3. Evaluate the extent to which the French Revolution and reign of Napoleon altered existing hierarchies in Europe.

4. Evaluate the extent to which modernism differed from Romanticism.

DOCUMENT-BASED QUESTION

Directions: Question 1 is based on the accompanying documents. The documents have been edited for the purpose of this exercise. You are advised to spend 15 minutes planning and 45 minutes writing your answer. In your response, you should do the following:

- **Thesis:** Make a defensible claim that establishes a line of reasoning and consists of one or more sentences found in one place.
- **Contextualization:** Relate the argument to a broader historical context.
- **Document Evidence:** Use content from at least six documents.
- **Outside Evidence:** Use one piece of evidence not in the documents.
- **Document Sourcing:** Explain how or why the point of view, purpose, situation, or intended audience is relevant for at least three documents.
- **Analysis:** Show the relationships among pieces of historical evidence and use them to support, qualify, or modify an argument.

1. Evaluate the extent to which attitudes toward leadership and political ambition changed in France from 1789 to 1795.

Document 1:

Source: Camille Desmoulins, speech at the Bastille, July 14, 1789

There is one difference between a monarchy and a republic, which alone should suffice to make people reject with horror all monarchical rule and prefer a republic regardless of the cost of its establishment. In a democracy, though, the people may be deceived, yet they at least love virtue. It is merit which they believe they put in power as substitutes for the rascals who are the very essence of monarchies. The vices, concealments, and crimes which are the diseases of republics are the very health and existence of monarchies. Cardinal Richelieu avowed openly in his political principles, that "kings should always avoid using the talents of thoroughly honest men." Long before him Sallust said: "Kings cannot get along without rascals; on the contrary, they should fear to trust the honest and upright." It is, therefore, only under a democracy that the good citizen can reasonably hope to see a cessation of the triumphs of intrigue and crime; and to this end the people need only to be enlightened. . . . There is yet this difference between a monarchy and a republic: the reigns of Tiberius, Claudius, Nero, Caligula and Domitian all had happy beginnings. In fact, all reigns make a joyous entry, but this is only a delusion.

Document 2:

Source: *Declaration of Rights of Man and of the Citizen*, August 26, 1789

Therefore, the National Assembly recognizes and proclaims, in the presence and under the auspices of the Supreme Being, the following rights of man and of the citizen:

Men are born and remain free and equal in rights. Social distinctions may be founded only upon the General Good.

The aim of all political association is the preservation of the natural and imprescriptible rights of man. These rights are liberty, property, security, and resistance to oppression. . . .

Liberty consists in the freedom to do everything which injures no one else; hence the exercise of the natural rights of each man has no limits except those which assure to the other members of the society the enjoyment of the same rights. . . .

Law is the expression of the General Will. Every citizen has a right to participate personally, or through his representative, in its foundation. It must be the same for all, whether it protects or punishes. All citizens, being equal in the eyes of the law, are equally eligible to all dignities and to all public positions and occupations, according to their abilities, and without distinction except that of their virtues and talents."

Document 3:

Source: *The Women's March on Versailles*, October 5, 1789

Credit: Wikimedia Commons/Bibliothèque nationale de France

Document 4:

Source: Henri Grégoire, a Jacobin member of the New National Convention, 1791

Not one of us would ever propose to retain in France the fatal race of kings.

We all know but too well that dynasties have never been anything else than rapacious tribes, who live on nothing but human flesh. It is completely necessary to reassure the friends of liberty. We must destroy this talisman whose magic power is still sufficient to stupefy many men. I move accordingly that you sanction, by a solemn law, the abolition of royalty.

Document 5:

Source: George Jacques Danton, 1792

At such a moment this National Assembly becomes a veritable committee of war. We ask that you concur with us in directing this sublime movement of the people, by naming commissioners who will second us in these great measures. We ask that any one refusing to give personal service or to furnish arms shall be punished with death. We ask that a set of instructions be drawn up for the citizens to direct their movements. We ask that couriers be sent to all the departments to notify them of the decrees that you proclaim here. The tocsin we are about to ring is not an alarm signal; it sounds the charge on the enemies of our country. To conquer them we must dare, dare again, always dare, and France is saved!

Document 6:

Source: Maximilien Robespierre, address at the National Convention, May 7, 1794

Now, in these circumstances, the first maxim of our politics ought to be to lead the people by means of reason and the enemies of the people by terror. . . . The basis of popular government in time of revolution is both virtue and terror.

Terror without virtue is murderous, virtue without terror is powerless. Terror is nothing else than swift, severe, indomitable justice – it flows, then, from virtue.

330   EUROPEAN HISTORY: AP® EDITION

Document 7:

Source: Illustration of Napoleon visiting the orphans of the legion of honor, date unknown

Credit: Getty Images

Napoleon visiting with the orphans of soldiers who received special recognition for their service to France

UNIT 6: Industrialization and Its Effects
c. 1815 to c. 1914

Topic 6.1

Contextualizing Industrialization and Its Origins and Effects

Essential Question: What was the context in which industrialization originated, developed, and spread in Europe?

The Age of Exploration and the Scientific Revolution greatly accelerated Europe's technological progress. Advances in manufacturing, transportation, and communications allowed European countries to develop a worldwide economic network, which helped transform its traditional agricultural economy to an industrial economy during the 18th and 19th centuries.

Origins of the Industrial Revolution In the mid 18th century, Britain's natural resources, together with its social, economic, and political structure, made it ideal for industrial development. Innovations such as new forms of energy, new inventions, and improved ways of organizing human labor resulted in significant increases in British textile production. These changes, paired with support from the British government, paved the way for an industrial revolution. By the mid 19th century, Britain had achieved industrial dominance in Europe and throughout the world.

Industrialization spread to the European continent, then to America, and other parts of the world. Continental European governments were for the most part more autocratic than Britain's government. When the continent industrialized, monarchs, military leaders, and aristocrats often held power over the process and were slow to change.

Industrialization and Daily Life Daily life in industrialized areas of Europe was profoundly affected by the Industrial Revolution. Social classes became more defined, with economic differences greater between the upper and lower classes. Jobs in the new factories required lower-class workers to follow specific schedules and work long hours at repetitive tasks for low pay. Many industrial workers labored in unsafe conditions.

The need for labor in the many new factories led to rapid urbanization. City infrastructure was not ready for such an influx of people, so poverty, crime, disease, and unsanitary living conditions were often the result. Factory work separated workers from their families, since the home was no longer the focus of working life as it had been on farms. Many of the people who continued to farm changed from growing crops for their own families to commercial farming, sometimes growing produce for distant markets. This change largely came about from improvements in transportation, including better roads, ships, and railroads.

The new middle class gained influence, creating a demand for consumer goods and causing industrialization to grow and spread. The middle class began to live in comfortable homes and attend schools and colleges that emerged in cities. Over time, education and literacy increased for both the middle class and the lower class. More available and progressive public health care, in addition to increased amounts of (and access to) food, helped to increase the average life span for those in industrialized locations. Both middle and upper class families had more leisure time. Public spaces such as libraries, parks, and museums became destinations for family leisure.

Industrialization Results in New Ideologies In Europe's industrialized societies of the 19th century, changing political thought resulted in revolutionary movements intent on upsetting traditional institutions. Governments responded by developing ideologies to maintain existing power structures. One of the ideologies was conservatism, a movement of people who opposed societal change and wanted to keep power in the hands of the aristocracy, the church, and the military. Conservatives believed that it was dangerous to give common people too much power, as was seen in portions of the French Revolution. On the other side, liberals and nationalists wanted reforms that would change political systems and borders, giving more power to the common people. These revolutionary movements threatened conservatism and created international tensions in Europe in the build-up to World War I.

ANALYZE THE CONTEXT

1. Explain the context in which industrialization originated in Europe.

2. Explain the context in which industrialization developed and spread in Europe.

Topic 6.2

The Spread of Industry Throughout Europe

The opening of a foreign trade, by making them acquainted with new objects . . . sometimes works a sort of Industrial Revolution in a country . . . inducing those who were satisfied with scanty comforts and little work, to work harder for the gratification of their new tastes. . .

—John Stuart Mill, *Principles of Political Economy*, 1873

Essential Question: What were the factors that influenced the development of industrialization in various parts of Europe from 1815 to 1860?

British philosopher John Stuart Mill lived through one of the greatest revolutions in European history. During his lifetime, new technological developments in manufacturing, transportation, and communications played a powerful role in transforming Europe's economy from one largely dependent upon agriculture to one that revolved around industry (the production of goods). Known as the **Industrial Revolution**, the era proceeded in two stages.

The first Industrial Revolution began in the textile (cloth) industry in Britain in the mid-18th century. It later spread across the European continent. Britain's natural resources, including coal and iron, combined with its social, economic, and political structure, made it ideal for industrial development. By the 1850s, Britain had achieved industrial dominance in Europe and the world. Between 1850 and 1870, France and Prussia were becoming more industrialized as well. Yet industrialization proceeded more slowly in those two countries, so governments took a more prominent role in supporting change.

Great Britain's Industrial Dominance

Great Britain established the lead in the Industrial Revolution through the mechanization of textile production, the development of steam power, increased mining of coal and iron ore, and the production of wrought iron (the molded form of iron used for building iron objects) and steel. The development of railroads in Britain sped the transportation of raw materials to factories and finished goods to consumers. Another key to Britain's industrialization was that no location was more than a few miles from a canal, a river, or the coast. The digging and maintenance of **canals**, in particular, were early signs of the British government's strong support for industrialization. In addition,

Britain's parliamentary democracy enabled manufacturers and industrialists to influence government policies through their representatives, or members of Parliament. Britain had a growing middle class, and the British social climate favored inventors, businesspeople, and entrepreneurs—those who could create wealth rather than inherit it.

The Textile Industry

In 1764, English inventor James Hargreaves developed the spinning jenny, which dramatically increased the production of cloth thread. Before the spinning jenny, women spun thread mostly at home, using a spinning wheel with a single spindle, or spool. Production was slow, and the demand for thread by textile weavers was often greater than the supply. Hargreaves's jenny, however, had eight spindles and thus allowed a single worker to produce eight times as much thread. Eventually, machines similar to spinning jennies were attached to waterwheels, and waterpower was used to spin thread. In 1785, Edmund Cartwright invented a water-powered loom to weave cloth.

Source: Getty Images

This wood engraving from about 1880 shows a woman using a more advanced spinning jenny.

Capitalism and the Rise of Factories With the use of water-powered spinning wheels and looms, textiles could be produced in large quantities, or **mass produced**. Textile workers no longer worked at home or in small workshops. Instead, they labored together in textile mills in groups as large as three or four hundred.

Opening a textile mill required **capital**, or money and other resources set aside for building a business. Often, new owners borrowed money from banks in the form of loans they would have to repay from the profits of the mill. Private individuals also invested in new companies or contributed money in exchange for a share of future profits. These individuals would receive a portion, or share, of the mill's profit at the end of the year. The mill owners generated profits by selling finished goods.

In Britain, private individuals, not the monarch or the state, owned the mills. This system of private ownership of industry and industrial resources became known as **capitalism**. The textile manufacturing industry created a new class of well-to-do factory owners. Unlike aristocrats, their wealth came from business, not inherited land. Eventually, textile mills became known as manufactories, or simply factories, because they manufactured goods.

Cotton Becomes King Britain had an abundant supply of wool from the country's many sheep. However, **consumers**—people who buy goods or services—increasingly favored cotton cloth. Compared to wool, cotton was lighter, cooler, and easier to dye bright colors and patterns.

Britain's colonies in India and the American South grew cotton. Raw, fluffy cotton bolls contained seeds and had to be cleaned, or combed, slowly by hand before they could be spun into thread. In 1794, American inventor Eli Whitney unveiled a machine called the cotton gin that removed seeds from cotton bolls, revolutionizing the production of cotton cloth. Large quantities of combed cotton could now be imported from the United States or India and woven in Britain. By the end of the 18th century, Britain was exporting finished cotton cloth to its American colonies and to the other countries of Europe.

Steam Power Changes Manufacturing In 1769, James Watt of Scotland patented the **steam engine**. This was a revolutionary technology that used steam from water heated by a coal fire to power numerous devices. The pressure from built-up steam moved a system of small plungers, or pistons, attached to gears and shafts to generate energy to operate machines.

By 1800, steam power had begun to replace water power in textile factories. Factories no longer had to be located near a stream or river. Instead, they could be anywhere there was a steady supply of coal to keep the steam engines moving. By 1835, there were more than 1,000 steam-powered looms in Britain.

Coal was transported to factories over land by carts or by water. In the early 19th century, the British Parliament sponsored the construction of canals expressly for the transport of coal. Steamboats carrying cargo traveled the nearly 2,000 miles of canals that had been dug by 1815.

Coal

Beginning in the 19th century, coal became the major source of energy in Britain. Coal stoves rather than wood-burning fireplaces heated homes and buildings. More important, railroads and factories needed coal for fuel.

Britain had abundant coal reserves, especially in the regions of northeast and central England, southeast Scotland, and Wales. Coal mining was a difficult and dangerous job. Workers often died in cave-ins or floods or from inhaling the poisonous gases that built up underground. The demand for coal, however, created millions of jobs for men and women in mines.

In 1750, Britain produced about 3 million tons of coal. By 1816, production reached 16 million tons. Then it approximately doubled every 20 years for the following century.

Iron and Steel

During the Industrial Revolution, demand for iron soared. Railroads needed iron to build tracks and locomotives. Steam engines, furnaces, and many types of tools were made of iron. The military needed iron for weapons, including cannons and cannonballs. Bridges were made of wrought iron, while buildings had iron staircases, railings, and other fixtures.

Coke Smelting Coal played an important role in the production of iron. Coke, a solid form of coal bricks, provided the steady burning fuel needed to smelt, or extract, iron ore from rocks and melt it into bars, called pig iron. These bars could then be bent, rolled, and molded into wrought iron to use in building machines and in construction. Since people often found iron deposits near coal seams, the iron industry became closely tied to coal-producing regions. Before 1860, Britain was able to mine all of the iron ore it needed domestically. But afterward, iron ore imports steadily rose and averaged about 30 percent of the ore consumed by the early 1900s.

The Growth of the Iron Industry Smelting and molding iron could be a time-consuming process. In 1783, Henry Cort, a former British naval officer, improved the production of wrought iron. He invented a puddling furnace and roller mechanism that could shape iron while it was still soft and malleable. Cort became known as the father of Britain's iron industry.

Between 1780 and 1790, Britain produced about 70,000 tons of iron. Between 1855 and 1859, it produced 3.5 million tons. By the early 20th century, Britain was the greatest iron-producing nation in the world, smelting more than 8.7 million tons between 1900 and 1904.

Steel In 1856, English inventor **Henry Bessemer** patented the **Bessemer process**. This is a method for mass-producing steel—a combination of iron and carbon that is more durable and more resistant to rust than pure iron. Bessemer relied on huge furnaces and hot air pumps that removed impurities from pig iron through a chemical process called oxidation. Bessemer's invention revolutionized the production of steel, and Britain became a leader in steel production.

Britain Celebrates Its Economic Might In 1851, Britain staged the Great Exhibition of the Works of Industry of All Nations. Known more commonly as the **Great Exhibition of 1851**, its centerpiece was the magnificent **Crystal Palace**, a multistory glass and steel structure the length of three city blocks.

As host country of the Great Exhibition, Britain created large exhibits and showed many inventions. Among the inventions displayed were a steam-powered hammer, a hydraulic press, early bicycles that were known as velocipedes, rubber-tubed hearing aids, a high-speed printing press, and a massive railway locomotive. More than 6 million people attended the exhibition. The palace and its exhibits were intended to impress the world with Britain's industrial strength.

Railroads

Steam power soon had another important use. In the early 19th century, George Stephenson invented a locomotive, powered by steam, that ran along iron rails. The railway industry would become a major part of the Industrial Revolution. By 1830, 51 miles of rails had been laid in Britain. Rail transport soon eclipsed canals. By 1850, more than 6,000 miles of British railways united all regions of the country. Trains carried raw materials to factories and goods from factories to consumers in cities, or to ports for export abroad.

People, as well as goods, traveled by rail. Improved transportation helped create a sense of common culture and national identity. Greater mobility led to increased trade and migration, which increased links between regions.

Source: Getty Images

George Stephenson's locomotive was a breakthrough in land transportation. Like steamships, it used the expansive power of steam to produce rotary motion.

In addition, the growth of mass production and mass consumption reduced differences in regional dialects, dress, and other customs.

Before the Industrial Revolution, all goods from cloth to soap to dishes to nails were produced by hand, so they were expensive. Manufacturing reduced the prices for many goods, so they became available to many people for the first time, and consumerism—promoting the buying of goods and services—became part of the economic fabric. Local variations of goods decreased, and people recognized that they had much in common with one another. While economic class differences remained strong, cultural differences declined. People increasingly identified with their country rather than with their city or region.

Banking

Britain's banking industry became particularly strong during the Industrial Revolution. The growth of industry most likely would not have been possible without banks willing to lend money to businesspeople for them to build factories. By the early 19th century, more than 800 licensed and unlicensed banks existed in Britain. Many of these loaned money for the construction of mines and workshops as well as factories.

The Invention of Savings Banks In 1810, British bankers established the first savings bank. A savings bank allows people to keep their money in a safe place and earn small payments called interest. When large numbers of people, even those with little money, use savings banks, their combined deposits can become a significant sum that bankers can lend to businesses. French and Dutch bankers soon established savings banks in their own countries.

Crises Bring about New Laws Despite these innovations, British banks experienced financial crises in 1825 and 1826. Experts blamed these crises on small banks lending too much money. In response, the Bank of England established regional branches in different parts of the country to make the British banking industry more stable. Over the years, British banks experienced a cycle of financial crises followed by new rules and laws to prevent more crises. Having a stable banking industry remains an essential part of any country's economic and political strength today.

Patents and Rewards for Inventors

The British government recognized the importance of inventors to the economy through its support of **patents**. These are licenses issued by the government that allow inventors to control and sell the rights to their inventions for a period of time. Patents enabled inventors to profit from their work, thus encouraging inventors to be creative. While the British patent system dated back to the Middle Ages, in 1852, new laws enabled inventors to obtain patents more rapidly. This gave inventors greater motivation to develop new devices and mechanisms.

Britain also supported inventors through the use of incentives, or financial rewards, given for new inventions or improvements to old ones. In 1754, William Shipley, a drawing teacher, established the Society for the Encouragement of Arts, Manufactures and Commerce. The society issued a challenge asking people to solve particular problems in fields such as manufacturing, chemistry, agriculture, or engineering, and offered cash prizes to people whose ideas proved most successful. Innovators developed better machinery for textile production and for lumber milling. The society started as a private organization and acquired government sponsorship through a royal charter in 1847.

Political Power and Social Class

The Industrial Revolution accelerated and increased differences in social class since many of the newly created factory jobs paid low wages. Gaps between the richest and poorest members of society meant that many people could not enjoy the benefits of prosperity. For many thousands of people, the Industrial Revolution led to a life of tedious work with long hours and little reward.

However, others found new opportunities for upward social mobility and education. And while life was especially harsh for the first generation or two that lived in cities, by the end of the 19th century, poorer city dwellers did see an improvement in their standard of living. Additionally industrialization made goods more available and affordable.

The Growth of the Middle Class The Industrial Revolution encouraged the growth in Britain of a **middle class**. These people were neither peasants, nobles, nor clergy. Instead, they were merchants, clerks, factory managers, and others. They were, in general, wealthier and better educated than peasants but without the traditional status and power of nobles and clergy. Compared to the working class, the middle class of the late 19th century led lives that seemed luxurious, living in comfortable houses often with servants waiting on them.

As middle-class people accumulated more wealth, they could pursue higher education. Literacy increased and with it the desire for books, newspapers, and magazines. People became more aware of events beyond their immediate geographical region. Improved transportation and communications helped create a greater sense of common culture and national identity.

The Repeal of the Corn Laws Reforms enacted by Parliament in 1832 gave more power to the House of Commons. This chamber represented merchants and manufacturers more than did the aristocratic House of Lords. By the 1840s, Britain's middle class was powerful enough to challenge the **Corn Laws**, which placed a high tariff on imported grains. These laws kept the price of wheat, also known as corn, high. High wheat prices benefited aristocratic landowners, but made bread expensive for everyone. In 1846, the Anti-Corn League, a reform movement led by Sir Robert Peel and members of the middle class, persuaded Parliament to repeal the Corn Laws. Removing the tariffs meant that the price of wheat would be based mainly on supply and demand.

Increasing Trade After the repeal of the Corn Laws, Britain began to import more grain from the United States and European nations. British farmers could not compete with the cheap imported grain. Many of them began to leave the countryside for factories, accelerating the dominance of manufacturing over agriculture in the British economy.

The Anti-Corn League also supported the larger issue of **free trade**, a policy of few restrictions or taxes on trade. The merchant class did not want Parliament to limit their right to import and export goods. The repeal of the Corn Laws led to the relaxing of trade laws in general and further increased the importance of industry. The change symbolized a major shift in power in British politics, from the land-based aristocrats to the merchants. Throughout the 19th century, British **tariffs**, or taxes on imported goods, decreased. By 1900, Britain led Europe in both manufacturing and trade.

Industrialization on the Continent

Industrialization took place more slowly on the European continent, in part because the British government protected its industries by closely guarding its inventions from foreign discovery. The British made it illegal for anyone to take blueprints for power looms, engines, and other devices outside the country. During the late 18th and early 19th centuries, continental Europe was also beset by revolutions, wars, and border disputes that made it difficult for governments to focus on economic development. Many nations also suffered from a lack of natural resources, especially coal and iron. Extreme focus on the aristocratic market left many of the middle and lower classes without growth and further slowed industrialization.

Continental European governments were more autocratic than democratic. When the continent industrialized, military leaders and aristocrats often took the lead in initiating economic and financial programs.

Industrialization in France

Industrialization in France took place mostly after 1815. Unlike Great Britain, France did not have large reserves of coal and iron ore. Most of the coal and iron fields were concentrated in the north, close to the Belgian border. France had experienced limited growth in manufacturing during the mid-18th century, especially around the region of Lyon. Luxury goods such as silk, woven tapestries, porcelain, and carved furniture formed the basis of France's modest industrial expansion. Wealthy aristocrats bought most of these goods.

The French Revolution of 1789, and the violence that followed, disrupted the country's economic development, and manufacturing declined. Though the revolution had promised democracy, the government proved too unstable to fulfill its aims. In 1799, the French general Napoleon Bonaparte seized power, turning the country into a military dictatorship.

Napoleon's Reforms Napoleon laid the groundwork for France's industrial growth. His army needed weapons and uniforms, so iron and cloth production increased to meet the demands of the military. In addition, Napoleon supported many innovations that helped modernize France, especially in education and transportation. His administration established schools that taught engineering, science, architecture, and mathematics. He initiated the construction of new roads, bridges, and canals that helped unify the nation.

Among his major achievements was the completion in 1810 of the Saint Quentin Canal, a waterway joining a network of rivers and other bodies of water that connected the coal and iron fields of northern France to the capital city of Paris. Other canals connected to ports and allowed barges to transport grain and other goods across the country.

Napoleon also established the Bank of France, the country's national bank and main financial institution. The bank helped fund government infrastructure projects, including the expansion of the railroad. As in Britain, government support helped industry develop.

British Technology Helps France After Napoleon's abdication in 1815, France entered a period of renewed industrial growth. Many French aristocrats who had escaped to England during the French Revolution returned, bringing English technology with them. During the 1830s, France finally acquired access to British weaving technology and started to use looms with multiple spindles, reviving the French silk industry. The cities of Lille and Rouen in northern France became centers for cotton manufacturing. The Alsace region of northeast France proved rich in deposits of coal and iron and began to attract manufacturers.

The introduction of the steam engine increased the demand for coal. Industrialist François de Wendel began to use steam engines to mine coal. He also introduced the British method of smelting iron, and his family became one of the major manufacturers of heavy machinery during the 19th century.

French Railroads The French began to build railroads shortly after the British introduced them in 1816. By 1827, France had constructed the first railway line on the continent. It ran about 11 miles (18 km), carrying coal and iron from mines to a nearby river. In 1832, it expanded and added passenger cars. Demand for iron increased as France's railroads grew. In 1838, French ironworkers completed the first locomotive made entirely in France.

THE SPREAD OF RAILROADS IN EUROPE

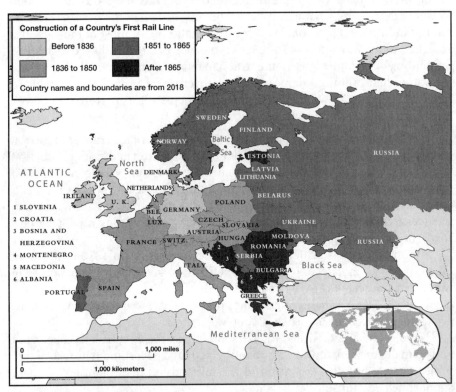

Source: FDV, Wikipedia Commons

Railroad lines expanded throughout France during the second half of the 19th century. The government, rather than private investors, sponsored most of the expansion. In 1879, the government launched the Freycinet Plan, a program that called for making railroads accessible to nearly every town and village in France.

Trade Agreements and Tariffs The French government tried to protect its industries from competition by controlling the importation of goods. To do so, the government put high tariffs on imports. Sometimes it banned the importation of certain goods. This changed in 1860, when a British member of Parliament, Richard Cobden, convinced the French government that free trade would improve their labor market. France and Britain signed a treaty easing trade between the two nations and reducing French tariffs on British goods. French-British free trade lasted until France returned to its earlier protectionist policies and imposed tariffs once more in 1892.

Nonindustrialized Europe

Compared to the industrialized areas of Northern and Western Europe, Southern and Eastern Europe remained more dependent on agriculture. Though serfdom had ended in the Habsburg Empire in 1848 and in Russia in 1861, most people remained poor and landless. They usually rented land from or were employed by a landlord, receiving "pay" in the form of food and shelter. The landowners formed an elite that continued to dominate politics and society. As the 19th century progressed, peasants suffered from famine, or extreme and widespread shortage of food, when crops failed because the region's economy offered few alternatives to agriculture.

Societies that depended mainly upon agriculture provided little financial cushion for most people when crops failed. In the mid-19th century, poor agricultural practices, combined with absentee landlords and a growing population, created conditions leading to famines.

Urban areas in Southern and Eastern Europe were smaller and more isolated than those of Western and Northern Europe. Manufactured goods were imported and available only to the wealthy elite. In many regions, relationships between peasants and aristocrats had changed little since the Middle Ages. The harsh economic conditions found in Southern and Eastern Europe, often combined with religious or political persecution, forced the poor and oppressed to migrate to places such as the United States and Latin America.

The Irish Potato Famine

Controlled by the English for centuries, Ireland was made a part of the United Kingdom in 1801 and governed as a colony. Ireland was located in Western Europe but was economically more similar to the nonindustrialized countries of Southern and Eastern Europe. With few sources of coal, the Irish relied on a substance called peat, a dense, dirt-like layer of partially decomposed plant matter dug out of the ground. Since the plant matter had not fully decomposed, it could be burned for fuel and heat. Although Ireland had a small linen industry based on the cultivation of the fibrous plant flax, there was little attempt at full-scale industrialization.

The British regarded Ireland as a source of produce for their own workers. Irish farms and estates cultivated grain, potatoes, and dairy products, most of which the English landlords exported to England. The Irish people, for the most part, remained poor. During the **potato famine** of the 1840s and 1850s, approximately a million Irish men and women migrated to the United States and Canada. (The potato famine and the high price of imported grains led to food shortages throughout Great Britain during this period. Referred to as the **"Hungry '40s,"** this period helped bring about the repeal of the Corn Laws.)

Causes of the Famine Potatoes originated in the Americas. They first arrived in Europe in the 1600s. Nutritious and easy to grow in Ireland's poor soil, they rapidly replaced other foods as a staple among the Irish poor farmers. By the 1840s, most rural Irish relied almost entirely upon potatoes for nourishment. Around 1846, a disease known as blight began to destroy the crops. In response, the British Parliament did little to aid the Irish. Food shortages drove up prices.

Most Irish land belonged to English aristocrats who spent little time in Ireland. They did little to ease the suffering of their tenants, whom many of the landlords viewed as an inferior people. Religion caused a further separation. Most English landowners were Protestants while nearly all Irish tenants were Catholics. For centuries, anti-Catholic laws had prohibited most Irish from owning land or voting. Some of these restrictions had been removed in the 19th century, but the legacy of religious discrimination persisted.

Even when the potato famine was at its worst, English landlords continued to demand rent regardless if crops failed. They evicted peasants who could not pay. Starving, homeless people wandered the Irish countryside. One form of aid was the workhouse, built to house homeless people and provide them work. The British government built 163 workhouses in Ireland, but with little industry in Ireland, there was nothing for people to do to earn a living. Most of the workhouses were overcrowded, leading to unsanitary conditions and the spread of disease. Death rates in Ireland soared.

The Effect of the Famine on Population The Irish potato famine lasted about four years, from 1845 to 1849. Between 1841 and 1851, Ireland's population decreased 20 percent. In the mid-1800s, nearly 1 million people died of starvation and disease. Nearly 2 million more people emigrated to the United States, Britain, Canada, or Australia. Many never reached their destination. Vessels carrying Irish immigrants were called "coffin ships" because so many passengers, weakened by hunger and sickness, died on the way. Economically, the country remained poor for many decades, with most people dependent on subsistence farming and fishing for a livelihood.

From Famine to Independence The famine worsened political tensions between Ireland and Britain. When starving Irish farmers rioted to protest the lack of British aid, the government sent armed troops to suppress them.

Irish anger at British treatment continued to simmer. In the later 19th century, many Irish joined a vigorous campaign demanding Home Rule, a policy allowing Irish self-government. A group called Irish Unionists, primarily Protestants who saw Home Rule as a threat to their power, opposed this movement. Finally, in 1914, after decades of Irish pressure, Parliament passed a Home Rule bill. However, when World War I broke out, the enactment of the bill was delayed and hostilities resumed. (See Topic 8.2.)

Slower Growth in Southern Europe

As much of western and central Europe industrialized to varying degrees, Southern Europe remained largely agrarian, with few factories and railroads. Portugal, Spain, southern Italy, and Greece lacked significant deposits of coal and iron. In addition, their economies featured large landowners who used peasants or serfs to work the land. Landowners had little interest in industrial development that might lure people to work in factories. Because the landed elites controlled the governments, these states had little desire to sponsor the construction of railroads.

Life in Southern Europe remained as it had been for hundreds of years. People rarely used cash, and banks had little role in the economy. During the 1800s, Britain, France, and Germany grew wealthier and stronger than did Southern European countries. This continued into the 20th and 21st centuries.

Slow Change in Russia

Tsar Alexander II recognized that serfdom undercut Russia's power. It reduced the incentive for people to work hard, try new farming techniques, and take initiative. It produced men who made poor soldiers, and it created little wealth to fund a strong military. So, despite the opposition of many nobles, he issued the **Emancipation Edict of 1861** that started gradually abolishing serfdom. It technically allowed ordinary people to own land and participate in local government. Most peasants, however, lacked money to buy land. They had little education. Many chose to remain on the estates where they were born and continued to work for the landowners by renting small plots of land. Overall, their lives changed little after emancipation.

In spite of the stagnation of its agricultural section, Russia eventually began to industrialize. It built railroads to connect major commercial centers. The Trans-Siberian Railroad transported goods and materials between Moscow and the Pacific Ocean, a distance of over 5,700 miles. It enabled Russia to trade more easily with East Asian countries. Russia's coal, iron, and steel industries developed along with its railways, mostly in the 1890s. Russia became the world's fourth-largest steel-producing nation by 1900. Still, Russia's economy remained largely agricultural until the Communists took power in 1917.

To accumulate the money needed to invest in railroads and factories, Russia increased its grain exports. It did so even in years when it had too little to feed its own people. One government minister noted that the peasants might starve but the country would export.

The Trans-Siberian Railway circa 1903 (left) and in recent years (right)

REFLECT ON THE ESSENTIAL QUESTION

Essential Question: *What were the factors that influenced the development of industrialization in various parts of Europe from 1815 to 1914?*

Factors	Influence on Industrial Development

KEY TERMS

Industrial Revolution	Henry Bessemer	free trade
canals	Bessemer process	tariffs
mass produced	Great Exhibition of 1851	potato famine
capital	Crystal Palace	"Hungry '40s"
capitalism	patents	Emancipation Edict of 1861
consumers	middle class	
steam engine	Corn Laws	

MULTIPLE-CHOICE QUESTIONS

Questions 1–3 refer to the following passage.

"The work of undermining the population is going on stealthily, but steadily. Each succeeding day witnesses its devastations—more . . . deadly than the plague. We do not say that there exists a conspiracy to uproot the 'mere Irish;' but we do aver [assert], that the fearful system of wholesale ejectment [removing people from their land], . . . which we daily behold, is a mockery of the eternal laws of God—a flagrant outrage on the principles of nature. Whole districts are cleared. Not a roof-tree [the ridge of a roof] is to be seen where the happy cottage of the laborer or the snug homestead of the farmer at no distant day cheered the landscape. . . ."

—Tipperary Vindicator, an Irish newspaper, quoted in
The Illustrated London News, December 16, 1848

1. The passage above reflects which of the following regarding the British government's response to Irish suffering during the potato famine?
   (A) It required landlords to stop ejecting Irish tenant farmers from their homes.
   (B) It spoke out clearly about the deplorable sufferings of the Irish.
   (C) It allowed the suffering of the Irish to get worse.
   (D) It organized a conspiracy to remove the Irish from their land.

2. Which historical development most directly created the context for the crisis discussed in the passage?
   (A) The Industrial Revolution because it encouraged British exploitation of Ireland
   (B) The French Revolution because it increased British fear of Irish republicanism
   (C) The Napoleonic wars because it made the British less concerned about human suffering
   (D) The Romantic movement because it led the British to focus on nature's beauty

3. Which of the following was the most direct consequence of the Irish famine?
   (A) The Irish became more dependent on potatoes as a food crop.
   (B) Irish Roman Catholics lost some of their influence in the country.
   (C) The Irish accepted English landowner's control of Irish land.
   (D) Irish nationalism increased political tensions with England.

SHORT-ANSWER QUESTION

Answer all parts of the question that follows.

1. a) Explain ONE reason why Britain industrialized faster and more efficiently than other European countries.
   b) Explain ONE cause for the delay in industrialization in France from 1780–1850.
   c) Explain ONE cause for the delay in industrialization in Russia from 1780–1850.

Topic 6.3

Second Wave Industrialization
and Its Effects

His creation was a sort of new religion...
—Émile Zola, describing a massive department store in
the novel *The Ladies' Paradise*, 1883

Essential Question: How did innovations and advances in technology during the Industrial Revolution lead to economic and social changes?

As technology and inventions spread, people began refining them. In many cases, they developed new ways to manufacture items, generate and transmit energy, and communicate. The world began to resemble today's world more closely as electricity, telephones, and other technologies emerged and took hold.

The Second Industrial Revolution, 1870–1914

From around 1870 to 1914, Europe underwent a dramatic expansion of manufacturing, transportation, and trade that became known as the **second industrial revolution**. Innovations in manufacturing increased the mass production of goods. Steel became a major industry. Electricity revolutionized urban centers and provided a new source of power for manufacturing. Chemical engineering introduced new materials including galvanized rubber and plastics. The invention of the **internal combustion engine** ushered in an age of vehicles powered by gasoline, diesel oil, and other liquid fossil fuels.

Mechanization and the Factory System

The expansion of factories increased the demand for the machines that created products. These machines needed to be standardized in size, shape, and function so that if one part broke down it could easily be replaced. The second industrial revolution saw a rise in the manufacture of machine tools—those used to shape metal and build other machines.

Manchester During the second industrial revolution, Manchester, England, became one of the world's most industrialized cities and a center for the manufacture of machines used in the production of textiles and other consumer goods. The construction of deep canals in the 1880s and 1890s brought cargo ships directly into Manchester to be loaded with export goods.

In 1898, Manchester created the world's first industrial park—an area designated expressly for manufacturing. In 1902, the British branch of the U.S.-based Westinghouse Electric Company opened a factory in the park. In 1911, the Ford Automobile Company opened its first British factory there. Manchester's role in industry gave rise to the term **Manchester capitalism**, the idea that free trade could raise the living standard of all workers.

The Krupps The **Krupp family** of Essen, Germany, began manufacturing steel in 1810, specializing in weapons. The government subsidized much of the Krupp business. In the 1840s, the Krupps invented a new method for making steel. In 1847, they produced the first steel cannon. Other countries began to buy Krupp weapons. Soon, Krupp was one of the world's wealthiest manufacturers. In 1862, the Krupps built the first Bessemer process furnace in continental Europe. (See Topic 6.2 for a description of the Bessemer process.) They added their own improvements to the process to develop purer steel. In the 1890s, the Krupps developed steel combined with nickel, thin enough for the construction of ships. These steel-sided vessels became models for ocean liners and cargo carriers. The family also became one of the world's largest railroad suppliers.

In 1872, Alfred Krupp, the company's president and owner, presented his *General Directive,* one of the first systematic plans for the management of a large modern company. It described the specific duties and responsibilities of all employees, established a formal hierarchy, and outlined employee benefits and regulations for working conditions.

Die Hüttenwerke von Krupp in Essen. (Nach Originalzeichnung.)

Source: Getty Images

While the steel industry took off first in Great Britain, other countries quickly followed. In Germany, the steel works owned by the Krupp family became enormous in the country's economic development and the rise of its military power in the 19th and 20th centuries.

Electricity

The second industrial revolution was also an electric revolution. For most of history, electricity, such as lightning strikes or sparks of static electricity, were sources of curiosity or danger. The first practical use for electricity was in communications. In the 1840s, the American inventor Samuel Morse introduced the **telegraph**, a method of sending messages along an electric wire using a series of taps that made long or short sounds—Morse code. For the first time, humans could transmit complicated information faster than a human or an animal could travel. It allowed almost instantaneous communication across hundreds or thousands of miles. In the 1870s, the laying of the first successful trans-Atlantic telegraph wire connected Britain with the United States.

Electrical Generators Transform Urban Life The development of electric generators in the 1880s led to the establishment of the **electric grid**, a system of supplying cities and towns with electric power for lighting, streetcars, and trolleys. With the use of electric light, offices, schools, libraries, restaurants, and factories could remain open at night. City life entered a 24-hour cycle of work and play.

Electricity Speaks Scottish American inventor Alexander Graham Bell patented the first **telephone** in 1876. Telephones did not become widely available, however, until the early 20th century. Telephone communications relied on a central "switchboard," or exchange where workers connected wires manually. As telephone lines spread, thousands of young women acquired jobs as telephone operators, making the telephone part of a new movement toward jobs and economic independence for women in the United States and Europe.

Wireless communication, or **radio**, first evolved in the 1890s. In 1894, Italian physicist and inventor Guglielmo Marconi invented a device he called the "wireless" telegraph. He received a British patent for his invention in 1896 and relocated to England. Marconi's wireless transmitted only signals, not human voices.

The first wireless voice transmission was accomplished by the Brazilian inventor Roberto Landell de Moura in 1900, and on December 25, 1906, Americans working for the Westinghouse Corporation broadcast the first radio program from a station on the coast of Massachusetts. Marconi capitalized on these new developments by opening the world's first radio factory in 1912. The new forms of communications enabled people to transmit ideas, inventions, and news rapidly across the globe, and the world became more interconnected.

Transportation

Even as new communication methods made the world smaller, new and improved transportation methods helped bring about the same goal. New inventions made transporting people and goods easier, safer, faster, and cheaper.

Bicycles What is today known as a bicycle had many precursors and failed forerunners throughout the 1800s. But after the 1870s, it began to resemble the useful, reliable form of transportation that exists today. As they became more practical, bicycles became a cheap, clean, reliable form of transportation for workers. And cycling was fun enough for royalty in Russia and Britain to take it up as a hobby.

Steamships The invention of **steamships** in the late 19th century meant that sailors no longer had to depend on favorable winds or river currents to take them where they wanted to go. Shipping times on some routes decreased by more than half. Farmers could ship crops longer distances without spoilage. And governments used steamships to move troops and supplies in wartime.

Streetcars A **streetcar**, also called a trolley or tram, is a multi-passenger vehicle that runs along a track set into a street. The first streetcars were horse-drawn. Later ones used batteries and then electricity. Over time, streetcars became the main method of transportation for people in many European cities. Streetcar companies extended their lines into suburbs, giving ordinary people the chance to comfortably travel further for less money.

Internal Combustion Engine This type of engine usually runs on gasoline or diesel fuel. Internal combustion engines in tractors and other farm equipment revolutionized farming and eventually led to higher crop yields and lower food prices. These engines became essential parts of "horseless carriages" (cars), motorcycles, buses, and trucks. People could travel far without having to limit themselves to streetcar routes, and they could travel much faster than on horseback. Although Britain led in earlier technological movements, advances in the internal combustion engine mostly came from Germany and the United States.

Airplanes In 1903, Wilbur and Orville Wright of the United States were the first to achieve a powered, controlled, sustained flight. The brothers' experience in bicycle sales and repair helped them as they developed the airplane. They began by building gliders and then added an internal combustion engine. Soon, airplanes had economic uses (such as quickly delivering mail) and military uses (such as getting a bird's-eye view of opposing troops).

Chemical Engineering

The second industrial revolution brought new uses for chemicals. Vulcanization, the process of hardening rubber by treating it with sulfur, made rubber far more durable and therefore valuable. It could be used to make many materials waterproof, including a coating for electrical wires.

In 1907, a chemist in New York, Leo Baekeland, developed a mixture of the chemicals phenol and formaldehyde to produce a hard, smooth material he named Bakelite. This material was the world's first plastic. Bakelite proved to be practical material for many modern devices including radios, telephones, phonographs, and cameras.

Chemical engineering also improved the textile industry. In 1894, Frederick Cross of England and his colleagues invented a fiber from wood pulp they called viscose. A little more than a decade later, the British textile manufacturing company Courtaulds opened the first factory devoted exclusively to the production of chemical, or synthetic, cloth.

Managing Markets

During the second industrial revolution, many countries experienced economic instability that led to a downward spiral or depression. Between 1873 and 1879, both Western Europe and the United States struggled with an economic crisis. Governments and corporations attempted to control unpredictable business cycles through a variety of methods.

The Long Depression

Several factors caused the economic crisis historians now call the Long Depression. Wars between Germany and France had destabilized both countries. Germany demanded monetary reparations from the defeated French, which the French had difficulty paying. Yet in a growing economy, people increasingly relied on money to buy and sell goods. However, the supply of money, which was based on the amount of gold each country held, did not increase fast enough. Money remained in short supply. Like anything in short supply, it became more valuable, and people had a hard time borrowing to expand or even operate a farm or business.

As a result of these economic strains, investment dried up for the railway building booms in Germany and the United States. Investors went into a panic over existing investments, and many workers faced unemployment. From 1873 to 1896, the rate of growth in production declined, unemployment rose, and prices in general fell. It was the world's most severe global economic crisis since the start of industrialization.

In need of cash, people sought to withdraw their money from banks, causing a "run" on the banks. Because banks had money out on loan before the crisis, they could not return all deposits and would sometimes go out of business. Although most nations had recovered somewhat by 1879, similar crises occurred periodically throughout the 1880s and 1890s. In response to these upheavals, both businesses and governments tried to develop strategies to survive economic uncertainty.

Responses to the Depression

Nations tried to stabilize their economies through **protectionism**, with high tariffs to protect their own industries. Tariffs had been a successful strategy for economic growth for countries as they began to industrialize. However, the lack of trade caused manufacturers and merchants to go out of business, leading to even more widespread unemployment and social unrest.

Tariffs and Other Government Policies Traditionally, governments tried to protect their native industries by placing tariffs on foreign imports. High tariffs, however, could lead to trade wars, with each country raising tariffs to punish the other. **Free trade agreements** between individual states could allow for the mutual exchange of goods with few or no tariffs. This meant a trading partner had a **most favored nation** status. Free trade agreements could also be used to support political and military alliances. While freer trade created more competition for producers, it often reduced prices for consumers.

Trusts and Monopolies During the Industrial Revolution, manufacturers tried to balance supply with demand. A surplus of goods would lead to a drop in price that would cut into profits. On the other hand, a shortage might raise the price beyond what consumers were willing to pay. Sometimes corporations would try to set prices by joining together in **cartels** or **trusts.** Rather than competing on the open market, these groups of companies would privately agree to set their prices at a certain level. Such price setting became illegal in many nations, and governments would punish companies that engaged in it.

A **monopoly** exists when one company limits or controls competition for a particular industry. That company would then control the entire market for the product and consumers would be forced to pay whatever price the company set. Governments tried to control monopolies by passing laws against them.

Not all monopolies were outlawed, however. The government might decide that in a certain industry one single company could provide better service than many companies, particularly when the cost of starting a business was very high. For example, electric companies and phone companies needed to build vast and costly networks of wires to carry electricity or phone calls. Once a company built such a network, other companies could rarely challenge its control of a market. Since those companies lacked competition, governments often regulated them.

Source: Getty Images

The high prices that monopolies set often angered people. This British political cartoon from 1890 shows a laborer, a mechanic, a farmer, and others feeding a beast called King Monopoly. The caption is "And still he wants more!"

The Influence of Banks The influence of banks grew as the economies of industrialized nations became more complex and sophisticated. Large banks gained considerable political and social influence. They could decide which companies and individuals were most worthy of loans and which would be denied credit.

Banks could also make loans to governments for infrastructure projects and other state-sponsored programs. In addition, banks helped international trade through currency conversion. Different nations used different monetary systems. If an American company sold goods to Britain, those goods would be purchased with British pounds. A bank would then convert the pounds into American dollars for the company to use.

Rise of Consumerism

During the last half of the 19th century, the industrialized nations of Europe experienced a dramatic increase in the number of consumer goods available on the market. Ready-made clothing, processed foods, books, furniture, and even toys spurred the rise of consumerism, a lifestyle that revolved around the purchase of consumer goods. In urban areas, **department stores**, sometimes called emporiums, appealed to middle-class shoppers by providing a wide array of goods within a single establishment. Shopping became a leisure activity for many middle-class women, and successful department stores catered to their tastes. Some stores even added restaurants, beauty salons, theaters, and toilets to their premises to make shopping an all-day experience for their customers.

Marketing and Advertising

As consumer culture grew in the second half of the 19th century, merchants developed new ways of reaching customers. Women, because they did most of the family shopping, became the prime movers of consumer culture. Advertisements in magazines and newspapers were often aimed toward women and used illustrations to promote products. These advertisements played upon the role the woman was expected to fulfill in the family, reminding her that a good wife and mother might want to purchase "only the best" soap, fabric, or canned foods for her loved ones.

Shopping by Mail

Railroads and steamships transported goods across countries and continents, and catalogs enabled merchants to reach consumers. Welshman Sir Pryce Pryce-Jones created the first known **mail-order catalog** around 1861. He established a company called the Royal Welsh Warehouse in the city of Newtown, Wales. From there he shipped clothing to customers as far away as Russia and Australia. Even the famous nurse and statistician Florence Nightingale and Queen Victoria were customers.

Consumerism and Innovations in the Home

The increase in consumer goods redefined home life, especially for the middle class. The invention of the first **refrigerated railroad cars** by William Davis of the United States in 1868 enabled fresh foods to be shipped from rural farm areas to cities. Once purchased, those foods could be stored in zinc-lined iceboxes designed to keep provisions cold even during the hottest days.

Women began to cook with time-saving canned foods and prepared mixes. Rubber and the plastic material known as linoleum were used to construct easy-to-clean counters and floors.

Other aspects of home life were also transformed:

- The gramophone, an early record player invented by Thomas Edison in 1877, changed how people interacted with friends. For the first time, people could hear recorded music, and "gramophone parties" became a popular form of entertainment toward the end of the 19th century.

- In the early 20th century, the introduction of mass-produced incandescent light bulbs and electrification further revolutionized home life. With artificial light, people could socialize at night as easily as they could during the day.

- The development of the radiator to distribute steam heat also made homes warmer in the winter. With light and heat, the middle-class family could enjoy evenings together.

By the early 20th century, the middle-class home had come to symbolize both progress and comfort. For many people, these consumer goods were indeed proof that the Industrial Revolution had created a better way of life.

Industrialization in Prussia

Before the age of Napoleon, the name "Germany" referred to a region in north central Europe that consisted of more than 300 separate kingdoms, free cities, and other states. Many were part of the Holy Roman Empire, but they maintained their separate identities. From 1815 to 1867, many of these states consolidated and became loosely united in the German Confederation. However, they did not form a single country.

One of the largest and most dominant kingdoms of the German Confederation was Prussia. In the 18th century, Prussia focused on building a strong military to protect itself from Europe's two most powerful armies, those of France and Russia.

Then, as the Industrial Revolution spread through Europe, Prussia became even stronger. Its large deposits of coal and iron helped it become the first German state to industrialize. Prussian textile mills, using British techniques, began operating in 1786. By 1837, Prussia had more than 1,000 mills. In 1794, the first coke-smelting furnace started operating in Silesia, a region in what is now southwestern Poland. A few years later, the Ruhr Valley, an area straddling the Rhine River in Western Germany, became a center of iron production. The introduction of the steam engine in the 1830s spurred the demand for iron and coal. By 1850, Prussia was producing around 529,000 tons of iron and mining 6 million tons of coal per year to support its railroads and manufacturing industries. Prussia had become a leader in industrialization.

The Zollverein Agreement

Political divisions reduced trade and slowed the economic growth of German states in the early 19th century. In 1834, guided by an ambitious Prussian monarchy, several German states signed the **Zollverein Agreement**. The goal of this arrangement was to promote German unity by eliminating the customs, or taxes, paid on goods traded among German states. When the government ended many of the trade barriers between German states, industrialization was possible on a large scale. The state of Prussia also invested in new technologies for silver mines and coal mines.

In 1871, Prussia finally united the numerous German states (except Austria) into the German Empire. Industrialization proceeded rapidly, and hundreds of thousands of Germans moved from rural areas to cities and towns. By 1900, Germany had the largest manufacturing economy in Europe. By 1914, Germany was making twice as much steel as Britain.

List's National System

In a set of ideas known as the **National System**, German economist **Friedrich List** (1789–1846) argued for government involvement in economic growth, including tariffs and investments in education and infrastructure. List, a supporter of German unification, believed that tariffs would protect German industries from English imports. But once Germany was on an equal footing with England, List believed, free trade could be gradually reintroduced. List's ideas provided the framework for later free trade agreements among European nations.

List also believed that an extensive network of government-controlled rail lines would help German unification and increase government power. The first German railroad line opened in 1835. In 1842, Prussia's government established the Railroad Fund to finance rail lines throughout German lands. Germany, like all of Europe except densely populated Great Britain, relied on government support to build its railway network. During the next decade, most major German cities became connected by rail, with Berlin emerging as a railway hub and leading urban center. By the time Germany unified in 1871, it had more than 11,000 miles of railway.

REFLECT ON THE ESSENTIAL QUESTION

Essential Question: *How did innovations and advances in technology during the Industrial Revolution lead to economic and social changes?*

Innovations and Technological Advances	Effects of Innovations and Technological Advances

KEY TERMS

second industrial revolution	telephone	free trade agreements
internal combustion engine	radio	most favored nation
industrial park	steamships	department stores
Manchester capitalism	streetcar	mail-order catalog
Krupp family	protectionism	refrigerated railroad cars
telegraph	cartels	Zollverein Agreement
electric grid	trusts	National System
	monopoly	Friedrich List

MULTIPLE-CHOICE QUESTIONS

Questions 1–3 refer to the table below.

OUTPUT OF COAL IN EUROPEAN COUNTRIES, 1820-1900					
Year	United Kingdom	France	Germany	Belgium	Russia
1820	18	1	1	Not available	Not available
1840	34	3	4	4	Not available
1860	81	8	17	10	Less than 1
1880	149	19	59	17	3
1900	229	33	150	23	16

Source: B. R. Mitchell, European Historical Statistics 1750–1970

Quantities of coal are in millions of metric tons.

1. One reason for the difference between coal production in the United Kingdom and France was that France
   (A) did not have a national bank to help finance industrial growth
   (B) lacked a strong agricultural sector to support a mining industry
   (C) could purchase coal cheaply from other countries
   (D) had fewer coal deposits to mine

2. Which of the following factors most directly explains how German government influenced the change in coal production shown in the table?
   (A) It opened its own mines to compete with privately-owned mines.
   (B) It removed trade barriers and it invested in mining technology.
   (C) It negotiated with British companies to encourage them to invest in German mines.
   (D) It ended the Zollverein Agreement which had limited the trade in coal.

3. The level of Russian coal production was most likely a result of which of the following?

    (A) Russia's agricultural-based economy

    (B) Russia's development of alternate sources of energy for mining

    (C) British use of patents to restrict the spread of steam engine technology

    (D) Inadequate population to sustain an industrial workforce

SHORT-ANSWER QUESTION

Use the passage below to answer all parts of the question that follows.

"No branch of political economy presents a greater diversity of views between men of theory and men of practice, than that which treats of international commerce and commercial policy. . . . We have seen in our century, Prussia, a continental nation, as yet imperfectly prepared for manufacturing industry, seeking her welfare in the prohibitory system so condemned by theorists. And what has been her reward? National prosperity.

On the other hand, encouraged by promises of theory, the United States of America, which had made a rapid growth under the protective system, have been induced to open their ports to the manufactures of England; and what fruits has this competition borne? A periodical visitation of commercial disaster."

—Friedrich List, *National System of Political Economy*, 1856
(first published in 1841)

1. a) Describe the historical context in which List made his claims about trade policy.

    b) Explain ONE element of List's point of view toward the group of people that he regarded as "men of theory."

    c) Explain ONE example of evidence that List used to support his claim about trade policy.

Topic 6.4

Social Effects of Industrialization

The first chimney I went up, they told me there was plum pudding and money at the top of it.

—William Cooper, 1818, describing becoming a chimney sweep at age 10

Essential Question: What were the causes and consequences of social developments resulting from industrialization?

Industrialization reshaped nearly every aspect of daily life, first in Northern and Western Europe and eventually throughout the world. Social classes became more distinct, and people in each class developed their own outlook based on their economic role. As many workers moved from farms to factories, they had to learn to follow strict schedules, working a set number of hours at a repetitive task, often in unsafe conditions and for very low pay. Factory work also separated workers from their homes and families, since the home was no longer the focus of working life.

Those who remained on farms were forced to change how they worked as well. Many became tenant farmers, growing crops for others on commercial farms. Improvements in transportation—including railroads, steamships, and better roads and harbors—prompted these commercial farms to produce for distant markets rather than for their own or local consumption.

Social classes were linked with each other through the processes of production and consumption of goods. Charles Dickens believed that many in the lower class produced far more than their low wages enabled them to consume. Dickens, the most famous English novelist of the mid-19th century, had been poor as a child. He sympathized with those who had little money. Many of his novels depict characters from the lower class who, against all odds, rise to the ranks of the middle class—something that rarely actually happened. In real life, **social mobility**, or moving from a poorer and less influential class to a wealthier and more prestigious one, was extremely difficult.

Rise of New Social Classes

Industrialization created new types of work. People filling these new jobs did not fit into the feudal classes, such as peasants and nobles.

The Working Class The members of the **working class**, or **proletariat**, worked largely in manufacturing, mining, and related industries, such as railroads and steamship travel. Many working-class people lived in homes they rented from their employers or in a new type of housing that first appeared during industrialization—multifamily dwellings called **tenements**, in which several families would crowd into buildings, often forced to share kitchen and toilet facilities. Few working-class families owned land. Working-class women and children often had to work to help support the family.

In England, as industrialization grew, the number of industrial workers skyrocketed during the 19th century. In 1750, about 60 percent of all males worked in farming, but by 1900 that had declined to about 12 percent, even though agricultural production (the amount of food being harvested) doubled during that period. By 1900, nearly 80 percent of the population in industrialized countries worked on commercial farms, in factories, or as domestic servants.

The Middle Class Members of the **middle class**, or the **bourgeoisie**, in contrast, worked in jobs such as business management, law, medicine, banking, government civil service, and higher education. Many middle-class families owned their own homes. Communities of single-family dwellings, or **suburbs**, on the edges of cities expanded to accommodate the growing middle class during the late 19th and early 20th centuries. Few middle-class women worked outside the home. Children attended school or were tutored at home.

This new middle class gained power and influence, creating a demand for consumer goods that further spurred industrialization. Urban areas became centers of education and culture that reflected middle-class interests and values. For this new middle class, a comfortable home served as a shelter from the larger society—a place where women and children could find shelter from the so-called masculine world of work.

A small number of middle-class families accumulated enormous wealth through the ownership of factories, mines, railroads, and steamship lines. Toward the end of the 19th century, these families began to form a new upper-class "aristocracy," buying large country estates and building mansions that rivaled those of the traditional aristocrats.

Class Identity Among Workers

The term **class identity** means that members of a social class were aware of which class they belonged to and consciously identified with that class and its interests. They spoke of themselves as members of a class and saw their lives through the lens of class distinctions. They might consider members of other classes as opponents or even enemies.

This class identity was especially true of the proletariat. Working-class people often left their homes to seek work in factories and mines. Without their extended family network nearby, they had to rely on their immediate families and one another for help and support. On their rare days off, workers would spend their much-valued leisure time together, often with their families. New activities to relax became popular:

- performances at **vaudeville** theaters, where audiences could see a variety of musicians, dancers, magicians, and actors in a single show

- sports, such as boxing matches, horse races, and team games such as rugby and football (known in the United States as soccer); often these were played in new arenas

- excursions, on bicycles or on foot, into the countryside or to a beach

- picnics and other leisure activities in new urban parks

- shopping at department stores (see Topic 6.3)

- visiting museums (Many new museums opened in Austria, France, and Britain in the second half of the 19th century. Some installed gas lighting or electric lighting so that people could visit in the evenings.)

- going to opera houses, which sprang up all over Europe and which could seat hundreds or even thousands of people

Spending both work and leisure time together created solidarity (a sense of unity) among people who did physical labor in factories and mines. They began to see themselves as a distinct social class, and they wanted political representation.

On August 16, 1819, about 70,000 people gathered in St. Peter's Fields in Manchester, England, to demand reforms in Parliament, such as expanding the right to vote. Efforts to break up the gathering resulted in 15 deaths. This event, known as the **Peterloo Massacre**, demonstrated to many working people that they needed to unite to defend their interests. They became more willing to join **labor unions**, also called **trade unions**, which are organizations of workers that can negotiate with employers to improve wages and working conditions. Many workers also formed **mutual aid societies**, groups that helped members in times of need.

Class Identity in the Middle Class

Members of the new middle class tried to distinguish themselves from the working class by adopting the styles and **social mores**, or customs, of the aristocratic classes as they became seen as the "new bourgeoisie." Middle-class families invested deeply in their homes. Luxury items such as works of art, china dishes, fine wooden furniture, woven rugs, and window drapes enhanced bourgeois homes as conspicuous consumption—the public display of luxury goods purchased—became part of the culture. Middle-class families often entertained at home and employed servants to cook and clean for them. The bourgeoisie even tried to act like the aristocracy by attending the theater, ballet, symphony, and horse races.

As did working-class families, middle-class families mainly socialized with those from the same class. When they traveled, members of the bourgeoisie chose resorts and hotels where they could socialize with other middle-class families. In England, the city of Bath, with its hot springs, was a traditional vacation spot for the bourgeoisie. In Germany, the town of Baden-Baden served a similar function. Social life was also a way to establish business connections, which would further solidify middle-class wealth.

Many middle-class men joined private clubs whose members shared investment opportunities and business advice with one another. Some joined **fraternal organizations**, also known as brotherhoods, or groups of people with common interests and ambitions. Once a man joined such an organization, he could depend on his "brothers" for a loan or a job reference. Many of these organizations, such as the Freemasons, started out as professional guilds for skilled workmen. As the guilds themselves declined and disappeared, the organizations continued to flourish as a means of mutual support. In this way, they helped strengthen the bonds among the middle class.

Middle-Class Philanthropy

As members of the middle class began to accumulate wealth, they had new opportunities to take on roles formerly carried out only by the elite. For example, middle-class people formed **philanthropic**, or charitable, organizations. Some of these organizations endowed museums, symphonies, schools, operas, and other cultural institutions.

Others worked directly with people who needed assistance. Many middle-class women provided aid at orphanages and helped the poor and working class by distributing food and clothing and training children for domestic service or factory jobs. While these charities did not lift people out of poverty, they did provide basic care at a time when there were few government programs in industrialized nations that addressed the needs of the poor.

Several charitable groups were religion-based. One of the best known was the Salvation Army, founded in London in 1865 to provide shelter to the homeless and unemployed. As part of the Social Gospel movement, it also encouraged the people it served to become Christians or to deepen their Christian faith. The Social Gospel movement encouraged people to apply Christian beliefs or values to problems in the world.

Population Growth and Urbanization

Industrialization brought rapid population growth to Europe, particularly in cities, and urbanization changed the face of Western Europe. Rural populations dwindled as cities grew.

These shifts led to changes in politics and economics. Political power became concentrated in cities. Governments began to invest in such projects as sewage systems to improve urban life. Rural areas, meanwhile, decreased in influence, and their people had less say in government policies. People saw cities as centers of opportunity and wealth. Even those with few resources were eager to make the transition from country to city in search of jobs and, ultimately, a better life.

Many people moved to cities because of "pull" factors, such as jobs and other opportunities. However, there were "push" factors as well. For example, in northern Scotland, landlords forced small farmers off the lands they rented so the landlords could use the lands for more profitable sheep farms. This movement, called the Highland Clearances, began in the late 18th century and lasted about a hundred years. As a result, some parts of Scotland were among the least populated in Europe.

THE GROWTH OF WESTERN EUROPE'S URBAN POPULATION, 1750-1900					
Year	Population Living in Urban Areas	Population Living in Rural Areas	London	Paris	Berlin
1800	20%	80%	1,200,000	580,000	172,500
1850	35%	65%	2,650,000	1,050,000	419,000
1900	55%	45%	6,500,000	3,500,000	1,500,000

Reasons for Population Growth

Despite the terrible living conditions in the growing cities, one important reason that the population grew was increased progress in agricultural productivity through better agricultural practices:

- Crop rotation increased harvests of grains and vegetables.
- The cast-iron plow (1803) allowed farmers to sow crops in deeper furrows, preventing seeds from being blown away.
- The mechanized reaper, developed by Cyrus McCormick (1837), enabled farmers to harvest crops faster and with less labor. In fact, McCormick had demonstrated years earlier that one worker using an early version of his reaper could do the work of 12 men with scythes.
- The steel plow (1837) made farming even more efficient.

Effects of Overcrowding

As cities grew, urban problems increased. Most city residents were poor and working class. Five or more people might live in a single tenement "flat," or apartment, of one or two rooms. Some rooms did not have windows, so fresh air and sunlight were scarce. Residents had to share bath facilities. Mice, rats, and other vermin proliferated. Contagious diseases such as tuberculosis, cholera, and typhus spread rapidly in such overcrowded conditions.

Lack of Housing Some people could not afford any housing at all and they lived on the margins of society as beggars. Such dire poverty forced many men into a life of crime, and women often turned to prostitution for survival. Orphanages, workhouses, and debtors' prisons served as last resorts for those who had nowhere else to go.

Poor Public Infrastructure Throughout much of the 19th century, cities did not have the infrastructure—the basic physical structures needed for a process—to provide clean water. Tenements lacked toilets and running water. People depended on public pumps and wells for drinking water. Raw sewage was often disposed of as it had been in the Middle Ages, dumped on the street. It then found its way into these water sources. Even if it was carried away from homes, it was often dumped in or near the rivers that provided the water people drank. This led to deadly outbreaks of cholera.

In the 1850s, multiple major cholera outbreaks in London led the British physician John Snow to research what caused the disease and how it spread. He accurately theorized the disease came from direct contact with germs living in human waste that got into the water supply. His 1855 work *On the Mode of Communication of Cholera* established him as the father of modern epidemiology—the study of how and why diseases spread through populations.

THE "SILENT HIGHWAY"-MAN.
"YOUR MONEY OR YOUR LIFE!"

Source: Getty Images

In the mid-19th century, the Thames, the main river flowing through London, was so polluted with industrial and human wastes that it was viewed as carrying death. The city had grown rapidly and did not have the public infrastructure to handle the increased sewage and discharge from factories.

Other Health Issues Cold and damp housing led to respiratory problems. Lack of access to sunlight was particularly hard on children. Sunlight produces the vitamin D needed for strong bones. With so little of it, children developed crippling bone diseases such as rickets. Cholera, tuberculosis, and typhoid fever sometimes reached epidemic levels of infection. Industrial accidents also took many lives.

For most urban dwellers, life was dangerous and difficult. Yet during the last half of the 19th century, trends in agriculture and health care enabled the population to grow. Despite the hardships, the standard of living began to improve by the end of the century, even for the working class.

The Persistence of Rural Economies and Elites

In some less-industrialized regions of Europe, aristocratic landholders continued to wield much of the power—even until the early 20th century. With few urban centers and few middle-class people in their regions, agricultural elites faced little pressure to share power or accommodate new social classes. In Eastern and Southern Europe, many peasants chose to emigrate to the Americas and other regions rather than stay where they had so little economic or political power.

Family Structure and Relationships

Over time, the Industrial Revolution altered the family structure and personal relationships for both bourgeois and working-class families. Overall, family units became smaller, and multigenerational households became less common. The norm became the nuclear family, which consisted mainly of two generations—parents and their children living in a single home.

In addition, in an industrialized society, family and work occupied separate spheres, or areas of life. Instead of everyone working at home and integrating work with family life, the adults increasingly worked outside the home. As a result, the home took on less of an economic function and more of a comforting and nurturing one. This separate-sphere arrangement was particularly true for men in middle-class families.

Changes for the Working Class

In a rural farming society, people had always depended on the family to work the land. Children learned skills from the adults. Craft workers, such as blacksmiths and furniture makers, often worked from home. Men could not marry until they either inherited land or could support a family with a skill; women had to have a dowry (an amount of money, goods, or land) to enter a marriage.

However, once people started working in factories, they were often separated from their families. Family members no longer worked together. Each employed individual brought his or her wages home. Workers' wages were low, and a family usually needed many workers just to pay for necessities like food, clothing, and shelter. Even apprentices left their rural families to live and work with masters in large cities.

Working-Class Childhood Children in factories labored at a single task all day long and rarely had the chance to learn new skills. Some working-class families relied heavily on the labor of their children. Many factory owners preferred child workers because they worked for less than one-half the wages paid to men. In some industries, the owners preferred children because smaller hands could perform the fine work needed in manufacturing textiles. Many young boys worked at the very dangerous job of bobbin boy, delivering empty bobbins to women spinning thread and removing bobbins when they were full. Some bobbin boys worked 14 hours a day, six days a week.

Once these children grew too old for their jobs, they might find themselves unemployed and unwanted. In urban areas, unemployed children were often expected to fend for themselves, by begging, scavenging for scrap material to sell, or even stealing to survive. Conditions for working children contributed to the growth of reform movements.

Working-Class Women Working-class women, too, were often expected to work for wages as well as cook, clean, and care for any young children in the home. When a mother worked outside the home, small infants were often left in the care of a neighbor rather than with a grandparent or relative. By the late 19th century, the most common jobs for working-class women were as domestic servants. Working-class men worked long hours, and many had little time for family life. As labor unions sought reforms in the late 19th century, many called for a shorter workday not just to give workers a break from physical labor but also to help them find time for family life.

Middle-Class Families Become the Social Ideal

Beginning in the late 19th century, many working-class people looked to the middle class as an example of the ideal family life. Like middle-class people, they tried to make their homes the center of their lives and to provide their children with greater education and the opportunity for social mobility.

As the 19th century progressed, the middle-class family developed clearly defined gender roles. A husband and father who worked outside the home supported the family. Women did not work outside the home. Rather, they stayed home and cooked, cleaned, and cared for the children. In what became known as the **cult of domesticity**, the main goal of the wife and mother was to make the home a shelter for her husband and children as well as for herself. A woman's intrinsic value was connected to her domestic role.

Home life revolved around the emotional relationships between family members. Middle-class people believed a home should provide a warm and caring atmosphere for the family. Children in middle-class homes often remained dependent upon their parents until their late teens or early twenties. Sons did not enter the workforce until they had graduated from secondary school or college. Daughters usually remained at home until they married.

Middle-Class Marriage and Family Life With the rise of the middle class during the 19th century, the "ideal" family was one whose members were bound to one another primarily by love and affection. The conditions in which most urban families lived made this ideal state of an attentive and loving family difficult to reach. However, it provided a powerful image of 19th- and 20th-century culture.

Novelists such as Jane Austen and Charlotte Brontë presented characters who married for love, not money. Young people, who grew up reading these novels, believed that they should have the right to marry whomever they chose, rather than let their parents arrange a marriage for them. Childbearing and child-rearing were the main roles for women, and motherhood was considered a woman's highest achievement.

For most of the 18th century, birth control was limited and highly controversial. However, new types of birth control began to become available beginning in the 1840s. And the introduction of other methods of birth control at the turn of the 20th century made it possible for some couples to limit the size of their families. Birth control was mainly available to middle-class people. With fewer children, parents could invest more time and money in each child. Education became increasingly important, and smaller families allowed greater social mobility for the middle class.

Economic Class Distinctions Continue Economic prosperity remained important to the middle class. Most people married within their own social class because the classes rarely mixed with one another. Marriages between middle-class and working-class people were relatively rare and frowned upon by most middle-class families. Even within the middle class, wealthier families tended to marry into one another. The daughter of a small shopkeeper, for instance, was not likely to wed the son of a man who owned a steamship line or railroad. Yet within these restrictions, men and women aimed for a companionate marriage—one in which both spouses regarded one another as friends and companions striving toward the same goals in life. This view of marriage, which diminished the view of marriage as an economic transaction, moved steadily from the middle classes to the working class over time.

Middle Class Benefits Industrialization did generate some improvements for all social classes. Mass production and improvements in transportation made obtaining material goods easier than ever. Progress in medicine and public health increased the average life span in industrialized areas. Education and literacy increased, first for the middle class and later for the working class.

Industrialization also resulted in more leisure time for many families. Parents and children could visit public spaces and institutions such as parks, libraries, and museums. For many families, these replaced the at-home activities common in agrarian communities.

Social Reform and Family Life

People responded to the problems that came with industrialization by demanding that the government impose reforms. The first reforms protected women and children, who were seen as the most vulnerable members of society. Reformers sought to limit the types of jobs women and children could perform and the number of hours they could work. During the first half of the 19th century, Britain's Parliament passed three acts regulating industrial work: the **Factory Act of 1833**, the **Mines Act of 1842**, and the **Ten Hours Act of 1847**.

The Factory Act of 1833 This was the first attempt to protect working children. The act declared that no child under the age of 9 could be employed in a factory or mine. Children between the ages of 9 and 13 could work up to nine hours a day. Children between 14 and 18 could work up to 12 hours a day. No child could work between 8:30 at night and 5:30 in the morning. In practice, these restrictions made little difference because lighting in factories was very limited before the widespread use of electricity. Further, children were supposed to receive at least two hours of schooling each day. They had to provide a certificate stating that they had the equivalent of that schooling the prior week.

The weaknesses of the act rapidly became obvious. Many families lied about the age of their children to get work certificates, and employers made little effort to verify the true ages of those they employed. Even a child as young as 4 or 5 could get a piece of paper giving a false age of 9 or 10. Children and teens old enough to work rarely had time for school, and schools for working children did little to prepare them for better jobs. Certificates for weekly education requirements were readily granted. When government factory inspectors found manufacturers violating the law, they had little power to punish them. Many owners employing underage children received only small fines or no punishment at all.

Nevertheless, the act did have some influence. It made people aware of the need to protect children from some of the worst aspects of industrialization. Further, it introduced the idea that the welfare of children was the government's responsibility.

The Mines Act of 1842 Like the Factory Act, the Mines Act of 1842 represented another attempt to regulate the treatment of women and children in industry. Under this act, no boy under the age of 10 could be employed in coal mines in Britain. In addition, women and girls were banned from working in mines entirely. Legislators felt that mine work was too difficult and even degrading for females. Rather than improving conditions for all workers, they simply chose to ban women. Although the ban was meant to protect them, many working-class women felt threatened by the new law. While work in mines was grueling and exceedingly dangerous, women in mining districts had few other job options. If they could not work in the mines, their families would suffer.

Source: Getty Images

This illustration from the early 1840s shows a woman and child dragging coal up a shaft.

As with the Factory Act, many workers and employers disregarded the rules. Small boys continued to work in the mines. Women sometimes dressed as men or came to the mines as "substitutes" when their husbands and sons were sick or injured. Only when the miners' unions secured higher wages for men in the early 20th century did it become economically possible for women and children to leave the mines entirely.

The Ten Hours Act of 1847 At the beginning of the Industrial Revolution, workers did not have any set hours. They worked as long as the employer needed them, and shifts of 12 to 15 hours were common.

During the 19th century, a campaign for the 10-hour day became a major theme for labor unions and reformers. In 1847, after several failed attempts, reform-minded members of Parliament finally passed a bill limiting the number of hours that children between 13 and 18 and women could work to 10 hours a day on weekdays and 8 hours a day on weekends. Children under the age of 13 were banned from working. As with previous laws, the Ten Hours Act proved hard to enforce. Economic need forced many women and children to work beyond the provisions of the act.

REFLECT ON THE ESSENTIAL QUESTION

Essential Question: *What were the causes and consequences of social developments resulting from industrialization?*

Causes	Consequences

KEY TERMS

social mobility	class identity	fraternal organizations
working class	vaudeville	philanthropic
proletariat	Peterloo Massacre	cult of domesticity
tenements	labor unions	Factory Act of 1833
middle class	trade unions	Mines Act of 1842
bourgeoisie	mutual aid societies	Ten Hours Act of 1847
suburbs	social mores	

For most of human history, people did not expect progress. Technology and ideas changed so little from one generation to the next that parents assumed their children would lead lives similar to theirs. This expectation changed during the Enlightenment.

Trust in Reason The Marquis de Condorcet was a prominent Enlightenment writer and philosopher. Condorcet popularized the idea that humankind had the ability to constantly improve. He expressed this view in his book *Sketch for a Historical Picture of the Progress of the Human Mind* (1795). He thought that the human mind had already evolved through nine stages. He predicted it would eventually reach a tenth stage of peaceful equilibrium around the world. Condorcet acknowledged that there were limits to the population the planet could handle and the amount of cooperation people of a civilization could reach. Yet he asserted that, by the time humankind reached that stage, science would have kept pace and would resolve such issues.

World War I Challenges Progress On the brink of another traumatic event, as World War I began, activist lawyer Victor S. Yarros pointed out how widespread, yet recent, the idea of progress was. Yarros explained that it was unheard of in the ancient world but popularized by Enlightenment thinkers such as Condorcet. From those thinkers stemmed the belief that progress was constant, steady, and certain—that the world would always get better. However, in 1913, scholars began to question that notion. Yarros referred to the work of French scholar Emile Faguet. In response to the idea of progress, Faguet wrote, "I think it is absurd by its very definition to know whether anyone is advancing toward a goal." Faguet argued that mere movement is not progress, and the theory that humanity constantly and consistently improves is "sheer delusion, a prejudice, not only useless, but dangerous."

But not all early 20th-century scholars were so critical of the idea of progress. American philosopher, educator, and social critic John Dewey presented a more measured analysis of progress. Although Dewey began his career viewing the world in the same terms as Condorcet, his views became more complex. He believed that progress could continue, but that people had to plan and work for it.

Dangers of Progress By the 21st century, some thinkers argued that the population might be about to outstrip the ability of the earth to support it. One such scholar is Ronald Wright. In *A Short History of Progress* (2004), he made the point that the belief in human progress is not predetermined nor necessarily positive. Instead, Wright described "progress traps" into which both large and small civilizations fell because their populations outstripped the ability of their environment to sustain them. Rather than believing, as Condorcet did, that humans become smarter over generations and develop the ability to think their way out of their environmental problems, Wright declared that some fall prey to the same traps time and again, such as by producing technology that destroys the very environment that nurtures progress. No civilization has ever ultimately dodged these traps and survived, although the Egyptians and Chinese each made the longest run at about 3,000 years.

Optimism However, the cognitive psychologist Steven Pinker resurrected the argument for progress in his 2018 book, *Enlightenment Now*. Pinker challenged the "progress traps" of Wright and suggested instead that humans have reached the point predicted by Condorcet. He believed that scientific, analytical thinking had improved life for most people, reduced the number of nuclear weapons in the world, and given people the capacity to resolve the challenges of global climate change.

1. In what ways did working-class and middle-class people experience progress in the time period from approximately 1815 to 1914?

2. Do you think Emile Faguet believed that the Factory Act of 1833, the Mines Act of 1842, and the Ten Hours Act of 1847 were examples of real progress? Explain.

MULTIPLE-CHOICE QUESTIONS

Questions 1–3 refer to the passage below.

"As far as Dickens's own response to the wonders of the industrial revolution goes, there is no doubt that he welcomed them at the beginning of the 1850s. Dickens had a pride in progress even though he opposed any mechanization of the spirit. It is no doubt true, as Herbert L. Sussman says, that 'although he saw the factories of England and America at first hand, his imagination never thrilled to mechanized manufacturing as it did to the railway.' . . .

George Orwell [a 20th century writer] may be right in saying that Dickens was 'not mechanically minded,' but he had to adapt to the machine age. That he did deserves to be recognized more clearly by those who now read Dickens's novels at all closely."

—K. J. Fiendling and Anne Smith, "Hard Times and the Factory Controversy: Dickens vs. Harriet Martineau," *Nineteenth-Century Fiction*, 1970

1. To which of the following would Dickens have been most opposed?

   (A) The Peterloo Massacre

   (B) The Factory Act of 1833

   (C) The Social Gospel movement

   (D) The Mines Act of 1842

2. According to Sussman's comment on Dickens, Dickens would have been most concerned about the switch from

   (A) water-powered textile mills to coal-powered textile mills

   (B) wool clothes for everyday wear to cotton clothes

   (C) work done on one's own schedule to work done based on a clock

   (D) coal stoves in home kitchens to electric stoves

3. The view of Dickens toward the economic and cultural changes of the 18th and 19th centuries was most similar to the views of

   (A) Jean-Jacques Rousseau because both believed that industrialization could harm people's spirits

   (B) Napoleon Bonaparte because both argued for more education in literature and art to help people respond to industrialization

   (C) Richard Cobden because both believed that free trade could solve the problems that industrial laborers faced

   (D) Alfred Krupp because both believed in the benefits of large, modern industrial factories

SHORT-ANSWER QUESTION

Answer all parts of the question that follows.

1. a) Describe ONE specific example of the changing role of women in the workplace in the second half of the 19th century.

   b) Describe ONE specific example of the changing role of men in the workplace in the second half of the 19th century.

   c) Explain ONE specific reason for the development of "separate spheres" that took place during the 19th century.

Topic 6.5

The Concert of Europe and European Conservatism

Democracy is a reality in America. In Europe it is a falsehood....it cannot end in a ripe, old age.

—Klemens von Metternich (1773–1859)

Essential Question: How was European political order reestablished and maintained in the period following Napoleon's defeat?

In Topic 6.4, you learned about economic, political, and scientific changes that led to societal change and progress. However, many of those in power believed that change could be damaging or even deadly. Monarchs and other leaders often worked to limit or even reverse changes that were taking place.

Conservatism and the Status Quo

In the 19th century, **conservatism** was a movement of people who believed that governments were most stable when based on traditional sources of power such as the monarchy, the church, and the army. They were suspicious of mass movements and resisted giving too much power to common people. Conservatives worried that people with little education and little property to protect might disrupt the economy and create social chaos. As a result, conservatives believed that authority was best concentrated in the hands of the upper classes. Change should happen slowly, and when it does, it should not be pushed by government.

One of the most fundamental differences between liberals and conservatives concerned human nature. Conservatives focused on the imperfections of humanity. In contrast, liberals were more optimistic that humans could improve themselves and the world.

Leaders of Conservatism

Many conservatives developed their ideology in response to the French Revolution (1789–1799). They watched in horror as a revolution that started as an attempt to reform a corrupt monarchy disintegrated into violence and civil war. Events in France, conservatives insisted, demonstrated that mass movements could not produce progress. Distrust of such movements was one of the beliefs developed by a series of conservative thinkers in the late 18th and 19th centuries.

Burke of Britain Born in Ireland in 1730, **Edmund Burke** is considered the father of modern British conservatism. In some ways, Burke was a progressive. Like John Locke, he agreed with the idea of a social contract between rulers and the ruled. He believed that even the king should obey the laws, a concept known as **limited monarchy**. He was sympathetic to the American colonies and believed that Britain could have avoided the American Revolution if the king had been more lenient and willing to listen to the colonists' complaints.

Burke stopped short of advocating true democracy, however. He did not believe most people were capable of governing themselves. In his book *Reflections on the Revolution in France* (1790), Burke argued that traditional authority was part of a **natural order** that enabled humans to flourish. Human society needed the structure imposed by a strong but responsible government. Without such authority, people would inevitably become selfish and violent. Freedom for the masses would lead only to civil strife. In Burke's view, respect for tradition and authority was the safeguard against chaos. Burke's vision of a well-regulated society under the leadership of a small group of elite rulers was shared by other European politicians.

Maistre of France Born in southeastern France in 1753, **Joseph de Maistre** attended Catholic schools and became a French politician and lawyer. At first, he supported the French Revolution. However, he quickly became alarmed by the violence and the anticlerical sentiments of the revolutionaries, who believed the Catholic Church was too powerful. Maistre believed that all political authority should be based on religious and moral teachings. After the Revolution, he supported a return to monarchy and declared that only a strong Christian leader could maintain social order in France.

Metternich of Austria One of the most powerful diplomats of the 19th century, **Klemens von Metternich** descended from an aristocratic family. He served as Austria's minister of foreign affairs for four decades beginning in 1809. Metternich was alarmed by both the French Revolution and Napoleon's rise to power. He opposed liberalism because he believed that it would weaken Europe and lead to costly revolutions and wars. Only a strong, centralized government, he argued, could result in prosperity and peace. Such a government could be effectively controlled only by a monarch.

Conservatives Reestablished Control

Though conservative in his political philosophy, Metternich had more progressive ideas about international cooperation to promote peace. To build international coalitions, he organized congresses, or formal meetings, at which European powers could discuss issues, decide on ways to act collectively to maintain their power, and settle their differences.

The most important of these meetings was the **Congress of Vienna** in 1814–1815 (see Topic 5.7), after the defeat of Napoleon. European leaders gathered under Metternich's leadership to try to end the centuries of war that had ravaged the continent. From the Congress of Vienna grew a system of conflict resolution known as the **Concert of Europe** (or the Congress System). It was an informal agreement by leaders to restore legitimacy and a "**balance of power**" to the continent based on the principles of 19th-century conservatism:

- the right of monarchies to rule
- the rights of landed aristocracies
- the need for an organized religion
- the danger of liberal nationalist movements

Congress of Vienna Preserves Conservatism A key element of promoting stability was to create a balance of power among the rival states of Europe, with no state strong enough to dominate all others. This required dividing territory in a way that made each state feel secure. (See Topic 5.7 for more on the division of territory that resulted from the Congress of Vienna.)

EUROPE AFTER THE CONGRESS OF VIENNA, 1815

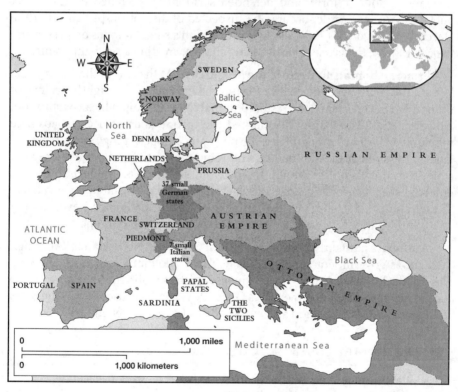

While the Congress of Vienna reestablished conservative control in Europe generally, it did not resolve all differences. Leaders tried to combat liberalism and nationalism in their own states.

The German Federation Preserves Conservatism In 1819, just a few years after the conclusion of the Congress of Vienna, a member of a radical student organization murdered the famous playwright August von Kotzebue. Because Kotzebue had traveled widely, some people thought he was a spy for Russia. In response to the murder, Metternich used people's widespread horror of the murder as a way to persuade the governments of Austria, Prussia, and several other states to issue the Carlsbad Decrees. These were designed to suppress liberal and nationalist tendencies within the German states. They banned nationalist organizations, expanded press censorship, and disbanded radical student organizations. Despite the repressive decrees, German nationalism grew stronger. The decrees were enforced until 1848. Conservatives reestablished or strengthened their control within the German Federation and elsewhere, including Russia, France, and the Kingdom of the Netherlands.

Russia Maintains an Autocratic State In the early 19th century, Russia remained one of the most conservative empires in Europe. Its rulers, called tsars, continued to claim they ruled by divine right. The country had a rural, agricultural economy. The tsars enforced strict censorship, suppressed demands for constitutional reform, and defended serfdom. They relied on the secret police to imprison or deport anyone suspected of dissent—especially after the Decembrist Revolt of 1825. (See Topic 6.6.) With a singular focus on preserving their authority, the tsars suppressed any change, creating a stagnant empire.

France Attempts to Restore the Monarchy At the end of the Napoleonic Wars, Europeans recognized the Bourbon Dynasty as the rightful rulers of France. For several years, the restored monarchy was limited by a constitution. However, in 1824, Charles X inherited the throne and ruled as an absolute monarch. Charles X strengthened his power by compensating nobles who lost land in the French Revolution and enforcing the death penalty for those who stole from the Catholic Church. In addition, he dissolved the legislature and enforced strict censorship, angering liberals. However, his rule was short lived. These actions led to the July Revolution, also called the French Revolution of 1830, and Charles X would be the last Bourbon monarch of France.

Authoritarianism in the Kingdom of the Netherlands Although William I's government allowed citizens many economic freedoms, the king was politically conservative. Government ministers reported to the king, not to the governing body called the States General. William's censorship of the press in Belgium led to a rebellion and eventually to Belgian independence.

REFLECT ON THE ESSENTIAL QUESTION

Essential Question: *How was European political order reestablished and maintained in the period following Napoleon's defeat?*

Political Order Reestablished	Political Order Maintained

conservatism	natural order	Congress of Vienna
Edmund Burke	Joseph de Maistre	Concert of Europe
limited monarchy	Klemens von Metternich	balance of power

MULTIPLE-CHOICE QUESTIONS

Questions 1–3 refer to the passage below.

> "The Governments, having lost their balance, are frightened, intimidated, and thrown into confusion by the cries of the intermediary class of society, which, placed between the Kings and their subjects, breaks the scepter of the monarch, and usurps the cry of the people—the class so often disowned by the people, and nevertheless too much listened to, caressed and feared by those who could with one word reduce it again to nothingness.
>
> We see this intermediary class abandon itself with a blind fury and animosity . . . to all the means which seem proper to assuage its thirst for power, applying itself to the task of persuading Kings that their rights are confined to sitting upon a throne, while those of the people are to govern, and to attack all that centuries have bequeathed as holy and worthy of man's respect—denying, in fact, the value of the past, and declaring themselves the masters of the future. . . . [This class] takes possession of the press, and employs it to promote impiety, disobedience to the laws of religion and the State, and goes so far as to preach murder as a duty for those who desire what is good."
>
> —Klemens von Metternich, letter to Tsar Alexander I of Russia, 1820

1. The ideas expressed by Metternich in the passage represent which of the following historical developments?

   (A) The development of the proletariat

   (B) They spread in labor unions

   (C) The growth of conservativism in Europe

   (D) The increase in social mobility

2. The situation described by Metternich was largely the result of which of the following developments?

   (A) The impact of the French and Industrial Revolutions

   (B) The defeat of Napoleon

   (C) The spread of the ideas of Edmund Burke

   (D) The outcome of the Congress of Vienna

3. Which of the following groups would have been most accepting of the ideas Metternich describes in the passage?

(A) Protestant Christians

(B) Peasants and serfs

(C) The middle class

(D) Fraternal organizations

SHORT-ANSWER QUESTION

Use the passage below to answer all parts of the question that follows.

"If we had never heard governments spoken of, and men were called upon to deliberate, for example, on hereditary or elective monarchy, we should justly regard one who would decide for the former as a madman: the argument against it appear so naturally to reason, that it is useless to repeat them. History, however, which is experimental politics, demonstrates, that an hereditary monarchy is the government which is most stable, the happiest, and the most natural to man; and an elective monarchy, on the contrary, is the worst form of government known.

It is written, 'By me, kings reign.' [Proverbs 8:15] This is not a phrase of the church, a metaphor of the preacher; it is a literal truth, simple and palpable. It is a law of the political world. God makes kings in the literal sense. He prepares royal races; maturing them under a cloud which conceals their origin. They appear at length crowned with glory and honor; they take their places; and this is the most certain of their legitimacy.

The truth is, that they arise as it were of themselves, without violence on the one part, and without marked deliberation on the other: it is a species of magnificent tranquility, not easy to express. Legitimate usurpation would seem to me to be the most appropriate expression, (if not too bold,) to characterize these kinds of origins, which time hastens to consecrate."

—Joseph de Maistre, "Essay on the Generative Principle of Political Constitutions," 1809

1. a) Describe the historical situation in which de Maistre was writing.

b) Explain the importance of the historical situation in which de Maistre was writing.

c) Explain ONE phrase in this passage that shows the difference between the ideas of Maistre and those of John Locke.

Topic 6.6

Reactions and Revolutions

The government has violated legality;
we are absolved [excused] from obedience.

—Paris journalists' response to French King Charles X's
conservative rule, July 26, 1830

Essential Question: How and why did various groups react against the existing order from 1815 to 1914?

Rebellions and revolutions do not always end in success. Many times, autocratic leaders use force to stamp out the rebellion and pass harsh new laws to prevent more rebellions. However, in the 19th century, many Europeans were willing to risk punishment or even death. They were seeking the right to vote, own land at a fair price, and speak and write freely, among other demands. The year 1848 was an especially tumultuous year for political and social upheaval.

Revolutionaries Battle the Status Quo

While monarchs wanted a return to conservative ideals, liberals and nationalists wanted various reforms in the early 19th century. Many of these movements had little success at first in their efforts to alter political systems, social inequalities, or national borders. However, by the second half of the 19th centuries, many liberal ideas were well established throughout the continent, and nationalism was such a strong force that it was accepted even by many conservatives.

Greek Independence Movement From 1821 to 1832, the **Ottoman Empire** experienced a continuous rebellion by Greek citizens who wanted independence. The Ottoman Empire, a conservative monarchy, had ruled Greece since the 15th century. While the Ottomans ruled with a measure of religious toleration, they required the Greeks to serve in the military and pay additional taxes. Starting in the 1700s, more conservative Ottoman rulers, or sultans, began ordering the destruction of ancient Greek temples and relics.

In 1821, a Greek nationalist group established a small military force. While defeated at first, the Greek cause later attracted the naval support of Great Britain, France, and Russia. Each of these states had its own reasons to try to weaken the Ottoman Empire. Russia, as always, wanted access to a warm-water port, while France and Great Britain were determined to thwart Russian ambitions and acquire land for themselves. After a series of battles, the coalition defeated the Ottoman Empire, which then recognized Greece as an independent state in 1832. The victory by the Greeks was the first of many nationalist secession movements that would disrupt the balance of power in Eastern Europe throughout the 19th century.

Decembrists Revolt in Russia Near the end of 1825, Tsar Nicholas I inherited the Russian throne. A secret society of Russian officers who had served in the Napoleonic Wars and had been influenced by liberal ideals saw the transition in rulers as a chance to establish a representative government. Known as the **Decembrists**, they and a few thousand soldiers attempted to overthrow the new tsar. They were crushed in less than a month. In response, the tsar intensified the Russian police state, further suppressing dissenters.

July Revolution in France In 1830, the French citizens became frustrated by the autocratic policies of King Charles X. (See Topic 6.5.) That summer, demonstrations began in the streets of Paris, and violence erupted. More than 500 citizens and soldiers were killed in three days. In response to the revolts and facing a hostile Chamber of Deputies, Charles abdicated and fled to England.

A distant cousin of Charles, Louis-Philippe, took the throne. Seeing what had happened to his relative, he assumed the title of Louis-Philippe, the "Citizen King." Louis-Philippe reigned as a constitutional monarch and extended civil liberties. Most importantly, he doubled the number of French men with access to voting rights to 170,000, which still represented only 5 percent of the population. (French women did not gain the right to vote until 1944.) While the **July Revolution** did not create a republic, it did move France from autocratic rule to a constitutional monarchy.

Source: Getty Images

Louis-Philippe (top), the last king of France, and his family. The king had six sons and three daughters.

Polish Rebellion Russia controlled numerous Polish territories after the 18th century partitions. Russian tsar Nicholas I angered the Polish people as he increasingly disregarded Polish rights and autonomy. When Nicholas announced his plan to use Polish troops to end the July Revolution in France (Nicholas considered himself a defender of conservativism across Europe), discontent turned to violence. A group of young soldiers led a rebellion in the city of Warsaw. They took weapons, used them to arm civilians, and took over the northern part of the city. However, lacking a clear plan, the young rebels were unable to get money or support from other countries.

Nicholas brought an army of 115,000. It overwhelmed the 40,000 Polish troops. After putting down the Polish rebellion, Russia increased its control over Poland.

Revolutions, War, and Reform

Throughout the 1800s, revolutionary movements, nationalistic leaders, and socialist demands challenged conservatism and the balance of power. By the late 1800s, nationalism and antagonistic alliances heightened international tensions in Europe directly before World War I.

Revolutions of 1848

While the beginning of the 19th century saw isolated regional resistance movements against conservative governments, the **revolutions of 1848** exploded all across the continent. These revolutions were spurred by economic hardship and political discontent and caused a breakdown in the Concert of Europe established by Metternich at the Congress of Vienna.

Revolution Strikes France First When Louis-Philippe became king of France in 1830, he promised to rule as a constitutional monarch. Yet, as king, he blocked many attempts at expanding voting rights. In response, opposition leaders organized and began demanding a more liberal government. At the same time, Paris experienced a bread shortage. Initially, workers, students, and the unemployed rallied together, built barricades, and protested the conservative king. After the military opened fire and killed 50 citizens, Parisians took to the streets, building more than 1,500 barricades. In 1848, Louis-Philippe abdicated the throne, and the provisional government declared a republic in France. The French Republic quickly passed laws creating a property tax, ending the death penalty, and allowing for freedom of the press.

While French citizens were excited to create a new government, the February Revolution, as it came to be called, failed because of class division. The working class became concerned the middle class was ignoring their demands for national workshops across the country, which provided work for the unemployed. In the summer elections, mostly middle-class professionals were elected to the National Assembly, and these men closed the national workshops. About 10,000 workers took to the streets and rioted.

While the French Army and National Guard defeated the workers, the National Assembly voted Louis-Napoleon, the nephew of Napoleon, president of France—a vote favoring order rather than liberty. In 1852, Louis-Napoleon declared himself Emperor **Napoleon III** and reestablished an authoritarian government in France.

Revolution in the German States Inspired in part by the 1848 uprising in France, demonstrators in Prussia and the German states began calling for civil liberties and constitutional reforms. The demonstrations spread to Berlin, where Frederick William IV used force to respond. By the middle of March, hundreds were dead. However, the king promised to create a constitutional monarchy. At the Frankfurt Assembly, delegates from each German state were sent to create a constitution and to unify the German states. The process in Frankfurt was slow, as delegates discussed what groups to include in this new German state. Meanwhile, in Berlin, the monarchy regained control, and the king crushed the remaining protesters, refusing to accept the Frankfurt Constitution.

UPRISINGS IN 1848–1849

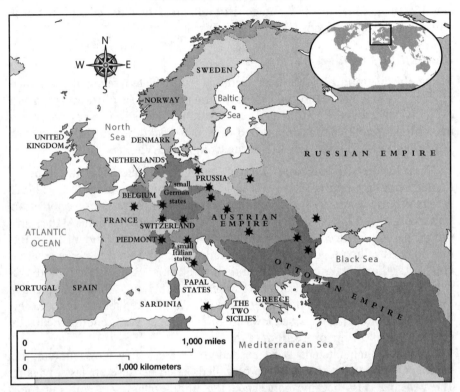

Revolution in Conservative Austria Austria also experienced rebellion in the summer of 1848. Austria's government struggled to maintain control of its multi-ethnic empire, as nationalities such as Hungarians, Poles, Czechs, Croats, and Serbs sought self-rule. In addition, students in Vienna demanded a more liberal government and began rioting in the streets. As a result, Metternich, resigned from office. His resignation led to further revolts:

- In Hungary, the dominant ethnic group, known as the Magyars, demanded autonomy under the leadership of Louis Kossuth.

- In Prague, Czechs also demanded self-rule.

- Italians fought to be part of the Italian Confederation in Northern Italy.

Austria's Habsburg monarchy, with Russian help, subdued the Magyar revolt, put down the Czech demands, and installed a conservative monarchy under Francis Joseph (ruled 1848–1916). In 1867, in what appeared to be a liberal reform, Francis Joseph established the "dual monarchy," which established the state known as Austria-Hungary. While seeming to put the two halves on even terms, the agreement that established the new entity mostly just maintained the status quo of Austrian rule. (See Topic 7.2 for more on the creation of Austria-Hungary.)

Source: Getty Images

The revolutions of 1848 drove Metternich from office after almost 40 years as one of Europe's most influential diplomats. His opposition to liberalism and nationalism first brought him success but then undercut his power.

Short-Term Results In the mid-19th century, the results of uprisings of 1848 and 1849 looked like a failure. The movements scattered throughout Europe did not share a clear ideology, nor were they coordinated with each other. They were divided by ethnicity. They did not have strong military backing and the rebels did not kept power for long.

In addition, most governments reacted by becoming more conservative. For example, in Russia, Tsar Nicholas I expanded the use of secret police. He hoped to uncover and crush any further attempts at rebellions before they started. In France, the government banned the writing of novelists, anarchists, and others considered dangerous.

In response to the harsher government policies, many people who were sympathetic to the uprisings emigrated. Some went to Great Britain, which was generally more tolerant of dissenters than most of Europe. Many moved to the United States. In the United States, German immigrants would later become important supporters of the Union in the American Civil War.

To some, the failures of 1848 provided more evidence that republicanism would not take hold in Europe. The English had tried a republican government in the 1640s under Oliver Cromwell, and it had ended in a terrible civil war. The French had also tried republicanism in the late 18th century, and again it had resulted in extensive bloodshed.

Long-Term Results The long-term impacts of 1848 and 1849 are more difficult to determine. The reforms advocated in 1848 included such changes as greater voting rights, more freedom for the press, and more self-rule for ethnic groups within empires. Eventually, advocates for these goals would be successful.

Russian Reforms under Alexander II

While Russia possessed a large empire and army, its defeat in the Crimean War demonstrated how far behind it had fallen compared with Western Europe. Russia lacked industrialization and innovation, and so it was becoming weak.

Russia's Tsar **Alexander II** (ruled 1855–1881) recognized these problems. He supported efforts to reform Russia's social system, infrastructure, and legal code in order to maintain the country's role on the international stage. However, aristocrats stubbornly resisted calls to end serfdom. In 1861, Alexander took action. He issued the Emancipation Manifesto, abolishing serfdom in Russia. The process for peasants actually obtaining land, however, was very complicated, with peasants having to remain on the land until payment schedules could be established. Most had to make "redemption payments" to the government over a lengthy period of time to actually receive the land.

More Local and National Reforms To increase autonomy at the local level, Alexander II created the Zemstvo, elected councils meant to address local issues. Unfortunately, the Zemstvo did not create social equality because the local nobility manipulated the system to maintain their power. Nonetheless, it represented a step towards local self-government.

At the national level, Alexander II implemented independent courts and demanded equality before the law. In order to modernize, he encouraged and financed the construction of the railroad industry. By 1916, the Trans-Siberian Railroad stretched from Russia's western border in Europe to its eastern borders in Asia. Alexander also set out to modernize the Russian military, introducing conscription, or a draft, for the first time in the Russian army.

Despite Alexander's power, reforms moved slowly. Many peasants were frustrated, and many working-class people felt that Russia needed more radical change. In 1881, a terrorist faction of radicals assassinated the tsar.

Russia Attempts Reform Again Following the assassination of Alexander II, his son, **Alexander III** (ruled 1881–1894), assumed the throne. While the new tsar rejected liberal political reforms, he did support industrialization. Under his finance minister, **Sergei Witte**, Russia modernized its economy:

- It passed a protective tariff to help Russian industry.
- It placed Russia on the gold standard (an economic policy that limits inflation and encourages international trade).
- It sped up construction of the Trans-Siberian Railroad.
- It improved education related to commerce and technology.

Witte's economic reforms brought changes, but most Russians continued to live in poverty under an oppressive government.

In 1905, Russia lost a war against Japan, and the defeat ignited the Revolution of 1905. Many Russians wanted a more liberal government, in part to compete in the modern age. Tsar Nicholas II (ruled 1894–1917) appointed Witte to frame liberal reforms. Witte crafted the October Manifesto, which gave Russians the right to citizenship, freedom of speech, and universal suffrage for men. Russia created a representative body, the **Duma**, in which leaders could express their grievances. Nevertheless, the tsar maintained his power with the right to veto any law, and within a short time suffrage was restricted and the power of the Duma was limited.

In the Duma, **Peter Stolypin**, a conservative monarchist, pushed for agrarian reform to help peasants. He wanted to end the open-field system and replace it with a system of small landowners, thus creating a higher standard of living for peasants. Stolypin believed that a prosperous peasant class would stabilize Russia and prevent a revolution.

REFLECT ON THE ESSENTIAL QUESTION

Essential Question: How and why did various groups react against the existing order from 1815 to 1914?

Revolutions and Reactions	Outcomes of Revolutions and Reactions

KEY TERMS

Ottoman Empire	Napoleon III	Duma
Decembrists	Alexander II	Peter Stolypin
July Revolution	Alexander III	
revolutions of 1848	Sergei Witte	

Questions 1–3 refer to the passage below.

"Not in sunk Spain's prolong'd death agony;

Not in rich England, bent but to make pour

The flood of the world's commerce on her shore;

Not in that madhouse, France, from whence the cry

Afflicts grave Heaven with its long senseless roar;

Not in American vulgarity,

Nor wordy German imbecility—

Lies any hope of heroism more.

Hungarians! Save the world! Renew the stories

Of men who against hope repell'd the chain,

And make the world's dead spirit leap again!

On land renew that Greek exploit, whose glories

Hallow the Salaminian [Salamis is a Greek island] promontories,

And the Armada flung to the fierce main."

—Matthew Arnold, "Sonnet to the Hungarian Nation," 1849

1. Which of the following statements about the historical context of the mid-1800s most influenced Arnold?

   (A) The Spanish Empire was in decline after colonization had made it large and wealthy.

   (B) The United States was growing stronger and beginning to challenge European countries.

   (C) The potato famine had decreased Ireland's population by 20 percent.

   (D) The Revolutions of 1848 had challenged conservative rulers and empires throughout Europe.

2. The phrase in the poem "repell'd the chain" refers to Hungary's efforts to

   (A) reduce the influence of Roman Catholic bishops

   (B) abolish serfdom as other countries were doing

   (C) avoid alliances with other European states

   (D) end the control of Austria and the Habsburgs over itself

3. Which previous event in European history is most like the one praised by Arnold?
   (A) The Greek independence movement because it was an uprising by an ethnic group
   (B) The English Civil War because it was a battle between legislative and monarchical power
   (C) The French Revolution because it was a war inspired by desires for representative government
   (D) The Thirty Years' War because it was a religious conflict

SHORT-ANSWER QUESTION

Use the cartoon below to answer all parts of the question that follows.

Source: John Leech, "Montagne Russe A Very Dangerous Game," wood engraving, *Punch* 27 (1854): 127

The figure in the toboggan represents Russian Tsar Nicholas I, who reigned from 1825 to 1855.

1. a) Describe the historical context that explains how the cartoonist viewed Tsar Nicholas I.

   b) Explain ONE event that occurred in the mid-1800s that could be used to modify or refute the main point of the cartoon.

   c) Explain ONE attempt a Russian tsar after Nicholas I made to prevent the outcome for Russian rulers depicted in the cartoon.

Topic 6.7

Ideologies of Change and Reform Movements

Workers, without women, you are nothing!

—French-Peruvian philosopher Flora Tristan (1803–1844)

Essential Question: How and why did different intellectual developments challenge the political and social order from 1815 to 1914?

The word *politics* refers to all activities relating to government, including the rivalries among those who vie for power. Greek philosopher Aristotle declared, "Man is a political animal." Aristotle recognized that a stable, functioning government needed the work of many citizens.

In Europe's rapidly growing industrialized societies, few people could avoid the influence of political movements. These movements played an enormous role in public life among all classes during the Industrial Revolution. To paraphrase Aristotle, man *and woman* truly proved to be political animals.

The Emergence of New Ideologies

In response to the turmoil of the Industrial Revolution and the French Revolution, Europeans explored many political theories and ideas of government. Some supported absolute monarchies while others promoted constitutional monarchies or republics. As the working class grew, people explored varieties of socialism and communism. A few people argued that the lack of any centralized government was the best system of all. In general, though, average citizens began taking on larger roles in public life than before.

Liberalism and the Rights of the Individual

One very influential new theory was **liberalism**, the political philosophy that emphasizes the rights of the individual and the idea that the government should have a limited role in the everyday lives of citizens. According to classical liberal theory, anything not expressly forbidden by law is allowed. Liberalism was introduced in England in the 17th century by the philosopher John Locke, who advocated the idea of the social contract, the theory that governments rule only with the consent of the governed.

Popular Sovereignty Locke's work inspired a movement toward **popular sovereignty**, the idea that the people, rather than just the monarch or nobles, should hold the greatest power in society. This idea conflicted with reality in 19th-century Britain. At that time, most people could not participate in government. The British Parliament consisted of two houses. The House of Lords was a group of aristocratic men who inherited their positions. The House of Commons consisted of male commoners, those who had no aristocratic titles or estates. Members of their districts elected representatives to the House of Commons. However, before 1832 only men over the age of 21 who owned land worth a certain amount of money could vote. These qualifications described less than 20 percent of the adult male population.

Reform Acts and Voting Rights As the middle class grew in the 19th century, its members began to demand greater freedoms. They argued, demonstrated, and sometimes rioted. In 1832, Parliament responded by passing the Great Reform Act of 1832. This bill extended the vote to some middle-class men who did not own property—those who paid at least 10 pounds (£10) a year in rent. As a result, about 20 percent of Britain's adult male citizens could vote. The act favored rural regions, as conservatives feared giving cities too much power. Over the following century, additional reform bills would expand voting rights to adults, including women.

THE ELECTION.

THE POLLING.

Engraved by J.C. Decembre from the Original Picture by W. Hogarth

This engraving by William Hogarth provides a lively look at the way elections took place in the 18th century. To vote, a person had to announce in public how they were voting. The right-hand side of the image shows a campaigner attempting to bribe a voter.

Victory over the Corn Laws As voting rights spread, the middle class began to exercise its power by pressuring Parliament to enact laws favorable to their class. In 1839, Richard Cobden, a textile merchant and writer, organized the **Anti-Corn Law League**, opposing high taxes on imported wheat and the laws that regulated the wheat trade. (Recall that wheat also was known as "corn" then.) The wheat taxes favored British aristocrats who rented their land to wheat farmers but raised the cost of wheat and wheat products for urban dwellers. When crops in England failed, the cost of imported wheat remained high, leading to scarcity and food riots.

Petitions were one of the main public-opinion tactics used by the Anti-Corn Law League to influence Parliament. A petition was a formal document signed by citizens requesting lawmakers to take action on a certain issue. Petitioning the government was an old and popular tradition in Britain dating back to the 17th century. In 1843, the House of Commons received approximately 34,000 petitions, most of which concerned the Corn Laws. In 1846, the League convinced British Prime Minster Peel to support the repeal of the Corn Laws, representing a major victory for the middle class and helping increase the power of the House of Commons. (See Topic 6.2 for more on the Corn Laws.)

Personal and Social Good Liberals argued that repeal of the Corn Laws was an example of **enlightened self-interest**, the idea that a person can see how acting for the good of society also benefits himself or herself. The middle class pushed for the repeal, but it also helped the poor and working classes by making food less expensive. The success encouraged middle-class politicians and the working class to join forces to get what they wanted.

Whig Party Most liberal politicians belonged to Britain's Whig Party. Founded around 1688, the Whig Party believed in limited government. The Whigs controlled Parliament when it passed the Great Reform Act of 1832 and when it repealed the Corn Laws in 1846. In 1859, the Whigs joined other groups to create Britain's Liberal Party. Liberals believed in free trade, voting rights, and social reforms—all of which they hoped would promote greater stability and economic prosperity for all classes.

Jeremy Bentham and Utilitarianism One British philosopher who contributed to the ideas later associated with liberalism and the Liberal Party was **Jeremy Bentham**. Born in London in 1748, he studied law at Britain's prestigious Oxford University. After receiving his degree, he abandoned his legal career to travel, write, and promote social reform. His writing focused on philosophy, politics, and economics.

In 1789, he published his first book, *An Introduction to the Principles of Morals and Legislation*, outlining his "theory of utility." The goal of all laws, he declared, "must be the greatest happiness of the greatest number" of people. Bentham thought that the government should pass laws that promoted and protected the well-being of most of the population. The value of every law, he believed, could be measured by how much good it accomplished. Bentham's idea became known as **utilitarianism**. According to utilitarianism, any action is "right" that promotes happiness or well-being for all those affected. Utilitarianism thus contradicted Christian teachings and other ideas about ethics that held certain acts as inherently or always wrong.

Acting upon his utilitarianism, Bentham supported many causes. Among these were prison reform, education for women, religious freedom, the decriminalization of homosexuality, and the humane treatment of animals. His ideas attracted many followers. Utilitarianism gave birth to the concept of the "greater good," which shaped many 19th-century social reform movements.

John Stuart Mill and Liberalism Among those influenced by Bentham's works was the politician and writer **John Stuart Mill**. One of his central beliefs was that everyone was entitled to seek happiness as long as he or she did no harm to others. He called this idea **social liberty**.

Mill joined the Liberal Party and was elected a member of Parliament in the House of Commons in 1865, becoming one of Britain's most influential liberal leaders. He worked to expand voting rights and to expose corrupt government practices. In addition, he supported free speech, equal rights for women, and the abolition of slavery. His book, *The Subjection of Women*, published in 1861, was the first work in the English language to assert that women should have the same rights as men to vote, hold property, and pursue professional careers. His other works include *Principles of Political Economy*, *On Liberty*, and *Considerations on Representative Government*.

Mill often called himself a utilitarian who considered the greatest good for the greatest number. However, he also believed that governments should protect individual liberties, even from a democratic majority.

Chartism and the Working Class

Bentham and Mill both came from wealthy families. However, working-class people also were heavily involved in political movements.

Chartism In Britain, a working-class movement known as **Chartism** campaigned for voting rights for all men regardless of wealth or property. The movement got its name from a document called the People's Charter, written by William Lovett in 1839.

Lovett, a self-educated cabinetmaker, had become involved in radical politics in London. His charter called for universal male suffrage, which would allow all men to vote regardless of wealth. Lovett and his followers sought to reform laws that they believed oppressed working people. The Chartists organized mass meetings that drew thousands of men and women.

In 1842, the Chartists presented Parliament with a petition bearing between 2 million and 3 million signatures calling for political reforms. Parliament ignored the petition. Around the same time, Chartists also engaged in violent clashes with police, and many Chartist leaders were imprisoned. The movement declined after 1850, but its influence continued in subsequent ideological movements such as socialism and Marxism. Many reforms advocated by the Chartists were eventually enacted in the last half of the 19th century.

Flora Tristan Advocates for Women and Workers One of the people inspired by the Chartists was **Flora Tristan**. The illegitimate child of an aristocratic Peruvian father and a French mother, Tristan was a social outcast. While still a teenager, she married her employer. He was very abusive, but French courts did not allow her to legally separate from him until after he shot and wounded her.

Tristan was an author and a vocal advocate for the rights of women and of workers in general. She was one of the early leaders in Europe in the fight to win the right of women to vote. She believed that the working class could not be free until women gained more rights and better treatment, including the right to divorce their husbands. She died relatively young, at the age of 41, and 8,000 people attended her funeral.

Alternatives to Capitalism

Socialism is a political and economic system under which the means of production—the ways people gather raw materials and manufacture goods— are owned or controlled by society and used for the public good. Socialism does not outlaw all private property, but it does promote laws and rules about how to acquire and distribute property. Unlike capitalism, in a socialist state, the economy is not governed primarily by the principle of supply and demand. Instead, the government is closely involved in the production and distribution of wealth. It might also promote social welfare and pass laws regarding health care, education, housing, and employment.

Utopian Socialism

Modern socialism originated during the early 19th century when social reformers tried to address the inequalities between workers and factory owners. Some of these reformers sought to create an ideal, or utopian, society.

The Ideals of Saint-Simon French writer and philosopher **Henri Saint-Simon** first introduced the idea of **utopian socialism** in the early 19th century. Saint-Simon was fascinated by science and engineering. He believed that scientists and engineers, working together with businesspeople, could transform society for the better. Factories would become clean, efficient, and safe places to work, and all manufacturing would be devoted to creating things useful to society. Saint-Simon was deeply religious and believed that his new society would be based on the Christian ideals of loving kindness, and charity.

Though Saint-Simon never had the opportunity to put his ideas into practice, his writing attracted a large following and became a major influence on socialism and social reform throughout Europe.

Intentional Communities Among Saint-Simon's most active followers were **Charles Fourier** of France and **Robert Owen** of Britain. Both advocated the establishment of intentional communities—small societies governed by the principles of utopian socialism. In these societies, all property would be owned communally. Every part of life, including work, education, and leisure time, would be governed by the rules of the community.

Owen set up a utopian community in New Lanark, Scotland, around 1800. He set eight-hour days in the community's textile mills, founded free public schools and day care for children, and opened a store that sold goods to workers at minimal cost. Though New Lanark attracted a great deal of interest, few people in Europe formed similar communities.

In the United States, where land was cheaper, people were more receptive of utopian socialist ideas. Among the American communities founded or operated with utopian socialist roots were New Harmony, Indiana; Brook Farm, Massachusetts; and Oneida, New York.

The Scientific Socialism of Karl Marx

German-born historian and economist **Karl Marx** shared some of the goals of the utopian socialists. However, he criticized them for failing to understand how capitalism worked in practice. He wanted to develop a model of socialism that reflected the same systematic approach that scientists used. Marx became one of the first close observers and critics of European capitalism. He and one of his supporters, Friedrich Engels, summarized their ideas in *Communist Manifesto*. Published in 1848, it was a short book written for a broad audience. Marx's more detailed analysis of the modern economy, *Capital* (1867), formed the basis of the body of thought known as **Marxism**.

Marx's View of History Marx based his predictions for a revolution on his study of the past. Most historians of his time focused on politics or religion. Unlike them, Marx emphasized the importance of technology. He thought technology shaped economics, which then shaped politics and other aspects of culture. That is, he thought a society based on handmade goods and horsepower would generate one type of political system. A society based on large factories and steam engines would produce another.

Marx also saw history as an unending story of class struggle. He defined a class by its relationship to how goods and services were produced. For example, some classes, such as slaves and peasants, performed physical labor. Others, such as merchants and lawyers, did mental labor.

Since technology was constantly evolving, economics and politics were always changing to catch up. This gap created contradictions in every social system. Resolving them could be violent but would always lead to a new system. This change was inevitable. How it happened would be affected by individual leaders and temporary conditions, but the underlying forces were unstoppable. Their belief that history followed laws, just as physics or chemistry did, became known as **historical determinism**.

Marx's View of His Era Marx was struck by the sharp contradiction between the impressive abundance capitalism produced and the dreadful misery many workers lived in. While he often supported reforms advocated by middle-class leaders, he saw them as weak efforts that failed to address the roots of inequality. He thought that the working class, which he labeled the proletariat, would gain class-consciousness, an awareness of their place in the socioeconomic structure and a recognition that they all shared a similar plight. The proletariat would then overthrow the middle-class industrialists, which he labeled the bourgeoisie, who profited from their labor.

The proletarian revolution would replace most privately owned factories, banks, and businesses with ones owned collectively. This socialism would be a step toward **communism**, in which all property used to produce goods would be owned collectively and all classes would disappear.

Since Marx believed that revolutions would be led by the proletariat, they would happen only in wealthy, industrialized countries, such as those in Western Europe. However, the development of labor unions and social reforms reduced the interest in revolution. The first major communist revolutions occurred in two relatively poor countries, Russia and China, in the 20th century.

Revolutionary Options

The ideas of Karl Marx spread throughout Europe in the late 19th century. While they challenged some of the basic ideas of capitalism, the theory of anarchism challenged the idea of government itself.

Women as Marxist Leaders

Marx and Engels believed that women and men should be equal. This idea attracted a number of women who supported both gender equality and labor reform.

Clara Zetkin Advocates International Socialism In Germany, **Clara Zetkin** became a leading advocate of Marxism. Born into a middle-class family, she was impatient with the limited roles for women in bourgeois society and felt more drawn toward the labor movement and workers' rights.

In 1878, she joined Germany's Socialist Workers' Party. A dedicated feminist, she supported women's suffrage and edited *Die Gleichheit* ("Equality"), a socialist newspaper for women. She later joined Germany's communist party. Zetkin was a strong advocate of international workers' movements, and she believed that all workers had the same interests regardless of where they lived. She opposed nationalism, and her resistance to the rise of Germany's fascist Nazi party in the 1930s made her a hero to many Europeans after World War II.

Rosa Luxemburg Rejects Nationalism One of the most famous women in the socialist movement, **Rosa Luxemburg** was born in Poland and became involved in socialist workers' movements in her teens. Her political activity attracted the attention of the authorities. To escape arrest, she fled to Switzerland, and later to Germany, where she became a citizen at the age of 28 and joined Germany's communist party.

Luxemburg was a dramatic speaker who believed that workers had the right to take up arms against a government that oppressed them. In 1914, she helped organize the radical socialist group, the Spartacus League. The League opposed Germany's participation in World War I and was part of the failed German Revolution of 1918–1919. Luxemburg was then murdered by conservatives who had taken over Berlin's police force.

Anarchism and Syndicalism

Anarchism is the theory that all forms of government should be abolished. Anarchists believe that society should be based on the voluntary cooperation of all members. The word *anarchy* comes from ancient Greek and means "without a chief or ruler."

The modern philosophy of anarchism evolved in the 19th century in response to industrialization. Like utopian socialists, anarchists believed that people could live without national governments or states to oversee them. However, unlike utopians, anarchists did not advocate withdrawal from society. Many thought that capitalism could be overthrown only by force and became swept up in violent underground movements.

Mikhail Bakunin Born into a noble family in Russia, **Mikhail Bakunin** was drawn to socialism and communism through his study of philosophy. As a young man he traveled to France, where he met many socialist leaders, including Marx. Bakunin supported the violent overthrow of established governments and the destruction of property owned by capitalists. His political activities landed him in prison many times. In 1849, Swiss authorities arrested him and sent him to Russia, where he was imprisoned and later exiled to Siberia. He was allowed to leave Siberia in 1861 and moved to Italy. While there, he developed what he called his "anarchist creed."

Bakunin had become disillusioned with socialism and communism. He believed that once capitalist governments were overthrown, socialist leaders would simply take over the government, and the power that came with it, for themselves. A socialist government, he declared, was no better than any other form of government. Bakunin wanted to see all forms of government and centralized authority abolished. He wanted all property controlled by groups of workers who ran their own communities. This idea became known as collective anarchism.

Bakunin also believed that revolution could be accomplished not by mass movements but by small, tightly knit groups that operated secretly or "underground." The larger socialist movement mostly rejected Bakunin's ideas. But his concept of anarchism remained influential in Spain and Italy, where anarchist groups flourished in the 1930s.

Georges Sorel and Syndicalism Born in France in 1847, **Georges Sorel** developed ideas that influenced anarchism as well as other social revolutionary movements. He believed that once capitalism was overthrown, all property should be transferred to labor unions. The unions would then organize workers into small, self-supporting groups. This idea became known as **syndicalism**.

IDEOLOGICAL RESPONSES TO INDUSTRIALIZATION			
Movement	Beliefs	Important Individuals	Examples of Significance and/or Impact
Liberalism	• Popular sovereignty • Individual rights • Social reform • Enlightened self-interest	• John Locke • Richard Cobden • Jeremy Bentham • John Stuart Mill	• Increased voting rights, Anti-Corn laws, rise of Whig and Liberal parties • Rise of utilitarianism
Chartism	• Universal male suffrage • Need for reform of poor laws and labor laws	• William Lovett	• Many Chartist reforms enacted in last half of 19th century
Utopian Socialism	• Redistribution of wealth	• Henri Saint-Simon • Charles Fourier • Robert Owen	• "Intentional communities" in France, Britain, and the United States
Marxist Socialism	• Worker control of the means of production	• Karl Marx • Friedrich Engels • Clara Zetkin • Rosa Luxemburg	• Communist revolutions in Russia and China in the 20th century
Anarchism	• Abolition of government • Creation of a society of voluntary cooperation from all members	• Mikhail Bakunin • Georges Sorel	• Violent underground revolutionary actions

REFLECT ON THE ESSENTIAL QUESTION

Essential Question: *How and why did different intellectual developments challenge the political and social order from 1815 to 1914?*

Intellectual Development	Challenge to Political and Social Order

KEY TERMS

liberalism	Flora Tristan	communism
popular sovereignty	socialism	Clara Zetkin
Anti-Corn Law League	Henri Saint-Simon	Rosa Luxemburg
enlightened self-interest	utopian socialism	anarchism
Jeremy Bentham	Charles Fourier	Mikhail Bakunin
utilitarianism	Robert Owen	Georges Sorel
John Stuart Mill	Karl Marx	syndicalism
social liberty	Marxism	
Chartism	historical determinism	

MULTIPLE-CHOICE QUESTIONS

Questions 1–3 refer to the passages below.

Passage 1

"There exists for Man a unitary destiny—a Divine social order to be established on the earth for the regulation of the social and domestic relations of the human race . . . . It is the height of folly to wish to improve a system that is radically defective in its nature! There is then but a very small minority who accept and adhere to the civilized state as now organized. This minority is composed of men of leisure and fortune. As to social liberty, the poor classes are wholly deprived of it."

—Charles Fourier, *Theory of Social Organization*, 1820

Passage 2

"Political power, properly so called, is merely the organized power of one class for oppressing another. If the proletariat [working class] during its contest with the bourgeoisie [middle class] is compelled, by the force of circumstances, to organize itself as a class, if, by means of a revolution, it makes itself the ruling class, and, as such, sweeps away by force the old conditions of production, then it will, along with these conditions, have swept away the conditions for the existence of class antagonisms and of classes generally, and will thereby have abolished its own supremacy as a class."

—Karl Marx and Friedrich Engels, *Communist Manifesto*, 1848

1. One difference between the authors of the two passages is that Marx and Engels rejected Fourier's claim in this source that capitalism
   (A) violated the principles of a Divine social order
   (B) was too flawed to be saved by small reforms
   (C) benefited only a small minority of people of leisure
   (D) deprived people in the poor classes of liberty

2. The authors of the passages would most likely agree with which of the following?
   (A) The Enclosure Movement fundamentally changed agriculture.
   (B) The Industrial Revolution increased production and class conflicts.
   (C) The Napoleonic Wars spread nationalism and liberal ideas throughout Europe.
   (D) Romanticism was important because of its impact on how people interpreted the world.

3. The ideas expressed in these passages were most clearly part of which of the following historical developments in the 19th century?

    (A) The reaction against the Enlightenment

    (B) The spread of nationalism

    (C) The movement for liberal reforms

    (D) The demand for a different distribution of wealth

SHORT-ANSWER QUESTION

Answer all parts of the question that follows.

1. a) Explain ONE political event or policy in the 19th century that was a response to a problem of industrialization.

    b) Explain ONE event or policy proposed by women in the 19th century to respond to a problem of industrialization.

    c) Explain ONE event or policy used by nongovernmental reformers in the 19th century in response to a problem of industrialization.

Topic 6.8

19th-Century Social Reform

We are here not because we are law-breakers;
we are here in our efforts to become law makers.

—suffragist Emmeline Pankhurst (1858–1928)

Essential Question: What were the movements and calls for social reform that resulted from intellectual developments from 1815 to 1914?

Who should hold political power, and what should they do with it? As industrialization spread, education levels rose, quality of life improved, and people who had previously been left out of political decision-making began to demand seats at the table. Social reforms and political changes meant that working-class people and women were more likely to have an impact on government decisions and actions.

The Development of Mass Political Parties

Industrialization and the rise of new social classes required new forms of government. People in both the middle and working classes wanted to influence government through public opinion and mass political parties. Generally, conservative parties favored the status quo, while more liberal parties favored increased suffrage and popularly elected governments. Labor unions became politically active as workers joined socialist parties or formed their own labor parties.

Conservatives, Liberals, and Labour in Britain

The **Conservative Party** in Britain worked to protect the interests of wealthy landowners. However, the party split over the issue of whether the Corn Laws should be repealed. (See Topics 6.2 and 6.7 for more about the Corn Laws.) Party leader and Prime Minister Benjamin Disraeli focused on social reforms and reducing inequality, which brought a wider range of voters to the party. "I must follow the people," Disraeli said. "Am I not their leader?"

In contrast, Britain's **Liberal Party** was the major source of opposition to the Conservatives until 1918. While in power, the Liberals were able to pass many social reforms, including creating a national education system and using secret ballots while voting. The **Labour Party** emerged when working-class Britons had trouble getting liberals to support certain candidates. Because the Liberal and Labour Party members had many goals in common, they at first informally agreed not to run candidates against each other. However, after

World War I, the Labour Party became stronger and better organized as liberals declined in influence.

Conflict and Reform in France

Like Germany and Britain, France had politically active working-class and middle-class movements. In the early 19th century, Napoleon had sought to create national unity in France by instituting public education, building infrastructure, and enacting a body of laws known as the Napoleonic Code. After Napoleon's exile in 1815, a series of monarchs and emperors ruled France. Reforms introduced in 1830 limited the power of the throne and created a constitutional monarchy. Laws expanded voting rights, allowing more men to vote for representatives to the nation's General Assembly. Overall, conservative parties in France favored the monarchy and tried to limit citizen participation in government, while socialist and liberal parties supported workers' rights and popular sovereignty.

The Revolution of 1848 As you learned in Topic 6.6, a series of liberal uprisings spread throughout Europe in 1848. Their causes varied, but all involved mass protests against established governments. In France, when the government tried to limit political gatherings by working-class and middle-class political groups, people rioted. The government collapsed. Replacing it was one known as the Second Republic. The leader of the new government was **Napoleon III**, nephew of Napoleon Bonaparte.

Knowing he had wide support, Napoleon III extended voting rights to all adult men. He also pledged financial relief to help unemployed workers. However, he was not committed to liberal government. Playing on conservative and middle-class fears of working-class movements, he declared himself emperor in 1852.

Source: Wikimedia Commons
1865 portrait of Napoleon III

His government became increasingly authoritarian. As workers felt more alienated from the government, the radical socialist and anarchist parties grew stronger. In 1860, losing popularity, Napoleon III again shifted his policies, hoping to regain support and increase French nationalism. Historians often refer to the period after 1860 as the "Liberal Empire" because he gave the legislature greater power, relaxed restrictions on civil liberties, and opened France to free trade and better relations with Britain.

The Paris Commune In 1870, Napoleon III believed war with Prussia would rally the country behind him and that France would be victorious. However, the war led to his downfall. Joining the battle himself, Napoleon III was taken prisoner and then overthrown in a bloodless revolution in Paris.

In 1871, elections supported a republican monarchy that called itself the Third Republic. However, a combined group of socialist and anarchist workers, fearing that the new government would be more monarchist than republican, barricaded streets in Paris in an attempt to create their own separate society, which they called the **Paris Commune**. They demanded reforms in education, welfare, and rights for women. After bloody clashes with the police, the Commune was defeated. But the determination of the Commune cannot be underestimated; up to 10,000 insurrectionists gave their lives in pursuit of reforms.

Few of the reforms the Paris Commune called for were enacted, but it did serve as an inspiration for later worker revolts in Russia. Many of the Commune's leaders remained in French politics and were elected to the National Assembly where they represented socialist parties.

Women's Rights in France French women had been active in politics since at least the French Revolution. For most French feminists, the campaign for women's rights was part of the larger struggle for workers' rights. One of the first women to call for female suffrage in France after Olympe de Gouges was Flora Tristan. As a young woman, she was drawn toward Saint-Simon's ideas of utopian socialism. Tristan believed that the political emancipation of women was essential for true social revolution. In 1843 she published an essay, "The Workers' Union," in which she called for a national union of all working-class men and women. (See Topic 6.7 for more on Flora Tristan.)

The Social Democratic Party in Germany

Two workers' parties combined in 1875 to form the **Social Democratic Party**. Despite this merger, struggles still remained within the party. Some Social Democrats believed that social, economic, and political changes were possible without violent revolution. However, other Marxists within the party were certain that class struggles would inevitably cause violent conflict. German elites were so panicked about the existence of a socialist party that they banned the Social Democratic Party from 1878 to 1890. But the party remained popular and still exists.

The Russian Social Democratic Party

A social democratic party took longer to develop in Russia than it did in Germany. The Social Democratic Party in Russia formed in 1898 to support workers and promote Marxism. The party itself was divided into several factions including the Bolsheviks and Mensheviks that were unable to come together. Ultimately, the Bolsheviks led the 1917 October Revolution, later changing their name to the Communist Party.

Philanthropy and Social Reform

In addition to efforts at reform through politics and labor unions, private **philanthropies**, or charitable organizations, also addressed poverty and inequality. Religious faith inspired many reformers. For example, some Christians joined the Social Gospel movement. (See Topic 6.4.) Rather than focusing directly on individual salvation, they focused on improving social conditions. They believed that feeding the hungry, improving housing for the poor, and organizing labor unions would enable people to become devout Christians.

Often, educated middle-class women spearheaded these efforts. In 1869, the English reformer **Josephine Butler** began her work on behalf of women and girls who had been forced into prostitution. Butler established industrial schools to give females vocational skills and campaigned against human trafficking through which women and girls were sold into sexual slavery.

Women also helped lead the **temperance movement**, an organized attempt to ban the sale and consumption of alcoholic beverages. Though the movement never achieved its aims, it did succeed in placing taxes on the sale of liquor.

Other social reforms supported by women included the **Sunday School movement**, founded in 1795, which provided basic education for working-class children. By 1850, more than 2 million children were enrolled in weekly Sunday school classes, most of which were taught by women. The Sunday School movement led to advances in science and other areas. For example, the paleontologist Mary Anning had no formal education other than learning to read and write in Sunday school. However, she educated herself and went on to discover, assemble, and correctly identify many dinosaur skeletons.

Feminism and Women's Suffrage in Britain

As women became more involved in reform, they began to question their own status. In 1850, a group of British women led by **Barbara Smith Bodichon** began to meet to discuss women's rights. Eventually known as "the Ladies of Langdon Place," they called for women's suffrage and also for married women to have the right to control their own property. In 1856, Bodichon gathered 26,000 signatures on a petition for women's property rights. A year later, in 1857, Parliament passed the Married Women's Property Act, which enabled married women to control their own property. In 1869, Bodichon helped Emily Davis found Girton College, in Cambridge, the first institution to offer higher education to women in Britain.

The Pankhursts Protest In the early 20th century, a strong women's suffrage movement emerged in Britain, picking up on the ideas of Flora Tristan. In 1903, the **Pankhurst family**, mother Emmeline and her daughters Christabel, Adela, and Sybil, formed the **Women's Social and Political Union (WSPU)** to promote women's suffrage. The Pankhursts went far beyond writing petitions. They organized huge rallies. In June 1908, nearly 500,000 women assembled in London's Hyde Park to demand the vote.

The Hyde Park demonstrators were physically attacked, harassed by police, and even arrested. In prison, the suffragists went on hunger strikes to protest their treatment. The wardens then fed them by force, a violent and degrading process intended to punish the women for their disobedience rather than to nourish them. Emmeline Pankhurst was arrested at least eight times during her campaign for the vote.

Gradual Expansion of Women's Suffrage While her militancy alienated some allies, Pankhurst forced the Liberal Party to take women's suffrage seriously and include it in their party platform. In 1918, Parliament passed an act allowing all men over the age of 21 and all women over the age of 30 to vote. In 1928, the act was amended to allow every citizen over 21 to vote, making voting a universal right for all adults in Britain.

Source: Getty Images

Suffrage supporters in Great Britain drew attention to their cause by getting arrested.

Abolitionist Movement

The abolition movement fought for an end to slavery. An English court ruled in 1772 that English law did not allow slavery. However, slavery still existed on a large scale in the West Indies, South America, and the United States. Even people who never saw an enslaved person benefited from consuming relatively inexpensive products—including sugar, rice, coffee, and cotton cloth—produced by enslaved people. "You may choose to look the other way," said abolitionist William Wilberforce, "but you can never say again that you did not know."

The abolitionist movement in Britain lasted for more than a century after the 1772 ruling, as some Britons worked to wipe out slavery around the globe. The slave trade to the British colonies ended in 1807. But people were still enslaved. In 1838, the British West Indies abolished slavery. Still, slavery remained legal in Cuba until 1886 and in Brazil until 1888.

The abolitionist movement in France had more setbacks than its British counterpart. France abolished slavery in 1794, during the French Revolution. Napoleon reinstated slavery throughout France's empire in 1802. In 1804, France lost its colony Saint-Domingue in a rebellion. Saint-Domingue renamed itself Haiti, and it was the first nation founded by formerly enslaved people. France abolished slavery again in 1848—also during a revolutionary period.

REFORMERS FROM THE LATE 18TH TO THE EARLY 20TH CENTURIES

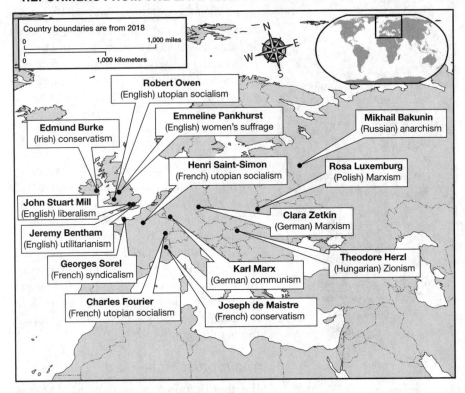

Country boundaries are from 2018

0   1,000 miles

0   1,000 kilometers

Robert Owen
(English) utopian socialism

Emmeline Pankhurst
(English) women's suffrage

Mikhail Bakunin
(Russian) anarchism

Edmund Burke
(Irish) conservatism

Henri Saint-Simon
(French) utopian socialism

Rosa Luxemburg
(Polish) Marxism

John Stuart Mill
(English) liberalism

Clara Zetkin
(German) Marxism

Jeremy Bentham
(English) utilitarianism

Georges Sorel
(French) syndicalism

Theodore Herzl
(Hungarian) Zionism

Karl Marx
(German) communism

Charles Fourier
(French) utopian socialism

Joseph de Maistre
(French) conservatism

REFLECT ON THE ESSENTIAL QUESTION

Essential Question: *What were the movements and calls for social reform that resulted from intellectual developments from 1815 to 1914?*

Reform Movements	Goals of Movement

KEY TERMS

Conservative Party	Social Democratic Party	Barbara Smith Bodichon
Liberal Party	philanthropies	Pankhurst family
Labour Party	Josephine Butler	Women's Social and
Napoleon III	temperance movement	Political Union (WSPU)
Paris Commune	Sunday School movement	

MULTIPLE-CHOICE QUESTIONS

Questions 1–3 refer to the photograph below.

Source: Wikimedia Commons

The photo shows a march in Hyde Park, London, June 21, 1908. Emmeline Pankhurst is the tall woman in the middle of the front row.

1. What is the purpose of the event shown in the photograph?
   (A) To celebrate the passage of a major bill by the British government
   (B) To protest against the lack of equality for women in British colonies
   (C) To demonstrate support for women's suffrage in Britain
   (D) To show that men supported causes led by British women

2. The historical process of the event shown in the photograph is best described by which of the following?
   (A) The increasing difference between Great Britain and the rest of Europe
   (B) The expansion of voting rights for both men and women
   (C) The greater reliance of reformers on mass events rather than violence
   (D) The growing spread of socialism and communism

3. Which of the following best describes the result of the event shown in the photograph?
   (A) It had little impact at the time because it was such a small event.
   (B) It slowed progress towards its goal because it upset many people.
   (C) It achieved its goal fairly quickly, within a year.
   (D) It was part of a movement that achieved its goal 20 years later.

Use the passage below to answer all parts of the question that follows.

"The SPD [German Social Democratic Party] also helped promote Germany's extensive system of welfare support giving Germany the most comprehensive system of social insurance in Europe by 1913. They pressed successfully for some constitutional changes like the secret ballot (1904) and payment of MPs (1906), which permitted lower middle and working-class men, with no other income, to put themselves forward as deputies for the Reichstag [Germany's legislative body]. In 1911, they supported measures whereby Alsace-Lorraine was given Reichstag representation and universal male suffrage at 21 years was introduced. They also successfully resisted the taxation proposals that would hit the working man harder and promoted progressive taxes, whereby those with the most would be forced to pay more."

—Sally Weller, *AQA History: The Development of Germany, 1871–1925*, 2014

1. a) Explain ONE historical process of which the founding of the SDP was a part.

   b) Explain ONE example of evidence used in the passage that would support an argument against support for the SDP.

   c) Describe ONE reason for the passage of the reforms mentioned in the passage?

Topic 6.9

Institutional Responses and Reform

*When thee builds a prison, . . . [remember] that thee
and thy children may occupy the cells.*

—Quaker minister Elizabeth Fry (1780–1845)

Essential Question: In what ways did governments and other
institutions respond to challenges resulting from industrialization?

The massive upheavals that industrialization brought changed the way many
people viewed society and government. In earlier eras, people with power and
money often favored **laissez-faire** economic policies. In other words, they
believed the government should leave things alone, allowing individuals to
buy, sell, hire, and fire as they wished. But in the 19th century and beyond,
people who had power or influence began to become more **interventionist**.
That means they began to make (or pressure politicians to make) more rules for
economies and societies. This interventionist approach showed up in different
ways in different countries.

The Growth of Government Intervention

Urbanization and industrialization created complex social issues, requiring
governments to expand their powers and increase the size of their bureaucracies.
In addition, the rise of nationalism made governments aware of the need
to secure their borders and maintain their laws, all leading to a stronger
government presence in the lives of ordinary people.

Police and Prison Reform

In the 1800s, London was one of the most important economic centers in the
world, allowing some people to acquire great wealth. Economic activity and job
opportunities caused the population to grow rapidly—meaning that problems,
such as poverty and crime rate, also rose. As a result of this growth and change,
movements arose to try to improve London and the rest of Britain.

A Professional Police Force An enormous, crowded city like London
could no longer get along with night watchmen hired by individuals and
a few constables (police officers) hired by local parishes. Therefore, in 1829,
the central government created a centralized police force—the first such

organization in the world. Many worried that this type of police force would support a military dictatorship and crush protests. For this reason, London police were not armed. In 1839, the government allowed counties to set up their own police forces.

Prime Minister Robert Peel, a member of the Conservative Party, established the Metropolitan Police as part of an overhaul of laws related to criminal behavior. Peel and many of the lawmakers who supported him believed that improving crime prevention would reduce London's crime rate.

A Professional Prison System Until the 1800s, British prisons were crowded and provided little food, clean water, or medical care. Groups of prisoners, male and female, were often locked in together. Reformers, including the Quaker minister Elizabeth Fry, led efforts to improve, standardize, and professionalize prisons. Fry recommended that male and female prisoners should be kept separate and that women should supervise female prisoners. She also believed that prisoners should have access to education, religious instruction, and employment.

Fry's efforts led to prison reforms not only in Britain but also throughout most of Europe. She observed conditions in French prisons and sent a report to the king of France about them. The report included the advice in the quotation at the start of this topic.

Liberalism and Reform in Britain

In Britain, the government promoted several liberal reforms that helped average citizens and increased their sense of national loyalty. Faced with the threat of worker revolts and increasing unrest, the British Parliament became increasingly involved in the day-to-day lives of its citizens. Further, by increasing voting rights, the government gave a wider range of citizens the sense that they had a voice in social policies.

Improving the Public Sector Several reforms addressed infrastructure, housing, public health, and education. Reforms were especially crucial in overcrowded and unsanitary urban areas. **Edwin Chadwick**, a follower of utilitarian Jeremy Bentham, led many efforts to reform the 16th century Poor Laws. These laws jailed people simply for being unemployed. He also helped establish public health standards. In particular, his report titled "Sanitary Conditions of the Labouring Population of Great Britain," published in 1842, was a landmark in the development of public support for the idea that the government in an industrial society should protect the health of its citizens.

Between 1848 and 1913, Parliament enacted a series of reforms that improved life for the working class. Reforms helped increase loyalty to the government and decrease the possibility of armed class struggle. Between 1880 and 1896, real wages (wages adjusted to inflation, or the relative amount of goods and services they could buy) rose approximately 45 percent. Reforms also gave the British Liberal Party a boost over the rival Conservative Party. (See Topic 6.8.) In 1906, the Liberal Party won a majority of seats in Parliament, mostly as a result of support from working-class voters.

ACTIONS IN RESPONSE TO INDUSTRIALIZATION IN BRITAIN	
Movement	**Examples of Significance and/or Impact**
1833	Abolition of slavery in the British Empire
1848	Public Health Act passed in response to cholera epidemic, paving the way for clean water and sewage control
1850	Public Libraries Act establishes free public libraries
1855	Work begins on London's infrastructure for a subway
1863	World's first underground rail line opens in London
1870	Education Act establishes free elementary schools for all children
1889	Employment of children under 10 is outlawed
1890–1892	Slums cleared for new housing in cities and towns
1908	National old age pensions introduced
1913	Sickness, maternity, and unemployment compensation benefits introduced

Reforms Transform Cities

In the 1850s, France enjoyed a period of relative peace and stability. Emperor Napoleon III decided to celebrate his reign by completely renovating the city of Paris, France's largest city and national capital.

The Transformation of Paris Paris was an old city, plagued by slums, narrow streets, poor water systems, and crumbling bridges. The emperor wanted to see the city become a more modern metropolis and hired **Georges Haussmann** to oversee the project.

In the largest urban renewal project up to that time, Haussmann, a civil servant, completely redesigned the Parisian infrastructure, creating wide boulevards, public parks and plazas, a system for gas lighting, and new water mains to bring fresh water to the city. The new water supply and drainage improved sanitary conditions for the working class and eliminated the city's foul odor. The wider boulevards allowed people and goods to move through the city more easily. The boulevards also had a military purpose, replacing many narrow streets where anti-government rebels might build barricades and allowing police and troops to move rapidly to any part of the city.

The main part of the construction work took nearly 20 years, and some parts were not completed until the 1920s. The huge financial costs of this **urban redesign** made Haussmann very unpopular with some legislators, but most historians agree that his work was a success. Haussmann was an urban visionary who turned Paris into one of the most attractive cities in Europe and made it a model for urban planners throughout the world. Haussmann went on to redesign Vienna and other cities as well.

Educational Opportunities Expand

As the political power of ordinary people gradually rose and governments began to intervene more in society, people began to demand other reforms.

One of the most influential of these movements focused on public education for children.

In Switzerland, a Focus on the Heart, Head, and Hands Swiss reformer Johann Heinrich Pestalozzi wrote extensively about educating young people. He urged the education of poor children. Pestalozzi suggested that children be grouped by ability rather than by age and that their learning should be hands on, including building models and going on field trips. He believed that education should equip students to make a living as well as to discover the joy of learning. Educators from Germany and elsewhere visited the school he ran and brought his methods to their countries. Many of the ideas Pestalozzi pioneered are still part of education today.

In Germany, a "Garden of Children" Influenced by Pestalozzi, German intellectual Friedrich Froebel pioneered kindergarten education. He also wrote an extremely popular book about how to use play and songs effectively in early education. The book was translated into other languages, and people in other countries began founding kindergartens of their own. Froebel believed that social reforms could not happen unless early childhood education became effective and common.

In France, a Move to Nonreligious Education Some reformers focused on what they believed were the best interests of children. Others saw widespread public education as a way to shape the future of their nations. Under Premier Jules Ferry, France made education of children required, free, and secular (nonreligious). These changes meant that the Catholic Church lost some of its influence in French society. Also, literacy rates in France rose dramatically. In 1870, about 60 percent of French men and women could read. By 1900, 95 percent could. Increased literacy in France and other countries provided important economic advantages to nations that had invested in universal public education. They also helped create populations that were hungry for new ideas and entertainment.

REFLECT ON THE ESSENTIAL QUESTION

Essential Question: *In what ways did governments and other institutions respond to challenges resulting from industrialization?*

Governmental/Institutional Responses	Effects of Responses

KEY TERMS

laissez-faire	Edwin Chadwick	urban redesign
interventionist	Georges Haussmann	

MULTIPLE-CHOICE QUESTIONS

Questions 1–3 refer to the passages below.

Passage 1

"That the various forms of epidemic, endemic, and other disease caused, or aggravated, or propagated chiefly amongst the laboring classes by atmospheric impurities produced by decomposing animal and vegetable substances, by damp and filth, and close and overcrowded dwellings prevail amongst the population in every part of the kingdom . . . .

The primary and most important measures, and at the same time the most practicable, and within the recognized province, and within the recognized province of public administration, are drainage, the removal of all refuse of habitations, streets, and roads, and the improvement of the supplies of water."

—Edwin Chadwick, Poor Law Commissioners' Report, 1834

Passage 2

"Gentlemen who supported the present measure . . . professed their object to be the welfare of the laboring community . . . held that the common sense of the working classes was capable of enabling them to take care of themselves; if it were not, let them be educated and better taught . . . . If the competition so created and going on were to continue, he apprehended that those who were asking for the limitation of labor to eight or ten hours, would find eight or ten hours to be much to their inconvenience... It was well known that after defraying the expenses of individual labor and interest on capital, owners of mills . . had to calculate, besides having the competition of the Continent and of America . . . whether they could . . . obtain a proper and fair amount of profit."

—Factories Bill (10-Hours Act) debate in the House of Commons, 1847

1. Problems such as those described in the passages were caused most directly by which of the following changes?
   (A) New agricultural techniques that reduced the frequency of famines
   (B) Changes in marriage patterns that resulted in lower birthrates
   (C) Overcrowding in the cities caused by rapid industrialization
   (D) Increased trade between Eastern and Western Europe because of lower tariffs

2. The reforms promoted by Chadwick in his report would have most helped
   (A) people who lived in rural communities near decomposing animals and vegetation
   (B) factory workers in cities who faced health and economic hardships
   (C) middle-class entrepreneurs who often lived in overcrowded dwellings
   (D) factory owners who faced regulation by the public administration

3. Reforms such as the ones proposed in the passages occurred within the context of
   (A) men taking more dangerous jobs while children attended school
   (B) women and children moving back to rural areas for work
   (C) the development of class-consciousness among both the working class and middle class
   (D) a sharp decrease in life expectancy for workers in the second half of the 19th century

Use the painting below to answer all parts of the question that follows.

Camille Pissarro, *Place du Théâtre-Francais and the Avenue de l'Opéra, Sunlight, Winter Morning*, 1898, Museum of Fine Arts, Reims, France

1. a) Describe ONE historical development that caused Napoleon III's government to want to change Paris as reflected in this painting.

   b) Describe ONE aspect of the historical context in France that enabled the country to rebuild Paris to look as it appears in this painting.

   c) Explain ONE point that might refute the claim that this painting provides useful information about Haussmann's influence on Paris.

Topic 6.10

Causation in the Age of Industrialization

There is but one law for all, namely that law which governs all law, the law of our Creator, the law of humanity, justice, equity—the law of nature and of nations.

—British member of Parliament Edmund Burke, regarding British imperial practices in India, c. 1794

Essential Question: What was the influence of innovation and technological development in Europe from 1815 to 1914?

During the Industrial Revolution, there were many innovations and technological developments that caused the advancement of manufacturing, transportation, and communications in Europe. These developments started in Britain and spread throughout the European continent. Industry changed daily life in Europe, especially in the heavily industrialized areas. The changes to daily life during this period also caused new political ideologies to emerge, as reform movements grew in response to industrialization.

Progress in Innovations and Technologies Britain led the way in industrialization with innovations in textile, iron, and steel production. This progress was enabled by developing steam power to run factories and trains and building railroads and improving waterways to transport raw materials to factories and finished products to markets—both domestic and foreign. The parliamentary democracy of Britain allowed industrialists to participate in government and shape policies through their representatives. In addition, the daily lives of inventors and businesspeople were influenced by their industrial advances and innovations. These influencers had the opportunity to become a part of a new middle class for the first time, earning money rather than inheriting it. All of this caused Britain to become the world's dominant industrial power by the middle of the 19th century.

Industrialization spread to the European continent, but slowly in some areas. Political disputes and revolutions caused European nations, particularly France, to focus their attention and resources elsewhere, while Britain became an industrial power. Europe's autocratic leaders and the aristocrats that held power were hesitant to implement political or industrial changes since it would weaken their control. The lagging development of an entrepreneurial middle class and the persistence of a primarily agricultural lower class meant that industry was slow to grow on the continent.

Industrialization Influences Daily Life The Industrial Revolution caused many changes to daily life in areas that were industrialized. In these areas, social classes became more sharply drawn and had new characteristics. The growing working class often came from farms to cities for new factory jobs that required them to work long hours at dangerous tasks for low pay. The new middle class was made of people who were business managers, lawyers, doctors, bankers, professors, and other professionals. Many middle-class families owned their own homes, attended schools that sprung up in industrialized cities, had progressive public health offerings, and had more leisure time than ever before. By the end of the 19th century, a small number of families who owned factories, railroads, shipping lines, and mines amassed a huge amount of wealth and became the new upper class of European industrial society.

Daily life in industrialized cities also changed because of fast population growth. Urbanization became the trend as workers moved from farms to cities to take factory jobs. Eventually, industrialization caused family patterns to change. Generally, family units became smaller and were made up of only two generations: parents and children. Traditional multigenerational families became a thing of the past. Also, family members often worked outside their homes, which also broke tradition.

Industrialization Causes New Ideologies and Reforms The Industrial Revolution and political upheavals such as the French Revolution caused new political ideologies to develop and take hold in Europe during the 19th century. Conservatism was one of the ideologies that was a response to the tremendous the political and social changes caused by industrialization. European conservatives wanted to keep or revert to traditional institutions of authority such as the land-and-title-based class system, the church, and the military. In their view, the common people were not well equipped to handle power.

European liberals wanted reforms to political institutions to match the societal changes caused by industrialization. To them, the common people had the right to hold power. Popular sovereignty is an example of the ideologies of the 19th century, expressing that people, not monarchs or the nobility, should hold the greatest amount of power in a nation. The liberal philosophy of utilitarianism, an idea from British philosopher Jeremy Bentham, advanced the idea that every law should be measured by how much good it could accomplish for people. Based on utilitarianism, many social reform movements of the 19th century came to be, including education for women, religious freedom, prison reform, and humane treatment of animals.

QUESTIONS ABOUT CAUSATION

1. What was the influence of innovations and technological developments in Europe from 1815 to 1914?

2. How did industrialization cause new ideologies and reform movements from 1815 to 1914?

UNIT 6 REVIEW: Industrialization and Its Effects
c. 1815 to c. 1914

WRITE AS A HISTORIAN: *IDENTIFY RELATIONSHIPS*

One effective way to extend an argument in a historical essay is to show the interrelationships among the different historical themes, for example, the connection of economic and commercial developments with cultural and intellectual developments such as Social Darwinism.

When making this type of connection, use a transition word or phrase, such as *similarly*, *also*, or *in addition to*. As you write, remember to explain your ideas thoroughly to establish clear connections between your thoughts.

Referencing the DBQ documents is another way to make connections. You may encounter a political cartoon or an excerpt from a law. Explaining the context and importance of diverse sources allows you to extend your answer and show mastery of more than just straightforward historical dates and events.

In the statements below, identify any transition words that signal a relationship to another field of historical study and identify the area of connection being made.

1. Europe experienced rapid urbanization during the Industrial Revolution as people moved to cities to take factory jobs. Technological advances transformed society in other ways as well. Self-conscious economic classes (such as the bourgeoisie and the proletariat) arose and led to social divisions between the working and middle classes.

2. Economic changes resulted in distinctive class-based cultures of dress, speech, values, and customs. Because middle-class women, in particular, embraced new socially conscious values, legislation changed in response. For the first time, society provided for universal schooling and protections for women and children laborers in mines and factories.

3. Family life evolved. Couples began to use birth control and had fewer children but were able to care for them better. Companionate marriages became common even among the working classes. As a result of these shifts, cities and philanthropists responded by creating family spaces: parks, beaches, sporting venues, libraries, theaters, and museums.

4. Industrialization and mass marketing increased both supply and demand for many consumer goods, including clothing, processed foods, and labor-saving devices. At the same time, new and efficient methods of transportation, such as steamships, railroads, and refrigerated railroad cars, all made it possible to distribute these goods, leading to improved quality of life for both sellers and consumers.

LONG ESSAY QUESTIONS

Directions: Suggested writing time is 40 minutes. In your response, you should do the following:

- Respond to the prompt with a historically defensible thesis that establishes a line of reasoning.
- Describe a broader historical context relevant to the prompt.
- Support an argument in response to the prompt using specific and relevant examples of evidence.
- Use historical reasoning (e.g., comparison, causation, continuity and change over time) to frame or structure an argument that addresses the prompt.
- Use evidence to corroborate, qualify, or modify an argument that addresses the prompt.

1. Evaluate the most significant factor that made Great Britain a leader in the Industrial Revolution.

2. Evaluate the most significant effect of the growth of the middle class during the Industrial Revolution.

3. Evaluate the extent to which the Industrial Revolution altered workers' positions within the family and society.

4. Evaluate the most significant difference in family life between countries that experienced industrialization and countries that remained agrarian.

DOCUMENT-BASED QUESTION

Directions: Question 1 is based on the accompanying documents. The documents have been edited for the purpose of this exercise. You are advised to spend 15 minutes planning and 45 minutes writing your answer. In your response, you should do the following:

- **Thesis:** Make a defensible claim that establishes a line of reasoning and consists of one or more sentences found in one place.
- **Contextualization:** Relate the argument to a broader historical context.
- **Document Evidence:** Use content from at least six documents.
- **Outside Evidence:** Use one piece of evidence not in the documents.
- **Document Sourcing:** Explain how or why the point of view, purpose, situation, or intended audience is relevant for at least three documents.
- **Analysis:** Show the relationships.

1. Evaluate the relative importance of the different factors that led to the development of industrial competition in Europe between 1800 and 1890.

Document 1:

Source: Napoleon Bonaparte, The Berlin Decree, November 21, 1806

That this monstrous abuse of the right of blockade has no other aim than to prevent communication among the nations and to raise the commerce and the industry of England upon the ruins of that of the continent. That, since this is the obvious aim of England, whoever deals on the continent in English goods, thereby favors and renders himself an accomplice of her designs. That this policy of England, worthy of the earliest stages of barbarism, has profited that power to the detriment of every other nation.

We have consequently decreed and do decree that which follows: All commerce and all correspondence with the British Isles are forbidden. Consequently letters or packages directed to England or to an Englishman or written in the English language shall not pass through the mails and shall be seized.

Every individual who is an English subject, of whatever state or condition he may be, who shall be discovered in any country occupied by our troops or by those of our allies, shall be made a prisoner of war.

Trade in English goods is prohibited, and all goods belonging to England or coming from her factories or her colonies are declared lawful prize.... Half of the product resulting from the confiscation of the goods and possessions declared a lawful prize by the preceding articles shall be applied to indemnify the merchants for the losses they have experienced by the capture of merchant vessel.

Document 2:

Source: Debate in Parliament on the British Corn Laws, 1814

The Petition characterized the Report of the committee as a proposition which had for its object the raising the import price of corn, and compromising the commercial interests of the country for the temporary interests of the landlords; and as "an unhallowed attempt to bring ruin and devastation on the country, to annihilate the manufactures, and force our artizans to emigrate to countries where the means of subsistence were more easily obtained." The greatest caution and deliberation in legislating upon this important subject. It was but last year that it was asked, could any person expect to live to see corn so low as 10s. 6d. a bushel. Gentlemen had only to look to the present price, and the change that took place would sufficiently prove the necessity of proceeding with all possible care.

Document 3:

Source: *The Peterloo Massacre*, 1819

On August 16, 1819, about 70,000 people gathered in St. Peter's Fields in Manchester, England, to demand reforms in Parliament. When officials tried to arrest the speakers, officers attacked the crowd, killing 15 people and injuring hundreds more.

Credit: Getty Images

Document 4:

Source: Resolutions of the Select committee of the House of Commons on Artisans and Machinery, 21 May 1824, Hansard's *Parliamentary Debates*, New Series, XI, 813-814

EUROPEAN ECONOMIC GROWTH, 1830-1890			
Country	**1830**	**1860**	**1890**
Great Britain	$375	$500	$800
Germany	$225	$325	$500
France	$225	$325	$500
Italy	$225	$250	$250
Russia	$200	$200	$200

Source: Adapted from Paul Bairoch, "Europe's Gross National Product: 1800–1975," Journal of European Economic History, 5 (2), 286.

Amounts are estimates of GDP per capita in 1960 U.S. dollars.

Document 5:

Source: Friedrich List, German economist, "The National System of Political Economy," 1841

I saw clearly that free competition between two nations which are highly civilised can only be mutually beneficial in case both of them are in a nearly equal position of industrial development, and that any nation which owing to misfortunes is behind others in industry, commerce, and navigation, while she nevertheless possesses the mental and material means for developing those acquisitions, must first of all strengthen her own individual powers, in order to fit herself to enter into free competition with more advanced nations. In a word, I perceived the distinction between cosmopolitical and political economy. I felt that Germany must abolish her internal tariffs, and by the adoption of a common uniform commercial policy towards foreigners, strive to attain to the same degree of commercial and industrial development to which other nations have attained by means of their commercial policy.

Document 6:

Source: Prince Albert, describing the Great Exhibition, 1851

Man is approaching a more complete fulfillment of that great and sacred mission which he has to perform in this world… to conquer nature to his use… In promoting [the progress of the human race], we are accomplishing the will of the great and blessed God.

Document 7:

TARIFF UNIONS IN GERMAN STATES, 1818 TO 1854

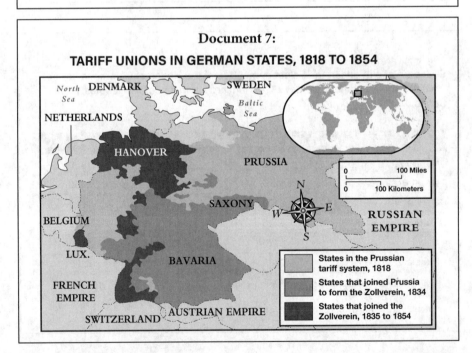

UNIT 7: 19th-Century Perspectives and Political Developments
c. 1815 to c. 1914

Topic 7.1

Contextualizing 19th-Century Perspectives and Political Developments

Essential Question: What was the context in which nationalistic and imperialistic sentiments developed in Europe from 1815 to 1914?

The changes in European society because of the Enlightenment, the French Revolution, and the Industrial Revolution were the context for a new Europe in the 19th century. In particular, industrialization had radically changed how goods were produced and how all classes of Europeans lived. By 1815, Europe's growing industrial working class and rising urban middle class had new ideologies, wanted more freedoms, and pushed for changes to existing political structures.

As the lives of Europeans changed, so did political beliefs. Liberal ideology held that individuals should be free from an overbearing government and able to own private property. Liberalism and socialism could be seen in the reform movements that wanted to extend voting rights and redistribute societies wealth and resources. As liberalism grew, conservatives sought to suppress reform movements and return to more traditional political and social structures.

Struggle for International Stability European nations began to unify under the ideology of nationalism, shifting the balance of power in the 19th century. Unified Italy and Germany challenged the traditional powers of Europe as nationalism continued to grow in both countries. Meanwhile, Austria, the Ottoman Empire, and Russia worked to put down nationalist revolutions. International conflicts and unsuccessful alliances among nations meant that tensions in Europe continued to grow throughout the 1800s. This international instability eventually resulted in a world war in the early 20th century.

Europe's Globalization Increases Tensions Among Powers A second wave of European imperialism began as industrialization greatly boosted Europe's economy. In the 19th century, strong European nations competed with each other to control Africa and Asia. This control would give them access to Africa's and Asia's raw materials. It would also give European nations a market in which to sell their mass-produced goods. Europeans justified taking advantage of less-developed nations as sharing their more advanced economic and political systems as well as civilizing native populations.

Colonized populations resisted European control and exploitation. This combined with the increasing economic competition among imperial European nations, caused international tensions to grow. During the 19th and early 20th centuries, European imperialism and the worldwide growth of nationalist sentiments set the stage for conflicts on regional and global scales.

Objectivity vs. Subjectivity Between the late 18th century and the early 20th century, there were many forces that influenced European culture and thought—economic and industrial growth, political upheaval, and globalization, to name a few. Art and literature responded to the changes of society. On one side, there was objectivity, scientific realism, and materialism in art, music, philosophy, and literature. On the other, subjectivity, human expression, and romanticism were the basis of artistic expression.

ANALYZE THE CONTEXT

1. Explain the context in which nationalistic sentiments developed in Europe from 1815 to 1914.

2. Explain the context in which imperialistic sentiments developed in Europe during this period.

Topic 7.2

Nationalism

Politics is the art of the possible.

—Otto von Bismarck, architect of a unified Germany

Essential Question: How did the development and spread of nationalism affect Europe from 1815 to 1914?

In Europe, **nationalism** emerged in the early 1800s as a strong, emotional attachment to one's ethnic or cultural group. In its emphasis on emotion, it was a challenge to the emphasis on reason associated with the Enlightenment. It began as a cultural movement, focusing on art, literature, and music. Ideas of cultural pride quickly took on political meanings as well. These were expressed in many ways, and what began as a positive movement emphasizing the culture of common people changed over time, taking on a number of divisive aspects.

The Evolution of Nationalism

Promoters of nationalism encouraged people to join the movement in different ways. These ways included romanticism, aggrandizement, discrimination, political unification, and liberal reforms.

Romantic Idealism

Nationalism grew through **romantic idealism** in the 19th century. Romantics, such as writers, poets, and musicians, idealized the past as a nobler time in which majestic heroes saved nations in battle. (See Topic 7.8 for more about Romanticism.) Folk traditions, music, and legends were treasured. The individual commoner was valued, and democracy and liberal reforms became goals.

The **Grimm brothers**, Jacob (1785–1863) and Wilhelm (1786–1859), were famous German scholars who compiled fairy tales and other folk stories, as well as folk music. German composer **Richard Wagner** (1813–1883) wrote romantic and nationalistic operas that became popular German traditional music. Traditional German culture was celebrated through the literature and music of these men and others. Various European nations emphasized nationalism through the arts, including Britain and France. The French writer **Victor Hugo** (1802–1885), for example, wrote of individuals struggling against cruel societies.

National Aggrandizement

German philosopher and nationalist **Johann Gottlieb Fichte** (1762–1814) espoused the special importance of German language and culture and felt that Germany, because of its outstanding qualities, had a duty to lead other nations. This was **national aggrandizement**, or promoting a nation to appear to have great powers. Fichte was an ardent German nationalist whose peaceful, universalist ideas were abused by nationalistic leaders who were **chauvinistic**, or had excessive and aggressive belief in their nations' superiority.

Racialism

The idea that some races of people are better than others is racism, or **racialism**. This racialism in which some people believed was used to promote nationalism in 19th-century Europe. Often, racialism and nationalism grew together.

Pan-Slavism In some instances, racialism was used to promote a race's interests. **Pan-Slavism** was a nationalist movement in which Slavic peoples of Eastern and east-central Europe strove to unite in furtherance of their mutual cultural and political aspirations. Pan-Slavists believed that Eastern and east-central Europe should belong to people of Slavic origin.

Pan-Slavism was especially popular in Russia by the mid-1800s. Russian Pan-Slavists wanted Slavic peoples in Turkish and Austrian territories to be liberated and independent of what they considered to be foreign rule.

Antisemitism Racialist beliefs and actions directed against Jewish people are known as **antisemitism**. By the 19th century in Western Europe, most constitutions and laws were written giving Jews equality and removing restrictions on where they could live or work. At the same time, antisemitism grew with nationalism. In Russia, in the late 19th and early 20th centuries, antisemitism sometimes took the form of **pogroms**. These were violent attacks of varying scales that were condoned (and often instigated) by governmental officials who found Jewish populations to be useful scapegoats. (There is more on European antisemitism later in this topic.)

Popular Nationalism Strengthens the State

A new generation of conservative leaders in France, Italy, and Prussia recognized the power of nationalism and used it to strengthen the state, and ultimately to unify their nations. These "neo-conservatives" used the cultural nationalism aroused by the Napoleonic conquest of Europe and transformed it into a political movement designed to achieve political unification.

France

Following the revolutions of 1848, the French attempted to establish another republic with a strong executive branch. In the elections of 1848, Louis-Napoleon, the nephew of Napoleon Bonaparte, campaigned on liberal reforms to "defend religion, property and the family, the eternal bases of all social order."

A dark-horse candidate, Louis-Napoleon won almost 75 percent of the vote. As president, he possessed the power to declare war, make laws, and sign treaties. However, the law barred him from running for a second term. So, in 1852, he used a direct vote, as his uncle had done, to approve his decision to crown himself Emperor **Napoleon III** of France (ruled 1852–1870). With his new title, he ruled as an autocrat even as he agreed on the importance of nationalism, liberal reforms, and political participation.

Napoleon III undertook the massive project of redesigning and modernizing much of Paris. He also promoted other liberal reform projects that he believed would modernize France and promote prosperity:

- building railroads, ports, and canals to stimulate trade
- increasing international trade by opening French markets
- supporting the creation of new banks
- encouraging shipbuilding
- backing the construction of the Suez Canal in Egypt

The emperor's public projects won him support. They created jobs that stimulated the economy. Further, since bread prices were low, people who worked could afford to eat. His political reforms, such as reinstating universal male suffrage, also made him popular. They looked impressive, even if they did not result in true political liberty.

Italy

Nationalism in Italy gained momentum throughout the 19th century. Several important leaders set the table for the politically fractured region's eventual unification.

Giuseppe Mazzini An ardent nationalist, **Giuseppe Mazzini** (1805–1872) envisioned all of the Italian peninsula united into one state. He faced several major obstacles to uniting the region:

- Austria controlled several Italian states and opposed losing its influence.
- Conservative leaders, particularly Russia's tsar and Prussia's king, feared the creation of any powerful state.
- The pope was opposed to Italian unification, and many Italian Catholics followed his lead.
- The people of the peninsula were divided by culture. There were significant differences between the industrialized, cosmopolitan north and the agrarian, almost feudal south.

In 1832, Mazzini founded the Young Italy movement that led several small uprisings as part of the broader Italian nationalist movement called the Risorgimento, or "resurgence." But these revolts had little success. His importance was his inspiration to later nationalists.

Camillo di Cavour In 1848, the strong Italian state of Piedmont-Sardinia established a liberal constitution, pushed by parliament member and nationalist **Camillo di Cavour** (1810–1861). In 1852, Cavour became the prime minister of Piedmont-Sardinia. Cavour was a powerful, influential statesperson and diplomat who worked to gain control of all of northern Italy. His goal, supported by the liberal Italian middle classes, was Italian unification. (See Topic 7.3 for more about Cavour and the final unification of Italy.)

Source: Getty Images

Prussian leader Otto von Bismarck in full military uniform

Prussia

Like Italy, Germany moved toward unification in the mid-1800s. This unification movement was led by **Otto von Bismarck** (1815–1898), who served as Prussian foreign minister and then prime minister.

Otto von Bismarck Bismarck began his political career as a staunch conservative but saw more opportunities for himself and Prussia through an embrace of selected liberal causes and in an increasingly nationalistic foreign policy. The German state of Prussia had a mostly German population, so it was united by nationalism. From there, Prussia expanded, taking over Austrian, French, and Hungarian states. Bismarck was the mastermind, deliberately starting wars to stoke nationalist feelings and develop a Prussian-dominated Germany. (See Topic 7.3 for more about Bismarck and German unification.)

Nationalism Affects Austria

For multiethnic empires, such as that of Austria, nationalism increased tensions. Ethnic groups that dominated a particular Austrian region advocated for self-determination. In addition, conservative leaders in Austria feared liberal and socialist reforms. Nevertheless, the revolutions of 1848 caused Austria to recognize the need for a change in its political, economic, and social systems in order to compete with nation-states of Western Europe.

Austria-Hungary's Dual Monarchy

Following the revolutions of 1848, the Austrian monarchy attempted to suppress Hungarian culture, but with little success. The *Ausgleich*, or Compromise of 1867, established the dual monarchy of Austria-Hungary under Francis Joseph. This dual monarchy recognized the political power of the Hungarians, the largest ethnic minority in the empire. Austria-Hungary shared the same ministers for foreign policy, finance, and defense. However, the dual monarchy provided autonomy for Hungary by creating two capitals and two official languages. The status of Hungary was made more complex by the diversity in that region. Most people in Hungary identified as part of one or another non-Hungarian ethnic group, such as Ruthenians, Romanians, or Slovaks, and did not speak the Hungarian language.

COMPARING AUSTRIA AND HUNGARY		
Trait	**Austria**	**Hungary**
Largest ethnic group	Germans	mostly Magyars (Hungarians), but not a majority
Capital	Vienna, which was also the main capital of the empire	Budapest, though divided into separate cities of Buda and Pest until 1873
Religion	mostly Roman Catholic	mostly Roman Catholic with significant Protestant and Orthodox minorities

While the dual monarchy recognized the Hungarians, both the Hungarians and Austrians continued to neglect the other minority groups. For example, while Hungarians voted and served in the Parliament, Croatians and Romanians lacked representation. In addition, Hungarian became an approved language in schools, but languages such as Czech and Polish were not permitted.

By establishing the dual monarchy, the empire had hoped to stabilize itself by reconfiguring national unity and recognizing Hungarians as an official minority group. While the empire lasted into the 20th century, the dual monarchy would collapse as a result of World War I, as other ethnic groups within the Austro-Hungarian Empire sought self-determination.

Jews and Antisemitism in Europe

Throughout most of European history, Jews were subject to antisemitism, or discrimination and persecution based on their religion, and often forbidden from owning property or practicing certain professions. Some municipalities, such as the city of Venice, required Jews to live in specified areas and forced them to obey a curfew at night.

The Enlightenment, with its emphasis on individual liberties and rights, brought wide-scale changes to Europe's Jewish population. During the French Revolution, the Revolutionary government issued an edict granting Jews full citizenship. After Napoleon took over the French government, he extended rights to Jews in all the countries he conquered.

By the mid-19th century, Jews in most Western European countries enjoyed equal rights and were fully integrated into the economy. However, antisemitism was not gone. In fact, it commonly grew along with nationalism.

The Christian Social Party

The German **Christian Social Party** was a conservative political party that drew much of its support from antisemitic elements of German working classes. The classes were united through shared nationalistic antisemitic beliefs.

The Austrian Christian Social Party's founder and leader, **Karl Lueger** (1844–1910), was also mayor of Vienna. The Austrian Christian Social Party was conservative, nationalistic, and antisemitic, like its German counterpart. A 20th-century admirer of Lueger was Adolph Hitler, who praised Lueger's accomplishments.

The Dreyfus Affair

Integration and emancipation for Jews by the mid-19th century did not mean that antisemitism had disappeared, though. Even if Jews did not face legal discrimination, they still faced suspicion and hostility from the majority who often regarded them as "outsiders." In 1894, Alfred Dreyfus, a Jewish captain in the French Army, was accused of passing sensitive military information to Germany. He was tried and convicted of treason, although the government had little evidence against him. However, because he was Jewish, he made a convenient scapegoat. Some people found blaming him easy because he belonged to a minority group.

Source: Getty Images

While some French magazines portrayed Dreyfus as a traitor, most French later looked back on the treatment of Dreyfus as a disgraceful example of antisemitism.

For more than ten years, the **Dreyfus Affair** split French society. Some people defended Dreyfus and condemned antisemitism. Others blamed Jews for social problems and claimed that Dreyfus showed that Jews could not be trusted. Advocates for religious liberty prevailed, and Dreyfus was pardoned in 1906. By that time, the issues raised by the Dreyfus Affair had spread beyond France to other regions of Europe. Jews throughout Western Europe, even in countries that seemed to accept religious diversity, found their loyalty questioned. Vienna's mayor openly appealed to antisemites and introduced laws restricting Jewish immigration from Russia and Eastern Europe.

Zionism

Other Jews determined that they should have a homeland of their own, a concept known as **Zionism**. The most important early leader of Zionism was **Theodore Herzl**. Born in Hungary in 1860, he grew up in an assimilated German-Jewish family—one deeply absorbed into German society. He admired German culture and believed that Jews should become part of the larger European society. The Dreyfus Affair, however, opened his eyes to the persistence of antisemitism in Europe. Herzl later claimed that his reaction to the Dreyfus Affair inspired his interest in Zionism. Some historians dispute this claim, stating that Herzl had explored the idea of a Jewish state even before the arrest of Dreyfus.

Herzl's book *Der Judenstat (The Jewish State)*, published in 1895, was one of the first documents to declare that Jews should have a nation-state of their own. Herzl felt that without their own state, Jews would remain at the mercy of others. He wanted a place where Jews would be guaranteed the right to practice their own religion and form their own government. At first, Herzl did not stipulate where the Jewish state should be, even speculating that it might be established in South America or Africa.

In the early 1900s, though, Herzl and his followers came to believe that the region known as Palestine was the most likely place for a Jewish state. Most Jews regarded the land around the city of Jerusalem as the traditional Jewish homeland. Jews had lived there for centuries, and many traveled there to see the ancient city. The British, who controlled Palestine, supported the creation of a "national home" for Jews there. The Zionist movement continued, even after Herzl's death in 1904, and Jewish immigration to Palestine grew throughout the 1920s and 1930s. In 1948, the Jewish state of Israel was established. Israelis considered Herzl one of their nation's founders and celebrate his birthday as a national holiday.

REFLECT ON THE ESSENTIAL QUESTION

Essential Question: *How did the development and spread of nationalism affect Europe from 1815 to 1914?*

Advocate for Nationalism	Effects of Advocate's Efforts

KEY TERMS

nationalism	chauvinistic	Camillo di Cavour
romantic idealism	racialism	Otto von Bismarck
Grimm Brothers	Pan-Slavism	Christian Social Party
Richard Wagner	antisemitism	Karl Lueger
Victor Hugo	pogrom	Dreyfus Affair
Johann Gottlieb Fichte	Napoleon III	Zionism
national aggrandizement	Giuseppe Mazzini	Theodore Herzl

Questions 1–3 refer to the passages below.

Passage 1

"In other nations humanity comes after nationality. Among the Slavs nationality comes after humanity. Scattered Slavs, let us be a unified whole, and no longer mere fragments. Let us be all or nothing. Who are you, a Russian? And you, a Serb? And you, a Czech? And you, a Pole? My children, seek unity! Say: I am a Slav!"

—Ján Kollár, Slovak poet and advocate of Pan-Slavism, 1829

Passage 2

"The danger that Austria has to face is the diversity of language and race in the empire. Our Slavic nationalities are likely at a moment of dangerous crisis to develop pro-Russian tendencies."

—Count Friedrich Ferdinand von Beust, former Austrian
foreign minister and imperial chancellor, 1887

1. The ideas expressed by Kollár most clearly show the influence of which of the following historical developments?

(A) Romantic idealism

(B) Marxist socialism

(C) Social Darwinism

(D) Antisemitism

2. The danger facing Austria described by von Beust was part of a larger trend that was also a danger for

(A) Germany

(B) France

(C) Italy

(D) the Ottoman Empire

3. The unification of several groups of Slavs into a single state would have been supported by

(A) both Kollár and von Beust

(B) neither Kollár nor von Beust

(C) only Kollár

(D) only von Beust

Use the passage below to answer all parts of the question that follows.

> "The idea which I have developed in this pamphlet is a very old one: the restoration of the Jewish State. The world resounds with outcries against the Jews, and these outcries have awakened the slumbering idea. . . .
>
> Everything depends on our propelling force. And what is our propelling force: The misery of the Jews. . . . We are one people. . . .
>
> Let the sovereignty be granted us over a portion of the globe large enough to satisfy the reasonable requirements of a nation; the rest we shall manage for ourselves."
>
> —Theodore Herzl, *A Jewish State: An Attempt at a Modern Solution of the Jewish Question*, 1904

1. a) Describe ONE cause that Herzl gave for his decision to advocate for the idea in this passage.

   b) Explain how the idea in this passage was situated within the broader historical context of changing ideas in Europe in the 19th century.

   c) Explain how Herzl's motives regarding the Jewish population were different than Bismarck's motives regarding the German population.

Topic 7.3

National Unification and Diplomatic Tensions

Forward, the Light Brigade!
Charge for the guns!" he said.
Into the valley of Death
Rode the six hundred.

—Alfred, Lord Tennyson, "The Charge of the Light Brigade," 1855

Essential Question: What factors resulted in Italian unification and German unification?

The charge of the Light Brigade was a failed attack by the British light cavalry against the Russians in October 1854, during the Battle of Balaklava in the Crimean War. Tennyson's poem commemorates the bravery of the brigade's soldiers who, following miscommunicated orders, made a frontal attack into the direct line of Russian fire, even though they knew they had little chance of survival. The battle itself was inconclusive: the Russians failed to capture the port of Balaklava, which Britain and its allies used to supply their armies, and the British lost control of its major supply route. Each side lost some 620 men. The battle was just one failure in a disastrous war that caused Austria to lose Russia's support in central European affairs, which in turn led to the unification of both Italy and Germany.

The Crimean War

While the revolutions of 1848 were mostly unsuccessful in creating political change across Europe, the uprisings did challenge the status quo and cause Europeans to question political systems and the balance of power in Europe.

Causes of the Crimean War

In 1853, the nations of France, Russia, Great Britain, and the Ottoman Empire met on the Crimean Peninsula to fight the bloodiest European war between the end of the Napoleonic conflicts in 1815 and the start of World War I in 1914. The **Crimean War** erupted for two main reasons:

- Religion: France had enjoyed a certain status as protectors of the Christians in the Ottoman Empire, and Russia wanted a similar position within the empire.

- Politics: Emperor Napoleon III of France and Tsar Nicholas I of Russia wanted to prove their military strength, and the weakening Ottoman Empire provided a way to do so. Great Britain did not support the expansion of Russian power and sought to maintain a balance of power in Europe. Furthermore, the Kingdom of Piedmont-Sardinia entered the war in order to gain support for nationalistic ambitions in northern Italy.

In October 1853, the sultan of the Ottoman Empire refused to cede territory to the Russian Empire and declared war. In response, the French and British came to the aid of the Ottoman Empire, hoping to intimidate Russia into backing down. Great Britain also opposed the increased territory Russia would gain if it were victorious, which would affect the balance of power.

Mass Politics and Warfare

Over the next 18 months, the Crimean War resulted in more than a million casualties. Critics attacked it as a useless war fought by incompetent generals. Compared to previous European wars, the conflict in Crimea was followed closely and quickly by civilians on the home front through newspapers. While the *London Times* provided the most detailed coverage, other papers also benefited from changes that brought in readers:

- Greater freedom of the press allowed journalists to write more freely.
- Increased literacy meant that more people could read news of the war.
- The telegraph allowed journalists to get news to the home front rapidly.
- The camera allowed people to see photos of battles.

As civilians knew more, governments had to be more sensitive to public perception and opinion.

Source: Getty Images

The medical care provided for wounded soldiers in the Crimean War by Florence Nightingale and others reflected the greater opportunities for women and the increasing use of scientific knowledge.

Effects of the War

The publicity given the Crimean War exposed the weakness of the Ottoman Empire, the growing importance of mass politics, and the increased importance of military technology. The war also demonstrated the struggle of European states to maintain stability in an age of nationalism.

It also demonstrated to Tsar Alexander II, who had succeeded Nicholas I in 1855, that Russia was comparatively backward and weak compared to its European counterparts. In response, Alexander launched a reform program to upgrade communication and transportation within the empire. His boldest and most important move was the abolition of serfdom in February 1861. (See Topic 6.6 for more on Russia's reform and modernization program.)

National Unification Movements

While nationalist movements would one day break up the Austro-Hungarian and Ottoman empires, they brought unification elsewhere. Nationalistic movements among Italians and among Germans led to the creation of the modern nations of Italy and Germany in the 1860s and the 1870s. As unified states, both emerged as important powers, both in Europe and on the world stage.

Cavour and Garibaldi Unify Italy

The process of Italian unification succeeded in the second half of the 19th century because a handful of leaders overcame foreign opposition and traditional regional loyalties. Giuseppe Mazzini's revolutionary Young Italy society made attempts to liberate Italian states from foreign rule as did Camillo di Cavour to unite northern Italy under Piedmont's rule. (See Topic 7.2.)

Cavour's Diplomatic Strategy In his role as minister of agriculture, Camillo di Cavour supported free trade through treaties with France, Belgium, and Great Britain. As prime minister under King **Victor Emmanuel II** (1820–1878) Cavour advanced the interests of Piedmont through skilled, if often dishonest, diplomacy. He carefully played Europe's most powerful states, particularly France and Austria, against each other. This style is known as **realpolitik**, the practice of acting for political power rather than for a religious, moral, or ideological goal. Through a series of wars, alliances, and betrayals, Piedmont won control over most of northern Italy.

Cavour managed to convince European nations that the continent's peace was threatened by Austrian dominance of much of Italy, the mismanagement of the Papal States of central Italy, and the presence of a Spanish Bourbon monarch in the south. In July 1858, he and Napoleon III of France planned to provoke a European war against Austria. In fact, Austria actually provoked the war by demanding that Piedmont disarm. As a result of the armistice, Piedmont acquired Lombardy (present-day Italy on Austria's southern border). Cavour had hoped to gain all of Austria's holdings in the Italian peninsula. He resigned his post in frustration, only to be returned to power the next year.

The war with Austria had inspired revolutionary movements in Tuscany and other regions of Italy, including the Papal States, and Cavour worked to annex those territories to Piedmont. In 1861, a national parliament proclaimed the Kingdom of Italy, with Victor Emmanuel II as its king. Cavour felt that Rome, which was still under the control of the pope, should be the capital of a unified Italy. He was attempting to establish the complete separation of church and state when he fell ill and died at the age of 50. His successes included improving banking practices, reducing the power of the Catholic Church, and increasing access to education.

The Heroic Garibaldi The third great Italian leader, along with Mazzini and Cavour, was a charismatic military figure, **Giuseppe Garibaldi** (1807–1882). He was known throughout the Atlantic world because of his exploits on behalf of various South American revolts. Later in his life, during the American Civil War, the Union considered offering him a position as a general. He declined because the Union refused to make the war explicitly about abolishing slavery.

RIGHT LEG IN THE BOOT AT LAST.

Garibaldi: "IF IT WON'T GO ON, SIRE, TRY A LITTLE MORE POWDER."

Source: Getty Images

Garibaldi, with a sword at his side, helps Victor Emmanuel II "fit into" the Italian boot. Besides his leading role in uniting Italy, Garibaldi fought alongside revolutionaries in Brazil and Uruguay in South America.

In Italy, his success came in the southern states. His rebel army, known as the Red Shirts, combined with his appeals to popular nationalism, unified the region. He considered attacking Rome, where French armies protected the pope. Instead, he chose to hand over Naples and all the lands in southern Italy to King Victor Emmanuel II, whom Cavour had made ruler of most of northern Italy. As a result, one monarch controlled almost the entire peninsula.

Italian Unification Completed In 1861, Victor Emmanuel II became king of a united Italy. The new country began to form a constitutional monarchy with a parliament. Rome was added when Napoleon III withdrew French forces to fight in the Franco-Prussian War. In 1871, Rome became the capital of the newly unified Italy, finalizing the unification process.

Bismarck's Realpolitik Unites Germany

Prussia's Otto von Bismarck was somewhat similar to Cavour. Both were masters of realpolitik—each used war and deceit to unify states under the leadership of his own region. However, compared to Cavour, Bismarck was far more conservative. He believed in authoritarian rule under a strong monarch. By relying on diplomacy, industrialization, and political manipulation, Bismarck created a German powerhouse that threatened the balance of power in Europe. Bismarck's goal was to create a united Germany without Austria being a part of it. This was known as *kleindeutsch* (lesser Germany) versus *grossdeutsch* (greater Germany). He was not eager to include Austria for several reasons:

- Bismarck was a devout Protestant, and Austria was mostly Roman Catholic.
- Austria was poorer than many of the northern German states.
- Bismarck believed an independent Austria could be a diplomatic ally for his German state.

Bismarck's Successful Foreign Policy

While the revolutions of 1848 had failed to create a united Germany, nationalism continued to grow in the German states. The Prussian monarchy led the movement. Bismarck emerged as the conservative politician to negotiate unification, relying on industrialized warfare to bring other German states together under Prussian leadership. These wars included the three in the table below.

PRUSSIAN WARS LEADING TO UNIFICATION	
War	Features
War with Denmark, 1864	• Bismarck provoked and won a short war with Denmark. • Prussia and Austria won control of the provinces of Schleswig and Holstein on the border between Denmark and northern Germany. • Popular support for Bismarck's coalition increased.
Seven Weeks War, 1866	• Bismarck provoked and won a short war with Austria. • Prussia unified northern and central German states. • A lenient peace treaty encouraged Austria's neutrality in future military engagements.
Franco–Prussian War, 1870	• Bismarck provoked and won a short but deadly war with France. • Prussia unified northern and southern German states. • France had to pay a heavy indemnity and lost the Alsace-Lorraine region on the German-French border.

Bismarck's Domestic Policy

While Bismarck employed a successful foreign policy, he also needed to maintain internal unity. From 1871 to 1890, Bismarck served as the chancellor of Germany. To create a modern industrial state, he instituted a new legal code and a national constitution. Under the new constitution, the king of Prussia became the emperor of the German Empire. Bismarck actively promoted economic innovation and growth. German inventors created the internal combustion engine and the electric train. Berlin installed a telephone network. Coal and iron production, as well as the size of the railroad network, increased sharply.

Source: Getty Images

In this 1878 painting, Otto von Bismarck (right) meets with French leader Napoleon III after France's surrender in the Franco-Prussian War.

In 1879, Bismarck concluded that high-tariff countries were more prosperous than low-tariff countries, so he passed the "iron and rye" tariff, which partially protected German manufacturers and farmers from foreign competition. Under Bismarck, cities flourished and the economy competed with other industrial European powers.

While Bismarck tried to create a conservative, centralized state, he met opposition from Catholics and socialists in Germany. First, Bismarck feared the power of the Catholics in the southern states, who represented 40 percent of the population. He sought to diminish the power of Catholicism by creating a program called *Kulturkampf* (culture struggle) and passing laws that expelled the Jesuits, ended Catholic education, and introduced civil marriage.

However, Bismarck soon backed off from the conflict with Catholics. He was increasingly concerned about socialist demands from the working class in response to industrialization. To reduce the spread of socialism, he passed laws that banned socialist newspapers and abolished trade unions. At the same time, he tried to undercut the appeal of socialists by implementing innovative programs such as nationalized health care and old-age insurance. These programs provided a model that other industrialized countries followed. Nevertheless, the socialist movement continued to gain support.

Bismarck's Dismissal

Earlier in his career, Bismarck had successfully used three wars to unify Germans under Prussian leadership. After unification, Bismarck's major goal in both domestic and foreign policy had been to consolidate and strengthen the power of Germany. Domestically, he had sometimes sided with liberals and at other times with conservatives.

In foreign policy, Bismarck viewed France as Germany's most significant rival. He thought France might want revenge after its defeat in the Franco-Prussian War. To prevent this, Bismarck created a web of alliances with other states in an effort to isolate France. For example, he negotiated agreements with Russia and Austria. He supported their influence in Eastern Europe. In return, he hoped they would not support a French war against Germany.

However, he was ultimately unable to overcome the political and religious divisions within the country. In 1890, **Kaiser Wilhelm II** (also known as Emperor William II) dismissed Bismarck and adopted a more aggressive foreign policy stance. The kaiser was determined that Germany would achieve the status he believed it deserved. In contrast, Bismarck promoted a restrained foreign policy designed to prevent conflict that could weaken Germany.

A New Diplomatic Order

The balance of power in Europe shifted under the force of nationalism. Germany and Italy emerged as new powers while Austria, Russia, and Turkey tried to crush nationalist uprisings. Bismarck had served as the initial architect of a complex system of alliances that attempted to maintain the status quo. Over time, conflicts in the Balkans and antagonistic alliances increased tensions in Europe, paving the way for the massive conflict now known as World War I.

Alliances Increase Tension

The European powers desired to maintain the balance of power in Europe. As nationalism and unification challenged the status quo, governments began making alliances to demonstrate their military might and assure their protection.

Bismarck's Alliance System To ensure the success of a unified Germany, Bismarck engineered a series of alliances that created a new diplomatic order in Europe. He also wanted to isolate Germany's longtime rival France so that Germany would not get pulled into a multinational war. To accomplish these goals, Bismarck negotiated several treaties.

EUROPEAN TREATIES CREATING ALLIANCES			
Alliance Name	**Nations Involved**	**Date**	**Purpose**
Three Emperors' League	• Germany • Austria-Hungary • Russia	1873–1887	Spheres of influence for Austria-Hungary and Russia were determined to avoid conflict in the Balkans. This also, this preempted an alliance of Austria-Hungary, Russia, and France, which could threaten Germany.
Reinsurance Treaty	• Germany • Russia	1887	A secret treaty after the collapse of the above treaty, it promised that Germany and Russia would remain neutral if the other went to war with another major party. Exceptions were if Germany attacked France or Russia attacked Austria.
Dual Alliance	• Germany • Austria-Hungary	1879–1918	Germany and Austria-Hungary promised to support each other if attacked by Russia.
Triple Alliance	• Germany • Austria-Hungary • Italy	1882–1915	Allies promised mutual support if attacked.

Congress of Berlin Bismarck organized the major powers of Europe in the **Congress of Berlin** of 1878 to solve the growing tensions in the Balkan states resulting from the Russo-Turkish War (1877–1878). Bismarck wanted to stabilize the Balkans in order to appease Great Britain, Austria-Hungary, and the Ottoman Empire while trying to diminish Russian gains.

As a result of the 1878 Congress, Romania, Serbia, and Montenegro gained independence, and Austria-Hungary occupied Bosnia and Herzegovina. Russia believed the Congress failed to sufficiently help the Slavic people, causing tension between Austria-Hungary and Russia. Bismarck had hoped to create stability and maintain the balance of power, but the Congress created more animosity in the region.

Alliances Create Tension The kaiser forced Bismarck to resign in 1890 so that he could achieve his goal of reviving royal executive authority. Meanwhile, Austria-Hungary and Germany drew closer, and Kaiser William II refused to renew the Reinsurance Treaty because it violated the spirit of the Dual Alliance. Russia responded by signing a defensive alliance with France in1894. Great Britain and France signed a series of agreements known as the **Entente Cordiale**, and in 1907, Britain and Russia signed an Anglo-Russian Convention, ending their rivalry in Central Asia. The system of alliances became an increasing source of tension as Europe divided into two main factions—the Triple Alliance of Germany, Austria-Hungary, and Italy and the **Triple Entente** of Great Britain, France, and Russia. Bismarck had created the alliance system to maintain the status quo and peace. However, by the early 20th century, the alliances created antagonism across Europe.

Individually, states could justify making these alliances. Germany feared a British naval blockade in the event of a war, while the British and French feared a growing German military. Together, the results of the alliances increased the danger for all of Europe.

Nationalist Conflicts in the Balkans

Bismarck had recognized the growing instability in the Balkans and hoped to create stability through the Congress of Berlin. Unfortunately, at the turn of the 20th century, tensions in the Balkans escalated as the Great Powers supported regional groups and nationalism threatened the stability of the Balkans.

Ethnic Tensions The **Balkans**, a peninsula in southeastern Europe, had always been a multiethnic region. For centuries, the Ottoman Empire and Austria-Hungary had competed for control of the territories in the region. As nationalism sparked unification movements in Europe, it also ignited independence movements in the Balkans. For example, the Slavic people throughout the region were unified under the policy of Pan-Slavism. (See Topic 7.2.) Russia supported Pan-Slavism, motivated in part by a desire to gain warm-water ports in the eastern Mediterranean.

Annexation of Bosnia-Herzegovina Austria-Hungary feared the growing power of nationalistic movements in the region. It expanded its influence in the Balkans by occupying **Bosnia-Herzegovina** in 1878 as a result of the Congress of Berlin before formally annexing the region in 1908. Reluctantly, both Serbia and Russia recognized the acquisition since they both lacked the military strength to win a war. This event empowered Austria-Hungary to take an aggressive stance in the Balkans.

Serbian Nationalism The French Revolution inspired Serbian and Greek nationalists in the Balkans to seek independence. Following two uprisings, in 1804 and in 1815, Serbia became an autonomous, or self-governing, principality within the Ottoman Empire in 1839. The Congress of Berlin recognized Serbian independence in 1878. Serbian nationalists dreamed of uniting all Slavs of the Balkan Peninsula in one nation, but newly independent Serbia was no match for the older Austro-Hungarian and Ottoman empires. Serbia recognized its weakness on the international stage, leading to the rise of radical nationalist groups. Organizations such as the terrorist group Black Hand called for action against Austria-Hungary in order to free Serbs outside Serbia from Habsburg rule.

The Balkan Wars In 1912 and 1913, two **Balkan Wars** erupted as the Ottoman Empire crumbled. Independent states such as Serbia, Greece, and Bulgaria fought alongside Russia to ensure independence for Ottoman territories in Europe. A month after the end of the First Balkan War, the Second Balkan War began among the former allies because of tensions over the borders created by the peace settlement. Bulgaria was defeated by an alliance of Balkan states. As a result, Bulgaria lost territory and nationalist tensions in the region escalated further.

REFLECT ON THE ESSENTIAL QUESTION

Essential Question: *What factors resulted in Italian unification and German unification?*

Factors in Italian Unification	Factors in German Unification

KEY TERMS

Crimean War	Kaiser Wilhelm II	Dual Alliance	Triple Entente
Victor Emmanuel II	Three Emperors'	Triple Alliance	Balkans
realpolitik	League	Congress of Berlin	Bosnia-Herzegovina
Giuseppe Garibaldi	Reinsurance Treaty	Entente Cordiale	Balkan Wars

---

HISTORICAL PERSPECTIVES: *WHAT CAUSED NATIONALISM?*

For most of human history, people felt their primary loyalty was to the local city or small region where they lived or to a particular monarch who ruled over them. In the past two centuries this changed. People began to identify more with their nation, all the people who shared their basic culture. The nation was larger than a city or region and more general than just one leader. Historians have disagreed on why this change occurred.

The Importance of Culture As liberalism and democracy spread in Europe during the 19th century, French historian Jules Michelet began to write history that focused more on common people than on great leaders. He saw the rise of nationalism as an expression of the demands of masses of people who shared elements of a culture, such as language, religion, ethnicity, and traditions that had existed far back into history. In his view, common people pushed their leaders to either break up or unite states so that cultural and political boundaries matched.

The Importance of Forgetting Another French scholar of the 19th century, Ernest Renan, saw nationalism quite differently. To him, it depended not only on shared history but also on forgetting events that had divided people. For example, before the French Revolution, France was a coalition of various regions and languages. Only after the event did people identify as French and begin to speak the same language. To achieve this, they had to leave behind the religious and regional conflicts that had long divided them.

The Importance of Elites In the 1960s, historians began to focus more on how common people lived and what they felt. They found that the common people—the poor and poorly educated—were not the first advocates of nationalism. Rather, the wealthy and well-educated elites were. They developed an idea of cultural unity and then worked to get others to accept it. In *Imagined Communities* (1983), political scientist and historian Benedict Anderson argued that nations were not natural but created. As they were, they took the place of religion in unifying people. He explained that "the symbolism and fervor of religion was replaced with the nation, and people were willing to make the ultimate sacrifice for their nation." These nation-states had become the key organizing principle of global politics and so ingrained in the understanding of the world that it became nearly impossible to imagine a world without them.

1. Which of these theories of nationalism best describes the unification of Italy? Explain your answer.

2. Which of these theories of nationalism best describes the unification of Germany? Explain your answer.

3. Which of these theories of nationalism best describes the nationalist conflicts that took place in the Balkans? Explain your answer.

MULTIPLE-CHOICE QUESTIONS

Questions 1–3 refer to the passages below.

Passage 1

"The intellectual life of the masses moves within a highly restricted circle of ideas. Of those which they can acquire, the most noble and elevating other than religious ones are the concepts of patriotism and nationality.

If the political circumstances of a country prevent these concepts from being manifest or give them false direction, the masses are plunged into a state of deplorable inferiority. But that is not all; if a people cannot be proud of nationality a feeling of personal dignity exists only incidentally among a few privileged individuals.

The majority, occupying the humblest social positions, needs a feeling of national greatness to acquire a consciousness of their own dignity."

—Count Camillo di Cavour, "On Railroads in Italy," 1846

"Italians! The Sicilians are fighting against the enemies of Italy and for Italy. To help them with money, arms, and especially men, is the duty of every Italian. . . .

A handful of brave men, who have followed me into battle for our country, are advancing with me to the rescue. Italy knows them; they always appear at the hour of danger. Brave and generous companions, they have devoted their lives to their country; they will shed their last drop of blood for it, seeking no other reward than that of a pure conscience."

—General Giuseppe Garibaldi, Italian patriotic leader, 1860

1. Which of the following historical concepts is best reflected in the passages?
   (A) Conservatism because of its emphasis on religion and history
   (B) Nationalism because of its emphasis on people who share a consciousness
   (C) Liberalism because of its emphasis on participation by the mass of people
   (D) Socialism because of its emphasis on economic reform

2. One way in which the ideas of Cavour and Garibaldi differed was over the issue of
   (A) who should lead a new Italy
   (B) what type of government they wanted for Italy
   (C) why they wanted Italian unification
   (D) how Italians should achieve independence

3. Which of the following European countries was most affected because of the work of the authors of these two passages?
   (A) Great Britain
   (B) Germany
   (C) Austria
   (D) Russia

SHORT-ANSWER QUESTION

Answer all parts of the question that follows.

1. a) Describe ONE cause of the Crimean War.
   b) Explain ONE effect of the Crimean War on the Russian Empire.
   c) Explain ONE effect of the Crimean War on the balance of power

Topic 7.4

Darwinism, Social Darwinism

[A]s all organic beings are striving, it may be said, to seize on each place in the economy of nature, if any one species does not become modified and improved in a corresponding degree with its competitors, it will soon be exterminated.

—Charles Darwin, *On the Origin of Species*, 1859

Essential Question: How did Darwin's theories influence scientific and social developments from 1815 to 1914?

During the Enlightenment, scientists viewed the world as stable and orderly. For example, Isaac Newton and others proposed unchanging laws to explain how planets moved. Biologists categorized species. However, the ideas of Charles Darwin undermined this view. His emphasis on gradual but nonstop change in living things caused scientists in all fields to rethink their focus on stability.

Science of Charles Darwin

English naturalist **Charles Darwin** (1809–1882) formulated a bold theory after returning from a voyage around the world in 1837 during which he closely observed geological phenomena and collected specimens, including prehistoric fossils and bones, to take back to England. More than two decades later, he published *On the Origin of Species* (1859), a book stating that species change, or evolve, by a process of **natural selection**—a theory adapted from Thomas Malthus's *Essay on the Principle of Population*. Malthus's essay argued that, as growing populations competed for finite resources, the unfit would be weeded out.

According to Darwin's theory, evolutionary changes occur as a result of struggles for existence and for mating opportunities. Members of a species that have traits which help them survive in a particular environment will have more offspring than members without those traits. Eventually, if those traits are inheritable, all members of the species will be born with them. Darwin's work became the foundation of modern evolutionary studies.

Darwin went on to apply his **theory of evolution** to humans in *The Descent of Man*, published in 1871. In that work, he argued that humans are descended from primate ancestors. This work initially shocked Victorian society by suggesting that animals and humans shared common ancestry. Many Christians thought his ideas about changes in species and shared ancestry went against the teachings of the Bible. However, his focus on evidence rather than religious tradition appealed to the rising class of professional scientists. By the time of his death in 1882, the theory of evolution had spread through all of science, literature, and politics.

Social Darwinism

One of the early advocates of Darwin's theory of evolution was the English sociologist and philosopher **Herbert Spencer** (1820–1903). He is best known today for his doctrine of **Social Darwinism**, which applied Darwin's theories of evolution and natural selection to human societies. Spencer used the phrase **"survival of the fittest"** to describe the struggle of humans in society for existence. Social Darwinism was used to support political conservatism and laissez-faire social and economic policies. Its proponents used the theory to justify class stratification. They believed that wealth was a sign of success, and the upper classes were inherently superior to the lower classes. The poor were poor because they were "unfit," and they should not be helped through charity or government assistance.

Source: Wikimedia Commons

Charles Darwin depicted as an ape in an 1871 cartoon in the British magazine *The Hornet*, with the caption "Venerable Orang-Outang: A Contribution to Unnatural History"

Social Darwinism was also used to justify imperialist and racist policies. Social Darwinists believed in the biological and cultural superiority of people of Anglo-Saxon or "Aryan" descent. They also believed they had a duty to conquer and "civilize" the peoples of Africa and Asia.

Another outgrowth of Social Darwinism was the practice of eugenics, which aimed to improve the human race by eliminating "undesirables." In the 20th century, Adolf Hitler's genocidal Nazi regime would be influenced by both Social Darwinism and eugenics. (See Topic 8.9.)

REFLECT ON THE ESSENTIAL QUESTION

Essential Question: *How did Darwin's theories influence scientific and social developments from 1815 to 1914?*

Darwin's Theories	Influence

Charles Darwin

On the Origin of Species

natural selection

theory of evolution

Herbert Spencer

Social Darwinism

"survival of the fittest"

MULTIPLE-CHOICE QUESTIONS

Questions 1–3 refer to the passage below.

"In demanding from a citizen contributions for the mitigation of distress . . . the state is . . . reversing its function and diminishing that liberty to exercise the faculties which it was instituted to maintain. . . .

Pervading all nature we may see at work a stern discipline, which is a little cruel that it may be very kind. That state of universal warfare maintained throughout the lower creation, to the great perplexity of many worthy people, is at bottom the most merciful provision that the circumstances admit of. . . . The poverty of the incapable, the distresses that come upon the imprudent, the starvation of the idle, and those shoulderings aside of the weak by the strong, which leave so many 'in shallows and in miseries,' are the decrees of a large, farseeing benevolence. It seems hard that an unskillfulness, which with all its efforts he cannot overcome, should entail hunger upon the artisan. It seems hard that a laborer incapacitated by sickness from competing with his stronger fellows, should have to bear the resulting privations. It seems hard that widows and orphans should be left to struggle for life or death.

Nevertheless, when regarded not separately, but in connection with the interests of universal humanity, these harsh fatalities are seen to be full of the highest beneficence—the same beneficence which brings to early graves the children of diseased parents, and singles out the low-spirited, the intemperate, and the debilitated as the victims of an epidemic."

—Herbert Spencer, *Social Statics*, 1851

1. This passage is most closely connected to scientific theories of the late 19th century and early 20th century about which of the following topics?

    (A) Marxist socialism

    (B) Natural selection

    (C) Germs and disease

    (D) Special and general relativity

2. The ideas in this passage most directly contributed to which of the following historical developments?

   (A) Political conservatism because it justified class stratification

   (B) Liberalism because it supported expanding the rights of citizens

   (C) Materialism because treated the human mind as physical matter

   (D) Psychoanalysis because it studied irrational motivations

3. Which of the following thinkers provided the most likely claims that people could use to support Spencer's argument?

   (A) John Locke because of what he wrote about how people formed social contracts

   (B) Adam Smith because of what he wrote about how individuals made economic decisions

   (C) Karl Marx because of what he wrote about how the bourgeoisies treated the proletariat

   (D) Victor Hugo because of what he wrote about how society treated individuals

SHORT-ANSWER QUESTION

Use the table below to answer all parts of the question that follows.

EUROPEAN TRANSLATIONS OF *ON THE ORIGIN OF SPECIES*			
Year	Language	Year	Language
1860	German	1872	Danish
1860	Dutch	1873	Polish
1862	French	1873	Hungarian
1864	Italian	1877	Spanish
1864	Russian	1878	Serbian
1871	Swedish		

1. a) Describe ONE claim about spread of scientific ideas in Europe between 1859 and 1878.

   b) Describe ONE claim about common traits among the first countries where *On the Origins of Species* was translated.

   c) Explain ONE way in which *On the Origins of Species* demonstrated continuity with Enlightenment thinkers.

Topic 7.5

Age of Progress and Modernity

We are living at a period of most wonderful transition, . . . [T]he realisation of the unity of mankind. . . . [T]he Exhibition of 1851 is to give us a true test of the point of development at which the whole of mankind has arrived in this great task, and a new starting point from which all nations will be able to direct their further exertions.

—Prince Albert of Great Britain on the Great Exhibition of 1851,
published in *The Illustrated London News*, 1849

Essential Question: How did science and other intellectual disciplines develop and change from 1815 to 1914?

By the middle of the 19th century, Great Britain was the most powerful nation on Earth. It had been spared the political upheavals of 1848, and Queen Victoria and her husband, Prince Albert, wanted to celebrate peace, progress, and the wonders of industry. Prince Albert chaired a royal commission to plan the exhibition, which would not just showcase British achievements but also include technological and scientific marvels from around the world. Among the exhibits were the mechanical looms that had revolutionized the textile industry, electric clocks, gas ranges, a submarine, and oddities like a kite-drawn carriage. Proceeds from the exhibition funded the creation of several London museums and still provide technical fellowships to British students. The exhibition attracted more than six million people from around the world and inspired future world's fairs.

Materialism in Philosophy, Science, and Economics

Romantic and liberal ideas inspired antimonarchical revolutions across Europe in 1848. The failure of the uprisings to replace royal authority is reflected in the name often given to the period from 1837 to 1901. In the English-speaking world, it is known as the **Victorian era**, after Queen Victoria of England, whose reign spanned these years.

Throughout the Victorian era, the concept of matter changed in the face of evolutionism, realism, and empiricism—the idea that all knowledge comes from sensory experience. **Materialism** is the philosophy that everything—including the human mind and consciousness—is matter, or inert substance. Materialism is closely related to **physicalism**, which acknowledges the fact that physics has shown that not everything is matter, but that there are forces such as gravity that are physical but not material in the usual sense of the word.

Positivism

The philosophy of **positivism** holds that science alone provides knowledge. It emphasizes the rational and scientific analysis of nature and human affairs. It is based on two principles:

- Knowledge of facts is based on sensory experience, not on intuition.
- Pure logic and pure mathematics exist beyond the realm of fact.

While hints of positivism can be seen in ancient philosophy and in some works of medieval European thought, the roots of positivism lie most clearly in the Enlightenment, with its clear focus on reason. Frenchman **Auguste Comte** (1798–1857) is recognized as the founder of positivism and as one of the founders of sociology.

Modernism in Intellectual and Cultural Life

Realism (see Topic 7.8) was most influential during the Victorian era, a period of strict morals and social conventions. In reaction to these limits, the modernist movement embraced industrialization, social change, and scientific advancement. **Modernism** rejected all traditional belief systems and moral codes as hypocritical or outdated. Modernists believed that individuals needed to free themselves of such restrictive baggage.

Because of new scientific discoveries and technological developments, the world was changing quickly and many people in society struggled to keep up. Because cultural change was constant, modernists did not want to commit to any system that would stifle their creativity. As science and technology changed the way people looked at themselves and the world, modernists pioneered new ideas in psychology and political theory. Their goal was to move beyond the realists' strict interpretations of the world around them to find less-literal modes of expression.

Philosophy

The philosophy of **irrationalism** moved beyond rational interpretations of humans and their surroundings to focus instead on their impulses. Irrationalists believed that conflict and struggle led to progress and suggested that life be explained not only by the rational methods of science but also by the spirit. Irrationalism explored humans' biological roots through evolution:

- **Friedrich Nietzsche** (1844–1900) was a German philosopher who questioned the fundamental cultural values of Western philosophy and morality. He influenced a wide range of artists and politicians with his examination of the ways in which individuals can lead meaningful lives. One focus of Nietzsche's thought was that of nihilism, which he used to describe decay of the traditional moral structure of European society.

- **Georges Sorel** (1847–1922) was a French philosopher who argued that social change required revolutionary action. Sorel was a "syndicalist"—a believer in the overthrow of church and state, replacing them with a government based on labor unions or "syndicats."
- **Henri Bergson** (1859–1941) was a French philosopher who emphasized change and evolution. He inspired a group of thinkers known as process metaphysicians who rejected established values and embraced the ideas of change and evolution in society.

Natural and Social Sciences

Developments in the natural sciences such as quantum mechanics and Einstein's theory of relativity undermined the physics of Isaac Newton as an objective way to describe nature. Modernist scientists placed human thought and presence at the center of their practices.

Sigmund Freud Austrian neurologist **Sigmund Freud** (1856–1939) was the founder of **psychoanalysis**, a therapeutic technique related to the study of the unconscious mind. Freud's work helped create psychology as an independent discipline, separate from either philosophy or neurology. Psychoanalysis led to investigations of human behavior that gradually revealed the need for more subtle methods of analysis. Freud delved into the human psyche through dream analysis, talk therapy, and hypnosis, and he wrote about the power of irrational motivations and humans' ongoing struggle between the conscious and subconscious parts of their minds.

Albert Einstein No figure looms larger on the 20th-century scientific scene than does **Albert Einstein** (1879–1945). Thought a failure by many as a young man, Einstein went on to produce some of the most stunning and important theories in the history of physics, if not science altogether. His theories of special relativity (1905) and general relativity (1915) forever redefined how people understand the elements and forces that make up and control the universe: space, time, gravity, energy, and matter.

Max Planck In the 1800s, scientists noticed that the colors of light radiated by hot objects did not always match those predicted by classical theories of thermodynamics. The German physicist **Max Planck** (1858–1947) came up with a way to match the theory with observations. He suggested that only certain amounts of energy, known as quanta, could be given off rather than all the values of energy that were possible, as classical physics predicted. Planck's idea is known as quantum theory. It revolutionized human understanding of atomic and subatomic processes. The practical application of the quantum theory is known as **quantum mechanics**, and it is behind many things people take for granted, including semiconductor-based electronics (computers, smartphones, cars, and appliances), lasers, atomic clocks, the Global Positioning System (GPS), and magnetic resonance imaging (MRI).

Essential Question: *How did science and other intellectual disciplines develop and change from 1815 to 1914?*

Development	Impact of Development

KEY TERMS

Victorian era	modernism	Sigmund Freud
materialism	irrationalism	psychoanalysis
physicalism	Friedrich Nietzsche	Albert Einstein
positivism	Georges Sorel	Max Planck
Auguste Comte	Henri Bergson	quantum mechanics

MULTIPLE-CHOICE QUESTIONS

Questions 1–3 refer to the passage below.

"To examine the effects of violence it is necessary to start from its long-term consequences and not from its immediate results. . . .

We have the right to conclude from this that [union-related] violence, perpetrated in the course of strikes by proletarians who desire the overthrow of the State, must not be confused with the acts of savagery. . . .

The immense successes obtained by industrial civilization ha[ve] created the belief that, in the near future, happiness will be produced automatically for everybody. . . .

The optimist in politics is an inconstant and even dangerous man, because he takes no account of the great difficulties presented by his projects; . . . He frequently thinks that small reforms of the political system and, above all, of government personnel will be sufficient to direct the movement of society in such a way as to mitigate those evils of the modern world which seem so hideous to sensitive souls. Yet men who are participating in great social movements always picture their coming action in the form of images of battle in which their cause is certain to triumph."

—Georges Sorel, *Reflections on Violence*, 1908

1. Which of the following best identifies Sorel's point of view about the role of violence in transforming society?
   (A) Proletariat strikes that attempt to overthrow the government are justifiable.
   (B) Acts of savagery that might seem hideous to sensitive people will slow down change.
   (C) Automatic changes without violence will gradually make people happier.
   (D) Changing government personnel is the most important step.

2. This passage best demonstrates which of the following historical developments?
   (A) Physicalism because it emphasizes material rather than spiritual factors
   (B) Positivism because it emphasizes logic and science
   (C) Modernism because it emphasizes individual freedom rather than restrictions
   (D) Irrationalism because it emphasizes spirit and impulse

3. This passage expresses an approach to understanding the world that is most similar to that of
   (A) Enlightenment thinkers
   (B) conservative politicians
   (C) Marxist revolutionaries
   (D) women's suffrage advocates

Use the passage below to answer all parts of the question that follows.

"In order to explain properly the true nature and peculiar character of the positive philosophy, it is indispensable that we should first take a brief survey of the progressive growth of the human mind as whole; for no idea can be properly understood apart from its history. . . . Each branch of our knowledge passes in succession through three different theoretical states: the theological or fictious state, the metaphysical or abstract state, and the scientific or positive state. . . .

In the theological state, the human mind directs its researches mainly toward the inner nature of beings. . . . It therefore represents these phenomena as being produced by the direct and continuous action of more or less numerous supernatural agents. . . .

In the metaphysical state, which is in reality only a simple general modification of the first state, the supernatural agents are replaced by abstract forces, real entities, or personified abstractions inherent in the different beings of the world. . . .

Finally, in the positive state, the human mind, recognizing the impossibility of obtaining absolute truth, gives up the search after the origin and hidden causes of the universe and a knowledge of the final causes of phenomena. It endeavors now only to discover, by a well-combined use of reasoning and observation, the actual laws of phenomena—that is to say, their invariable relations of succession and likeness. The explanation of facts, thus reduced to its real terms, consists henceforth only in the connection established between different particular phenomena and some general facts, the number of which the progress of science tends more and more to diminish."

—Auguste Comte, *Introduction to Positivism*, c. 1851

1. a) Describe the historical context in which Comte wrote this passage.

   b) Explain how ONE person, idea, or development in the 18th and 19th centuries could be used as evidence to support Comte's claim in this passage.

   c) Explain how ONE person, idea, or development in the 18th and 19th centuries could be used as evidence to refute Comte's claim in this passage.

Topic 7.6

New Imperialism: Motivations and Methods

Gentlemen, we must speak more loudly and more honestly! We must say openly that indeed the higher races have a right over the lower races. . . . I repeat, that the superior races have a right because they have a duty. They have the duty to civilize the inferior races. . . .

—French Premier Jules Ferry, "On French Colonial Expansion," speech to French Chamber of Deputies, 1884

Essential Question: What were the motivations and technological advances that helped advance European imperialism from 1815 to 1914?

At the beginning of the **Age of Imperialism**, expansion by European powers into Asia and Africa increased global tensions. During the Berlin Conference of 1884–1885 (see Topic 7.7), the European powers established guidelines for the "carving up" of Africa for colonization. Germany's Otto von Bismarck had called the conference to maintain peace and stability among the European powers. Bismarck's role as a broker for stability eventually led to his dismissal in 1890 by Kaiser Wilhelm II. The kaiser sought a more aggressive foreign policy than Bismarck desired.

European nations and businesses also sought access to raw materials and new markets in Asia. By the turn of the 20th century, colonial exploitation, global markets, and resistance movements created increased tensions throughout the world while European countries established new colonial empires.

Motives of Imperialism in Africa and Asia

The Industrial Revolution had a dramatic impact on Europe's economy. Industrialized powers desired access to raw materials such as oil, diamonds, rubber, and manganese (which was used in steel production) to enrich their merchants and fuel their factories. They also desired new markets in which to sell their mass-produced goods. In the 19th century, imperialist European states competed with each other to control Africa and Asia in order to obtain resources and sell finished products.

Search for Raw Materials and Markets

As colonies in North America and South America sought and acquired their independence, European governments and capitalists focused on new territories in Asia and Africa. They provided Europeans with access to needed natural resources, labor, markets to sell their manufactured goods, and sources for investment to improve infrastructure, such as building railroads.

Trade with China Since the 18th century, European powers had been trading in Asia. In China, they hoped to create a favorable **balance of trade**—a total value of exports greater than the value of imports—in order to gain fair prices on Chinese goods such as tea, silk, and porcelain. Tea accounted for 60 percent of England's trade with China. However, the British produced no goods that the Chinese wanted to buy, making it difficult to achieve a favorable balance of trade. But then the British began smuggling the addictive drug opium from India into China in the early 1800s. Chinese leaders protested, but the British defended their actions on the principle of free trade. When a Chinese official destroyed a large quantity of opium seized from British traders, the British started the Opium War against the Chinese. The British won the war, and the Chinese were forced to accept the following terms in the Treaty of Nanking in August of 1842:

- The British took control of Hong Kong, which lasted until 1997.
- China opened five ports of trade to the British.
- China compensated Britain with $21 million in silver.

From this point on, China gradually became more and more accessible to European powers. While China became a vital market to Europeans, many Chinese never forgave their government for failing to protect them from the opium trade. China's humiliating defeat in the Opium War would contribute to what was known as the Boxer Rebellion, an unsuccessful uprising against European imperialism in the late 1890s, and to the overthrow of the Qing Dynasty in 1911.

England in India Following the Seven Years' War, the British East India Company acquired sole rights to trade in India. In 1857, Indians rebelled unsuccessfully against British dominance in the Sepoy Rebellion. The British government then took direct control of India in order to protect this vital territory, allowing Britain to profit greatly from the export of India's tea, indigo, coffee, cotton, and opium. Moreover, with more than 300 million Indian subjects, the British were able to sell manufactured goods to the Indian people, creating additional profit for Great Britain. While Britain exploited India's natural resources and subjects, it also invested in railroad construction and increased access to education for the people of India.

Looking to Africa For centuries, Europeans had considered Africa south of the Sahara to be something of a mystery because they lacked accurate maps and knowledge of the interior. Attempts to colonize Africa failed because of the prevalence of diseases such as malaria and sleeping sickness. The British and Dutch began to explore Africa in the 19th century. By 1914, Europeans controlled all of Africa except Liberia and Ethiopia. (See Topic 7.7.) They used Africans as poorly paid miners or farm workers. In central Africa, King Leopold II of Belgium used the Congolese as slave labor.

Myths of Cultural and Racial Superiority

As the European powers expanded into Africa and Asia, imperialists justified this expansion and subjugation by claiming cultural and racial superiority. Europeans believed they were civilizing the world by spreading their Western ideals to "less-developed" peoples. Europeans assumed that other cultures were less civilized.

The White Man's Burden   In the late 19th century, Herbert Spencer, a British sociologist and anthropologist, began applying, however incorrectly, Darwin's principles of evolution to social groups. Spencer used Darwin's idea of "survival of the fittest" in comparing cultures. Spencer stressed that different ethnicities and classes had progressed to be more advanced and sophisticated than others. This idea, called Social Darwinism (see Topic 7.4), provided European nations with the rationale that they were actually *helping* less-developed Asian and African peoples by colonizing them.

Rudyard Kipling, a British subject living in India, exemplified this attitude in his poem **"The White Man's Burden"** in 1899. Kipling described the native people as "half-devil and half-child," insisting that European powers must "Send forth the best ye breed" to end famine, laziness, and disease in less-developed parts of the world.

THE SURVIVAL OF THE FITTEST.

Source: Getty Images

The creator of this drawing suggested that over time, Darwinism would make people taller, smarter, and more attractive.

Mission Civilisatrice Imperialists stressed that the colonization of Africa and Asia was a civilizing mission, as Europeans spread the ideals of Western nations across the world. The French term *mission civilisatrice*, meaning "the civilizing mission," was not a new concept. It had been employed in the Age of Exploration and supported during the Enlightenment. Europeans stressed the importance of indoctrinating indigenous peoples around the world to accept Western ideals of religion and government.

For example, the French, under the leadership of Jules Ferry, wanted to civilize France's West African colonies by teaching Christianity, requiring people to speak French, and encouraging the adoption of French fashion. The French colonial administration hoped that if African people adopted French culture, they would also share French values about equality and liberty.

While initially occupied with West Africa, the French government also saw an opportunity to colonize Southeast Asia. This region, heavily influenced by Indian and Chinese culture, was known as Indochina. Today, it includes the countries of Southeast Asia.

Technological and Industrial Developments

As the second half of the 19th century progressed, technological and industrial developments in Europe aided the expansion of global empires. In particular, during the second industrial revolution (see Topic 6.3), Europeans acquired the technological tools and scientific means to more effectively establish empires in Asia and Africa.

Military Technologies

While European powers possessed smaller armies than native peoples, they were able to conquer large amounts of land because of developments in weaponry and medicine.

Advances in Weaponry Military technology gave relatively small European armies the ability to conquer vast territories that were home to huge populations which used comparatively primitive weaponry. Europeans' technology allowed for the use of less manpower and fewer economic resources in the process of building global empires. There were two important phases in this revolution in weaponry:

- The muzzle-loading musket was upgraded to a rifled barrel—a spiraled barrel, spinning the bullet and thus creating greater accuracy. These new rifles used a **Minié ball**. Invented in 1849, this oblong bullet improved accuracy and had greater range.

- Two new weapons—the **breech-loading rifle** (or breechloader) and the **machine gun**—increased firing speed and accuracy. The breechloader was faster and easier to load than the musket. By the 1870s, one model could fire ten shots consecutively. By the 1880s, a model of the British-made Maxim machine gun could fire 500 rounds per minute.

Source: Getty Images

The development of weapons such as the Maxim gun made war more deadly than previously. The British used it widely in colonial conflicts.

Medical Technologies

In the 19th century, medical science expanded rapidly as scientists employed the scientific method and research to develop new medicines and medical procedures. European nations also enacted public health initiatives to prevent diseases and reduce the mortality rate.

Public Health Projects The Industrial Revolution was accompanied by a decline in the health and welfare of workers. As cities grew, death rates soared. In Great Britain, the Public Health Act of 1848 created a General Board of Health. It was responsible for protecting the health of the public through education and the removal or prevention of causes of disease. Local boards were responsible for regulating sewage and the disposal of refuse and for maintaining a safe water supply. The French focused on using scientific methods to identify, treat, and control infectious diseases. In Germany, hygiene emerged as an experimental laboratory science.

European powers introduced new health services in their colonies, although colonial health care and public health measures were often put in place primarily to meet the needs of the colonial regimes and their armies. In many cases, town jails doubled as hospitals for the native population, and racism sometimes led Europeans to conduct dangerous and unethical medical experiments on natives. Europeans tended to disparage native medical practices. Christian missionaries often provided medical services to natives.

Advances in Medical Care Research by **Louis Pasteur** (1822–1895) and **Joseph Lister** (1827–1912) was groundbreaking. Pasteur was a French chemist and one of the founders of medical microbiology. He formulated the **germ theory** of fermentation and disease, which held that both were caused by microorganisms. This led, in turn, to the development of pasteurization to kill germs in foods and beverages and of vaccines against rabies and anthrax. Lister was a British surgeon and medical scientist. He began to look for the cause of "hospital disease," which caused nearly 50 percent of people who had limb amputations die as a result of infections. His research led him to believe that these infections were caused by contamination, and he used Pasteur's germ theory to formulate rules for **antiseptic** surgery. As a result, mortality rates plummeted.

The development of **anesthesia** helped reduce the trauma of surgery. The British chemist Sir Humphrey Davy suggested in 1798 that gases such as nitrous oxide could be used to relieve pain during surgery. It was not until the 1840s that American doctors began using ether during surgery and childbirth. When England's Queen Victoria gave birth to Prince Leopold in 1853, she was administered ether to alleviate the pain. After that, women lobbied for pain-free deliveries.

Advances in medical care had an important impact on military power. They allowed European militaries to vaccinate troops and provide a safer surgical environment for injured soldiers. Microbiology thus decreased battlefield mortality rates, which made the military more efficient.

Preventing Malaria In Africa, the disease **malaria** had prevented Europeans from exploring the interior of the continent—limiting exploration and trade to coastal areas. While dysentery and yellow fever also contributed to European mortality, malaria was the primary disease that killed Europeans. In the 19th century, French scientists discovered a treatment for malaria by extracting **quinine** from the bark of a tree found in South America. With the mass production of the medicine, Europeans were able to enter the African interior without fear of contracting malaria. Medical science provided European explorers and capitalists with the biological tools to exploit the African interior.

Improving Communication and Transportation

As their colonial empires expanded across Asia and Africa, Europeans developed innovations in communication and transportation, allowing them greater access to colonial territories.

Advances in Transportation Technology

To improve access to colonial possessions, European powers increased their speed and navigation with the railroad and steamship. The steamship gave European soldiers, explorers, and capitalists the ability to travel up and down rivers without relying on wind or currents. Macgregor Laird, a British explorer and proponent of steam power, noted, "By his [James Watt's] invention every river is laid open to us, time and distance are shortened." Over time, European powers armed the steam-powered boats, turning them into gunboats.

Expanding Railroads Once European powers acquired colonial possessions, they invested time and money into building infrastructure—in particular, railroads. Railroads allowed Europeans to create rapid transportation networks within colonial territories in order to move raw materials and resources to ports more quickly. In India, the British Empire built 22,000 miles of railroad. In Africa, the railroad allowed Europeans to connect rivers and lakes with a clear transportation route. By 1907, the industrial powers had built 168,000 miles of railroad tracks beyond Europe and the United States.

Opening the Suez Canal Europeans had begun using canals to connect waterways in the early 19th century. In 1869, the Suez Canal opened, connecting the Mediterranean Sea with the Red Sea and Indian Ocean. European ships no longer needed to travel around Africa to gain access to Asian ports. Instead, a three-day trip through the Suez Canal shortened the voyage to India by more than 5,000 miles, allowing easier movement of goods and troops.

Advances in Communication Technology

The **telegraph** and undersea cable transformed European communications with their colonial empires. In the early 19th century, people used the system of "dashes" and "dots" known as Morse code (see Topic 6.3) to transmit messages by telegraph over long distances. While the telegraph was initially used only across land, European and American capitalists and inventors developed undersea cables to communicate across bodies of water such as the Atlantic Ocean. By the 1860s, people on the European continent could communicate relatively rapidly with their counterparts in North America, and by 1890, Great Britain could communicate with all of its Asian and African colonies. A sender could relay a message from India to England in only five hours. European powers had nearly "instant" communication with their colonies.

The first practical means of capturing photographic image (the daguerreotype process), developed in France in 1839. By the end of that year, photographs of famous monuments in Egypt, Israel, Greece, and elsewhere were available for purchase. By the 1840s, photographers were following imperial administrators and armies to European colonies, where they photographed "exotic" native leaders, landscapes, and buildings. The camera became indispensable in cataloging colonial possessions and the civilizing mission that helped justify colonial rule. Photographs were used to contrast "civilized" Europeans and "uncivilized" natives as a tool to justify racist policies. But they were also used by international activists to document atrocities, such as those committed by Leopold II's regime in the Congo, to bring about reforms.

REFLECT ON THE ESSENTIAL QUESTION

Essential Question: *What were the motivations and technological advances that helped advance European imperialism from 1815 to 1914?*

Motivations	Technological Advances

Age of Imperialism   breech-loading rifle   antiseptic
balance of trade   machine gun   anesthesia
"The White Man's Burden"   Louis Pasteur   malaria
mission civilisatrice   Joseph Lister   quinine
Minié ball   germ theory   telegraph

MULTIPLE-CHOICE QUESTIONS

Questions 1–3 refer to the image below.

Georges Dascher, "The French Colonies," the front page
of a French school notebook, c. 1900

1. Which of the following led most directly to the spread of ideas such as those represented in the image?

(A) The desire to share the ideals of the French Revolution

(B) The influence of Romantic writers and artists

(C) The beliefs of Jesuit missionaries who wanted to teach about Roman Catholicism

(D) The competition among countries for markets during the second industrial revolution

2. Which of the following 19th century theorists would be most likely to support the ideas expressed in the image?

(A) John Stuart Mill

(B) Karl Marx

(C) Herbert Spencer

(D) Charles Darwin

3. The artist's purpose in drawing this image was to emphasize that France's colonial subjects generally

(A) invited the French to rule over them

(B) benefited from adopting aspects of French culture

(C) shared many cultural traits with other French colonies

(D) opposed French rule with violent resistance

SHORT-ANSWER QUESTION

Use the passage below to answer all parts of the question that follows.

"Owing to greatly increased and cheaper supplies of the cinchona-bark, from which quinine is extracted, and to the employment of new and more economical processes, by which more quinine can be made in from three to five days than could be in twenty under the old system, the markets of the world in recent years have been overwhelmed with supplies of this article, and its price has declined in a most rapid and extraordinary manner. . . .

But recently the large manufacturers in Europe have made an arrangement to put up quinine (pills) protected by gelatin, and introduce and offer it so cheaply in the East Indies and other tropical countries, as to induce its extensive consumption on the part of a vast population inhabiting malarious districts which has hitherto been deprived of the use of this valuable specific by reason of its costliness."

—David Wells, "The Economic Outlook—Present and Prospective,"
The Popular Science Monthly, March 1888

1. a) Explain ONE way that the Industrial Revolution influenced the production of quinine.

   b) Explain ONE way that the change in the production of quinine influenced imperialism.

   c) Explain the point of view of the author of this passage toward imperialism.

Topic 7.7

Imperialism's Global Effects

What the partial occupation of his soil by the white man has failed to do;

what the mapping out of European political "spheres of influence" has failed to do;

what the Maxim [machine gun] and the rifle, the slave gang, labour in the bowels of the earth and the lash, have failed to do;

what imported measles, smallpox and syphilis have failed to do;

whatever the overseas slave trade failed to do,

the power of modern capitalistic exploitation, assisted by modern engines of destruction, may yet succeed in accomplishing.

—E. D. Morel, *The Black Man's Burden*, 1903

Essential Question: How did imperialism affect European and non-European societies?

In his 1920 book *The Black Man's Burden*, the British journalist E. D. Morel drew attention to the abuses of imperialism in Africa. The worst atrocities were carried out in the Congo Free State, a colony owned personally by Belgium's King Leopold II. Leopold created a private army made up of African soldiers under European officers to carry out the ruthless exploitation of the Congolese people. Families were kidnapped and the men were forced to work in mines or plantations to enrich the Belgian king. Failure to do so could mean mutilation or even death. The army slaughtered the families of those who rebelled and burned their villages. Over 23 years, the Congo's population declined from an estimated 20 million to 8 million.

Imperial Tensions and Debate

Imperial conquest affected European society and diplomacy by increasing domestic and international tensions. While diplomacy initially allowed for the "peaceful carving up" of Africa, over time, imperialism strained relations between the European powers. In Europe, critics began to question the ethics and economic value of imperialism, while writers other influential people challenged the effects on indigenous poulations.

National Rivalry

The Industrial Revolution that began in Great Britain spread to Belgium in the early 19th century, to France by mid-century, and to Germany after unification in 1871. Rivalries among European nations fostered imperial competition as a result of industrialization as the great powers of Europe competed for markets and fought for strategic locations that offered human capital (workers), geographic advantages, and natural resources. In particular, there was intense imperial competition between Great Britain, France, and Germany (after Kaiser Wilhelm II dismissed his chancellor Bismarck) for territories in Asia and Africa.

The Berlin Conference In 1884–1885, Otto von Bismarck of Germany hosted the **Berlin Conference** to ensure the peaceful expansion of European powers into Africa. As industrialized European nations sought the natural resources available in Africa, tensions mounted among European nations such as Belgium, Great Britain, and France because each nation wanted valuable land in Africa. This competition became known as the **"Scramble for Africa."**

Bismarck, considered an honest broker with little interest in African territory for Germany, negotiated a peaceful and orderly conference to divide up the African continent. Bismarck sought stability in order to consolidate German strength and keep France from forming threatening alliances.

CURRENT NAMES OF FORMERLY COLONIZED AFRICAN COUNTRIES	
Imperial Power	**Countries Today**
Great Britain	• Egypt • Sudan • Nigeria • Zimbabwe • South Africa
France	• Algeria • Morocco • Niger • Mali
Germany	• Namibia • Tanzania
Portugal	• Angola • Mozambique
Belgium	• Congo
Italy	• Somalia

During a series of meetings in Berlin, the leaders of the European powers peaceably agreed to colonial boundaries and trade arrangements in Africa. In addition, the powers agreed to the free movement of goods on Africa's major rivers such as the Niger River and the Congo River.

Nationalistic Motives With more than 11 million square miles of territory, Great Britain possessed the largest empire in the world by the beginning of the 20th century. Britain had acquired valuable territory in strategic locations such as India, Egypt, and South Africa. Despite its power, Britain faced competition from the French and Germans for overseas power:

- During the Scramble for Africa, France had solidified its claims on most of West Africa. In addition, it acquired large parts of North Africa, which contained vital natural resources such as iron ore and petroleum.

- At the Berlin Conference, Bismarck negotiated for territory on the east and west coasts of Africa. Germany exploited the mining industry in German South West Africa (Namibia), while German East Africa (Tanganyika, or most of present-day Tanzania) blocked Britain's hopes of creating a railroad from Cairo, Egypt, to Cape Town, South Africa.

As each European power became stronger, tension over the control of colonies increased. In particular, Germany began to threaten Britain's dominance. Germany was rapidly building its industrial base. This made it more dependent on international trade and a stronger potential military foe. In addition, after Kaiser Wilhelm II dismissed Bismarck in 1890, Germany adopted a more aggressive foreign policy.

The Pan-German League As you learned in Topic 7.3, there were two choices for German unification—*grossdeutsch* and *kleindeutsch*, and Bismarck chose the *kleindeutsch* approach. Supporters of the *grossdeutsch* approach wanted to include Austria in the new German nation. Some advocated including all speakers of Germanic dialects, including Dutch and Flemish, even going so far as to suggest including the Scandinavians. Many supporters of the *grossdeutsch* approach considered German or Nordic people to comprise a superior "Aryan" race. In 1894, Ernst Hasse, a professor and member of the Reichstag, or parliament, organized the **Pan-German League**. The league had two main goals:

- raise German nationalist consciousness
- promote German expansion in Europe

The Pan-Germanism did not only appeal to Germans, but also to German-speaking people outside Germany. Supporters of the Pan-German League in Austria-Hungary, for example, attacked Jews and Slavs, as well as capitalism. The ideas of the Pan-German League would greatly influence Adolf Hitler.

Diplomatic Tensions Increase

In spite of the agreements struck at the Berlin Conference, diplomatic tensions among Great Britain, France, and Germany had become strained. These strains resulted in conflicts in Sudan and Morocco.

Fashoda Crisis In 1898, British-French tensions escalated in Africa over railroads. France wanted rail lines to unify an African empire from the Niger River in West Africa to the Nile River in East Africa. Britain wanted to create a railroad network from Cairo, Egypt, to Cape Town, South Africa.

The two great powers came into conflict in Fashoda, Sudan, in what became known as the **Fashoda Crisis**. There, British and French colonial authorities disputed the ownership of the territory, and both nations sent military forces into the region. Within a few days, France withdrew its military and conceded the territory to Britain, recognizing the strength of Great Britain's military as well as the need for a strong European ally in future wars, given the increasing competition from Germany. In 1904, France and Britain agreed to the Entente Cordiale (see Topic 7.3), recognizing French and British colonial territories and formally acknowledging the British-French friendship.

Moroccan Crises Tension between Germany and France escalated over a territorial dispute in **Morocco**. Since the 19th century, France had wanted to control North African territories, as evidenced by their acquisitions at the 1884 Berlin Conference. As part of the 1904 Entente Cordiale, Britain recognized France's sphere of influence in Morocco, and France recognized Great Britain's sphere of influence in Egypt. A **sphere of influence** is an area of control over a foreign territory, often for commercial purposes.

Germany disliked the British-French agreement and in 1905 and 1911, supported Moroccan rebellions against French rule. The crisis ended with Morocco becoming a *protectorate*—a country that is controlled and protected by a more powerful country—of France. The dispute over Morocco did not bring war, since Germany did not have the support of its allies, while France had backing from Britain. However, tensions between Germany and France intensified as a result of the conflict, further strengthening the alliance between France and Britain.

Debates over Colonial Acquisition

While many Europeans supported imperialism, disagreements about it affected European society and culture while writers and artists debated the necessity and ethics of colonial empires. Writers like Joseph Conrad and E. D. Morel documented the mistreatment of Africans and questioned the morality of imperialism. J. A. Hobson and Vladimir Lenin wrote about and debated the economic viability of imperialism.

Joseph Conrad While European capitalists and governments benefited from the new markets and abundance of raw materials, others debated the ethics of imperialism. In the 1890s, novelist **Joseph Conrad** (1857–1924) visited the Congo, at that time under the personal control of King Leopold

II of Belgium, and witnessed the harsh realities of imperialism. In 1899, he published the novella *Heart of Darkness* depicting the immoral treatment of the Congolese by Leopold's private army. Conrad described how European colonizers abused and starved the native peoples of Africa.

E. D. Morel At the same time, **Edmund D. Morel** (1873–1924), a shipping clerk in England, recognized unethical trading practices in the Congo. The Berlin Conference had set the rules for the Congo as a "free trade" region, yet Morel discovered the Belgians were shipping large amounts of illegal military supplies. After further investigation, Morel noted that Belgian capitalists were stripping the Congolese of their economic autonomy by restricting free trade and abolishing fair wages. In 1902, Morel made his first public speech on the mistreatment of the Congolese.

The Congo Reform Association In 1904, Morel founded the **Congo Reform Association (CRA)** with the financial backing of the Quaker and chocolate entrepreneur William Cadbury. He recruited many notable authors and political and religious leaders in Europe and the United States, including Joseph Conrad, Sir Arthur Conan Doyle, Mark Twain, Booker T. Washington, Anatole France, and Roger Casement. The CRA exposed the brutality of King Leopold II's regime to the world through publications and Lantern Lectures that featured photographs by Alice Seely Harris, an English missionary and early documentary photographer. Their efforts to inform the public led to widespread indignation in Europe and the United States, eventually forcing Leopold to transfer the Congo to the Belgian government in 1908. The Congo Reform Association led the way for future human rights organizations, including Amnesty International and Human Rights Watch.

John Hobson While figures such as Conrad and Morel objected to imperialism from an ethical standpoint, some economists criticized imperialism because they believed it was not a profitable or sound economic policy. In 1902, British economist **John A. Hobson** (1858–1940) published *Imperialism: A Study*, arguing that imperialism "jeopardized the entire wealth of the nation" and insisting that imperialism made the European economy dependent on unstable markets. Moreover, Hobson believed that imperialism required European nations to invest in foreign infrastructure as well as spend larger amounts on the military. Hobson thus believed that imperialism was not beneficial in the long run for European powers.

Vladimir Lenin While Hobson outlined the detrimental economic effects of imperialism on capitalist nations, **Vladimir Lenin** (1870–1924) stressed philosophical arguments against imperialism. Lenin declared that imperialism was "the monopoly stage of capitalism." As a prominent Communist Party leader in Russia in the early 20th century, Lenin wanted to expose the exploitation of colonized people. In his essay "Imperialism, the Highest Stage of Capitalism," Lenin insisted that European nations plundered the world for their own self-interest and that imperialism would inspire a global revolution against capitalism.

Colonial Challenges to Imperialism

While imperialism had both positive and negative effects on the colonizing European nations, they were not the only regions affected by change. Asian and African nations may have benefited to some extent from modernized societies and economies, but not without a wide range of devastating and long-lasting repercussions. Nationalist movements in colonized regions challenged European imperialism and sought self-determination with varying degrees of success.

Resistance in Africa

African nations and localized groups experienced varied levels of success as they resisted European imperialism. In the case of the Zulus, their attempts to rebel against the British eventually failed, while Ethiopians defeated Italian troops.

Zulu Resistance In 1843, the British occupied Natal and Zululand in Southern Africa. **Zulu** miners there worked in Britain's profitable diamond mines. In 1872, the leader of the Zulu people decided to resist British rule and organized 40,000 men into a disciplined army. The British demanded the Zulus disarm, but by 1879, when the Zulus continued to maintain a defensive posture, the British sent in military personnel to suppress the rebellion. Initially, the British suffered defeats by the native forces, but after six months, the British forced a Zulu surrender. By the end of the century, Great Britain formally annexed Natal and Zululand, and Zulu resistance to British imperialism ended.

Ethiopia Resists Successfully The East African nation of **Ethiopia** represents one of the most successful attempts to resist European imperialism in Africa. The emperor of Ethiopia recognized that European nations, especially Italy, wanted to control East Africa. To ensure that Ethiopia could defend itself, the emperor purchased modern weapons such as rifles from France and Russia, which profited from the sale of these weapons. However, Italy claimed Ethiopia as a protectorate, and Italian troops began to occupy parts of the region. Ethiopia declared war on Italy. At the Battle of Adwa (1896), Ethiopian forces defeated the Italian troops, leading to Italy's eventual withdrawal. Ethiopia maintained its independence into the 20th century.

Resistance in Asia

Similar to nations in Africa, Asian nations resisted European imperialism, most notably in India and China. Japan represented one of the few successful efforts to prevent European occupation through imitation of Western modernization.

Sepoy Rebellion and the Congress Party Since the 1600s, the British East India Company had operated profitable trading ports in India. The Industrial Revolution made India especially important to the British economy because India provided raw materials such as cotton for British factories. India also provided markets for British manufactured goods. India was the Jewel in the Crown of the British Empire.

Over time, the British gained powerful influence over Indian politics. By 1857, the British East India Company staffed a private army with British officers and **sepoy**, or Indian soldiers, who were mostly Hindus or Muslims. British officers had little contact with the sepoy.

The sepoy were discontented with the growing presence of Christian missionaries and felt that Great Britain was attempting to undermine their Hindu and Islamic faiths. Yet the discontent went well beyond the sepoy. Much of Indian society resented British rule, the rapid pace of Westernization, and the degrading of their own rulers and traditions.

In 1857, the sepoy mutinied after hearing unconfirmed rumors that the British started to issue rifle cartridges to sepoy that were coated in beef or pork fat as a lubricant. While holding the rifle, a soldier often had to tear open the cartridge with his teeth. This would have violated the sacred tenets of Hindus (cows are sacred) and Muslims (pigs are unclean). The mutiny began in March 1857 with a single attack. It spread across Delhi, Agra, Kanpur, and Lucknow. Initially, the British military had only 23,000 troops, which limited their ability to suppress the mutiny. Eventually, however, they were successful. The British defeated the sepoy and officially declared peace in July 1858.

However, reprisals may have continued for as long as a decade. Historians do not agree on the number of deaths during the rebellion, but some estimate that 100,000 Indians may have been killed during reprisals.

While the mutiny was unsuccessful, it caused the British to increase their political and military presence in India. As a result of the rebellion, however, the British government took direct control of India from the British East India Company, making India an official colony.

An Indian nationalist movement for independence from British rule began in the 1850s. In 1885, the first Indian National Congress convened. In its early years, the **Congress Party** passed a number of reform resolutions. As poverty and hardship increased under British imperialism, however, many members of the party became radicalized. In the early 20th century, they called on Indians to boycott British imports and eventually, under Mahatma Gandhi, began to advocate civil disobedience. The Congress Party became the country's most influential political party after India gained independence in 1947.

Boxer Rebellion By the late 19th century, European powers and Japan were "carving up" China, each seeking a sphere of influence. While the Qing Empress still ruled, she felt threatened by these foreign assaults on her country. In 1898, she gave some support to attacks on foreigners in port cities.

Carrying out these attacks were members of the Society of Righteous and Harmonious Fists. Since this group was also known as the Boxers, their actions became known as the **Boxer Rebellion**. They recruited economically depressed peasants angered by growing foreign power in their country. Many were particularly offended by Christian missionaries, who they felt disrespected their traditions.

Source: Wikimedia Commons

Eight countries sent forces into China to put down the Boxer Rebellion: Japan, Russia, the United States, Great Britain, France, Germany, Austria, and Italy.

In 1900, the Boxers attacked the capital city of Peking, today known as Beijing, targeting signs of European culture, such as Christian churches. In response, an international force of about 19,000 soldiers, made up mostly of Japanese and Russians, put down the rebellion by late 1901. The uprising had significant results:

- Deaths in the rebellion may have totaled 100,000 people.

- The involvement of Japan marked a turning point in Japanese imperialism in the core of China. This imperialism would continue until World War II ended in 1945.

- Europeans forced the Chinese government to pay more than $330 million in reparations, a tremendous sum. It was the equivalent of about a year's income for China's central government.

Source: Getty Images

France awarded medals to soldiers who helped defeat the Boxer Rebellion in China.

Japan Modernizes Japan's involvement in China was part of its rapid development into a world power. Starting in the 17th century, Japan had mostly isolated itself from trade with Western powers. Then, in 1853, heavily armed American ships, led by Commodore Matthew Perry, sailed into Edo, now called Tokyo. They threatened that they would return and attack Japan if it did not allow more foreign trade. Unprepared for battle, the Japanese submitted. They opened two ports for trade with European and American merchants.

Within Japan, the concession to foreigners set off a furious debate. How could Japan protect itself from industrialized powers while keeping its own culture? The debate led to the overthrow of the government, an event known as the **Meiji Restoration**. It restored direct rule to the emperor in 1868. Under him, Japan sent officials to Europe and America to learn how to grow strong enough to protect itself. The government built schools, factories, railroads, a navy modeled on Great Britain's, and an army modeled on Germany's. Between 1894 and 1905, Japan's military power enabled it to defeat China and Russia in wars, as well as to help crush the Boxers.

Japan also learned from Europeans that powerful countries should possess colonies. It formally seized Korea in 1910. This was the first step in creating an East Asian empire—a move that would contribute to the start of World War II.

REFLECT ON THE ESSENTIAL QUESTION

Essential Question: *How did imperialism affect European and non-European societies?*

Effects on European Societies	Effects on Non-European Societies

---

KEY TERMS

Berlin Conference	Edmund D. Morel	Zulu
"Scramble for Africa"	Congo Reform Association (CRA)	Ethiopia
Fashoda Crisis	John A. Hobson	sepoy
Morocco	Vladimir Lenin	Congress Party
sphere of influence	Pan-German League	Boxer Rebellion
Joseph Conrad		Meiji Restoration

MULTIPLE-CHOICE QUESTIONS

Questions 1–3 refer to the passage below.

"Seeing that the Imperialism of the last three decades is clearly condemned as a business policy, in that at enormous expense it has procured a small, bad, unsafe increase of markets, and has jeopardized the entire wealth of the nation in rousing the strong resentment of other nations, we may ask, 'How is the British nation induced to embark upon such unsound business?'

The only possible answer is that the business interests of the nation as a whole are subordinated to those of certain sectional interests that usurp control of the national resources and use them for their private gain. This is no strange or monstrous charge to bring; it is the commonest disease of all forms of government. The famous words of Sir Thomas More [a 16th century Roman Catholic leader in England] are as true now as when he wrote them: 'Everywhere do I perceive a certain conspiracy of rich men seeking their own advantage under the name and pretext of the commonwealth.'

Although the new Imperialism has been bad business for the nation, it has been good business for certain classes and certain trades within the nation. The vast expenditure on armaments, the costly wars, the grave risks and embarrassments of foreign policy, the stoppage of political and social reforms within Great Britain, though fraught with great injury to the nation, have served well the present business interests of certain industries and professions."

—John A. Hobson, British economist, *Imperialism: A Study*, 1902

1. The claim about the colonial system that Hobson refutes most directly is that
   (A) the ideas of Social Darwinism were correct
   (B) the mission civilisatrice was succeeding
   (C) the success of European colonization was based on superior technology
   (D) British prosperity relied on natural resources from colonies

2. Which of the following most accurately describes one of Hobson's claims about imperialism and shows a limit to its use?

(A) His claim that imperialism reflects what More called "a certain conspiracy" is based on religious beliefs, and it might not appeal to people who are not Roman Catholics.

(B) His claim that imperialism rouses "the strong resentment of other nations" is based on ethical values, and it might not influence leaders who care only about those who can vote.

(C) His claim that imperialism "has been bad business for the nation" is based on economic analysis and it might not apply to other countries.

(D) His claim that imperialism results from the self-interest of "certain classes and certain trades" is based on political goals, and it might not concern most people in Great Britain.

3. Which of the following groups carried out policies that demonstrated the most continuity with Hobson's conclusion about imperialism?

(A) Bismarck because of his desire to promote European stability

(B) Japanese leaders of the Meiji Restoration because of their involvement in Korea and China

(C) European leaders at the Berlin Conference of 1884–1885 because of their dividing up of Africa

(D) Belgium's King Leopold II because of his brutal rule over the Congo

SHORT-ANSWER QUESTION

Use the passage below to answer all parts of the question that follows.

"New Imperialism has long been the object of controversy among historians because of its extraordinary speed and scope; by one account, the land area of the world controlled by Europeans increased from 35 percent in 1800 to 84.4 percent in 1914. . . . In their fascination with the motivations of the imperialists, most historians took for granted that the European powers and the United States had the technical . . . means to turn their ambition into reality. . . . Technology is now widely recognized as a necessary, if not sufficient, explanation for the New Imperialism in Africa and Asia."

—Daniel Headrick, *Tools of Empire*, 1981

1. a) Explain how ONE piece of evidence supports Headrick's argument regarding the reason for New Imperialism from 1870–1914.

b) Explain how ONE piece of evidence undermines Headrick's argument regarding the reason for New Imperialism from 1870–1914.

c) Explain ONE example from the Age of Exploration in the 15th or 16th century that provoked a similar argument described by Headrick.

19th-Century Culture and Arts

I cannot send you my explanation of the word "Romantic," because it would be 125 sheets long.

—Friedrich Schlegel, in a letter to his brother Wilhelm, 1793

Essential Question: What were the continuities and changes in European artistic expression from 1815 to 1914?

The 150-year period from the late 18th century through the early 20th century featured an ideological struggle between two worldviews. Objectivity emphasized facts with little interpretation. Subjectivity encouraged emotions with more interpretation. Each part of the period was a direct response to, and a reaction against, the period immediately before it. In art, literature, and music, when objective, universal ways of thinking became the norm, the pendulum would soon swing back toward subjective, skeptical questioning.

Throughout this period, some artists acively sought societal reforms. Musicians created masterpieces that transcended notes on a page. Philosophers developed social and economic theories that continue to be tested and questioned. The tension between objectivity and subjectivity only served to propel great art and thinking forward.

Romanticism in Art, Music, and Literature

The Enlightenment emphasized the principles of logic, reason, and rationalism. It was followed by the Romantic period, which lasted from the late 18th to mid-19th century. **Romanticism** was a backlash against the Enlightenment's rationalism and materialism (see Topic 7.5), foreshadowed by Rousseau's interest in introspection and feelings. Romanticism chose subjective emotion and creativity over objective logic and reason.

Romanticism was also a rejection of the neoclassical style—a popular movement during the Enlightenment that employed classical themes and linear design. Romanticism rejected neoclassicism's standards of order and balance, replacing them with a greater appreciation of imagination and emotion.

Looking Inward Romantics of the 19th century tended to avoid the fields of politics and science, instead expressing themselves through art, music, and literature. They also were historians, but they documented the world around them in more creative and expressive ways. Romantics encouraged introspection, or a deep focus on the self and one's emotions. They examined human personality and moods, and they were fascinated by the personalities of exceptional figures such as mythic heroes. The great figures of the Romantic period focused on the purity of nature as a way to abandon what they considered to be the corruption of their modern society.

Individual Expression By the end of the Romantic era, a new view of the artist had emerged. Artists of all kinds—from painters and sculptors to composers and authors—now were seen as supremely individual creators. Their work was not dictated by the church or a state and was limited only by their own imaginations. Creative spirits were valued over a strict adherence to formal rules and traditional procedures. There was now a new emphasis on imagination as a gateway to a higher spiritual truth.

Romanticism in Art

Artists of the Enlightenment attempted to depict reason and order. Their compositions were filled with traditional mythological figures and symbolism that exalted logic and reason. Romantic artists broke from such conventions to emphasize less-tangible subjects such as emotion, nature, and individuality.

Landscapes The German painter most famous for his landscapes was **Caspar David Friedrich** (1774–1840). He preferred to show vast, mysterious landscapes and seascapes. For example, *The Wanderer Above the Sea of Fog* (1818) portrays a solitary individual looking outward over a turbulent sea. Friedrich shows the individual from behind. As a result, the viewer cannot see the individual's face to know whether he is feeling awe, fear, anxiety, or some other emotion.

English landscape artists **John Constable** (1776–1837) and **J. M. W. Turner** (1775–1851) glorified nature. Constable's favorite subject was the local countryside, with its ancient castles, working farms, waterways, and agricultural laborers. He used a broader color palette than was typical at that time, trying to represent the *chiaroscuro*—the contrast between *chiaro* (light) and *scuro* (dark)—that he saw as a principle feature in nature. Likewise, Turner favored a radical color palette and innovative techniques, some of which laid the groundwork for modern Impressionism. Turner is known for his expressive depictions of turbulent, storm-swept seas and luminous skies.

Source: Andrew W. Mellon Collection, National Gallery of Art

John Constable's painting (*Salisbury Cathedral from Lower Marsh Close,* 1820) demonstrates the interest of Romantic painters in elements of nature, including trees, clouds, and shadows.

Politics While many Romantics were more fascinated by nature than by human events, others focused on individual heroism, battle scenes, and dramatic conflict. Some expressed strong feelings of nationalism in their works:

- **Francisco Goya** (1746–1828), a Spanish painter, portrayed dramatic, sometimes violent scenes of historical conflict. Among his best-known works was *The Third of May 1808* (1814). It shows Spanish rebels being executed by a French firing squad during the Napoleonic wars.

- **Eugène Delacroix** (1798–1863) of France often painted contemporary scenes in vibrant colors. His painting *Liberty Leading the People* (1830) reflected the zealous commitment to equality and liberty of the revolutionaries in France in 1830.

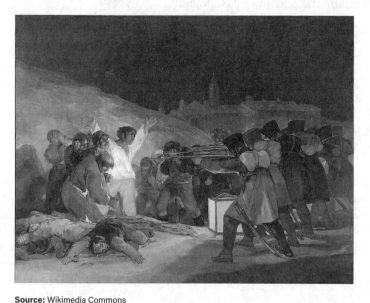

Source: Wikimedia Commons

Francisco Goya's *The Third of May 1808* (1814) commemorates the Spanish resistance to Napoleon's armies during the Peninsular War.

Romanticism in Music

Just as Romantic artists strove to free themselves from the confines of the preceding Enlightenment period, so did Romantic composers and musicians. They prized originality and individuality in their compositions. They worked to be less formulaic, and they freely experimented with various styles that could showcase personal emotional expression:

- **Ludwig van Beethoven** (1770–1827) was trained in the classical style. However, his increasing use of dramatic changes in pitch and volume and innovative harmonies marked him as one of the first composers in the Romantic style. His nine symphonies and many sonatas remain widely performed today.

- **Frédéric Chopin** (1810–1849) was a Polish composer and skilled virtuoso on the piano. He wrote numerous concertos, mazurkas (Polish folk dances), ballades (piano compositions), nocturnes (pieces that evoke the spirit of the night), and three sonatas that are still among the most popular classical works. Often turbulent and passionate, Chopin's music stands out for its intimacy and expressiveness.

- Building on the work of early Romantics, Russian composer **Pyotr Ilyich Tchaikovsky** (1840–1893) wrote impressive symphonies and other works, including ballets such as *The Nutcracker* and *Swan Lake*. Like many Romantics, he was influenced by national pride. His best-known work may be the *1812 Overture*, a tribute to Russian bravery in stopping the invasion by Napoleon.

Historical Influences and Wagner Beethoven, Chopin, Tchaikovsky, and other Romantic composers often included folk melodies in their works. Using these tunes was one more expression of nationalism in the 19th century. Few composers drew upon traditional culture as much as **Richard Wagner** (1813–1883). Wagner combined Germanic and Nordic mythology, expressive music, and the cult of the hero to create operas that represented German nationalism. Because of this, long after his death, he became a favorite among extreme German nationalists, including many Nazis.

Although Wagner drew upon the past for content, the form of his music was innovative. Compared to previous composers, he used far larger orchestras and choruses, wrote much longer pieces, and used unusual harmonies. Listeners found his works awe-inspiring, even if they found them exhausting and, at times, filled with clashing sounds they were not used to hearing. His most famous work was the *The Ring of the Nibelung*, a set of four operas. A performance of the full *Ring* cycle takes about 15 hours spread over four days.

Romanticism in Literature

Much of the inspiration for literature during the Romantic period came from premodern times. Writers looked back to a world before industrialization, and the emphasis on reason reshaped how people related to each other and to the natural world. Writers such as Sir Walter Scott were attracted to the medieval romance, and folklorists such as the Grimm brothers resurrected traditional tales. Others, including William Blake, William Wordsworth, Percy Bysshe Shelley, and John Keats, emphasized their emotional reactions to beauty, nature, or the spiritual world. Mary Shelley wrote *Frankenstein*, a novel that explored emotional and supernatural realms, representing another move away from the Enlightenment's reason and science.

Many Romantic writers took inspiration from the growth of cultural nationalism and encouraged it throughout their work:

- **Johann Wolfgang von Goethe** (1749–1832) was one of the most influential German writers in history. People considered his works, such as his play *Faust*, as expressions of an essential and distinctive spirit of the German people.

- **William Wordsworth** (1770–1850) was a dominant figure in Romantic literature. Wordsworth argued for "common speech" in poetry and decried the old emphasis on epic poetry, preferring an emphasis on emotion and the imagination. Published anonymously in 1789, *Lyrical Ballads* was a joint collection of poetry that is recognized as Wordsworth's masterpiece.

- George Gordon Byron, better known as **Lord Byron** (1788–1824), was an English poet and satirist who admired both nationalism and classical Greek culture. His beliefs inspired him to fight on behalf of the Greeks in their war for independence from the Ottoman Turks. He died in the conflict in 1824, at the age of 36.

- **Percy Bysshe Shelley** (1792–1822) was a social reformer and pamphleteer before turning more to poetry. His lyrical drama *Prometheus Unbound* and the poems "Ode to the West Wind" and "To a Sky-Lark" expressed several Romantic themes: the quest for love and beauty, social justice and political rights, and hope arising from natural beauty.

- **John Keats** (1795–1821) often expressed his emotional response to nature in his poems. However, his most famous work, "Ode to a Grecian Urn," reflected his interest in classical culture.

- **Victor Hugo** of France (1802–1885) was a prolific writer whose novel *Les Misérables* provided a sympathetic account of the lives of the poor and outcast people of France.

Source: Getty Images

In 2012, the United States issued a stamp commemorating Boris Karloff's famous portrayal of the monster created by Dr. Frankenstein in a 1931 film based on Mary Shelley's novel.

- **Mary Shelley** (1797–1851), the wife of Percy Bysshe Shelley, was an English novelist. She is best known for her first novel, *Frankenstein; or, The Modern Prometheus* (1818), but many consider her best novel to be *The Last Man* (1826), a futuristic tale of the extermination of the human race by a plague.

Realist Art and Literature

While Hugo's *Les Misérables* expressed the drama typical of Romantic literature, it also pointed toward a new development. Writers and painters were examining the struggles of common people in their own country. They created realist art and literature, giving an accurate, detailed depiction of nature and contemporary life. **Realism** rejected imaginative fantasies in favor of strict observation. Materialist ideas stressing the centrality of physical things and processes also influenced realist artists. Painters and writers of the realist style depicted the lives of ordinary people. Creating a clear depiction of the world around them meant that realists also drew attention to the social problems of their time.

Realist Art

Artists in the Romantic period prized emotion over subject matter, but the pendulum swung back during the realist period. Realist artists of the later 19th century strove to depict life as accurately as possible. Some used their work to make political statements about the living conditions of those around them, especially the working poor.

France was the center of European realism, especially through the work of **Gustave Courbet**. In works such as *Burial in Ornans*, he emphasized the material nature of life. This was in contrast to the long tradition of European painting that showed the influence of the spiritual world. Courbet was strongly opposed to any idealization in his art, and he urged other artists to make the commonplace and contemporary their focus as well. From France, the movement spread to other parts of Europe, especially Russia and Germany. It then crossed the Atlantic to the United States.

REALIST PAINTERS AND PRINT ARTISTS			
Individual	Country	Works	Legacy
Gustave Courbet 1819–1877	France	*The Artist's Studio* *The Stone Breakers*	Incorporated political views into his art
Jean-François Millet 1814–1875	France	*The Gleaners*	Portrayed the dignity of French peasants
Ilya Repin 1844–1930	Russia	*Barge Haulers on the Volga*	Connected Russian art to the European mainstream for the first time
Adolph von Menzel 1815–1905	Germany	*History of Frederick the Great* *Iron Rolling Mill*	Developed illustration as an important art form
Honoré Daumier 1808–1879	France	*The Laundress* *Gargantua*	Created satirical caricatures, paintings, sculptures, and lithographs

Source: Getty Images

The Gleaners (1857) by French painter Jean-François Millet is among the most famous realist paintings. It portrays the hard labor of women working in the fields.

Realist Literature

Just as realist painters wanted to show the world the actual conditions of those of the lower social orders, so too did novelists. Honoré de Balzac, for example, attempted to create an almost encyclopedic portrait of the whole range of French society. His series *La Comédie humaine,* or *The Human Comedy,* pioneered the realist movement in literature.

Realism entered the mainstream of European literature during the 1860s and 1870s. Authors emphasized strict objectivity, avoiding implausible and exotic elements. They detached themselves from their subject matter, unlike the deeply connected Romantic authors who preceded them. Realist writing provided a very clear, emotionally restrained criticism of the social environment and values of the time.

One significant result of literary realism was **naturalism,** a late 19th- and early 20th-century movement that aimed at an even more accurate representation of reality. Naturalistic authors emphasized **scientific determinism,** or the belief that all natural events and social changes are exclusively the result of the events that preceded them. The French novelist Émile Zola was the leading author of the naturalist movement in his 20-novel series *Les Rougon-Macquart.*

REALIST WRITERS			
Individual	Country	Works	Legacy
Honoré de Balzac 1799–1850	France	• *The Human Comedy* • *The Unknown Masterpiece*	Helped establish the traditional form of the novel
Fyodor Dostoevsky 1821–1881	Russia	• *Crime and Punishment* • *The Brothers Karamazov*	Noted for his psychological novels that also treat philosophical and political issues
Charles Dickens 1812–1870	England	• *A Tale of Two Cities* • *A Christmas Carol* • *David Copperfield*	Portrayed the lives of the poor, sometimes based on his own childhood
George Eliot (Mary Ann Evans) 1819–1880	England	• *Middlemarch* • *Silas Marner*	Described the emptiness of middle- class domestic life and marriage

REALIST WRITERS			
Leo Tolstoy 1828–1910	Russia	• *War and Peace* • *Anna Karenina*	Delved deeply into the psychology of his characters
Émile Zola 1840–1902	France	• the *Les Rougon-Macquart* series • *J'Accuse...!*	Depicted social injustice and promoted political liberalization in France
Thomas Hardy 1840–1928	England	• *Tess of the d'Urbervilles* • *Jude the Obscure* • *Wessex Tales*	Wrote about his native Wessex and the rural working class with sympathy

Modern Art

Realist artists sought to depict their subjects accurately. However, in a world with photography, painters felt less need to portray the world exactly as it appeared. This shift led to **modern art**, a style that was more subjective, abstract, and expressive than most European art throughout history. It included several movements.

The rapid evolution of art made the late 19th and early 20th centuries a time of experiment and controversy. Traditional content, such as portraits of aristocrats and landscapes, gave way to depictions of the activities of common people. Then artists began to downplay the importance of content altogether, emphasizing light or color or emotion. Art became nonrepresentational. The shifts in style and content excited some museum goers and angered others:

- **Impressionism** emphasized light and color as the true subjects of their work. It reflected the influence of Japanese traditions.

- **Post-Impressionism** used symbolic motifs, unnatural colors, and visible brushstrokes to convey emotion rather than realism.

- Expressionism focused on portraying the internal feelings of the artists rather than showing a subject accurately. The content often looked somewhat realistic, but modified in order to focus on a mood.

- Fauvism featured simplified forms, bold but nonnaturalistic colors, and violent brushwork often resulting in wild dabs of paint.

- **Cubism** abandoned the need for subject matter altogether in an attempt to depict three-dimensional subjects on a two-dimensional plane.

The bold colors and forms of Expressionism, Fauvism, and Cubism were all influenced by African art, which was being discovered by Europe at a time when Western artists were searching for new forms of artistic expression.

Source: Getty Images

Van Gogh's series of paintings of sunflowers, like those of many modern artists, focused more on the process of creativity than on the subject matter.

MODERN ARTISTS			
Individual and Country	**Style**	**Works**	**Legacy**
Claude Monet (1840–1926) France	Impressionism	• *Impression, Sunrise* • *Water Lilies* (series) • *Haystacks* (series)	Focused on the use of light and color by painting the same scene at different times of day
Edgar Degas (1834–1917) France	Impressionism	• *Woman with Chrysanthemums* • *The Dance Class*	Depicted everyday life in Paris
Henri Matisse (1869–1954) France	Fauvism	• *Woman with a Hat* • *La Danse*	Used brilliant colors to evoke strong reactions among viewers
Paul Cézanne (1839–1906) France	Post-Impressionism	• *The Bathers* • *The Card Players*	Took a step toward representational art with paintings that emphasized the painting itself rather than the subject matter
Vincent Van Gogh (1853–1890) Netherlands and France	Post-Impressionism	• *The Starry Night* • *Sunflowers*	Used forceful brushwork to express emotion more than subject matter
Pablo Picasso (1881–1973) Spain and France	Cubism and others	• *Les Demoiselles d'Avignon* • *Guernica* • Untitled sculpture in Daley Plaza, Chicago	Represented multiple perspectives in one painting

REFLECT ON THE ESSENTIAL QUESTION

Essential Question: *What were the continuities and changes in European artistic expression from 1815 to 1914?*

Continuities in Artistic Expression	Changes in Artistic Expression

KEY TERMS

Romanticism
Caspar David Friedrich
John Constable
J. M. W. Turner
Francisco Goya
Eugène Delacroix
Ludwig van Beethoven
Frédéric Chopin
Pyotr Ilyich Tchaikovsky
Richard Wagner
Johann Wolfgang von
   Goethe
William Wordsworth
Lord Byron

Percy Bysshe Shelley
John Keats
Mary Shelley
Victor Hugo
realism
Gustave Courbet
Jean-François Millet
Ilya Repin
Adolph von Menzel
Honoré Daumier
naturalism
scientific determinism
Honoré de Balzac
Fyodor Dostoevsky

Charles Dickens
George Eliot
Leo Tolstoy
Émile Zola
modern art
Impressionism
Post-Impressionism
Cubism
Claude Monet
Edgar Degas
Henri Matisse
Paul Cézanne
Vincent van Gogh
Pablo Picasso

MULTIPLE-CHOICE QUESTIONS

Questions 1–3 refer to the passage below.

Gustave Corbet, *The Wheat Sifters*, 1854, Museum of Fine Arts, Nantes, France

1. *The Wheat Sifters* is example of the artistic movement known as
   (A) Romanticism
   (B) realism
   (C) Impressionism
   (D) Cubism

2. The painting reflects a change from Enlightenment principles art because it emphasizes
   (A) the heritage of the classical world
   (B) the values of balance and order
   (C) the use of reason to guide decisions
   (D) the emotions of individual people

3. Which of the following writers had an approach to artistic expression most similar to that shown in the painting?
   (A) Mary Shelley because she wrote about supernatural forces
   (B) Victor Hugo because he wrote very dramatic tales
   (C) Honoré de Balzac because he wrote about everyday life
   (D) Émile Zola because he wrote about the forces determining human actions

SHORT-ANSWER QUESTION

Answer all parts of the question that follows.

1. a) Explain ONE change between the music of Wolfgang Amadeus Mozart and the later works of Ludwig van Beethoven.

   b) Explain ONE continuity between the music of Richard Wagner and Pyotr Ilyich Tchaikovsky.

   c) Explain ONE continuity between the music of Frédéric Chopin and the writings of William Wordsworth.

Topic 7.9

Causation in 19th-Century Perspectives and Political Developments

We will not have failure—only success and new learning.

—Queen Victoria of Great Britain (1819–1901)

Essential Question: What was the influence of nationalist and imperialist movements on European and global stability?

New political ideologies developed and existing ones were reshaped in Europe during the industrial age. Growing nationalist movements were one of the most powerful forces on the continent during the 19th century. At the same time, imperialist motivation dominated European nations' actions as they sought control over Africa and Asia in order to obtain raw materials and create new markets for manufactured goods. Both nationalist and imperialist movements affected the balance of power and stability in European and on a global scale.

Nationalism Causes International Instability After the French Revolution, many European leaders feared that the liberal ideas fought for in the revolution would lead to revolutions elsewhere. This possibility caused conservative leaders in 1815 to agree to the Concert of Europe, which was designed to re-establish the traditional rights of monarchs, landed aristocrats, and organized religion. The plan also sought to keep down liberal nationalist movements. However, the Concert of Europe failed to control the growth of nationalism. While the rise of nationalism was linked with a growing middle class and democracy, it also caused competition among nations and led to war.

During this time, Italy and Germany became strong nations with clear identities because of their nationalist movements. Italian states were culturally and politically fractured and had a history of being ruled by foreign powers. However, growing nationalist sentiment and astute political maneuvering caused the Italian states to unify as one nation in 1861. Capitalizing on nationalist movement, Prussian leader Otto von Bismarck used industrialization, warfare, and realpolitik to pull the many German states together as one nation by 1871. The unification of Italy and Germany made both strong, changing Europe's balance of power. However, nationalist revolutions in other European states, including Austria, the Ottoman Empire, and Russia, were less successful.

Imperialism Increases Tensions among Powers The Industrial Revolution boosted Europe's economic activity and led to a European Age of Imperialism in the second half of the 19th century. Nations reached across the globe with the intention of becoming or strengthening their imperial status by colonizing Africa and Asia. Competition for the resources and markets of these continents caused conflicts among European powers. Native people of colonized lands resented the exploitation and often rebelled against imperial powers, further increasing tensions international instability.

Objectivity vs. Subjectivity Forces such as imperialism and nationalism reshaped Europe, and artistic expression represented these changes. Neoclassical styles of the Enlightenment, which demonstrated reason, order, and balance, caused Romanticism to grow into the dominant style in the late 18th and 19th centuries. Subjectivity, creativity, and emotion were the focus of Romantic artists, composers, and writers. Cultural, political, and economic struggles of the time caused art to swing back to a more realist approach as accurate depiction of life, especially life of the poor, came to be common subjects of art and literature.

QUESTIONS ABOUT CAUSATION

1. What were the effects of nationalist movements on European and global stability?

2. What were the effects of imperialism on European and global stability?

WRITE AS A HISTORIAN: *IDENTIFY CONTINUITY AND CHANGE*

Historians often write about continuity and change over time—what remains constant and what evolves. One historian might view European imperialism as evidence of continuity in history: people have been fighting and exploiting others as far back in history as we have evidence for. Another historian might view imperialism in the context of change: the weapons and tactics of 19th-century Europeans differed greatly even from those of 17th-century Europeans. Some have argued violence of all sorts, including imperialism and war, has been slowly decreasing in human society. Writing clearly and powerfully about continuity and change over time is a required skill on the AP exam.

To think and write like a historian, practice understanding historical events in terms of continuity and change over time. Look for ways that people or societies stay the same. Look for the turning-point events that signal important shifts. Then consider how these two forces of continuity and change interacted. International trade was an example of continuity during the period of imperialism. However, the development of steam-powered ships and locomotives brought change as these technologies revolutionized trade.

Also examine "ripple effects"—the series of changes that spread out from a main effect. How often have merchants, armies, or missionaries moved into a region and affected its history in ways both large and small? Such details often set into motion the big patterns that keep repeating, such as the rise of empires, forced migrations, the spread of diseases, and exchanges of ideas and cultures.

Which three of the statements below best illustrate continuity?

1. The search for raw materials and markets for manufactured goods fostered imperialist expansion in Asia and Africa, much as it had earlier in the Americas.

2. This latest wave of imperialist expansion was once again fueled by economic rivalries among European powers.

3. Revolutionary advancements in weaponry combined with the development of capitalism combined to ensure European domination over less-developed regions.

4. Even as European former colonies in Central and South America gained independence, new colonial uprisings took place, such as the creation of India's Congress Party and the Boxer Rebellion in China.

5. Thanks to better medical techniques such as quinine for malaria and use of antiseptics, Europeans were more successful at adapting to life overseas.

Which of the following topic sentences best addresses the reasoning skill of continuity and change over time?

6. a. The "new imperialism" of the late 19th and early 20th centuries was promoted in European nations by interest groups that included politicians, military officials and soldiers, missionaries, explorers, journalists, and intellectuals.

    b. Millions of Europeans carried their culture abroad to the Americas and elsewhere through emigration and helped create a variety of mixed cultures around the world.

    c. The European imperial outreach of the 19th century was in some ways a continuation of three centuries of colonization, but it also resulted from the economic pressures and necessities of a maturing industrial capitalist economy.

LONG ESSAY QUESTIONS

Directions: Suggested writing time is 40 minutes. In your response, you should do the following:

- Respond to the prompt with a historically defensible thesis that establishes a line of reasoning.
- Describe a broader historical context relevant to the prompt.
- Support an argument in response to the prompt using specific and relevant examples of evidence.
- Use historical reasoning (e.g., comparison, causation, continuity and change over time) to frame or structure an argument that addresses the prompt.
- Use evidence to corroborate, qualify, or modify an argument that addresses the prompt.

1. Evaluate the most significant reason for a change in European attitudes toward imperialism after 1870.

2. Evaluate the extent to which European expansion changed from the period of the Age of Exploration (16th–18th centuries) to the New Imperialism of the 19th century.

3. Evaluate the extent to which scientific advancements influenced artistic expression and the search for truth during the 19th century.

4. Evaluate the extent to which modernism differed from Romanticism.

DOCUMENT-BASED QUESTION

Directions: Question 1 is based on the accompanying documents. The documents have been edited for the purpose of this exercise. You are advised to spend 15 minutes planning and 45 minutes writing your answer. In your response, you should do the following:

- Respond to the prompt with a historically defensible thesis that establishes a line of reasoning.
- Describe a broader historical context relevant to the prompt.
- Support an argument in response to the prompt using at least six documents.
- Use at least one additional piece of specific historical evidence (beyond that found in the documents) relevant to an argument about the prompt.
- For at least three documents, explain how or why the document's point of view, purpose, historical situation, and/or audience is relevant to an argument.
- Use evidence to corroborate, qualify, or modify an argument that addresses the prompt.

1. Analyze the extent to which the arts of the 19th century represented a change in European artistic expression.

Document 1

Source: Caspar David Friedrich, German artist, *The Monk by the Sea*, 1808–1810

Document 2

Source: William Wordsworth, English poet, *I Wandered Lonely as a Cloud*, 1807

I wandered lonely as a cloud
That floats on high o'er vales and hills,
When all at once I saw a crowd,
A host, of golden daffodils;
Beside the lake, beneath the trees,
Fluttering and dancing in the breeze.

Continuous as the stars that shine
And twinkle on the milky way,
They stretched in never-ending line
Along the margin of a bay:
Ten thousand saw I at a glance,
Tossing their heads in sprightly dance.

Document 3

Source: Francisco Goya, Spanish painter, *The Third of May 1808*, 1814

Document 4

Source: Charles Kingsley, Anglican priest and Christian Socialist reformer, *Cheap Clothes and Nasty*, 1850

At the honourable shops, the work is done, as it was universally thirty years ago, on the premises and at good wages. In the dishonourable trade, the work is taken home by the men, to be done at the very lowest possible prices, which decrease year by year. . . . For at the honourable shops, the master deals directly with his workmen; while at the dishonourable ones, the greater part of the work, if not the whole, is let out to contractors, or middle men - "sweaters", as their victims significantly call them...who have to draw their profit. And when the labour price has been already beaten down to the lowest possible, how much remains for the workmen after all these deductions, let the poor fellows themselves say! . . .

And now comes the question - What is to be done with these poor tailors, to the number of between fifteen and twenty thousand? Their condition, as it stands, is simply one of ever-increasing darkness and despair. The system which is ruining them is daily spreading, deepening. While we write, fresh victims are being driven by penury into the slop-working trade, fresh depreciations of labour are taking place. . . . What can be done?

Document 5

Source: Richard Wagner, German composer, note to his friend Mathilde Wesendonck, written while working on his opera *Tristan und Isolde*, 1859

Child! This Tristan is turning into something dreadful!

That last act!!!

I'm afraid the opera will be forbidden unless the whole

thing is turned into a parody by bad production: only mediocre

performances can save me! Completely good ones are bound to drive

people crazy, I can't imagine what else could happen. To such a

state have things come!!! Alas!

I was just going full steam ahead!

Document 6

Source: Bram Stoker, English author, *Dracula*, 1897

Beyond the green swelling hills of the Mittel Land rose mighty slopes of forest up to the lofty steeps of the Carpathians themselves. Right and left of us they towered, with the afternoon sun falling full upon them and bringing out all the glorious colours of this beautiful range, deep blue and purple in the shadows of the peaks, green and brown where grass and rock mingled, and an endless perspective of jagged rock and pointed crags, till these were themselves lost in the distance, where the snowy peaks rose grandly. Here and there seemed mighty rifts in the mountains, through which, as the sun began to sink, we saw now and again the white gleam of falling water. One of my companions touched my arm as we swept round the base of a hill and opened up the lofty, snow-covered peak of a mountain, which seemed, as we wound on our serpentine way, to be right before us:—

"Look! Isten szek!"—"God's seat!"—and he crossed himself reverently.

Document 7

Source: Emile Zola, French journalist, *J'Accuse...! (I Accuse...!),* a letter to the president of France, published in the Paris newspaper *Aurore,* January 13, 1898

Unscathed by vile slander, you have won the hearts of all. You are radiant in the patriotic glory of our country's alliance with Russia, you are about to preside over the solemn triumph of our World Fair, the jewel that crowns this great century of labour, truth, and freedom. But what filth this wretched Dreyfus affair has cast on your name - I wanted to say 'reign' -. A court martial, under orders, has just dared to acquit a certain Esterhazy, a supreme insult to all truth and justice. And now the image of France is sullied by this filth, and history shall record that it was under your presidency that this crime against society was committed....

I accuse Lt. Col. du Paty de Clam of being the diabolical creator of this miscarriage of justice - unwittingly, I would like to believe - and of defending this sorry deed, over the last three years, by all manner of ludicrous and evil machinations....

I accuse General Billot of having held in his hands absolute proof of Dreyfus's innocence and covering it up, and making himself guilty of this crime against mankind and justice, as a political expedient and a way for the compromised General Staff to save face.

UNIT 8: 20th-Century Global Conflicts
c. 1914 to present

Topic 8.1

Contextualizing 20th-Century Global Conflicts

Essential Question: What was the context in which global conflict developed in the 20th century?

The tensions and instability that built up in the 19th century among European nations and other powerful states exploded into conflicts in the 20th century. Many catalysts came together as the context for wars, including nationalism, imperialism, alliances, economic competition, territorial disputes, and the rise of totalitarian regimes. Growing European militarism, or the build-up of military strength also contributed greatly to this already turbulent situation. Technological advances and industrialization made an arms race a reality in a tense world. The 20th century's two world wars resulted in unprecedented destruction.

World War I and World War II Devastate Europe What started as a small regional conflict in 1914, quickly ignited into a global war. Complete mobilization of resources by participating nations led to a total war that changed the relationship among European nations and with others, such as the United States and Russia. The 1919 Versailles Treaty that brought the "Great War" to a close ended up being disliked by many nations and set the stage for another conflict less than two decades later.

A global economic crisis, the emergence of totalitarian governments, and the terms of the World War I treaty, among other reasons, plunged the world back into chaos in the 1930s. Industrialized warfare, extreme nationalism, and increasingly dangerous weapons made the results of this war even more devastating than the first.

Economic Weaknesses and Ideological Struggles The internal conflicts that European states experienced can be understood in the context of political upheaval, severe economic problems, and ethnic tensions. By the end of World War I, the Russian, German, Austro-Hungarian, and Ottoman empires had collapsed. Political boundaries were redrawn, and new states were established after both world wars. These changes often heightened tensions between political entities and created conflicts among different ethnic, cultural, and political groups.

One conflict was the emergence of disparate and competing political and economic ideologies. Political differences revolved around the amount of authority the state should have as well as the level of participation individuals should have in governance. These theories coalesced into communist, democratic, and fascist ideologies. Also, competing economic beliefs developed around who should own businesses and the means of production within society. These ideologies clashed with one another, providing context for international conflicts through the end of the century.

Intellectual and Cultural Developments Science and technology greatly improved the standard of living for many in the 20th century while at the same time, providing the possibility of immense destruction. Advances in various academic disciplines, such as physics, paved the way for era of extraordinary inventions but led people to question much about the universe and their place in it.

The successes and tragedies of the first half of the 20th century led many Europeans to question their traditional social beliefs and economic patterns. While life improved in many countries, others struggled with widespread suffering and even genocide. Opportunities and expectations for women widened during the 20th century, particularly in the workplace. New democracies were created out of the world wars, while other nations and peoples lost the ability to self-govern.

ANALYZE THE CONTEXT

1. Describe the context in which World War I developed?

2. Describe the context in which World War II developed?

Topic 8.2

World War I

I am a Yugoslav nationalist, aiming for the unification of all Yugoslavs, and I do not care what form of state, but it must be freed from Austria.

—Gavrilo Princip, at his trial for assassinating Austrian
Archduke Franz Ferdinand and his wife

Essential Question: What were the causes and effects of World War I?

A number of factors converged to cause World War I. Although Europe had been more peaceful in the 19th century than it had been for many centuries, France was eager to regain the provinces of Alsace and Lorraine near the French-German border. The provinces had changed hands as a result of France's humiliating defeat in the Franco-German War in 1871.

Germany's desire to expand its territory and influence alarmed Britain and Russia for years as well. A series of agreements among France, Russia, and Britain became, in effect, an alliance to counter growing German power. Germany and Austria-Hungary had been allied to one another for many years. Smaller nations in Europe felt pressured to take sides.

Militarism and Nationalism in Europe

Militarism, the arming of European countries, grew as nations began to accumulate arms for both offensive and defensive purposes. Using raw materials that poured in from imperial colonies, the ever-increasing efficiency of factories as a result of the continued Industrial Revolution fueled an arms race that reflected nationalist notions of superiority. From 1890–1910, defense expenditures had more than doubled among major European powers.

Nationalism had dramatically increased, especially since the unifications of Italy and Germany in the second half of the 19th century. In addition, movements such as Pan-Slavism had caused unrest, especially within the Balkan region of the Habsburg Empire. Citizens wanted a strong government that would protect and promote their interests.

Imperialism became a source of tension among European nations in the 19th and 20th centuries. Countries were in competition to colonize Asia and Africa, at times getting close to declaring war on one another. This **imperial competition** increased nationalism and militarism, pushing rivalries to new heights.

World War I Begins

The war began with a chain of events starting with the assassination of Austrian **Archduke Franz Ferdinand** by Serbian nationalist **Gavrilo Princip** in Sarajevo on June 28, 1914. A month later, Austria-Hungary declared war on Serbia. In response, Serbia's ally Russia mobilized its forces, thereby heightening tensions around Europe. Germany, hoping to gain a quick victory over unprepared adversaries, declared war on Russia on August 1 and on France on August 3. Germany's subsequent invasion of neutral Belgium brought Great Britain into the war on France and Russia's side.

Ultimately, 32 states fought in the war. The two sides were known as the Central Powers and the Allies. The **Central Powers** consisted of Germany, Austria-Hungary, and the Ottoman Empire, soon joined by Bulgaria. France, Britain, and Russia led the **Allies**; Italy (which had been allied with Germany and Austria-Hungary) joined the Allies in 1915, as did the United States in 1917.

In Europe, the war was fought largely on two fronts. The **Western Front** stretched for more than 400 miles from Belgium through France. The **Eastern Front** extended for 1,000 miles from the Baltic Sea in the north, to the Black Sea in the south.

The Eastern Front

The war on the Eastern Front began on August 17, 1914, when Russia invaded Germany. Austria-Hungary rapidly joined on the side of the Germans and invaded Poland (part of the Russian Empire at the time). Although the Russians repelled the Austrian advance, Germany increased its forces on the Eastern Front.

Source: Getty Images

Horse-mounted cavalry, such as these Russian Cossacks on the Eastern Front, played a significant role in World War I. By the time of World War II, only approximately 20 years later, the use of horses in battle was all but eliminated.

By 1915, Germany and Austria-Hungary had seized all or most of the Russian territories of Poland, Latvia, and Lithuania. The offensive stalled, however, as the Germans fell short of supplies, and the Russians were able to establish a nearly 800-mile defensive line stretching southeast from the Baltic Sea to the border with Romania.

In mid-1916, the Russian army rallied and regained much of its lost territory, but victory was costly. About 1 million Russian soldiers died, were wounded, were taken prisoner, or deserted. As the hardships of war mounted, Russian soldiers began to refuse to fight and even rise up against their officers. The political turmoil that followed led to an overthrow of the Russian government and Russia's withdrawal from the war in 1917.

The Western Front

Germany invaded (neutral) Belgium in August 1914 and swiftly overwhelmed the small country. By the end of the month, German forces had invaded France, but the offensive bogged down, causing the extensive use of **trench warfare.** Each side dug protective trenches into the ground from which they could emerge to attack the other. The space between the trenches was called no-man's-land. Trenches could stretch for miles. Soldiers might live in the trenches for months at a time. They endured cold, wet, and unsanitary conditions. Contagious diseases spread easily. Many men suffered from trench foot, a crippling foot condition caused by the damp and cold.

Between 1914 and 1916, the German army confronted British and French forces in a series of battles in central France. Major engagements included the Marne, Verdun, Ypres, and the Somme. Both sides suffered staggering numbers of soldiers killed and wounded. Soldiers dug in on each side, and the war seemed to reach a **stalemate,** or standstill. In 1917, the United States entered the war, tilting the advantage toward the Allies.

Beginning in March 1918, Germany launched a series of attacks in France on the Western Front, hoping to gain the upper hand before the imminent arrival of massive numbers of U.S. troops. But after some early successes, Allied counterattacks restored most of the pre-March status quo by early August. The German army was exhausted and demoralized. Facing a desperate situation at home and on the front, Germany signed an **armistice** treaty with the Allies on November 11, 1918, bringing World War I to an end.

WORLD WAR I TIMELINE	
Date	**Event**
1914–1915	
June 28, 1914	Archduke Franz Ferdinand assassinated
August 1–4, 1914	Germany declares war on Russia and France, invades neutral Belgium; Britain declares war
September–October 1914	Battles of the Marne and Ypres begin
November 1914	War expands to Turkey

WORLD WAR I TIMELINE	
Date	**Event**
May 7, 1915	German submarines sink the ocean liner *Lusitania*, killing 1,198 civilians (128 Americans)
1916–1917	
February 1916	Battle of Verdun begins
July 1916	Battle of the Somme begins
March 15, 1917	Tsar Nicholas II of Russia abdicates
April 6, 1917	United States enters war against Germany
December 1917	Russia withdraws from the war
1918–1919	
November 11, 1918	Germany signs armistice agreement
January 1919	Versailles Conference

New Technologies in Weapons

New technologies contributed to the mass casualties of World War I. **Machine guns** killed and maimed thousands of soldiers. **Poison gas** blinded and suffocated its victims. Gas masks became part of every soldier's equipment. **Barbed wire** protected trenches. Attacking soldiers slowed by or entangled in the spiky wire were easy targets for enemy machine gunners. Armored **tanks** could cross open terrain, crushing anyone and anything in their path.

Armies deployed **airplanes** in combat for the first time. By the end of they war, pilots engaged in one-on-one combat with machine guns mounted in the cockpit and both sides used planes to drop small bombs on enemy targets—the first form of aerial bombardment. At sea, German **submarines** sank enemy warships and merchant vessels. The Germans expertly developed their submarine, or U-boat, program, deploying more than 100 of the vessels during the course of the war. Wired communication technologies, such as the telephone and telegraph, helped orders and results move farther and more quickly on the battlefield.

Source: Getty Images

A French Renault FT-17 tank blasting through a trench, heading toward the German front line in France in 1918

Protest and Insurrection

Stalemate on the battlefront demoralized the troops. On both sides, soldiers began to feel abandoned by their respective leaders. Some men mutinied and openly refused to fight. Others began to sabotage equipment or desert their posts. One of the largest mutinies took place among French soldiers during the Second Battle of the Aisne in 1917. Soldiers in 136 regiments refused to man the front lines. Thousands deserted. Around 40,000 men participated in various acts of mutiny. General Henri Petain finally brought the rebellion to a halt. Twenty-six men were executed. The rest returned to their posts.

The cost of the war sparked unrest at home too. In Russia and Ireland, revolutions began to remake European society and politics.

Easter Rebellion in Ireland

For centuries, the Irish had sought to free their island from British rule. Despite their differences with Britain, though, thousands of Irish soldiers enlisted to fight with the British in World War I. Heavy losses in the trenches increased resentment at home. Many Irish believed that the British had no intention of honoring the Irish Home Rule Bill that had been passed by the British parliament but "temporarily" suspended with the outbreak of the war. On April 23 (Easter Sunday), 1916, the **Easter Rebellion** broke out in Dublin, Ireland's capital. A week of street fighting between Irish rebels and British troops ended with the uprising crushed. About 1,350 people had been killed or wounded. The British executed 15 rebel leaders. In 1922, a treaty divided Ireland into two parts: the Irish Free State and British Northern Ireland. Conflict would continue to plague Ireland for most of the 20th century. (See Topic 9.5.)

Russian Revolution

Russia's war with Germany left the country drained and impoverished. Workers went on strike. Riots broke out. After going to the Eastern Front to personally command the war effort, **Tsar Nicholas II** returned home to find his capital in revolt. As a result of the **Russian Revolution**, Tsar Nicholas II abdicated his throne in March 1917, and a provisional government took over. However, the new government's weak leadership and insistence on continuing the war effort made it vulnerable. In November, the Bolshevik Party seized power. **Vladimir Lenin**, a communist leader, controlled the new government.

In December 1917, Russia and Germany negotiated an armistice, a cessation of fighting, and the March 1918 Treaty of Brest-Litovsk officially marked the end of Russia's war. In 1922, Russia formed the **Soviet Union**, a confederation of communist republics. Relations between the Soviet Union and Germany were sometimes tense in the years that followed, and the two countries would confront one another again in World War II.

Global Conflict

The war in Europe quickly spread to the Middle East, North Africa, and Asia. Japan declared war on Germany and seized Germany's colony in China. Arabs began to revolt against the Ottoman Empire in the Arabian Peninsula. By the end of 1914, World War I was truly a global conflict.

Armenian Genocide

In 1915, the Ottoman government began a systematic program to seize Armenian land and deport Armenians from Turkey. Armenians were a Christian minority who lived mainly in northeastern Turkey. Turkey's Muslim rulers feared that Armenians were potential traitors who would betray the empire if they had a chance to win autonomy.

Ottoman authorities encouraged ethnic Turks to rise up against their Armenian neighbors. Many Armenians were murdered outright, while others died of hunger, thirst, and disease on the forced march from their homes to camps in the deserts of Syria and Iraq. Between 1915 and 1916, an estimated 1 million or more Armenians died. Many Armenians and their supporters have described the actions of the Turks as **genocide**, an attempt at complete extermination of all people in an ethnic or religious group. The Turkish government has denied the charge of genocide.

Arab Revolt Against the Turks

Although both Arabs and Turks were Muslim, Arabs regarded Turks as oppressors. As the Ottoman Empire weakened, Arab tribes in the Arabian Peninsula organized attacks on Ottoman posts. The British supported the Arabs against their common enemy the Turks and supplied them with weapons and advisors led by the famous Lawrence of Arabia, Colonel T. E. Lawrence. Emir Faisal of Arabia drove the Ottomans from the cities of Mecca and Medina. In Syria and Lebanon, Arab nationalists overthrew Ottoman rulers.

After the war, however, Britain betrayed earlier promises to support Arab nationalism, and the Arabs failed to establish independent states.

Japanese Aggression in the Pacific

Japan declared war on Germany in 1914. Japanese troops seized many of Germany's island territories in the South Pacific as well as territory on mainland China. In 1916, Russia helped Japan extend its reach into Manchuria. Japan attended the Peace Conference in Paris but did not gain any territory. Anti-Japanese sentiment forced the Japanese out of China. These frustrations of Japan's territorial ambitions fueled its desire for an empire. In 1931, Japan returned to Manchuria, beginning its imperialist collision course with the United States and World War II in the Pacific.

The Balance of Power Shifts

After World War I, the balance of power shifted. The United States emerged as a world leader. The Austro-Hungarian Empire disbanded and split into several smaller states. The dissolution of the Ottoman Empire led to the creation of the modern state of Turkey, under the leadership of **Kemal Ataturk**, in 1923. Although sympathetic to the Allies, it did not participate in World War II.

A defeated and weakened Germany lost its staus as a dominant power in Europe and worldwide. Britain, France, and Belgium took control of Germany's former possessions in Africa and in the Pacific as a part of the **mandate system**. Under this system, victor nations governed the colonies of the defeated nations. The mandate system was also applied to Middle Eastern territories once ruled by the Ottoman Empire. France and Britain controlled the regions of Palestine and Syria.

REFLECT ON THE ESSENTIAL QUESTION

Essential Question: *What were the causes and effects of World War I?*

Causes of World War I	Effects of World War I

KEY TERMS

militarism	stalemate	Tsar Nicholas II
imperial competition	armistice	Russian Revolution
Archduke Franz Ferdinand	machine gun	Vladimir Lenin
Gavrilo Princip	poison gas	Soviet Union
Central Powers	barbed wire	genocide
Allies	tank	Kemal Ataturk
Western Front	airplane	mandate system
Eastern Front	submarine	
trench warfare	Easter Rebellion	

MULTIPLE-CHOICE QUESTIONS

Questions 1–3 refer to the passages below.

Passage 1

> "The Bishop tells us: 'when the boys come back
>
> They will not be the same; for they'll have fought
>
> In a just cause: they lead the last attack on Anti-Christ. . . .'
>
> 'We're none of us the same!' the boys reply.
>
> 'For George lost both his legs; and Bill's stone blind;
>
> Poor Jim's shot through the lungs and like to die. . . .'"

—Siegfried Sassoon, "They," October 31, 1916

Passage 2

> "And men will not understand us—for the generation that grew up before us, though it has passed these years with us here, already had a home and a calling; now it will return to its old occupations, and the war will be forgotten—and the generation that has grown up after will be strange to us and push us aside. We will grow older, a few will adapt themselves, some others will merely submit, and most will be bewildered;—the years will pass by and in the end we shall fall into ruin."

—Erich Maria Remarque, *All Quiet on the Western Front*, Germany, 1928

1. The author of the passage in Passage 1 is suggesting the disillusionment was caused by
   (A) anti-imperial sentiment
   (B) political unrest
   (C) new weapon technology
   (D) British colonial losses

2. The views represented in these two passages both refer to
   (A) the destruction caused by "fire-bombing"
   (B) Armenian genocide
   (C) German blitzkrieg
   (D) the horrors of World War I

3. The author of Passage 2 is likely to find which of the following most responsible for many postwar problems?

(A) The Versailles Treaty

(B) The Schlieffen Plan

(C) The New Imperialism

(D) The Industrial Revolution

SHORT-ANSWER QUESTION

Use the passage below to answer all parts of the question that follows.

"The cannon fodder loaded onto trains in August and September is moldering in the killing fields of Belgium. . . .

Across the ocean stretch thousands of greedy hands to snatch it up. Business thrives in the ruins. Cities become piles of ruins; villages become cemeteries; countries, deserts; populations are beggared; churches, horse stalls. International law, treaties and alliances, the most sacred words and the highest authority have been torn in shreds. Every sovereign 'by the grace of God' is called a rogue and lying scoundrel by his cousin on the other side. Every diplomat is a cunning rascal to his colleagues in the other party. Every government sees every other as dooming its own people and worthy only of universal contempt. There are food riots in Venice, in Lisbon, Moscow, Singapore. There is plague in Russia, and misery and despair everywhere. Violated, dishonored, wading in blood, dripping filth—there stands bourgeois society. . . .

Today's world war is entirely a competitive struggle amongst fully mature capitalisms for world domination, for the exploitation of the remaining zones of the world not yet capitalistic."

—German communist leader Rosa Luxemburg, *The Crisis in German Social-Democracy (The Junius Pamphlet)*, 1915

1. a) Identify Luxemburg's audience for this passage.

   b) Explain how ONE word or phrase indicates Luxemburg's point of view about World War I.

   c) Explain ONE example of a historical development or process that Luxemburg is basing her claims on.

Topic 8.3

The Russian Revolution and Its Effects

Workers of the world, unite; you have nothing to lose but your chains.
—Karl Marx, *Communist Manifesto*, 1848

Essential Question: What were the causes and effects of the Russian Revolution?

The power of central governments increased throughout Europe during World War I. By the end of the war, the Russian, German, Austro-Hungarian, and Ottoman empires had collapsed. The new democratic governments that followed tended to be weak, because there was no history of democratic institutions in these countries. These political changes led to internal conflicts in many European states, exacerbated by severe economic problems and ethnic tensions. Different ideas soon emerged about the relationship between the individual and the state.

Responses to Industrialization

Among these ideas, **communism** advocated ownership of the means of production by the **proletariat**, or working class, with the ultimate goal of a classless society. As these ideals became reality, communists believed individuals would be freed from oppressive labor to develop their full human potential, and the state would eventually cease to exist.

Communism is an extreme form of **left-wing** ideology. On the opposite side, **fascism** espoused a strong central government with dictatorial control over the economy and the lives of individuals. Fascism is an extreme form of **right-wing** ideology. Both of these ideologies conflicted with **liberal democracy**, which characterized the governments of several Western European states. In liberal democracies, individuals were free to elect government leaders and develop their individual self-interests through a capitalist economy. These ideological conflicts led to World War II and continued throughout the 20th century.

THREE APPROACHES TO MODERN INDUSTRIAL SOCIETY			
Policy Area	Communism	Capitalism	Fascism
Economics	Belief that businesses should be owned or managed by the government	Belief that businesses should be owned privately and compete with each other	Belief that businesses should be owned privately, and government should restrict competition
Internationalism and Nationalism	Supports internationalism by opposing colonialism and calling for global worker solidarity	Supports a mixture of nationalism and internationalism	Strongly supports nationalism by urging each nation to pursue its unique interests
War and Peace	Belief that international peace would follow the defeat of capitalism through violent revolution	Expresses mixed attitudes toward war and peace	Often pursues a policy of nationalist expansionism
Equality	Supports both political and economic equality	Supports political equality but not economic equality	Opposes both political and economic equality
Religion	Rejects religion and advocates atheism	Allows individual religious liberty	Views religion as a way to promote national unity

The Russian Revolution and Lenin

In Russia, both reformers and revolutionaries were influenced by the German intellectual **Karl Marx** (1818–1883). Among these was a lawyer, Vladimir Lenin. Even before he studied Marx closely, Lenin was a revolutionary, committed to overthrowing the tsarist government. While he adopted most of Marx's ideas, he modified them in important ways. For example, Marx thought that a socialist revolution could happen only in a wealthy, highly industrialized country. Lenin disagreed. He believed that even Russia, a poor, peasant-dominated country, could become socialist. Further, Lenin thought that a successful revolution would always depend on a small group of dedicated revolutionaries who could lead the masses. His modifications of Marx's ideas became known as **Marxist-Leninist theory**.

Lenin led the **Bolshevik** faction of the **Russian Social Democratic Party**, an early Russian Marxist organization. While some socialists believed in gradual, peaceful change, the Bolsheviks called for immediate, violent change. They became the basis for the modern **Communist Party**, which controlled Russia through much of the 20th century.

War Spurs Revolutionary Change

A peaceful march to the tsar's palace led to violence and revolution in 1905. In order to quell the violence, Tsar Nicholas II finally agreed to create a **duma**, or elected legislature. However the duma never gained the power to create a true constitutional monarchy since it was ultimately under the tsar's control.

Political and economic problems continued. Russian society remained hierarchical with extreme social inequality. The incomplete industrialization that began in the 1890s created many social problems, with people living and working in poor conditions in the crowded cities of Moscow and St. Petersburg. Land and food distribution excluded many people. Most peasants did not own land, and food shortages were common. The demands of World War I made these long-standing problems worse and brought Russia to the brink of collapse. Because of this weakened condition, a revolutionary minority, the Bolsheviks, was able to gain control of the country.

The March Revolution Russian industries were unprepared for wartime production. With so many men in the military, women held many factory jobs. After working long hours, these women then had to stand in long lines to buy meager amounts of food. On March 8, 1917, about 10,000 women demonstrated under the banner "Peace and Bread" on the streets of the capital city of Petrograd (formerly, and again today, known as St. Petersburg). A general strike shut down the city's factories on March 10. When the tsar ordered troops to disperse the crowds, many of the troops joined the demonstrators instead.

After the duma met on March 12, the tsar agreed to abdicate on March 15. The moderates in the duma then established the **Provisional Government**, which represented the middle class and liberal aristocrats rather than workers and peasants. The government wanted to continue the war as a matter of national honor. However, the lower classes wanted the war to end immediately.

At the same time, the Provisional Government faced competition from the **Soviets**, councils that represented workers, peasants, and soldiers. The first Soviet formed in Petrograd in March. Others quickly formed within the army and then other areas. These Soviets, composed mainly of radical socialists, represented the interests of the lower classes.

Lenin Returns to Russia Lenin had been involved in antigovernment activity since 1887 and active in Marxist organizations since 1893. In 1897, the government had punished him by sending him for a number of years to Siberia, a remote region with extreme climate in the eastern part of Russia. After 1900, he lived mostly in exile in Switzerland. Lenin saw the formation of the Provisional Government as an opportunity

Source: Getty Images

Vladimir Lenin had a reputation as a powerful speaker.

for the Bolsheviks to seize power. He returned to Russia in April 1917 and laid out his plans for revolution. Lenin believed that the Bolsheviks could use the Soviets to overthrow the Provisional Government. He had the Bolsheviks gain control of the largest Soviets in Petrograd and Moscow. At the same time, the Bolsheviks began to use propaganda to gain the support of the people. Propaganda uses emotional language, distortion of facts, or scare tactics to persuade others to support a particular point of view. Bolshevik propaganda revolved around three slogans:

- Peace, Land, Bread
- Worker Control of Production
- All Power to the Soviets

The Bolshevik Revolution

The Petrograd Soviet promoted insurrection in the military by directing soldiers to obey only orders that came from newly elected committees of soldiers rather than from the officers who had been in charge. This action created chaos in the army. The Provisional Government was unable to undertake a new military offensive in July as many peasant soldiers deserted and returned to their homes. Although an attempt by soldiers and workers to overthrow the government failed at that time, conditions revealed how weak the government was.

By late October 1917, the Bolshevik Party's membership had grown substantially, and the Bolsheviks had gained slim majorities in the Petrograd and Moscow Soviets. Lenin believed that the time was right for the Bolsheviks to seize control. He overcame resistance in his party with the help of **Leon Trotsky** (1877–1940). Trotsky had once been a member of the more moderate Menshevik faction of the Social Democratic Party but had become an ardent supporter of revolution. On November 6–7, the Bolsheviks easily took control of the Winter Palace in Petrograd, where the Provisional Government had its headquarters.

Lenin soon established the Council of People's Commissars, which held true power in the country. He quickly enacted laws to give peasants control of land and workers control of factories in order to keep the masses of people supporting the Bolsheviks, who soon became known as **communists**. Lenin then disbanded the Constituent Assembly, which had been elected under the Provisional Government and in which the Bolsheviks had a minority of seats.

On March 3, 1918, Bolshevik-led Russia agreed to give the Baltic territories and some other lands that were part of the Russian empire to Germany in the Treaty of Brest-Litovsk, which ended Russia's involvement in World War I. Shortly after this treaty was signed, Lenin moved the Russian capital to Moscow because it was farther from Germany. In July 1918, Tsar Nicholas II and his family were executed. In about one year, Russia had moved from an autocratic government led by the tsar to a new form of authoritarian rule under the Communists.

Civil War

Although lower-class Russians wanted peace, the treaty that ended their country's involvement in World War I did not bring it to them. Instead the country was plunged into a long civil war because numerous forces opposed the Bolsheviks, who were called the Reds because of the color of the Communist flag. Opponents, called the Whites, included not only members of the bourgeoisie and aristocracy who opposed communism but also other socialist factions that opposed Lenin. This included the Mensheviks and the Social Revolutionaries. Troops from the Allies fighting in World War I also became involved. Their initial goal was to bring Russia back into the war against Germany, although they remained in the country after World War I ended in November 1918.

Source: Wikimedia Commons

Red Army troops in Moscow, 1919

For a time, the Whites seemed close to success. By 1921, however, the Communists had regained control of the country. There were several reasons why the Communists were ultimately successful:

- The Red Army was more disciplined and effective under the leadership of Leon Trotsky and had better field positions.

- The Whites could not agree on a united political strategy. Some wanted the return of the tsarist government; others wanted a more democratic form of government.

- The communists were unified around the goal of creating a new order in Russian society.

- The communists established **war communism** in order to win and maintain their power. They took steps such as nationalizing banks and industries, forcibly taking grain from peasants, and creating a centralized government bureaucracy controlled by the Bolsheviks. In addition, they used a secret police force to eliminate all opposition to the party.

- The communists appealed to Russians' patriotism to fight against Allied troops that were portrayed as foreign invaders.

Lenin's New Economic Policy

In 1921, Lenin saw that Russia was on the brink of economic collapse after years of war and strict government control of the economy. Peasants and workers threatened to revolt against the policies that had been put in place during the civil war. For example, peasants began holding back food from the government. A two-year drought that began in 1920 resulted in widespread famine that killed millions of people.

To address these conditions, Lenin introduced his **New Economic Policy (NEP)** in March 1921. The NEP was basically a modified form of a free-market or small-scale capitalist economy. Peasants were allowed to sell their produce on the open market. Private ownership of retail shops and other small businesses was permitted. The state retained control of larger industries, banks, and mines. By 1922, the economy and harvests had improved, and the country was more stable.

REFLECT ON THE ESSENTIAL QUESTION

Essential Question: *What were the causes and effects of the Russian Revolution?*

Causes of the Russian Revolution	Effects of the Russian Revolution

---

KEY TERMS

communism	Karl Marx	Provisional Government
proletariat	Marxist-Leninist theory	Soviets
left-wing	Bolshevik	Leon Trotsky
fascism	Russian Social Democratic	communists
right-wing	Party	war communism
liberal democracy	Communist Party	New Economic Policy
	Duma	(NEP)

MULTIPLE-CHOICE QUESTIONS

Questions 1–3 refer to the passage below.

"The situation in the army has not changed and may be described as a complete lack of confidence in the officers and the higher commanding personnel. The belief is growing among the soldiers that they cannot be punished for what they do. . . . To this must be added a general weariness, an irritability, and a desire for peace at any price. . . . The press of the political parties is no longer influencing the soldier masses. Again and again one hears the orders of the Provisional Government severely criticized. The committee of the 95th Regiment . . . declared Kerensky a traitor . . . ."

An intensive agitation is being conducted in favor of an immediate cessation of military operations on all fronts. Whenever a whole regiment or battalion refuses to carry out a military order, the fact is immediately made known to other parts of the army through special agitators. . . ."

—Russian Army intelligence report, October 1917

1. The conditions referred to in the passage led most immediately to
   (A) the abdication of Tsar Nicholas II
   (B) the creation of a liberal republic in Russia
   (C) the Bolshevik takeover of the government
   (D) Stalin's purges of political and military rivals

2. The report best supports which of the following claims?
   (A) The backing for revolutionary change was largest in Russia's major cities.
   (B) The Provisional Government's commitment to the war effort undermined its legitimacy.
   (C) Widespread domestic discontent led to the collapse of the Soviet Union.
   (D) The Bolsheviks' victory in the Russian Civil War resulted from the military weaknesses of their opponents.

3. The situation in the Russian army in 1917 was similar to the situation in
   (A) the Decembrist Revolt (1825) because members of the military were opposed to government policies
   (B) the Napoleonic Wars (1812 to 1815) because the military carried out a scorched-earth policy
   (C) the Crimean War that began (1853–1856) because the military wanted to demonstrate its strength
   (D) the Polish uprising (1830) because the military was sent out to defeat an internal rebellion

SHORT-ANSWER QUESTION

Answer all parts of the question that follows.

1. a) Describe ONE way that communism, capitalism, and fascism all developed in response to the same historical context.
   b) Explain ONE economic policy of Lenin's that supported his claim that he supported communism rather than capitalism or fascism.
   c) Explain ONE foreign policy of Lenin's that supported his claim that he supported communism rather than capitalism or fascism.

Topic 8.4

Versailles Conference and Peace Settlement

It is far easier to make war than peace.

—French Prime Minister Georges Clemenceau, speech at Verdun, 1919

Essential Question: How and why did the settlement of World War I fail to resolve political, economic, and diplomatic challenges of the early 20th century?

In the aftermath of World War I, the **Versailles Conference** was organized to negotiate the terms of peace. The conference convened in Paris on January 4, 1919. The United States, Great Britain, France, and Italy led the negotiations. These countries, known as the "big four," wanted to establish long-term peace in Europe and beyond, but they did not necessarily share a unified vision for how that would be achieved.

The Peace Settlement

At the forefront of this effort to gain long-term peace was U.S. President **Woodrow Wilson** (1856–1924). In early 1918, Wilson had introduced his Fourteen Points, an idealistic vision for postwar peace and security in Europe and worldwide. In many ways, the points delivered what Wilson called "peace without victory"—a resolution to the war in which humiliation, resentment, and a desire for revenge could be avoided.

However, the stunning ravages of the war (see the table below) put Prime Minister **David Lloyd George** (1863–1945) of Great Britain and Prime Minister **Georges Clemenceau** (1841–1929) of France in a much less charitable frame of mind. They insisted Germany accept guilt for starting the war and pay heavy **reparations**—money paid for the cost of the war and the damages it caused—to the victorious nations. They hoped to cripple Germany's ability to wage war in Europe ever again.

MAJOR COMBATANT COUNTRIES' MILITARY CASUALTIES, WORLD WAR I			
Country	**Total Forces**	**Killed/Died**	**Wounded**
British Empire	8,900,000	908,000	2,090,000
France	8,400,000	1,360,000	4,266,000
Russia	12,000,000	1,700,000	4,950,000

MAJOR COMBATANT COUNTRIES' MILITARY CASUALTIES, WORLD WAR I			
Country	Total Forces	Killed/Died	Wounded
United States	4,355,000	116,500	204,000
Austria-Hungary	7,800,000	1,200,000	3,620,000
Germany	11,000,000	1,775,000	4,216,000
Turkey	2,850,000	325,000	400,000
Total	**55,305,000**	**7,384,500**	**19,746,000**

The Terms of the Treaty

The **Treaty of Versailles** required Germany to give up 10 percent of its land and all of its foreign colonies. The nation was forced to disarm. The Germans had to officially accept responsibility for the war and pay a total amounting to $33 billion U.S. dollars to the victorious nations. Germans resented these terms. Economic difficulties made it almost impossible for them to meet their payments. The German democratic **Weimar Republic**, established after the war, could not immediately rebuild the economy or stabilize German society.

Effects on the Weimar Republic

Daily life was especially challenging for the German people after World War I. Germany was already in debt during the war, so the Treaty of Versailles that ended World War I left them in economic ruins. The treaty not only forced Germany to pay billions of dollars in reparations, it humiliated the country by forcing it to accept full responsibility for the conflict.

To pay the staggering reparations and support German workers who went on strike after France and Belgium took over the industrial Ruhr region in 1923, the Weimar Republic inflated the value of German currency to the point that it became worthless. Even wheelbarrows of cash were not enough to buy food. Political and social unrest were the predictable results of such circumstances, and extreme nationalist groups readily

Source: Library of Congress

Under the Weimar Republic, German currency declined so much in value that burning it was cheaper than purchasing firewood or coal.

exploited the unrest. Although Germany recovered from this crisis, the stage was set for the country's move toward fascism—a dictatorial form of government marked by violent repression, hypernationalism, and racism.

The League of Nations

Created as part of the Treaty of Versailles, the **League of Nations** was intended as a forum where nations could work to resolve their differences. Its charter, or covenant, was based in part on Wilson's Fourteen Points. Wilson believed an international organization supported by a majority of nations could prevent future wars. One of the league's main goals was international **disarmament**, for without weapons, nations could not fight wars. Both the treaty and the covenant went into effect on January 10, 1920.

The first meeting of the league's General Assembly took place in Geneva, Switzerland, on November 15. The league never lived up to its high ideals. The assembly was plagued by suspicion. No nation trusted the others enough to give up its arms. Wilson refused to take any U.S. Senators to Paris with him, so he could not convince the Senate to ratify the Versailles Treaty and the United States did not join the League of Nations. Without U.S. support, the league remained weak. Germany and the Soviet Union were excluded. Though the league continued to exist legally, it had little influence. The League of Nations officially disbanded in 1946 after its weaknesses were exposed by World War II. It was replaced by the United Nations. (See Topic 9.3 for more on the United Nations.)

New States Emerge in Europe

The collapse of the Austro-Hungarian Empire after World War I led to the formation of several new states. Poland, Czechoslovakia, Hungary, and Yugoslavia all emerged from parts of the former empire. Though most of these states wanted to be democratic, political unrest and economic crises created instability and left them vulnerable to authoritarian movements:

- **Poland** became an independent republic in 1918. In 1926, Józef Pilsudski overthrew the government and became dictator. Many Poles welcomed his rule, believing he could enforce order and unity.

- **Czechoslovakia** was formed by the unification of the Czech Republic and Slovakia. Of all the new nations formed after World War I, it was the most democratic and prosperous.

- **Hungary** split from Austria in 1918. In 1920, the victorious nations of World War I forced Hungary to surrender most of its territory. The country became increasingly **totalitarian**—a centralized government led by a dictator, allowing no opposition.

- **Yugoslavia** emerged over time. After the war, this area of the Balkans was called the Kingdom of Serbs, Croats, and Slovenes and was ruled by the Serbian dynasty. Dissatisfaction and struggle among the ethnic groups led to the declaration of a royal dictatorship in 1929 and renaming the country Yugoslavia.

WORLD WAR I BATTLES AND POSTWAR BOUNDARIES

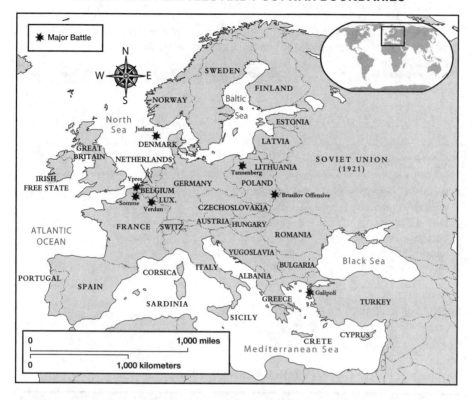

Mandate System Changes the Balance of Power

The League of Nations created the mandate system. (See Topic 8.2.) In this new system, League of Nations members on the winning side of World War I took control over mandates, or colonized terrotories, that had been ruled by defeated nations in the war.

Specifically, Britain and France took control over Middle Eastern territories once ruled by the Ottoman Empire, which no longer existed. Britain was granted control of **Iraq** and **Palestine** (in what is now Israel and Jordan). France was granted control of **Syria** and **Lebanon**. The balance of power had shifted from the Ottoman Empire to Western Europe. This meant that Britain and France had a new strategic interest in the oil produced in the Middle East.

Additionally, the League of Nations took over Germany's colonies in Africa and the Pacific. Britain, France, Belgium, Japan, and Australia now controlled Germany's former African colonies.

The League of Nation's plan was for the controlling nations to stay in charge only until the mandates were judged by the League of Nations to be ready for independence. This meant that controlling nations were not allowed to turn their mandates into their own colonies. Many people in the new territories were upset by the mandate system, fearing it was another name for continued colonialism rather than a road to independence.

REFLECT ON THE ESSENTIAL QUESTION

Essential Question: *How and why did the settlement of World War I fail to resolve political, economic, and diplomatic challenges of the early 20th century?*

Political Failures	Economic Failures	Diplomatic Failures

KEY TERMS

Versailles Conference	Weimar Republic	totalitarian
Woodrow Wilson	League of Nations	Yugoslavia
David Lloyd George	disarmament	Iraq
Georges Clemenceau	Poland	Palestine
reparations	Czechoslovakia	Syria
Treaty of Versailles	Hungary	Lebanon

MULTIPLE-CHOICE QUESTIONS

Questions 1–3 refer to the map below.

THE BALKANS, 1913

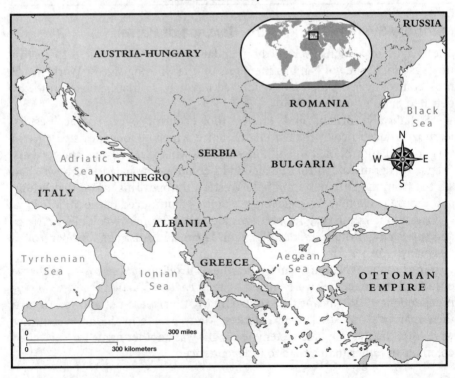

1. Comparing this map with one of the same region a century earlier would highlight the importance of
   (A) conservativism as a reaction against the Enlightenment
   (B) nationalism as a reaction against multiethnic empires
   (C) socialism as a reaction against capitalism
   (D) anarchism as a reaction against the growth of government

2. How did a map of this region look different following post-World War I treaties?
   (A) Serbia, Montenegro, and parts of Austria-Hungary would combine to form a new state.
   (B) Serbia, Bulgaria, and part of Greece would be part of the Ottoman Empire.
   (C) Serbia and Montenegro would be part of Austria-Hungary.
   (D) Serbia, Albania, and Romania would each be divided into smaller states.

3. The changes that occurred after World War I in the region shown on the map differed from the changes in the Middle East because the ones in the region shown
   (A) resulted in independent countries rather than mandates
   (B) were supported by Russia rather than opposed by it
   (C) weakened the empires that lost in World War I rather than strengthened them
   (D) increased the influence of nationalism rather than weakened it

SHORT-ANSWER QUESTION

Use the passage below to answer all parts of the question that follows.

"Not many people noticed at the time, but World War I ended this year. Well, in a sense it did: on Oct. 3, Germany finally paid off the interest on bonds that had been taken out [from foreign investors, including ones in the United States] by the shaky Weimar government in an effort to pay the war reparations imposed by the Treaty of Versailles.

While the amount, less than $100 million, was trivial by today's standards, the payment brought to a close one of the most poisonous chapters of the 20th century. It also, unfortunately, brought back to life an insidious historical myth: that the reparations and other treaty measures were so odious that they made Adolf Hitler's rise and World War II inevitable.

In truth, the reparations, as the name suggests, were not intended as a punishment. They were meant to repair the damage done, mainly to Belgium and France, by the German invasion and subsequent four years of fighting. They would also help the Allies pay off huge loans they had taken to finance the war, mainly from the United States. At the Paris peace talks of 1919, President Woodrow Wilson was very clear that there should be no punitive fines on the losers, only legitimate costs. The other major statesmen in Paris, Prime Ministers David Lloyd George of Britain and Georges Clemenceau of France, reluctantly agreed, and Germany equally reluctantly signed the treaty."

—Margaret MacMillan, "Ending the War to End All Wars,"
The New York Times, December 25, 2010

1. a) Describe ONE similarity in how Great Britain, France, and Germany felt about signing the treaty at Versailles, according to MacMillan.

   b) Explain ONE piece of additional evidence that refutes MacMillan's observation about the similarity in how Great Britain, France, and Germany felt about the Versailles Treaty.

   c) Explain ONE example of how banks and investors in the United States benefited from the reparations plan.

Topic 8.5

Global Economic Crisis

The difficulty lies, not in the new ideas, but in escaping from the old ones.

—British economist John Maynard Keynes, *The General Theory of Employment, Interest and Money,* 1936

Essential Question: What were the causes and effects of the global economic crisis of the 1920s and 1930s?

In October 1929, the U.S. stock market crashed, setting off the **Great Depression**. It quickly spread to Europe, which was still economically recovering from World War I. Weaknesses in international trade also contributed to the Depression. As citizens faced rising unemployment and hunger, radical political responses to the crisis spread throughout Europe. Before it was over, the Depression became a major factor in undermining Western European democracies.

Worldwide Economic Weaknesses

One reason for the rapid spread of the Great Depression to Europe was that most countries determined the value of their currency based on its worth in a fixed amount of gold, a monetary practice known as the **gold standard**. There was no flexibility to let the value of a currency and its exchange rate with other currencies change as economic conditions changed.

There were many causes of weak economies throughout the world after World War I. Tied to the gold standard, the currencies of countries had **depreciated**, or declined in value, after the war. European countries had spent billions of dollars waging the war, leading to massive debt and the need to borrow for rebuilding. Countries on the losing side, especially Germany, were burdened by the requirement to pay huge reparations to the victors, especially France and Britain. European economies had barely started recovering from the war by 1922. Other problems weakened the economies further.

Overproduction

Countries geared up agriculture and manufacturing production to meet the requirements of total war. When demand fell after the war, overproduction led to declining prices. Farmers and businesses had to cut back production to adjust. Many had gone into debt to increase production during the war and now did not have the revenue to pay off that debt.

Tariffs and Trade

By the mid-1920s, many European countries began to impose tariffs, or taxes on imported goods, to protect their domestic agricultural and manufacturing sectors, interfering with the free flow of goods and hindering trade. These nationalistic tariff policies led to higher prices for imported goods or closed markets to some foreign goods completely.

In addition, countries in Europe that had their factories and infrastructure damaged during the war lost out on trade to the United States. For example, heavy industry in the Wallonia region of Belgium (the country's southern half) was almost totally destroyed during German occupation. This region had historically produced iron, steel, woolen goods, glass, and weapons.

Speculation

In the United States, stock prices rose faster than other prices during the 1920s; investors began to put more money into the stock market in the hopes of reaping huge returns. Stock prices rose rapidly, and more and more people were tempted to invest in the market. This led to **speculation**, which is making high-risk investments hoping that they will eventually pay off well. People often bought on margin, which meant they were borrowing a large portion of the money needed to buy stocks. Such investors believed they could pay back their borrowing from the profits they made. Stock prices rose beyond the value of the companies' worth, revealing the underlying weakness in the economy.

Source: Getty Images/Frederic Lewis

The front page of the *The Philadelphia Inquirer* newspaper published one day after the Wall Street Crash of Black Thursday (October 24, 1929)

Financial Collapse

The Dawes Plan of 1924 reduced German war reparations and provided a $200 million loan for German recovery. The plan had also encouraged U.S. investment in Europe. American bank loans to Germany created prosperity from 1924 to 1929. In 1928, investors began diverting capital from Europe to invest in the U.S. stock market. When stock prices started to decline, investors lost confidence and pulled their money quickly out of the market. This selling off of stocks caused the 1929 stock market crash in October.

As a result of the crash, capital stopped flowing from the United States to Europe. This loss of capital in turn led to the collapse of major banks in Germany and other parts of central Europe. Without American funds, trade and industry declined and unemployment increased. Individual countries' economies were affected by the problems of international banks.

Attempts to Overcome the Great Depression

Western democracies tried a variety of economic and political strategies to overcome the Great Depression. However, their results fell short. Extremist movements weakened democracy throughout the continent.

Rethinking Economic Theories and Policies

The traditional government response to a typical economic depression was a policy of balanced budgets, which required lowering wages and raising protective tariffs, in order to let the depression run its course. During the Great Depression, however, this approach tended to make the situation worse. Britain changed one policy by going off the gold standard in 1931; this change produced some recovery.

The British economist **John Maynard Keynes** (1883–1946) proposed a new and different economic approach. Instead of balanced budgets and tariffs, he advocated increased government spending to increase consumer demand, even if this spending resulted in budget deficits. For example, he stated that government spending on infrastructure projects could help create jobs, giving consumers more money to spend and thus provide a reason for other businesses to hire workers to produce more products. Such a program required greater government involvement in the economy, but British politicians did not have the will to do that in the 1930s.

Forging Political Alliances

Several European governments found it necessary to forge political alliances among parties that usually competed rather than cooperated. For example, in Britain, a **national government** was formed in 1931 that was a coalition of all three parties—Conservative, Liberal, and Labour. This coalition government was successful in cutting unemployment from about 3 million in 1932 to about 1.6 million in 1936, using traditional economic policies.

France felt the effects of the Depression later than other countries because its economy had more balance between agriculture and industry. However, fascist groups in France became stronger as the Depression worsened. The French **Popular Front** government, formed in 1936, was a response to the rise of fascism. This coalition government included Communists, Socialists, and Radicals—all left-wing groups. The Popular Front introduced new policies that favored workers, such as a 40-hour work week, paid holidays, and collective bargaining. However, these policies did not effectively solve France's economic problems. By 1939, France and Britain were the only major European countries with democratic governments.

Source: Getty Images/ Keystone

Members of the Front Populaire (French Popular Front) carrying a huge portrait of Socialist leader Léon Blum during a gathering in the Place de la Republique, Paris, to protest high unemployment.

Cooperative social action in Scandinavia under socialist leaders successfully dealt with the Great Depression. Capitalists and socialists worked together to increase social welfare benefits, including retirement pensions, maternity allowances, subsidized housing, and unemployment insurance. In Sweden, they used large-scale deficits to finance public works and promote employment. However, the eventual price for all of the spending was high taxes on most Scandinavians.

German Extremism

Germany suffered more from the Great Depression than any other European nation due to the high reparations and German dependence on American investment as a result of the Dawes Plan. By the end of 1930, almost 4.5 million people were unemployed; the number had increased to 6 million two years later. The Weimar Republic's inability to deal with this level of economic suffering and the fear that followed in its wake opened the door for Hitler's Nazi Party to come to power. The Nazis held out the hope of restoring Germany to order and prosperity.

REFLECT ON THE ESSENTIAL QUESTION

Essential Question: *What were the causes and effects of the global economic crisis of the 1920s and 1930s?*

Causes	Effects

Great Depression   speculation   Popular Front
gold standard   John Maynard Keynes
depreciate   national government

MULTIPLE-CHOICE QUESTIONS

Questions 1–3 refer to the table below.

CHANGE IN INDUSTRIAL OUTPUT, 1928 TO 1932	
Country	**Percentage of Change**
Sweden	+10%
Norway	–2%
France	–10%
Netherlands	–15%
Great Britain	–17%
Belgium	–29%
Austria	–40%
Czechoslovakia	–40%
Germany	–42%

Source: "Change in Industrial Output in Selected European Countries from 1928 to 1932 and from 1928 to 1937/8, Following the Great Depression," statista.com

1. One similarity among countries listed in this table where industrial production declined was that they were
   (A) the first countries to industrialize
   (B) the lowest in population or small in area
   (C) the most dependent on agriculture in the 1930s
   (D) the ones located in central Europe

2. The historical context that most directly influenced the changes shown in the table was that Europe faced economic problems because of
   (A) the results of World War I and the treaties that ended it
   (B) the new technology developed during and after World War I
   (C) the threat of the spread of Russian communism into other countries
   (D) the impact of disarmament agreements on employment

3. The changes shown in the table were most directly a result of which of the following?

   (A) Consumers could not afford to purchase all that companies could produce, so companies eventually reduced production.

   (B) Investors were reluctant to purchase stocks in the 1920s, so companies had less money to invest in making new products.

   (C) Old empires were breaking apart, so trade became more difficult and production became less efficient.

   (D) Countries were beginning to adopt the gold standard for the first time, so the value of currency declined.

SHORT-ANSWER QUESTION

Use the cartoon below to answer all parts of the question that follows.

'PHEW! THAT'S A NASTY LEAK. THANK GOODNESS IT'S NOT AT OUR END OF THE BOAT' (1932)

Source: Wikimedia Commons, David Low, Great Britain, 1932

The boat is labeled "World Money Problems." The label on the left side of the boat is "Middle Europe." The labels on the right side are "Britain," "France," and "U.S.A."

1. a) Describe the historical development portrayed in this cartoon.

   b) Explain ONE cause of the conditions portrayed in this cartoon.

   c) Explain ONE response in dealing with the issues shown in the cartoon.

Topic 8.6

Fascism and Totalitarianism

Before mass leaders seize the power to fit reality to their lies,
their propaganda is marked by its extreme contempt for facts,
as such, for in their opinion fact depends entirely on the power of man
who can fabricate it.

—political scientist and philosopher Hannah Arendt (1906–1975),
The Origins of Totalitarianism (1951)

Essential Question: What factors led to the development of fascist and totalitarian regimes in the aftermath of World War I?

Essential Question: What were the consequences of Stalin's economic policies and totalitarian rule in the Soviet Union?

After World War I, political uncertainty arose as European countries tried to transition to democracy in the context of economic instability. These conditions led to an increase in the popularity of fascism.

Fascism and Authoritarian Rule

The roots of fascism could be seen in the heightened nationalism and increasing militarism in Europe in the pre–World War I era. During that era, the rise in socialism and the increase in labor strikes alarmed conservative leaders. Though they appreciated how capitalism created great wealth, they worried that it created great instability and bitter social conflict.

After the war, there was bitterness over the Treaty of Versailles, especially in Italy and Germany. The revolution in Russia sparked fears that communism was a threat to other countries. All of this political uncertainty and unrest led to an increase in popularity for the promises of fascism.

Mussolini in Italy

The results of World War I made Italians bitter. The war had been costly for Italy, both financially and in human lives. Though Italy was on the winning side, the Treaty of Versailles did not give Italians all the land they desired. Then postwar economic problems caused severe inflation and unemployment.

Rise of the Blackshirts In 1919, **Benito Mussolini** (1883–1945), a former socialist, formed a political group, the *Fasci di Combattimento* (League of Combat), whose name later gave rise to the term *fascism*. Mussolini saw that if he switched from left-wing to right-wing positions, he could take advantage of the fear caused by instability in the country. The postwar parliament was unable to govern successfully, and strikes by industrial and agricultural workers created a climate of violence and class warfare. Mussolini gained the support of middle-class business owners and large landowners by opposing communism and strikes and appealing to Italian national pride. The **Blackshirts**, squads of armed supporters, violently attacked labor organizations and workers. The government supported the Blackshirts as a way to oppose communism.

The Promise of Order The fascists portrayed themselves as the party that would bring order to the country, and they soon gained power. In 1922, the king named Mussolini prime minister after the fascists had marched on Rome and threatened to take it by force. The fascists won 65 percent of the vote in a national election in 1923 and gained a majority in parliament. Although the fascists had manipulated the election, the large victory seemed to indicate the growing popularity of fascism. By the end of 1926, Mussolini established a complete dictatorship as the free press and other political parties were eliminated. Although the army, the monarchy, and the Catholic Church retained some independence from the fascist state, Mussolini ruled Italy as a totalitarian dictator until his death near the end of World War II.

Hitler in Germany

The defeat of the German empire in World War I led to the creation of the democratic Weimar Republic. The republic lacked strong leadership and was unable to control such institutions as the army, judiciary, and government bureaucracy. Wealthy aristocrats and business owners still wanted an imperial government. Germans were bitter about the burden of paying war reparations demanded in the Treaty of Versailles. In addition, severe inflation in the early 1920s caused many people to lose their life savings. Members of the middle class were increasingly attracted to right-wing parties, especially when the Great Depression created severe economic hardship.

Hitler's Emergence Amid the postwar political and economic weakness of Germany, extremism became the path for **Adolf Hitler** (1889–1945) and his supporters to rise to power. As an unsuccessful young artist living in Vienna from 1908 to 1913, Hitler came in contact with such men as Karl Lueger, mayor of Vienna, who influenced his ideas about German nationalism, antisemitism, and leadership of a mass movement through emotional manipulation.

After serving in World War I, Hitler entered politics in Munich. He gained control of a small right-wing party and in 1921 changed its name to the National Socialist German Workers' Party or **Nazi Party**. In November 1923, Hitler and the Nazis staged an armed uprising, the Beer Hall Putsch, in Munich, hoping to cause the collapse of the Weimar Republic. The uprising was unsuccessful, and Hitler was arrested, charged with treason, and sentenced to five years in prison.

Finding Supporters While in prison, Hitler concluded that the way to overthrow the republic was to manipulate its democratic institutions. During his imprisonment, he wrote *Mein Kampf (My Struggle)*, in which he laid out his antisemitic ideas and his plans for expanding German territory.

Hitler also showed an understanding of how to organize mass movements through propaganda. After serving one year in prison, Hitler quickly reestablished himself as the unquestioned leader of the Nazi Party. He first focused on establishing the party organization throughout the country and increasing its membership. By 1929, Hitler realized that the Nazis' greatest success would come from appealing to the middle class in small towns and rural areas rather than workers in large cities.

As Germany began to experience severe economic problems and unemployment in the early 1930s, extremist parties such as the Nazis and communists won support. The Reichstag, or German parliament, was no longer able to govern effectively. Increasingly, right-wing elites in business, the aristocracy, the military, and the bureaucracy saw Hitler as the leader who could restore order and prestige to Germany through a totalitarian government. These elites persuaded President Hindenburg to appoint Hitler as chancellor in January 1933.

Taking Power Once in power, Hitler quickly created the governmental framework for Nazi control over Germany. A key supporter, Hermann Göring, took control of the police. He replaced non-Nazis with members of Hitler's Storm Troops, making Nazi terror part of the government. Hitler persuaded the president to give the government emergency powers after a fire in the Reichstag building in February. Under these powers, citizens lost their rights. Then, after elections in March 1933, Hitler pushed the Reichstag to pass a law suspending the constitution for four years so he could address Germany's problems. The parliament thus gave Hitler the powers of a dictator under the appearance of democracy. The Nazis held totalitarian control under Hitler's rule until his death at the end of World War II in 1945.

Dictatorships and Propaganda

As communist leaders had done in Russia, fascist dictators also used propaganda to attract followers from those who were disillusioned about conditions in their countries. These dictators of the 1920s also used modern technology such as radio and movies to spread their propaganda quickly to wide audiences. In their messages, they rejected democratic institutions, promoted charismatic leaders, and glorified war and nationalism. They presented fascism as the system that would bring order and glory to their countries.

Charismatic Leaders Both Mussolini in Italy and Hitler in Germany were charismatic leaders who created a **cult of personality** around themselves. Both men assumed a title that meant *leader*. Mussolini called himself *Il Duce*, a leader with the strength of iron whose decisions were always correct. Hitler was the *Führer*, a visionary leader who demanded unconditional loyalty from his followers, including a willingness to die for him.

Both men wore military uniforms, had special symbols, and surrounded themselves with elite squads of soldiers and police—known as the Blackshirts in Italy and the Brownshirts in Germany—who terrorized the population. At mass rallies, their speeches whipped crowds into frenzies. The Italian and German states became identified with their supreme leaders who put themselves above the country's democratic institutions.

New Methods of Propaganda Hitler was more successful than Mussolini at using the new technologies of radio and film to spread his propaganda, although both men used newsreels—government-produced propaganda movie shorts that were shown to captive audiences in theaters before popular films—to convey stories that showed them in a most positive light. Hitler soon learned that the sound of his voice over the radio was sufficient to create the feelings of fervent enthusiasm that he achieved among crowds present at mass rallies, allowing millions of people to feel they were present at the rallies.

Hitler's minister of propaganda, **Joseph Goebbels** (1897–1945), used film as an important tool in his work. For example, *The Triumph of the Will* was an important documentary about the 1934 Nazi rally at Nuremberg. The director **Leni Riefenstahl** (1902–2003) used 32 different cameras to capture images of Hitler flying into the city for the rally, driving through the streets while cheered by adoring crowds, and addressing crowds of soldiers and civilians. Such images reinforced Hitler's claims about the widespread support for his ideas.

Architecture, too, became an avenue of propaganda for the Nazis. They disapproved of modern buildings that had been constructed in the Weimar Republic. Hitler wanted new buildings to emphasize the Nazi Party's power and to intimidate the German people. The idea was to build monuments, using flat roofs, uniformity, and no decorative elements.

Italy and Germany were on different sides during World War I, but similar conditions in both countries after the war allowed fascist dictators to come to power. Both Mussolini and Hitler exploited postwar bitterness and economic instability, used terror to control the population, and manipulated the new democracies in their countries, which were generally unpopular.

Franco and the Spanish Civil War

After World War I, the Spanish parliamentary monarchy was weak. A military dictator, General Miguel Primo de Rivera, controlled the country between 1923 and 1930 with support from the Spanish king Alfonso XIII. The beginning of the Great Depression, combined with a multitude of other political, social, and economic issues, led to a loss of support for the monarchy. Alfonso XIII abdicated and the Spanish republic was formed. The government of the republic was extremely unstable as parties on the left and right fought for control. In 1936, the Popular Front, a coalition of left-wing groups, took control. The army, the Catholic Church, and the aristocracy refused to accept the authority of the Popular Front. Under the leadership of General **Francisco Franco** (1892–1975), the army led a violent revolt against the government. The bloody **Spanish Civil War** resulted.

In a number of ways, the Spanish Civil War was a testing ground for World War II. It was a clash between fascists and the Popular Front's left-wing republicans, workers' groups, and communists. This anticipated the clash in World War II between an alliance of Fascists and an alliance of Western democracies and communists. Though it was a war between opposing factions within Spain, other countries became involved:

- Franco received weapons, money, and troops from right-wing fascist governments in Italy and Germany.

- The Popular Front received some support from the Soviet Union, and 40,000 volunteers from Western democracies fought for it. However, the governments of Western democracies did not intervene in the war.

The Spanish Civil War provided both sides the opportunity to test new weapons and tactics they would use in World War II.

Over time, Franco's forces prevailed over the Popular Front, and the war came to an end in March 1939. Franco then instituted a totalitarian government in Spain that lasted until the mid-1970s. Although Spain's government was not exactly fascist, Franco exhibited the characteristics of a fascist dictator, and Spain largely supported the fascist governments in Italy and Germany without joining the Axis powers.

SPREAD OF FASCISM IN EUROPE, 1922–1944

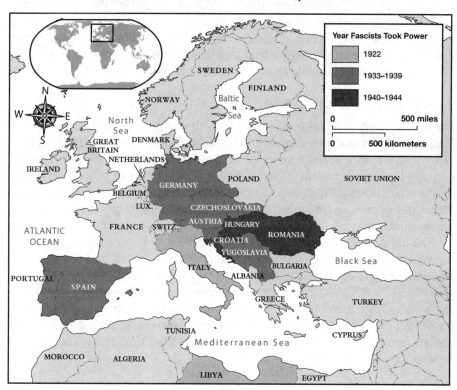

Authoritarian Dictatorships

World War I created a number of new states in Central and Eastern Europe from the dismantled empires of Austria-Hungary and Germany, including Austria, Czechoslovakia, Poland, and Yugoslavia. These new states established parliamentary democracies. Several existing countries, including Bulgaria, Greece, Hungary, and Romania, also established more democratic forms of government in the early 1920s. However, most of these new democracies soon gave way to authoritarian dictatorships.

In general, these states had little tradition of democracy and weak middle classes. Many of these countries were largely rural, and large landowners were not in favor of peasants' rights or the redistribution of land. Ethnic differences were also a source of conflict in many states. Many people, especially the landowners and the churches, saw authoritarian governments as a way to maintain the old social order. For example, the kings of Bulgaria and Yugoslavia established authoritarian governments in the 1920s.

The fascist governments in Italy and Germany provided attractive models for other states. A strong fascist movement grew up in Romania. The king responded by establishing authoritarian rule. A military dictatorship then took control of the country with the outbreak of World War II.

Between 1920 and 1944, Hungary was ruled by head of state and former naval officer, Miklos Horthy. He was a conservative leader who had defeated revolutionary forces in Hungary after World War I. In Poland during this time, Józef Pilsudski took control and fought against Russian aggression. Pilsudski eventually became dictator of Poland from 1926 to 1935. Czechoslovakia was the only state in the region that remained democratic. It had a stronger democratic tradition, middle class, and industrial economy.

The Soviet Union Under Stalin

During Lenin's NEP era, Russia joined with three other territories to form the **Union of Soviet Socialist Republics (USSR)** or **Soviet Union** in 1922. In that same year, Lenin suffered a series of strokes, and he died in 1924. Before his first stroke, Lenin appointed **Joseph Stalin** (1879–1953) as general secretary of the Communist Party. Before his death, Lenin expressed doubts about Stalin, but Lenin's declining health prevented him from removing Stalin from his position.

Lenin's death set off a power struggle within the Politburo, a group of seven men that controlled the Communist Party. One group, led by Leon Trotsky, wanted an end to the NEP and favored the rapid industrialization of the Soviet Union and "international revolution"—the expansion of communism around the world. Other members of the Politburo, including Stalin, wanted to focus on developing "socialism at home"—creating a strong communist state in the Soviet Union—and supported the continuation of the NEP. Stalin and Trotsky were fierce political rivals.

As general secretary, Stalin made thousands of political appointments at the local and regional levels. These appointees became Stalin's strong supporters because they depended on him for their jobs. Eventually, Stalin declared his decision to focus on creating a strong communist state in the Soviet Union and forced all his rivals out of the party. By 1929, Stalin had complete control of the party and established a dictatorship of unprecedented power over the country that lasted until his death.

Rapid Economic Modernization

Although Stalin disagreed with Trotsky on the idea of a worldwide communist revolution, he did favor a program to push for the Soviet Union's rapid modernization. Stalin's first **Five Year Plan**, launched in 1928, was designed to transform the Soviet Union from a mainly agricultural country to an industrial powerhouse. A second plan followed in 1933. Under these plans, the government took control of industry and emphasized production of chemicals, heavy equipment, and weapons rather than consumer goods such as clothing. The steel and oil industries were particularly important. New cities for these industries quickly grew in areas with large iron ore and coal deposits. The rate of economic growth was 14 to 20 percent per year. The Soviet Union also built the largest electric power plant in Europe during this period. This rapid growth and change had severe repercussions for the Soviet people.

Consequences of Economic Modernization

Such rapid industrial growth caused millions of new workers to join the labor force and move into industrial cities. Millions of people lived in terrible conditions because the government spent too little on housing for workers during this period. In addition, workers' wages fell by 43 percent between 1928 and 1940. The government also passed laws that limited workers' ability to move freely about the country. The government used propaganda to encourage workers to sacrifice for the good of the socialist state they were creating.

The government also reorganized agricultural production to finance industry and feed the huge numbers of urban workers. These changes led to suffering for millions in the countryside. In his repressive actions, Stalin made it clear he would stop at nothing to achieve his goals.

Liquidation of the Kulaks Under the NEP, the class of wealthy landowning peasants known as **kulaks** came under greater scrutiny. About two million kulaks employed other peasants to farm on their land for wages. Communists saw the kulaks as capitalists who did not belong in their society. Stalin's response was the **collectivization** of agriculture, eliminating private farm ownership and forcing people onto large collective farms controlled by the state.

Source: Wikimedia Commons

Propaganda stressed the importance of communal values. The text of this 1933 poster from Uzbek, Tashkent, is "Strengthen working discipline in collective farms."

The peasants strongly resisted the move to collective farms. They hid or destroyed their crops and even killed their livestock rather than turn them over to state control. Stalin responded by expanding the process of collectivization to include all private farms, not just the wealthiest kulaks. By 1934, virtually all of the Soviet Union's 26 million peasant households had been moved to 250,000 collective farms. Most of the crops grown on these farms were sold to the state at low prices. Peasants were allowed to have very small private plots to grow food for themselves. The peasants' actions and the state's response had devastating consequences.

Famine in the Ukraine The destruction of crops and livestock led to famines that were created by human action rather than by weather or crop failures. These famines in 1932 and 1933 were especially devastating in the Ukraine, one of the Soviet Union's most fertile farming regions. An estimated 7 to 10 million peasants died as a result of these famines. The government took much of the crops that were grown to feed industrial workers or use for industry. Although peasants starved, industry grew.

Purges of Political Rivals Stalin was determined to eliminate anyone who stood in the way of his policies and goals. He especially focused on his political rivals, termed *Old Bolsheviks*, who had supported Lenin and might oppose Stalin's decisions. During the period of terror known as the Great Purge of 1936–1938, many of these Old Bolsheviks were put on trial and condemned to die. Other perceived enemies of the state were also purged at this time, including members of the Communist Party, five Marshals of the army (the highest-ranking members), and leaders of labor unions. Also, diplomats, intellectuals, and even ordinary citizens were often seen as enemies of the state. As many as eight million people may have been arrested; millions were sent to Siberia where many died in one or another of the systems of forced labor camps known as the **Gulag**.

Repression Under Stalin Stalin's actions resulted in an oppressive political system. He strengthened the Communist Party organization, and anyone who tried to stand in his way could be exiled to Siberia. In a climate of fear, people were encouraged to spy on one another, and the secret police arrested millions of people. Stalin's government also ended the liberal social policies instituted after the 1917 revolution. It outlawed abortion, made divorce more difficult, and treated homosexuality as a crime.

Women in Stalin's Russia Stalin encouraged families to have more children in order to increase the Soviet population. However, at the same time, the government encouraged Soviet women to take jobs outside their homes. The Russian newspaper *Pravda* took pride, in 1929, of how the Russian woman "stands in the most advanced ranks of our working collective . . . [i]n the factory workshop and at the controls of the state ships, in the cooperatives and at the shooting range, in the nursery school and at the thundering machinery, everywhere the tractors of our increasingly strong state farms and collective farms go . . . in none of these places have the working women of the Soviet Union been forced into last place."

WOMEN IN HIGHER EDUCATION IN THE 1930S				
Type of Institution	Soviet Union	Germany	England	Italy
All higher education	38%	14%	26%	14%
Industrial institutes	2%	4%	2%	1%
Agricultural institutes	32%	2%	13%	1%

Source: Adapted from "Women in the Soviet Union and Capitalist Countries," *Zhenshchina v USSR* (Moscow, 1936)

REFLECT ON THE ESSENTIAL QUESTIONS

Essential Question: *What factors led to the development of fascist and totalitarian regimes in the aftermath of World War I?*

Essential Question: *What were the consequences of Stalin's economic policies and totalitarian rule in the Soviet Union?*

Causes of Fascist and Totalitarian Regimes	Effects of Stalin's Policies

HISTORICAL PERSPECTIVES: *WHAT WAS THE APPEAL OF FASCISM?*

When Italian fascism first emerged in the early 20th century, Mussolini focused on regaining the lost glory of the Roman Empire from two millennia earlier. Similarly, other fascist-style leaders often looked to the past for inspiration. However, historians have argued that the appeal of fascism was more than just returning to a time in the past.

Fascism's Connections to Traditions In his book *The Fascist Revolution* (1999), George L. Mosse argued that fascism did not win support by looking at the distant, premodern past. Nor did it offer a revolutionary new ideology. Rather, it combined elements of 19th- and 20th-century ideologies, including Romanticism, liberalism, socialism, Social Darwinism, and modern technology. Because it picked up ideas that were already spreading, it attracted followers quickly. It promised a better future and created an illusion of political participation. Mosse noted that fascism had not originally included racism, nor was racism essential to it.

Fascism's Appeal to Modernists Roger Griffin, in *The Nature of Fascism* (1991) and *Modernism and Fascism: The Sense of a Beginning under Mussolini and Hitler* (2007), focused on how fascism appealed to fear. In the aftermath of World War I, people were anxious that the modern world was becoming decadent. To Griffin, early 20th-century Europeans were desperate for a better world, rejecting the failing one. In this environment, the modernist styles of Mussolini and Hitler and their calls for social revitalization proved attractive. Fascism offered strength and confidence to people who felt little of either.

Fascism at the Right Place and Time Robert O. Paxton wrote *The Anatomy of Fascism* (2004) as a culmination of a lifetime of study of European history. While Mosse and Griffin emphasized cultural concerns, Paxton looked more closely at the influence of changes in political, social, and economic structures. Paxton noted first that although political participation was on the rise, most people still lacked a voice. Fascists criticized this failure of democracy and welcomed the voiceless to their mass politics. Paxton was careful to point out that the fascist movement was possible only because existing political alternatives to capitalism—communist or socialist—failed to provide people with real hope. Existing policies were also unable to solve the economic and social crises of the time.

However, even this cluster of circumstances was not enough for fascism to arise, according to Paxton, since Mussolini and Hitler were around for a number of years before people found their messages attractive. It was only when they combined their message with the nationalism resulting from frustrations after World War I that the fascists gained traction, while existing political elites continued to struggle.

1. Explain Mosse's argument that the appeal of fascism depended on a combination of existing ideologies.

2. Explain how World War I boosted the popularity of fascism.

MULTIPLE-CHOICE QUESTIONS

Questions 1–3 refer to the poster below.

Source: Getty Images

This poster was created by the Soviet government in 1932 and shows Joseph Stalin. It describes how collectivization should be accomplished at the end of the Five Year Plan.

1. The poster best reflects which of the following goals of the Soviet government during the 1930s?

   (A) To encourage migration from the countryside to the cities

   (B) To increase agricultural efficiency by establishing centralized state-run farms

   (C) To prioritize agricultural development over heavy industry

   (D) To win the support of rural residents by redistributing land to individual families

2. The developments reflected in the poster can best be seen as a continuation of

(A) Alexander II's emancipation of the serfs

(B) the expansion of the social welfare state

(C) Lenin's mixture of socialism with free-market principles

(D) the increase in state control over the economy

3. The policy represented in the poster had which of the following effects in the Soviet Union?

(A) It ended the era of centralized economic planning.

(B) It increased the political influence of the kulaks.

(C) It expanded the use of state repression.

(D) It eliminated famine in the countryside.

SHORT-ANSWER QUESTION

Use the passage below to answer all parts of the question that follows.

"Totalitarian movements use and abuse democratic freedoms in order to abolish them. This is not just devilish cleverness on the part of the leaders or childish stupidity on the part of the masses. . . . Above the state and behind the facades of ostensible power, in a maze of multiplied offices, underlying all shifts of authority and in a chaos of inefficiency, lies the power nucleus of the country, the superefficient and super-competent services of the secret police. The emphasis on the police as the sole organ of power, and the corresponding neglect of the seemingly greater power arsenal of the army, which is characteristic of all totalitarian regimes, can still be partially explained by the totalitarian aspiration to world rule and its conscious abolition of the distinction between a foreign country and a home country, between foreign and domestic affairs."

—Hannah Arendt, *Origins of Totalitarianism,"* 1951

1. a) Explain how ONE piece of evidence supports Arendt's argument regarding the rise of totalitarianism from 1917–1939.

b) Explain how ONE piece of evidence modifies or refutes Arendt's argument regarding the rise of totalitarianism from 1917–1939.

c) Explain ONE difference between absolute monarchies of the 16th, 17th, and 18th centuries and totalitarian leaders of the 20th century as described in Arendt's argument.

Topic 8.7

Europe During the Interwar Period

Fascism is the complete opposite of Marxian socialism. . . .
Fascism combats the whole complex system of democratic
ideology, and repudiates it, whether in its theoretical
premises or in its practical application.

—Benito Mussolini, 1932

Essential Question: How and why did political and ideological factors result in the catastrophe of World War II?

During the 1920s and 1930s, the societies of Europe faced growing levels of social, political, and economic instability. The psychological and emotional devastation of what Europeans still regarded as the War to End All Wars was still fresh in most people's minds. The Great Depression hit Europe hard. In the grip of this economic disaster, the countries who won the war hardly felt victorious, and the countries who lost spoke of betrayal and revenge.

In this atmosphere, one of the winners of the war, Italy, and one of the losers, Germany, turned to the authoritarian ideology known as fascism. Italy's fascist leader Benito Mussolini and his German counterpart Adolf Hitler, realizing their common methods and goals, formed the Rome-Berlin Axis in 1936, an agreement allying the two nations. The Pact of Steel, agreed in May 1939, further solidified their political and military ties. The rise of fascism placed the free nations of Europe and the rest of the world in grave danger.

Appeasement and Expansion

One of Hitler's initial diplomatic moves was to withdraw Germany from the League of Nations in 1933. At about the same time, he began rebuilding the German armed forces—in secret at first, but then publicly after March 1935. Germany's rearmament and troop buildup were direct violations of the Versailles Treaty, but halting these actions was a difficult task.

The war-weary French and the British feared another costly war with Germany. Neither country wanted to sacrifice a new generation of soldiers to combat. As a result, both countries followed a policy of **appeasement** toward Hitler. They granted him what he wished in return for peace.

The United States, too, had little interest in confronting the German dictator. Americans wanted to focus on their own problems. The economic depression of the 1930s left the country struggling with high unemployment and business and bank failures. Isolationist policies restricted immigration and encouraged people to turn away from Europe and its conflicts.

In addition, deep distrust and political differences between the Soviet Union and the democratic, capitalist nations of the United States and Western Europe made it difficult to present a united front against the fascist states. Germany and Italy took advantage of the fear, isolationism, and discord to continue expanding their militaries and begin annexing new territory.

Italian Invasion of Ethiopia

Italy had maintained colonies in East Africa since the late 19th century. In October 1935, Italy invaded the independent state of **Ethiopia**. The Italian conquest of Ethiopia threatened the British, who controlled the Suez Canal in Egypt. Although the League of Nations condemned Italy's actions, member nations enacted only token economic sanctions against Italy.

Remilitarization of the Rhineland

The Treaty of Versailles forbade Germany from arming the **Rhineland**, a German region bordering France and Belgium. In March 1936, Hitler sent troops to occupy the area. He wanted to test whether Britain and France were committed to enforcing the treaty. When neither nation challenged him, he accelerated his drive toward rearmament and focused his plans for expansion into Austria and Eastern Europe.

Annexation of Austria

On March 12, 1938, Germany finalized its **annexation**, or formal takeover, of Austria. Nazis had influenced Austrian politics for several years, and Nazi propaganda had generated strong support for Germany in Austria. Many Austrians welcomed the German soldiers when they arrived in 1938. In a plebiscite, or referendum, conducted in April, a near total majority of Austrians declared themselves in favor of unification with Germany, a dubious result that merely reinforced an established fact.

Source: Wikimedia Commons

Crowds of Austrians welcome the Nazis into Vienna, Austria, in 1938.

The Munich Agreement

Next, Hitler set his sights on Czechoslovakia, where he sought to absorb the region that bordered Germany, the Sudetenland, which had about 3 million people of German heritage. Nazi-aligned Sudeten Germans helped his cause by accusing the Czech government of discrimination and oppression. Hitler's continuing demands and threats put Czechoslovakia's allies France and Britain on alert, but neither was willing to go to war for Czechoslovak territorial integrity. Through much of 1938, a series of conferences between Britain, France, and Germany resulted in ever-increasing German demands that were met with continual appeasement from France and especially Britain. Finally, on September 30, 1938, Britain, France, Italy, and Germany all signed the **Munich Agreement**. (Czechoslovakia was all but excluded from participation.) Great Britain and France agreed to let Germany annex the Sudetenland. In return, Germany promised to maintain peace in Europe and leave the rest of Czechoslovakia alone. These promises, of course, were hollow.

Fearing it would be the next target of German aggression, Poland turned to France and Britain for protection. Both nations pledged to defend Poland's borders if it was attacked by Germany.

Nazi–Soviet Non-Aggression Pact

The Soviet Union was not ready to engage in another major war with Germany. It also distrusted Britain and France. On August 23, 1939, Germany and the Soviet Union signed what is referred to as the **Nazi–Soviet Non-Agression Pact**, promising that they would not attack one another for ten years. They also agreed that they would divide Poland between them. This pact essentially gave Germany the freedom to invade Poland a week later without fear of any opposition from the Soviet Union. In return, Germany allowed the Soviet Union to take control of the eastern part of Poland and did not protest the Soviet invasion of Finland or the Soviet annexation of the Baltic states and Romania. The pact dissolved with the German invasion of the Soviet Union in 1941.

REFLECT ON THE ESSENTIAL QUESTION

Essential Question: How and why did political and ideological factors result in the catastrophe of World War II?

Political and Ideological Factors	Results

KEY TERMS

appeasement	Rhineland	Munich Agreement
Ethiopia	annexation	Nazi–Soviet Non-Aggression Pact

Questions 1–3 refer to the cartoon below.

Source: British Cartoon Archive, "Increasing Pressure," by David Low, in the *Evening Standard*, a British newspaper, February 18, 1938

1. The British policy depicted in the cartoon had which of the following effects on European politics in the period before World War II?

   (A) It helped European economies recover from the Great Depression.

   (B) It reaffirmed the peace settlement made by the Treaty of Versailles.

   (C) It allowed fascist states to rearm and expand their territory.

   (D) It encouraged loyalty from subjects of the British Empire.

2. Which of the following was the most significant part of the historical context in explaining the British attitude in the cartoon?

   (A) The losses and devastation during World War I

   (B) The confidence in the diplomatic influence of the League of Nations

   (C) The establishment of a British alliance with the Soviet Union

   (D) The presence of a significant German population in Britain

3. Which of the following best describes the purpose of the cartoon?

   (A) To mock the weakness of other European countries

   (B) To encourage British isolationism

   (C) To criticize the British policy of appeasement

   (D) To glorify German military strength

SHORT-ANSWER QUESTION

Use the passages below to answer all parts of the question that follows.

Passage 1

"Many British politicians regarded Communism as a greater threat than Nazi Germany. Their negative views were reinforced by the brutal show trials of the 1930s in Stalin's Soviet Union. A common saying at the time was 'better Hitlerism than Communism.'

During the 1930s, Britain had a National Government. This was formed from members of the Conservative, Liberal and Labour parties. The largest group came from the Conservative party. The Conservatives believed that Hitler's Germany could be a strong defense against possible Soviet plans to invade Europe. Soviet involvement in the Spanish Civil War (1936–1939) raised suspicions about their aims."

—BBC, "British and French Appeasement, to 1938"

Passage 2

"In analyzing appeasement, it is necessary to examine the role of the British prime minister, Neville Chamberlain, who was not as foolish as some have imagined. . . . The Western democracies have been denounced for their failure to go to war against Germany before 1939. Such accusations fail to take into account the public mood and the lack of military preparedness on the part of France or Great Britain. It is important to realize that the Western leaders who had to make the decision for war or peace had grave doubts about the capabilities of their armed forces."

—Keith Eubanks, *The Origins of World War II*, 1969

1. a) Describe ONE major difference between the two interpretations of the origins of World War II.

   b) Explain ONE historical event or development from 1930 to 1939 that could be used to support the first interpretation.

   c) Explain ONE historical event or development from 1930 to 1939 that could be used to support the second interpretation.

Topic 8.8

World War II

I have nothing to offer but blood, toil, tears, and sweat. We have before us an ordeal of the most grievous kind. We have before us many, many long months of struggle and of suffering. . . . You ask, what is our aim? I can answer in one word: It is victory.
—Winston Churchill, speech to the British people, May 13, 1940

Essential Question: How did technology and innovation affect the course of World War II and the 20th century?

World War II took place in two major regions of the globe, or theaters of war—the European theater and the Pacific theater. The war pitted the **Axis powers** against the **Allies**.

The Axis powers consisted mainly of Germany, Italy, and Japan. All had fascist governments dedicated to military conquest. Adolf Hitler of Germany, Benito Mussolini of Italy, and General Hideki Tojo of Japan led the Axis nations.

The major nations of the Allies were Great Britain, the United States, and the Soviet Union. France's exiled government continued to assist the Allies even after its surrendered and the country was occupied by Germany. Other European governments-in-exile supported the Allies as well. The British Commonwealth nations of Canada, Australia, and New Zealand also fought with the Allies. **Winston Churchill** of Britain, **Franklin D. Roosevelt** of the United States, and Joseph Stalin of the Soviet Union led the Allies. Britain and the United States were both democracies, while the Soviet Union was a Communist dictatorship. The three nations decided to put their political differences aside, however, to combat a common enemy.

World War II Begins

In 1937, Japan invaded and conquered a large part of eastern China, instigating the initial phase of the war in the Pacific. In Europe, Germany prepared to seize Poland. Germany relied on a strategy called **blitzkrieg**, or lightning war. Blitzkrieg used a combination of tanks, troops, and air power to overwhelm the opposition's defenses as rapidly as possible. Once the Germans broke through enemy lines, they used maximum force to intimidate the civilian population and crush the opposing army. German officers became experts in blitzkrieg tactics. Between 1939 and 1941, Germany conquered Poland, Yugoslavia, Greece, and most of Western Europe including France, Belgium, Norway, Denmark, and the Netherlands.

Polish Campaign of 1939

World War II began in Europe with the German invasion of Poland on September 1, 1939. In the face of such blatant Nazi aggression, Britain and France could no longer avoid war. Honoring their commitment to Poland, they declared war on Germany two days later on September 3. They could do little to help Poland, though. In line with the Molotov-Ribbentrop Pact, Germany's nonaggression treaty with the Soviet Union, the Soviets had invaded Poland from the east on September 17, quickly occupying that half of the country. On September 27, Poland surrendered.

France Surrenders

From October 1939 through April 1940, there was very little actual fighting in the west, during what historians refer to as the Phony War. However, in April 1940, the Germans used blitzkrieg tactics in the west. After quickly gaining control of the Low Countries (Belgium, the Netherlands, and Luxembourg), Germany invaded France in May 1940. France surrendered to Germany on June 24, 1940. Marshal Pétain signed the armistice on behalf of France. In return for his cooperation, Hitler gave him official control of southern France, which became known as Vichy France, named for the town that was home to Pétain's collaborationist government. Germany controlled northern France, including the city of Paris. In theory, Vichy was a free state. In reality, it was a puppet state of the Nazis. Pétain simply enacted Nazi laws. After France's surrender to Germany, General Charles de Gaulle began to organize a French army in exile. In France, a strong resistance movement worked to undermine German rule and helped the Allies by providing intelligence on German movements.

Operation Barbarossa

On June 22, 1941, Germany launched **Operation Barbarossa**, a three-pronged invasion of the Soviet Union. Hitler had never intended to honor his non-aggression pact with Stalin. He needed Russia's natural resources, especially iron, coal, and oil, to support his army. He also saw the Soviet Union as a threat to his control of Eastern Europe. More than 3 million soldiers attacked the Soviet Union. The Eastern Front stretched nearly 1,500 miles from the Baltic Sea in the north to the Black Sea in the south.

Source: Wikimedia Commons

German troops battle Russian forces in Kharkov in 1941.

Germany anticipated an easy victory. The Soviets, however, rallied after a series of initial losses and put up surprising resistance, forcing the Germans to endure a Russian winter. Soviet forces repelled a German attack on Moscow in the winter of 1941. Germany continued to occupy parts of the Soviet Union until 1944, but they were never able to subdue the country completely.

Path to the Allied Victory

The United States entered World War II with the Japanese bombing of the U.S. naval base at **Pearl Harbor**, Hawaii, on December 7, 1941. Immediately after the attack, the United States declared war on Japan; Germany and Italy declared war on the United States, which then responded in kind.

Although Germany had a highly trained army, the Allies enjoyed significant advantages. The United States was rich in natural resources, especially oil. The United States also had a large population that could be mobilized for war and manufacturing industries that could produce weapons and other war material.

Britain Holds Out

Under the leadership of Winston Churchill, the British had proven that they had the will to resist Germany. They withstood severe aerial bombardment during the Battle of Britain from July to November 1940. The battle took place almost entirely in the air, and Britain's Royal Air Force demonstrated it had the skill and determination to protect the British Isles from German invasion.

Russian Endurance

Russians also resisted the German onslaught. In December 1941, Soviet forces drove Germans from Moscow. During the Siege of Leningrad, which lasted from September 1941 to January 1944, Soviet civilians and military endured brutal conditions rather than surrender to the Nazis. The most significant battle took place at Stalingrad. The Germans launched a massive attack in the summer of 1942 in an effort to seize the Volga River and the oil fields of the Caucasus. By the spring of 1943, the Germans had lost the entire 6th Army (more than 750,000 casualties) and the Soviet Union held Stalingrad. From that point, the Germans were on the defensive on the Eastern Front.

The War in North Africa

Hitler regarded the conquest of North Africa as key to the control of the shipping lanes of the Mediterranean and the Suez Canal. He wanted access to the oil fields of the Middle East in order to fuel German tanks and planes, and he wanted to deny that oil to the British. After a four-year battle for North Africa, the Allies won control of the region in 1943.

The War in Italy

After the conquest of North Africa, the Allies turned to Italy. If they could seize the airfields in Rome, they could launch bombing raids on Berlin from there instead of London. The shorter distance would conserve fuel and lives. British and American troops invaded the island of Sicily in July 1943, a few months before Mussolini was overthrown. After a year of hard fighting, the Allies controlled Rome.

WORLD WAR II TIMELINE	
Date	**Event**
January 1933	Hitler appointed chancellor of Germany
October 1936	Germany and Italy sign the Rome-Berlin Axis
March 1938	Germany annexes Austria
September 1938	Munich Agreement signed
September 1939	Germany invades Poland; World War II begins
May–June 1940	Germany invades and defeats France
September 1940	Germany, Italy, and Japan sign the Tripartite Pact
June 1941	Germany invades Soviet Union
December 1941	United States enters the war
August 1942–February 1943	Battle of Stalingrad wages
June 1944	Allies land in France
February 1945	Allied leaders hold the Yalta Conference
May 7, 1945	Germany surrenders
August 6 and 9, 1945	United States drops atomic bombs on Japan
September 2, 1945	Japan formally surrenders; World War II ends

The War in Western Europe

On June 6, 1944, Allied troops, led by U.S. General Dwight D. Eisenhower and British General Bernard Montgomery, landed on Normandy Beach on the coast of France. Known as D-Day, the invasion was the first step in the Allied effort to liberate Western Europe from Nazi control and ultimately defeat Germany. Approximately 175,000 Allied troops faced 850,000 German soldiers. The two sides fought for more than a month. Air support tipped the battle in the Allies' favor. Allied bombing raids pushed the Germans back.

On July 25, the Allies broke through German lines. Within a month, Allied forces had liberated most of France, Belgium, and the Netherlands. In December, the German army attempted to stop the Allied advance at the Battle of the Bulge in Belgium. Although the Allies suffered about 75,000 casualties, the German toll was even higher, and the assault failed. The Allies continued their advance on Berlin from the west.

Meanwhile, Soviet forces drove the Germans out of Eastern Europe. They marched toward Berlin from the east. Facing certain defeat, Hitler and several of his high-ranking officers committed suicide. On May 7, 1945, the German army surrendered to Allied forces. The war in Europe was over.

The Yalta Conference

On February 4, 1945, Roosevelt, Stalin, and Churchill met at the **Yalta Conference** in the state of Crimea in order to discuss the Allied occupation and treatment of Germany and how to deal with liberated countries. They agreed on the following:

- France should take part in the administration of Germany after the war.

- Germany as a whole, and Berlin in particular, would be divided into four occupation zones administered by Great Britain, the Soviet Union, the United States, and France.

- Eastern European countries liberated from Germany would be allowed to hold free elections.

Stalin also agreed that the Soviet Union would join the Allies in the war in the Pacific against Japan.

All parties agreed that Germany would be required to pay reparations, but the reparations would not be excessive, and the civilian population would be allowed to rebuild their country as long as they accepted the terms of the Allied victory.

However, the Soviets did not fully honor the promise of free elections in Eastern Europe. Stalin wanted pro-Soviet governments in that region to serve as a buffer between the Soviet Union and Germany. Even before the end of the war, it became clear to Roosevelt and Churchill that Eastern Europe would become part of the communist bloc of nations. Nevertheless, the Yalta Conference did foster peaceful cooperation among the Allies in Western Europe and helped set the terms for the German surrender.

The End of the Pacific War

In July 1945, the Allied Powers met at Potsdam, Germany, to discuss issues regarding occupied Europe as well as the final defeat of Japan. The Allies and some Japanese leaders recognized that Japan was almost defeated. In August, the United States dropped atomic bombs on Hiroshima and Nagasaki. Japan formally surrendered on September 2.

Unprecedented Casualties

The death toll both on and off of the battlefield in World War II was astounding. There had never been a war with so many losses. See the table on the following page to comparing casualties in World War I and World War II.

ESTIMATED CASUALTIES IN WORLD WAR I AND WORLD WAR II		
Category	World War I	World War II
Military Deaths	10 million	23 million
Military Injuries	22 million	25 million
Civilian Deaths	9 million	49 million

Source: www.nationalww2museum.org/students-teachers/student-resources/research-starters/research-starters-worldwide-deaths-world-war

The Technology of Industrial Warfare

What made World War II so much more deadly than any other war in history? The main players in the war devoted every aspect of their societies to the war effort. In this atmosphere of "total warfare," new military technologies could be produced, and established technologies could be enhanced at a pace never before imagined.

MILITARY TECHNOLOGIES OF WORLD WAR II	
Tanks	Faster, better armored, more powerful guns
Aircraft (fighters and bombers)	Faster, longer range, able to carry more bombs and weaponry
Ships	Aircraft carriers able to transport a concentrated aerial attack anywhere in the world; submarines able to stay below surface longer, dive deeper to avoid detection, and deliver deadlier torpedoes
Bombs	Bigger and more deadly (from planes, from ships, and artillery); the nuclear bombs dropped on Japan, which showed the greatest example of increased lethality

Out of this atmosphere of industrialized warfare, the Nazis created an efficient mechanism for the wholesale murder of the majority of Europe's Jews, as well as that of other "undesirables"— the Roma people, Poles, Communists, people with disabilities, homosexuals, and others. (See Topic 8.9. for more about the genocide perpetrated by Nazi Germany during World War II.)

After World War II, the Allied cooperation continued between the United States and Europe. However, the Soviet Union broke away from its wartime allies and hostility replaced cooperation. This led to a long-standing "cold war" between the superpowers—the United States and the Soviet Union. The superpowers' development and proliferation of nuclear weapons in the 1940s became a threat to all countries. Nuclear war became the next possibility, and that threat continues.

REFLECT ON THE ESSENTIAL QUESTION

Essential Question: *How did technology and innovation affect the course of World War II and the 20th century?*

Technological Advances and Innovations	Effects

KEY TERMS

Axis powers

Allies

Winston Churchill

Franklin D. Roosevelt

blitzkrieg

Operation Barbarossa

Pearl Harbor

Yalta Conference

MULTIPLE-CHOICE QUESTIONS

Questions 1–3 refer to the passage below.

"In his prison cell at Nuremberg [after the end of the war], Hitler's foreign minister, Joachim von Ribbentrop, wrote a brief memoir in the course of which he explored the reasons for Germany's defeat. He picked out three factors that he thought were critical: the unexpected 'power of resistance' of the Red Army; the vast supply of American armaments; and the success of Allied air power. . . .

Soviet resistance was in some ways the most surprising outcome. . . . The transformation in Soviet fighting power and morale has a number of explanations.

In the first place the Red Army learned a great deal from German practice and from their own mistakes. . . . The pre-war experience of economic planning and mobilization helped the regime to run a war economy on an emergency basis, while the vast exodus of workers (an estimated 16 million) and factories (more than 2,500 major plants) from in front of the advancing Germans allowed the USSR to reconstruct its armaments economy in central and eastern Russia with great rapidity.

The second factor lay with politics. Until the summer of 1942 Stalin and the Party closely controlled the Red Army. Political commissars worked directly alongside senior officers and reported straight back to the Kremlin. Stalin came to realize that political control was a dead hand on the army and cut it back sharply in the autumn of 1942."

—Richard Overy, "World War Two: How the Allies Won," 2011

1. Which of the following reasons most limits the value of Ribbentrop's point of view?
   (A) As a prisoner of the Allies, he would not have information about the end of the war.
   (B) As the foreign minister, he would have known little about military issues.
   (C) As a subordinate of Hitler, he would have a reason to avoid offending his commander.
   (D) As a top Nazi leader, he would have reason to ignore German mistakes.

2. This passage most directly supports which of the following arguments?
   (A) The Soviets were the primary reasons the Allies won the war in Europe.
   (B) The Soviet army played a vital role in controlling North Africa.
   (C) Germany should have realized in 1939 that it had no chance to win the war.
   (D) Germany lost the war because it failed to learn from Soviet successes.

3. Which of the following best identifies Overy's purpose in this passage?
   (A) To show that Ribbentrop analyzed the conditions accurately
   (B) To praise the bravery of the Soviet soldiers
   (C) To identify the Soviets' ability to make changes during the war
   (D) To demonstrate that communist economies were more adaptable than capitalist ones

SHORT-ANSWER QUESTION

Answer all parts of the question that follows.

1. a) Describe ONE similarity in the causes of World War I and World War II.
   b) Describe ONE difference in the causes of World War I and World War II.
   c) Using a specific example from the period 1914 to the present, explain how the results of World War I and World War II differed.

Topic 8.9

The Holocaust

Around us, everyone was weeping. Someone began to recite the Kaddish, the prayer for the dead. I do not know if it has ever happened before, in the long history of the Jews, that people have ever recited the prayer for the dead for themselves.

—Elie Wiesel, Holocaust survivor, Nobel Laureate

Essential Question: How and why were cultural and national identities affected by war and the rise of fascist/totalitarian powers from 1914 to the present?

Antisemitism had a long history in Europe before 1800. In the 19th and 20th centuries, the problem became more intense. The legacy of the Enlightenment supported tolerance, so some people opposed discrimination against Jews. However, as societies focused more on the concept of race, people began to believe and spread the idea that some people were racially superior to others. For Hitler and the Nazis, antisemitism was a core part of their belief that Germans were Aryans, northern Europeans who formed a superior race. They viewed Jews as inferior, and they blamed Jews for Germany's economic problems after World War I. Nazis referred to the **Jewish Question**—the issue of how to end Jewish influence in Germany.

Nazi Persecution Intensifies

Beginning in 1935, Hitler's government enacted a series of laws that denied German Jews their citizenship and civil rights. Known as the **Nuremberg Laws**, these acts forbade marriages between Jews and non-Jews. Jews could no longer employ non-Jews or work in certain businesses. Jewish doctors could not treat non-Jewish patients. Eventually the laws were extended to mean that Jews could not attend public schools or universities or mingle in public places with non-Jews. Jews had to carry identity cards at all times. Later, the Nazi government required all Jews in Germany and German-occupied territories to wear a yellow star on their clothes.

On the night of November 9–10, 1938, the Nazi government unleashed a wave of pogroms, or organized assaults on Jews. In Germany, Austria, Poland, and Czechoslovakia, mobs attacked Jewish homes, businesses, and synagogues. They smashed windows, looted goods, and burned buildings. Called **Kristallnacht**, or the Night of Broken Glass, these attacks left many Jewish communities in ruins. At least 91 individuals died, and about 30,000 Jewish men were rounded up and deported to concentration camps. An estimated 7,500 Jewish-owned businesses were destroyed and at least 270 synagogues were burned. By the end of 1939, more than 100,000 Jews had fled Germany and Austria.

Antisemitism was so accepted in Europe and the United States that other governments did little to stop the Nazis. However, Jews resisted when they could, and some non-Jews tried to help them escape to other countries. Some countries, including the United States, accepted only a small number of refugees. Most Jews who did leave went to nearby countries that were later overrun by the Nazis. By October 1941, Jewish emigration was officially forbidden.

Source: Getty Images/Hulton Archive

People view a smashed Jewish shop window in Berlin following riots of Kristallnacht (November 10, 1938)

Wannsee Conference and the Final Solution

On January 20, 1942, Nazi officials met in Wannsee, a neighborhood near Berlin, to plan the "final solution" to the Jewish Question. They decided to murder all Jews. Their plan was an example of genocide.

Labor Camps and Death Camps

During World War II, the Nazis operated about 40,000 **concentration camps**. Most were prisons and slave labor sites where people were worked until they died. Camp inmates died of starvation, cold, sickness, beatings, and gunshot wounds. In several camps, Nazi doctors performed cruel experiments designed to see how people reacted to brutally cold temperatures, drowning, diseases, and other deadly conditions.

A few of the sites were death camps, which were designed solely for the purpose of killing human beings. In the largest of these camps, Auschwitz, Nazis murdered more than 1 million Jews. Nazi allies such as Romania and collaborationist regimes in Nazi-conquered nations such as France, Hungary, Yugoslavia, and others handed over many of their Jewish citizens to German control. Many of these unfortunate people met the same sad fate as the Jews of Germany, Poland, and anywhere else under Nazi rule.

Further Persecution and Resistance

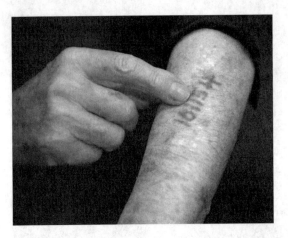

Source: Getty Images

The Nazis tattooed an identification number on people sent to concentration camps.

Many Jews were killed in gas chambers in the concentration camps. Others died in mass executions, especially in the Soviet Union and Eastern Europe. These were perpetrated by Nazi mobile killing squads that rounded up and executed hundreds, even thousands, of Jews at a time. On September 29–30, 1941, Nazi forces shot 33,771 Jews and buried them in a mass grave at Babi Yar, outside the city of Kyiv (Kiev) in Ukraine. In several cities, Jews were forced into overcrowded areas called **ghettos**. Walled off from the larger city, they were denied food, water, and basic sanitation services.

In Warsaw, Poland, approximately 400,000 people were packed into an area of 1.3 square miles. At least 83,000 died of starvation and disease. Thousands of others were deported to death camps. In April 1943, several hundred resisters staged a revolt, attacking German soldiers with homemade grenades and weapons smuggled in from the outside. The uprising took the Germans by surprise, temporarily driving them away. The revolt lasted four weeks. In the end, the Germans captured and killed almost all of the rebels. A few were able to escape and find shelter outside the ghetto. When the Soviet forces liberated Warsaw from Nazi control in 1945, approximately 11,500 Jews in the entire city had survived out of an original population of around 350,000. While the uprising had failed, it served as an inspiration to Holocaust survivors throughout Europe and is still commemorated in Israel today.

Before Hitler's rise to power, approximately 9 million Jews lived in Europe. Between 1933 and the end of the war in 1945, an estimated 6 million, or two thirds, died. Jews referred to this slaughter as the *Shoah*, a Hebrew word meaning destruction. In the 1950s, historians translated this as the **Holocaust**, a word derived from Greek meaning "sacrifice or burnt offering."

In addition to murdering Jews, Nazis murdered approximately 5 million other people. They singled out for death groups they viewed as inferior. Among these were Slavs (including Poles and Soviet prisoners of war), Roma (formerly known as Gypsies), gay men, lesbians, and people with mental and physical disabilities. The Nazis also massacred socialists, communists, and others politically opposed to them.

Essential Question: *How and why were cultural and national identities affected by war and the rise of fascist/totalitarian powers from 1914 to the present?*

Cultural Identities	National Identities

KEY TERMS

Jewish Question	Kristallnacht	ghetto
Nuremberg Laws	concentration camp	Holocaust

MULTIPLE-CHOICE QUESTIONS

Questions 1–3 refer to the passage below.

"A new way of approaching the study of the Holocaust is implicit in much of the unparalleled, widespread public discussion about various aspects of the Holocaust that has been taking place for the last two years. The old paradigm consists of abstract, faceless structures and institutions . . . and allegedly irresistible external forces (totalitarian terror, the exigencies of war, social psychological pressure). This paradigm effaces [eliminates] the human actors and their capacity to judge what they were doing and make moral choices. . . .

This is being challenged by a view that recognizes the Holocaust was brought about by human beings who had beliefs about what they were doing, beliefs which they developed within a highly specific historical context, and who made many choices about how to act.

The heretofore [previously] dominant question of 'What compelled them to act against their will?' is being replaced by the question of 'Why did these people choose to act in the ways that they did?' "

—Daniel Jonah Goldhagen, American historian,
"The Paradigm Challenged," 1998

1. Goldhagen's point of view on the Holocaust is that historians should assume that

   (A) people did not want to participate in the Holocaust

   (B) a person's culture determines their behavior

   (C) people in all cultures make similar decisions

   (D) people have the power to choose how to act

2. Goldhagen's emphasis in his study of the Holocaust is most similar to which of the following ways of thinking?

   (A) Romanticism because it also highlighted individual action

   (B) Darwinism because it also studied slow change over a long time

   (C) Communism because it also demonstrated the importance of class

   (D) Fascism because it also emphasized the importance of order

3. Which decisions in the earlier wars involving Germany were most directly comparable to the ones studied by Goldhagen?

   (A) Ones made by individual Germans in the Thirty Years' War because they had to decide how to treat people based on their religion

   (B) Ones made by German intellectuals about Napoleon because many changed their minds about him over time

   (C) Ones made by Bismarck in unifying Germany because he was motivated by a desire to unify Germany under Prussian leadership

   (D) Ones made by the German government in World War I because they were based on diplomatic and political reasons

SHORT-ANSWER QUESTION

Use the passages below to answer all parts of the question that follows.

Passage 1

> "Accordingly, I have placed my death-head formations in readiness—for the present only in the East—with orders to send to death mercilessly and without compassion, men and women of Polish derivations. Only then shall we gain the living space which we need. Who, after all, speaks today of the annihilation of the Armenians?"

> —Adolph Hitler, speech in Obersalzberg, Germany, August 22, 1939

Passage 2

> "Never again."

> —phrase used beginning in 1945 to remember the Holocaust

1. a) Identify ONE similarity between the main ideas of the two sources.

   b) Identify ONE difference between the main ideas of the two sources.

   c) Explain how the attitude expressed by Hitler contributed to the need for the second source.

Topic 8.10

20th-Century Cultural, Intellectual, and Artistic Developments

Prediction is very difficult, especially about the future.

—physicist Niels Bohr (1885–1962)

Essential Question: How did the events of the first half of the 20th century challenge existing social, cultural, and intellectual understandings?

European thought and culture in the 20th century reveals a change from the optimism and belief in progress that characterized much of the 19th century. Science and reason had made great strides in solving human problems since the Age of Enlightenment. A variety of intellectual and cultural movements throughout the 20th century, however, began to question whether objective knowledge about the world was possible. These movements ushered in an "Age of Anxiety." Many saw the limits of reason in reaching the truth, especially about human experiences. In addition, organized religion's role in determining standards of morality was called into question.

Challenges to the Belief in Progress

Before World War I, most Europeans were still confident that science and technology could solve problems and answer questions that affected people's lives. This confidence was based on personal experience of an improved standard of living, which included better schools and urban environments, as well as new inventions such as electric lights and automobiles.

However, some philosophers, writers, and artists began to question Europeans' widely held belief in progress. These cultural leaders explored the weaknesses in European life and saw that some kind of disaster was approaching. After two world wars, the sense of anxiety spread to more people. Although new scientific and psychological theories created some uncertainty, confidence persisted because the new ideas at first touched only a relatively small group of intellectuals. By the end of the 20th century, more intellectual frameworks for understanding the world had emerged.

New Theories About Atoms

Throughout the 19th century, most scientists saw their work as the application of existing scientific laws to solve problems in a mechanical universe. The laws were based on Isaac Newton's conception of the universe. Matter, space, and time were thought to be objective realities independent of the scientists studying them. The atom, which was perceived as hard and solid, was considered the smallest unit of matter.

Around the turn of the 20th century, however, scientists began to question whether atoms were the basic building blocks of matter when they discovered **subatomic particles** such as protons and electrons. These discoveries created uncertainty about the Newtonian view of the universe.

Albert Einstein In 1905, these discoveries were pushed even further when **Albert Einstein** (1879–1955) published a paper that included his **theory of relativity**. Einstein's theory claimed that space and time were not independent of human observers and were linked together in what he called the space-time continuum. Einstein also posited that matter was not something solid but was a different form of energy. Although Einstein's ideas were not generally accepted until the 1920s, they led to exploration into the energy contained in the atom, opening the door to the atomic age later in the century. After World War I, the challenges continued to expand, as scientists gained increased knowledge about the atom and the potential energy that it contained.

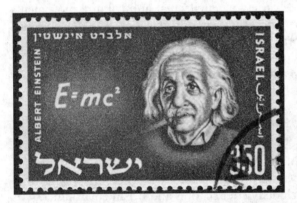

Source: Getty Images

Albert Einstein, with his unruly hair and bushy mustache, became one of the best-known faces in the world in the 20th century. His formula summarizing the relationship among energy, mass, and the speed of light became famous, though hard for many people to fully understand.

Werner Heisenberg Earlier scientists and ordinary people believed that with enough knowledge, accurate predictions could be made about the way the world worked. In 1927, however, **Werner Heisenberg** (1901–1976), a German physicist, questioned this belief. He argued that scientists could not accurately predict the path of an electron's movement because the act of observing that movement with light affected the electron's path. His conclusion was known as the **uncertainty principle**.

Erwin Schrödinger Austrian physicist **Erwin Schrödinger** (1887–1961) contributed to the wave theory of matter, among other important concepts of quantum mechanics. According to his wave theory, different energy states of an atom's electrons could be described via wave equations. Instead of predictable movements, Schrödinger thought energy waves were more abstract and, based on probability, not a set sequencing.

Enrico Fermi Italian American **Enrico Fermi** (1901–1954) was a nuclear physicist active in the 1930s and 1940s whose experiments splitting atoms led to the nuclear reactor and the first controlled nuclear chain reaction. From 1942 to 1945, Fermi worked with other U.S. physicists on the Manhattan Project—the successful U.S. government research project to develop an atomic bomb.

Niels Bohr The work of Danish physicist **Niels Bohr** (1885–1962) and his concept of the atomic nucleus led to the understanding of nuclear fission. Nuclear fission is the division of an atom's nucleus into two parts, which releases an enormous amount of energy. Bohr had been a contributor to the development of the atomic bomb during World War II, but later worked for arms control.

The New Physics By the mid-1970s, so-called "new physics" provided alternative frameworks for understanding the physical sciences that acknowledged chaos and uncertainty in the behavior of particles. More concretely, the new physics also provided the framework from which both nuclear weapons and nuclear power facilities were created. Nuclear weapons became and remain a dark cloud hanging over European (and world) society, while nuclear power is a much-debated issue in Europe.

Psychology

The physical world was not the only realm in which new ideas began to create a sense of uncertainty and anxiety. In 1900, **Sigmund Freud**, a physician from Vienna, published new ideas about the human mind in *The Interpretation of Dreams*. In this work, Freud presented the theory that human behavior was not always motivated by reason but was often driven by unconscious forces, including past experiences or inner urges of which people are generally unaware. According to Freud, the *ego*, the center of human reason, and the *superego*, the higher realm of conscience and social norms, struggled to control the unconscious forces of the *id*.

Freud thought that much of this struggle revolved around the repression of sexual urges, stemming from experiences in childhood. Through hypnosis and analysis of dreams, Freud began the practice of **psychoanalysis**, in which therapists help patients become aware of the contents of their unconscious and resolve psychological conflicts. These ideas about the irrational foundation of much human behavior undermined the optimistic belief that human reason would lead to unending progress in society. As with physics, however, these ideas had a limited impact before World War I.

Women's Lives Transformed

During World War I, women's lives began to transform from traditional to modern. Women needed to take on new roles in their families and for their countries in order to support the war effort. They worked in jobs that were previously considered to be "men's only." As a result, after the war, there was a growing number of women seeking education and professions in business, medicine, journalism, and other nontraditional women's roles.

Their success at these jobs made it possible for women to successfully push for the right to vote. After World War I, women could lawfully vote in many European countries and the United States.

This new power for women helped change cultural expectations. Wanting to be modern, many women moved away from the extremely modest, dark, and heavy fashions of earlier generations. They rejected restrictive clothing, wanting shorter, lighter dresses. Hairstyles changed, too. Many women cut their hair short so it was easier to care for. Feeling more independence, it became fashionable for women to wear makeup, smoke, drink alcohol, and drive cars, all having been deemed inappropriate by earlier generations of men and women.

Working Through World War I and Interwar

During World War I, women left textile and commercial food processing jobs for employment in metalworking and munitions factories. This surge of women in the workplace was short-lived, however. When men returned from the war, they reclaimed the jobs taken by women. For example, in 1917, women made up more than 40 percent of France's industrial workforce. However, by 1926, that percentage had dropped to just under 29 percent. Nonetheless, the experience of women during the war had opened the door to women in the workforce.

Working Through World War II

Women on both sides of the conflict during World War II joined the armed services in large numbers. Hundreds of thousands of women served in auxiliary—or support—positions such as nurses, ambulance drivers, and office workers. They also played significant roles in resistance movements, which often took them into enemy territory. Women in Yugoslavia even fought alongside men on the front lines. In Russia, almost 800,000 women served in the armed forces, some as pilots and snipers. In Britain, more than 640,000 women served in the armed forces during World War II. At first, only single women, aged 20 to 30, were called to serve, but by mid-1943, almost 90 percent of single women and 80 percent of married women were working in factories or directly with the armed forces.

War also brought an increased demand for labor on the home front. Women made up much of the shortfall. The British workforce grew by half a million between 1939 and 1943, and women—many of whom had previously been unemployed—contributed 80 percent of that. This surge of women into the workforce happened during World War I as well, but women left the workforce as soon as men returned from war. After World War II, however, the change was more lasting. Unemployment in Britain was wiped out. In the Soviet Union, where women were already widely employed before World War II, more than half the labor force was female by 1942.

World War I's Effects on Society

Many people who lived through World War I became disillusioned by the devastation and changes brought by the war. They questioned traditional ideas about rational progress in societies.

Democratization of Societies

Following World War I, many European societies moved toward democracy. One of the ways this happened was when countries that were either on the losing side of war or had gained their independence as a result of war became democratic. Germany and Austria declared themselves democratic republics, and the following countries established new constitutions upon being freed from control from the old empires: Georgia, Latvia, Lithuania, Estonia, Finland, Poland, Czechoslovakia, Yugoslavia, and Romania.

Another way European societies became democratized was through the spread of universal suffrage in Europe in the interwar period. The following European countries adopted universal suffrage following World War I: Austria, Czechoslovakia, Estonia, Georgia, Germany, Hungary, Ireland, Latvia, Luxembourg, the Netherlands, Poland, and the United Kingdom. Some of the countries that established universal suffrage did not establish new constitutions, which shows that there was a limit to the democratization.

Lost Generation

The young adults of Europe and America during World War I became known as the **Lost Generation**. They were "lost" because many of them were cynical or disillusioned with the world after the war and were either unwilling or unable to establish a settled life. The values this generation inherited from their parents were no longer relevant in the postwar world. The new society they were suddenly a part of seemed hopelessly materialistic and without a moral compass.

The term "Lost Generation" was coined by American writer Gertrude Stein and made popular by American writer Ernest Hemingway in his novel *The Sun Also Rises*, which captures this postwar disillusionment. The Lost Generation also refers to Stein, Hemingway, and other American writers who came of age during World War I, settled in Europe after the war, and established themselves as writers in the 1920s.

REFLECT ON THE ESSENTIAL QUESTION

Essential Question: *How did the events of the first half of the 20th century challenge existing social, cultural, and intellectual understandings?*

Challenges to Social and Cultural Understandings	Challenges to Intellectual Understandings

subatomic particles	uncertainty principle	Sigmund Freud
Albert Einstein	Erwin Schrödinger	psychoanalysis
theory of relativity	Enrico Fermi	Lost Generation
Werner Heisenberg	Niels Bohr	

MULTIPLE-CHOICE QUESTIONS

Questions 1–3 refer to the passage below.

"What intellectuals found most difficult to accept about the war was its mechanical and impersonal quality. Death and wounds were not ordinarily doled out in hand-to-hand combat, but in the whizzing and hissing and booming of shells fired by an unseen foe. Soldiers lay huddled like animals in craters and dugouts for hours and sometimes for days expecting death and praying for survival. . . . The men of the front came to view themselves as lepers who had been struck down by fate, cordoned off from the healthy population, and consigned to caves to die.

Conceptions of heroism had to be abandoned, then refashioned out of new materials. [As one German soldier Ernst Toller wrote,] 'Instead of heroes, there were only victims; conscripts instead of volunteers. . . . We were all of us cogs in a great machine which sometimes rolled forward, nobody knew where, sometimes backward, nobody knew why. We had lost our enthusiasm, our courage, the very sense of our identity.' . . .

Eventually, soldiers even lost their ability to react to death."

—Robert Wohl, *The Generation of 1914*, 1979

1. The impact of World War I on male soldiers as described in this passage and on female civilians in their families and in work was similar in that both men and women
   - (A) reacted to wartime changes by asserting the values they had held before the war
   - (B) found that their wartime experience gave them new opportunities in work and education
   - (C) felt disillusioned by the wartime tasks they felt their country needed them to do
   - (D) concluded that their prewar values and practices did not apply during and after the war

2. The political context of the immediate postwar world facing the men who had experienced combat as described in this passage is best described by which of the following?

(A) Many political leaders became more influential because people had greater trust in them.

(B) Many cities' governments became more powerful because more people advocated the idea of self-determination.

(C) Many countries became more democratic because they expanded suffrage.

(D) Old empires became stronger because they consolidated their rule over rebellious regions.

3. The experiences described in the passage contributed to formation of the Lost Generation because so many young men

(A) were killed or wounded that Europe lost a generation of young men who would have become husbands and fathers

(B) became disillusioned with their civilization that Europe lost a generation of people with hope for the future

(C) gave up writing during the war that Europe lost a generation of poets and novelists

(D) were unable to work after the war that Europe lost a generation of economic progress

SHORT-ANSWER QUESTION

Answer all parts of the question that follows.

1. a) Identify ONE similarity between ideas of physicists such as Werner Heisenberg and Erwin Schrödinger and the ideas of psychologists such as Sigmund Freud.

   b) Identify ONE difference between the ideas of physicists such as Werner Heisenberg and Erwin Schrödinger and the ideas of psychologists such as Sigmund Freud.

   c) Explain ONE impact of new ideas in physics and psychology in the early 20th century on how people thought about society.

Topic 8.11

Continuity and Change in an Age of Global Conflict

The man who tries to make the flag an object of a single party is a greater traitor to that flag than any man who fires at it.

—David Lloyd George, Prime Minister of the United Kingdom, 1916–1922

Essential Question: How did Europe's economic challenges and ideological beliefs during the 20th century influence prior conceptions about the relationship between the individual and the state?

During the first half of the 20th century, European nations and many others around the world experienced significant change. A map of Europe from before the start of World War I in 1914 looks very different from a map of the continent at the end of Second World War in 1945. By the end of this period, the way that many Europeans lived changed greatly as well. Political turmoil and economic uncertainty seemed to be the only constants during this time.

Unsettled Interwar Period At the Versailles Conference in 1919, representatives of Allied nations gathered to work out a peace agreement to conclude World War I—the Treaty of Versailles. The representatives wanted to establish long-term peace in Europe and beyond, but they did not agree on how to attain that peace. The United States sought a treaty that provided security and fostered economic cooperation, while Britain and France wanted to punish the war's losers politically and economically. The treaty left Germany weak and vulnerable.

In the years after the war, European nations wanted to guarantee safety and promote rebuilding with protectionist and nationalist policies, such as protective tariffs. This type of action and others acted as catalysts for the Great Depression and ultimately heightened its effects.

More Economic Challenges The currencies of European countries had declined in value after World War I. In addition, these countries were in massive debt from the war and needed money during the 1920s to rebuild their war-torn countries. European nations came to rely on a steady flow of American capital, but when the U.S. stock market crashed in 1929, this source of money was shut off. European economies were still struggling from the effects of World War I; the Depression magnified these problems.

Severe inflation, high unemployment, food shortages, and other problems caused radical political responses that destabilized many democracies in Western Europe. The extreme nationalism and grand promises to restore their nations to greatness from men like Adolf Hitler in Germany and Benito Mussolini in Italy appealed to many.

New and Conflicting Ideologies The interwar years saw the emergence authoritarian states—fascist Germany, Italy, and Spain, and the communist Soviet Union. The ideological beliefs of these countries led to a changing relationship among countries and between the individual and the state. Democracies in Europe and around the world were challenged by the militarization and expansion of these totalitarian states. The isolationism of the United States and weak responses by the leaders of European democracies emboldened fascist aggression and expansion, leading to World War II.

The suffering and death as a result of this war far exceeded that of the First World War. Estimates of military and civilian casualties, combined with those killed in the Holocaust, are often significantly more than 60 million.

Intellectual and Cultural Developments Exponential growth in science and technology made for a world very different during the first five decades of the 20th century. Many scientists contributed to a greater understanding of the universe and humans' place in it. Even during two global wars and an unprecedented economic crisis, the lives of many people improved, and their rights expanded.

QUESTIONS ABOUT CONTINUITY AND CHANGE

1. What were some of Europe's economic challenges in the age of global conflict?

2. How did Europe's economic challenges and ideological beliefs of the 20th century change conceptions about the relationship between the individual and the state?

UNIT 8 REVIEW: 20th-Century
Global Conflicts
c. 1914 to present

WRITE AS A HISTORIAN: *MARK HISTORICAL CHANGES*

Demonstrating that you understand the basis for continuity and change is essential when writing an AP essay. There are a variety of ways to track and mark continuity and change.

- By a concept, such as the Cold War
- By historical events, such as World War II
- By years, such as the 20th century or the 1950s
- By influential individuals, such as the Stalin era
- By developments in historical evolution, such as capitalism or communism
- By geographically specific events, such as Francisco Franco's fascist regime in Spain
- By comparative label, such as the more industrialized countries

Marking the start of a significant change is an attempt to make sense of historical time periods and to determine an era's beginning and end points, its characteristics, and its causes and effects. Periods may reflect major trends in technology, science, religion, the arts, or popular culture. Or periods may be concrete, such as the beginning and end of a specific war or political reign. Sometimes, a single individual is so powerful that an era is based entirely on that person's influence.

Choices about identifying the bases for change in history can actually shape the way we think about it. These choices might give higher value to one group, one narrative, or one geographic region over another. Thinking critically about how subjective the basis for identifying change is can enrich the content of your essay.

In the statements below, which words indicate various models of marking time periods?

1. Military and worker insurrections in Russia set the stage for Lenin's Bolshevik Revolution and the establishment of a communist state.

2. Under Stalin, the Soviet Union engaged in rapid economic modernization, as demonstrated by Collectivization and the Five Year Plan.

3. Fascism gained hold in the environment of bitterness and economic instability of the post-World War I era.

4. The Great Depression undermined Western European democracies and fomented radical political responses throughout Europe.

5. During the Marshall Plan years, the United States financed extensive reconstruction of Western and Central Europe.

6. The expansion of cradle-to-grave social welfare programs in the post-World War II era was funded by high taxes, which became a contentious political issue in Europe.

7. Following a long period of economic stagnation, Mikhail Gorbachev's internal reforms of *perestroika* and *glasnost* attempted to prevent the collapse of the Soviet Union.

8. The rise of new nationalisms in the late 20th century resulted in war and genocide in the Balkans and instability in some former Soviet republics.

LONG ESSAY QUESTIONS

Directions: Suggested writing time is 40 minutes. In your response, you should do the following:

- Respond to the prompt with a historically defensible thesis that establishes a line of reasoning.
- Describe a broader historical context relevant to the prompt.
- Support an argument in response to the prompt using specific and relevant examples of evidence.
- Use historical reasoning (e.g., comparison, causation, continuity and change over time) to frame or structure an argument that addresses the prompt.
- Use evidence to corroborate, qualify, or modify an argument that addresses the prompt.

1. Evaluate the extent to which developments in the Balkans were the most significant factor leading to World War I.

2. Evaluate the extent to which the Germans and French viewed the Versailles Treaty differently.

3. Evaluate the extent to which Lenin fostered change in Russian society and economics.

DOCUMENT-BASED QUESTION

Directions: Question 1 is based on the accompanying documents. The documents have been edited for the purpose of this exercise. You are advised to spend 15 minutes planning and 45 minutes writing your answer. In your response, you should do the following:

- **Thesis:** Make a defensible claim that establishes a line of reasoning and consists of one or more sentences found in one place.
- **Contextualization:** Relate the argument to a broader historical context.
- **Document Evidence:** Use content from at least six documents.
- **Outside Evidence:** Use one piece of evidence not in the documents.
- **Document Sourcing:** Explain how or why the point of view, purpose, situation, or intended audience is relevant for at least three documents.
- **Analysis:** Show the relationships among pieces of historical evidence and use them to support, qualify, or modify an argument.

1. Analyze how the Great War contributed to the "Age of Anxiety" during the interwar years of 1919–1939.

Document 1:

Source: Eduard Beneš, Czechoslovakian statesman, *The Rationale for The Little Entente*, 1924 [The Little Entente, a treaty creating an alliance between Yugoslavia, Romania, and Czechoslovakia, was signed on April 23, 1921.]

[T]his policy was criticized, belittled, and distorted from its true meaning. At first it was not welcomed in Western Europe. We quietly went on, and later events have proved that we were acting on the right lines. One section of the Opposition at home said that the Little Entente was imperialistic and militaristic; another section saw in it a weapon for European reaction against Soviet Russia; some considered it to be hostile to Italy, others said that it meant discord with France, declaring nevertheless, when it was convenient to say so, that the Little Entente was in vassalage to France; finally, others thought that it was merely out for self-advertisement and was no more than a piece of bluff. This is what was said to me here (in Bucharest) on one occasion even in the Czechoslovak Commission for Foreign Affairs. Today after three years the group of these three States has shown great vitality; it has shown an example of close cooperation, loyalty and genuine friendship and has achieved considerable results in its policy; it has preserved the peace of Central Europe in the most critical moments, acted as a moderating influence in a series of conflicts, and brought about such a degree of consolidation in its neighborhood and within its own States that there is no important international statesman today who would not openly recognize its value.

Document 2:

Source: Adolf Hitler, *Mein Kampf*, 1925

The fact that intelligent sections of the community regard the German collapse primarily as an economic catastrophe, and consequently think that a cure for it may be found in an economic solution, seems to me to be the reason why hitherto no improvement has been brought about.

No improvement can be brought about until it be understood that economics play only a second or third role, while the main part is played by political, moral and racial factors. Only when this is understood will it be possible to understand the causes of the present evil and consequently to find the ways and means of remedying them. . . .

The most facile [simplistic], and therefore the most generally accepted, way of accounting for the present misfortune is to say that it is the result of a lost war, and that this is the real cause of the present misfortune. The apostles of world conciliation habitually asserted the resurgence of the German people—once "militarism" had been crushed. Did not these self-same circles sing the praises of the Entente and did they not also lay the whole blame for the sanguinary [bloody] struggle on the shoulders of Germany? Without this explanation, would they have been able to put forward the theory that a military defeat would have no political consequences for the German people? Is not that so, you miserable, lying rascals? That kind of impudence which is typical of the Jews was necessary in order to proclaim the defeat of the army as the cause of the German collapse.

Document 3:

Source: Albert Camus, *The Stranger*, 1942

Nothing, nothing had the least importance and I knew quite well why. [The priest], too, knew why. From the dark horizon of my future a sort of slow, persistent breeze had been blowing toward me, all my life long, from the years that were to come. And on its way that breeze had leveled out all the ideas that people tried to foist on me in the equally unreal years I then was living through. What difference could they make to me, the deaths of others, or a mother's love, or his [the priest's] God; or the way a man decides to live, the fate he thinks he chooses, since one and the same fate was bound to "choose" not only me but thousands of millions of privileged people who, like him, called themselves my brothers. Surely, surely he must see that? Every man alive was privileged; there was only one class of men, the privileged class. All alike would be condemned to die one day; his turn, too, would come like the others'. And what difference could it make if, after being charged with murder, he were executed because he didn't weep at his mother's funeral, since it all came to the same thing in the end?

Document 4:

Source: Paul Valéry: *The European Mind*, 1922

We are a very unfortunate generation, whose lot has been to see the moment of our passage through life coincide with the arrival of great and terrifying events, the echo of which will resound through all our lives. One can say that all the fundamentals of the world have been affected by the war, or more exactly, by the circumstances of the war; something deeper has been worn away than the renewable parts of the machine. You know how greatly the general economic situation has been disturbed, and the polity of states, and the very life of the individual; you are familiar with the universal discomfort, hesitation, apprehension. But among all these injured things is the Mind. The Mind has indeed been cruelly wounded; its complaint is heard in the hearts of intellectual man; it passes a mournful judgment on itself. It doubts itself profoundly.

Document 5:

Source: Sigmund Freud, *Civilization and Its Discontents*, 1930

It is impossible to escape the impression that people commonly use false standards of measurement—that they seek power, success and wealth for themselves and admire them in others, and that they underestimate what is of true value in life. And yet, in making any general judgment of this sort, we are in danger of forgetting how variegated the human world and its mental life are. There are a few men from whom their contemporaries do not withhold admiration, although their greatness rests on attributes and achievements which are completely foreign to the aims and ideals of the multitude. One might easily be inclined to suppose that it is after all only a minority which appreciates these great men, while the large majority cares nothing for them. But things are probably not as simple as that, thanks to the discrepancies between people's thoughts and their actions, and to the diversity of their wishful impulses. . . .

This brings us to the more general problem of preservation. The subject has hardly been studied as yet; but it is so attractive and important that we may be allowed to turn our attention to…a destruction of the memory-trace—that is, its annihilation—that everything is somehow preserved and that in suitable circumstances it can once more be brought to light. Let us try to grasp what this assumption involves by taking an analogy from another field. We will choose as an example the history of the Eternal City. Historians tell us that the oldest Rome was the *Roma Quadrata*, a fenced settlement on the Palatine. . . .

Of the buildings which once occupied this ancient area he will find nothing, or only scanty remains, for they exist no longer. The best information about Rome in the republican era would only enable him at the most to point out the sites where the temples and public buildings of that period stood. Their place is now taken by ruins, but not by ruins of themselves but of later restorations made after fires or destruction.

Document 6:

Source: Gino Severini, *The Accordion Player*, 1919

Document 7:

Source: W. H. Auden, "Dance of Death," 1933

It's farewell to the drawing room's civilised cry The professor's sensible where-to and why

The frock-coated diplomat's social aplomb Now matters are settled with gas and bomb.

The works for two pianos, the brilliant stories Of reasonable giants and remarkable fairies The pictures, the ointments, the frangible wares And the branches of olive are stored upstairs. For the Devil has broken parole and arisen

He has dynamited his way out of prison Out of the well where his Papa throws The rebel range, the outcast rose. . . .

The fishes are silent deep in the sea: The skies are lit up like a Christmas tree

The star in the west shoots its warning cry "Mankind is alive but mankind must die."

So good-bye to the house with its wallpaper red, Good-bye to the sheets on the warm double bed Good-bye to the beautiful birds on the wall,

It's good-bye, dear heart, good-bye to you all.

UNIT 9: Cold War and Contemporary Europe
c. 1914 to present

Topic 9.1

Contextualizing Cold War and Contemporary Europe

Essential Question: What was the context in which the Cold War developed, spread, and ended in Europe?

Two super powers arose from World War II—the United States and the Soviet Union. Although these nations allied to fight fascist Germany, their ideologically opposed systems led the nations to the Cold War which lasted for more than four decades.

As Europe rebuilt from World War II, alliances and organizations fostered unity and integration among European nations rather than the nationalism of previous years. By combining European cooperation with economic growth, technological advancement, and globalization, Europe transformed itself in the second half of the 20th century and beyond.

The Cold War Develops Even before the end of World War II, the United States and the Soviet Union attempted to work together with the creation of the United Nations, a peacekeeping organization. These efforts to cooperate were short lived. Both countries wanted to dominate Europe's political and economic post-war rebuilding which led to a division of the continent. The Soviet Union's plans included establishing communist governments in Eastern Europe to protect itself from Western European threats. U.S. plans involved financial support for Western Europe and the cultivation of democratic governments in Eastern Europe. This would politically stabilize these nations (providing more allies for the United States) and strengthen their economies (providing additional U.S. trading partners).

The Cold War Spreads The Cold War between the Soviet Union and the United States put the rest of the world under pressure to choose a side. In 1949, the United States formed an alliance with ten Western European countries and Canada known as the North Atlantic Treaty Organization (NATO). In 1955, the Soviet Union responded by establishing its own alliance, called the Warsaw Pact, with the Eastern European nations that were under its control. The Cold

War continued to spread in the form of military conflicts, or proxy wars, in Asia, Africa, Latin America, and the Caribbean.

An intense competition to develop and stockpile nuclear weapons developed between the United States and the Soviet Union. In addition to this arms race, the super powers wanted to demonstrate their technological superiority in space exploration—the space race. The spending necessary for the arms and space races showed the economic weaknesses of the Soviet Union. Those weaknesses combined with political inflexibility caused the collapse of the Soviet Union (and the end of the Cold War) in the early 1990s, which freed many European nations to pursue more democratic governments and capitalistic economies.

20th-Century Changes and Movements A new type of colonization, the mandate system, which developed after World War I, began to be dismantled after World War II. Nationalist movements around the world gained momentum and numerous countries freed themselves from European political and economic control.

European nations started to set aside their nationalistic sentiments in the postwar era. They formed various groups for economic and political benefits, and eventually the European Union was formed with the aim of greater prosperity and security.

Globalization spread European culture and products to the rest of the world through technological advances in communication and transportation. Europe also received cultural influences through increases in immigration, which at times led to conflict brought about by anti-immigrant groups. By the end of the century, social movements worked to expand civil rights for groups, such as women and the LGBTQ community.

ANALYZE THE CONTEXT

1. What was the context in which the Cold War developed in Europe?

2. What was the context in which the Cold War spread, then ended, in Europe?

Topic 9.2

Rebuilding Europe

[Europe] must have substantial additional help or face economic, social, and political deterioration of a very grave character.

—U.S. Secretary of State George C. Marshall (1880–1959)

Essential Question: How did postwar developments result in economic changes after World War II?

After the destruction and devastation of World War II, it was unclear which European countries would align themselves with the United States and liberal democracy and which would align with the communist **Soviet Union**, also known as the **Union of Soviet Socialist Republics (USSR)**. This Cold War polarization eventually led to efforts for transnational unity in Europe—or linking participants across boundaries.

Devastation and Recovery

In Europe, even countries that had been victorious in World War II were in tatters. Between 40 million and 50 million people died in World War II, many of them European. For example, nearly 6 million Poles died, which was one-fifth of Poland's prewar population. Around Europe, survivors often had injuries that prevented them from working. Homes, factories, ships, and transportation networks had been destroyed. There was a real danger of famine because workers and transportation were both lacking.

Source: Getty Images

This 1945 photograph shows the destruction of buildings and trolley tracks in the city of Koblenz in western Germany. Also, it shows people lined up for food rations.

Would people in devastated countries turn to communism to address these issues? How much more suffering could people take after a world war? Although the United States had endured slightly more than 400,000 deaths in the war, its factories, farms, and markets remained largely intact.

The United States Influences Western Europe

The United States wanted to support the countries of Western Europe that had democratic governments. For this reason, in 1947 it announced the **Marshall Plan** to provide economic support to help European countries rebuild. The plan was named after its architect and Secretary of State, George C. Marshall. As a former general and Army chief of staff during World War II, Marshall had been responsible for coordinating more than 8 million troops.

An Invite to the USSR The United States invited the Soviet Union and the countries under Soviet influence (called **satellite nations**) to take part in the Marshall Plan. However, these communist nations declined. They considered the economic regulations that would come with Marshall Plan money to be a form of U.S. imperialism—an infringement on their national sovereignty.

Marshall Plan Stimulates Growth

U.S. President Harry Truman signed the Marshall Plan into law as a way to help Europe rebuild its infrastructure and industry. Marshall and others believed that restoring economic stability in Europe would prevent communism from becoming stronger and keep European countries from falling under the influence of the Soviet Union. The plan offered $13 billion for economic recovery programs.

Western Europe Recovers For the countries of Western Europe, funds from the United States under the Marshall Plan provided a strong stimulus for rapid economic recovery and growth. Countries used the funds to buy new equipment and raw materials for construction projects, leading to the revival of industry. By 1950, European industry was producing 30 percent more than it had before World War II. The steel industry's output was 70 percent higher than before the war. This economic growth continued through the 1960s. It was aided, in part, by the nations' economic cooperation.

Economic Cooperation Between Friendly Nations

The Marshall Plan encouraged the countries of Western Europe to cooperate with one another to maximize the benefits of U.S. aid and boost postwar recovery. Early cooperative efforts expanded over time. In 1951, France, West Germany, the Netherlands, Belgium, Luxembourg, and Italy created an organization, the European Coal and Steel Community (ECSC), to eliminate trade barriers on steel and coal. In 1957, the same six countries signed a treaty that created the **European Economic Community (EEC)**, often known as the **Common Market**, which promoted free trade within the EEC. By the 1960s, the Common Market was a trading force that was close in size to the United States.

An "Economic Miracle" The postwar economic recovery in Germany has often been referred to as an "economic miracle." West Germany was smaller than prewar Germany, yet by 1955 its gross national product (GNP), or total economic output, was higher than prewar GNP. Unemployment was low, and wages doubled between 1950 and 1965. In Italy, the economy recovered in a similar fashion. Italian growth in producing automobiles, electrical appliances, and office machinery was an example of the increasing importance of consumer goods to the new economy.

As countries recovered economically, their citizens began to wonder what this new postwar world should look like. In many nations, governments began to improve the social safety net (government assistance programs in times of crisis) for ordinary people. Individuals also bought large and small luxuries to improve their quality of life.

Economic Growth and the Welfare State

Even in the democracies of Western Europe, governments became more involved in managing economic decisions during World War I, the Great Depression, and World War II. This practice continued after World War II as governments actively managed their economies and used the benefits of postwar growth to provide increased social welfare benefits to their citizens. The growth of the welfare state revealed a new relationship between individuals and the state—one in which the state assumed some responsibility for basic needs of individuals. Economic hard times later in the 20th century led to some criticism and limitation of the welfare state.

Rise of Consumerism As Europe's economy grew stronger, consumerism, the theory that individuals should buy more goods in order to expand the economy, grew in importance both economically and culturally. Being able to buy more became a key sign of upward mobility. The middle class grew as large numbers of people took jobs as supervisors, administrators, and technicians, creating a larger market for consumer goods. At the same time, wages for all workers increased so that working-class families were able to acquire some of the trappings of a middle-class lifestyle, such as televisions and home appliances. Buying on installment by making monthly payments for purchases allowed more people to buy these expensive goods. An increase in automobile ownership was the main indicator of the growth of consumerism. Between 1948 and 1960, the number of automobiles in Europe grew from 5 million to 45 million.

GDP PER CAPITA, 1960 AND 2020		
Country	1960	2020
Denmark	21,076	60,908
Italy	10,868	31,676
Portugal	4,506	22,439
Spain	7,360	27,057
United Kingdom	13,827	40,284
Countries now using the euro	10,809	40,089
World	3,697	10,925

Source: Adapted from the World Bank at data.worldbank.org

Data given in constant 2010 U.S. dollars

REFLECT ON THE ESSENTIAL QUESTION

Essential Question: *How did postwar developments result in economic changes after World War II?*

Development	Economic Result

Soviet Union (or USSR,   Marshall Plan   European Economic
   Union of Soviet Socialist   satellite nations   Community (EEC)
   Republics)   Common Market

MULTIPLE-CHOICE QUESTIONS

Questions 1–3 refer to the passage below.

"The world situation is very serious. . . . In considering the requirements for
the rehabilitation of Europe, the physical loss of life, the visible destruction
of cities, factories, mines and railroads was correctly estimated, but . . .
this visible destruction was probably less serious than the dislocation of
the entire fabric of European economy . . . . [T]he rehabilitation of the
economic organization of Europe quite evidently will require a much
longer time and greater effort than had been foreseen. . . .

The truth of the matter is that Europe's requirements for the next three or
four years of foreign food and other essential products—principally from
America—are so much greater than her present ability to pay that she must
have substantial additional help, or face economic, social and political
deterioration of a very grave character. . . .

It is logical that the United States should do whatever it is able to do to
assist in the return of normal economic health in the world, without which
there can be no political stability and no assured peace. Any assistance that
this Government may render in the future should provide a cure rather
than a mere palliative."

—George C. Marshall, speech at Harvard University, 1947

1. Which of the following descriptions of Europe most accurately
   describes the economic context in which Marshall gave this speech?

   (A) World War II had devastated the infrastructures of many countries.

   (B) Many governments had accumulated money to finance
       construction projects.

   (C) The creation of the welfare state had spread poverty and starvation.

   (D) A decline in consumerism had reduced the market for goods.

2. The excerpt above expressed ideas that, in the 1950s, contributed to
   - (A) increased conflicts between the United States and Great Britain
   - (B) greater tensions between France and Germany
   - (C) greater cooperation among the countries in Western Europe
   - (D) closer ties between Western Europe and Eastern Europe

3. Which European country viewed the ideas expressed in the speech above as a threat to its economic and political status?
   - (A) Great Britain because it was a close ally of the United States
   - (B) France because it wanted to be the dominant country in Europe
   - (C) Germany because it had been an opponent in World War II
   - (D) The Soviet Union because it was a rival to the United States

SHORT-ANSWER QUESTION

Use the passage below to answer all parts of the question that follows.

"After World War II the German economy lay in shambles. The war, along with Hitler's scorched-earth policy, had destroyed 20 percent of all housing. Food production per capita in 1947 was only 51 percent of its level in 1938, and the official food ration set by the occupying powers varied between 1,040 and 1,550 calories per day. Industrial output in 1947 was only one-third its 1938 level. Moreover, a large percentage of Germany's working-age men were dead.

Observers thought that West Germany would have to be the biggest client of the U.S. welfare state; yet, twenty years later its economy was envied by most of the world. And less than ten years after the war people already were talking about the German economic miracle."

David R. Henderson, "German Economic 'Miracle,'"
The Concise Encyclopedia of Economics

1. a) Explain ONE piece of evidence that supports Henderson's argument regarding the German economic miracle following World War II.

   b) Explain ONE piece of evidence that supports an argument regarding the lack of an economic transformation in a European country other than Germany following World War II.

   c) Account for the differences in your arguments in your responses in parts a. and b.

Topic 9.3

The Cold War

[A]n iron curtain has descended across the continent . . .
—Winston Churchill (1874–1965), speech in Fulton, Missouri, March 5, 1946

Essential Question: How did the conflict between the United States and the Soviet Union play out in global politics?

During World War II, Western democracies in Europe and the United States allied with the communist Soviet Union to defeat Nazism. The Allies put aside political differences between liberal democracy and communism to focus on their main goal. As the defeat of Germany became certain in 1945, Allied leaders began to talk about the peace process and these differences once again became prominent. The United States and the Soviet Union emerged from the war as the two political and military super powers, and they had very different visions for the postwar world. Neither side was willing to engage in another massive battle on the ground. Instead, tensions led to a **Cold War** in which conflicts played out in propaganda campaigns, secret operations, limited military conflicts, and an arms race. The Cold War lasted for nearly 50 years.

The Division of Europe

U.S. President **Franklin Roosevelt** and British Prime Minister **Winston Churchill** made the establishment of the **United Nations (UN)** a priority during World War II. They hoped this new international organization would be more effective than the League of Nations had been in mediating disputes among nations. **Joseph Stalin** of the Soviet Union negotiated with the other Allied leaders on certain aspects of the UN's makeup. In the end, the founding countries made concessions and created the UN Charter. Divisions between West and East were soon reflected, however, in the workings of the UN. The United States and the Soviet Union each have veto powers in the Security Council (as do the the three other permanent member nations) and would not approve decisions that conflicted with their interests. Several specific issues soon led to the division of Europe.

Eastern Europe For the United States and Great Britain, the principle of **self-determination** was most important. They advocated for free elections in the countries of Eastern Europe that the Soviet Union had liberated from the Nazis. Stalin insisted that the nations of Eastern Europe remain under Soviet influence. "Everyone imposes his own system as far as his army can reach," Stalin said. "It cannot be otherwise." He recognized that free elections would potentially result in governments that were less than friendly to the Soviets. He also believed that Soviet security depended on buffer states in Eastern Europe to protect the USSR from Western aggression. Therefore, by 1948, the Soviets put pro-Soviet governments in place in Poland, Czechoslovakia, Romania, Bulgaria, and Hungary.

Source: Getty Images

This monument in Hungary recalls the period when Soviet power divided Eastern European.

Following Winston Churchill's speech (quoted at the start of Topic 9.3), people in the West referred to the countries under Soviet domination as the **Iron Curtain** countries. After communist Yugoslavia supported communists in a civil war in Greece, in 1947, the United States proclaimed the **Truman Doctrine**. This policy offered financial aid to any country threatened by communist takeover. Truman and his advisors embraced an idea called the domino theory. It held that the "fall" of any one nation to communism would cause neighboring countries to also fall. Further, the U.S. policy of containment meant that, short of war, the United States and its allies would aid countries fighting a communist takeover. As a result, the distinct division of Europe into West and East—noncommunist and communist—continued.

Germany The question of what to do with Germany was also a source of conflict among the Allies. All agreed that the country and the city of Berlin would be partitioned among France, Great Britain, the United States, and the Soviet Union. The three Western Allies wanted to combine their three zones into one state under democratic principles. In Berlin, the three Western zones would become a free city that was located within the Soviet zone of Germany.

In contrast, the Soviets wanted to stop these Western plans and control all of Berlin. To this end, they set up a blockade of the Western zones in Berlin to prevent the West from moving supplies into the area by land. The Western Allies did not want to risk a military confrontation with the Soviets and ultimately began the Berlin Airlift. Through this operation, the United States and Britain flew supplies into the Western zones every day between June 1948 and May 1949, when the Soviets finally lifted the blockade. After that time, two states emerged in Germany: the West German Federal Republic and the German Democratic Republic, generally referred to as East Germany. The division of Europe into East and West was complete.

The Cold War on a Global Stage

In 1949, communists gained control of the government of China. This increased the West's concerns about the spread of communism. The United States and the Soviet Union never fought direct military battles against one another. Instead, the war involved four major types of conflict.

Arms Race

When the Soviets exploded their first atomic bomb in 1949 in response to the atomic bombs developed by the United States, a **nuclear arms race** became a key part of the Cold War. Both sides were intent on developing increasing numbers of and more powerful weapons. The nations knew that if they launched a nuclear attack, the other side would be able to retaliate and destroy them. Therefore, neither side wanted to risk an unwinnable nuclear war that would devastate much of the world.

The Cuban Missile Crisis The threat of nuclear war reached its peak during the Cuban Missile Crisis. The Soviets had supported the government of Fidel Castro on the island of Cuba since 1959, and the United States had been unsuccessful in its efforts to overthrow Castro. In 1962, the Soviets decided to place nuclear missiles in Cuba—only 90 miles off the coast of Florida. When a U-2 spy plane photographed Soviet missiles in Cuba, President John F. Kennedy ordered a blockade of the island and demanded the removal of the missiles already there. Ultimately, the Soviet leader Nikita Khrushchev agreed to recall the ships carrying the missiles if Kennedy agreed not to invade Cuba. Kennedy also agreed that the United States would remove missiles in Turkey, a key U.S. ally and member of NATO, which bordered the Soviet Union.

After this scare, the two countries established a telephone hotline to allow rapid communication. In 1963, they also agreed to ban the testing of nuclear weapons in the atmosphere. However, the arms race continued for most of the period until the collapse of the Soviet Union in 1991.

The Space Race The unofficial competition known as the "space race" was another area in which each country tried to prove its technological superiority. This race did not have the potential for global catastrophe that the arms race had, but each side recognized the potential for military applications in space exploration. In October 1957, the Soviet Union successfully launched *Sputnik*, the first man-made object to enter into Earth's orbit. They followed this success with the first manned orbit of Earth by cosmonaut Yuri Gagarin in March 1961.

This shocked the U.S. public, spreading fears that the Soviets could spy on, or even attack, the United States from space. The U.S. response to this setback was to establish the National Aeronautics and Space Administration (NASA). Through massive funding and effort, the United States "won" the race to land humans on the Moon when Apollo 11 touched down in July 1969. In truth, victories in the space race for both sides were as much about propaganda as they were about military or technological superiority, but satellite technology would become increasingly important for strategic and economic reasons in the decades to come.

Propaganda Campaigns

Because the Cold War was a war between different ideologies, an important part of the "fight" was the effort to persuade people around the world of the superiority of each side's ideas and values. For the West, those values were focused on democracy, political freedom, and the benefits of a capitalist economy. The Soviets promoted the values of a communist system, such as the end of class differences and the benefits of a planned, collective economy. Both sides used a variety of means to promote their messages.

The United States used mass media to promote the benefits of a Western lifestyle to people in Eastern Europe and the Soviet Union. Voice of America and Radio Free Europe were two government-sponsored programs that broadcast Western news and culture throughout the Soviet bloc. These programs provided an alternative to the messages from state-sponsored media in communist countries. The Soviets made every effort to jam these radio signals but were largely unsuccessful.

Soviet messages focused on the corruption and greed of Western countries, portraying them as economic imperialists. They pointed to problems of class and race in the United States. Stalin saw efforts by the United States to supply aid to European countries to rebuild after World War II as efforts to make those countries dependent on the United States. Soviet propaganda posters often showed images of Lenin and other early communist leaders to encourage citizens in the East to make sacrifices for communist ideals. The Soviets also emphasized their strengths in developing weapons and space technology.

Covert Actions

The nature of the Cold War led to **covert actions**—secretive or shadowy operations that were not openly carried out by the governments of the nations involved. Much of this activity was in the form of espionage, or spying. The main intelligence agencies involved in spying were the Soviet KGB, the American Central Intelligence Agency (CIA), and the British Secret Intelligence Service (SIS), usually referred to as MI6. All of these agencies grew out of organizations that had been active during World War II.

Each agency recruited people to infiltrate its counterpart in other countries to gain secret information, such as plans for weapons development or Cold War strategies. For example, before World War II, the Soviets recruited four college students from Cambridge University in England who supported the communists in the fight against fascism. During the Cold War, these young men gained influential positions within the British government but were actively working for and supplying information to the KGB. One of the top double agents, Harold "Kim" Philby, was asked why he betrayed his own country for the Soviet Union. "To betray, you must first belong," he answered. "I never belonged." In addition to gathering foreign intelligence, the KGB spied on and terrorized its citizens who might be opposed to the Soviet regime.

The CIA influenced the internal politics and governments of a number of countries. For example, it intervened in Italian elections in 1947 and 1948 to prevent communists from taking control of the Italian government. In a similar way, it sought to weaken the Communist Party in France.

Limited "Hot Wars"

The ideological Cold War was accompanied by actual "hot wars" in Asia, Africa, and Latin America. A hot war is one that includes military fighting. These conflicts resulted in the deaths of many millions of people. They were sometimes referred to as *proxy wars* because the armies of other countries were proxies, or stand-ins, for the two super powers. Most focused on spreading or stopping the spread of communism. For example, in the 1970s, the United States supported anti-communist forces in a civil war in Angola in southwest Africa, while the Soviet Union and Cuba supported the communist forces.

Conflicts in Korea and Vietnam Two of the biggest confrontations were the **Korean War** and **Vietnam War** in Asia. Both countries were split into a north with a communist government and a south with a pro-U.S. government. When North Korea invaded South Korea in 1950, the United States, with the support of the United Nations, sent troops to counter the move. North Korea received support from the Soviet Union and later China. The opposing sides fought to a stalemate. An armistice in 1953 left the Korean peninsula divided.

The division in Vietnam occurred in 1954 after the Vietnamese succeeded in defeating the French, who had controlled the country for almost a century. The United States supported the weak and corrupt government of South Vietnam and in the 1960s began to send increasing numbers of military advisors and troops to fight communist guerrillas, the Viet Cong, as well as troops sent from North Vietnam. (A guerrilla is a fighter who is not part of a country's official military forces.) Both the Soviet Union and China supported the Vietnamese communists. The United States was unsuccessful in defeating the communist forces. It withdrew from the country in 1973; North Vietnam soon gained control, uniting the country under a communist government in 1975.

Yom Kippur War A conflict in the Middle East, the **Yom Kippur War**, brought the United States and the Soviet Union into indirect contact with each other. In 1973, on the Jewish holy day of Yom Kippur, Syria and Egypt both attacked Israel. The attack also took place during the Muslim holy month of Ramadan. The Soviet Union had long been a supplier of military and other materials to Syria and Egypt, and it ramped up these efforts when the war commenced. The United States, which was at first reluctant to send aid to Israel, changed its position in light of the Soviet actions and began to supply Israel—in spite of opposition from a number of its allies. The war lasted 20 days. Although Israel won, it suffered many casualties. In a broader geopolitical sense, the war temporarily increased tensions between the two super powers.

The USSR Invades Afghanistan In 1979, the Soviet Union sent troops into Afghanistan. The goal was to support the communist government against anti-communist Muslim guerrillas. In response, the United States backed the guerrillas. The Soviets sent in 100,000 troops, of which 15,000 died. Although the United States did not send in troops, it provided antiaircraft missiles and other weapons. After years of stalemate, the war grew increasingly unpopular among the Soviet people. The USSR, crumbling from within, finally withdrew from Afghanistan in 1989.

Non-Aligned Movement Some countries, such as India, Indonesia, and Yugoslavia, wanted to avoid taking sides in the U.S.–Soviet conflict. Known as the **Non-Aligned Movement**, they stayed out of military alliances with either super power and tried to benefit from good relationships with both.

THE GLOBAL COLD WAR

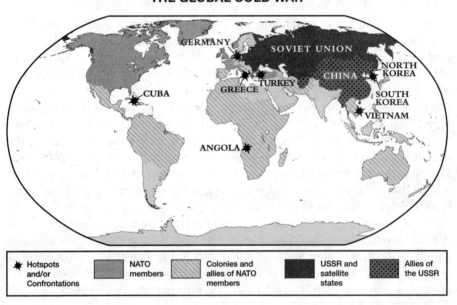

| ✴ | Hotspots and/or Confrontations | | NATO members | | Colonies and allies of NATO members | | USSR and satellite states | | Allies of the USSR |

REFLECT ON THE ESSENTIAL QUESTION

Essential Question: *How did the conflict between the United States and the Soviet Union play out in global politics?*

Conflicts	Effects on Global Politics

KEY TERMS

Cold War	self-determination	Korean War
Franklin Roosevelt	Truman Doctrine	Vietnam War
Winston Churchill	Iron Curtain	Yom Kippur War
United Nations (UN)	nuclear arms race	USSR invasion of Afghanistan
Joseph Stalin	covert actions	Non-Aligned Movement

Questions 1–3 refer to the passage below.

"While [U.S. secretary of state] Kissinger was trying to sort out the cease-fire, he met with his State Department senior staff to give them his assessment of the situation since the war broke out. This gave him a chance to vent some steam about issues that troubled him, such as the question of his advice on preemption and the attitude of West European allies who, he argued, were behaving like 'jackals' because they 'did everything to egg on the Arabs.'

Kissinger reviewed the immediate prewar intelligence estimating on the Arab-Israeli conflict ('no possibility of an attack'), the 'new elements' in Arab strategy, overall U.S. strategy, interpretations of Soviet conduct, the decision for a major U.S. airlift, U.S. early efforts toward a cease-fire, and Resolution 338. On the basic U.S.-Israeli relationship during the war, Kissinger explained his balancing act: 'we could not tolerate an Israeli defeat' but, at the same time, 'we could not make our policy hostage to the Israelis.' Thus, 'we went to extreme lengths to stay in close touch with all the key Arab participants.' The progress of the war, so far, had been a 'major success' in part because it validated the importance of détente: 'without the close relationship with the Soviet Union, this thing could have easily escalated.'

Washington, however, not Moscow, was in the catbird seat [the best position]; the Israelis had won, Soviet clients had lost, and a peace settlement depended on Washington. The United States was in a 'position where if we behave wisely and with discipline, we are really in a central position.'"

—Henry Kissinger, staff meetings transcript, October 23, 1973

1. According to the passage, prewar intelligence indicated that Arab countries were
   (A) trying to coordinate an attack on Israel
   (B) being encouraged by Russia to attack Israel
   (C) in danger of being attacked by Israel
   (D) unlikely to attack Israel anytime soon

2. The passage claims that the relationship between which countries was extremely important in limiting the Israeli-Arab conflict?
   (A) The Soviet Union and the United States
   (B) The Soviet Union and the Arab countries
   (C) Western Europe and Israel
   (D) Western Europe and the Arab countries

3. Which of the following statements best explains the Arab-Israeli conflict in the context of the Cold War?

(A) It was a cold war because it was diplomatic maneuvering rather than military fighting.

(B) It was a guerrilla war because it was fought by small military units.

(C) It was a proxy war because it was part of a rivalry between more powerful countries.

(D) It was a trade war because it was based on economic differences.

SHORT-ANSWER QUESTION

Use the passage below to answer all parts of the question that follows.

"From Stettin [a German-Polish city] in the Baltic to Trieste [a city in Italy] in the Adriatic, an iron curtain has descended across the Continent. Behind that line lie all the capitals of the ancient states of Central and Eastern Europe. Warsaw, Berlin, Prague, Vienna, Budapest, Belgrade, Bucharest and Sofia, all these famous cities and the populations around them lie in what I must call the Soviet sphere, and all are subject in one form or another, not only to Soviet influence but to a very high and, in many cases, increasing measure of control from Moscow. Athens alone-Greece with its immortal glories-is free to decide its future at an election under British, American and French observation.

The Russian-dominated Polish Government has been encouraged to make enormous and wrongful inroads upon Germany, and mass expulsions of millions of Germans on a scale grievous and undreamed-of are now taking place. The Communist parties, which were very small in all these Eastern States of Europe, have been raised to pre-eminence and power far beyond their numbers and are seeking everywhere to obtain totalitarian control. Police governments are prevailing in nearly every case, and so far, except in Czechoslovakia, there is no true democracy."

—Winston Churchill, "Iron Curtain" speech, Westminster College, Fulton, Missouri, March 5, 1946

1. a) Describe the historical process behind Churchill speech.

b) Explain ONE piece of evidence not mentioned in the passage that could be used to support Churchill's argument in the passage.

c) Explain ONE piece of evidence not mentioned in the passage that could be used to refute Churchill's argument in the passage.

Topic 9.4

Two Super Powers Emerge

Whether you like it or not, history is on our side. We will bury you.
—Soviet premier Nikita Khrushchev (1894–1971), November 18, 1956

> **Essential Question:** What are the economic and political consequences of the Cold War in Europe?

The emergence of the United States and the USSR as **super powers** during the Cold War affected many nations. Most nations chose to align with one of the powers which brought the advantages of military protection, economic benefits, and political assistance.

U.S. Influence in Western Europe

During the Cold War, European nations could not act independently in the area of foreign policy because they were so closely tied to the super powers. No one country in Western Europe could stand up to aggression from the Soviet Union. As a result, many of these nations sought alliances with the United States.

The North Atlantic Treaty Organization (NATO)

In 1949, 10 nations of Western Europe signed a treaty with the United States and Canada to form the **North Atlantic Treaty Organization (NATO)**. The member countries pledged to support one another if any of them were attacked. This was primarily a defensive alliance against the Soviet Union.

Early Monetary and Trade Systems

A conference to plan for the economy after the end of World War II took place at Bretton Woods, New Hampshire, in July 1944. The United States and Great Britain led the conference, and representatives of 44 countries, including the Soviet Union, attended. The purpose of the conference was to avoid the economic problems that developed after World War I, which led to the rise of fascism and the Great Depression. Out of the conference came the **World Bank** to provide loans for trade and rebuilding and the **International Monetary Fund (IMF)** to help with currency exchange and trade.

As of 2021, about 180 countries were members of the IMF. Each country pays a fee to the IMF depending on its level of wealth. Countries that pay more get more voting power. Although the United States has had the most voting power within the fund, IMF tradition is that the fund does not select Americans to the all-important managing director role. Since the early 1970s, the IMF has focused on lending money to poor countries. The fund has come under criticism from some experts who believe it approves loans that are too risky and others who believe its loan terms exploit poor nations.

GATT In 1948, 23 countries signed the **General Agreement on Tariffs and Trade (GATT)** to reduce barriers to world trade. At the time, it was the largest trade negotiation ever attempted. The idea was that it would be a temporary arrangement and that a United Nations agency would form so GATT would no longer be needed. However, this never happened. Largely due to GATT, many of the barriers to international trade dropped in the second half of the 20th century. The organization succeeded because any country that took part in the agreement had to open its markets equally to any other GATT country. The goal was for no country to have a trading advantage over any other. Average tariff rates dropped from 22 percent in 1947 to less than 5 percent in 1993. In general, tariffs mean lower prices for consumers, but they also include the risk of jobs moving to other countries where the cost of living is lower.

WTO In 1995, the **World Trade Organization (WTO)** replaced GATT. With about 164 member nations, the WTO currently controls about 96.4 percent of international trade. WTO's mission is for trade to flow smoothly. When trade disputes arise, the WTO works to solve the problems. The group has the power to conduct negotiations and impose sanctions. In 2021, Dr. Ngozi Okonjo-Iweala of Nigeria became director-general of the WTO—the first woman and the first African to hold that position.

Anti-WTO demonstrations have erupted in the United States, Canada, and Switzerland. Many participants in these demonstrations have contended that the WTO is a type of global government that interferes with the rights of individual nations. Some point out that countries (especially poorer countries) may not be able to pass laws protecting their workers and the environment because doing so might be considered a violation of free trade.

The Soviet Union Dominates Eastern Europe

The Soviet Union responded to the efforts of the United States in to promote democracies in Western Europe by establishing their own organizations to integrate the countries of Eastern Europe. The Soviets dominated the European countries east of the Iron Curtain militarily, politically, and economically.

Council for Mutual Economic Assistance (COMECON)

As you learned in Topic 9.2, the Soviets refused to participate in the Marshall Plan. In 1949, they created the **Council for Mutual Economic Assistance (COMECON)** to strengthen economic ties among the countries in the Soviet bloc. Later, other countries in Eastern Europe and other communist countries, including Cuba and Vietnam, became part of COMECON. After Stalin's death in 1953, the Soviets used COMECON to promote industrial specialization among member countries as part of the planned economy. The purpose was to minimize duplication of production and competition in manufacturing.

Warsaw Pact

In 1955, after West Germany was admitted to NATO, the Soviets signed a treaty known as the **Warsaw Pact** with Albania, Bulgaria, Czechoslovakia, East Germany, Hungary, Poland, and Romania. This pact created a military alliance with the satellite countries of the USSR. Through it, the Soviet Union increased its dominance over satellite countries. The pact forced all member nations to supply a certain number of troops each year and gave control of those forces to the Soviet Union. In 1956, when Hungary began to reject Soviet policies, the Soviets reacted with force. The Soviets also cited the Warsaw Pact when it used troops to crush an uprising in Czechoslovakia in 1968.

The Soviet Bloc

Western European governments were actively involved in managing their economies and even had national control over some industries. However, their economies also maintained many aspects of free-market capitalism. The situation was quite different in the **Soviet bloc**, nations of Eastern Europe that were closely bound to the Soviet Union, which exerted tremendous control over all aspects of life in the region. Albania and Yugoslavia were the only countries of Eastern Europe that had communist governments but were independent of the Soviet Union to varying degrees. At times, Soviet control was very repressive. At other times, it included limited economic and social reforms.

Centrally Planned Economies

Soviet-bloc countries all featured **planned economies** in which a central committee of the Communist Party in Moscow determined what was produced, how much was produced, and where it was produced and sold. Joseph Stalin's five-year plans of the 1930s were prime examples of planned economies in the Soviet Union. After World War II, Stalin returned to these policies in order to rebuild industry in the Soviet Union. Once again, the state's plans focused on the growth of heavy industry at the expense of working and living conditions for ordinary people. These plans put little emphasis on consumer goods. Prices were kept low, but food, medicine, and consumer goods were often in short supply. Shoes and clothing were often of poor quality.

Source: Getty Images

Source: Getty Images

One of the most common symbols used in the Soviet Union was the hammer, representing industry, and the sickle, representing agriculture. Together, factory workers and farmers were to build a strong, prosperous country. (See image on previous page.)

Planned Economies in the Stalinist Era Communist leaders in the Soviet-bloc countries of Central and Eastern Europe followed Stalin's model in their own countries with similar five-year plans focused on heavy industry and collectivized agriculture (as opposed to privately owned farms). The Soviet Union itself controlled certain features of the economies in Soviet-bloc countries. COMECON (1941–1949) was set up to ensure that the economies of the Soviet bloc benefited the Soviet Union. For example, after the war, the Soviets confiscated factories, railroad equipment, and livestock in East Germany, Romania, Poland, Bulgaria, and Hungary and shipped them to the Soviet Union. In addition, each country was directed to focus on certain industries. One five-year plan in Czechoslovakia, for example, focused on machine building, chemical production, and metallurgy. The Soviet Union also set trade terms with the satellite nations that forced the satellites to increase their trade with the Soviet Union on terms that benefited the Soviets more than the satellites.

Social Welfare Programs As part of these planned economies, the state provided extensive social welfare programs, such as affordable housing and health care. However, the quality of these social services was often poor and the quantity insufficient. Affordable housing consisted of huge apartment buildings that were generally poorly constructed and extremely crowded. Often more than one family shared a small apartment. However, people who had experienced conditions before and during World War II still saw these conditions as an improvement. In the early years after the Russian Revolution, the Soviets improved life expectancy. But the health care system deteriorated over time as governments failed to continue to make improvements to an aging system.

The Soviets greatly improved education with special emphasis on science and technology. Students attended free public schools that included communist indoctrination along with their studies. Students were educated to fill the jobs needed in the state-run industries. Generally, only children of elite members of the Communist Party had access to a university education.

Weaknesses of Planned Economies The Soviets' centrally planned economy achieved some rapid industrial growth, but at a great cost. The government restricted the freedoms of individual citizens, giving priority to what it decided was the good of the state. For example, people often had a limited choice about where they could live or work. The system was slow to respond to changes in technology and in demand for goods, so it became less efficient.

Suppression of Dissent

Communists suppressed dissent by anyone who disagreed with their ideas and policies. The Communist Party soon became the only political party allowed in Soviet-bloc countries. Yet only a small percentage of the population belonged to the party. All forms of intellectual expression in art, literature, and science had to conform to the state's political goals. Communists threatened to close any private organizations, such as soccer or chess clubs, that they feared could be used to organize political opposition to them. This level of suppression of dissent was reinforced by state terror. Stalin made the recruitment of secret police a priority in the governments of Eastern Europe.

Limits on Travel

The governments of the Soviet bloc also severely limited freedom of travel and emigration. A prime example of this policy is the construction of the **Berlin Wall** in 1961. As people in East Germany began to experience the reality of the Soviet-planned economy, many of them wanted to emigrate to the West. Moving from East Berlin to West Berlin provided the easiest way out. An estimated 2.5 million people fled East Germany through Berlin between 1949 and 1961, many of them skilled workers and professionals.

The East German leaders realized that the loss of these individuals would threaten their economy, so they built a barrier to prevent freedom of movement. The original wall, built in August 1961, was later strengthened into a 15-foot-high concrete barrier topped with barbed wire, monitored by armed guards, and supplemented by electrified fences. The wall eventually stretched 28 miles across the city of Berlin and 75 miles around West Berlin to create a barrier between the city and the Soviet-bloc country of East Germany in which it was located. Between 1961 and 1989, only about 5,000 people successfully fled East Berlin by crossing the wall.

Czechoslovakia Other Soviet-bloc nations also limited emigration. After rescuing Czechoslovakia from the Nazis, the USSR nationalized Czechoslovakian industries and destroyed internal opposition. This process was called sovietization. The Czech government maintained electric fences at the country's borders with Austria and West Germany. At least 276 people were electrocuted or shot to death as they tried to cross over. The borders stayed electrified until the Velvet Revolution in 1989, when the country's Communist Party gave up power.

Hungary In the late 1950s, after political turmoil, strikes, and the execution of a former leader, about 200,000 Hungarians escaped to Western Europe and the United States. These included many people who were young, well-educated, or both, and their loss harmed the country economically. Hungary did not completely lift travel restrictions until 1988.

Changes under Khrushchev

Stalin's death in 1953 led to a struggle for leadership of the Communist Party in the Soviet Union. By 1956, **Nikita Khrushchev** emerged as the supreme leader. However, Khrushchev ruled in a very different way from Stalin.

De-Stalinization Policies Khrushchev gave a speech at a closed session of the 20th Party Congress in 1956. He denounced many of Stalin's most abusive practices, such as purges of his political enemies and his oppressive leadership style. He then embarked on a series of new policies called **de-Stalinization**. Under these policies, Khrushchev eased some political restrictions:

- allowing greater freedom of expression by artists and writers
- allowing people to read what they wanted
- decreasing the power of the secret police
- releasing some political prisoners

In addition, Khrushchev also revised some economic policies to make the system more flexible and more rewarding to average Soviets:

- shortening the workweek to about 40 hours
- giving workers more freedom to move from place to place
- allowing certain people to change jobs
- putting more resources into producing consumer goods in order to improve people's standard of living
- allowing more local decision-making about agriculture
- planning to grow corn and increase farming in the region east of the Ural Mountains

However, these economic policies failed to meet their goals. The Soviet Union's growth rate slowed dramatically between 1953 and 1964.

Revolts in Eastern Europe As part of his de-Stalinization policies, Khrushchev agreed that the Soviet government in Moscow would give more autonomy to the communist governments in Eastern Europe. In addition, he eased travel and trade restrictions in Eastern Europe. However, the slowing down of the Soviet economy and people's growing frustrations over restrictions of their individual rights led to a series of revolts in Eastern Europe.

REVOLTS IN EASTERN EUROPE, 1956–1968			
Country	**Leader**	**Causes**	**Result**
Poland, 1956	Władysław Gomułka	• Workers staged protests. • Poland rejected the Soviet choice for prime minister.	• Gomułka supported the Soviet Union. • Poland remained in the Warsaw Pact.
Hungary, 1956	Imre Nagy	• Hungary wanted to be a non-communist, independent, and neutral country with free elections.	• Soviet troops invaded Hungary. • Soviets executed Nagy and installed Janos Kador as leader.
Czechoslovakia, 1967–1968	Alexander Dubček	• Writers protested censorship. • The government eased censorship during the **Prague Spring**. • Czechs wanted their own form of socialism.	• The Soviets sent Warsaw Pact troops to put down the revolt. • The Soviets announced they would intervene to defend communism—the Brezhnev Doctrine.

Communist Repression

Soviet control was not limited to military interventions, economic controls, and travel restrictions.

Communist Regimes Repress Art The USSR controlled art and science as well. The approved art form was "socialist realism," which showed optimistic scenes from everyday life under communism. Artists in the USSR, Central Europe, and Eastern Europe rebelled, creating—and hiding—abstract art and expressing ideas about forbidden subjects.

Totalitarian Regimes Repress Science In a similar way, the Soviets dictated what scientists would study and publish. In the 1940s and 1950s, the government of the USSR supported Lysenkoism, which held that the science of genetics was worthless, that farmers should not use fertilizer, and that humans could manipulate seeds to grow lemon trees outdoors in the coldest regions. The embrace of Lysenkoism led to persecution of scientists (especially geneticists) as well as famines.

Communist Regimes Repress Religion The USSR considered religion a threat to communism, so it tried to wipe out churches and other religious institutions. In Poland, which was almost entirely Catholic, religious leaders worked out a deal with the Soviets. The Catholic Church would keep some religious freedoms in exchange for supporting communist rule. Communist officials spied on priests and sharply criticized them in the media. The election of a Pole, Karol Wojtyła, as Pope John Paul II in 1978 helped to unify Poles in their struggles against communism.

Communist Regimes Beyond the USSR Leaders in some other nations, including China, embraced totalitarianism even if they didn't always follow Soviet policies. One Soviet-bloc country was relatively independent politically but followed the Soviet model of extreme control and repression. Under Nicolae Ceausescu (ruled 1965–1989), Romania greatly reduced its participation in the Warsaw Pact. However, Ceausescu, a devoted communist, tightly controlled the government, the media, and the lives of ordinary people. In 1966, he outlawed nearly all contraception and abortion. This led to a drastic rise in the deaths of women as they used illegal and dangerous forms of birth control and abortion. Severe shortages of food and medicine also caused unrest. After an uprising, a firing squad shot Ceausescu to death in 1989.

The Integration of Eastern and Western Europe

The ultimate rejection of communist rule in many of the Eastern-bloc countries began in 1989 after Soviet leader Mikhail Gorbachev introduced the policies of *glasnost*, or openness, and *perestroika*, or restructuring. A variety of political and economic factors, including the costs of the Cold War arms race, led to the final collapse of the USSR in 1991.

With the collapse of communism, the Cold War ended and the Warsaw Pact dissolved. For the most part, the countries of the Warsaw Pact peacefully transitioned to independent nationhood. But the same was not true for the numerous republics that made up the Soviet Union. (See Topic 9.7 for more on the end of the USSR and the struggles of the former Soviet republics.)

THE COLD WAR IN EUROPE

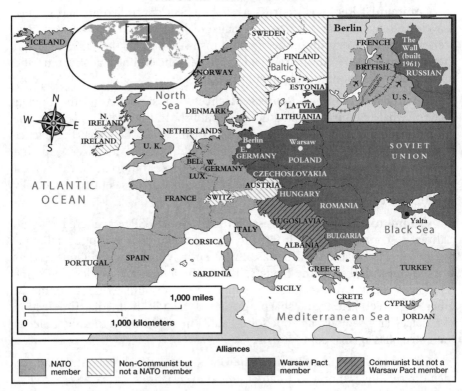

After the collapse, countries in Eastern Europe rejected the planned economies of the Soviet era and began to establish capitalist economies. The transition to market economies was difficult. As consumers, citizens grappled with higher prices as state subsidies ended. As workers, citizens faced unemployment as state planning ended. However, the expansion of economic freedom allowed for more innovation and opportunities for people to make decisions about their own careers.

As former Eastern-bloc countries moved toward greater political and economic freedom, many applied to join the European Union. Between 2004 and 2007, 10 former Eastern-bloc countries became members. (See Topic 9.10 for more about the European Union.)

In the realm of politics, the end of Soviet dominance in Eastern Europe led to both greater integration and new divisions. East and West Germany were reunited even before the official collapse in 1991, beginning with free elections held in March 1990. The countries merged their economies in July and their governments in October of that year.

In Czechoslovakia, ethnic differences led to the separation of the country into two states, the Czech Republic and Slovakia, in 1993. The separation was peaceful.

REFLECT ON THE ESSENTIAL QUESTION

Essential Question: *What are the economic and political consequences of the Cold War in Europe?*

Economic	Political

KEY TERMS

super power
North Atlantic Treaty Organization (NATO)
International Monetary Fund (IMF)
World Bank
General Agreement on Tariffs and Trade (GATT)

World Trade Organization (WTO)
Council for Mutual Economic Assistance (COMECON)
Warsaw Pact
Soviet bloc
planned economies

Berlin Wall
Nikita Khrushchev
de-Stalinization
Prague Spring
glasnost
perestroika

The causes of the nearly five-decade struggle between the United States and the Soviet Union after World War II are many. Historians continue to weigh them.

The Soviet Union In the 1940s and 1950s, the orthodox, or mainstream, historians of the Cold War argued that Stalin and his uncompromising totalitarian ways caused the conflict. Arthur Schlesinger Jr. expressed this view in numerous works throughout the 1960s, including the article "Origins of the Cold War" (1967). He saw capitalism and communism as incompatible ideologies. Schlesinger pointed to Lenin's view that all capitalist societies were destined to follow the road to communism and to Stalin's creation of a totalitarian state as the key factors in causing the Cold War. Schlesinger recognized changes in the Soviet Union after Stalin's death. The process of de-Stalinization, he thought, might lead to the Soviets' willingness to compromise, which would reduce tensions.

The United States By the 1960s, the Cold War spread to the developing countries, such as Vietnam. As a result, historians became more critical of the American role in the cause and course of the Cold War. These revisionist historians focused on the U.S. pursuit of a capitalist agenda that made diplomatic decisions based on economic needs and a desire to dominate the global economy.

Among the most controversial revisionists were Gabriel and Joyce Kolko. They argued that the demands of a growing capitalist economy depended on an expansionist American foreign policy. Further, economic pressures demanded resistance to leftist movements everywhere because they threatened this system. The Kolkos considered the role of the United States in Eastern Europe in the aftermath of World War II to be evidence of this behavior. Some revisionists argued that if the United States had recognized the Soviet need for security, Stalin would have been more willing to compromise.

Refocusing on the Soviets In the later years of the Cold War, the most famous of Cold War historians, John Lewis Gaddis, shared the post-revisionist view that misunderstandings on both sides escalated the Cold War. However, once the wall came down and access to the Soviet archives became available, Gaddis revisited his views in 1998 and again in 2005, stating that it was in fact Russia's fault. In his 2005 book, *The Cold War*, Gaddis finds much evidence in telegrams to justify American policy decisions. Based on his research in the Soviet archives, Gaddis placed blame for the Cold War squarely on the internal workings of the Soviet system: "Soviet leaders had to treat the outside world as hostile because otherwise they could not excuse the dictatorship without which they did not know how to rule."

1. What caused John Lewis Gaddis to reevaluate his opinion on the causes of the Cold War?

2. According to Gabriel and Joyce Kolko, why did the United States oppose leftist governments in other countries?

3. In what way did Arthur Schlesinger Jr. have limited access to evidence in the 1960s when he did his research and writing on the causes of the Cold War?

MULTIPLE-CHOICE QUESTIONS

Questions 1–3 refer to the passage below.

"The statements contained in the North Atlantic treaty [that created NATO] that it is designated for defense and that it recognizes the principles of the United Nations organization serve aims which have nothing in common, either with the tasks of self-defense of the parties to the treaty or with real recognition of the aims and principles of the United Nations organization.

Of the great powers, only the Soviet Union is excluded from among the parties to this treaty, which can be explained only by the fact that this treaty is directed against the Soviet Union.

The North Atlantic pact is designed to daunt the states which do not agree to obey the dictate of the Anglo-American grouping of powers that lay claim to world domination, though the untenability of such claims was once again affirmed by the second World War which ended in the debacle of fascist Germany, which also had laid claim to world domination."

—*Soviet Monitor*, April 1949

1. Which of the following statements could best be used to support the point of view in the passage about the relationship between the "Anglo-American grouping of powers" and "Fascist Germany"?

   (A) The Soviet Union had an alliance with fascist Germany between 1939 and 1941.

   (B) The governments of Great Britain, the United States, and fascist Germany were generally anti-Communist.

   (C) Fascist Germany had been an ally of Japan during World War II after the attack on Pearl Harbor.

   (D) The leader of the Non-Aligned Movement had organized the United Nations, and Great Britain, the United States, and fascist Germany had been reluctant to join.

2. The development of which organization or agreement most directly countered the concerns about NATO reflected in the passage?

   (A) The Non-Aligned Movement because it was a reaction to the growth of super powers

   (B) The European Economic Community because it promoted free trade in Western Europe

   (C) The World Trade Organization because it included countries around the world

   (D) The Warsaw Pact because it was a military alliance that included the Soviet Union

3. The writer's point of view in the passage was mostly clearly part of which development after the Second World War?

   (A) The formation of the United Nations

   (B) The rebuilding of European roads, rail lines, and factories

   (C) The emergence of the U.S.-Soviet Cold War

   (D) The outbreak of deadly wars in Korea and Vietnam

SHORT-ANSWER QUESTION

Use the passage below to answer all parts of the question that follows.

> "The Hungarian Revolution of 1956 is one of the great historical events of the twentieth century. It was an unplanned, leaderless, spontaneous explosion brought on by a confluence of fateful errors. In late October and early November of 1956, the world's attention was riveted on the uprising in Budapest and the revolution which quickly enveloped the whole country; even more so when it was all brutally crushed by the Soviet Union in what seemed like just a few days."
>
> J. P. Matthews, *Explosion*, 2007

1. a) Describe ONE other event from Eastern Europe that was similar to the actions of Hungary or the Soviet Union described in the passage.

   b) Describe ONE event from *outside* Eastern Europe that was similar to the actions of Hungary or the Soviet Union described in the passage.

   c) Explain ONE reaction from the Soviet Union or a Warsaw Pact member that had a result different from the one described.

Topic 9.5

Postwar Nationalism, Ethnic Conflict, and Atrocities

If you are not confused you don't understand the situation.
—graffiti on walls in Belfast, Northern Ireland

Essential Question: What are the causes and effects of mass atrocities from the end of World War II to the present?

Just because a ruling authority decides that a country has certain borders doesn't mean that everyone agrees with those borders. After World War II, nationalist movements bubbled up in different parts of Europe. Members of different ethnic, cultural, and religious groups sought recognition, respect, power, and authority—sometimes by force.

Nationalist and Separatist Movements

In the postwar era, Europe outwardly appeared to be a relatively stable place, the Cold War notwithstanding. But long-simmering ethnic and nationalist desires led to separatist movements of varying lengths and intensities.

Western Europe

Numerous separatist movements took place in Western Europe in the 20th century. The success of these movements varied.

Northern Ireland Irish Protestants and Catholics both fought on the British side during World War I. However, religious, political, and economic differences sparked conflicts. In the early 1920s, the area split into Ireland, where the majority of people were Catholic, and Northern Ireland, where majority of people were Protestant.

About half a million Catholics lived in Northern Ireland, and hundreds of thousands of Protestants lived in Ireland. In Northern Ireland, the Protestant majority governed in its own interest. Many Protestants in Northern Ireland discriminated against Catholics, denying them equal employment, housing, and education.

By the mid-1960s, Catholics in Northern Ireland had launched a civil rights movement. Britain sent in troops. In 1969, the Irish Republican Army (IRA), a group which had advocated for complete Irish independence split into two factions. One of the factions began a violent campaign with the goal of destabilizing Northern Ireland and reuniting the country with Ireland. Some

Protestants—called unionists because they wanted to continue being part of the United Kingdom—created their own paramilitary groups. People called this violence **the Troubles**.

In 1972, Britain's prime minister suspended Northern Ireland's parliament and constitution. From then until 1999, Northern Ireland was under direct British rule. In 1994, after decades of attempts at new governments, paramilitary groups on both sides agreed to a cease-fire. In 1998, the Good Friday Agreement held that an elected board of local officials would control most of the government of Northern Ireland. Ninety-four percent of Irish voters and 71 percent of Northern Irish voters formally approved the agreement. Some violence continued, but in 2007, Protestant and Catholic hard-liners in Northern Ireland formed a government in which both sides shared power and Britain reduced the number of its troops there.

The Basque Region The ethnic **Basque** people of northern Spain and southwestern France have a language and culture distinct from the rest of Spain and have historically enjoyed a certain level of autonomy. However, the Spanish dictator Francisco Franco, who came to power in the 1930s and ruled until 1975, took this away. Later Spanish governments returned some of the autonomy.

The group **ETA**, whose name stands for Basque Homeland and Liberty, formed in the 1960s to resist Franco and fight for an independent Basque state. During and after the Cold War, ETA engaged in attacks that resulted in the deaths of more than 800 people. Support for ETA decreased in the 21st century. In May 2018, the group announced its intention to formally disband. The last known head of ETA faced terrorism charges in France in 2020.

Belgium The country of Belgium in northwestern Europe has two main cultures. The **Flemish** make up about half of the population and mostly live in the north in an area called Flanders. They have traditionally spoken Flemish, a language similar to Dutch. The **Walloons** make up about one-third of the population and mostly live in the southern part of the country. They speak French.

Tensions between the two groups have existed for the entire history of Belgium, which was founded in 1830. In 2020, the leader of one of the moderate Flemish parties complained that his party and another party had been shut out of the parliamentary government. "Sixty percent of Belgians are Flemish," Peter De Roover said. "Two-thirds of the national wealth is created in Flanders. And their majority is not reflected in this government."

Yugoslavia

The country of **Yugoslavia** was created during the peace process after World War I. One of its most powerful leaders was Josip Broz Tito, who took power after World War II. He tightly controlled the country until his death in 1980, keeping the many ethnic and national groups at bay. Although a communist country, Yugoslavia under Tito had always followed a policy of nonalignment, refusing to follow Soviet doctrine.

Ethnic Cleansing and Disintegration After Tito's death, nationalists on the Balkan Peninsula wanted to establish the independent republics of Slovenia, Croatia, Bosnia-Herzegovina, and Macedonia. The violent dissolution of Yugoslavia in the 1990s was fueled by ethnic conflict and nationalist and separatist movements. The dissolution began with declarations of independence from both Slovenia and Croatia in June 1991. Serbian nationalists under the leadership of Slobodan Milošević fought to maintain and expand Serb areas of Croatia and Bosnia-Herzegovina, which declared its independence in March 1992.

In their efforts to drive **Bosnian Muslims** from the territory, the Serbian army killed 250,000 people and forcibly removed approximately two million people from their homes. This effort to create an ethnically homogeneous territory through violence was called **ethnic cleansing**. In a similar effort in the late 1990s, Milošević's forces drove hundreds of thousands of ethnic Albanian Muslims from the province of **Kosovo**.

Milošević opposed nationalist efforts in the name of protecting Serb minorities within those republics. Under his leadership, the Serbian army attacked Croatia and Bosnia-Herzegovina, violently taking control of large tracts of territory and carrying out genocide against Bosnian Muslims who were massacred by Bosnian Serb forces. Some Croatian forces were also accused of ethnic cleansing of Serbs and Muslims, including attacks on refugees.

COUNTRIES FORMED FROM YUGOSLAVIA

War's End and Aftermath The war finally ended with a peace agreement in 1995 that resulted in new boundaries being drawn. In 2002, Milošević went on trial for war crimes. He died in 2006 before the court reached a verdict. In 2011, a war crimes court convicted two Croatian generals of atrocities against Serbs, but the next year an appeals court overturned the verdict and freed the generals. In 2016 and 2017, United Nations tribunals convicted some of the top Serbian leaders and generals of genocide and sentenced some of them to life in prison.

Chechnya

The breakup of the Soviet Union in 1991 led to independence for many former Soviet republics, including Ukraine, the Baltic states, and the Caucasus countries of Azerbaijan, Armenia, and Georgia. The small, petroleum-rich, and mostly Muslim republic of **Chechnya** in the southwestern part of Russia also declared its independence in November 1991. Leaders advocated for Chechen nationalism and opposed Russian influence. Russian troops invaded Chechnya in 1994 to forcibly bring the republic back into the Russian Federation, formed after the dissolution of the Soviet Union. By 1997, when a peace treaty was signed, about 100,000 Chechens had been killed and 400,000 had been made homeless.

Russian troops returned in 1999, when the Russian government accused Chechens of bombings that killed Russian civilians. Though Chechen involvement was not proved, Russia maintained control over the republic. In 2003, the new Chechen constitution reaffirmed the republic's membership in the Russian Federation. Russian officials have appointed the presidents of the republic since that time.

REFLECT ON THE ESSENTIAL QUESTION

Essential Question: *What are the causes and effects of mass atrocities from the end of World War II to the present?*

Causes	Effects

KEY TERMS

the Troubles	Walloons	Kosovo
Basque	Yugoslavia	Chechnya
ETA	Bosnian Muslims	
Flemish	ethnic cleansing	

Questions 1–3 refer to the passage below.

Credit: Getty Images

The graveyard at Srebrenica includes more than 6,000 Bosnian Muslims who died in July 1995.

1. Which challenge in maintaining a government does the photo above reflect?

    (A) The danger of famine from inefficient use of agricultural resources

    (B) The violence that could occur in multi-ethnic regions

    (C) The risks faced by countries that did not align with the Soviet Union

    (D) The consequences of emphasizing rapid industrial development

2. Which best describes the historical context in which events represented by the photo above occurred?

    (A) The power vacuum left in the Balkans by the death of Josip Broz Tito

    (B) The Russian attempts to increase its influence in nearby Muslim regions after 1991

    (C) The conflict between supporters and opponents of Communism in the former Yugoslavia

    (D) The conflict fought along religious lines known as "the Troubles"

3. Which was the most direct result of the general conflict that resulted in the photo shown above?

(A) The Soviet Union broke apart, with Russia becoming the largest of the new states.

(B) The country of Yugoslavia disintegrated into a handful of smaller countries.

(C) Slobodan Milošević signed a peace treaty with Croatia and Bosnia-Herzegovina.

(D) United Nations tribunals convicted several leaders of genocide.

SHORT-ANSWER QUESTION

Use the passage below to answer all parts of the question that follows.

"I was then taken into what I can only guess was another room and made to stand with my feet wide apart with my hands pressed against a wall. During all this time I could hear a low droning noise, which sounded to me like an electric saw or something of that nature. This continued for what I can only describe as an indefinite period of time.

I stood there, arms against the wall, feet wide apart. My arms, legs, back and head began to ache. I perspired freely, the noise and heat were terrible. My brain was ready to burst. What was going to happen to me? Was I alone? Are they coming to kill me? I wished to God they would, to end it. My circulation had stopped. I flexed my arms to start the blood flowing again. They struck me several times on the hands, ribs, kidneys and my kneecaps were kicked. My hood covered head was banged against the wall. As I have said this particular method of torture lasted for an indefinite period, but having consulted other men who suffered the same experience I believe this period to have been about two days and nights."

Patrick McClean, an Irish activist imprisoned by the British during the Troubles, 1971

1. a) Describe ONE similarity between the movement represented by McClean and another movement in post-World War II Europe.

b) Describe ONE difference between the movement represented by McClean and another movement in post-World War II Europe.

c) Describe ONE similarity between the movement represented by McClean and another movement in 19th century Europe.

Topic 9.6

Contemporary Western Democracies

And now win the peace.

—Slogan of the Labour Party of Britain, 1945
(The party won in a landslide.)

Essential Question: What were the state-based economic developments following World War II and what were the responses to these developments?

After World War II, many European economies experienced an extended period of growth. Improvements in technology and greater access to resources meant that each European (on average) was producing finished goods and services at three times the rate he or she used to. People and countries began asking a bigger question: What should postwar societies look like? Who should benefit from this increasing wealth?

To improve the lives of everyday people and reduce the chances of violent rebellion, governments began providing more resources and services to citizens. However, these benefits were expensive. During economic downturns, some people questioned whether the benefits should continue.

Economic Cooperation

After the war, bombed cities, infrastructure, and factories needed rebuilding. And rebuilding countries began cooperating with each other economically:

- In 1952, Western European countries established the European Coal and Steel Community (ECSC) so that their coal and steel industries would work together more efficiently. France, West Germany, Italy, Belgium, the Netherlands, and Luxembourg were the original members, and other countries joined later. The organizers dreamed of a "United States of Europe"— a new power that would rival the United States economically, they believed.

- The dream of a United States of Europe became closer to reality with the establishment of the European Economic Community (EEC). The EEC began in 1957 with Belgium, France, Italy, Luxembourg, the Netherlands, and West Germany, later joined by the United Kingdom, Denmark, and Ireland and then Greece, Portugal, and Spain.

- The final step to unite Europe economically was the European Union. (See Topic 9.10.)

Expansion of Social Welfare Programs

European economic growth gave governments funds to help provide welfare benefits for their citizens. Although these programs were politically popular when times were good, changing economic conditions led to contentious political debates about social welfare in the late 20th century.

Creation of the Welfare State Even before the Marshall Plan was introduced, Britain's newly elected Labour Party government began implementing a **welfare state** that provided a wide range of social benefits to all citizens. In 1946, laws were passed to provide benefits for subsidized health care, unemployment insurance, and old-age **pensions**—a set amount of money paid to someone on a regular basis after they retire. These comprehensive benefits are sometimes called **cradle-to-grave** social welfare programs.

The British system became the model for other European states. Sweden required pensions for all employees beginning in 1959. France either built or helped pay for 90 percent of all housing constructed there between the end of the war and 1970. States in Western Europe, Romania, and the Soviet Union provided benefits for children in the form of direct payments to families for each child. European countries also sought to increase educational and employment opportunities by creating more universities and providing free or low-cost tuition. The idea was that a country with more university graduates would be more economically prosperous and better able to compete with other countries.

These social programs required high taxes and high government expenditures, which grew over time. By 1980, many European governments were spending more than 20 percent of their countries' GDPs on social programs. Most people accepted the high taxes that resulted because they liked the benefits that the programs provided. The welfare state not only increased the role of the government in people's lives but also showed that the state wanted to promote better lives for its citizens.

Challenges to the Welfare State Decades of economic growth in Europe came to an end with recessions from 1973 to 1974 and 1979 to 1983. As countries around the world experienced difficult economic times, demand for European goods declined, which led to job losses. Rising life expectancies also meant there were more senior citizens who required care. During such challenging times, European governments began to face difficult choices about continuing the high level of spending on social welfare programs. For example, in 1982, West Germany's coalition government split apart over the question of reducing such spending. When a conservative government came to power in Denmark, its leaders cut social security benefits.

Thatcher Changes Britain When the Conservative Party's **Margaret Thatcher** became prime minister of Britain in 1979, she vowed that she would cut taxes and limit social welfare programs. She did not do away with basic health and welfare benefits but cut government spending to curb inflation. These spending cuts were seen as harmful in the northern industrial parts of the country, where unemployment increased as the government began to end its substantial subsidies to businesses.

In her second term, she battled the National Union of Mineworkers over the closing of 20 coal mines that the government said were unproductive. The strike lasted for a year, but in the end, the miners returned to work with no concessions being made. Probably Thatcher's main legacy was the privatization of many industries, often with mixed results. Privatization means that a government allows an industry or service it once controlled to become privately owned instead. Thatcher privatized the airline, telecommunications, steel, and gas industries in Britain.

Thatcher rejected the idea that it was a society's duty to protect and nurture its citizens. In 1987, she said, "There is no such thing as society. There are individual men and women and there are families. . . . It is our duty to look after ourselves and then, also, to look after our neighbors."

REFLECT ON THE ESSENTIAL QUESTION

Essential Question: *What were the state-based economic developments following World War II, and what were the responses to these developments?*

Economic Developments	Responses

KEY TERMS

welfare state	pensions	cradle-to-grave	Margaret Thatcher

MULTIPLE-CHOICE QUESTIONS

Questions 1–3 refer to the passage below.

"The Nordic nations—Finland, Iceland, Norway, Denmark and Sweden— have similar approaches to social welfare. Government programs in these nations tend to offer high levels of social support, but at the cost of high taxes. As Western societies grapple with challenges ranging from technological disruption to climate change, from immigration to globalization, examining the Nordic model of social welfare may help. The model can offer insights about providing a social 'safety net', reforming the public sector and supporting economic competitiveness in the face of disruption.

Increased productivity is the main contributor of economic growth and increased prosperity. Measuring the GNI [gross national income] per hour worked indicates the extent to which a country can generate income for every hour worked. . . . The Nordic countries are among those with the strongest ability to generate income.

Although the size and role of the public sector generates much attention in Nordic countries and is at the core of ongoing reforms, defining elements of the Nordic model's sustainability are often considered a competitive private sector and favorable business environment. These are designed to enhance productivity and, thus, income.

The Nordic countries are all ranked within the top 30 internationally in terms of competitiveness, ease of doing business, economic freedom, entrepreneurship and lack of corruption. Often, they're ranked in the top 10. . . . The Nordic countries score relatively low in terms of economic freedom, compared to the other categories, but are generally still ranked high globally."

—Deloitte Insights, "The Nordic Welfare Model," c. 2020

1. The source states the claim that the Nordic approach to social welfare works because countries have
   (A) avoided the challenges of technological disruption
   (B) reformed their public sectors
   (C) kept taxes low to encourage entrepreneurship
   (D) encouraged favorable business environments

2. Which of the following individuals or groups implemented ideas that could be seen as early versions of the Nordic social welfare model?
   (A) Mercantilists because they discouraged imports
   (B) Robert Owen because he supported utopian communities
   (C) Bismarck because of his support for nationalized health care and old-age insurance
   (D) Stalin because of his policies on collectivization

3. Which of the following statements best identifies one similarity between the goals of Margaret Thatcher and the policies of the Nordic countries as described in the passage?
   (A) Both supported the idea of economic freedom.
   (B) Both emphasized reducing the size of government in order to lower taxes.
   (C) Both rejected the idea that a society had a duty to protect its citizens.
   (D) Both opposed large social welfare programs.

Use the passage below to answer all parts of the question that follows.

"We consider the efficacy of her policies from the point of view of Thatcher's and her government's stated aspirations. It is often assumed that Thatcher's goals were purely economic, the re-establishing of the principles of free-market fundamentalism. . . . However, that is to underestimate the scale of her ambition. Thatcher sought to 'change the soul' of the British people: and believed 'Economics is the method' by which this might be achieved. . . .

The data do not support the hypothesis that Thatcher's policies were successful in reducing unemployment or increasing employment. Despite welfare reform, it was dependency, not employment, that increased during the 1980s. . . .

Ultimately, Thatcher's policies failed to build a living tapestry of individuals. Furthermore, her policy regime did not facilitate the UK's living within its means. Under [her policies], the typical Briton became more, not less, dependent on debt and benefits. Rather than promoting ethics and family values, [according to political scientist P. J. Deneen], her ideology 'has ruthlessly drawn down a reservoir of both material and moral resources that it cannot replenish.'"

—Kevin Albertson and Paul Stepney, "1979 and All That: A 40-year Reassessment of Margaret Thatcher's Legacy on Her Own Terms," *Cambridge Journal of Economics*, 2020

1. a) Identify ONE example of a Thatcher policy that she hoped would "change the soul" of people in Great Britain.

   b) Explain the significance of the point of view that the writers used in this passage to study the success of Thatcher's policies.

   c) Explain ONE aspect of the context of Thatcher's time in office that could modify or refute the conclusions in the passage.

Topic 9.7

The Fall of Communism

Communism . . . suppresses individual initiative, and the 21st century is all about individualism and freedom.

—Lech Walesa, union leader and president of Poland from 1990 to 1995

Essential Question: What were the causes and effects of the end of the Cold War?

The Soviet Union remained one of the world's two super powers throughout the 1970s and early 1980s. Under the leadership of **Leonid Brezhnev** (1906–1982), the head of the Communist Party after Khrushchev's forced retirement in 1964, the Soviet Union retained economic and political control over the countries of Eastern Europe in the Soviet bloc. Brezhnev favored the status quo rather than experimentation or reform. He advocated the Soviet Union's right to use military force to hold off threats to socialism in socialist countries. Intervention in Czechoslovakia in 1968 showed this policy in action.

In the 1970s, the United States and the Soviet Union pursued the policy of *détente*, which means an easing of tensions between nations. They and 33 other nations signed the Helsinki Accords in 1975. Under this nonbinding agreement, participating nations agreed to respect one another's sovereign equality and refrain from using force. As Brezhnev believed that Russia's diplomatic relationships with the United States had become more relaxed, he allowed more access to Western popular culture. There was still little tolerance for dissent, however. Communism seemed strong, and its rapid collapse in the late 1980s surprised many. Economic problems were a major reason for this collapse.

Soviet Decline

Brezhnev continued to emphasize heavy industries in the Soviet economy. The Soviets surpassed the United States in producing cement, coal, iron, and steel, but overall, the Soviet economy slowed down. Weaknesses in the nature of planned economies, including the huge bureaucracy needed to manage the economy, led to inefficient use of resources and a lack of productivity. Also, Soviet workers were guaranteed jobs, so they had little incentive to work hard or innovate. Similar problems led to declines in agricultural productivity, which worsened when severe weather led to bad harvests in the mid-1970s. The Soviet Union was forced to import grain from the United States in order to feed its people.

After this long period of economic stagnation, by 1980 the Soviet Union was in serious trouble. Economic decline combined with a decline in overall health, including increases in the rates of alcoholism and infant mortality, led to a sense within the nation that the communist system was starting to fail. The expensive and longstanding arms race between the two super powers also taxed the Soviet economy to a great degree. In the 1980s, when U.S. military planners openly discussed a space-based defense system against Soviet missile attack—referred to in the press as "star wars"—the Soviet Union appeared both inwardly and outwardly to be well behind in its economic ability to maintain the contest.

After Brezhnev's death in 1982, the Soviet Union remained stagnant. In 1985, Mikhail Gorbachev (b. 1931), whose formative years were spent under the rule of Krushchev, became the leader of the Soviet Union and introduced far reaching reforms to reform the communist system; however, his policies could not prevent the demise of the Soviet Union.

Gorbachev's Reforms

The Soviet Union continued to be strong in technology related to space exploration and weapons. However, it fell behind the United States in the development of computers and remained far behind in the production of consumer goods. The Soviet people were aware that their standard of living had declined. In 1986, Gorbachev spoke about the need for changes in Soviet society. His program of reforms was built around the idea of *perestroika,* or economic restructuring. He wanted to introduce elements of a free-market economy to the Soviet Union, including some private property. It was difficult to implement his ideas because some people wanted rapid and widespread change, and others wanted to introduce change more slowly. Trying to implement change halfway was not successful.

Gorbachev realized he could not change the economy without changing Soviet society. He then introduced the idea of *glasnost,* or openness. He encouraged members of the Communist Party and ordinary people to discuss openly what was working and what wasn't working in the Soviet system. State news media and artists presented information about problems and protests.

Glasnost also led to changes in the political system. Authorities freed dissidents from prison. Elections became competitive as political parties other than the Communist Party became legal. The Soviet state was no longer identified with the Communist Party, and Gorbachev established the new position of president of the Soviet Union. This position became more powerful than that of general secretary of the Communist Party. Gorbachev became the first president of the Soviet Union in March 1990. (See Topic 9.4 for more about *perestroika* and *glasnost.*)

The Soviet Union's Collapse

Gorbachev's reforms had been designed to make the Soviet system more flexible. However, these reforms had unexpected effects that weakened the Soviet Union and ultimately led to its collapse. For example, the Soviet Union was made up of 15 different republics, which included 92 nationalities and 112 languages recognized by the state. When the Communist Party was strongly in control, it kept ethnic tensions in check. With *glasnost*, ethnic groups began protesting examples of discrimination, and violence often erupted. Many of these ethnic republics also began to develop feelings of nationalism and desired independence from Soviet control. These feelings were especially strong in Azerbaijan and Georgia between the Black and Caspian seas; Estonia, Latvia, and Lithuania on the Baltic Sea in the northwest; landlocked Moldavia; and Uzbekistan in the southeast. Lithuania declared its independence in March 1990.

COUNTRIES FORMED FROM THE SOVIET UNION

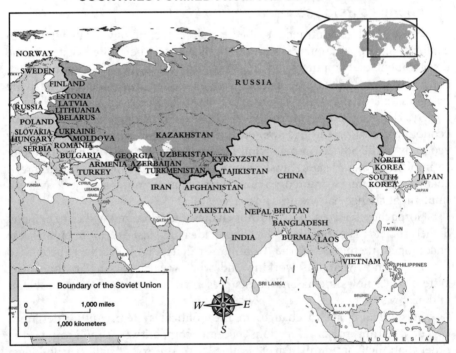

Gorbachev tried to find a balance between conservative and liberal forces in Soviet society. Under the new electoral system, **Boris Yeltsin** (1931–2007) became the first popularly elected leader of the Russian republic in June 1991. In August, conservative forces attempted a coup by arresting Gorbachev. However, Yeltsin and thousands of others resisted, and the coup was unsuccessful. Nonetheless, the republics' push for independence accelerated. By December, the Soviet Union began to unravel, and by the end of the month, it simply ceased to exist.

Satellites Break Free

Perestroika and *glasnost* had consequences within the Soviet bloc as well as within the Soviet Union itself. In 1989, Gorbachev stated that the Soviet Union would no longer intervene with its military to support communist governments in Soviet-bloc countries as it had done earlier in Hungary and Czechoslovakia. With the collapse of the Soviet Union, there was an end to its ability to control the satellite countries of Eastern and Central Europe. As change happened in the Soviet Union in the late 1980s, it also happened throughout the Soviet bloc.

Poland Severe economic problems in Poland in the 1970s led to the rise of **Solidarity**, a labor movement led by Lech Walesa (b. 1943) that represented almost one-third of the Polish population. This movement had the support of the Catholic clergy and Pope John Paul II, a Pole who became the first non-Italian pope in hundreds of years when he was elected in 1978.

In 1981, the communist government arrested Walesa and established military rule. Walesa won the Nobel Prize for Peace in 1983. However, economic problems continued to grow, and workers demonstrated in large numbers in 1988. At that point the government had to agree to free elections, which had not been held in Eastern Europe since 1948. In 1990, Solidarity formed a new coalition government with Lech Walesa as president.

Germany The division between East and West in Germany, symbolized and enforced by the Berlin Wall, was one of the most visible examples of Soviet control in Eastern Europe. East Germany's extremely repressive communist government, was headed in the 1970s and 1980s by Erich Honecker—the man who was in charge of building the Berlin Wall back in 1961.

In 1988, severe economic problems and the repressive government motivated huge numbers of people to leave East Germany. Demonstrations and the flight of refugees from the country continued to grow throughout 1989. Honecher was deposed in October 1989, but his replacement was yet another hardline communist. Regardless, the communist government soon lost its ability to function—even with a show of support from Gorbachev in a visit to East Berlin—and gave in to this popular pressure. On November 9, 1989, the border to the West was opened, and the Berlin Wall began to fall. The Christian Democrats won the free elections held in March 1990 and favored rapid unification with West Germany. By October 1990, the reunification of Germany was complete.

Czechoslovakia The country of Czechoslovakia formed after World War I, when the victorious powers broke up Austria-Hungary. The two main ethnic groups, Slovaks and Czechs, had similar languages, religions, and cultures. Czechoslovakia became prosperous but then suffered under Nazi occupation in World War II and after that under Soviet domination until 1989. Even after peaceful multiparty elections in the 1990s, Czechs and Slovaks disagreed on how rapidly government-run industries should be privatized. In 1993, Czechoslovakia peacefully split into two nations: Slovakia and Czechia (also called the Czech Republic).

At about the same time that Czechoslovakia was dissolving, Yugoslavia also disintegrated—but in a much more violent way. (See Topic 9.5 for more about the breakup of Yugoslavia.)

Source: Getty Images

In 2008, Czechs posted replicas of posters and graffiti first made in the 1968 protest against the Russian invasion of their country. "Hanba" means "shame." Notice the star (a red star was a traditional symbol of Russian communism) being equated with a Nazi swastika.

REFLECT ON THE ESSENTIAL QUESTION

Essential Question: *What were the causes and effects of the end of the Cold War?*

Causes	Effects

KEY TERMS

Leonid Brezhnev	Mikhail Gorbachev	Solidarity
détente	Boris Yeltsin	

MULTIPLE-CHOICE QUESTIONS

Questions 1–3 refer to the passage below.

Passage 1

"Unfortunately, at this congress of Green parties, our friends working in the independent Green initiatives in East Germany, Hungary, Poland, the Soviet Union, and Czechoslovakia are missing, unable to join us. 'Glasnost' must also include them and their right, as well as ours, to travel and consult one another. . . . There can be no peace if there is social injustice, if there is suppression of human rights."

—Petra K. Kelly, "Towards a Green Europe, Towards a Green World," 1987

Passage 2

"The Berlin Wall has collapsed. This entire era in the history of the Socialist system is over. Following the [Polish United Socialist Party] PUWP and the [Hungarian Socialist Workers' Party] HSWP, Honecker [the Communist leader of East Germany] has left. But the main thing is the GDR [East Germany], the Berlin Wall. For it has to do not only with 'socialism' but also with the shift in the world balance of forces. That is what Gorbachev has done. And he has indeed turned out to be a great leader."

—Anatoly Chernyaev, diary, November 10, 1989

1. In Passage 1, the author refers to a term, glasnost, which is most closely related to which other idea supported by Mikhail Gorbachev?

   (A) *Détente*

   (B) Solidarity

   (C) *Perestroika*

   (D) De-Stalinization

2. One main idea that is similar in these passages is that both

   (A) were written after people took down the Berlin Wall

   (B) implied that Gorbachev supported green policies in Russia

   (C) viewed changes in Eastern Europe as part of broader changes

   (D) connected changes in politics with changes in environmental policies

3. One main idea that is indicated in one of these passages but not the other is that

(A) *glasnost* was working poorly at the time the passage was written

(B) Eastern Europe needed to be more like Western Europe in some ways

(C) Gorbachev was moving Russia in a positive direction

(D) communist governments in Eastern Europe needed to be reformed or replaced

SHORT-ANSWER QUESTION

Use the passage below to answer all parts of the question that follows.

"*Gorbachev*: I thank you, Mr. President, for this information. I am also glad to talk to you. . . . We would support the direction in which the situation is moving now, with the exception of one aspect. I have in mind all the excitement that has been raised in the FRG around the issue of German unification.

Mitterrand: I understand what you are saying. . . . The French position is as follows: we would like to avoid any kind of disruption. We realize that it is necessary to take into account the real feelings that exist among people both in West and East Germany. At the same time, I do not think that the issue of changing borders can realistically be raised now—at least until a certain time.

Our two countries are friends of East Germany. I plan to visit the GDR in the near future. I am convinced that they should not undertake any hasty actions which could destabilize the situation. There is a certain equilibrium that exists in Europe, and we should not disturb it. . . . .

I would like to find out your assessment of the evolution of the situation in Europe, and to tell you that for my part, I plan to keep my cool.

Gorbachev: . . . we should not allow any artificial stimulation and forcing of the events."

—Mikhail Gorbachev and François Mitterand (French president 1981–1995), telephone call, November 14, 1989

1. a) Identify ONE phrase in the passage the supports the claim that Gorbachev's primary concern in this phone call was the stability of existing borders.

b) Identify ONE phrase in the passage the supports the claim that Mitterand's primary concern was the stability of existing borders.

c) Explain ONE development in Russia that contributed to the fall of the Berlin Wall.

Topic 9.8

20th-Century Feminism

Man is defined as a human being and woman as a female—whenever she behaves as a human being she is said to imitate the male.

—philosopher Simone de Beauvoir (1908–1986)

Essential Question: How have women's roles and status developed and changed throughout the 20th and 21st centuries?

As Europeans moved beyond the conflicts and settled into the second half of the century, women began to have opportunities and choices as never before. Feminist movements emerged throughout Europe as women's advocates fought for their causes. Women demanded entry into colleges, universities, and medical and law schools that had once been off-limits to them. Gradually, women became prominent in jobs that had once been mostly or entirely held by men, such as lawyers, professors, economists, and elected politicians

The Influence of Feminism

During the early 20th century, daily life in Europe was focused on survival. Many women left their traditional roles as mothers and caretakers to work in munitions factories and other male-dominated fields.

Feminists in the West

World War I brought about women's suffrage, or the right to vote, through much of Europe. The recognition of the vital contribution women made to the war effort led to the widespread belief that women should be granted the right to vote. The battle was harder fought in some countries than others. France allowed women the right to vote in 1944, Italy in 1946, Belgium in 1948, and Greece in 1952. In neutral Switzerland, women didn't gain the right to vote until 1971.

But beyond voting rights, women's status at home and in the workplace was little changed in the early 20th century. Society after World War I was male-dominated. Women were still largely discriminated against in the labor market, especially married women. If paid employment was available, it was usually only in "women's jobs," such as nursing, teaching, and secretarial work. In education, too, women continued to struggle. While more women began to study at universities between 1900 and 1940, the percentage was still small. In Spain and Greece, for example, only about 7 percent of university students were female.

Second-Wave Feminism The first wave of feminism in the 19th and early 20th centuries focused mostly on public issues, such as women's suffrage and legal rights. Building on these achievements, **second-wave feminism**, also called the women's movement, addressed more personal issues, including family, sexuality, and professional ambition. It was largely a response to the postwar ideal of the domesticated housewife and the inherent limitations that ideal placed upon women. Second-wave feminism peaked in the 1960s and 1970s, after women used it to expand choices for themselves both inside their homes and in the workplace.

Third-wave feminism emerged in the 1990s. Many of its proponents were the children of second-wave feminists. In general, third-wave feminists grew up with the idea that they deserved the same rights and opportunities as men. However, third-wave feminists critiqued earlier feminists and often focused on race as well as gender.

Simone de Beauvoir French writer, philosopher, and feminist **Simone de Beauvoir** is best known for her 1949 book *Le Deuxième Sexe*, or *The Second Sex*. In it, she writes about the need to abolish what she called the myth of the "eternal feminine." To her, this myth was the traditional view of women that limited their opportunities for intellectual development and for work opportunities. She also wrote about the need for women to be politically active, to engage in debate, and to advocate for equality. De Beauvoir advanced the concept that all individuals—regardless of gender—should be afforded the same opportunities. Her works became an essential part of literature.

Source: Getty Images

Women throughout Europe protested inequality in the workplace. The German words on this sign say "Equal pay for equal work for men and women."

Eastern Europe and the Soviet Union

Stalin encouraged families to have more children in order to increase the Soviet population. However, at the same time, the government encouraged Soviet women to take jobs outside their homes. The Russian newspaper *Pravda* took pride, in 1929, of how the Russian woman "stands in the most advanced ranks of our working collective . . . [i]n the factory workshop and at the controls of the state ships, in the cooperatives and at the shooting range, in the nursery school and at the thundering machinery, everywhere the tractors of our increasingly strong state farms and collective farms go . . . in none of these places have the working women of the Soviet Union been forced into last place."

In the USSR, women made great progress in some fields. For example, by the early 1960s, about 75 percent of doctors in the Soviet Union were women. However, men continued to hold the most powerful and influential jobs in medicine—and in government.

WOMEN IN HIGHER EDUCATION IN THE 1930S				
Type of Institution	Soviet Union	Germany	England	Italy
All higher education	38%	14%	26%	14%
Industrial institutes	2%	4%	2%	1%
Agricultural institutes	32%	2%	13%	1%

Source: Adapted from "Women in the Soviet Union and Capitalist Countries," *Zhenshchina v USSR* (Moscow, 1936)

In some communist countries, women faced a double burden. The state controlled them politically and economically, just as it controlled men and children. However, the state also controlled women's reproduction. For example, in Romania, abortion was banned in 1966. Women who had or tried to have abortions faced imprisonment or even death.

The author Slavenka Drakulić pointed out that under communism, many women worked full-time jobs while obeying the state and caring for husbands, parents, and children. She traveled Eastern Europe in the early 1990s. She wrote, "Each and every woman I spoke to, whether in Bulgaria or Poland, in Czechoslovakia or Hungary, could point out where communism had failed them: from shortages of food and disposable diapers to a scarcity of apartments and toilet paper. It was these banal, everyday things that defeated communism, long before 1989, and not, I am sorry to say, people's desire for freedom, human rights and democracy."

Options for Women

Many states throughout Europe created job opportunities for women. Initially, these jobs were in fields traditionally dominated by females. For example, right after World War II, Britain's newly created National Health Service first employed women as nurses, midwives, and clerical staff. Opportunities soon emerged throughout Britain in fields such as banking, textiles, and light industries such as electronics. The overall proportion of women in the British workforce increased from 46 percent in 1955 to 51 percent in 1965. Still, jobs were typically segregated by gender, with work categorized as "women's work" typically paying less money than other jobs. Many women also still faced the "marriage bar," which prevented married women from entering the workforce.

By the 1960s, attitudes toward women—both in employment and in general—started to shift noticeably. Employers began to allow married women to work for wages, at least part-time. Countries passed laws making it illegal to fire a woman if she became pregnant. Divorce laws became more lenient throughout Europe, and women's studies programs emerged at colleges and universities. Record numbers of women ran for—and started winning—political office. Women were becoming more integrated into the workforce, a trend that continued into the 21st century.

The Pill In the 1950s, family planning advocate Margaret Sanger raised $150,000 to fund research for a **birth control pill**, a pill that a woman could take to greatly reduce the chance of pregnancy. In 1960, the pill, as it became known, was approved for use in the United States. It was soon available throughout much of Europe. The pill provided women with much greater control over their own fertility and helped families plan when to have children. However, it was controversial. The Roman Catholic Church and some other religious groups opposed the use of the pill.

Scientific Fertilization Alternate methods of fertilization gave women a different type of freedom. The process of **in vitro fertilization (IVF)** fertilizes the egg outside the woman's body and then implants the embryo. Couples who are unable to conceive children biologically have IVF as an option. Also, women who wish to have children on their own are able to do so without a male partner, needing only a male donor.

Women in Politics

Thanks in large part to suffrage movements and second-wave feminism, women in the latter half of the 20th century began to achieve political power. Throughout Europe, women attained political positions previously held only by men.

Margaret Thatcher of Great Britain Margaret Thatcher led the Conservative Party in Britain and became the country's first female prime minister in 1979. Her stated goal was to break with what she considered to be the failed practices of the Labour Party. The term **Thatcherism** became synonymous with her economic policies, including cuts in public spending and tax cuts for high-income earners.

Another of Thatcher's goals was to make Britain more competitive in the global marketplace by reducing the number of trade unions. Her attempts to privatize such institutions as the National Health Service were not popular, though she was still elected to a third term. She ultimately resigned in 1990 amid conflicts within her own party over European integration. (See Topic 9.6 for more about Margaret Thatcher.)

Gro Harlem Brundtland of Norway In 1981, Gro Harlem Brundtland was appointed the first female prime minister of Norway. She went on to win two more terms. A physician, she later became director general of the World Health Organization, which is part of the United Nations.

Mary Robinson of Ireland In 1990, **Mary Robinson** became the first female president of Ireland. As president, Robinson worked to convey to the rest of the world a more modern image of Ireland, and she did so by taking on a more prominent role than had past presidents. Robinson was strongly committed to human rights. She was the first head of state to visit Somalia after its civil war in 1992. Two years later, she was the first to visit Rwanda after a period of genocide.

Shortly before Robinson's term as president expired, she took up the post of United Nations High Commissioner for Human Rights (UNHCHR). In that role, she made human rights at both the national and regional levels priorities of her office.

Édith Cresson of France During her stint as the first female premier of France, serving from May 1991 to April 1992, **Édith Cresson** worked to improve France's industrial competitiveness and to reduce social inequities. She was replaced after just one year, however, because of rising unemployment and declining support for her Socialist Party.

In 1995, Cresson was appointed to serve as European Commissioner for Science, Research, and Education. She and the entire European Commission resigned in 1999 because of alleged fraud and corruption.

Hanna Suchocka of Poland From 1992 to 1993, former law professor Hanna Suchocka was the first female prime minister of Poland. Although her time as the head of government was brief, she was respected for her ability to forge alliances between conservatives and moderates.

Reneta Indzhova of Bulgaria In 1994, Indzhova, an economist, was appointed interim prime minister after a previous government coalition broke down. She was popular for taking a stand against organized crime, but she served as prime minister for less than a year.

Angela Merkel of Germany When Angela Merkel was a university student in the 1970s, the Stasi, or East German secret police, tried to recruit her as an informant. She refused. She earned a doctorate in quantum chemistry in the 1980s. After Germany's reunification, she began a career in politics, becoming the first female chancellor of Germany in 2005, serving until 2021.

REFLECT ON THE ESSENTIAL QUESTION

Essential Question: *How have women's roles and status developed and changed throughout the 20th and 21st centuries?*

Changes in Women's Roles and Status	Effects of Changes

second-wave feminism   in vitro fertilization (IVF)   Édith Cresson
Simone de Beauvoir   Thatcherism
birth control pill   Mary Robinson

MULTIPLE-CHOICE QUESTIONS

Questions 1–3 refer to the passage below.

Passage 1

> "According to French law, obedience is no longer included among the duties of a wife, and each woman citizen has the right to vote . . . . A woman . . . is not emancipated from the male because she has a ballot in her hand. . . . It is through gainful employment that woman has traversed most of the distance that separated her from the male."
>
> —Simone de Beauvoir, *The Second Sex: Existential Feminism*, 1949

Passage 2

> "WE ORGANIZE . . . to break through the silken curtain of prejudice and discrimination against women in government, industry, the professions, the churches, the political parties, the judiciary, the labor unions, in education, science, medicine, law, religion, and every other field . . . . We believe that a true partnership between the sexes demands . . . equitable sharing of the responsibilities of home and children and of the economic burdens of their support."
>
> —National Organization for Women (NOW),
> Statement of Purpose, 1966

1. Which of the following best describes the relationship of these passages to the broader context of feminism?
   (A) Both statements reflected first-wave feminism.
   (B) Beauvoir's statement reflected first-wave feminism while the NOW statement reflected second-wave feminism.
   (C) Both statements reflected second-wave feminism.
   (D) Beauvoir's statement reflected second-wave feminism while the NOW statement reflected third-wave feminism.

2. Both passages reflect a reaction against which idea or development?
   (A) The failure of women to win the right to vote after World War I
   (B) The ideal of the domesticated housewife after World War II
   (C) Discrimination against women who were living under Communist governments
   (D) The lack of attention to racial issues by women within the feminist movement

3. Which of the following best describes a difference between these two passages?
   (A) Beauvoir emphasizes women's independence from male control while NOW focuses on equal opportunities for women and men.
   (B) Beauvoir emphasizes the importance of voting while NOW focuses on equality in work.
   (C) Beauvoir emphasizes how much feminism has achieved while NOW focuses on how little feminism has accomplished.
   (D) Beauvoir emphasizes the importance of wives continuing to carry out their traditional duties while NOW does not.

SHORT-ANSWER QUESTION

Use the passage below to answer all parts of the question that follows.

"Around 1950, participation in higher education worldwide was still very low for both sexes but, still, enrollment rates for men were more than double those for women. From the 1960s onwards, participation in tertiary [post-secondary] education rapidly expanded. Initially, this expansion disproportionately involved men, leading to a widening of the gender gap in higher education. However, from the 1970s onwards, the gap began to shrink."

—Jan Van Bavel, "The Mid-Twentieth Century Baby Boom and the Changing Educational Gradient in Belgian Cohort Fertility," *Demographic Research*, March 2014

1. a) Describe ONE cause for low female participation in post-secondary education in Europe prior to 1950.

   b) Describe ONE cause for the increase in female participation in post-secondary education in Europe after 1950.

   c) Explain ONE political, social, or economic factor that contributed to the cause you identified in part b.

Topic 9.9

Decolonization

We are determined that our nation and the world as a whole shall not be the plaything of one small corner of the world.

—Sukarno, first president of Indonesia

Essential Question: What were the various ways in which colonial groups around the world sought independence from colonizers in the 20th and 21st centuries?

European colonial empires, amassed in Asia and Africa during the 18th and 19th centuries, finally came apart in the 20th century. Decolonization took decades in many cases, as European imperialist states had varying reactions to the process—ranging from cooperation to interference and violent resistance. The two world wars played a major role in the move to end European control over their empires.

Decolonization Replaces European Empires

Nationalist forces were among the causes of World War I. At the end of the war, four major empires were dismantled: the German, Austro-Hungarian, Ottoman, and Russian. In Europe, some former territories within these empires became independent states. (See Topic 8.4.)

National Self-Determination

During the peace process, U.S. President **Woodrow Wilson** advocated the principle of national **self-determination**. He believed that the people of a given territory should be able to decide their own form of government without interference from outside states.

Though he was not successful in getting this principle included in the charter of the League of Nations, Wilson's ideas struck a chord with many nationalists around the world. These nationalists believed that they would benefit from new policies and freedoms. People in French and British colonies were disappointed when it soon became clear that reality did not match the promises of self-determination.

British India The **Indian National Congress** was the main group in India advocating for national independence. After World War I, many argued that India's wartime service to the empire strengthened its case for independence. Almost 1.5 million Indians had volunteered, providing troops and support services for the British, mostly in Africa and the Middle East. Britain promised a gradual increase in self-governance but always insisted that India remain part of the empire. Indian nationalists refused to accept what they saw as insufficient concessions.

French African Colonies In a similar way, France used hundreds of thousands of colonial subjects from West Africa and North Africa to fight on the Western Front during World War I. Many Africans also worked in French factories as battle losses created a shortage of French workers. The French often drafted Africans into the French armed forces. Also, French reforms after World War I did little to encourage nationalists in its African colonies.

The Mandate System

The League of Nations tried to establish some international control over colonies after World War I. The **mandate system** was set up so that League-supervised European powers would take administrative responsibility for former colonies of the German and Ottoman empires. The Middle East was a key region where the mandate system took effect. (See Topics 8.2 and 8.4 for more about the mandate system.)

Middle East Mandates During World War I, the Allies had promised independence to many Arab territories in the Middle East in exchange for their support in fighting the Ottoman Empire. Yet when the empire was dismantled during the peace process, Great Britain and France were awarded control of these former Turkish territories as mandates. As a result of the mandate system, Turkey's power in the Middle East was severely limited while that of France and Great Britain grew.

The British mandates in the Middle East were Iraq and Palestine, which included present-day Jordan and Israel. The French mandates in the region were Syria and Lebanon. These mandates were all considered to be close to independence, yet the British and the French remained actively involved in the region until after World War II.

Mandates and Oil One major reason for the ongoing presence of these European powers was the recognition of the strategic importance of the Middle East and its oil. As World War I progressed, oil became increasingly important to fuel ships, trucks, tanks, and planes. Countries also realized oil would be important after the war as a fuel and a lubricant for the civilian economy.

Before World War I, German and British oil companies had invested in the Turkish Petroleum Company (TPC), which was exploring for oil in the region that became Iraq. During the peace negotiations, Germany lost all rights to this company. The victors in the war—Great Britain, France, and the United States—negotiated with one another for control of the oil. In 1928, private oil companies in the three countries agreed that they would work together to develop the oil fields in the Middle East region that the Ottoman Empire had formerly controlled.

Nationalist Movements and Delayed Independence

Indigenous nationalist movements in many Asian and African colonies began before World War I and grew stronger immediately after it. These movements were generally repressed until after World War II. In 1945, the principle of national self-determination became part of the United Nations Charter. In addition, most European states were so weakened by World War II that they could no longer maintain control over their colonies. For example, after Britain resisted the move for decades, India achieved independence in 1947. But for a variety of reasons, independence for many colonies was delayed for decades.

Indochina The French had been reluctant to relinquish control of their colonies in Indochina, a region in Southeast Asia that later became the countries of Cambodia, Laos, and Vietnam. In Vietnam, the **Viet Minh**, a strong nationalist guerilla group under the leadership of **Ho Chi Minh**, defeated the French in 1954 at the battle of Dien Bien Phu. Laos and Cambodia then achieved independence from the French. The French divided Vietnam into two countries until elections could be held in 1956. However, Vietnam then became the site of a long proxy war between the United States and the Soviet Union. Vietnam finally became independent under a communist government in 1975.

Indonesia At different times, the British, French, and Dutch controlled what is now Indonesia. Indonesian nationalists formed organizations in the early 1900s. As World War I was ending, the Dutch established a People's Council in Indonesia, but this group had no real power. Nationalists tried to gain more traction by focusing their efforts around religious freedom for Muslims and communist beliefs but both failed to attract popular support.

Source: Getty Images

The Martyrs' Memorial in Algiers, Algeria, opened in 1982 to pay respect to all the Algerians who died in the fight for independence from France.

In 1942, the Japanese invaded. They made an Indonesian named **Sukarno** their chief adviser. He negotiated with the Japanese and declared Indonesian independence in 1945. Sukarno became the country's first president in 1949. He suppressed the new country's parliament, destroyed free enterprise, and ruled as an authoritarian until 1966, when the Indonesian army deposed him and installed another leader in his place.

North Africa Though France granted independence to Morocco and Tunisia in 1956, it was reluctant to do the same for Algeria, in large part because two million French citizens had settled there. In Algeria as in Vietnam, nationalist guerillas, the **National Liberation Front (FLN)**, fought the French in a long war that deeply divided citizens in France. Algeria won independence from France in 1962.

Southern Africa In southern Africa, several countries gained independence peacefully. By 1960, the French, British, and Belgians had given up direct control of most of their colonies. However, Portugal fought longer to keep control of its African colonies, including Angola. After 14 years of fighting, Angola declared its independence in 1975 when a coup disrupted the Portuguese government. However, Angola lacked stability. Three different groups had been fighting for independence, with groups being supported by the Soviet Union and Cuba, the United States, China, and Zaire (now the Democratic Republic of the Congo). Much of this international interest resulted from the Cold War and the spread of communism. After independence, Angola endured a long civil war that ended in the mid-1990s.

Effects of Decolonization Even after decolonization, European influence remained strong in many former colonies. As these countries dealt with poverty and factional disputes, they remained dependent on the West and Japan for technology and financial aid. In addition, many former colonial subjects migrated to Europe seeking economic opportunities. Migration due to decolonization especially affected Great Britain, France, and the Netherlands.

In the first decades after World War II, Europe needed migrant labor to help it rebuild. About 10 million people migrated to Western Europe between 1950 and 1973. However, when economic times grew tighter in the 1970s, many European countries found that workers they considered temporary residents wanted to become permanent citizens. Ethnic and racial tensions between immigrants and native populations grew over time as Europe found its ideas about its identity changing.

REFLECT ON THE ESSENTIAL QUESTION

Essential Question: *What were the various ways in which colonial groups around the world sought independence from colonizers in the 20th and 21st centuries?*

Efforts for Independence	Results

KEY TERMS

Woodrow Wilson	mandate system	Sukarno
self-determination	Viet Minh	National Liberation Front
Indian National Congress	Ho Chi Minh	(FLN)

Questions 1–3 refer to the passage below.

"For the past three years Algeria has been the theatre of an atrocious war. Blood flows profusely, increasing both mourning and hatred. . . . Before anything else, you must know the truth that they are trying to hide from you.

[T]he demands of a people to its own national life is natural and legitimate. . . . The Algerians will not stop fighting until they are free. . . . Despite the presence of 500,000 French soldiers, despite the horrible repression . . . 'pacification' has failed. . . .

The Algerians aren't making war on the French people or the Europeans of Algeria, but on FRENCH COLONIALISTS. Besides, isn't it true that many European Algerians participate in this struggle alongside their Moslem [Islamic] brothers? They are Communists, liberals, Christians.

No! The Algerians don't want to throw you into the sea! . . .

Contrary to what colonialist propaganda wants you to believe, the future Algerian Republic will not be theocratic. The different Algerian national organizations have expressed this: it will be democratic and social. . . .

Who is responsible? . . .

It is the colonialists, the big bosses, the big landowners . . . and financiers.

Yesterday they served Hitler and Vichy in the name of French Sovereignty. Today, fearing defeat, they are preparing their fall-back position, exporting their capital, buying land in France and South America. . . .

This horrible face of colonial war explains the fact that exasperated patriots answer by the bomb and the grenade. And how can we forget that there were several tens of victims of these attacks, while colonialist barbarism has already caused SEVERAL HUNDRED THOUSAND DEAD, among the Algerians?"

—Algerian Communist Party, message to
Europeans in Algeria, 1957

1. Which of the following best describes a main purpose of the Algerian communists as expressed in this source?
   (A) Establishment of an Islamic-ruled state
   (B) Expulsion of French citizens from Algeria
   (C) Elimination of colonial rule by France
   (D) Seizure of estates belonging to large landowners

2. In this passage, Algerian communists defend violent tactics as
   (A) a powerful means of demonstrating Algerian resolve
   (B) a rational effort to force the Nazis out of Algeria
   (C) an essential method for achieving economic equality
   (D) a justified response to French brutality

3. The main audience for this letter is the group of people who are living in
   (A) Algeria and do not support the Communist Party
   (B) Algeria and are of French ancestry
   (C) France and are of Algerian ancestry
   (D) France and who do support the Communist Party

SHORT-ANSWER QUESTION

Use the passage below to answer all parts of the question that follows.

"Similarly, resistance to the United States and the Soviet Union did not grow exclusively out of anti-American and anti-Soviet sources. Quite the contrary, many of the most effective critics of the superpowers emerged from Cold War institutions, especially political parties and universities. Postcolonial personalities certainly had their roots in local traditions and experiences, but they also drew on rhetoric, ideas, and resources from dominant international institutions. Decolonization was, at least in part, a product of the Cold War."

—J. Suri, "The Cold War, Decolonization, and Global Social Awakenings: Historical Intersections." *Cold War History*, 2006

1. a) Describe ONE way in which the Cold War contributed to decolonization.

   b) Describe ONE cause other than the Cold War that contributed to decolonization.

   c) Explain ONE result of decolonization in a specific African or Asian location.

Topic 9.10

The European Union

Our British friends have decided to leave us—which is very sad for all of us—but life goes on and the European Union as well goes on.

—Italian politician Federica Mogherini (b. 1973)

Essential Question: How has the formation and existence of the European Union influenced economic developments from the end of World War II to the present?

After decades of global conflict, several factors contributed to European countries' desire for greater cooperation. For the French in particular, such cooperation was a means to keep an eye on Germany, a country that had occupied it twice in the 20th century. There was also a growing sense that economic rationalization and collaboration were needed to end wasteful competition and ease tensions between nations. Concerns about the Soviet Union further encouraged unity.

European Integration

After World War II, Europeans took explicit steps toward reducing nationalism. The measures European leaders put into place were designed to promote both economic and political integration. Leaders hoped that integration would lead people to see peace as in their self-interest. Further, these measures were intended to change how people thought about themselves. The goal was to establish a shared European identity. Just as the development of nationalism in the 19th century had overcome regional divides, internationalism might overcome national divides.

To aid in Europe's postwar economic recovery, the United States provided $13 billion, or roughly $140 billion in modern-day currency. As part of the Marshall Plan, the United States stipulated that European nations must spend the money cooperatively. The first step in European unification, the **Organization for European Economic Cooperation (OEEC)**, was established to administer Marshall Plan funds.

Member states France, West Germany, Italy, Belgium, Luxembourg, and the Netherlands continued to work together toward postwar economic recovery. The **European Coal and Steel Community (ECSC)** was established in 1951. It combined and administered Europe's vital steel and coal resources and also established an assembly—later named the **European Parliament**—as well as a court. The ECSC also collected tax income. The main architect of the ECSC was Robert Schuman of France, who hoped that it would make war between France and Germany "not merely unthinkable, but materially impossible."

In 1957, the original member nations of the ECSC signed the Treaty of Rome, which established the **European Economic Community (EEC)**, often referred to as the **Common Market**. Britain, Ireland, and Denmark joined the EEC in the early 1970s. The agreement lifted almost all trade restrictions among the member states. In 1986, the Single European Act allowed citizens to move freely among the member nations. West Germany had been a member of the EU since 1958, but German reunification in 1990 meant that former East German territory became part of the EU. German politician Constanze Krehl said, "The European Parliament was one of the first institutions which clearly stated that they support this process of reunification in a peaceful way. It was the first step towards overcoming the division of the whole continent."

The Maastricht Treaty of 1991 led to the establishment of a common currency, the **euro**, though the actual paper currency and coins didn't go into circulation until 2002. The treaty also allowed European nations to cooperate in areas such as security and environmental affairs and resulted in a name change from EEC to the **European Union (EU)**.

The EU Expands In 2004, ten countries joined the EU. Eight of them were from Eastern and Central Europe. This was significant because it reunited large parts of Europe that had been divided after World War II.

21ST CENTURY EXPANSION OF THE EUROPEAN UNION	
Year	**Country**
2004	Czechia (also called Czech Republic), Estonia, Latvia, Lithuania, Poland, Slovakia, Slovenia, Cyprus, Malta
2007	Bulgaria, Romania
2013	Croatia

Modern Europe

Membership in the EU became a perpetual balancing act. Leaders and citizens in each country had to weigh the benefits against the costs.

Positive Outcomes

EU membership provided countries with many advantages. For example, tax-free trade allowed businesses to sell their products more easily in a wider market. Free movement for citizens across borders made travel for work and tourism easy. Sharing a common currency made every financial transaction simpler. Greater political cooperation made addressing cross-border problems, such as pollution, more effective. These advantages help explain why Europe under the EU had its most peaceful and prosperous period in many centuries.

Ongoing Challenges

Many countries struggled with the challenges to their national sovereignty that came with being a member of such an economic and political union.

Legal Requirements The EU requires all countries to obey certain rules and laws. For example, no EU member may use the death penalty. "We oppose capital punishment in all times and under all circumstances," a 2021 EU statement reiterated. People in some countries object to the degree of oversight from the European Parliament.

Movement Through Borders Most countries within the European Union allow EU residents to travel, work, and live in other EU countries without special papers or arrangements. However, critics say that an EU without internal borders allows criminals and terrorists to roam freely. Migrants from outside the EU have also presented challenges. People fleeing conflicts in Syria, Iraq, Afghanistan, and Eritrea have sought safety in the EU. So have economic migrants from the Balkans region, Nigeria, and Pakistan. Many migrants want to settle in Germany and Sweden, but those nations want their EU partners to share the costs and challenges of supporting so many new residents. In 2021, twelve EU member states formally requested improved physical barriers at borders within the EU.

Economic Requirements Wealthier countries sometimes resented helping support poorer ones. Economic integration brought greater stability and prosperity overall, but it also meant that an economic change that helped one EU country could harm others. Also, economic difficulties harmed some member countries more than others. For example, in the financial crisis of 2007 and 2008, Greece, Spain, Italy, and Portugal suffered more than many other EU countries did.

Vanishing Cultures Some countries feared the loss of their own distinct culture. They wanted to protect their language and their traditions from becoming just part of a general European one. In response, the EU has taken measures to protect what it calls regional and minority languages, including Basque, Welsh, Kashubian, Scots, Livonian, and Cornish.

Leaving the European Union

Another difficulty EU member nations faced was determining if, when, and how to leave. In 2016, British citizens voted to leave the EU. This move became known as **Brexit** (short for "British exit"). Britain's prime minister, David Cameron, opposed Brexit and resigned the day after it passed. Negotiations between Britain and the rest of Europe over separation proved complicated. Another prime minister, Theresa May, also stepped down after failing to negotiate a Brexit deal within the British parliament. In January 2020, Britain officially left the European Union.

Ever since Brexit was suggested, many people have wondered if other countries would leave the EU. Political scientist Markus Gastinger suggests that the EU will survive as long as Germany is committed to staying in it. Germany's economic power, size, and influence will continue to bolster the EU. However, countries such as Italy, Sweden, Denmark, and Greece may follow Britain out the door if they believe doing so would be advantageous to them.

Source: Getty Images

The vote on whether to remain in the European Union was hotly contested in the United Kingdom. Some viewed the EU as a continuation of Churchill's policies of working closely with European allies. Others supported leaving because they thought membership infringed on the country's independence.

REFLECT ON THE ESSENTIAL QUESTION

Essential Question: *How has the formation and existence of the European Union influence economic developments from the end of World War II to the present?*

EU-Related Event	Effects on Economic Development

KEY TERMS

Organization for European Economic Cooperation (OEEC)

European Coal and Steel Community (ECSC)

European Parliament

European Economic Community (EEC)

Common Market

euro

European Union (EU)

Brexit

MULTIPLE-CHOICE QUESTIONS

Questions 1–3 refer to the passage below.

Passage 1

"The movement of coal and steel between member countries will immediately be freed from all customs duty. Conditions will gradually be created which will spontaneously provide for the more rational distribution of production at the highest level of productivity."

—French Foreign Minister Robert Schuman,
Schuman Declaration, May 9, 1950

Passage 2

"British citizens are able to travel, study, work, retire, get fairer legal redress and obtain free medical help anywhere in Europe, without restrictions. We work together better to stop international gangs bringing drugs, terrorism, and illegal immigrants into our country. It provides a network of trade, aid and cooperation that covers most of the world, giving us greater influence, stability and prosperity."

—British Foreign Secretary Jack Straw, message to
House of Commons, June 16, 2004

1. The organization discussed in the first passage was formed because of a desire to
   (A) prevent France and Germany from going to war for a third time in the 20th century
   (B) stop the smuggling of drugs and other illegal goods throughout Europe
   (C) offer countries an alternative international organization to the United Nations
   (D) respond to the growing economic power of the Soviet Union after World War II

2. One difference between the organizations discussed by Schuman and Straw is that the one described by Straw
   (A) focused on forming a military force that fought in areas such as Bosnia
   (B) reached out to Eastern European countries, including the Czech Republic
   (C) required that the United Kingdom end its use of its own currency
   (D) included the United States and Canada as members

3. A historian could use these two passages to support which argument about Europe between 1945 and 2004?

(A) National governments were growing weaker as ethnic groups were demanding more regional power.

(B) Europeans were identifying more strongly with their nation and less strongly with the rest of Europe.

(C) Local governments were taking over functions that national governments had performed before World War II.

(D) Nation-states were becoming less important and international organizations were becoming more important.

SHORT-ANSWER QUESTION

Answer all parts of the question that follows.

1. a) Explain ONE economic cause of increased integration among countries in Western and Central Europe after World War II.

   b) Explain ONE economic effect of increased integration among countries in Western and Central Europe after World War II.

   c) Explain ONE result of economic integration on political relationships among the countries in Western and Central Europe.

Topic 9.11

Migration and Immigration

We will fight until every woman can play the sport that she wants to play, how she wants to play it.

—Hawa Doucouré, age 19, a soccer player protesting a
French sporting organization's decision to forbid
women from covering their hair while on the field

Essential Question: What have been the causes and effects of changes to migration within, and immigration to, Europe from the end of World War II to the present?

As Europe became richer and travel became easier, more people began to immigrate to Europe and within Europe. These changes have affected European religion, economics, and politics.

Immigration and Religion

A variety of factors affected Europe's religious makeup in the 20th century, which had traditionally been characterized as Judeo-Christian. The Holocaust and repression in the Soviet Union led to the death or emigration of millions of Jewish citizens from Europe during and after World War II. At the same time, decolonization after World War II brought many people from the former colonies into Europe seeking better economic opportunities. For example, immigrants came to the United Kingdom from India, Pakistan, and the Caribbean and to France from North and West Africa. In the 1950s and 1960s, many European nations encouraged immigrants to come to Europe as guest workers to meet a severe labor shortage. Many of these newcomers practiced Hinduism, Buddhism, and Islam.

Starting in the early 1970s, economic conditions caused governments to discourage immigration. Yet from the 1980s onward, economic, political, and ecological conditions in many parts of Asia, Africa, and the Middle East led to an increase in immigrants and refugees coming to Europe. In 2015, hundreds of thousands of migrants, many from Syria, Afghanistan, and Iraq, massed in Turkey, seeking permission to live in Europe. Some migrations ended in tragedy. In 2018, the United Nations reported that more than 2,000 migrants drowned that year while trying to reach Europe.

THE MUSLIM POPULATION OF EUROPE, C. 2017

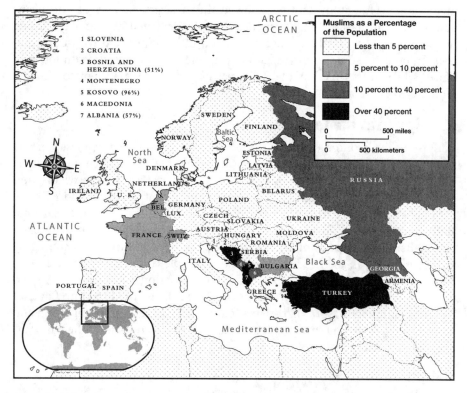

Source: World Factbook

Growth of the Muslim Population The minority religion that grew the most with increased immigration to Europe was Islam. Muslims (those who practice Islam) made up about 1 percent of the population of many European countries in 1970, although France's Muslim population was 3.9 percent of the total. In 2016, the overall Muslim population of Europe was about 5 percent, with France having the highest proportion at 8.8 percent. Germany and the United Kingdom each had slightly more than 6 percent.

Debates About Religion In spite of increased immigration, Europe remained predominantly Christian, with about 75 percent of the population identified as Christians in 2010. However, nearly 20 percent identified as "unaffiliated," marking a growth in Europe's secularism. In 2018, an extensive survey of people in Western Europe revealed that 64 percent of the population identified as Christian, but only 18 percent said they went to church at least once per month.

Europe's secularism created a strong separation between church and state. The rapid growth of Islam as a larger minority religion caused debate and conflict about the role of religion in social and political life. For example, Muslim girls are prohibited to wear headscarves in public schools in France. (Islamic rules about modesty apply to the clothing and behavior of men and women. Many Muslims believe that women should cover their hair as a sign of modesty.) One study in 1997 showed that a large majority of Europeans agreed that immigrants who wished to be fully accepted into society needed to give up any part of their religion or culture that conflicted with European laws. In politics, some countries allowed immigrants to vote and run for local office, while others have made it increasingly difficult for them to become naturalized citizens.

Immigrants as Targets

Because of the economic growth of the 1950s and 1960s, many guest workers from southern Europe, Asia, and Africa immigrated to Western and Central Europe. After the economic downturn of the 1970s, these workers and their families often became targets of anti-immigrant agitation and extreme nationalist political parties. In France, for example, the right-wing **National Rally** political party (formerly known as the National Front) supports French nationalism and controls on immigration. It has been accused of encouraging **xenophobia**, or an intense fear or dislike of people from other countries, and antisemitism. In 2020, a French court fined the National Rally and jailed two of its leaders for defrauding the party's own candidates. The **Freedom Party of Austria**, founded in 1956, also argued for stricter controls on immigration and has warned against the "over-foreignization" of Austrian society. The party has become increasingly anti-Muslim over the years.

Source: Wikimedia Commons

A 2015 anti-Islam protest in Poland by the National Radical Camp

---

REFLECT ON THE ESSENTIAL QUESTION

Essential Question: *What have been the causes and effects of changes to migration within, and immigration to, Europe from the end of World War II to the present?*

Causes	Effects

MULTIPLE-CHOICE QUESTIONS

Questions 1–3 refer to the passage below.

Passage 1

"All of France's children, whatever their history, whatever their origin, whatever their beliefs, are the daughters and sons of the republic. . . . It cannot be tolerated that under the cover of religious freedom, the laws and principles of the republic are challenged. Secularism is one of the great achievements of the republic. We cannot allow it to be weakened. In all conscience, it is my view that the wearing of clothes or of symbols which conspicuously demonstrate religious affiliations must be banned in state schools."

—French President Jacques Chirac, speech, December 17, 2003

Passage 2

"[This] is not a religious constraint since it is not laid down in Islam or the Qur'an. . . . It is my personal choice. . . . When [French] President Sarkozy said, 'The burqa [a garment that covers the entire body] is not welcome' . . . [he] opened the door for racism aggression, and attacks on Islam. . . . [I]t has created enormous racism and Islamophobia that wasn't there before. . . . I will go all the way to the European court of human rights and I will fight for my liberty."

—Kenza Drider, *The Observer*, a British newspaper, April 2011

1. Which of the following best describes the historical context for these two passages?
    (A) European countries were becoming more closely connected.
    (B) Immigrants from former colonies were moving into Europe.
    (C) Communism was collapsing in Eastern Europe.
    (D) Christianity was becoming less influential in Western Europe.

2. The main ideas of these two passages both reflect a conflict in France between
   (A) an older generation and a younger generation of people
   (B) traditions of secularism and individual liberty
   (C) supporters and opponents of feminism
   (D) attitudes in the first and second decades of the 21st century

3. The basic issue represented in these passages makes it most similar to which of the following events in French history?
   (A) The Fronde that began in 1648
   (B) The July Revolution of 1830
   (C) The Paris Commune of 1871
   (D) The Dreyfus Affair that began in 1894

SHORT-ANSWER QUESTION

Use the table below to answer all parts of the question that follows.

EUROPEAN POPULATION DIVERSITY, 2019			
Country	Number of Immigrants per 1,000 Inhabitants	Percentage of Non-National Residents from EU Countries	Percentage of Non-National Residents from Non-EU Countries
Malta	56	10	10
Ireland	17	7	6
Estonia	14	2	14
Austria	12	9	8
Germany	11	5	7
France	6	3	5
Slovakia	1	2	1
European Union	6	---	---

Source: Eurostat, "Migration and Migrant Population Statistics." ec.europa.eu/eurostat

1. a) Describe how Estonia's immigration pattern is unlike that of the other countries listed in the table.

   b) Explain how Malta's location as an island in the Mediterranean Sea relates to its percentage of immigrants.

   c) Explain how the data in the table can be used to modify or refute the Freedom Party's immigration fears about "over-foreignization" in Austria.

Topic 9.12

Technology

Essential Question: How have innovations and advances in technology influenced cultural and intellectual developments from 1914 to the present?

In 2019, European average life expectancy at birth was 78.5 years for men and 84 years for women. This was a tremendous improvement over 1950, when European life expectancies hovered around 65. The gains were largely due to advances in technology and medicine. However, medical and technological advances brought controversies with them.

The Benefits and Costs of Science and Technology

Science and technology made life better for many people. Inventions such as home appliances made life easier. Improvements in transportation included the railroad, the automobile, and the airplane. From the assembly line to computers, people used technology to make workplaces more efficient. However, all of these technological advances had costs, leading many people to question whether the benefits outweighed the costs—especially in the areas of medical advances and military technology.

Medicine became increasingly scientific in the 20th and 21st centuries. New medical theories and technologies improved the quality of life for many and increased life expectancy:

- The development of antibiotics, medications that fight bacteria, allowed for the successful treatment of many types of infection.

- Continued development of chemotherapy drugs improved cancer treatment and increased survival rates.

- Knowledge about the genes that make up an individual's hereditary traits led to new diagnostic tests and treatments that could be tailored to individual patients.

These advances, however, raised a variety of questions, and people did not always agree on how to address them. These questions—and responses to them—ranged across religious, political, and philosophical perspectives.

Social Questions

As life expectancy increased, the percentage of the population that was elderly also increased. The aging population, along with new but expensive drugs and technologies, increased the cost of health care. Because most European nations had established some sort of national health system, health care costs were a high cost for governments. For example, in Germany, by the early 21st century, health care accounted for more than 10 percent of the country's gross domestic product, and 77 percent of that was financed through the government. National health systems were designed to provide care to everyone. Europeans debated how to finance advanced technologies and treatments and allocate them fairly.

A related social issue was unequal medical care within the European Union. Each country set its own health care policies. For example, in countries such as Greece, Spain, and Portugal that faced government cutbacks during the economic crisis that began in 2009, life expectancy decreased, and doctors sought better opportunities in other countries. For these reasons, patients often traveled throughout Europe seeking better care than they could find in their home countries.

Moral Questions

Changes in philosophy and technology raised questions about truth and morality. If all knowledge was relative to the observer, could any moral standard apply to all people in all circumstances? The lack of agreement on morality and truth sometimes ignited fierce controversies over new technologies that enabled people to intervene in the basic processes of life.

Birth Control By the 1990s, contraceptive pills were the most common **birth control** method used by Europeans to greatly reduce the chances of pregnancy. Often, government health programs provided these pills for free or at low cost.

Abortion In the 1960s and 1970s, many countries in Europe reduced restrictions on **abortions**. In most countries, women could obtain abortions, but the conditions varied widely. Strongest opposition to abortion came from the Roman Catholic Church on moral grounds.

Eugenics In the early 20th century, some people began to advocate policies, known as **eugenics**, which they argued would improve the genetic quality of the human race. For example, they supported forced sterilization for people with disabilities. The Nazis adopted this policy as part of their plan for "racial hygiene" to promote the Aryan "master race." Because of the association of eugenics with the Nazis, most people strongly rejected the idea as immoral.

Fertility Treatments Medical efforts to help couples conceive children, or **fertility treatments**, began in the 19th century. In England in 1978, the first child was born through in vitro fertilization. In this process, an egg is fertilized outside a woman's body and then placed inside her uterus to develop. While some people thought the process was unethical, others welcomed the possibility of helping couples have children.

Genetic Research European researchers were leaders in genetic research to explore how changes in a person's genes might be used to cure certain diseases such as cystic fibrosis and leukemia. This research generated debate about the possibility of dangerous side effects of **genetic engineering** (changing a living thing's characteristics by modifying or replacing genes). Some feared it would lead to human cloning—the production of human embryos that are genetically identical to a parent.

Stem Cell Research Other aspects of genetic research, such as stem cell research, have been debated as well. Stem cells are general cells that can divide and change into specialized cells such as blood cells or skin cells. Some scientists saw in stem cells the potential to treat many diseases. Others objected to the use of human embryos that had been discarded during fertility treatments in stem cell research.

Military Technologies

As in other fields, science and technology changed the nature of warfare in the 20th and 21st centuries. European countries strove to develop weapons and surveillance technologies that would give them advantages over their rivals. However, these new technologies resulted in devastation and dangers for not only Europe but also for the world.

Development of Nuclear Weapons Development of the atomic bomb took military technology to a new level. As scientists learned more about the secrets of the atom, they were developing the knowledge necessary for the production of nuclear weapons and power. Once they understood how to split the atom into its component parts, they learned to release the energy that resulted in a variety of ways. Atomic weapons, first used by the United States against Japan in World War II, had a destructive potential far beyond other types of weapons. In the 21st century, the European countries that possess nuclear weapons are the United Kingdom, France, and Russia.

Electricity from Nuclear Power Although the first use of nuclear energy was destructive, its use to provide power generation had great potential to meet a growing demand for electricity. Nuclear power plants were first developed in Europe in the late 1950s. In 2019, about 26 percent of electricity in the European Union came from nuclear power. However, nuclear power comes with risks. These include the release of radioactive material from waste disposal and accidents at nuclear power plants. The 1986 disaster at the Chernobyl nuclear power plant in Ukraine released more radioactivity into the atmosphere than the bombs at Hiroshima and Nagasaki. Contamination of soil and water from Chernobyl had long-lasting effects on people and livestock.

Nuclear Weapons Concerns The devastation of Hiroshima and Nagasaki in 1945 showed the destructive power of nuclear weapons technology. The Soviet Union developed its first atomic bomb in 1949. Soon the United States and the Soviet Union became involved in a nuclear arms race as each sought to move ahead of its rival in the growth of its nuclear arsenal.

The two super powers recognized the tremendous danger posed by a nuclear war. They came to believe that the best way to prevent a war was to protect the ability of a country to retaliate. They reasoned that a country would not use nuclear weapons first if it understood that its opponent could launch a nuclear attack in response. The desire to prevent war led to several arms control agreements that limited the testing, location, and number of nuclear weapons to varying degrees.

During the Cold War, **nuclear proliferation**, the spread of nuclear weapons, became a growing concern. In 1968, the United States, the Soviet Union, France, the United Kingdom, and China signed the **Nuclear Nonproliferation Treaty** to try to limit the spread of nuclear weapons to other countries. The treaty did not limit peaceful uses of nuclear technology. However, according to the Union of Concerned Scientists, as of 2021, nine countries had nuclear weapons: the United States, Russia, France, China, the United Kingdom, Pakistan, India, Israel, and North Korea. The threat of nuclear war remained. More than 100 countries have officially approved the Comprehensive Nuclear-Test-Ban Treaty, which forbids all nuclear explosions. However, several powerful countries have refused to sign the treaty.

REFLECT ON THE ESSENTIAL QUESTION

Essential Question: *How have innovations and advances in technology influenced cultural and intellectual developments from 1914 to the present?*

Innovations and Technological Advances	Influence on Cultural and Intellectual Developments

KEY TERMS

birth control	fertility treatment	Nuclear Nonproliferation
abortion	genetic engineering	Treaty
eugenics	nuclear proliferation	

MULTIPLE-CHOICE QUESTIONS

Questions 1–3 refer to the passage below.

"With European energy prices skyrocketing and pressure growing on the European Union to cut carbon emissions more quickly, it was only a matter of time before the debate over zero-carbon nuclear power came back to the fore—and with it, old divisions among EU member states.

On New Year's Eve, the European Commission presented the 27 EU member states with a draft regulation designating natural gas and nuclear power as "green" fuels for electricity generation. . . .

The moment the proposed EU regulation was leaked, battle lines were drawn along the Rhine. France, with 56 power reactors and nuclear weapons, is by far the EU's leading atomic state. . . . Germany, on the other hand, permanently turned off three of its remaining six reactors on the same day the commission sent out the proposed regulation—in line with Berlin's 2011 commitment to phase out nuclear power. . . . Joining Germany is even more fiercely anti-nuclear Austria and a small number of other countries, while France's most vocal support in favor of nuclear power comes from Finland and the Czech Republic.

If it were solely about climate policy and carbon emissions, the debate would long be settled. France, where 70 percent of electricity comes from nuclear power, has the lowest emissions from electricity generation per capita among the major EU economies. Germany, where both coal use and emissions rose in 2021, significantly exceeds the EU average—and produces more than six times the per-capita emissions from electricity generation of France, even though Germany styles itself as a green forerunner."

—Mark Hibbs, "Amid Energy Crisis, EU Fights Over Whether Nuclear Is Green," *Foreign Policy* (U.S. news magazine), January 13, 2022

1. Which of the following statements best describes the context for the debate over nuclear power in Europe?
   (A) The German-French rivalry that resulted in World War I and World War II continues.
   (B) Divisions on energy policy are reviving divisions within Europe along Cold War lines.
   (C) Several countries in Europe have nuclear weapons that endanger the peace.
   (D) Scientists argue that global warming threatens people throughout Europe and the world.

2. One example of evidence that supports Germany's position is that nuclear power
   (A) can produce radioactive leaks and wastes that endanger public safety
   (B) provides very little of Europe's electrical power overall
   (C) is unpopular in Europe, except in France
   (D) can also contribute to global warming

3. One example of evidence that supports France's position is that nuclear power

 (A) produces lower carbon emissions than do coal plants

 (B) provides 70 percent of Europe's electrical power

 (C) is popular throughout Europe, except in Germany

 (D) can cause problems, but these problems have only short-term effects

SHORT-ANSWER QUESTION

Use the passage below to answer all parts of the question that follows.

"Today is my 40th birthday. Like most people, I would probably rather keep that fact to myself.

But, around the world, the celebration of my birthday will also see celebrations that mark the 40th anniversary of IVF [in vitro fertilization]—the procedure that led to my birth.

New research released last month claims there have been eight million people born through IVF since its invention. An exhibition at the Science Museum, London, talks of six million—nobody is really sure of the exact numbers as there are babies being born every day now through assisted reproductive techniques.

When I was born, Patrick Steptoe and Robert Edwards, the two men who came up with the technique, suggested my middle name be Joy. They said my birth would bring joy to so many people. . . .

My mum, Lesley Brown, went to the doctor suffering from depression. At the heart of it was her inability to have a child with my dad, John. When they heard about this experiment it gave them hope. Even though it had never worked before it was something to cling on to—and happily led to me being born. . . .

Forty years on, other scientists are pushing the boundaries, embryologists are inventing new techniques and moral questions are still being raised."

—Louise Brown, *The Independent* (British newspaper),
July 25, 2018

1. a) Describe how ONE word or phrase indicates Brown's point of view about the procedure of invitro fertilization.

 b) Describe ONE other procedure or technology that raised similar moral questions to the ones referred to in the passage.

 c) Explain ONE reason for the moral concerns referred to in the passage.

Topic 9.13

Globalization

People have accused me of being in favor of globalization. This is equivalent to accusing me of being in favor of the sun rising in the morning.

—Clare Short (b. 1946), British politician

Essential Question: What have been the technological and cultural causes of increasing European globalization from 1914 to the present?

The rise of Europe's middle class and its involvement in an increasingly global economy exposed people to new goods, ideas, and practices. Many people welcomed **globalization** because it allowed consumers to access a wider variety of items at lower prices. However, concerns persisted that those lower prices would mean exploited workers and a single "global" culture that wiped out the individual cultures and art forms of less-powerful nations.

Consumer Culture

After World War II, mass production technologies that were perfected in munitions factories were turned to producing consumable products at rates never before seen. A new consumer culture was emerging. In it, domestic comforts such as electricity, indoor plumbing, plastics, and synthetic fibers made life easier.

Many historians attribute the rise in a consumer-driven Europe to a desire to emulate American-style consumerism. The postwar years saw unprecedented prosperity both in the United States and Europe. That, coupled with ongoing and rapid industrialization, only fueled the European consumer boom. The era has been called the Age of the Automobile because of the widespread availability of commodities and the new liberated, mobile style of life.

Communication and Transportation

Two world wars had devastated Europe and demanded full attention on survival. During the second half of the 20th century, however, Europeans' focus was no longer on survival on the home front or victory at war. Rather, people focused on the ease of domestic life and the technology that could achieve it.

Radios and Television Technology in the home became a great social equalizer. No longer did people need to visit the theater or cinema for entertainment, which only the affluent could afford. Instead, mass production of radios and televisions in the 20th century brought entertainment directly to living rooms, regardless of social class or standing. Millions of people from all walks of life could enjoy the same entertainment experience simultaneously. Tastes converged across classes and cultures, from the most remote rural areas to the busiest city centers. The 1954 World Cup, for example, was broadcast throughout Europe by the newly created Eurovision network. The wide audience for those soccer games demonstrated not only the proliferation of the television in the lives of all Europeans, but also the common way people chose to spend their new abundance of leisure time.

Telephones and Computers Other technological innovations also swept through Europe after the wars. The telephone made it easier for individuals to communicate and for businesses to be productive. Later, the cell phone made such communication even easier and more widespread. Few innovations were as influential as the computer. Early computers existed as early as the 1940s, but they were large, cumbersome, and slow. From the late 1950s to the mid-1970s, the computer grew from a purely scientific instrument to an integral part of enterprises. Computers made for home use became widespread in the 1980s.

The computer's related technology, the Internet, emerged in the United States in the 1970s, but it was not available to the general population until the 1990s. As unifying as radio and television may have been, the Internet is an unparalleled equalizer. In most countries, many people have access to a wide range of information and can connect with other people at any time. According to the United Nations, as of 2021, about 4.9 billion people had accessed the Internet, mostly on cell phones. However, nearly 3 billion people (about 37 percent of the global population) had never used the Internet as of 2021—almost all of them in poor countries.

Concerns about U.S. Influence In the second half of the 20th century, U.S. movies, television shows, music, video games, and other technology became popular throughout Europe and much of the world. In response, some Europeans became concerned that the United States might have too much cultural influence on other countries. Laws and rules that financially support and protect European filmmakers, musicians, and authors are popular with many European voters.

Transportation As advances in communication connected people remotely, transportation advances connected them physically. Throughout Europe at the beginning of the 20th century, populations clustered around railroad destinations. With automobile ownership, populations became even more mobile. Infrastructure that once built airplanes to bomb enemies instead built airplanes to transport leisure travelers across countries and over oceans. The world was becoming smaller, and social movements that united people across borders were beginning to take shape.

New Voices in Society

As feminism found its foothold in the world that emerged after two world wars, so did many other political, intellectual, and social movements. As individuals became more empowered, new voices found a place in European society.

Environmentalism and Green Parties By the 1960s, the rapid industrialization and increased farm production of the previous century had created significant environmental problems, including oil spills and negative effects from pesticides. Environmentalists argued that Europe was bound for ecological disaster if it failed to adopt practices that were more sustainable. They challenged the traditional economic and political establishment to adopt policies that were sensitive to the environment.

This movement included not only environmental conservation but also broader issues of lifestyle. The oil crisis of 1973, for example, in which a ban on oil trade drove down fuel supplies and drove up prices, helped spark the European environmental movement.

To try to gain a voice in political policy, environmentalists formed Green Parties—political parties whose main focus is on the environment or ecology-oriented ideals. Such parties began to form in the 1970s. An umbrella organization known as the **European Greens** was founded in Brussels, Belgium, in January 1984.

The first and most successful Green Party was **die Grünen**, founded in West Germany primarily by Herbert Gruhl and Petra Kelly in 1979. The party was formed by a collective of roughly 250 separate environmental groups. Its primary goal was to rally public support around the issues of nuclear energy and pollution. By the end of the 1980s, almost every country in Western and Northern Europe had its own version of the Green Party. Green Parties moved into the mainstream in parts of Europe in the 2000s and 2010s as more people became concerned about climate change.

REFLECT ON THE ESSENTIAL QUESTION

Essential Question: *What have been the technological and cultural causes of increasing European globalization from 1914 to the present?*

Technological Causes	Cultural Causes

KEY TERMS

globalization	European Greens	die Grünen

MULTIPLE-CHOICE QUESTIONS

Questions 1–3 refer to the table below.

GREEN PARTY ELECTORAL SUPPORT AMONG GERMANS		
Year	Percentage of Votes in German Parliamentary Elections	Percentage of Vote in European Parliamentary Elections
1994	6.5	10.1
1998	5.0	No European election
1999	No German election	6.4
2002	5.6	No European election
2004	No German election	11.9
2005	5.4	No European election
2009	9.2	12.1
2013	7.3	No European election
2014	No German election	10.7
2017	8.0	No European election
2019	No German election	20.5
2021	14.0	No European election

1. The information in the table above best supports the claim that between 1994 and 2021, the Green Party in Germany generally had

   (A) increasing support in both German and European elections

   (B) increasing support in German elections but not in European elections

   (C) stronger support in German elections than in European elections

   (D) stronger support in European elections than in German elections

2. Which of the following changes in attitudes helps explain the changes shown in the table?

   (A) Decreasing fear of communism because of the fall of the Berlin Wall

   (B) Decreasing interest in being part of the European Union because of economic problems facing poorer members

   (C) Increasing desire among Germans to reject older parties because they were associated with the welfare state

   (D) Increasing concern among voters about environmental issues because of global climate change

3. Which best describes the context in which the German Green Party existed?

(A) It was one of several active Green parties that developed in Europe.

(B) It was the only Green Party of importance in Europe.

(C) It was consistently a weak party within the German Parliament.

(D) It was consistently one of the most powerful parties within the German Parliament.

SHORT-ANSWER QUESTION

Answer all parts of the question that follows.

1. a) Describe ONE continuity between the consumer culture of post-World War II Europe and earlier trends in Europe.

   b) Describe ONE change between the consumer culture of post-World War II Europe and earlier trends in Europe.

   c) Explain ONE way that rural and urban cultures became more similar after World War II.

Topic 9.14

20th- and 21st-Century Culture, Arts, and Demographic Trends

Modernism was born in part out of the need . . . to describe a new world that was unlike anything that had gone before.

—Margaret MacMillan (b. 1943), author and professor

Essential Question: How and why has European culture changed from the end of World War II to the present?

After two world wars and worldwide economic depression, people's confidence in science and reason was profoundly shaken. As a result of this new way of looking at the world, new ideas emerged in visual art, architecture, literature, theater, music, and popular culture. Technological improvements made it possible for more people than ever to witness and react to these new ideas.

Challenges to Reason from New Philosophies

The catastrophic events of World War I and World War II revealed beyond doubt that science could lead to destruction as well as progress, and human beings could act in irrational and cruel ways. After World War II, these feelings of despair were expressed in new philosophical ideas that challenged the optimistic ideas of rational science.

Existentialism

The underlying premise of **existentialism** is that God is no longer present in the world. The German philosopher **Friedrich Nietzsche** (1844–1900) had already expressed this premise in the late 19th century when he proclaimed the death of God and along with it the values and purpose of life associated with God. According to his **nihilist** viewpoint, life had no purpose or meaning. Without God's presence and universal moral standards, humans could rely only on themselves. The work of two French thinkers reflected the ideas of existentialism in slightly different ways.

The French philosopher and author **Jean-Paul Sartre** (1905–1980) said that human beings first existed and then created who they were through their actions. To Sartre, existentialism emphasized that individuals should take responsibility for their lives. People must decide on their own values and then act accordingly. How people interacted with one another was central to the ethics of existentialism. Sartre himself fought in the Resistance against the Nazis in Paris; it is no surprise that he felt that "never were we freer than under the German occupation." What he meant was that he found meaning through struggle and purpose in his own actions.

Postmodernism

In the 1950s, intellectuals began using the term **postmodernism** to mean the general reaction to the ideas of modernism, which had begun in the late 19th century and was itself a reaction to Victorian morality and optimism. In addition to its use in philosophy, postmodernism referred to movements of the late 20th century in architecture, art, and literature.

In philosophy, postmodernism was a reaction to the certainty about the world expressed in the ideas of the Enlightenment. Postmodernism was skeptical about humans' ability to know anything for certain about the world apart from the individual's perception of it. Therefore, it questioned the existence of objective truth and the ability of reason to discern it. In general, postmodernists claimed that language, scientific theories, and historical analysis do not represent universal principles or objective truths but constructs by particular minds in a particular time and place. In addition, they saw that the application of science and technology did not always make society better. Postmodernists saw that logic and reason had used these tools for terrible purposes, especially in the atrocities of World War II.

EVOLVING ATTITUDES TOWARD REASON		
Philosophy	**Years**	**Ideas**
Enlightenment	c. 1685–1815	• Application of reason and the scientific method to political, social, economic, and religious institutions • A rational questioning of prevailing institutions and patterns of thought • A general belief that human progress was possible
Modernism	c. 1900–1970	• Doubt that reason was sufficient to explain people and nature • A belief that people need to take responsibility for their lives • A sense of despair and anxiety about a depersonalized world
Postmodernism	c. 1970–present	• Questioning of objective truth and the role of reason in determining it • A belief that ideas once thought objective were instead the creation of humans in a social and political context • A belief that science and reason were not inherently a force for good

Modern Challenges to Religion

As European society modernized in the 19th century, the role of organized religion in people's lives declined. As more people moved into urban environments, they became detached from the village churches that had been central to their lives. In addition, many European rulers in the late 19th century sought to curb the power of the churches.

Europe continued to become more secular as science and reason grew in importance. Some biblical scholars used new scientific and historical information to challenge the literal truth of the Bible. While some churches looked for ways to incorporate new ideas, others sought to maintain traditional beliefs. In the 20th century, as new ideas in science and philosophy questioned the belief in a rational, orderly universe, religious renewal provided an alternative viewpoint.

Christian Responses to Totalitarianism

Totalitarian governments in Central and Eastern Europe sought to replace Christianity with the ideologies of fascism and communism. These governments found different ways of dealing with the churches, and the churches responded in a variety of ways.

Fascism and the Church When Mussolini came to power in Italy in 1926, he established a totalitarian government. However, he found that he needed to work with existing institutions, including the Catholic Church. In 1929, the fascist state recognized the independence of Vatican City and declared the Catholic Church as the only official religion in Italy. The Catholic Church also received grants of money. In exchange, the pope recognized Mussolini's government and encouraged Italians to support it.

Germany As Hitler rose to power, some Protestant German clergy spoke out against him. **Dietrich Bonhoeffer** and **Martin Niemöller** first objected to the state's interference in matters of religious organization. Then they began to take strong stands against the state's anti-Christian and antisemitic views as well. Both were sent to concentration camps for their opposition. Bonhoeffer was executed, and Niemöller only narrowly escaped execution.

The Soviet Union Communism was an atheistic ideology that opposed all religion. (Karl Marx is often quoted as writing, "Religion is the opiate of the people.") Lenin and Stalin systematically attacked the Russian Orthodox Church, the largest in the Soviet Union, closing churches and sending clergy to labor camps or killing them. However, during World War II, Stalin reopened thousands of churches to appeal to people's patriotism in the fight against the Nazis. Khrushchev renewed attacks on Russian Orthodoxy, and thousands of churches were closed. After the collapse of the Soviet Union, Russians were again able to worship. The Russian Orthodox Church thrived despite the decades of opposition to it by the communist government.

Poland During Stalin's era, the Roman Catholic Church in Poland was persecuted just as the Russian Orthodox Church had been. After 1956, however, Poland's communist government and the Catholic Church reached a compromise. The government agreed to allow the Church to conduct its religious mission as long as it stayed out of politics. Although the Church was still strongly anti-communist, it accepted these terms.

When dissidents began to speak up against the communist government in the 1970s, the Church was in a difficult position. However, more clergy began to sympathize with dissidents and workers. In 1978, a Polish cardinal became **Pope John Paul II**. The following year, the pope made an eight-day visit to Poland and drew huge, enthusiastic crowds. The pope was a strong supporter of social justice and peace, and the Catholic Church in Poland became a strong supporter of the Solidarity movement that emerged in 1980. The support of the Catholic Church was an important factor in Solidarity's ultimate success and the downfall of the communist government in 1989.

Reform in the Catholic Church

The meeting of the **Second Vatican Council** (often referred to as Vatican II), the first such meeting of the Roman Catholic Church since 1870, was the major instrument of Catholic reform in the 20th century. **Pope John XXIII** (pope from 1958–1963) called the council, which began in 1962 and was continued under **Pope Paul VI** (pope from 1963–1978) until 1965. One of the main goals of the council was to make the Church more responsive to concerns of the modern world.

To that end, the council redefined some of the Church's doctrine and practices. For example, the Church allowed the celebration of the mass in vernacular languages rather than in Latin and encouraged greater participation by laypeople in the liturgy and in the Church. (Laypeople are those who follow a religion but are not priests, monks, nuns, or other religious leaders.) The Church also emphasized the Bible as the foundation of its teachings and encouraged Catholics to read the Bible rather than relying on clergy to interpret it for them. In addition, bishops were given a more active role in advising the pope.

The council also began to redefine the Church's relations with other religious communities. Many non-Catholic observers attended the council. The pope affirmed the close relationship between Christianity and Judaism and condemned antisemitism. Catholics were allowed to attend services and pray with other Christian denominations and were encouraged to be friendly with non-Christian faith communities. In 1965, the Roman Catholic and Eastern Orthodox churches, divided since the 11th century, issued a proclamation expressing a desire for some reconciliation between them.

Experimentation and Subjectivity in the Arts

Trends in 20th-century art followed the patterns seen in science, psychology, and philosophy, questioning objective knowledge and rational truth. Emphasis on the individual's perspective led to a growth of subjectivity and self-expression. As science challenged beliefs about the universe, artists in all fields experimented with new forms and subjects. After 1945, the United States replaced Europe as the dominant influence in both elite and popular culture.

New Movements in the Visual Arts

The visual arts, architecture, and music showed many similarities as they evolved throughout the 20th century. In all three fields, artists radically shifted aesthetics—principles governing the nature of beauty—by introducing new ideas of what was beautiful. Following the lead of psychologists such as Sigmund Freud, artists explored subconscious and subjective states in a variety of media. Many artists also satirized Western society and its values in their work. A major theme in new movements in the visual arts was an independence from Realism and a break with the past.

Source: Getty Images

The eggs sitting on top of the Dalí Theatre-Museum, located in the northeast corner of Spain, reflect Dalí's playful view of the world.

Cubism One style, **Cubism**, began in 1907 and became very influential. In this art form, the artist takes apart a subject and reassembles it to show many perspectives, often through the use of geometric shapes. Pablo Picasso became the most famous Cubist artist.

Futurism This style is an Italian art movement from between 1909 and 1916 that glorified the machine age. Representing different perspectives as the Cubists did, Futurist painters used multiple images and splashes of vibrant color to capture the frenzy of modern life. Although **Futurism** lasted only a short time, it had a strong influence on the movements that followed.

Dadaism A movement that began in Switzerland in 1916, and whose name origin is uncertain, **Dadaism** was a form of protest against the perceived purposelessness of life in the midst of World War I. It became strongest in Germany. This art movement created a type of anti-art by satirizing traditional aesthetics. For example, French artist Marcel Duchamp used the image of the famous *Mona Lisa* by Italian Renaissance artist Leonardo da Vinci and drew a mustache on her. Like Cubism and Futurism, Dadaism incorporated overlapping images, including photomontages, in an experimental way.

Surrealism In Paris in 1924, Dadaism gave rise to **Surrealism**, which also protested against older forms of art and Realism. Rather than focusing on the external world, Surrealism, influenced by the psychological theories of Freud, focused on the emotions and the unconscious mind by portraying objects with unusual shapes and relationships as they might appear in dreams and fantasies. The most well-known Surrealist painter was **Salvador Dalí** (1904–1989) from Spain.

Abstract Expressionism Like Surrealism, **Abstract Expressionism** explored the emotions and the unconscious but with even less of a connection to Realism. This movement began before World War I. One of its founders was the Russian artist Vasily Kandinsky (1866–1944). Abstract Expressionism became the dominant art movement after World War II. By then, New York City had replaced Paris as the capital of the Western art world, reflecting the growing influence of the United States on elite culture. The American painter Jackson Pollock (1912–1956), a leading Abstract Expressionist, was best known for his paintings consisting of drips of color that created explosive patterns. Although some artists embraced postmodernism and a return to Realism in painting, Abstract Expressionism remained strong throughout the century, with European artists such as Anselm Kiefer (b. 1945) showing that American artists were not as dominant in the 1980s as they had been earlier.

Pop Art After World War II, the United States and Britain led the way in the **Pop Art** movement. Pop artists sought a break from both traditional and contemporary art and turned to the world of popular culture—movies, TV, and advertising, for example—for inspiration. Iconic works from the Pop Art movement include American Andy Warhol's series of paintings of Campbell Soup cans.

Architecture

Change in architecture in the first half of the 20th century was largely driven by the slogan "form follows function," which expressed the idea that design flowed from a building's purpose. The **Modernist** movement in architecture rejected the more elaborate styles of the past and generally focused on clean lines and the use of modern materials, such as steel and reinforced concrete. Efficiency and lack of extraneous ornamentation were the hallmarks of this architecture.

For example, the **Bauhaus** school founded in 1919 in Berlin by Walter Gropius sought to integrate fine arts and crafts into sleek designs. Many of Gropius's buildings looked like boxes made of stainless steel and glass.

Source: Getty Images

The Nazis closed the Bauhaus building in Dessau, Germany, when they came to power. Bombings during World War II damaged it. However, the building was restored and designated a landmark because of the influence Bauhaus architects had on modern design.

In the 1960s, postmodernism became an important influence in architecture. Many architects and designers rebelled against what they saw as the sterile and boring qualities of many modern buildings. Architects referred back to historical styles and incorporated ornamentation on the outside of buildings, sometimes in a playful or satirical way. The American architect Robert Venturi was an early thinker and designer of this style. Postmodernism spread from the United States to Europe and the rest of the world. The Spaniard Santiago Calatrava was one of many influential European architects who embraced postmodernism.

Music

On the eve of World War I, the Russian composer **Igor Stravinsky** (1882–1971) shocked the musical world with his composition *The Rite of Spring*. Stravinsky's music included primitive rhythms and dissonant sounds that challenged the traditional aesthetics of Western musical forms used for centuries. Stravinsky's work also reflected an interest in the irrational that characterized other art forms of the period. He had a great influence on composers throughout the century.

In the interwar period, **Arnold Schoenberg** (1874–1951) from Vienna took experimentation even further. He began to write *atonal* music, which was built on 12 notes and was not written in a particular key. His work was similar to the emergence of abstract painting.

Richard Strauss (1864–1949) was a German composer and conductor whom some regarded as backward-looking for his use of traditional tonalities, in contrast to Schoenberg. However, he extended the boundaries of traditional harmonies and pioneered orchestration techniques that had a great influence on other composers, especially those of film scores. Strauss's composition *Also Sprach Zarathustra*, inspired by a philosophical novel of Nietzsche, was famously used as the opening to the film *2001: A Space Odyssey*.

Writers Challenge Conventions

Writers also challenged the conventions of their art form throughout the 20th century. **Franz Kafka** (1883–1924), a German-speaking Jew who was born in Prague, challenged convention by combining lucid prose with fantastical elements. The beginning of his novella *The Metamorphosis* demonstrates this combination: "When Gregor Samsa woke up one morning from unsettling dreams, he found himself changed in his bed into a monstrous vermin." Many other writers questioned traditional Western values, especially in the face of wars and new ideas about the human mind and human behavior. In their work, they often chose to address controversial social and political issues.

Response to War After serving in the German army during World War I, **Erich Maria Remarque** (1898–1970) wrote his famous novel *All Quiet on the Western Front*, an emotionally accurate and critical portrayal of the experiences of German soldiers in the war. After moving to Switzerland in 1930, Remarque wrote a number of other works critical of unquestioning patriotism and the horrors of war. The Nazis burned his works, and he moved to the United States in 1939.

Stream of Consciousness Another literary trend that emerged in the 1920s came from an interest in exploring the unconscious, as Surrealism had done in the visual arts. Writers used a technique known as stream of consciousness, which presented a character's inner thoughts as they occurred in the form of an unspoken monologue. Readers often had to piece together the meaning that the author conveyed in this way.

For example, the Irish writer **James Joyce** (1882–1941) used this technique to explore the minds of ordinary people in Dublin in the course of a single day in his novel *Ulysses*. The British author **Virginia Woolf** (1882–1942) used her own version of this technique in novels such as *Mrs. Dalloway* to reveal the world in which her characters lived. In her work, Woolf also challenged traditional roles for women, who were generally expected to be wives and mothers rather than artists.

Theater The philosopher Jean-Paul Sartre was also a playwright. His play *No Exit*, written in 1944, was a dramatic expression of his existentialist ideas, which he had articulated in the same year in his nonfiction *Being and Nothingness*. In *No Exit*, three characters are confined in a hotel room representing hell. They must face themselves through the perceptions of the others, creating an environment of eternal pain.

After World War II, the disillusionment with life in Europe was strongly expressed in literature in the Theater of the Absurd movement, which Sartre's work inspired. The Irish playwright Samuel Beckett (1906–1990) challenged the conventions of theater in works such as *Waiting for Godot*, in which nothing seemed to happen as two characters waited for the mysterious Godot to appear. It was clear to the audience that the action was not intended to portray reality. Beckett and other playwrights even questioned whether language was capable of accurately communicating about the real world.

American Cultural Influences

After World War II, the United States emerged as one of two world super powers—a leader economically, militarily, and politically. It also became an increasingly strong influence on European culture—at the elite level of fine art and at the popular level too. In elite culture, American influence was particularly strong in the visual arts and architecture. Technology and popular culture from the United States generated both enthusiasm and criticism.

Movies Film was a primary medium for bringing American popular culture to Europe. Charlie Chaplin's *Modern Times*, for example, was a slapstick comedy from 1936 that skewered industrialization and provided escapism during the Great Depression. It earned more money in other countries, especially Great Britain, than it did in the United States. By the 1960s, the European market accounted for 40 percent of the income for Hollywood filmmakers. At the same time, many European filmmakers made movies that were popular in art houses and independent cinemas in both Europe and the United States. Directors in Sweden, Italy, and France made movies that were more experimental than those that came out of Hollywood.

Television This new technology became widely available in the United States after the war and spread to Europe and other parts of the world in the 1960s. Along with private automobiles and home ownership, television became the hallmark of a middle-class American lifestyle. As the technology spread, American broadcasters sold their programming to European countries at very low prices. For example, the British Broadcasting Corporation (BBC) could buy American programs for a small fraction of what it cost to produce their own programs. Most European governments had state-controlled television and eventually established quota systems to limit the amount of American programming, which continued to be very popular. However, commercial television began to grow in Western Europe in the 1980s. In the early 2020s, the U.S.-based streaming platforms Amazon Prime, Netflix, and Disney+ were extremely popular with European audiences.

Popular Music While European composers such as Stravinsky and Schoenberg led the revolution in classical music in the 20th century, several innovations in popular music came from America and were based on African American music. These styles included blues, jazz, rock and roll, rap, house, and hip-hop. For example, rock and roll began in the United States in the 1950s. It built on the rhythm and blues music of Black performers, including Little Richard and Chuck Berry, and was adapted by performers such as Elvis Presley, Buddy Holly, and many others. In the 1960s, rock and roll became a worldwide phenomenon as American music inspired British groups, including the Beatles, who became wildly popular in the United States and elsewhere. This reciprocal influence also occurred in the 1970s when the punk movement that started in New York spread to Britain and back to the United States.

New Technologies In addition to art and architecture, technology shaped culture and everyday life in new ways:

- Indoor plumbing made life cleaner and more comfortable.
- Electricity and refrigeration meant that foods were cheaper, more varied, and more widely available.
- Plastics protected foods and medicines and made them safer to consume.
- Synthetic fibers meant that clothing and furnishings could be cheaper as well as more durable, colorful, and plentiful.

These innovations quickly became such integral parts of modern life that it became difficult to imagine existence without them. They helped fuel a **consumer culture** in Europe and the United States in which people came to expect that products would continuously improve and would delight users instead of merely satisfying them.

Political and Social Movements

You learned about feminist movements in Topic 9.8. Other political and social movements existed alongside the feminist movement. In each case, members of a particular group sought respect, power, and guarantees of their civil rights.

Population Growth One way for a country to become more powerful is for its population to increase. Therefore, some European governments followed a policy of **neonatalism**. They encouraged people to have more children by subsidizing many of the expenses that children bring. They also provided nutrition programs for young children and opened government-run or government-funded childcare facilities. Europe experienced a baby boom after World War II as people who had put off having children decided to have them. That boom tapered off as birth control methods became more reliable in the 1960s and later. The increase in the youth population in Europe had significant political and social effects.

Youth Revolts of 1968 A generation that had experienced neither economic depression nor total war came of age in the 1960s. It was also the first generation to grow up under the threat of nuclear destruction. The combination of forces created tensions between older and younger people around the world known as the generation gap.

As a movement, young people criticized existing institutions and beliefs while also calling for greater political and personal freedoms. Many students believed that leadership—either of their governments or educational institutions—was more interested in global security than in providing opportunity. In this period, echoes from the United States had an important effect on student action in Europe.

Several events led to massive student unrest in 1968. The year opened with young people in Czechoslovakia protesting Communist Party rule. Their action inspired movements in Rome and Paris. In France, the May student revolts against consumerism, capitalism, and traditional values sparked labor strikes as well, with 11 million workers walking off their jobs. Other student outbreaks soon followed, from London to Yugoslavia. The student movements produced few immediate concrete gains, but they raised awareness of persistent class divisions that seemed to prevent real democracy from taking hold in Europe. The students' efforts also highlighted gender divisions that would spark the women's movement.

GOALS OF UPRISINGS IN EUROPE IN, 1968

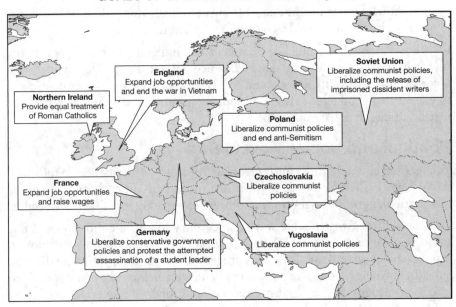

Gay and Lesbian Movements Organized movements for gay, lesbian, bisexual, transgender, and queer (LGBTQ) people may have started after other movements in Europe, but individuals in this group had a long history of struggle. Discrimination was widespread and legal. Aversion therapy—or the practice of attempting to rid an individual of homosexual tendencies—was practiced in most Western countries from the 1950s to the 1960s, often using painful electric shock therapy.

In France, the beginning of the gay liberation movement is commonly identified as May 1, 1971. A small group of protestors interrupted France's popular May Day celebrations. A decade later, in 1981, there were mass demonstrations against laws that supported discrimination against LGBTQ people. Since 1995, gay and lesbian people have obtained full legal rights throughout Europe, although social rights have not been achieved everywhere. In the early 2020s, opposition to gay rights was particularly strong in parts of Italy, Poland, and France.

REFLECT ON THE ESSENTIAL QUESTION

Essential Question: *How and why has European culture changed from the end of World War II to the present?*

How European Culture Changed	Why European Culture Changed

KEY TERMS

existentialism	Pope Paul VI	Igor Stravinsky
Friedrich Nietzsche	Cubism	Arnold Schoenberg
nihilist	Futurism	Richard Strauss
Jean-Paul Sartre	Dadaism	Franz Kafka
postmodernism	Surrealism	Erich Maria Remarque
Dietrich Bonhoeffer	Salvador Dalí	James Joyce
Martin Niemöller	Abstract Expressionism	Virginia Woolf
Pope John Paul II	Pop Art	consumer culture
Second Vatican Council	Modernist	neonatalism
Pope John XXIII	Bauhaus	

Questions 1–3 refer to the passage below.

"Even very recently, the elders could say: 'You know, I have been young and you never have been old.' But today's young people can reply: 'You never have been young in the world I am young in, and you never can be.' This is the common experience of pioneers and their children. In this sense, all of us who were born and reared before the 1940s are immigrants in today's culture. Like first-generation pioneers, we were reared to have skills and values that are only partly appropriate in this new time, but we are the elders who still command the techniques of government and power. And like immigrant pioneers from colonizing countries, we cling to the belief that the children will, after all, turn out to be much like ourselves. But balancing this hope there is the fear that the young are being transformed into strangers before our eyes, that teen-agers gathered at a street corner are to be feared like the advance guard of an invading army. . . .

Today, suddenly, because all the peoples of the world are part of one electronically based, intercommunicating network, young people everywhere share a kind of experience that none of the elders ever have had or will have. Conversely, the older generation will never see repeated in the lives of young people their own unprecedented experience of sequentially emerging change. This break between generations is wholly new: it is planetary and universal."

—Margaret Mead, *Culture and Commitment,*
1978, based on lectures given in 1969

1. The historical development that Mead describes in this passage is best described as
   (A) a competition between immigrants and native-born people occurring in several countries
   (B) a gap between people based on when they were born and raised
   (C) a conflict among groups of people who control government and power
   (D) a rivalry between countries based on their experiences in and right after World War II

2. Which of the following aspects of the historical context does Mead emphasize in this passage?

   (A) The changes in birthrates between older and younger generations

   (B) The advances in technology in communication and transportation

   (C) The movements around the world for feminism, LGBT rights, and racial equality

   (D) The development of international organizations such as the United Nations

3. Which of the following best describes Mead's point of view about the changes she describes in this passage?

   (A) An advocate who wants to encourage the changes taking place

   (B) An observer who sees similar changes in many countries at the same time

   (C) A skeptic who wonders if the changes are worthwhile

   (D) An opponent who thinks the changes are happening too quickly

SHORT-ANSWER QUESTION

Answer all parts of the question that follows.

1. a) Describe ONE way in which the Christian churches challenged modern secularism in the second half of the 20th century.

   b) Explain ONE similarity between the role of organized religion in Eastern Europe and in Western Europe from 1950 to 1991.

   c) Explain ONE difference between the role of organized religion in Eastern Europe and in Western Europe from 1950 to 1991.

Topic 9.15

Continuity and Change in the 20th and 21st Centuries

Our society is run by insane people for insane objectives. I think we're being run by maniacs for maniacal ends and I think I'm liable to be put away as insane for expressing that. That's what's insane about it.

—John Lennon, British musician and peace advocate

Essential Question: How did the challenges of the 20th century influence what it means to be European?

In the 20th and 21st centuries, Europe has dealt with many challenges. The chaos of two world wars, economic crises, the break-up of several multiethnic states, and the uncertainty of the Cold War led to significant changes in Europe. Ideological battles developed and intensified, which led to a polarized continent. In spite of this division and the occasional rise of virulent nationalist sentiments, political and economic unity among nations grew over time. The transition Europe was experiencing was reflected in its social and intellectual movements.

Conflicts and Political Instability From 1945–1991, a Cold War simmered between the United States and the Soviet Union based on political and economic differences. The Cold War grew into a global conflict forcing many nations to choose a side for the sake of security and prosperity. Europe divided between the democratic West and the communist East. Conflict among the countries of Europe represents a continuity over time. However, beginning slowly in the 1950s and accelerating after the fall of Communism in the early 1990s, Europe has made strides to reunify through various economic and political organizations such as the European Parliament and the European Union. Although European countries had long engaged in alliances and made other efforts toward continental unity, such as the Concert of Europe in the post-Napoleonic era, this level of Europe-wide cooperation and solidarity represents a decided change.

Continuity is evident in the various smaller-scale 20th-century conflicts that took place in Europe, as long-standing issues attached to ethnicity and political and/or military domination came to a head. In Spain, Basque separatists sought autonomy, while in Ireland, those who sought to unite the island fought to get the British out. In southeastern Europe, the multiethnic state of Yugoslavia disintegrated into its component countries when festering economic and political issues helped bring out age-old divisions along ethnic and religious lines. Even in Belgium, where Brussels is the seat of government and de facto capital of the European Union, centuries-old divisions between the Flemish- and French-speaking populations flared up.

Ideological Challenges Economic crises, ethnic tensions, and internal disagreements are not new to Europe. However, the response by European nations to these problems represent a change. Ideologies were shaped and redesigned by European leaders during the second half of the 20th century. The democracies of Western Europe, with the help of U.S. capital, developed the welfare state to rebuild a war-torn Europe. Communist nations of Eastern Europe expected the Soviet Union to respond to their changing political and economic needs. Soviet decline was apparent as satellite nations, such as Czechoslovakia and Poland, pushed for opportunities to explore democratic governments and capitalist economies. This foreshadowed the collapse of the Soviet Union and the end of the Cold War.

Diverse Intellectual and Cultural Movements The devastation of World War I and World War II, the worldwide economic collapse of the Great Depression, and the political and ideological divide of the Cold War led to significant changes in European thought and culture. Science and technology had long been seen as purely positive, holding the promise of progress for societies and individuals. However, modern warfare and the specter of nuclear annihilation seriously challenged this view. Two long-held pillars of European thought, reason and religion—often portrayed as opposites—were challenged as well. To many Europeans, the tragedies of the 20th century defied explanation through traditional logic or theology. Existentialism and postmodernism developed as a result, and religious belief and participation declined.

These changes in ways of thinking led to the liberalization of society, especially in Western Europe, for traditionally marginalized groups—particularly women and members of the LGBTQ community. New and evolving artistic endeavors in all fields flourished during the 20th century, often drawing inspiration from the century's tragedies and the resulting lack of moral and intellectual certainty. Traditional ideas of what constitutes "art" were challenged by writers such as Joyce and Woolf, composers such as Stravinsky, and visual artists such as Picasso and Dalí.

QUESTIONS ABOUT CONTINUITY AND CHANGES

1. How did the violent challenges of the 20th century influence the lives of Europeans?

2. How did the intellectual and cultural challenges of the 20th century influence the lives of Europeans?

WRITE AS A HISTORIAN: *ORGANIZE AN ESSAY*

When writing an essay answering a historical question, analyze the sources and use your knowledge of their context to explain big ideas and create defensible arguments. Organize your thoughts so they are clear to the reader.

The following questions are based on this prompt: Evaluate the extent to which the Cold War changed Europe's relationship with the rest of the world.

1. Which statement is the better thesis statement?

   a. During the Cold War struggle between the United States and the USSR. European countries used their wealth to continue exerting their power in international affairs even as they developed new ways to work together through international institutions.

   b. Although the Cold War has been seen by some historians as an ideological fight only between the two super powers, it also sustained established patterns in European traditions of dealing with other countries.

2. Select the *three* ideas that could best be the basis of topic sentences.

   a. An examination of new Cold War alliances and how they compared to alliances and military build-ups leading to both world wars

   b. An explanation of how the Cold War divided Europe into opposing factions, noting how economic differences shaped foreign policies

   c. A survey of America's political climate during the Cold War, including the McCarthy hearings and spy scandals

   d. An analysis of how European countries continued to have close relationships with lands they had once colonized

   e. A review of the events leading up to the construction of the Berlin Wall and to its destruction

3. Which reasoning process does this prompt focus on?

4. If you were to explain how World War I, the rise of communism, and World War II laid the groundwork for the Cold War, which reasoning skills would you be using?

LONG ESSAY QUESTIONS

Directions: Suggested writing time is 40 minutes. In your response, you should do the following:

- Respond to the prompt with a historically defensible thesis that establishes a line of reasoning.
- Describe a broader historical context relevant to the prompt.
- Support an argument in response to the prompt using specific and relevant examples of evidence.
- Use historical reasoning (e.g., comparison, causation, continuity and change over time) to frame or structure an argument that addresses the prompt.
- Use evidence to corroborate, qualify, or modify an argument that addresses the prompt.

1. Evaluate the various ways that nationalism caused instability within Europe from 1914 to 2014.

2. Evaluate the different goals of nationalist movements during the 20th century.

DOCUMENT-BASED QUESTION

Directions: Question 1 is based on the accompanying documents. The documents have been edited for the purpose of this exercise. You are advised to spend 15 minutes planning and 45 minutes writing your answer. In your response, you should do the following:

- **Thesis:** Make a defensible claim that establishes a line of reasoning and consists of one or more sentences found in one place.
- **Contextualization:** Relate the argument to a broader historical context.
- **Document Evidence:** Use content from at least six documents.
- **Outside Evidence:** Use one piece of evidence not in the documents.
- **Document Sourcing:** Explain how or why the point of view, purpose, situation, or intended audience is relevant for at least three documents.
- **Analysis:** Show the relationships among pieces of historical evidence and use them to support, qualify, or modify an argument.

1. Evaluate the extent to which Cold War politics affected international affairs during the period 1949–1989.

Document 1:

Source: Fidel Castro, speech to a group of farmers and farmworkers, February 24, 1959

Let us not speak about promises but about realities. The peasants had always lived under terror, they did not have faith because they had been deceived, they did not have hope. While the enemy [the troops supporting Batista] took away everything, stole everything, and did not pay for what they took, in spite of the many millions they had, the Rebel Army did the opposite. Nothing stopped Batista's Army from stealing personal belongings from the peasants, which were sold later. When they did not find anything to take, they just burned the houses. How little they thought about the efforts that had been needed to build them!

How easily they burned houses! How easily they murdered people! The conduct of the Rebel Army gained little by little the peasants' confidence, their love, and gave them faith in the final victory. We never took anything from the peasants without paying for it, we never invaded their houses. The Rebel Army never took anything that had not been spontaneously offered. Never a rebel soldier humiliated a peasant.

Document 2:

Source: Winston Churchill, speech, Fulton, Missouri, March 5, 1946

A shadow has fallen upon the scenes so lately lighted by the Allied victory. Nobody knows what Soviet Russia and its Communist international organization intends to do in the immediate future, or what are its limits, if any, to their expansive and proselytizing tendencies. I have a strong admiration and regard for the valiant Russian people and for my wartime comrade, Marshal Stalin.

. . . It is my duty, however . . . for me to state the facts as I see them to you.

. . . From Stettin in the Baltic to Trieste in the Adriatic, an iron curtain has descended across the continent. Behind that line lie all the capitals of the ancient states of Central and Eastern Europe, Warsaw, Berlin, Prague, Vienna, Budapest, Belgrade, Bucharest and Sofia, all these famous cities and the population around them lie in what I must call the Soviet sphere, and all are subject in one form or another, not only to Soviet influence but to a very high degree . . . of control from Moscow. If the Western democracies stand together in strict adherence to the principles of the United Nations Charter . . . no one is likely to molest them. If however they become divided or falter in their duty . . . then indeed catastrophe may overwhelm us all.

Document 3:

Source: Lord Ismay, Secretary General of NATO, Rome, October 18, 1952

[Unity] binds the 14 nations of the Atlantic Alliance together. I stress the word unity because that is what matters more than anything else: that is the real answer to the threat of aggression, that is what potential enemies fear more than anything else; that is what they want to destroy more than anything else. We must be on guard against the sometimes persuasive whispers and insinuations of propagandists who seek to magnify our differences and try to drive a wedge in our unity. Nations cannot afford to stand alone to be picked off one by one. We have the eloquent evidence of countries that formerly were free, independent, and important members of the Western European community, who now have fallen under the domination and imperialistic exploitation of the Soviet. Clearly we must arm up to the limit in order to be as strong as possible as rapidly as possible, but not at the expense of national bankruptcy. We cannot afford, through excessive haste to avert the hot war, to lose the cold one. Our alliance, it cannot be too often repeated, is purely defensive. Not a ship, not a plane, not a gun will ever be used except in self-defense. And no one knows better than the Soviet General Staff that the forces we plan are of a magnitude which can never be put to offensive or aggressive purposes.

Document 4:

Source: Hans M. Kristensen and Robert S. Norris, "Global Nuclear Stockpiles, 1945–2006," *Bulletin of the Atomic Scientists*, July 1, 2006 (data for 2015 from Arms Control Association, armscontrol.org)

NUCLEAR WEAPONS STOCKPILES, 1945 TO 2015		
Year	United States	Soviet Union
1945	6	0
1955	3,057	200
1965	31,982	6,129
1975	27,826	19,055
1985	24,237	39,197
1995	12,144	27,000
2005	10,295	17,000
2015	7,100	7,700

Document 5:

Source: Belgrade Declaration, the first conference of the Non-Aligned Movement, 1961

Imperialism is weakening. Colonial empires and other forms of foreign oppression of peoples in Asia, Africa and Latin America are gradually disappearing from the stage of history. Great successes have been achieved in the struggle of many peoples for national independence and equality . . .

The governments of countries participating in the Conference resolutely reject the view that war, including the "cold war," is inevitable as this view reflects a sense both of helplessness and hopelessness and is contrary to the progress of the world. They affirm their unwavering faith that the international community is able to organize its life without resorting to means which actually belong to a past epoch of human history.

Document 6:

Source: A West German soldier is standing in front of the Berlin Wall, with an armed East German soldier sitting on top of the wall

Credit: Library of Congress

Document 7:

Source: *Izvestia*, the newspaper for expressing views of the Soviet government, March 13, 1947

On March 12, President Truman addressed a message to the U.S. Congress asking for 400 million dollars to be assigned for urgent aid to Greece and Turkey, and for authority to send to those countries American civil and military personnel, and to provide for the training by Americans by specially picked Greek and Turkish personnel. . . .

Commenting on Truman's message to Congress, the *New York Times* proclaims the advent of "the age of American responsibility." Yet what is this responsibility but a smokescreen for expansion? The cry of saving Greece and Turkey from the expansion of the so-called "totalitarian states" is not new. Hitler used to refer to the Bolsheviks when he wanted to open the road for his own conquests. Now they want to take Greece and Turkey under their control, they raise a din about "totalitarian states." This seems all the more attractive since, in elbowing in itself, the U.S.A. is pushing non-totalitarian Britain out of yet another country or two.

AP® European History
Practice Exam

Section 1

PART A: MULTIPLE-CHOICE QUESTIONS

Directions: Each of the questions or incomplete statements below is followed by four suggested answers or completions. Select the one that is best in each case.

Questions 1–4 refer to the chart below.

COPIES OF BOOKS PRINTED IN WESTERN EUROPE		
Period	**Total Number**	**Number per Person**
1301–1400	3 million	fewer than 0.1
1401–1500	5 million	fewer than 0.1
1501–1600	210 million	0.2
1601–1700	540 million	0.5
1701–1800	990 million	0.8

Source: Adapted from www.OurWorldInData.org/data/media-communications/books; data from Eltjo Buringh and Jan Luiten van Zanden, "Charting the 'Rise of the West,'" *Journal of Economic History*, 2009

1. Which trend in Europe provides the most important part of the context for the trend shown on the table?
   - (A) The increased use of Latin as the primary written language for scholars
   - (B) The spread of humanist ideas into northern Europe
   - (C) The rising power of the Holy Roman emperor
   - (D) The expansion of educational opportunities for women

2. A historian might use the data in the table to support the claim that the number of printed books was
   - (A) a significant factor in the spread of the ideas of Martin Luther and John Calvin
   - (B) one sign of the development of centralized nation-states after the Peace of Westphalia
   - (C) a major cause in the expansion by European states of their overseas colonial empires
   - (D) a direct result of the spread of industrialization from Great Britain to other parts of Europe

3. The information in the table describes a change that contributed most directly to which development?

(A) The expansion of capitalist investment through written agreements to form joint-stock companies

(B) The establishment of republican governments based upon written constitutions

(C) The movement of people from rural to urban areas

(D) The publication of scientific writings that challenged classical learning

4. Which claim is best supported by the change in the number of books printed per person in Western Europe between 1300 and 1600?

(A) The number of books printed per person was increasing because the total population was decreasing.

(B) The total number of books printed was increasing because monarchs used books to spread their influence.

(C) The demand for books per person changed little because few people needed to read books for their work.

(D) The total demand for books was increasing because more people were learning to read.

Questions 5–7 refer to the following passage.

"The chief cause that I fell out with the pope was this: the pope boasted that he was the head of the Church, and condemned all that would not be under his power and authority; for he said, although Christ be the head of the Church, yet, notwithstanding, there must be a corporal head of the Church upon earth. With this I could have been content, had he but taught the gospel pure and clear, and not introduced human inventions and lies in its stead. Further, he took upon him power, rule, and authority over the Christian Church, and over the Holy Scriptures, the Word of God; no man must presume to expound the Scriptures, but only he, and according to his ridiculous conceits; so that he made himself lord over the Church, proclaiming her at the same time a powerful mother, and empress over the Scriptures, to which we must yield and be obedient; this was not to be endured. They who, against God's Word, boast of the Church's authority, are mere idiots. . . .

We, through God's grace, are not heretics, but schismatics, causing, indeed, separation and division, wherein we are not to blame, but our adversaries, who gave occasion thereto, because they remain not by God's Word alone, which we have, hear, and follow."

—Martin Luther, *Against Catholicism*, 1535

5. Which statement best describes the historical context in which Luther wrote this passage?

   (A) German rulers were resisting the power of the pope.

   (B) Nation-states were emerging throughout Europe.

   (C) The condition of peasants was improving because serfdom was being abolished.

   (D) The economy was changing because the Industrial Revolution was beginning.

6. Based on this passage, which of the following would Luther most likely have supported?

   (A) Replacing priests with volunteer ministers so that each local church would become its own authority

   (B) Breaking up the Holy Roman Empire so that each political state could develop its own version of Christianity

   (C) Making the pope into a political leader rather than a religious leader

   (D) Reading the Bible during worship services so that individuals could hear the words for themselves

7. Which individual would most likely share the point of view expressed by Luther in this passage?

   (A) Christopher Columbus because of his role spreading Christianity

   (B) Desiderius Erasmus because of his writings about religious reforms

   (C) Charles V because he was a Holy Roman Emperor

   (D) Mary Tudor because of her policies on religion while queen of England

Questions 8–10 refer to the following passage.

"The Thirty Years' War was extraordinarily violent and was the first war in European history to involve most European powers in one way or another. Indeed, some scholars have seen the war as merely a part of one or more much larger and longer international conflicts involving especially the French Bourbons, the Spanish and Austrian Habsburgs, the Dutch, the Scandinavian powers, Poland-Lithuania, and England. . . . The Ottoman Turks were also extremely interested in the progress of the war, as were the English, though neither were direct combatants. Given such international connection, the very name 'Thirty Years' War' could be misleading, since it suggests an artificial time limit for a much broader series of struggles over control of Europe itself.

Yet the Thirty Years' War, while clearly and strongly connected to the broader international scene, was also very much a distinct and inwardly focused civil war. This is the view supported by contemporary residents of the empire who saw their war as different from the other international conflicts of the time, and who began call it 'the Thirty Years' War' as soon as it was over. . . . In this volume I pursue this narrower understanding of the war, focusing on the empire itself and its residents."

—Tryntje Helffrich, *The Thirty Years War: A Documentary History*, 2009

8. Helffrich supports how her point of view on the Thirty Years' War differs from the one expressed by other historians by stating which of the following?

   (A) She reminds people of how violent the war was.

   (B) She explains how the war pulled in most European powers.

   (C) She says that some people find the name of the war misleading.

   (D) She notes how people at the time described the war.

9. Which of the following events refutes the interpretation Helffrich proposes in the second paragraph?

   (A) Forces of the Roman Catholic Emperor Ferdinand II defeated the forces of the Calvinist King of Bohemia Frederick I at the Battle of White Mountain.

   (B) Forces of the Roman Catholic Emperor Ferdinand II occupied part of Lutheran Denmark for a time.

   (C) Roman Catholic Cardinal Richelieu of France funded the Protestant forces under Gustavus Adolphus.

   (D) Roman Catholic Spain supported the Roman Catholic Holy Roman Emperor in battles in northern German states.

10. Which of the following results of the Thirty Years' War most directly supports Helffrich's main point about the war?

(A) Millions of people in central Europe died from the war, most because of famine and disease.

(B) The Peace of Westphalia weakened the Holy Roman Empire and strengthened French, Swedish, and German rulers.

(C) The war and treaties ended hopes that Roman Catholics and Lutherans in Europe would unite in one interpretation of Christianity.

(D) States agreed that other states could recognize Calvinism as valid religious faith.

Questions 11–13 refer to the following passages.

Passage 1

"Others again have propounded other reasons why there are more superstitious women found than men. And the first is, that they are more credulous; and since the chief aim of the devil is to corrupt faith, therefore he rather attacks them. . . .

The second reason is, that women are naturally more impressionable, and more ready to receive the influence of a disembodied spirit; and that when they use this quality well they are very good, but when they use it ill they are very evil.

The third reason is that they have slippery tongues, and are unable to conceal from the fellow-women those things which by evil arts they know, and since they are weak, they find an easy and secret manner of vindicating themselves by witchcraft. . . . All wickedness is but little to the wickedness of a woman."

—Heinrich Kramer, *Malleus Maleficarum*, 1487

Passage 2

"It is amazing to see so many demons and evil spirits and so many male and female witches confined to the Labourd, which is but a little corner of France, and to see that it is almost like a nursery [for the witches]; nowhere else in Europe, as far as we know, is there anything that approaches the vast number of them that we found here. . . .

And in order to show clearly that natural conditions are in part to blame for the presence of so many witches, it is important to note that this is a mountainous country that shares borders with three kingdoms: French, Basque, and Spanish. . . . All this diversity affords Satan excellent opportunities for organizing his assemblies and sabbaths in this area, especially since the seacoast makes the people rustic, rough, and badly controlled. . . . They are a people who for the least bit of strangeness that they observe will run after you and put their knife to your throat."

—Pierre de Lancre, *On the Inconstancy of Witches*, 1612

11. Which of the following accurately describes the ideas of both Kramer and Lancre?
    (A) Both argue that individuals begin the process of practicing witchcraft by seeing out the devil to teach them.
    (B) Both state that the religious conflicts in Europe contributed to the spread of witchcraft.
    (C) Kramer emphasizes the influence of traits a person is born with while Lancre focuses on the environment a person lives in.
    (D) Kramer asserts that witches are more common in some parts of Europe while Lancre believes that witches are equally common throughout Europe.

12. Which of the following developments was most directly connected to the ideas expressed by Kramer and Lancre?
    (A) The number of convents and monasteries increased, so people had more opportunities to study, write, and show leadership.
    (B) European Christians became more united in their beliefs, so they became more effective fighting common enemies.
    (C) People began to feel more power to fight against evil, so they became more willing to confront religious disagreements.
    (D) The development of capitalism decreased the control people felt over their land, so they felt more insecure economically.

13. How did the writings of Kramer, Lucre, and others affect the numbers of people accused of and convicted of witchcraft during the 16th and early 17th centuries?
    (A) Accusations and convictions both increased
    (B) Accusations increased but convictions decreased
    (C) Accusations decreased but convictions increased
    (D) Accusations and convictions both decreased

THE EXPANSION OF THE AUSTRIAN HABSBURG EMPIRE, 1525–1805

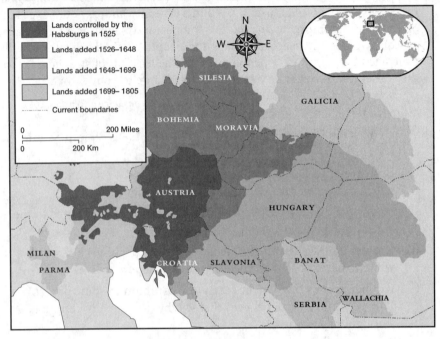

14. Which of the following best explains the context for the changes in Habsburg Empire shown on this map?

    (A) The growth of Russia power in the 17th and 18th centuries limited the eastward expansion of the empire

    (B) The Peace of Westphalia strengthened the power of countries west and north of the empire

    (C) The decline in the power of the Swedes in the early 18th century allowed for the expansion of the empire

    (D) The partitions of Poland in the late 18th century weakened the empire

15. Which event or trend within the Habsburg Empire contributed to the shift shown on this map?

    (A) The religious goals of Philip II in Europe and overseas

    (B) The Habsburg's successful defense of Vienna against an Ottoman attack in 1683

    (C) The desire of the Habsburgs' for peaceful relations with the tsars who controlled Russia in the 18th and 19th centuries

    (D) The Habsburg monarchy's failure to implement absolutist government in the 18th century

16. The map reflects which of the following 18th- and 19th-century developments?

    (A) The growing power of the Ottoman Empire helped them solidify their control over Hungary.

    (B) Economic development in Western Europe attracted attacks by less wealthy countries in central and Eastern Europe.

    (C) Despite France's victories in the Thirty Years' War, its army was weakened for much of the following century.

    (D) Despite the rise of nation-states, the dynastic interests of ruling families continue to shape diplomacy significantly.

17. The change in the Austrian Habsburg Empire shown on this map was most like the change in which other state in the same time period?

    (A) Great Britain because it created an empire based on a strong navy

    (B) Germany because it consolidated people who spoke variations of the same language under one ruler

    (C) Italy because it consolidated several regions under one government

    (D) Russia because it expanded its influence over neighboring but ethnically diverse regions

Questions 18–21 refer to the following passage.

"I think that in discussions of physical problems we ought to begin not from the authority of scriptural passages but from sense experiences and necessary demonstrations; for the holy Bible and the phenomena of nature proceed alike from the divine Word the former as the dictate of the Holy Ghost and the latter as the observant executrix [a female who carries out orders of another] of God's commands. . . .

From this I do not mean to infer that we need not have an extraordinary esteem for the passages of holy Scripture. On the contrary, having arrived at any certainties in physics, we ought to utilize these as the most appropriate aids in the true exposition of the Bible and in the investigation of those meanings which are necessarily contained therein, for these must be concordant [in agreement] with demonstrated truths. I should judge that the authority of the Bible was designed to persuade men of those articles and propositions which, surpassing all human reasoning could not be made credible by science, or by any other means than through the very mouth of the Holy Spirit. . . .

But I do not feel obliged to believe that the same God who has endowed us with senses, reason and intellect has intended us to forego their use and by some other means to give us knowledge which we can attain by them. He would not require us to deny sense and reason in physical matters which are set before our eyes and minds by direct experience or necessary demonstrations."

—Galileo Galilei, letter to the Grand Duchess of Tuscany, 1615

18. This passage most clearly demonstrates the influence of which development in how people thought about the world?

    (A) The reliance on classical Greek and Roman sources by Renaissance scholars

    (B) The desire for more accurate translations of the Bible by humanists

    (C) The promotion of reasoning and experimentation by thinkers during the Scientific Revolution

    (D) The emphasis on the authority of scripture by Protestant reformers

19. This passage best supports which of the following claims about scholars in the 17th century?

    (A) Most combined religious worldviews with the study of the natural world.

    (B) Most were Roman Catholic priests or bishops.

    (C) Most began their research to test the truth of statements in the Bible.

    (D) Most rejected the role of divine forces in the creation of the universe.

20. Ideas such as the ones conveyed in this passage contributed most directly to which of the following developments?

    (A) The Enlightenment because of its philosophies of skepticism and deism

    (B) Romanticism because of its emphasis on intuition and emotion

    (C) Social Darwinism because of its belief in the natural superiority of Western civilization

    (D) Positivism because of its application of science to solve social problems

21. Which change in the 17th century was based on a change or conflict most similar to the one that made writing this letter dangerous for Galileo?

(A) The development of mercantilism in England

(B) The rise to power of Louis XIV, who became known as the Sun King, in France

(C) The types of beliefs that led to the Thirty Years' War in central Europe

(D) The spreading influence of the Austrian Empire in southeastern Europe

Questions 22–25 refer to the following passage.

"Women, wake up; the tocsin [alarm] of reason is being heard throughout the whole universe; discover your rights. The powerful empire of nature is no longer surrounded by prejudice, fanaticism, superstition, and lies. The flame of truth has dispersed all the clouds of folly and usurpation. Enslaved man has multiplied his strength and needs recourse to yours to break his chains. Having become free, he has become unjust to his companion. Oh, women, women! When will you cease to be blind? What advantage have you received from the Revolution? Unite yourselves beneath the standards of philosophy; deploy all the energy of your character, and you will soon see these haughty men, not groveling at your feet as servile adorers, but proud to share with you the treasures of the Supreme Being. Regardless of what barriers confront you, it is in your power to free yourselves; you have only to want to."

—Olympe de Gouges, *Declaration of the Rights of Woman and Female Citizen*, 1791

22. Which statement about the Declaration of the Rights of Man is most useful in explaining the context in which de Gouges was writing?

(A) France had declared strong support for the rights of all women.

(B) France had proposed rights just for women of the nobility.

(C) France had encouraged wives to support their husbands.

(D) France had failed to extend equal rights to women.

23. Which group of women were the audience of de Gouges in this passage?

(A) All women of France

(B) Women of the French peasantry

(C) Women of the French bourgeoisie

(D) Women of the French royal court

24. Which of the following most accurately describes de Gouges's point of view about an ideal society?

(A) Women leading the government with men supervising life at home

(B) Women supervising life at home with men leading the government

(C) Women and men sharing control of government and life at home

(D) Women having full control of both government and life at home

25. Which individual was known for holding views about the rights of women most similar to those in this excerpt?

(A) Catherine de Medici

(B) Mary Wollstonecraft

(C) Maria Theresa

(D) Marie Antoinette

Questions 26–28 refer to the following passage.

"A little before noon on the 16th August, the first body of reformers began to arrive on the scene . . . in the town of Manchester. These persons bore two banners, surmounted with caps of liberty, and bearing the inscriptions, 'No Corn Laws,' 'Annual Parliaments,' 'Universal Suffrage,' 'Vote by Ballot." . . . The congregated multitude now amounted to a number roundly computed at 80,000. . . . The cavalry dashed into the crowd. The people began running in all directions; and from this moment the yeomanry lost all command of temper; numbers were trampled under the feet of men and horses; many, both men and women were cut down by sabers; several, and a peace officer and a female in the number, slain on the spot. The whole number of persons injured amounted to between three and four hundred."

—The Peterloo Massacre, *The Annual Register*, 1819

26. Followers of which ideology or movement would have been most in support of the actions taken against the reformers?

(A) Conservatism

(B) Liberalism

(C) Romanticism

(D) Democracy

27. Manchester was a likely location for the gathering described in the above passage because it

(A) was a center of the Agricultural Revolution

(B) was a port for mass emigration of people leaving England

(C) had grown rapidly as an industrial center

(D) had a radical newspaper that fomented protest

28. One long-term result of the event described in the passage and similar later events was which of the following?

(A) A steady decline in the trade union movement

(B) A gradual increase in unemployment

(C) A decrease in the free press

(D) An expansion in the right to vote

Questions 29–32 refer to the image below.

Front page of *Votes for Women*, a British newspaper published by the Women's Political and Social Union, June 1913. Below each figure is a list of the states in the United States and the countries in which women had the right to vote.

29. This image could best be used to illustrate which of the following historical development?

   (A) The growth of a cult of domesticity because it reflects the changing role of women in society

   (B) The rise of marketing because it reflects the increasing importance of women as consumers

   (C) The shift away from laissez-faire policies because it reflects a greater role for government

   (D) The emergence of mass politics because it is about expanding the number of people eligible to vote

30. Based on the imagery and intended audience, what was the most likely purpose for the newspaper?

   (A) To show women that full suffrage would never be achieved

   (B) To convince women that success at winning suffrage was achievable

   (C) To demonstrate to women that suffrage would make them more successful in business

   (D) To appeal to working-class women to join the suffrage movement

31. Which of the following contributed most directly to the continuation of the trend shown in this newspaper page?

   (A) The influence of World War I on gender roles

   (B) The impact of the Great Depression on employment

   (C) The growth of the welfare state after World War II

   (D) The desire to secure women's loyalty during the Cold War

32. Which of the following statements describes the context in which the changes shown in the image occurred?

   (A) Second-wave feminism was reaching its peak of influence.

   (B) The number of women studying in universities was rapidly increasing.

   (C) The status of British women at home and in the workplace was changing little.

   (D) Families were growing in size because they were having more children.

Questions 33–34 refer to the map below.

ITALIAN STATES PRIOR TO 1861 UNIFICATION

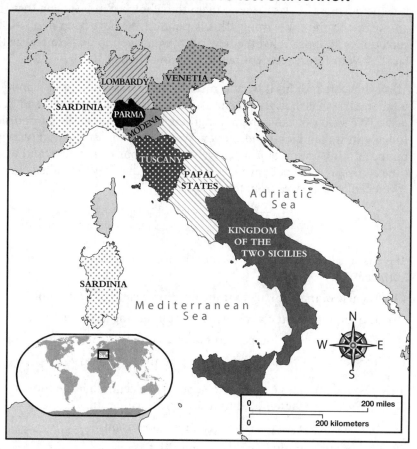

33. The changes that occurred by the end of 1861 for the states shown on the map most directly demonstrate

(A) the spread of nationalism in politics

(B) the interest in socialist ideas on the economy

(C) the importance of conservatism in culture

(D) the influence of industrialization on society

34. The states shown on the map went through a process in the 1850s and 1860s that was most similar to what was occurring at that time in

(A) France, which was also experiencing internal wars

(B) Germany, which was also unifying small states into a larger one

(C) The Hapsburg Empire, which was also facing conflicts among ethnic groups

(D) Russia, which was also expanding its influence into new territories

"Every Englishman knows that they are a mere handful in this country and it is the business of every one of them to befool you in believing that you are weak and they are strong. This is politics. We have been deceived by such policy so long. What the new party wants you to do is to realize the fact that your future rests entirely in your own hands. . . .

This is boycott and this is what is meant when we say, boycott is a political weapon. We shall not give them assistance to collect revenue and keep peace. We shall not assist them in fighting beyond the frontiers or outside India with Indian blood and money. We shall not assist them in carrying on the administration of justice. We shall have our own courts, and when time comes we shall not pay taxes. Can you do that by your united efforts? If you can, you are free from tomorrow."

—Indian nationalist Bal Gangadhar Tilak, speech to the
Indian National Congress, 1907

35. The passage best illustrates which of the following trends in the early 20th century?

   (A) The use of mass media to influence European public opinion
   (B) The growing financial burdens of maintaining a colonial empire
   (C) The resistance by indigenous nationalist movements to imperialism
   (D) The conscription of colonial troops in the world wars

36. This passage provides evidence to support the claim that the Indian National Congress attempted to resist British rule using

   (A) the tactic of resistance through noncooperation
   (B) the creation of intentional communities
   (C) the abolition of all centralized authority
   (D) the right to use arms in self-defense

37. This passage was part of a pattern in the 20th century of colonial subjects who wanted to win independence

   (A) by using economic and political pressure
   (B) by starting a violent revolution to overthrow colonial rule
   (C) by attracting Europeans to lead the resistance movement
   (D) by depending on a small colonial elite to achieve independence

Questions 38–40 refer to the image below.

Source: Wikimedia Commons/George Elgar Hicks, *The Sinews of Old England* (1857)

38. The scene in the painting most directly reflects which of the following historical developments?

   (A) The building of tenements in large cities

   (B) The construction of large homes on manorial estates

   (C) The decline of the cult of domesticity

   (D) The importance of the nuclear family model

39. Based on when the painting was created, which of the following best explains why the artist placed the figures at the threshold of a cottage?

   (A) It represented the meeting of rural and urban life.

   (B) It showed that higher living standards were emerging.

   (C) It showed the growing equality of men and women.

   (D) It marked the boundary between the spheres of women and men.

40. Which of the following most directly describes one way that this painting shows the influence of Romanticism in art?

(A) The organization shows balance and order

(B) The scene is something mysterious and possibly supernatural

(C) The emphasis is more on emotion than on reason

(D) The content is less important than the use of light and color

Questions 41–43 refer to the following passage.

"IRISHMEN AND IRISHWOMEN: In the name of God and of the dead generations from which she receives her old tradition of nationhood, Ireland, through us, summons her children to her flag and strikes for her freedom. . . .

Having resolutely waited for the right moment to reveal itself, she now seizes that moment, and supported by her exiled children in America and by gallant allies in Europe, but relying in the first on her own strength, she strikes in full confidence of victory. We declare the right of the people of Ireland to the ownership of Ireland and to the unfettered control of Irish destinies, to be sovereign and indefeasible. The long usurpation of that right by a foreign people and government has not extinguished the right, nor can it ever be extinguished except by the destruction of the Irish people. . . . Standing on that fundamental right and again asserting it in arms in the face of the world, we hereby proclaim the Irish Republic as a Sovereign Independent State."

—Proclamation of the Irish Republic, Easter 1916

41. Which of the following best explains why the writers of this proclamation believed the Irish were prepared to support them?

(A) European allies had secretly provided the Irish with military training.

(B) The British had failed to implement the Irish Home Rule bill.

(C) The German military had encouraged the Irish to rebel.

(D) The Irish had extensive experience in local constabulary actions.

42. Which of the following was the most important part of the historical context that led the Irish revolutionaries to claim it was the "right moment" for insurrection?

(A) Irish rebel leaders thought they had trained enough soldiers to be successful.

(B) Irish citizens resented how many Irish were fighting and dying for the British in World War I.

(C) The United States had indicated that it would allow Irish-Americans to support a rebellion.

(D) Easter was a time when many previous Irish rebellions had been launched.

43. The conflict started by the 1916 proclamation reflected the most historical continuity with

(A) the Greek War of Independence that began in 1821 because both were primarily nationalist movements

(B) the Decembrist Revolt in 1825 because both were ignited primarily to create a more liberal government

(C) the July Revolution in France in 1830 because both were primarily rebellions against autocratic monarchs

(D) the Revolutions of 1848 because they were all unsuccessful

Questions 44–46 refer to the table below.

UNEMPLOYMENT RATE IN BRITAIN AND GERMANY, 1920-1940		
Year	Britain	Germany
1920	2.0%	3.8%
1930	11.2%	15.3%
1932	15.6%	30.1%
1934	11.9%	14.9%
1936	9.4%	8.3%
1938	9.3%	2.1%
1940	3.3%	not available

Source: https://www.encyclopedia.com/education/news-and-education-magazines/global-impact-1929-1939

44. Which contributed most to the change in German unemployment between 1930 and 1932?

   (A) An increase in state spending on social welfare programs

   (B) The dependence on American loans and investment to settle reparations after World War I

   (C) The introduction of laborsaving machinery

   (D) An increase in labor strikes and factory shutdowns

45. Which caused the change in the German economy shown on the chart between 1932 and 1938?

   (A) The emigration of large numbers of Germans to the United States

   (B) The expansion of Germany's colonial markets

   (C) The Nazis' rearmament and remilitarization program

   (D) The establishment of the European Coal and Steel Community

46. Which of the following most accurately reflects the relationship between British and German unemployment in the years shown in the table?

   (A) British unemployment was caused by factors different from those causing unemployment in Germany.

   (B) British unemployment was less of a problem that was unemployment in Germany

   (C) British unemployment rose faster and declined faster than did unemployment in Germany.

   (D) British unemployment was never as high as unemployment in Germany, but it was slower to decline.

Questions 47–49 refer to the image below.

Source: Wikimedia Commons

Replica in Spain of the painting by Pablo Picasso, *Guernica*. Guernica was heavily bombed by Franco's forces in the Spanish Civil War.

47. Based on the painting *Guernica*, Picasso shows the most continuity with which of the following movements among writers?

(A) The neoclassicalism of Jane Austen and others because of how they expressed order and balance

(B) The Romanticism of Mary Shelley and others because of how they treated the supernatural

(C) The Romanticism of Victor Hugo and others because of how they connected art and politics

(D) The naturalism of Émile Zola and others because of how they represented reality

48. *Guernica* best exemplifies the reactions in 20th-century art against Realism known as

(A) Dadaism, which protested against the perceived purposeless of life

(B) Cubism, which showed one subject through many perspectives in a single painting

(C) Surrealism, which portrayed objects as they might appear in dreams or fantasies

(D) Pop art, which used works of popular culture such as movies, TV, and advertising

49. Which of the following best describes the most important part of the setting in which Picasso painted *Guernica*?

(A) The increasing use of radio and air travel were transforming events in one city into global news stories.

(B) A severe economic depression was causing high unemployment around the world.

(C) Artists, including painters, were experimenting with new ways of portraying reality.

(D) Both Mussolini in Italy and Hitler in Germany were giving military aid to the Spanish nationalists during Spain's Civil War.

Questions 50–51 refer to the map below

WORLD WAR II IN EUROPE, JANUARY 1942

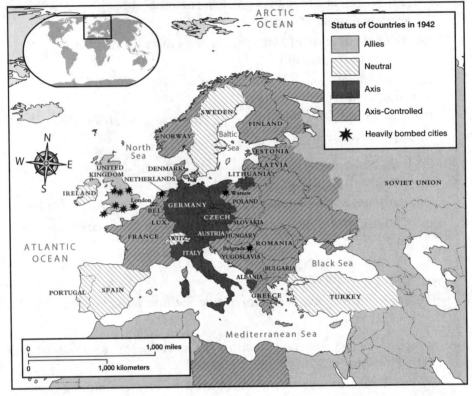

Source: thinglink.com

50. Which of the following contributed most directly to the pattern of Axis conquest shown on the map?

(A) The Axis countries had greater resources of iron and oil than did other European countries.

(B) Germany used tanks and planes to attack rapidly and with overwhelming power.

(C) Nazis found strong support within the countries they conquered.

(D) The British remained neutral in the war up until 1942.

51. Which of the following contributed most directly to a reversal of the patterns shown on the map?

(A) The creation of the Marshall Plan

(B) The actions of the League of Nations

(C) The military mobilization of the Soviet Union

(D) The use of nuclear weapons by the Allies

Questions 52–53 refer to the following passages.

Passage 1

"Soon after the end of the war, more and more tension arose between the victorious great powers, between the USSR on the one hand and the Western Allies, mainly the USA, on the other. The reason was the increasingly blatant imperialist drive of the USSR, which imposed the Bolshevist system of rule on one occupied country after another."

—Hans Ebeling, *The Journey into the Past*, a German history textbook, 1961

Passage 2

"At the end of the Second World War, the Soviet Union had lost more than 20 million people, and was devasted to a large extent. But the Red Army had occupied almost all of Eastern Europe and moved as far as Germany. . . In the long run, the Soviet head of state, Stalin, feared a conflict with the USA and other capitalist states. . . . [The United States] was the only country among the great powers not to suffer devastation. Its factories were producing more than ever before. . . . But the Americans also wanted to secure their economic dominance, and to reach this goal they needed free access to the markets and resources of the entire world."

—Dieter Burkard, *Travels Back in Time*, a German history textbook, 2010

52. Which of the following statements best explains the context in which the two sources were written?
    (A) Both authors wrote during the Cold War between the Western Allies and Germany.
    (B) Both authors wrote while Germany was united as one country
    (C) Ebeling wrote while Germany was divided and Burkard wrote while all of Germany was part of the European Community.
    (D) Ebeling wrote before the Cold War began and Burkard wrote after it ended.

53. Which of the following statements most accurately compares the main ideas in the two sources?
    (A) Both writers are critical of both the Western Allies and the Soviets.
    (B) Ebeling is more critical of the Soviets while Burkard is more critical of the Western Allies.
    (C) Ebeling is more critical of the Western Allies while Burkard is more critical of the Soviets.
    (D) Neither author is critical of either the Western Allies or the Soviets.

Questions 54–55 refer to the following passage.

"Simone de Beauvoir is seldom recognized by critics as a political thinker. . . . [Yet] we notice that Beauvoir was always thinking about political questions and responding to the historical-political events that unfolded in her lifetime (1908–1986). In essays, novels, and longer theoretical reflections, she discussed Stalinism, the disappointments of communism, and the purge trials; German occupation of France and the politics of collaboration and resistance; post World War II trials for collaborators and the articulation of crimes against humanity; racism in America; France's war in Algeria and the politics of colonization . . . .

Of all her writings, however, Beauvoir is by far best-known for The Second Sex. Her seven-hundred-plus page magnum opus on male theorization of 'Woman' and the challenges women's lived experience poses to any attempt to fix a feminine essence launched her reputation as a specifically feminist, rather than a more broadly political, thinker. The intense focus on this one book ironically served to obscure the importance of her other work, and its organic links to her political ideas. In the sixty-plus years following publication of The Second Sex, Beauvoir's reputation has been even more firmly associated specifically with feminist theory, and her work has been mostly ignored by other political theorists."

—Lori J. Marso, "Thinking Politically with Simone de Beauvoir
in *The Second Sex*," *Theory and Event*, 2012

54. Marso's main purpose in this passage is to show that Beauvoir
    (A) wrote about many political issues in addition to feminism
    (B) based her ideas on current political issues on her feminism
    (C) intended for people to read *The Second Sex* ironically
    (D) would be better known if she had not written *The Second Sex*

55. From the point of view of Marso, which of the following thinkers was Beauvoir most similar to in her ideas about liberty and equality?
    (A) Jerry Bentham because of his view on the theory of utility
    (B) John Stuart Mill because of his view on liberalism
    (C) Herbert Spencer because of his view on inherited traits of people
    (D) Mikhail Bakunin because of his views on anarchism

Section I

PART B: SHORT-ANSWER QUESTIONS

Directions: Use the passage below to answer all parts of the question that follows.

"The Germans accepted [Nazism] as a last act of desperation. A nation which appreciated its own excellent qualities and high abilities thought its existence menaced by chaos. It could not understand the reasons for this plight and refused to acquiesce. Millions of Germans from all classes and occupations felt the crisis to be so acute that the Nazis were quickly transformed from a small group of crackpots into a mass party led by a messiah determined upon action to restore the vigor and rightful glory of the German people. The ingredients of [Nazism] were derived in sufficient strength from the German past to be acceptable as German."

—Eugene N. Anderson, "Freedom and Authoritarianism in German History" in *The Struggle for Democracy in Germany*, 1949

1. a) Explain how ONE piece of evidence supports Anderson's argument regarding the causes of the success of the Nazis in Germany.

   b) Explain how ONE piece of evidence refutes Anderson's argument regarding the causes of the success of the Nazis in Germany.

   c) Explain ONE example of a development in another European country that resulted in a development similar to those described by Anderson.

Use the passage below to answer all parts of the question that follows.

"Our blood is too hot; we prefer to wear armor which is too heavy for our slender body; but we should use it nonetheless. The eyes of Germany are fixed not upon Prussia's liberalism but upon her armed might. Bavaria, Wurttemberg, and Baden [three German states] may indulge in liberal experiments; therefore no one will assign to them Prussia's role. Prussia must harbor and maintain her strength for the favorable moment—a moment which has already, on one occasion, slipped by; Prussia's boundaries, as drawn by the Vienna treaties, are not suitable for a healthy state life. The great questions of the day will not be decided by speeches or by majority decisions—that was the mistake of 1848 and 1849—but by blood and iron!"

—Otto von Bismarck, speech to the Prussian House of Representatives, 1862

2. a) Describe ONE significant change in German history represented by the ideas stated by Bismarck.

   b) Describe ONE significant continuity in German history represented by the ideas stated by Bismarck.

   c) Explain ONE significant effect of the changes in German history that resulted from the ideas stated by Bismarck.

Choose EITHER Question 3 OR Question 4.

3. a) Identify ONE significant cause of the rise of commercial capitalism starting in the 1600s.

   b) Identify ONE significant effect of the rise of commercial capitalism starting in the 1600s.

   c) Explain how the expansion of global trade influenced the early development of capitalism.

4. a) Identify ONE significant cause of the growth of imperialism starting in the 1800s.

   b) Identify ONE significant effect of the growth of imperialism starting in the 1800s.

   c) Explain how the growth of imperialism influenced international relations starting in the 1800s.

Section II

PART A: DOCUMENT-BASED QUESTION

Directions: Question 1 is based on the accompanying documents. The documents have been edited for the purpose of this exercise. In your response, you should do the following:

- Respond to the prompt with a historically defensible thesis or claim that establishes a line of reasoning.
- Describe a broader historical context relevant to the prompt.
- Support an argument in response to the prompt using at least six documents.
- Use at least one additional piece of specific historical evidence (beyond that found in the documents) relevant to an argument about the prompt.
- For at least three documents, explain how or why the document's point of view, purpose, historical situation, and/or audience is relevant to an argument.
- Use evidence to corroborate, qualify, or modify an argument that addresses the prompt.

Source: AP® European History Course and Exam Description, fall 2020

1. Evaluate the extent to which Enlightenment ideas supported the development of liberal ideas in European society from the late 17th century to the late 18th century.

Document 1

Source: John Locke, *An Essay Concerning Human Understanding*, 1689

Since it is *the understanding* that sets man above all other animals and enables him to use and dominate them, it is certainly worth our while to enquire into it. The understanding is like the eye in this respect: it makes us see and perceive all other things but doesn't look in on itself. To stand back from it and treat it as an object of study requires skill and hard work. Still, whatever difficulties there may be in doing this, whatever it is that keeps *us* so much in the dark to *ourselves*, it will be worthwhile to let as much light as possible in upon our minds, and to learn as much as we can about our own understandings. As well as being enjoyable, this will help us to think well about other topics

Document 2

Source: Baron de Montesquieu, *The Spirit of Laws*, 1748

There is no word that has admitted of more various significations, and has made more different impressions on human minds, than that of Liberty. Some have taken it for a facility of deposing a person on whom they had conferred a tyrannical authority; others for the power of choosing a person whom they are obliged to obey; others for the right of bearing arms, and of being thereby enabled to use violence, others in fine for the privilege of being governed by a native of their own country or by their own laws. . . .

There is ultimately a formula: a large state must be an autocracy, a medium sized state must be ruled as a kingdom and a small state can be ruled as a Republic. . . . There is also an ultimate formula that the English have achieved after their Glorious Revolution: an ultimate balance of power between the Monarch as an Executive power, the Parliament as the Legislative and the Judicial Branch.

Document 3

Source: Voltaire, *Candide*, 1759

"Do you believe," said Candide, "that men have always massacred each other as they do to-day, that they have always been liars, cheats, traitors, ingrates, brigands, idiots, thieves, scoundrels, gluttons, drunkards, misers, envious, ambitious, bloody-minded, calumniators, debauchees, fanatics, hypocrites, and fools?"

"Do you believe," said Martin, "that hawks have always eaten pigeons when they have found them?"

"Yes, without doubt," said Candide.

"Well, then," said Martin, "if hawks have always had the same character why should you imagine that men may have changed theirs?"

Document 4

Source: Jean-Jacques Rousseau, *Emile, or On Education*, 1762

Hold childhood in reverence, and do not be in any hurry to judge it for good or ill. . . .

You are afraid to see him spending his early years doing nothing. What! Is it nothing to be happy, nothing to run and jump all day? He will never be so busy again all his life long. . . . What would you think of a man who refused to sleep lest he should waste part of his life? You would say, "He is mad; he is not enjoying his life, he is robbing himself of part of it; to avoid sleep he is hastening his death." Remember . . . that childhood is the sleep of reason. . . .

Although memory and reason are wholly different faculties, the one does not really develop apart from the other. Before the age of reason the child receives images, not ideas; and there is this difference between them: images are merely the pictures of external objects, while ideas are notions about those objects determined by their relations.

Document 5

Source: Adam Smith, *The Wealth of Nations*, 1776

The greatest improvements in the productive powers of labor, and most of the skill, dexterity, and judgment with which it is directed or applied, seem to be results of the division of labor.

It will be easier to understand how the division of labor affects society in general if we first look at how it operates in some particular manufactures. . . .

In the large manufactures that are destined to meet the needs of the great body of the people, every branch of the work employs so many workmen that they can't be collected into a single workshop; so that we can't see more at one time than those employed in one branch. In such manufactures the work may be divided into many more parts than in the smaller ones, but the division is much less obvious and has accordingly been much less noticed.

Document 6

Source: Immanuel Kant, "What is Enlightenment," 1784

Enlightenment is man's leaving his self-caused immaturity. Immaturity is the incapacity to use one's intelligence without the guidance of another. Such immaturity is self-caused if it is not caused by lack of intelligence, but by lack of determination and courage to use one's intelligence without being guided by another. *Sapere Aude* [which is Latin for "dare to know"]! Have the courage to use your own intelligence! [This] is therefore the motto of the enlightenment.

Document 7

Source: *The Tennis Court Oath*, Jacques Louis David, early 1790s

Credit: Wikimedia Commons

PART B: LONG ESSAY QUESTIONS

Directions: Answer question 2 OR question 3 OR question 4. In your response, you should do the following:

- Respond to the prompt with a historically defensible thesis or claim that establishes a line of reasoning.
- Describe a broader historical context relevant to the prompt.
- Support an argument in response to the prompt using specific and relevant examples of evidence.
- Use historical reasoning (e.g., comparison, causation, continuity or change over time) to frame or structure an argument that addresses the prompt.
- Use evidence to corroborate, qualify, or modify an argument that addresses the prompt.

Source: AP® European History Course and Exam Description, fall 2020

2. Evaluate the extent to which the idea of the divine right of monarchs differed from the idea of the social contract.

3. Evaluate the extent to which the organization of empires in mid-19th century Europe differed from the organization of nation-states in mid-19th century Europe.

4. Evaluate the extent to which the ideology of fascism differed from the ideology of communism.

Index

Deism, 223
Democracy, 9
Democratization, 557
Demographic catastrophe, 60
Demographic foundation, 241
Demographic pattern, 230, 231
Demographic
  definition of, 60
Departments, 290
Department stores, 354
Depreciated, 517
Descartes, René, French
  philosopher, 206, 172
Desmoulins, Camille, 328
de-Stalinization, 590, 594
Détente, 608
Diamond, Jared
  Guns, Germs, and Steel
    (book), 56
Dias, Bartolomeu, 52
Dickens, Charles, 359
Diderot, Denis
  Encyclopédie, 219
Dien Bien Phu, battle, 624
Diet (assembly of leaders), 90
Diet of Augsburg, 30
Directoire, 294
Directory, 294, 299
Disarmament, 512
Divine right, 175
Domesticity, 244
Dominant faiths in Western
  Europe, 103
Dominicans, 43
Domino theory, 578
Donatello, 9
Donation of Constantine, 4
Double-entry bookkeeping, 67
Dowry, 118
Dreyfus affair, 428, 429
Dreyfus, Alfred, 428
  scapegoat, 428
Duma, 385, 504, 505
  provisional government,
    505
Dürer, Albrecht, 15
Dutch East India Company
  (VOC), 67–68, 171, 272
  joint-stock company, 171
Dutch Revolt, 177
Dutch War, 180
  Dutch War for
    Independence, 177,
    198

Dutch, trading companies, 46
  Dutch East India
    Company, 46
  Dutch West India
    Company, 46

E

East India Company, 273, 275,
  276
East Indies, 36, 272, 325
Easter rebellion, 498
Eastern-bloc countries, 593
Ecological disaster, 647
Economic miracle, 573
Edict of Nantes, 29, 104, 258
Edict of toleration, 255
Edison, Thomas
  gramophone, 355
  incandescent light
    bulbs, 355
Edo, now Tokyo, 470
Eighty Years' War, 170
Einstein, Albert, 554
Elect, 92
Electorate of Hanover, 278
Electric grid, 350
Elizabeth I (reigned 1558–
  1603), 27, 98
Elizabethan Settlement (1559),
  27, 98
Elton, G. R., 94
  *The New Cambridge
    Modern History, Vol.
    II, The Reformation*,
    94
Emancipation Edict of 1861,
  345
Empiricism, 214
Enclosure (also called
  inclosure), 72
Enclosure Acts, 232
Enclosure movement, 152, 232
Encomienda, 43
England's Parliament
  House of Commons, 188
  House of Lords, 188
English Civil War, 98, 144, 147,
  178, 215, 216
  timeline, 146
Enlightened absolutism, 253
Enlightened despot, 191
Enlightened monarchs, 253
Enlightened self-interest, 390

Enlightenment , 204, 205, 214,
  215, 221, 241, 252, 269
Enslaved Africans, 63f
Entente Cordiale, 439, 465
Entrepreneurs, 66
Epidemics, 233
  bubonic plague (Black
    Death), 233
  smallpox, 233
Equiano, Olaudah, 268
Erasmus, Desiderius, 17
  Praise of folly, book, 17
Erwin Schrödinger, 554
Estates-General, 171, 285
  First Estate: the Catholic
    clergy, 285
  Second Estate: the
    nobility, 285
  Third Estate: everyone else
    in French society,
    285
ETA (Basque Homeland and
  Liberty), 598
Ethiopia, invasion, 467, 536
Ethnic cleansing, 599
Eugenics, 444, 640
  "racial hygiene", 640
Euro, 629
Europe's commercial
  revolution, 167
Europe's secularism, 635
European Christianity, 22
  Protestant reformation, 22
European Coal and Steel
  Community (ECSC), 573,
  603, 628
European Commercial
  Revolution, 162
European Community
  (EC), 604
European diseases
  immunity, 55
  measles, 55
  smallpox, 55
European Economic
  Community (EEC), 573,
  603, 629
  common market, 573
European exploration, impact
  of, 56
European Greens, 647–649
  die Grünen, 647
European Parliament, 628

European Union (EU), 629, 630
  21st century expansion, 629f
European Union, countries that joined, 611f
European woolen industry, 66
Eve, 119
Evolving attitudes toward reason, 651f
Existentialism, 650
External tariff, 152
Eyck, Jan van, 15, 18f

F

Factory Act of 1833, 367
Fascism in Europe, 527f
Fascism, 503
  right-wing, 503
Fashoda crisis, 465
Father of humanism, 4
Fauvism, 480
Feast of Saint Mark (Festa di san Marco), 122
February revolution, 381
Feminist movements, 615
Ferdinand, Archduke Franz, 29, 495
Fermi, Enrico, nuclear physicist, 555
Fichte, Johann Gottlieb, 424
  national aggrandizement, 424
Ficino, Marsilio, 4
Final Act of the Congress of Vienna, 315
Final solution, 549
First Consul, 303
Fischer, David Hackett
  The Great Wave, 203
Five year plan, 529
Flanders, 189
Flemish, 598, 598
Florence Nightingale, 433f
Foljambe, Joseph, plows, 151
Folk ideas, 121
Fonte, Moderata, 140
Fouché, Joseph, 304
Foundling hospital, 235
Fourier, Charles, 392
France's West African, 456
Francisco Franco, general, 526
Franco-German War, 494

Franco-Prussian War, 435, 436f
Frankfurt assembly, 382
Fraternal organizations, 362
  "brothers", 362
  Freemasons, 362
Frederick II, 254, 279
Frederick III of Brandenburg
  "king of Prussia", 181
Frederick the Great, 181, 267
Frederick William I, 181, 254
Frederick William IV, 381
Free trade, 340
Free trade agreements, 352
Freedom Party of Austria, 636
  over-foreignization, 636
Freemasonry, 221, 221
French and Indian War, 280, 324
French colonialists, 626
French declaration, 289
French East India Company, 272, 324
French National Convention, 298
French popular front, 520f
French Revolution, 256, 270, 272, 284, 287f, 288, 292, 297, 294, 299, 318, 324, 325, 341, 421
Freud, Sigmund, 449
  Civilization and Its Discontents, 567f
  psychoanalysis, 449
  psychoanalysis, 555
  The Interpretation of Dreams, 555
Freycinet plan, 343
Friedrich, Caspar David, 474
  German artist, 488f
  landscapes, 474
  list, 356, 420f
  The Wanderer Above the Sea of Fog, 474
Froebel, Friedrich
  kindergarten education, 410
Fronde, 178, 188
Fry, Elizabeth, 408
  professionalize prisons, 408
Fuggers, 67, 68
Futurism, 654, 655

G

Gainsborough, Thomas
  The Portrait of Isabelle Bell Franks, 236
  The Blue Boy, 236
Galen, physician, 209
Galileo Galilei,
  mathematician, 208
  guilty of heresy, 209
  telescope, 208
  The Starry Messenger, 209
Gandhi, Mahatma
  civil disobedience, 468
Garibaldi, Giuseppe, 435
  red shirts, 435
Gentileschi, Artemisia, 131
George, David Lloyd, 510
GDP per capita, 574f
Gendarmerie, 309
General Agreement on Tariffs and Trade (GATT), 586
General directive, 349
Genetic engineering, 641
  stem cell, 641
Geneva, 100
Genocide, 499
Gentry
  definition of, 29, 31
Geocentric universe, 212f
Geometric perspective, 8
Germ theory, 457
German Peasants' War, 93
Ghettos, 550
Girondins, 291
Glasnost, or "openness", 592, 609
Global cold war, 582
Globalization, 645
Glorious Revolution, 145, 156, 199, 216, 253, 278, 178
GNI (gross national income), 606
God and gold, 35
Goebbels, Joseph, 526
Gold coast, 52
Gold standard, 517
Golden age, Dutch, 246
Good Friday Agreement, 598
Gorbachev, Mikhail, 592, 609
  glasnost, or "openness", 592
  glasnost, or openness, 609

Indian National Congress,
468, 622
Indians, 42
Individualism, 4
Indochina, 624
Inductive and deductive
reasoning, examples, 207f
Inductive reasoning, 206
Indulgences, 89
Industrial Revolution, 238,
332, 334, 414
Indzhova, 619
Inflation, 71
Intellectual developments, 642
Intelligence agencies, 580
American Central
Intelligence Agency
(CIA), 580
British Secret Intelligence
Service (SIS), 580
Soviet KGB, 580
Internal combustion engine,
348
Internal tariffs, 152
International Monetary Fund
(IMF), 585
Internet, 646
Interventionist, 407
Invisible hand, 227
Irish, 344
Irish Home Rule Bill, 498
Irish Unionists, 345
Iron curtain, 578, 586
Irrationalism, 448
Isaac Newton, 207
Isabella's, 29
Ismay, Lord, Secretary General
of NATO, 669f
Italian renaissance, 12
Izvestia, newspaper, 671f

J

Jacobins, 291
Jacquard, Joseph-Marie, 165
James I, 188
Jamestown, 46
Jenner, Edward
"father of immunology",
234
world's first vaccine, 234
Jesuits, 36, 112
missionary work, 36
Jewel, John, 139
Jewish question, 548

Jews in Europe, c. 1800, 257f
anti-Semitism, 427
Joint-stock company, 67, 171
dividends, 67
stock, 67
Joseph, Francis
"dual monarchy", 383
Austria-Hungary, 383
Joseph II, 255
Joyce, James, 657
Ulysses, novel, 657
Jubilee indulgence, 89–90
July Revolution, 376, 380

K

Kafka, Franz, 657
The Metamorphosis, 657
Kaiser Wilhelm II, 437, 439
Kandinsky, Vasily, artist, 655
Karranos, 28
Katherine of Aragon, 25
Mary Tudor, female, 25
Kennedy, John F., president
US, 579
Kepler, Johannes,
astronomer, 208
Keynes, John Maynard,
economist, 519
Khrushchev, Nikita, 590
de-Stalinizatio, 590
King Charles I, 215
King Charles X, 380
King Ferdinand, 28, 42
King Francis I, 99
King George I, 278
King George's War, 279
King Henry VIII, 114
King Louis XIII, French, 106
King Philip I, king, 104
Kleindeutsch (lesser Germany),
435, 464
Kingsley, Charles, Anglican
priest, 490f
Knox, John, 138
Koblenz, photograph, 571f
Korean war, 581
Kosovo, 599
Kristallnacht, 548
Krupp family, 349
Bessemer process furnace,
349
Kulaks, 529
Kulturkampf (culture
struggle), 437

L

L'Ouverture, Toussaint, 297,
298, 299
La Querelle des Femmes, 119
Labor unions, 361
Labour Party, 399
Lady Mary Wortley Montagu,
234
Laissez-faire, 226, 407
Land reclamation, 231
Landlord
definition of, 69
Languages
Arabic, 4
Greek, 4
Hebrew, 4
Last Supper, 10
Lateen sails, 38
Le Chapelier Law, 155
League of Nation, 512, 513,
535, 622
League's General Assembly,
512
Learning centers of the day
Bologna, 4
Florence, 4
Padua, 4
Paris, 4
Leeuwenhoek, Antonie van,
microbiologist, 172
Left-wing, 503
Legislative assembly, 290
Lémery, Louis
A Treatise of all Sorts of
Foods..., 202
Lending libraries, 221
Lenin, Vladimir, 466, 498, 505
Communist Party, 499
Lent, 121, 122
Leopold I, 180
Lesbian, bisexual, and
transgender (LGBT),
660, 661
Letters to Atticus, 4
Levée en masse, 292
Leviathan, 216
Liberal arts curriculum at
european universities, 5f
Medieval Universities,
(13th century), 5
Renaissance Universities,
(15th century), 5
Liberal democracy, 503

Middle-class, 340, 360, 361, 400
  families, 415
  philanthropic, 362
Middle-class women, 362
  aid at orphanages, 362
  training children, 362
Middle passage, 61–62, 163
Migrants, 237, 630, 634
Migrated, 230
Militarism, 494
Military revolution, 176f
Mill, John Stuart, 391
  Considerations on Representative Government, 390
  Principles of Political Economy, 391
  social liberty, 391
  The Subjection of Women, 391
Mines Act of 1842, 367, 368
Minh, Ho Chi, 624
Miracle of Saint Mark, 129
Mirandola, Giovanni Pico della, 4
Mission civilisatrice, French term, 456
Mixed farming, 151
Modern art, 480, 481f
Modern industrial society, 504f
Modern state, 28
Modernism, 448
Modernist, 655
Molotov-Ribbentrop pact, 541
Mona Lisa, 10
Monarchies, 143
Monetary systems, 354
Money economy, 67
Mongols, 193
Monopoly, 353
  British political cartoon, 353f
Montesquieu, 219
  The Spirit of Laws, 219
More, Thomas, 17
  Utopia, 17
Morel, Edmund D., 466
  Congo free state, 462
  The Black Man's Burden, book, 462
Morocco, 465
Morse code, 350, 459
Morse, Samuel, 350

telegraph, 350
Most favored nation, 353
Moura, Roberto Landell de, 350
Movable type, 20
Multiethnic empires, 426
Munich agreement, 537
Muslim Granada in 1492, 28
  Reconquista, 28
Muslim population of Europe, 635f
Mussolini, Benito, 523–525, 652
  "League of combat, 523"
  fascism, 523
  Il Duce, 525
Mutiny, 468
Mutual aid societies, 361

N

Nader, Helen
  The End of the Old World (article), 57
Napoleon Bonaparte, 237, 269, 294, 297, 302, 308f, 418f
  heroic, 308
  an opportunist, 309
  favorite dictator, 309
  visiting the orphans, 331f
Napoleon III, 381, 400, 401, 425
Napoleon's empire, 1812, 306f
Napoleonic code, 302, 305
Napoleonic wars, 164, 305
National aggrandizement, 424
National Assembly, 286–289, 381
  Declaration of the rights of man and of the citizen, 289
National convention, 291, 293, 302
National government, 519
  conservative, liberal, and Labour, 519
National Health Service, 617
National Liberation Front (FLN), 624
National rally, 636
National system, 356
National Union of Mineworkers, 605
Nationalism, 421, 423, 440f

Nationalist movement, 484, 597, 624
Nationalistic movements, 434
Native Americans, 162
Naturalism, 8
Natural laws, 207, 215
Natural order, 374
Natural rights, 216
Natural selection, 443
Natural worlds, 1
Naturalism, 479
Navigation, 38
  portolani, 38
  acts, 165
Nazi, 548, 549, 550
  Party, 524
Nazi–Soviet Non-Agression Pact, 537
Neoclassical authors, 249f
Neoclassicism, 247, 248
Neonatalism, 659
Nepotism, 90
New Amsterdam, 46
New Economic Policy (NEP), 508
New France, 46
New monarchies, 28
New physics, 555
New Spain, 42
New technologies, World War I, 497
  airplanes, 497
  barbed wire, 497
  machine guns, 497
  poison gas, 497
  submarines, 497
  tanks, 497
New Testament, 17, 97
New world, 42, 54, 55, 153, 207
New York, 46
Newton, Isaac, 209, 213
  law of gravitation, 209
  Principia, 209
Niemöller, Martin, 652
Nietzsche, Friedrich, philosopher, 448, 650
  nihilist, 650
Nine Years' War, 180
95 Theses, 98
Nobles (*also* called boyars), 190, 118
  of the robe, 31
Nogarola, Isotta, 6
Non-Aligned Movement, 581

Union of Soviet Socialist
Republics
(USSR), 571
Sovietization, 589
Soviets, 505
Space race, 579
Apollo 11, 579
National Aeronautics
and Space
Administration
(NASA), 579
Sputnik, 579
Spaniards, 44
Spanish Armada, 105, 187
Spanish Civil War, 526, 527
Spanish Habsburgs, 105
Spanish in the Americas and
the Pacific, 45f
Speculation, 518
Spencer, Herbert, 444, 455
"survival of the fittest", 444
Social Darwinism, 444
Sphere of influence, 465
Spice Islands, 45
Spinning jenny, 335f
St. Bartholomew's Day
Massacre, 103
St. Francis Xavier, 86
St. Peter's Basilica, 90
St. Petersburg Academy, 191
Stadholder, 171
Stalemate, 496
Stalin, Joseph, 528, 577
Stanisław II, 182
Star chamber, 30
Star wars, 609
States general, 376
Steam engine, 155, 336
Steamships, 351
Steen, Jan
The Merry Family
(painting), 117f
Stephenson, George, 338
invented a locomotive,
338f
Sternpost rudder, 38
Stoker, Bram, English author,
491f
Stolypin, Peter, 385
Strauss, Richard, 657
Also Sprach Zarathustra,
657
Stravinsky, Igor, composer
The Rite of Spring, 656

Streetcar, 351
Stuart monarchs
Charles I, 98
James I, 98
Subatomic particles, 554
Submarines, 497
Subsistence agriculture, 70
Suburbs, 360
Suchocka, Hanna, 619
Suez Canal, 459
Suffragists, 403
Sukarno, 624
Sunday School movement, 402
Superpowers, 585
Suppression of dissent, 589
Surrealism, 655
Survival of the fittest, 444
Swift, Jonathan
"The Lady's Dressing
Room", poem, 245
Syndicalism, 395

T

Tabula rasa, 235
Taille, 29
Tanks, 497
Tariffs, 340
Taverns, 243
"public houses" (pubs),
243
inns, 243
Tchaikovsky, Pyotr Ilyich
The Nutcracker and Swan
Lake, 476
Tea, 166
Technological innovations, 646
cell phones, 646
computers, 646
Internet, 646
Telegraph, 350
Telephone, 350
"switchboard", 350
Telescope, 208
Temperance movement, 402
Temple of reason, 291
Ten Hours Act of 1847, 367
Tenements, 360
Tennis Court Oath, 287, 288
Tenochtitlán, 42
Teresa of Avila, 112
Testaments, old and new, 114
Tetzel, Johann, 90
Textile industry, new
technologies, 155f

Thatcher, Margaret, 604
Thatcherism, 618
Theaters, 243
Theology, 78
Theory of evolution, 443
Theory of relativity, 554
Theresa, Empress Maria,
181, 237, 255
Thermidorian reaction, 293
Thinkers of the time
Leon Battista Alberti, 6
Leonardo Bruni, 6
Niccolò Machiavelli, 6
Third-wave feminism, 616
Thirty Years' War, 106, 108,
110, 135, 177
Thirty-Nine Articles (1571), 98
Three polish partitions, 183f
Three-field system, 71
Thresher, 151
Tintoretto, 129
Titian, Renaissance painter,
129
The Miracle of Saint
Mark, 129
Tito, Josip Broz, 598
Toleration Act, 256
Total warfare, 545
Totalitarian, 512
Trade networks, 41, 51
Trade unions, 361
Trans-Atlantic telegraph, 350
Transportation methods
airplane, 351
bicycle, 350
internal combustion
engines, 351
steamships, 351
streetcar, 350
Trans-Siberian railway, 346f
Transubstantiation, 91
Treaty of Aix-la-Chapelle, 279
Treaty of Brest-Litovsk, 498
Treaty of Lubeck (1629), 106
Treaty of Nanking, 454
Treaty of Paris, 280
Treaty of Tordesillas, 42, 43,
48, 52
Treaty of Versailles, 511, 523,
524
Treaty of Westphalia, 175
Trench warfare, 496
Triangle trade, 61, 62f, 163
middle passage, 61

Triple Entente , 439
Tristan, Flora, 392, 401
 "The Workers' Union", 401
Trotsky, Leon, 506
Troubles, 598
Truman doctrine, 578
Trusts, 353
Tsars, 190
Tsar Alexander II, Russia,
 384, 433
 emancipation manifesto,
 384
Tsar Nicholas I, 380, 383
Tsar Nicholas II, 385, 498
Tudor dynasty, 26
Tudor, Mary, 27, 98
Tuileries palace, 290
Tull, Jethro
 Horse-Hoeing
 Husbandry, 202
Turgot, Anne Robert
 Jacques, 226
 laissez-faire, 226
Turkish Petroleum Company
 (TPC), 623
Twelve Articles, 93
Two-field system, 71

U

UN Charter, 577
Uncertainty principle, 554
Understanding the prompt, 80
Unification, 434, 435, 436f
Union of Soviet Socialist
 Republics (USSR), 528,
 571
Union of Utrecht, 170
United Kingdom, 344
United Nations (UN), 577
 Charter, 624
United States Constitution
 bill of rights, 147
United States of Europe, 603
Universal suffrage, 557
University of Erfurt, 89
Urban financial centers, 68
 Amsterdam, 68
 Genoa, 68
 London, 68
Urban gentry, 171
Urban population, growth,
 363f
Urban redesign, 409
Ursulines, 112

Utilitarianism, 390, 391, 415
Utopian socialism, 392, 401

V

Valéry, Paul: The European
 Mind, 566f
Valla, Lorenzo, 4
Van Gogh's painting, 481f
Vaudeville, 361
Velásquez, Diego, artist
 Las Meninas, 246
Velvet revolution, 589
Vermeer, Johannes
 Girl with the Pearl Earring,
 247
 The Milkmaid, 247
Vernacular, 4
Vernacular Bibles, 97
Vernacular literature, 21
Verrazano, Giovanni de,
 navigator, 46
Versailles conference, 510
 treaty, 535, 536
Very subtle wit, 36
Vesalius, Andreas, 210
 On the Fabric of the
 Human Body, 210
Vespucci, Amerigo, 42, 83
Victor Emmanuel II,
 434, 435
Victorian era, 447, 448
Viet Minh, 624
Vietnam War, 581
Voltaire, 218
 "crush the loathsome
 thing," slogan, 218
 Candide, short novel, 218
 Letters on the English, 218
 Treatise on Toleration, 218
Vondel, Joost van den, poet,
 201
Voyages of discovery, 160

W

Wagner, Richard, 423, 476,
 490f
 nationalistic operas, 423
 The Ring of the
 Nibelung, 476
Walesa, Lech, 611
War of the Austrian
 Succession, 272, 279
War of the Grand Alliance, 277

War of the Spanish Succession,
 48, 180, 277, 280
War of the Three Henrys, 104
Wars of the Roses, 29
Warsaw Confederation Act, 98
Warsaw Pact, 587, 592
Washington, George, 158
Water meadows, 153
Watt, James
 steam engine, 336
Wave of pogroms, 548
Wedgwood, Josiah,
 entrepreneur
 imitation ceramics, 242
Wedlock, 235
Weimar Republic, 511, 524
Welfare state, 604
 cradle-to-grave, 604
 pensions, 604
Welshman Sir Pryce
 Pryce-Jones
 mail-order catalog, 354
 Royal Welsh
 Warehouse, 354
Wesley, John, 224
 Methodist, 224
 Holy Club, 320
 The Nature, Design, and
 General Rules of the
 United Societies, 320
West Indies, 42
 Indians, people as, 42
Western allies, 578
Western and Northern
 Europe, 343
Western European serfdom
Western front, 495, 496
Westinghouse Corporation,
 350
Whig Party, 390
Whipping and branding, 123f
White Man's Burden, 455
Whitney, Eli, 336
William Davis
 refrigerated railroad
 cars, 355
 zinc-lined iceboxes, 355
William III, 145
William of Orange, 145, 277
 Mary Stuart, 278f
Wilson, Woodrow, U.S.
 President, 622
 "fourteen points", 510

"peace without victory",
510
self-determination, 622
Witchcraft, 123, 124
Witte, Sergei, 384
Wollstonecraft, Mary, 218
   A Vindication of the Rights
      of Woman, 218
Woman and child dragging
   coal, 368f
Women movements
   Sunday School movement,
      402
   temperance movement,
      402
Women's Social and Political
   Union (WSPU), 402
Woolf, Virginia
   Mrs. Dalloway, novel, 657
Wordsworth, William, English
   poet, 489f
Working class, 359, 365, 399
   women, 366
World Bank, 585
World economy, 54
World in 1750, 162f, 273f
World Trade Organization
   (WTO), 586
World War I time line, 496f,
   497f
World War I, 345, 432, 495,
   503, 511
   Allies, 495
   Central Powers, 495
   military casualties, 510f,
      511f
   Western Front, 495
World War II, 394, 540, 571
   military technologies,
      545f
   Theater of Europe, 540
   Theater of the Pacific, 540
   timeline, 543f
Wright, Ronald
   A Short History of
      Progress, 370
Wright brothers, Wilbur and
   Orville, 351
   first airplane, 351
Wycliffe, John, cleric and
   scholar, 87

X

Xavier, Francis, 112
Xenophobia, 636

Y

Yalta conference, 544
Yeltsin, Boris, 610
Yeoman farmers, 152
Yom Kippur, 581
Yugoslavia, 598
   countries formed from,
      599f

Z

Zetkin, Clara, 394
   Die Gleichheit, 394
   joined Germany's Socialist
      Workers' Party, 394
Zionism, 428
   Jerusalem, 429
   Palestine, 429
Zola, Emile, French journalist,
   491f
   Les Rougon-Macquart, 479
Zollverein agreement, 356
Zong, slave ship, 163
Zulu, 467
Zwickau, 94
Zwingli, Huldrych, 91